War, Foreign Affairs,
and Constitutional
Power: 1829–1901

War, Foreign Affairs, and Constitutional Power: 1829–1901

by
Henry Bartholomew Cox

A Report of the American Bar Association Steering Committee
on War, Foreign Affairs, and Constitutional Power

Ballinger Publishing Company ● **Cambridge, Massachusetts**
A Subsidiary of Harper & Row, Publishers

International Standard Book Number: 0–88410–956–9

Library of Congress Catalog Card Number: 76–15392

Printed in the United States of America

Library of Congress Cataloging in Publication Data
(Revised for volume 2)

Sofaer, Abraham D.
  War, foreign affairs, and constitutional power.

  Vol. 2— by Henry Bartholomew Cox.
  "A report of the American Bar Association, Steering
Committee on War, Foreign Policy, and Constitutional
Power"—V. 2, t.p.
  Includes bibliographies and indexes.
  CONTENTS: [1]. The origins.—[2]. 1829–1901.
  1. War and emergency powers—United States—History.
2. United States—Foreign relations—Law and legislation
—History. 3. Separation of Powers—United States—
History. I. Cox, Henry Bartholomew. II. American Bar
Association. Steering Committee on War, Foreign Policy,
and Constitutional Power. IV. Title.
KF5060.S6   342.73'0412   ˙ 76–15392
ISBN 0–88410–222–X (v. 1)   347.302412
ISBN 0–88410–956–9 (v. 2)

The opinions and conclusions expressed by the author are his own, and as such do not constitute policy of the American Bar Association.

For my parents

Table of Contents

Illustrations

Preface and Acknowledgments

This is the second volume of a study of the war powers of the President and Congress sponsored by the American Bar Association. Volume I, which carried the story to 1829, was *War, Foreign Affairs, and Constitutional Power: The Origins,* by Abraham D. Sofaer published in 1976. This volume covers the years 1829 to 1901.

The core of the book is primary evidence culled from examination of all volumes of the *Congressional Globe* and *Record* that cover the last three-quarters of the nineteenth century. Over seventy years rich in American political and diplomatic history have been reviewed for the light they can shed on the power of the branches of government to make war and peace.

Analysis of war powers problems leads to the conclusion that few apparent crises in the present have not had relevant analogues in the past. Early congressmen were just as troubled as those of the present day by their perceived loss of power over emergencies in the war powers arena. In their own time, they sought to define the criteria of what they conceived to be the powers of the branches, and either granted or withheld delegations of authority. The potential totality of today's means of destruction may seem more threatening to civilization than certain perils of a century ago, but it does not render irrelevant the reactions of those who perceived that control of the power to negotiate involves the mightiest power of all—the means of making war. Even in the nineteenth century, Congress frequently claimed that its right to exercise power was threatened in areas that practice and precedent have long since accorded to the executive branch—*i.e.,* in the area of appointment and removal of officers and of defense of national territory.

Reconsideration of the "twilight zone" of executive-congressional prerogatives has revealed that legislative objections to intrusion on many powers over domestic and foreign activities that Congress considered its fundamental rights were most frequently advanced from the standpoint of the power over war that the executive would gain if the power were forfeited.

Both familiar and unfamiliar political and diplomatic controversies have been highlighted. Introductions are brief glosses on a few key issues and should suffice to refresh the recollection of more general readers as well as to guide students in supplementing their other readings. The periodization should help undergraduates find their way through a standard text, while more detailed subject matter headings and organization are designed to assist the specialist in constitutional history and law.

While there are doubtless more nineteenth century incidents illustrative of the war power problems, and though no book can hope to be all-inclusive, it was early deemed more important that the examples used here be discussed from the standpoint of all significant contemporary views expressed upon them. Substantial reliance has been placed on congressional debates covering the period examined by this work. Each volume of these proceedings has been summarized, and memoranda were drafted as appropriate covering the relevant problems. For those interested in further study, the complete text of our research can be found in the War Powers Study papers at Columbia University.

Funding for the volume was generously provided by the National Endowment for the Humanities, the Ford Foundation, and the American Bar Association. The project is especially indebted to John A. Williams of the National Endowment For the Humanities for his advice. In addition, I wish to express the thanks of the War Powers Steering Committee for financial assistance from the William Nelson Cromwell Foundation and the law firm of Cleary, Gottlieb, Steen, and Hamilton. The chairman of the Steering Committee, Lyman M. Tondel, Jr., deserves special recognition for his valuable comments, encouragement, and help at every turn, as do other members of that committee, especially Judge Abraham D. Sofaer and George Wade, for their guidance as the manuscript progressed. Judge Sofaer, while director of the study at Columbia Law School, also drafted portions of Chapter I. Countless but important details of administration were monitored by Katherine McG. Sullivan, assistant executive director of the American Bar Association, whose help throughout the production of the volume was indispensable.

Among the staffs of the institutions whose assistance is gratefully acknowledged are those of Columbia Law Library and Butler Library, whose Rare Book and Manuscripts Librarian Kenneth R. Lohf helped me to establish the War Powers Papers at Columbia. The kind assistance of the George Washington University's National Law Center and Gelman Library is particularly noted. The National Archives staff and members of various divisions of the Library of Congress guided us to documentary, narrative, and photographic materials: I especially wish to thank National Archives specialists Dale Floyd, George Perros, and Gibson Smith.

A volume such as this is a collective enterprise. The members of the War Powers Study staff at Columbia at the time of the preparation of this volume deserve the highest recognition for their vitally important digests of the record of debates: these included Patricia Atwater, Edith Bershadsky, Margaret Cullinan, Milton Henry, Judith Lewis, Eleanor Tejirian, and Brian Weiss. Outstanding memoranda were provided by Columbia law students Robert Lawrence, George Hritz, Richard Eade, David Lesser, Rena Seplowitz, Richard Seeborg, Jonathan Vinson, Joyce Perlmutter, Lee Pelzman, and Amos Hugh Scott. I especially thank Flora Paoli for her helpfulness with the manuscript, including proofreading and editorial suggestions.

The assistant director and staff attorney of this project was Enid Sterling, whose decade of superb legal-historical craftsmanship has helped immeasurably to shape the results of our research. Her drafts of important events such as the Schofield mission and the Falkland Islands incident have added new interpretations to American legal and diplomatic history.

My wife, Hannah Caffery Cox, has contributed unending encouragement to a task that would have been far less rewarding without her help.

Henry Bartholomew Cox
Department of History
The George Washington University

Introduction

The Constitution, Professor Edward S. Corwin once observed, "is an invitation to struggle for the privilege of directing American foreign policy."[1] Since war—the calculated use of violence—is the ultimate sanction in furthering foreign policy goals, that "invitation" has had significant consequences for the American constitutional order. In the first volume of the American Bar Association's important series on the relative war powers of Congress and the president, Professor (now Judge) Abraham D. Sofaer examined the origins of the war-making power and its use to 1829.[2] When Judge Sofaer was no longer available to continue the work, fortunately Henry Bartholomew Cox was prevailed upon to use his considerable talents as both historian and lawyer to carry the study to the end of the nineteenth century. His analysis shows that there was no clear winner in the struggle between the political branches of government. This volume is a worthy addition to the first; taken together, they are indispensable additions to the library of anyone interested—as all should be—in war and foreign affairs.

Clio may be an uncertain muse, but history surely is not irrelevant to one of the great constitutional questions not only of American history but of the present day. Current American involvement in Central America and elsewhere poses the same constitutional conflicts that Dr. Cox carefully delineates as having taken place in the nineteenth century. Justice Oliver Wendell Holmes once remarked that adherence to the past was not a duty but merely a necessity. So it is here. Nevertheless, those who read history to provide precise answers to modern constitutional problems are certain to be disappointed. Implicit in this volume, as well as its predecessor, are certain truths about the nature of American constitutionalism. They include:

volume, as well as its predecessor, are certain truths about the nature of American constitutionalism. They include:

First, there is little dispute over presidential use of violence *defensively.* Arguments erupt when the chief executive seeks to do so affirmatively. Compare, in this respect, what President Lincoln did at the beginning of the Civil War with what President Johnson did in Indo-China and, indeed, with what President Reagan seeks to do in Central America. In the spring of 1861 Lincoln took action of the most dubious legality;[3] when Congress finally convened, it speedily ratified the presidential acts. The president justified his action in this manner: "It became necessary for us to choose whether, using only the existing means, agencies, and processes which Congress had provided, I should let the Government fall into ruins or whether, availing myself of the broader powers conferred by the Constitution in cases of insurrection, I would make an effort to save it, with all its blessings, for the present age and for posterity."[4] The hard fact is that he acted as a "constitutional dictator," as the late Professor Clinton Rossiter maintained.[5]

Second, throughout American history, the presidency has steadily, albeit discontinuously, aggrandized power. This does not mean that the president is all-powerful. On the contrary, he must still reckon with Congress and, in practical effect, "negotiate treaties" with that body. What it does mean is that the executive has become much stronger than was originally envisaged by those who drafted the Constitution. The Founding Fathers attempted to balance the powers of government, perhaps proceeding on the assumption that conflicts between the branches would not only help prevent despotism but would also through some mysterious means ensure that the common good would be furthered. The Framers thus adapted Adam Smith's notion of the "invisible hand," an economic principle that he enunciated in his then and now influential *The Wealth of Nations,* to the political order.

Third, whether that principle of balance in governmental affairs, which can be traced to the Newtonian-Cartesian cosmological paradigm, is any longer sufficient to the need has begun to be doubted. Some students of the constitutional order—a leading example is the well-known Washington lawyer and presidential adviser, Lloyd Cutler—have recently called for revision in the balance of powers between president and Congress.[6] One may safely forecast that as the United States counts down to the two hundredth anniversary of the Constitutional Convention of 1787, a growing number of voices will ask the same question. For those observers, this and Judge Sofaer's studies are required readings.

Fourth, when the president uses violence without Congress's express consent, he implicitly but not expressly relies on one of the great silences of the fundamental law: constitutional reason of state (*raison d'état*). That concept has been defined as "the doctrine that whatever is required to insure the survival of the state must be done by the individuals responsible for it, no matter how repugnant such an act may be to them in their private capacity as decent and moral men."[7] John Locke, the "father" of the Constitution, called it the prerogative: the power to act "according to discretion, for the public good, without the prescription of the law, and sometimes even against it, is that which is called the prerogative.... There is a latitude left to the executive power, to do many things of choice, which the laws do not prescribe."[8] Congress, speaking generally, has often disagreed with the use of the presidential prerogative and has fought rear-guard actions against the president.

Fifth, Congress has acted affirmatively in recent years by enacting the War Powers Resolution of 1973 in an effort to curb use of the prerogative; at other times, it has specifically forbidden use of public funds in designated areas that the president considers important. The Supreme Court declared in June 1983 that some of these congressional actions are unconstitutional devices invented to rein in what Congress believes are excessive exercises of presidential power.[9] This decision will require lawmakers to reevaluate the methods they may use in the future to encourage executive accountability.

Sixth, in final analysis, politics, rather than law, rules in the struggle between president and Congress. It may be a harsh and perhaps unpleasant truth, but law is not and cannot be a substitute for politics. Throughout known human history political philosophers, including those who wrote the *Federalist Papers,*[10] have tried to create societies in which government is by laws and not by men. On the record, as this volume demonstrates, it is an unattainable ideal. Presidents can, and do, take such actions as the routine operations of the political process permit. The most important feature of our written Constitution is not that it *by itself* interdicts what political officers want to do in foreign policy matters but, rather, that it provides a framework—a structure of government—for the operation of the political system. In this connection, it should be remembered that the so-called doctrine of separation of powers is far less a doctrine than a political theory and, further, that it is only by an indefensible fiction that answers to questions of the relative powers of president and Congress can be logically deduced from the Constitution.

Seventh, the courts have little to say about the struggle between the other branches of government. By a self-imposed limitation, the Supreme Court usually carefully avoids having to rule on the calculated use of violence. When it does so, it is more likely than not to sustain the use of force.[11]

All of these matters are either explicit or implicit in the American Bar Association's illuminating study. By perusing the primary sources, this project has cast much light upon obscure corners of American history. That is a singular service, not only to academics but also to government officers who must deal routinely with emergent problems of foreign policy—including war.

The Constitution of 1787 is essentially an instrument for the resolution of domestic rather than external matters. Its ambiguities and silences were left to gather content from experience. Dr. Cox relates almost three-quarters of a century of that experience. He is telling us that the Founding Fathers tacitly informed each generation of Americans to solve its own problems, particularly when they concern such portentous matters as war and peace. Our international problems are not headaches; they will not vanish with a magic potion, a legal aspirin tablet. Participation in world affairs is "a process, not a conclusion [and] its commitments are unending. . . . We will not arise one morning to find all problems solved, all need for further strain and struggle ended."[12] Dean Acheson said it well.[13]

> It is a long tough job and one for which we as a people are not particularly suited. We believe that any problem can be solved with a little ingenuity and without inconvenience to the folks at large. We have trouble-shooters to do this. And our name for problems is significant. We call them headaches. You take a powder and they are gone. These pains about which we have been talking are not like that. They are like the pain of earning a living. They will stay with us until death. We have got to understand that all our lives the danger, the uncertainty, the need for alertness, for effort, for discipline will be upon us. This is new to us. It will be hard for us. But we are in for it and the only real question is whether we shall know it soon enough.

Acheson was not quite correct. The condition he describes is really not "new"—as Bart Cox so well describes in this volume. This book should be read, and heeded, by all who care about the problems of foreign policy in an increasingly interdependent world.

Arthur S. Miller
Professor Emeritus of Law
The George Washington Unversity

War, Foreign Affairs,
and Constitutional
Power: 1829–1901

Chapter 1

The Jacksonian Era, 1829–1845

INTRODUCTION

John Quincy Adams remarked during a debate over President Tyler's use of the appointment power that questions of constitutional authority were "immortal."[1] His comment went to the heart of issues such as the war and peace powers of the president and Congress that have been analyzed by generations of statesmen before and since his time.

The operation of the American government under the Constitution has tended to raise major recurring questions concerning the authority of its branches. Though law and practice have shaped the branches' prerogatives over some areas where allocation of the war power is incompletely defined, others have remained "immortal"—and are the subject of this book. For example, why did presidents engage in military commitments without congressional authorization? Which controls over warmaking were reserved for Congress? By what criteria were delegations of discretionary authority made to the president? Why did Congress either willingly—or not so willingly—forfeit its authority? What attempts did legislators make to dominate the course of foreign relations, and why? Answers to these and many more queries exemplify the dynamics of jurisdictional problems between the president and Congress that had arisen earlier but matured and were more sharply defined after the first quarter of the nineteenth century.

"Necessity" and "emergency" called for significant restatements of major questions regarding the war powers, frequently in the form of important presidential messages and vigorous debates. Classical nineteenth century analyses of constitutional issues in the war powers arena did not arise in a vacuum. Congress perceived there was a distinct danger of hostilities involving the United States upon the resurgence of the European conservative impulse after the Congress of Vienna in 1818 and heightened revolutionary activities in Latin America during the 1820s. The United States was encircled by potential adversaries England and Spain on three sides during the first half of the nineteenth century. Its statesmen, therefore, had to consider that any dispute with even one nation could possibly bring about military engagements with other countries. Also, Congress forcefully demonstrated a need to participate in decisions where commercial questions clearly implied future military involvement. The surge of new technology at the beginning of the nineteenth century that made the seeming miracles of the industrial revolution a practicality by 1830 meant that rights to build railroads and canals, settle western lands to keep pace with territorial acquisition, and relocate Indians would call into play complex domestic and international legalities. Congress's increased involvement in advising upon and regulating the domestic activities of the executive moved into the sphere of military affairs and foreign relations. Although the president continued to function as the principal organ for foreign relations and the chief officer in the government for the execution of U.S. military affairs, Congress's sharing in the shaping of foreign policy operated as a curtailment of executive activity more than it had during the previous half-century.

Problems of conflict of authority over the war powers also were used by political parties as vehicles for assertion of power. In any given case, it is often difficult to sift the rhetoric of political fervor expressed in debate from Congress's genuine, perceived need to oppose certain executive activity, substitute its own policies, or delegate authority to act. Moreover, in an "extreme case," Congress and the president each claimed that it was required to exercise power in the "public interest." Regardless of the outcome of a short-run political battle, neither branch suffered any real loss of lawful authority. Presidents at times faced diminution of standing even with their political supporters, and parties lost elections; nevertheless, the officers of the branches of government successfully managed to exercise their prerogatives in the war powers sphere. Because the extent and site of such powers remained unsettled, neither a politically dominant president nor Congress could subsume or appropriate the claimed war powers of the other branch for any extended period. The Framers' lack of specificity in the war power grants and the allocation of the war power between the branches, when tested during the nineteenth century, produced recognition by the coordinate branches that compromise rather than conflict would best promote resolution of the scope of their shared authority.

The so-called age of Jackson spanning the years 1829 to 1845 is one of the more important periods in American history relevant to a study of levels of authority under a "dominant" presidency. Of the three attorneys turned politician who were destined to shape and define executive authority, Andrew Jackson most clearly reflected the image of the nation that elected him; yet his apparent ruggedness, stubbornness, and simplicity overlay a mastery of politics that many of his predecessors could not equal. Some might conclude that Jackson did not expand the presidency merely because to do so was politically expedient but that he conceptualized the increased authority he proposed as a natural function of the office itself. His opponents surely agreed that governmental power had coalesced in the executive. For example, Representative John Bell (Wh. Tenn.) claimed that citizens did not ask what Congress planned to do about pending national business, but demanded instead, ". . . what will the *President* do? what will the *Executive* do? what will *Andrew Jackson* do?"[2] On the other hand, President Jackson's unquestioned energy in using the powers of his office may be seen as a reaction to congressional prerogatives. His vetoes were probably more a defense of his programs than a bold or newly charted course toward an imperial presidency.

Jackson survived party challenges, such as a severe reaction to his repudiation of states' rights in the Nullification controversy, because his opposition lacked his organization. His successor, Martin Van Buren, tried to project an image of continuity with Jackson's policies,[3] yet maintained a narrower concept of the role of the government in a military crisis. The contrast in their handling of foreign affairs was exemplified in dealings with Mexico: Jackson's administration set a scene for war that Van Buren finally translated into a peace maneuver because Congress refused to act precipitously. This incident in diplomacy illustrated the contention of certain of the members of the Constitutional Convention that the Constitution should contain a requirement for the president to come before Congress for authority to engage in warlike acts and should thus make going to war more difficult.[4]

Though the balance of political power during John Tyler's tenure shifted into the legislative sphere,[5] President Tyler carved out specific benchmarks of executive strength that would serve as precedent for future chief executives faced with similar imperatives. For example, Tyler succeeded in getting most of the treaties negotiated by his administration approved by the Senate and displayed skill in imposing the executive will on foreign policy. He also exerted executive privilege to withhold information from Congress more firmly than any former chief executive, and made it clear that he was not obliged to send materials at Congress's request, even if the possibility of war was involved.

This volume highlights these and other noteworthy examples of vigorous independence of the executive on critical issues, even during subsequent periods in American history when politics apparently set in motion a long-range diminution of presidential power.

EXECUTIVE-CONGRESSIONAL RELATIONS

The Appointment and Removal Power

American leaders since the Constitutional Convention of 1787 knew that the relative power of the legislative and executive branches would depend significantly on the dispensing of federal offices. Control of policy depended on subordinates' accountability and thus was linked inseparably to the appointment and removal of civil servants.* States-men of the Jacksonian era (1828–48) regarded these powers as the heart of the president's capacity to govern the nation, at peace or war. The questions that exercise of appointment powers raised are central to the war power. Even when the offices in question were entirely domestic, the legal issues involved represented precedents and conduct that were studied and followed by subsequent presidents and Congresses in deal-ing with foreign and military affairs.

Practice during the forty years preceding Andrew Jackson's presi-dency appeared to have settled several important questions. The presi-dent's power to appoint was freely exercised, and every president favored members of his own political party to some extent. Congress did not interfere with executive establishment of diplomatic offices as the need arose. On the other hand, Congress expanded its control over many offices and appointments by establishing the principle of rotation in the

---

*The Constitution divides the powers to appoint federal officers between the executive and legislative branches, granting the president the power to "nominate" certain officers but requiring that their appointment be by and with "the Advice and Consent of the Senate. ..." Congress must approve appointment of incumbents for all offices, except appointments to "inferior offices," which the Constitution permits Congress to delegate to either the president, the courts, or the heads of government departments. Congress may further limit the president's appointment power by refusing to create offices other than those created by the Constitution. Finally, the president has power to fill any vacancy occurring during Senate recess, with such appointments expiring at the end of the first complete session of Congress following the vacancy.

Removal power is not mentioned directly in the Constitution. Article II, section 4, provides for impeachment, and Article III establishes judges' tenure "during good behav-ior," leaving the subject otherwise open to considerable interpretation. Since it is inciden-tal to the power to appoint, the question arose whether removal of officers was, like appointments, subject to Senate approval or whether any independent authority could be found that lodged this power exclusively with the executive. Though the First Congress decided to provide for department secretaries' removal by the president, the settlement was not definitive.

Tenure of Office Act of 1820.* The Senate exercised its power to reject proposed appointments infrequently, but its authority to do so was never questioned on those occasions when it was exercised.

Principles and practices governing appointment and removal were questioned and considerably modified after Jackson's election in 1828. The offering of offices as prizes necessary to consolidate political victory—a practice repeatedly advanced by early Republicans as one of the great dangers posed by a growing national government—was recognized and accepted by Jacksonian Democrats as a political creed.†

Jackson announced himself in favor of rotation in his first annual message,[6] ostensibly in order to recommend that Congress consider limiting the terms of office for many more positions.** In effect, he was defending his policy of not reappointing many officers who had served under former President John Quincy Adams, regardless of whether they merited reappointment, in order to replace them with partisans. Van Buren and Tyler followed suit.

The Congressional Challenge to Executive Appointments Congress's most serious problems with uninhibited executive appointment power were related to diplomatic and consular commitments that the executive could make by sending representatives abroad prior to House or Senate action. Such commitments carried high potential for misunderstandings and hostility. Because of slow methods of communication, agents and ministers in Europe's capitals often bore extraordinary responsibilities, not the least of which was to exercise care not to give affronts. Therefore, to hedge executive power, Congress delayed and questioned, often unsuccessfully, the need for numerous diplomatic missions during the Jacksonian era. For example, a House attempt to

---

*In the Tenure of Office Act of 1820 (Act of May 15, 1820, 3 Stat. 582) Congress greatly expanded the number of offices with terms of limited duration (four years)—allegedly to secure the advantages of rotation but thereby increasing the occasions for the exercise of legislative influence and power over appointments.

†Edward Everett is quoted in L. White, *The Jacksonians: A Study in Administrative History; 1829–1861,* at 317 (1954):

> What then ... binds the mass of the parties together. ... Indubitably the hope of office, and its honors and emoluments. The consequence is, that the moment any Administration is formed, every man out of office, and desirous of getting in, is arrayed against it. If the Administration then discards the principle of bestowing patronage on their political friends, they turn against themselves not only the expectants but the incumbents. ... For an Administration then to bestow its patronage, without distinction of party, is to court its own destruction.

**Jackson removed many officers, especially during the first eighteen months of his administration. The extent of his removals has been exaggerated. His removal rate (about 10 percent of all offices) was no greater than Jefferson's, but the absolute number of offices involved was much higher. White, *The Jacksonians* 308.

withhold payment to an officer legally appointed to fill a vacancy was defeated, largely due to James Buchanan's determination that the appointment of foreign ministers was peculiarly an executive province.[7] Unlike the House, however, which Democrats controlled throughout Jackson's terms in office, the Senate began rejecting appointments in December 1829.* Virginia's Littleton Tazewell severely challenged the recess appointment of three commissioners to Turkey to negotiate most-favored-nation treatment for American trade.[8] Tazewell admitted that "in an extreme case," the president might appoint to a new office "without any direct authority ... provided he laid such an appointment before the Senate afterwards." But the argument of "state necessity" was inapplicable to ordinary transactions, such as the business of the Turkish mission.[9] Tazewell noted that Jackson had not even followed the constitutional direction to submit permissible appointments made during recess to the Senate's next session.[10] Such unauthorized missions, Tazewell warned, could in some contexts provide "just cause of war," thereby enabling the president alone "by the mere exercise of this trifling power of dispatching a minister to a new State, ... to bring about that very state of things which the wise authors of that instrument certainly intended to commit to the discretion of Congress only."[11]

Loyal Jacksonians, however, argued that these "commissioners" were mere "agents";† required no senatorial confirmation; had "no fixed public diplomatic powers"; were not subject to impeachment; and were unable to commit the nation by treaty without the Senate's consent.[12] Jackson's long-time supporter Edward Livingston (La.) pointed out that the Constitution had not restricted the president's appointment of such agents.**[13] Others argued that Congress had provided a contingency

*Among the many rejected nominations were some of great prominence. On 25 January 1832, a tied Senate vote gave Vice-President Calhoun the opportunity to deny his rival Martin Van Buren the post of minister to Great Britain. 4 *Senate Executive Journal* 199. On 24 June 1834, Roger B. Taney was decisively rejected as secretary of the treasury (*id.* 427), and on 3 March 1835, his nomination as an associate justice of the Supreme Court was postponed "indefinitely." *Id.* 484. Only with the more cooperative Twenty-fourth Congress did Jackson manage to secure Taney's confirmation, this time as chief justice. *Id.* 520.

†During a similar debate in the Tyler administration, Thomas Hart Benton (Mo.) objected to appointment of a minister to China whom the president had called an "agent" and " ... thus, by imposing a false name upon the minister, defraud[ing] the Senate out of their control over the appointment." 12 *Congressional Globe* 391–92. Though an amendment to the bill funding the Chinese mission passed, stating that no agent was to be appointed without Senate consent (*id.* 392), Tyler circumvented it by appointing Caleb Cushing during a Senate recess, even though a newly created office could not be lawfully filled, asserted Benton, by a temporary appointment during a Senate recess. Benton, 2 *Thirty Years' View* 514 (1856) U.S. Const., art. II, §2.

**Some in accord with Livingston argued that the power of appointing confidential agents to confer about commerce was deducible from this duty imposed by the Constitution on the president. 7 *Register* 271.

fund to pay them and had granted the president "a sound discretion, both as to the individuals employed, and the amount of their salaries, whether $500 or $5,000 a year." If he exceeded the amount authorized, no payment could be made without Congress's approval.[14]

Tazewell rebutted that he had not challenged the executive's power to appoint "private agents," but noted that Jackson had signed formal appointment papers from the Department of State. On the other hand, Livingston, who had defended Jackson for declaring and enforcing martial law in New Orleans in 1814, regarded the risks of a unilateral power to appoint as natural and acceptable. The appointment power, like any other power, was subject to abuse:

> [T]here is no power confessedly given to the President, that is not liable to greater and more fatal abuse than this. You fear *war* from his sending a minister to one of those new Powers which are yet unacknowledged by the rest of the world; and yet you cannot deny that he has the power to receive a minister from one of those Powers, without consulting the Senate or House of Representatives. You will not trust him with sending a minister, lest he should involve you in a war; and yet you confess that he has the uncontrolled command of your army and your navy—instruments, if he wishes war, infinitely better fitted to produce it. . . . You are obliged to swallow the camel—why strain at the gnat?[15]

After prolonged battle, the final bill provided for payment of the commissioners. The bill in its final form represented the Twenty-first Congress's reluctant but expedient acquiescence in certain presidential prerogatives arising out of the appointing power, although its exact nature was not well defined.*

Jackson and his predecessors gave due weight to congressmen's views on appointments to offices within their respective states. Congressmen were systematically asked their views on prospective appointments to all inferior offices. Although they became persistent in pressing recommendations as the party system created pressures on them to obtain for their supporters the prizes of political victory, Jackson was equally insistent upon exercising his prerogative to make the final choice for all these appointments. The constitutional framework remained unchanged, but legislative influence grew so markedly that the doctrine of senatorial courtesy was emerging by the time of Abraham Lincoln's presidency.[16]

---

*The issues remained, as the history of future administrations attests. *See infra* pp. 89–90. For example, Jackson's allies conceded that Congress retained the power to disagree by rejecting the outcome of any negotiation and (where the contingency fund was inadequate to cover the cost) to deny the persons involved any salary for their efforts.

Martin Van Buren's appointments also received congressional scrutiny but escaped challenges that both houses made to John Tyler. By repeated rejections of his Cabinet nominations, the Senate signaled Tyler that it regarded participation in the selection of Cabinet members as a senatorial prerogative based on the Whig view of the Cabinet's parliamentary role.* Tyler widened the breach with his own party by insisting, as Jackson had done, that he alone possessed the final authority in both selection and removal of subordinates.†

Removal Authority: The Struggle for Control   The power to remove civilian, diplomatic, and military officials was often examined during the early national period from the standpoint of the warmaking authority of the branches. A large minority of legislators claimed that the removal power was granted to both the president and Senate by implication from the grant of the appointing power. The majority, however, recognized sole presidential authority to remove department heads and other subordinates—some on the ground that there was practical need for presidential authority over all policy advisers, others, because they found in the Constitution independent authority to lodge exclusive control in the executive.

Although presidents prior to Jackson exercised greater restraint in

---

*Tyler had been formally written out of the Whig party by a party manifesto issued in September 1841 after his veto of the Second Bank Bill (see infra p. 13; see also R. Morgan, A Whig Embattled: The Presidency under Tyler 157 (1954)), and had unquestionably become the victim of virulent partisanship. One commentator has termed Senate refusal to concur in his recess appointments for secretaries of war and navy "the most remarkable violation in our constitutional history of the custom that the President's choice of cabinet members is not ordinarily to be fettered by senatorial rejection." Id. 86. Tyler's opponents were primarily Whigs who believed that Jackson's use of the informal "Kitchen Cabinet" violated relationships intended by the Constitution. Whig conception of a proper Cabinet was an assembly of constitutional advisers—preferably drawn from outstanding party members in Congress—whose decisions would help to link the executive and legislative branches. 2 W. Goldsmith, The Growth of Presidential Power 660–61 (1974); W. Bagehot, The English Constitution 14–15 (1955); Morgan, A Whig Embattled 58–60.

†Tyler's own view of his authority was in turn influenced by the peculiar circumstances of his assumption of the presidency. In order to avert conflict, Tyler retained Harrison's Cabinet. Morgan, A Whig Embattled 57, 58, 61–62. But their expressions of equality with him at the first meeting caused him to tell the members that their function was solely to counsel him, not to have an equal vote in setting administration policy. W. Binkley, The President and Congress 113 (1962); O. Chitwood, John Tyler, Champion of the South 270 (1964). Whenever there was any serious difference between the president and party leaders in Congress over Whig programs, Tyler became aware that because he had succeeded an elected president, many congressmen regarded Harrison's Cabinet as a fuller expression of the popular will. G. Poage, Henry Clay and the Whig Party 36 (1936). Hence, Tyler was adamant in insisting that he was president in his own right—not merely an "acting" president simply because he was the first vice-president to succeed to the presidency. He took the oath of office, delivered an inaugural address, and formally declared his authority over the Cabinet, whose members, he declared, could resign if they disapproved his chieftainship. Morgan, A Whig Embattled 6–16.

removing officers,[17] all assumed that they possessed a unilateral power of removal and exercised it. Like their predecessors, Jackson and Tyler believed that this authority flowed from the executive power as well as from the duty to execute the laws. The decision of 1789,* moreover, had not been seriously questioned and provided the support of legislative interpretation and years of practice for their contentions. Contemporary legal commentators noted that a strong historical and theoretical case could be made for a legislative power to require Senate consent to removals, but they concluded that any such power had been surrendered in practice.†

Jackson's opponents insisted that the reasons for all removals other than cabinet officers be properly motivated. They pointed to Congress's constitutional right to create offices and to check executive conduct short of impeachment as establishing their authority to see those reasons.[18] Yet impeachment was hardly a realistic weapon when the president was leader of the legislature's majority party. "Was ever the miracle achieved," asked David Barton (Mo.), "of inducing a majority, in the springtide of success, to impeach themselves, in the person of their leader, for deeds of despotism done to accommodate themselves and their friends?"[19] The practical effect of such requests was simply to serve as a restraint on the president in the wanton use of office for political gain.[20] Livingston agreed that presidents could abuse the removal power if left unchecked—but weren't the president's powers in foreign and military affairs virtually uncontrollable?

> [I]t has been said that this power is liable to abuse; the President may remove from caprice, prejudice, or a worse motive. No doubt, sir, he may; he may do worse; he may embroil you with foreign nations, by his abuse of the

*This decision was based on an expansive view of executive power espoused by James Madison at the early point when both houses of Congress extensively debated and narrowly approved executive removal of high-ranking officers without Senate consent. See A. Sofaer, *War, Foreign Affairs and Constitutional Power: The Origins* 64 (1976) (hereinafter "Sofaer, *Origins*").

†Joseph Story concluded that existing practice enabled the president to dismiss officers unilaterally. But Congress could, he suggested, when creating "inferior offices," limit the president's power to dismiss by specifying that Senate consent was necessary. J. Story, *Commentaries on the Constitution of the United States* §§1530, 1538 (1833). Other commentators, such as Bayard and Upshur, likewise recognized that practice had settled on the question of the president's power to remove. J. Bayard, *A Brief Exposition of the Constitution of the United States* 114 (1833). Abel P. Upshur did not contest this view of executive practice, but he criticized at length the effects of executive removal, predicting that it would make the president too powerful, with all officers serving him rather than the nation. A. Upshur, *A Brief Inquiry into the True Nature and Character of Our Federal Government* ... 117–20 (1833). And both Rawle and Sergeant maintained that the president may dismiss officers without Senate consent. W. Rawle, *A View of the Constitution of the United States of America* (1825); Sergeant, *Being a View of the Practice* ... *and of Constitutional Points Decided* (1830).

treaty making power; he may cause your fortifications to be dismantled and your army to be dispersed in time of war; he may destroy your revenue by the appointment of corrupt men in the management of the treasury; but what argument can be drawn from this? That he has not the constitutional power? Certainly not.[21]

Furthermore, said Livingston, ". . . if the President might abuse the power of removal, may not the Senate abuse the control with which it is attempted to invest them [its members]? If he has enemies to displace, may not they have friends to keep in?" The Senate was no less likely than a president "to be actuated by political feelings," and, he was "inclined to believe, the warmth that has been expressed arises only from a feeling for political friends, who have lost their places. . . ."[22]

Further Senate concerns over executive removal policies* presaged growing sentiment to attempt some far-reaching remedy. The most institutionally significant challenge to Jackson's removal practice came during the second session of the Twenty-third Congress. In February 1835, John C. Calhoun proposed a select committee on executive patronage. The committee of six, including Calhoun, Daniel Webster, and Thomas Hart Benton, drafted a bill that included a provision amending the 1820 Tenure of Office Act in order to require the president to give his reasons for all removals even though they would implicitly be accepted as final.[23] Henry Clay then moved an amendment that required Senate concurrence on all removals of officers to whose appointments the Senate had consented. This amendment was derived from a series of resolutions that he had submitted during the first session.†[24] Webster recognized how radical a change Clay proposed. "The power of removal had been supposed to lie with the President since the discussion of 1789," he said. "It was then fully and ably discussed by the great lights

*These concerns included, among others, Ohio Senator Thomas Ewing's two resolutions in 1832 condemning removal for any reasons except "sufficient" cause or securing faithful execution of the laws. 8 *Register* 181, 182. They erupted also when Jackson's removal of a minor official appeared to be aimed at undermining a Senate investigation into the officer's conduct. 4 *Senate Executive Journal* 74, 158; 2 *Public Documents*, Doc. No. 22, pp. 23, 69–70; 4 *Public Documents*, Doc. No. 151, p. 65; 4 *Senate Executive Journal* 465–66; 3 *Messages and Papers* 1351–53.

†The first of Clay's four resolutions read:

1. *Resolved*, That the Constitution of the United States does not vest in the President power to remove, at his pleasure, officers under the Government of the United States, whose offices have been established by law.
2. *Resolved*, That, in all cases of offices created by law, the tenure of holding that is not prescribed by the Constitution, Congress is authorized by the Constitution to prescribe the tenure, terms, and conditions, on which they are to be holden.

S. Doc. No. 155, 23d Cong., 1st Sess., 10 *Register* 836. There was no action on these resolutions, but their influence was apparent in the appointment and work of the select committee.

that formed the constitution, and decided in favor of the Executive. . . ."
Hardly one to be cowed by the judgment of even the Framers, however,
Webster announced that he "believed the minority to have been right on
that occasion,"* and others agreed.[25] They reasoned similarly: The
executive had grown too powerful, and some check was needed; the
power to remove was at the heart of the president's capacity to control
the nation; and since so important a power had not been delegated
expressly, it should be treated as shared between the president and
Congress, as was the power to appoint and many other important
constitutional powers.†[26]

Clay's amendment was agreed to on 16 February by a vote of 26 to
15.[27] On 21 February the bill passed the Senate 31–16.[28] But the House
was far less sympathetic. The bill was introduced 21 February but never
debated** and subsequently disappeared in the press of other business.[29]

Though candidate William Henry Harrison took a lofty ground concerning removals of his predecessors, as president, Harrison faced the
dilemma of continuing Jackson's and Van Buren's men in office and
undermining Whig policy, or else abandoning his high principles and
replacing Jacksonians with Whig party faithful.[30] Thereafter, Tyler
removed officials†† and laid claim to executive authority to do so despite
Senate inquiry into his dismissal of both military and civilian personnel. Tyler, for example, restationed General Matthew Arbuckle from
Arkansas to Baton Rouge, Louisiana, where there were no federal
troops. Arkansas Democrat Ambrose Sevier supported Congress's right

---

*Webster succinctly expressed the minority opinion in the 1789 debate—that since the
power of removal was nowhere expressly delegated, it could be found, and exercised, only
by construction, as an incident of the appointment power. "And since the President could
not appoint without the consent of the Senate, so he ought not to remove without the
consent of the Senate. . . . " 2 *Congressional Globe* 251.

†Other supporters of Webster's position, like John Clayton (Natl. Rep. Del.) believed
that the senators in 1789 had based their opinion on the necessity of enabling the
executive to remove negligent, unfaithful officers. But, added Clayton, "That was the only
use they expected. . . ." Jackson's use of the power "to remove for party purposes . . . was
an abuse never apprehended. . . ." *Id*. 256. Congress, he concluded, possessed authority,
under its power to legislate to carry into effect the Constitution's provisions, to remove the
power from the president's hands, where the earlier legislative decision had placed it. *Id*.;
U.S. Const., art. I, §8, cl. 18.

**The heavily Democratic House leadership stated its views on the issue some two years
later in reporting on a proposed constitutional amendment to require congressional
regulation of removals, except as provided in the Constitution. It reiterated both the
constitutional and practical reasons for leaving the removal power where it had been
placed after the debate of 1789. H.R. Rep. No. 296, 24th Cong., 2d Sess. This committee
report was never debated.

††Tyler justified his own removals as necessary in case the active partisanship of the
officeholder prevented him from a "steady and impartial discharge of . . . official duties."
5 *Messages and Papers* 1941–42.

to inquire into the disgrace of a military officer with a request for Tyler's reasons. William Preston (S.C.), however, characterized inquiry into the commander-in-chief's military orders such as locating of officers as "unfit and inexpedient."[31] Sevier rejoined that there was a congressional right to know the reasons for every order given by every executive officer in public service, from the president down; a refusal from any officer except the president was just ground for impeachment.[32] Henry Clay, however, disagreed. Though he had supported Congress's right to participate in the removal process, he balked at inquiring into executive disposition of commanding officers, troops, or vessels in time of peace because Congress might then claim the same procedural practice in time of war, when the speed and secrecy of decision making were critical.[33] Other senators, Richard Bayard (Wh. Del.) and William C. Preston (Null. S.C.), asked if circumstances of removal were important to the discharge of legislative duties and powers, since it was not within Congress's province to explore the "secret recesses of the executive mind."[34] These arguments prevailed, and the Sevier resolution was tabled.

As noted above, Whigs under Tyler were finally convinced that some rotation in civilian office was necessary despite their pledges for reform.* It was apparent by 1841 that executive practice would continue further to define Congress's "decision of 1789" and that Congress was unlikely to circumscribe presidential exercise of removal power.

Planning Function

Under Jackson and his successors, Congress frequently sought executive assistance in planning—since it lacked the technical information and capacity to develop complex legislation such as military bills.† Both Jackson and Van Buren proposed important legislation, as their prede-

---

*A House select committee reported a bill requiring that persons to be removed be furnished with reasons and that all removals be publicly reported. The bill was never acted upon. *H.R. Jour.* 1171, 27th Cong., 2d Sess. Similar attempts to prescribe the method of removal from office were equally fruitless. *E.g., H.R. Jour.* 369–70, 28th Cong., 1st Sess.

†On 26 April 1830, the House adopted a resolution (85 to 44) asking the secretary of war to report whether the number of army officers could be reduced "without injury to the public service" and, if so, to provide "a plan for the most efficient organization of the army in conformity with the reduction proposed." 6 *Register* 819. During December 1832, a motion for the secretary of the treasury's "opinion" on what articles of foreign origin duties ought to be reduced and other matters failed to pass the Senate after at least one member (Samuel Smith) objected to calling for opinions instead of facts. 9 *Register* 815. Many other objections were raised, however, particularly that the matter was one that should initially be considered by the House, to which body the secretary had already proposed legislation. 9 *Register* 14–16.

cessors had done, such as Jackson's emergency request to use the army and navy to collect customs duties if judicial process were obstructed[35] and Van Buren's urging of Congress to augment the regular armed forces on the maritime frontiers, which had been stripped of men during the Seminole War.[36]

Tyler altered earlier practice by failing to draft legislation. Like Jackson, he vigorously used the veto* and, in effect, curtailed legislative participation in foreign policymaking. Tyler's reluctance to outline legislative programs† was reflected in his messages; almost none offered details or plans to implement the specific recommendations he made** concerning such matters as the slave trade, repair of fortifications, or providing for organization and discipline of the militia.[37] Nor did any Tyler supporter hold a key committee chairmanship, from which vantage point he might have drafted and introduced bills for the president.[38] However, Tyler substantively expanded the executive's ability to influence legislation, despite the fact that he was politically ostracized for refusing to approve bills that promoted internal improvements or that looked like an attempt to resuscitate the Bank of the United States.[39] He did so by adopting Jackson's pattern of vetoing legislation that he deemed unsound, inexpedient, and unconstitutional.††

Andrew Jackson's sharing in the legislative process would have been a difficult example for a chief executive coming after him to avoid. In more than one instance, Jackson clearly showed that he was unwilling

---

*Tyler used the veto ten times; Jackson, twelve. *See generally* volumes 3 and 4 of *Messages and Papers of the Presidents.* In the forty years prior to their administrations there had been only nine vetoes, three of which turned on public policy. E. Mason, *The Veto Power: Its Origin, Development and Function in the Government of the United States* 142–207 (1890) (hereinafter "Mason, *The Veto Power*").

†Only once, during the banking and economic policy dispute, did Tyler offer such a plan, drafted by Treasury Secretary Thomas Ewing, that proposed a "fiscal" rather than "national" bank with branching power in the states conditioned on their consent. 2 Goldsmith, *The Growth of Presidential Power* 664. He did offer, however, to send over plans drawn up by department heads if Congress wanted them. 5 *Messages and Papers* 1902.

**After experiencing the frustrations of dealing with the trial of Canadian citizen Alexander McLeod in New York State for allegedly violating the law of nations (*infra* p. 49), Tyler recommended to Congress that legislation be drafted that would transfer such cases from state to federal courts. 5 *Messages and Papers* 1927, 1928 (first annual message); *id.* 1956 (special message). Without official authority and unknown to Tyler, Secretary of State Webster sent Georgia Senator John Berrien the draft of such a bill. The draft came in response to Berrien's request, and Webster emphasized that Tyler had not seen it—it was a "private and wholly unofficial act." 2 G. Curtis, *The Life of Daniel Webster* 86 (1870).

††Presidents before the Jacksonian era used the veto sparingly and primarily for reasons of alleged unconstitutionality. *See generally* Mason, *The Veto Power.*

to permit either the Supreme Court* or Congress to govern his exercise of executive power. The principal vehicles for Jackson's expression of power included a more expanded use of the veto; nonenforcement of judicial decisions; and the issuance of a proclamation that had the effect of a military ultimatum.[40]

Jackson believed that when he approved legislation, he was performing a legislative function granted the executive under the Constitution. Roger Taney commented in a letter to Martin Van Buren[41] that Jackson had viewed his rights and duties when a bill was presented to him for signature "as purely legislative as that of a member of Congress, when he is called on to vote for or against a bill. . . ." He based his veto of recharter of the Bank of the United States† on the Jeffersonian idea that each department had the right to decide the meaning of the Constitution in cases submitted for its action.[42] Jackson also concluded that an executive's enforcement of any measure that he considered contrary to the Constitution would be an abuse of the trust of the people in their president.

His theory that the president alone might determine constitutionality of statutes was just as easily converted into a finding that a state had transgressed the Constitution. He followed his independent course of thinking in the nullification controversy, in which Jackson threatened force if the state of South Carolina refused to obey federal law. In asserting the right to challenge a South Carolina statute as contravening the U.S. Constitution, he swung away from an earlier states'-rights posture with respect to certain Supreme Court decisions. Both positions are harmonized, however, by his claim of right to determine constitutionality alone.

Three criteria in the president's thinking involved elements of war powers analogues he apparently was ready to apply in case the controversy over nullification broke out into hostilities. First, any legal precedent that the president considered a dangerous shackle on individual or personal liberty was not to be accepted or followed. Thus, if a state statute was dangerous to popular liberty, it should be invalidated

---

*An intense states' rights predilection aligned Jackson against the Supreme Court in its decisions in *Cherokee Nation v. Georgia*, 30 U.S. (5 Peters) 1 (1831), and *Worcester v. Georgia*, 31 U.S. (6 Peters) 515 (1832). Perhaps more important than his dislike of Indian self-government or John Marshall was his knowledge that in order to carry out the Court's mandate against the state of Georgia, federal armed intervention would have been unavoidable. Jackson feared that such intervention would alienate Georgia from the Union and cause her to ally herself with the South Carolina Nullifiers. *See infra* p. 28.

†In his bank veto message of 10 July 1832, Jackson stated that the president's final decision on constitutionality must not be permitted to be controlled by Congress or the Supreme Court. 3 *Messages and Papers* 1139, 1145. Apparently, he was thinking of earlier bank legislation that had been clearly approved by both Congress and the Supreme Court. *McCulloch v. Maryland*, 17 U.S. (4 Wheaton) 316 (1819).

by executive action. Second, any major national issue required instantaneous executive response. Finally, the president was the officer required to take necessary action, since he was the representative of all the people.

Tyler also developed the concept that the president should be the governmental decisionmaker. For example, he claimed that he was exercising the independent judgment in regard to all bills that was "plainly implied in the responsibility of approving them."[43] Under this interpretation, he found authority to veto on the ground that certain bills were unwise.[44]

Congress vigorously protested "executive legislation"; and House members in a select committee report complained that President Tyler was "not only separated from the legislative power, but made dependent and responsible to it."[45] This and other attempts to counter Tyler's expansive use of the veto power were unsuccessful. John Quincy Adams in the House and Henry Clay in the Senate each went so far as to champion fruitless motions to amend the Constitution in order to permit a veto override by a simple majority rather than a two-thirds vote.[46] Even an impeachment resolution was defeated, 127 to 84, by a lame-duck House.[47] The principal effect of Tyler's use of the veto was practical: it operated not only subsequently on enacted legislation but also prospectively—congressmen in the course of deliberations carefully weighed the possibilities of veto. Presidential ability either to eradicate or strongly influence legislation affecting executive war powers was thus substantially increased during the second quarter of the nineteenth century.

Delegation of Discretionary Authority

Presidents Jackson and Van Buren exercised discretionary authority granted by Congress in making decisions involving military affairs, foreign affairs, and appropriations.* Though he frequently acted on his own, Jackson often asked his attorneys general to advise him as to the scope of the delegations, and in most instances, they concurred that he possessed broad powers. In one foreign affairs emergency,† however, Jackson did not attain the breadth of discretion that Congress ultimately bestowed on Van Buren.

Jackson was frequently required to exercise military authority to remove intruders from U.S. lands. In one instance, Attorney General

---

*Tyler's administration gives no example of Congress granting broad delegations, undoubtedly because of the bitter division he suffered with his party.

†This crisis involved the French spoliation claims controversy with the French government, in which Jackson sought reprisal authority. *See infra* p. 17.

Roger Taney cited the Act of March 3, 1807,* as the basis of the military authority supporting the president's duty to enforce a treaty made with a foreign nation. In contravention of an 1832 treaty, white settlers had attempted to settle on lands ceded to the United States by the Creek Indians.[48] Taney concluded that "the President may employ such military force as he may judge necessary and proper to remove persons who may intrude . . . in respect to the land in question."†[49]

In cases where Congress failed to approve funds for various military activities, Jackson found implicit authority in existing statutes. For example, Attorney General John M. Berrien examined the basis of the president's discretionary authority regarding extra appropriations for the navy.[50] Berrien pointed out that the "President has . . . the duty of fitting out and directing the employment of the public armed vessels; and where Congress fails to provide for . . . the performance of this branch of public duty, he may make such allowances to officers acting in higher stations than those to which they were appointed by their warrants or commissions."[51] Berrien also indicated that increased pay and other allowances had been granted for a series of previous years by annual appropriations. Accordingly, he maintained that the president's power to make the increased allowances had already received the sanction of Congress.[52]

On another occasion, Jackson paid state and territorial militiamen without specific authority to do so, after he called them up to repel Indian attacks in Missouri, Michigan, and Indiana. Attorney General Taney found implied discretionary authority in an earlier statute. He informed the secretary of war that Jackson's act was justified since in its Act of June 15, 1832, Congress expressed the intent to provide for payment of militia properly called out when a state or territory was in "imminent danger" of invasion.[53]

However, Congress hedged Jackson with many restrictions on his exercise of both domestic** and military authority. For example, when

---

*This statute authorized the president to use federal troops to protect against domestic insurrection and invasion, and to execute the laws. Act of March 3, 1807, 2 Stat. 443. *See also* Act of February 28, 1795, 1 Stat. 424; and U.S. Const., art. I, §8.

†Attorney General Benjamin Butler in 1837 rendered a similar conclusion on parallel facts. 3 *Official Opinions of the Attorneys-General of the United States* 255, 257 (hereinafter "*Official Opinions of the Attorneys-General*").

**Discretionary authority over domestic affairs was often limited by specific contingencies. When Congress specifically expressed its determination that the state of Ohio must obligate itself to complete a canal on federal land if the U.S. government was to transfer the land to Ohio, Taney warned Jackson not to deed the land after he had received Ohio's express refusal to assume Congress's conditions. 2 *Official Opinions of the Attorneys-General* 550, 551, 552. Taney often stressed that the president must be guided by the restrictions and qualifications of the delegation. He advised Jackson that even when he

Seminole Indians reacted angrily to efforts to remove them beyond the Mississippi, as agreed by treaty, a House bill offered to provide $80,000 "for the expenses attending the repressing of hostilities commenced by the Seminole Indians in Florida." Congressman John Quincy Adams moved to add the words "under the direction of the Secretary of War, *conformably to law*" because the bill was "rather too indefinite." He particularly wanted to emphasize that the bill gave the president no new authority to raise an army. His amendment was accepted and became part of the bill as passed.[54]

Frustration of Attempt to Seek Reprisal Authority　In one instance, both houses refused to grant Jackson the reprisal authority—a power tantamount to war—since reprisals would have avenged the nation's honor but probably would have provoked war. They also denied him a large appropriation of funds to prepare the nation's defenses. Both these denials occurred during a crisis with France over unpaid claims.

In 1833, Jackson became increasingly impatient at France's refusal to pay liquidated damages due the United States and formally obligated by treaty between the two powers in 1831.* Finally, in December 1834, he recommended to Congress that the president be authorized to order "reprisals upon French property" if the debt was not paid.[55]

Representative Augustin Clayton (Ga.) called the president's proposal "nothing more or less than a declaration of *war* against France. . . . The field of battle would be the high seas; and there we had a commerce afloat to the value of two hundred millions. . . ."[56] The president's message clearly contained "a *menace*" to France, he said, and he proposed sending that portion of the message to the House's Committee on Foreign Affairs with instructions to report "that it is expedient to await the further action of the French Chambers. . . ."[57] To delegate the power of reprisal requested, said Nathaniel H. Claiborne, would "be virtually conferring upon the President unconstitutional power—a power to declare war."[58] But others insisted that "[r]eprisals, though sometimes leading to war, are more frequently the means of

---

was executing an Indian treaty, if its contents involved terms and conditions defined and regulated by Congress, he could not exercise his own interpretations of those terms. *Id.* 563, 564.

*Jackson's most interesting diplomatic effort involved this attempt to collect the claims owed Americans by France for seizures of vessels as a result of Napoleon's Berlin and Milan decrees of 1806–07. After years of negotiation, a French-American treaty was signed on 4 July 1831 under which France agreed to pay 25 million francs in six annual installments. The first installment was due on 2 February 1833, one year after the treaty was ratified, but nothing was paid by December 1834, when Jackson reviewed and criticized France's failure to fulfill its treaty obligations. 2 *Congressional Globe* 4.

preventing it" and that the "code of civilized nations expressly recognizes the right of reprisal in a nation from which a just debt is withheld, as a mode of redress compatible with the continuance of peace."[59] What other way, they asked, could the nation's honor be preserved? Clayton thereupon withdrew his proposal, apparently resigned to awaiting the committee's report.[60] The committee's four resolutions were tabled.* When Henry Clay's Senate Committee on Foreign Relations reported on the president's message,† it concluded it was "inexpedient" to authorize the president to make reprisals.[61]

This was not the end of the attempt to provide Jackson with discretionary reprisal authority. John Quincy Adams successfully moved a qualified resolution for copies of the correspondence, "not hitherto communicated," relating to France's noncompliance with the claims treaty of 4 July 1831.**[62]

Jackson sent only extracts of some dispatches, and examination of the materials he communicated reveals extensive deletions.[63] He refused to transmit the "residue" of the correspondence for the period that the House specified. Adams immediately moved to have the documents†† committed to the House Committee on Foreign Affairs with instructions to report on the problem "forthwith."[64] He had reported that Livingston's dispatches counseled energetic government action as the only way to convince the French legislature to appropriate funds for the claims, but also expressed grave doubts about passage of such funding.[65] As the opposition to his motion grew, however, Adams retreated. He insisted that he had no intention to dictate any particular response; and once the language in his motion instructing the committee to report had been struck, the message and documents were referred without further opposition.[66]

The House resolution as finally adopted called for the treaty of 4 July 1831 to be "maintained and its execution insisted on," but it struck the bold formulation "at all hazards," which Adams had urged, as involving a threat of war. The remaining two resolutions discharged the commit-

---

*They affirmed the justness of the claims but asserted that the United States should rely on France's sincerity and therefore should not "at this time" adopt any legislative measure. *Id.* 162–63.

†Clay told his colleagues that he hoped France would not react with passion to the president's message but would "prudent[ly]" wait to see if Congress seconded the message. *Id.* 95.

**Adams apparently believed that if his colleagues studied correspondence from France, they would realize hope for treaty compliance was lost and would vote the necessary authority.

††Additional letters received from Minister Livingston subsequent to the 6 February transmittal were sent the House on 25 February and were therefore in the committee's hands when it delivered its report on the twenty-seventh. 3 *Messages and Papers* 1354–61; 4 *Messages and Papers* 1362–64.

tee from further consideration of reprisals but urged instead that preparations be made to meet any emergency with France.*[67]

Discretionary Military Funding A major Senate debate developed during the French spoliation crisis over the extent to which Congress could or should provide large sums to be spent on military and naval preparations at the president's discretion. House members voted without objection to amend the bill providing appropriations for fortifications during 1835, to provide $3 million to be expended by the president, in the recess of Congress, "if he should deem it expedient, for the military and naval service, including fortifications, ordnance, etc."[68] The Senate balked, however, and voted down the amendment, 29 to 19.[69] Both Houses refused to recede from their positions, and a compromise appropriation of $300,000 for fortifications and $500,000 for the navy came after the House had lost its quorum.[70] Thus, no measures whatever were adopted in response to the House's policy resolution that steps should be taken "to meet any emergency growing out of our relations with France."

All agreed the nation's defenses badly needed attention, but both pro- and anti-Jackson forces sought to blame each other for the situation. Jackson's opponents regarded the discretion sought as unconstitutional and argued that he should have requested specific means for specific purposes.[71] Jacksonians claimed, on the other hand, that ample precedent existed to support the constitutionality of a lump sum appropriation for defense. For example, Felix Grundy (D. Tenn.) stated that funds provided by Congress in 1794 authorizing President Washington to use $1 million not otherwise appropriated for foreign relations were to be accounted for "as soon as may be."[72] He added that an Act of 1806 appropriating $2 million for any "extraordinary" expenses relating to foreign affairs conferred "greater and broader discretionary powers [on Jefferson] than were contained in the proposition for the three million appropriation."[73]

Hugh L. White (Tenn.) rebutted that the Washington and Jefferson precedents were distinguishable: Congress's expenditures for foreign relations were easier to evaluate than the president's spending on a large number of items for many fortifications. Moreover, the 1794 statute had received close committee and congressional scrutiny, which was not true of the $3 million amendment. In 1806, the purpose of the

---

*France's Chamber of Deputies appropriated funds to carry the treaty of 1831 into effect. But insulted by Jackson's reprisal message of December 1834, it added an amendment providing no monies were to be paid until it received satisfactory explanation of the president's message. The French Ministry recalled their minister at Washington and suspended all diplomatic intercourse with the United States. 12 *Register,* app. 4.

monies granted Jefferson was to induce Spain to sell Florida, and this object had been divulged in secret session.[74] The delegation sought for Jackson was "unknown at former periods and under former Executives," maintained New Jersey's Samuel L. Southard. It violated both the spirit and meaning of the constitutional prohibition that "No money shall be drawn from the treasury but in consequence of appropriations made by law" and enabled the president to raise armies and to make war.*[75] Kentucky Representative Benjamin Hardin (Wh.) agreed that $3 million should not be left to the president to use for war preparations "at his pleasure."[76]

The threat of war with France dissipated rapidly. On 8 February 1836, Jackson announced that Britain had offered to mediate the dispute with France and that he had accepted the offer. He suspended his recommendation of prohibiting the entry of French goods and vessels but twice repeated his request for defensive preparations.[77] Only after payments were received in May 1836[78] did Congress finally respond to Jackson's request for defensive preparations. Appropriations were increased for both the army and navy, and a fortification bill was adopted with a view to protecting not only the coast but also the western and Texas boundaries.[79] But Congress had not delegated authority in a timely fashion to meet what the president conceived to be an emergency. Its carefully limited delegation permitted the president only to transfer unexpended funds from one fortification to another for similar purposes.[80]

With the military threat regarding France at a standstill, Congress's attention moved to potentials for hostilities in both the northern and southern United States. Legislators met what they perceived to be a warlike threat of the British in Canada by gradually opening the door to enlarged presidential discretion to act before hostilities. For example, as Canadian rebel outbursts threatened to involve American sympathizers in an all-out revolt against the British government in Canada,[81] President Van Buren attempted to enforce existing laws in order to maintain strict neutrality along the extensive and unfortified U.S. boundary with Canada. However, late in December 1837, a daring

*There were several responses to Southard's claim that the president could cause, and might have caused, war by his request for reprisals. James Buchanan reiterated Jackson's belief that he was required to give Congress "all the information which may be necessary to enable them to act...." without fear of offending a foreign government. *Id.* 351. Tennessee's Grundy stated that everyone knew the power to declare war was vested exclusively in Congress and that the president could only propose and discuss war measures. Thus, if Jackson made war-like sounds or requests, they had no significance under the Constitution; "until some resolution or act has passed the Senate and House of Representatives, and been approved by the President, the interests of no foreign nation can be affected." *Id.* 313. There was no recorded disposition of Benton's resolution.

party of Canadian nationals seized an American vessel, the *Caroline,* and sank it, clearly violating U.S. sovereignty by seizing the boat on the American side of the Niagara River.* Van Buren immediately asked Congress for "full power" to prevent injuries on neighboring nations by unlawful acts of U.S. citizens,[82] and a Senate bill was introduced in response.[83]

Henry Clay agreed with the president's recommendation, stating that any citizen interference with a rebellion in a country with whom the United States was at peace should be met promptly. Other senators regretted that a "rigid" course of neutrality had not been pursued in certain cases.[84] The neutrality bill,† intended to prevent U.S. citizens from aiding revolution in Mexico, Texas, and Canada, was passed by the Senate on 18 January without controversy.[85] After energetic debate, a House bill passed on 2 March that retained the president's authority to use the army, navy, and militia for enforcement. It provided for prompt judicial review but did not criminalize infractions of the law.[86]

The Senate accepted the House's minor changes but placed a two-year limitation upon the life of the act. Senator Buchanan commented that the reason for the limitation was the many imperfections of the legislation, not the least of which was the vast power it lodged in the executive. Buchanan probably expressed the uneasiness of many legislators who saw no other way to handle emergencies than to delegate broad discretionary powers.[87]

Congress's delegation of discretion in 1839 was prompted by the threat of a war over the northeast boundary, and it became one of the broadest accorded any nineteenth century president. The bill gave Van Buren prospective authority to resist British attempts to secure her claims of "exclusive jurisdiction" in the disputed Aroostook River area.[88] Van Buren was clothed with power to resist any British attempt to enforce claims to disputed territory, using whatever regular military force that "he may deem it advisable to call into service."[89] In addition, if there were imminent danger of invasion "in his opinion," the president could ask for up to 50,000 volunteers[90] as well as for funds to complete warships under construction.[91] This authorization not only would have permitted Van Buren to go to war before the British attacked U.S. positions but allowed him the latitude to judge when Congress's stated

---

*See *infra* pp. 49–50. Only a week before the *Caroline* incident, the president had obtained broad authority to deploy vessels along the coastline of the two countries and to use either regular armed forces or militia to enforce it. Act of December 22, 1837, 5 Stat. 208.

†The bill provided for seizure and retention of vessels and/or arms and munitions that could be used to aid in hostilities of neighboring powers. No criminal penalties were imposed. 6 *Congressional Globe* 103.

contingencies had occurred. Congress's ratification of the 42,000 volunteers Lincoln called into action more than twenty years later[92] came after the South formally sundered its allegiance by starting military action.[93] Van Buren was granted the use of 50,000 volunteers before any attack on the United States had taken place.

John Tyler, by contrast, apparently received only routine delegations due to his estrangement from Congress. Yet study of the particular authorizations he received to spend for military purposes indicates that the purposes to which the moneys could be directed, and the accounting for their use, were not always restricted. For example, late in his administration Tyler obtained power to transfer up to $200,000 from unexpended appropriations for the naval service. This delegation provided no guidelines or contingencies for the president's decision to increase the navy and its armament.[94] In earlier administrations, provision of expanded military and naval force encouraged both their actual use as well as potential for use.[95] Tyler also was granted the use of a sum of $40,000 to establish commercial relations with China but did not have to report how it was used.*[96]

Such discretionary use of the contingency fund as well as unexpended appropriations created the regular practice by successive presidents of going outside appropriated funds to further foreign relations. While increased use of the practice may be traced to Tyler, President Fillmore was later able to capitalize on lenient account requirements in dispatching Matthew Perry to China.[97] Fillmore gave Perry great latitude in his instructions, including the use of force to implement them.† These executives, as did others before and since, knew that a successful mission would evoke little or no criticism of the means employed to accomplish its objectives.

Control of Information

Executive release of information that Congress felt it needed to conduct the public business was generally quickly accomplished during the decade of the 1830s. Legislative committees routinely sent inquiries to the executive with no suggestion of criticism but simply for assistance. The agencies responded with special, often technical reports, which legislators used to draft bills knowledgeably.[98] During John Tyler's administration, statutes required certain annual reports in the

---

*The accounting requirement of the Act of July 1, 1790, which created an annual $40,000 contingency fund for foreign intercourse, required the president to account for amounts spent, unless in his judgment he felt it advisable to note only total amounts. 1 Stat. 128, 129.

†*See, for example,* descriptions of Perry's instructions and the threats of force they engendered, *infra* pp. 111–115.

same way that earlier Congresses institutionalized a regular reporting system to present agency data.*

On the other hand, Congress did not effortlessly obtain all information it considered necessary. For instance, senators complained in 1836 that Jackson sought funds to defend against Indians in Florida and on the western and Texas borders without any background information. How has this war "burst forth"? asked Henry Clay concerning the Florida troubles. Daniel Webster said he was equally surprised "that no official communication had been made to Congress of the causes of the war."[99] Congress reluctantly passed the funding bills, aware there was no time to issue and receive information in the face of urgent circumstances.[100] The Senate did not wait for voluntary communications the following year. It twice demanded a report from the secretary of war on military operations in Florida,[101] but the president still did not reply.

Foreign Relations Requests and the "Public Interest" Proviso It was customary, since the beginning of the republic, for congressmen to include a proviso along with their requests for information from the president, specifying that he transmit only so much information as in his judgment might be disclosed without damage to the "public interest."[102] Congress usually omitted this kind of qualification from all but foreign affairs requests, and it was even eliminated from queries dealing with foreign relations if no reason existed to assume that sensitive material might be revealed.† Its absence, on the other hand, connoted an "unqualified" request; it implied that Congress's judgment concerning impairment of the public interest was at least equivalent to that of the president, so that Congress might also balance the public interest against the need for relevant facts before enacting particular legislation or making a recommendation.

Ongoing negotiations with foreign powers were traditionally considered as the most sensitive information. President Van Buren, in a break with the custom that executives rarely transmit the substance of negotiations in progress, satisfied Senator Henry Clay's qualified request that he report on ongoing negotiations with Mexico over unsatisfied claims of U.S. citizens.[103] He probably hoped that Congress would respond favorably to the hint in his message of 5 December 1837 that he be allowed to conduct reprisals against Mexico in order to break the

---

*For example, the Act of August 16, 1842, 5 Stat. 507, required an annual report of all modifications in the commercial systems of other nations, whether by treaties, duties, or other regulations. *See* H.R. Doc. No. 1, 23d Cong., 2d Sess., setting forth the reports to be made to Congress.

†Some congressional inquiries to Tyler concerning fairly routine foreign affairs matters were unqualified. *E.g.,* the Senate request for information relating to progress of the Mexican claims commission, 5 *Messages and Papers* 1909; 10 *Congressional Globe* 133.

deadlock over Mexican intransigeance.[104] On the other hand, President Jackson claimed that suspended negotiations were to be considered ongoing. He had mentioned a dispute with Buenos Aires* in his annual message for 1832 but sent no documents because diplomatic bargaining was underway.[105] John Quincy Adams asserted that since the negotiations had failed, Congress was entitled to information about the matter; it was Congress's duty to determine whether measures were necessary to protect American commerce. A qualified information request was adopted on 21 December but failed to change Jackson's policy.[106] He replied on 28 December that negotiations had not "broken off, but are suspended only until the arrival of a minister." This, he believed, "will justify the opinion I have formed, that it will not be consistent with the public interest to communicate the correspondence and instructions . . . so long as the negotiation shall be pending."[107] The House took no further action in either this case or an instance of parallel circumstances brought before President Tyler, who similarly refused to convey data on the ongoing negotiations with England over the Maine boundary controversy.†[108]

A demonstration of the propriety of qualifying requests for foreign affairs information took place early in Van Buren's administration. On 12 September 1837, John Quincy Adams proposed that the House adopt three requests for information. Two were limited to disclosures the "public interest will permit," but the third, which contained no reservation, demanded to know whether Texas had requested annexation and, if so, sought the American answer and "all other" related correspondence. Adams's first and second resolutions easily passed,[109] but the third evoked controversy.

Representative Adams made it clear that the language had been intentionally omitted. He reasoned that since annexation was a proposition that neither the president nor Congress could constitutionally entertain but that only the people were competent to effectuate, it was impossible for the president to find it incompatible with the public interest to answer.[110] Waddy Thompson (S.C.) contested Adams's constitutional argument, noting that Adams as secretary of state had favored accepting ceded territory by treaty.**[111]

---

*See the Falkland Islands incident, *infra* pp. 60–61.

†This was the only *refusal* of President Tyler to comply with a request for information directly involving a foreign relations matter. The House had passed a qualified resolution asking that the president communicate the state of negotiations between the United States and Great Britain in relation to the Maine boundary. 11 *Congressional Globe* 256. The president, in his reply five days later, availed himself of the traditional reservation. *Id.* 265. The message was received without comment.

**The House refused to adopt a resolution proposed by Adams declaring that the power of annexing an independent foreign state was reserved to the people. 5 *Congressional Globe* 42.

Others agreed that an unqualified request would be wholly improper since it suggested the House possessed a power reserved exclusively to the president. Yet it could not compel a disclosure that might prevent the government from concluding an "advantageous arrangement."[112] The House restored "the usual proviso,"[113] and the president complied on 3 October.[114]

Many Senate requests to learn facts regarding foreign relations matters that were to be acted on in the future were both enacted and answered in secret* and were usually unqualified. For example, when the Senate became concerned that the king of the Netherlands had been selected as arbitrator of the Maine boundary dispute, it passed an unqualified request for information on this designation giving the president the option to send his response to secret or open session of the Senate.[115] President Jackson complied in confidence, "omitting nothing that may enable the Senate to give the advice requested by my message of 7th December [1831]. . . ."†[116]

Adjustment of Claims with France A significant incident demonstrates clearly what Jackson considered to be the public interest and why the executive department believed that indefinite retention of certain information was occasionally necessary. When France refused to pay the Napoleonic spoliation claims,** Jackson's anger at the delay came to a head in his December 1834 message to Congress, in which he suggested that U.S. honor could be upheld by Congress's permitting him to conduct reprisals.[117] Congressmen repeatedly requested information concerning execution of the treaty and France's refusal to pay. Jackson responded promptly to the first series of requests.[118] However, he deleted portions of further transmittals†† and also withheld numerous

---

*The confidentiality of Senate executive proceedings had been the subject of a special committee report issued on 24 March 1830. The committee first recommended that presidential communications to the Senate in executive session be treated as secret only when the president specifically designated them "confidential." Also, it suggested that all proceedings in connection with treaties be considered confidential. It concluded that an injunction of secrecy be attached to any remarks or information touching the character or qualifications of both nominees and persons (other than those nominated) and that the individual votes of Senators amounted to an expression of opinion that also should be kept secret. On the other hand, the facts of nomination, confirmation, rejection, or the overall vote could all be made public. Finally, the committee recommended procedures for removing the injunction of secrecy, which could be achieved only by a resolution declaring "that object in positive terms." *Senate Executive Journal* 21st Cong., 1st Sess., 122–25. The Senate ordered this report printed, *id.* 78, but on 29 March 1830, it was tabled on the motion of Daniel Webster. *Id.* 85.

†The Senate's request should also be evaluated in light of Jackson's invitation for Senate advice. 3 *Messages and Papers* 1122.

**See R. McLemore, *Franco-American Diplomatic Relations, 1816–1836* (1941).

††This request and the presidential response are dealt with in detail *supra,* "Delegation of Discretionary Authority," pp. 17–18.

dispatches that he claimed could not be placed immediately before the House. However, Jackson added that he would transmit subsequent communications exhibiting "any change" in France's failure to pay the claims.[119] He did so voluntarily but withheld a note of French Minister Sérurier that he implied would be sent later.*[120]

The French were offended at Jackson's message to Congress, and Edward Livingston, U.S. minister to France, attempted to explain[121] why the French government should not consider the message either an affront or a "menace."† Secretary of State Forsyth termed Livingston's final communication before he left Paris "a sincere effort to remove ill-founded impressions."[122] But French Foreign Minister de Broglie in a private letter to A.J.Y. Pageot, French *chargé d'affaires* in Washington, indicated that the effect of publication of Livingston's correspondence really had been the reverse of what had been intended.[123] He wondered why the president could not simply explain that he had not intended to menace France by his address of December 1834 or, if he wished, make the point by simply declaring that Livingston's notes contained such a declaration.

Pageot made very effort to publicize de Broglie's letter as "the real dispositions of my Government to the President...."[124] He read the note to Secretary Forsyth, who refused to receive it.[125] Then he discussed it with Henry Clay as chairman of the Committee on Foreign Relations, who thereupon decided to bring the matter officially into the open.** On the Senate floor, Clay complained that since relations with France were rapidly approaching a crisis, Congress should be given all available information:

> According to the theory of our constitution, our diplomatic concerns with foreign countries are intrusted to the President of the United States, until

*Sérurier's note was communicated with other correspondence in response to a Senate resolution of 12 January 1836. Sérurier, in a letter to Secretary of State Forsyth on 23 February 1835, referred to the president's complaint about the "pretended non-fulfillment" of engagements made by France in the claims controversy. Forsyth protested that the qualifying expression, "pretended," conveyed the idea that the president knew that his complaint was in error but had alleged it nonetheless. He instructed Livingston to seek explanation or disavowal. 3 *Messages and Papers* 1354; 4 *Messages and Papers* 1427, 1429–31.

†Livingston said that the president should never alter his duty to report to Congress his view of foreign affairs out of fear of offending a foreign power. He denied the right of nations to examine each other's governmental acts and language, directed to coordinate branches of government, for the purpose of finding injury and demanding explanation. Foreign powers, he declared, could rightfully take exception to and demand explanation of one another's completed and official acts, but not those in an "inchoate state." Livingston to Foreign Minister Duke de Broglie, 25 April 1835, *id.* 1397–1400.

**The New York Times* as an administrative organ denied the charge that de Broglie's note had been "suppressed" in December 1834. McLemore, *Franco-American Diplomatic Relations* 191–92. But *The National Intelligencer* stated that the executive was engaged in conspiracy to withhold information from Congress.

they reach a certain point involving the question of peace or war, and then Congress is to determine on that momentous question. In other words, the President conducts our foreign intercourse; Congress alone can change that intercourse from a peaceable to a belligerent one. This right to decide the question of war carries along with it the right to know whatever has passed between our own Executive and the Government of any foreign Power.[126]

Clay knew that the material he sought was an "informal" communication. This, he claimed, made no difference. "No matter what may be the nature of the correspondence—whether official or not—whether formal or informal—Congress has the right to any and all information whatever which may be in the possession of the other branch of the Government."[127] The Senate adopted Clay's qualified requests to see officially what he already knew regarding French overtures and U.S. responses.[128]

On 15 January, President Jackson sent the Senate a message accompanying what purported to be a voluntary transmittal of relevant dispatches. He asserted that he was fulfilling his design of keeping Congress informed. But since de Broglie's note had sought private explanations of the reprisal message, Jackson did not send it, explaining that it had not officially been received by the U.S. government.* The president indicated, however, that certain dispatches in his transmittal conveyed the substance of de Broglie's note.[129] Jackson's maneuver thus undercut the impression Clay attempted to create that the executive was not receptive to opportunity for reconciliation with France and had suppressed information. Congress generally approved Jackson's communication, although some newspapers criticized rejection of the note as a discourtesy to France and a blundering error.[130]

Jackson did not actually reply to the Senate's resolution for information for three more days. On 18 January, he forwarded papers that when added to those accompanying his special message were "believed to contain all the information requested."[131]

There was no further critical reaction in Congress. The president had successfully maintained his right to determine the mode of foreign intercourse, even when relations were at a critical and dangerous state. He had defused charges that he had suppressed information and, indeed, had withheld nothing, since the note had not been received and he had "voluntarily" informed Congress of the circumstances of its rejection. The administration's emphasis immediately shifted to mediation and eventual swift resolution of the dispute. Through this war of etiquette, some precedents were established for presidential control of

---

*Although Forsyth alone made the decision to refuse the note, he had later conferred with Jackson, who agreed with Forsyth's reasoning. 4 *Messages and Papers* 1418–19.

information, and criteria for release of information to Congress were
clarified.

Military Affairs Requests   Congress's war power was the focus of controversy over the need for a discretionary clause in requests for instructions to military officers. Toward the end of the nullification crisis in
February 1833, Senator George Poindexter (Miss.) moved on 7 February
that the president be requested to supply copies of all military and naval
orders issued concerning forces in and near Charleston, South Carolina,
particularly any orders given to resist the "constituted authorities" of
South Carolina.[132] Since Poindexter had not included the "public interest" reservation, Felix Grundy, Jackson's ally from Tennessee, complained that the resolution failed to "leave to the President that
discretion, as to the extent and bearing of the information to be communicated. . . ." Grundy apparently knew that one of the orders covered
by the request involved a private arrangement between Jackson and
Joel Poinsett, which Jackson undoubtedly wanted to withhold from
Congress. Poinsett, then a private citizen acting as Jackson's confidential agent in Charleston, had proposed to the president that local
Unionists be armed as a *posse comitatus* to enforce federal law, and
Jackson had authorized Poinsett to requisition up to 500 muskets and
100 rifles. This agreement would have been revealed if the paragraph
authorizing arms requisition were given the Senate. Jackson seems to
have concluded that release of these facts would have caused Poinsett
considerable inconvenience if not physical harm.*

Grundy justified adding a discretionary clause and moved "to put it in
the power of the Executive, without being subject to the imputation of
refusing to comply with a request of the Senate, to withhold any thing
connected with the papers called for which might involve private
individuals." He was confident that all military orders would be produced and that the Senate would be satisfied.[133]

Poindexter, however, treated Grundy's proposed amendment as an
attempt to evade disclosure generally. He denied the proposition that in
time of peace, "it had been usual, or was proper, to make any exception
whatever in calls upon the Executive" for orders to army or navy
officers. Exceptions were authorized only during diplomatic negotiations or to avoid warning an enemy of military actions. At present,
Poindexter concluded, the nation was at peace, and the Senate had the
right to know why troops had been assembled in and near South
Carolina and what they were to do. Grundy's opposition, he said,
"seemed to be indicative of a disposition to shroud in secrecy the

*See infra, "Military Authorizations," p. 50.

movements of the Executive authority. . . ." If the amendment were made, "he should take the liberty, in future discussion, of drawing his own inference as to the nature of the orders which the gentleman dare not call for."[134]

Grundy responded on 9 February. "It had been said," he noted, "that the President could withhold any information he chose, without the qualification proposed to be given to the resolution." And the president, he agreed, "was not afraid of responsibility." Yet, he argued, the president should be asked for information carefully, so as "not to seem to require from him more than he ought to communicate." And what is it "that we wish not to be communicated? Only . . . the names of private individuals, if any such are connected with the information. . . . There was no necessity for any such disclosure. Whatever the Executive had done, he would communicate; and why he had done it." Grundy wanted only "to prevent private individuals from being compromitted. . . . Was not party excitement already high enough in South Carolina? . . . Did the gentleman want to add fuel to the flame?"[135]

Jackson prepared to communicate the requested material. On 11 February, Grundy suddenly announced that he would withdraw his proposed amendment, "[h]oping that the evils which he had originally feared from the adoption of the resolution without amendment might not happen. . . ." Poindexter's resolution was thereupon agreed to without qualification.[136] And on 12 February, Jackson sent copies of all the military orders involved. "No order has at any time been given," he added carefully, "in any manner inconsistent therewith. There is a part, however, of the letter of the Secretary of War, dated December 3rd, 1832, omitted, which, being conditional in its character, and not relating to the operations of the troops, it is deemed improper, in the present state of service, to communicate."[137]

The paragraph withheld was that authorizing Poinsett to requisition firearms. Jackson's explanation was, consequently, misleading. The order withheld was not consistent with the orders revealed to the Senate, since the private individuals received different instructions. Furthermore, there was nothing really "conditional" in the omitted instruction; Poinsett had only to ask for the arms to receive them. Finally, the fact that the secret authorization did not relate "to the operations of the troops" was precisely its significance. The very question it would have raised was whether the president could use private individuals to put down state authority in a situation where doubt existed as to his right to use the armed forces.

Grundy had accurately assessed the reason Jackson withheld his order to Poinsett. Jackson wished to avoid "add[ing] fuel to the flame" while a settlement of the crisis was being worked out in Congress; therefore, it was critical to prevent the revelation of a controversial action of his own. After he transmitted the announcement that he had withheld material despite the absence of a clause expressly permitting him to do so, no further comment or action occurred concerning the issue.

House requests for information concerning the past conduct of military officers and their orders were usually unqualified and adopted without controversy. When a request related to ongoing matters, the reservation was included. For example, among its resolutions of 4 October 1837, one desired all documents and correspondence relating to the recall of General Winfield Scott, who had commanded American forces against the Seminoles in Florida. A second sought the proceedings of a court of inquiry into Scott's conduct and the decisions rendered by Jackson and Van Buren. A third requested the orders issued Scott concerning the terms that he was authorized to offer the enemy. The fourth resolution, however, requested orders issued to, and correspondence with, the then-present commander, General Jessup, and was limited to material "not injurious to the public service to communicate."[138] Van Buren, however, refused to respond to any of them, despite the fact that these requests had been made twice previously.*[139] The House thus demonstrated its belief that it had the right to seek information relating to the past conduct of military affairs but was unwilling generally to risk confrontation with the president by asking for the disclosure of ongoing military plans.

When legislators perceived that there existed a military threat to the peace and safety of the United States, they made an effort to elicit facts from the executive concerning military preparedness. For example, Martin Van Buren's peace effort in the controversy with Britain over the Maine boundary[140] spurred requests for information that some believed implied congressional dissatisfaction with executive action. Maine Senator John Ruggles, for example, desired to know what precautions had been taken under an 1839 act to remove the British from disputed territory and to establish military posts.[141] Although opponents of his qualified resolution said it implied censure of the president, Ruggles ably defended it as not being so intended, and the measure was adopted.[142] President Van Buren was fully responsive to both the Senate and the equally critical House requests for facts on the northeastern defense system.[143]

---

*There is no record of reply to these inquiries. The sole reply to this comprehensive House request was transmission of proceedings of a court of inquiry into Brigadier General John Wool's conduct in Cherokee country, proposed by Representative Benjamin Howard (Md.). 4 *Messages and Papers* 1589.

Executive Withholding and Congressional Censure John Tyler's assertion of power to withhold information was perhaps the strongest made
during the federal government's first sixty-five years. Controversy
erupted in the summer of 1842 over Tyler's efforts to control, in the
public interest, the flow of information.

In May 1842, the House sought to see the field reports of Lieutenant
Colonel Ethan Allen Hitchcock to Secretary of War John C. Spencer on
the subject of the status of the Cherokee Indians, as well as a report
alleging land fraud on the part of Indian agents.[144] Spencer refused to
send the material because some reports related to ongoing negotiations,
while the land fraud report dealt with unverified criminal charges.[145]
Congressmen James Cooper (Wh. Pa.) and John Quincy Adams then led
the fight to require President Tyler to release this information. Cooper
asserted the House's prerogative as "the grand inquest of the nation" to
deal evenhandedly with information.[146] Adams agreed: If the House
lacked knowledge that the laws were in fact being executed, it could not
perceive abuses or tend to correct them through the impeachment
process. Since negotiations with Indians led, in Adams's view, to laws
being imposed on them, it could not be maintained that the negotiations
were subject to harmful reversal or interruption if their substance were
revealed to Congress.[147]

Arguing from the administration's standpoint, Caleb Cushing placed
the issue of releasing the report in its largest perspective: did the House
have an absolute right to demand production of all papers? Could the
president thereupon absolutely refuse "according to reasons of state
known only to himself"?[148] He denied that the House possessed such a
right since the branches' powers were correlative; thus, it could not
compel the president to communicate or do anything the Constitution
did not "warrant." House members could easily interrogate individuals,
should the president choose not to communicate what he possessed.[149]

Despite Cushing's opposition, the House Committee on Indian Affairs
insisted it could demand the requested materials.*[150] Tyler did not
respond for nearly eight months, demonstrating an assertiveness not

---

*The committee report claimed that the House possessed implied power to secure all
information needed to create legislation. *H.R. Jour.* 916–19, 27th Cong., 2d Sess. The
report contained a series of "condemnatory" resolutions, which the House overwhelmingly approved. 11 *Congressional Globe* 810, 888–89. Appraisal of these resolutions must
take into account the hostility in Congress against Tyler for his vetoes of two bank bills in
the fall of 1841 and two tariff measures on 29 June and 9 August 1842. 5 *Messages and
Papers* 1916, 1921, 2033, 2036. John Quincy Adams announced on 10 August that Tyler's
latest veto had placed the executive and legislative branches "in a state of civil war." 11
Congressional Globe 871.

unlike Andrew Jackson's. A president without party, he had only his view of the Constitution to guide him. Since negotiations were concluded, he sent Colonel Hitchcock's reports because the reason for withholding no longer existed. The president omitted character evaluations of personnel, however, and data that concerned propositions still to come from the Indians. Tyler also sent the report concerning possible fraud among Indian agents, again asserting that he did so because the earlier reasons for withholding were no longer operative, such as witnesses' unavailability. Nonetheless, he asked the House to treat it as confidential and postpone publication until a committee determined how to handle the charges made against individuals.*

Tyler declared that he did not concur with Congress's premise that it was entitled to all information at the president's disposal; indeed, he maintained, the president's own evaluation of the conduct of departmental officials was solely an executive function.[151] He referred the House to many instances in which presidents had exercised discretion to decline information to its members, among them an example of James Monroe's failure to transmit correspondence relating to U.S. military activities in the Pacific[†] on the ground that it might "excite prejudices."[152] Relying on various evidential principles, Tyler concluded by saying that there were occasions in which "the general authority to compel testimony must give way ... to the paramount rights of individuals or of the Government," citing as examples the confidential nature of clients' professional relationships to their advisers and the protection of the names of those who communicate state information to the government.[153] But the committee to which Tyler's message was referred disagreed. It claimed that release of information to Congress vastly differed from disclosure of material to a jury, with its attendant publicity. Information sent to Congress was transmitted to a parlia-

---

*The president had no further funds to conduct any investigation on his own (see infra, 37 "Presidential Investigative Authority"), so he placed the entire matter of determining answers to incomplete areas of investigation in Congress's hands.

†The committee did not accept Tyler's example of Monroe's refusal as satisfactory grounds for withholding, since it claimed that in that case, Congress, by including the qualifying clause, had itself merely continued a long-standing practice of investing the president with a right to refuse to convey information by permitting him to judge what materials not to release in the public interest. Because Monroe had exercised discretion in a case where it had been conferred, the committee concluded, it was not to be assumed he would have exercised it in situations in which it was not conferred. H.R. Rep. No. 271, pp. 13–14, 27th Cong., 3d Sess. In an earlier argument on the same subject, Daniel Webster had similarly insisted that the discretionary clause conferred real discretion and was not mere formality or courtesy. Others differed, stating that the president had a constitutional duty to withhold information, which he must exercise even if the request were "wholly unqualified." See Sofaer, Origins 245–46; 2 Register 1212–78, passim.

mentary tribunal, charged with the public welfare. Perhaps in issues between private individuals the public's safety could require suppression of information, the committee concluded, but abuses in an executive administration required exposure.[154] Beyond filing this report, however, Congress made no further comment.

At times, President Tyler sent Congress extracts of diplomatic correspondence from which he had excised certain portions without the physical notation of an omission and without informing the legislature, despite the general executive practice of indicating omissions.* There is nothing in the record, however, to suggest that Congress was aware of Tyler's deletions.

The sole example of Congress's recording a resolution of censure against a president who refused to transmit information occurred early in 1834 when the Senate passed Henry Clay's motion to censure both Andrew Jackson and Secretary of the Treasury Roger B. Taney.[155] The cause of this stern rebuke was Jackson's successful assertion of the power to deny Congress access to the content of Cabinet discussions. Partisan congressmen, however, were reacting more generally against President Jackson's determination to destroy the Bank of the United States.

The constitutional questions of the bank war concerned an entirely domestic issue, but in their application they represented precedents for arguments and conduct that were followed by subsequent presidents in foreign and military affairs. Undoubtedly, Jackson's veto of the bank recharter bill added significantly to presidential power. None before him had exercised ultimate control over the secretary of the treasury on a matter vested by Congress in the secretary's discretion. Jackson was

---

*For example, Tyler sent the Senate a dispatch from Waddy Thompson, U.S. minister to Mexico, without stating that a lengthy argument favoring the acquisition of California had been omitted. Thompson to Webster, 29 April 1842, National Archives Microfilm, Department of State, *Dispatches from the United States Ministers to Mexico, 1823–1907*, M97, roll 11; *cf.* manuscript of S. Doc. No. 325, 27th Cong., 2d Sess. 80 leaves, RG 46, National Archives (the message and papers sent 15 June 1842, in response to the Senate request of 29 March). *See* 5 *Messages and Papers* 2010.

Another instance of an unnoted deletion occurred when portions of a report were cut before it was sent to Congress. Two naval commanders recommended that both Britain and the United States be permitted limited search of suspicious vessels "to determine [their] national character," as a means of suppressing the slave trade. Both Tyler and Secretary of State Webster knew, however, that Congress would protest such a suggestion. Report of Navy Commanders Charles Bell and James Paine, 10 May 1842, in 4 *Treaties and Other International Acts of the United States of America, 1776–1863*, at 440–41 (1931–48) (hereinafter *"Treaties"*). The executive sent the deleted passage to the British, indicating it had been erased from the report sent to Congress. British Minister Ashburton, in deference to the fact that the executive department had stricken the information, did not publish it. It is not published in Department of State records. *Id.* 440.

unilaterally assuming control of the nation's treasury,* believing that the people's having placed him in the highest office in the land constituted full authorization of his conduct. According to this president, Congress did not possess the sole power of the purse.

Jackson implemented his plans for removing the treasury deposits. He named William J. Duane to the treasury in June 1833, assuming that Duane's opposition to the bank would lead him to cooperate in authorizing removal at the proper time. Duane promised to resign in the event he could not support removal.

The proper time, as far as Jackson was concerned, was before Congress would reconvene in December because it was unlikely to authorize removal of the deposits—the House having expressly found them safe as recently as 2 March 1833.[156]

On 18 September, Jackson read to the Cabinet a long paper, prepared with the assistance of Attorney General Taney and developing in detail the reasons for removing the deposits. He saw no need to consult Congress, since "the power of the Secretary of the Treasury over the deposits is unqualified."[157] The law required that the secretary give his reasons for removal to Congress, but this, to Jackson, was "no limitation" on the secretary's discretion. Although Duane had not yet agreed to order the removal, Jackson nevertheless set 1 October as the date to order the shift of government funds. Without waiting for Duane to state his opinion, Jackson ordered his paper on removal to be published in the administration newspaper, *The Washington Globe.*[158] Since Duane refused to order removal or to resign, Jackson dismissed him on 23 September and replaced him the next day with Taney. On 26 September Taney ordered removal of the deposits effective 1 October.[159]

Congress reconvened on 6 December 1833. Jackson announced the removal of deposits, and Taney sent the required report giving his reasons. On 10 December, Clay proposed an unqualified resolution asking the president whether the paper concerning removal, "alleged to have been published [in *The Washington Globe*] by his authority, be genuine or not; and if it be genuine, that he also be requested to lay a copy of said paper before the Senate."[160] "If the President had merely read the paper to his Cabinet, without promulgating it, it might be a doubtful matter whether we had the right to call for its communication to us," Clay conceded. "But we have certainly the right to know from the

---

*Jackson's stance demonstrated that he believed economic democracy was the harbinger of political and social democracy. The bank bill veto in 1832 advanced the argument that each public official must support the Constitution as he understood it, not as the Supreme Court interpreted it. With four years to run on the 1816 charter, he then withdrew federal deposits until the bank was rechartered as a state bank. G. Van Deusen, *The Jacksonian Era, 1828–1848*, 80–87 (1959).

highest source whether the paper is genuine or not, and if it is, . . . to be put in possession of it."[161]

Senator John Forsyth (Va.) disagreed, since the paper was addressed to the president's confidential advisers. Why "depart from the rules which have heretofore governed us in relation to such papers, in order to obtain a paper which we do not want?" If the House needed the document as evidence of the president's "criminality," the Senate would see the original if he were placed on trial. But otherwise the Senate had access to it from the newspapers and had no proper use for it in any event.[162] Thomas Hart Benton (D. Mo.) concurred with Forsyth. If the right to such documents existed merely because they were overheard and published, he asked, "where shall we stop?" Benton saw no objection to treating the published paper as genuine and objected to the request, "not to protect the President, but to protect ourselves from the reproach of making a demand upon a coordinate branch of the Government which we had no right to make."[163]

Others such as George Poindexter (D. Miss.) and Daniel Webster viewed the paper as one of great importance. Webster did not regard it "in the nature of a private letter, but rather as a public document, and designed for the public eye . . . , like a proclamation." Poindexter claimed it was the Senate's responsibility to consider whether the president should have ultimate control of the purse, and Clay saw it "the duty of Congress to look into the source of the removal of the deposits. . . ."[164]

At Webster's suggestion, the resolution was modified to omit the question whether the published version was genuine and to ask simply for a copy of the paper. The Senate voted 23 to 17 in favor of the resolution as modified.[165]

Jackson replied the very next day, 12 December.[166] "I have yet to learn," he wrote, "under what constitutional authority that branch of the legislature has a right to require of one an account of any communication, either verbally or in writing, made to the heads of departments, acting as a cabinet council." The paper was published in order, he explained, to inform the people of the grounds of his conduct. He was willing "upon all *proper* occasions" to give Congress any information "useful in the execution of the appropriate duties confided to them." Sworn to uphold the rights of the executive, "I am constrained . . . by a proper sense of my own self-respect, and of the rights secured by the Constitution to the Executive branch of the Government, to decline a compliance with your request."[167]

Clay asserted immediately that Jackson's denial entitled him to assume that the published version was accurate—that "the President don't deny the genuineness of the paper."[168] But Felix Grundy (Tenn.)

reminded Clay that both "friends and enemies" would have been willing all along to concede the published paper was accurate and that the call had been entirely unnecessary. He moved to table the president's reply, which was agreed to.[169]

Jackson rested his refusal to provide the information on the president's absolute right to control Cabinet communications, even when they were published. The refusal's value as precedent, however, is limited to that category of material.

On 19 December, Clay demanded that Taney furnish the Senate additional information, particularly the terms on which state banks would perform services formerly performed by the Bank of the United States. He pronounced Taney's response[170] to be an "argument" instead of information because Taney claimed that Clay had demanded materials previously transmitted to Congress and that therefore the information could be found among official printed documents.* The enraged senator from Kentucky then introduced resolutions on 26 December 1833 condemning President Jackson's assumption of an extraordinary power over the treasury not granted by the Constitution (by dismissing secretaries who would not perform "contrary to their sense of duty") and also censuring Taney.[171] After eight weeks of debate the Senate adopted Clay's amended resolutions—the second of which (adopted by a vote of 26 to 20) read:

> Resolved, that the President, in the late Executive proceedings in relation to the public revenue, has assumed upon himself authority and power not conferred by the Constitution and laws, but in derogation of both.†[172]

The Senate also refused to acknowledge a right in the president to protest** any of its proceedings and adopted two resolutions asserting that in his protestation Andrew Jackson was exerting executive power inconsistent with the U.S. Constitution.[173] Only in 1837 did senators agree that condemnation of the president by resolution did not comport with constitutional practice. In support of Thomas Hart Benton's resolu-

---

*Subsequent to the uproar in the first session of the Twenty-third Congress over lack of information on the Bank of the United States, on 11 December 1834, the House requested the secretary of the treasury to report upon his correspondence regarding bankdrafts. 2 *Congressional Globe* 29. Compliance took place on the following day (*id.* 33–36), with a second installment two weeks afterward. *Id.* 78. On 16 December 1834, the House required the secretary to report on the official proceedings of the directors of the Bank of the United States (*id.* 43), and it received a response on 25 December 1834. *Id.* 8C.

†The Senate also adopted Clay's other resolution asserting Secretary Taney's reasons for removing the deposits were insufficient. 1 *Congressional Globe* 271.

**On 17 April 1834, President Jackson sent a "Protest" to the Senate regarding the Clay resolution charging him with exercising unconstitutional power. *Id.* 311.

tion to expunge the censure resolution of 1834 from the Senate record, Buchanan of Pennsylvania claimed the president stood judged without trial:

> Until the accused is brought before us by the House, it is a manifest violation of our solemn duty to condemn him by a resolution.[174]

On 16 January 1837, Senators voted 24 to 19 to expunge the censure of 1834.

Power to Investigate   It was predictable during the Jackson era that Congress would seek to probe more deeply into the nature of executive activities than mere reliance on answers to requests for information would provide. Having developed no techniques to coerce executive compliance, legislators often found presidential refusals to inform to be an embarrassment as well as an impediment to intelligent lawmaking.[175] As a result, investigations were used more widely than in prior administrations by the Jackson and Tyler Congresses, which desired to examine the propriety and constitutionality of particular demonstrations of executive power.* President Tyler also claimed an executive right to initiate investigations and to withhold the results from Congress, although legislative reaction to his assumption did not strengthen this position for succeeding presidents.

Presidential Investigative Authority   When the House inquired in 1842[176] why Tyler had unilaterally instituted a commission to investigate certain "concerns" regarding the management of the New York Custom House, the president replied that he had thus acted because of his power to faithfully execute the law. He explained that he also possessed a broad power to determine what measures he should recommend to Congress for its consideration.†[177] But he was careful to claim that it was not his duty to forward the commission's reports no matter what they said.[178]

---

*The investigation of the bank by a select committee in 1832 was controlled by antibank forces who used it as a device to attack bank officials, depositors, and customers. Their activities were criticized in detail by John Quincy Adams in a lengthy minority report that argued that the committee had exceeded its authority and had violated the privacy and constitutional rights of depositors and witnesses. Adams's report was ignored, and while the majority's recommendation against rechartering the bank was rejected, their report contributed to the overall Jacksonian strategy to undermine the bank among the people. *See generally* J. Macoll, "The Second Bank of the United States: 1832," in A. Schlesinger, Jr. and R. Bruns, *Congress Investigates* 591–684 (1975).

†Tyler also referred to an Act of 1799 providing for collectors of customs to submit their records to persons properly appointed, as evidence that Congress expected the executive to investigate abuses. 5 *Messages and Papers* 1952–53.

The House, however, directed Tyler to send the full report,[179] fearing that he might submit only selected portions.[180] Tyler then forwarded all of it without making any recommendations for reforms.[181]

Many members wanted to explore further the substantive issue of presidential investigatory power. Kentucky's Joseph Underwood condemned presidential appointment of agents at public expense to investigate abuses without statutory authority.[182] Massachusetts Congressman Caleb Cushing undertook to defend Tyler's claimed investigating authority. He argued that the constitutional provision for execution of the laws did not prescribe the manner in which duties were to be performed; therefore, the president might lawfully appoint agents to an investigating commission—as virtually every prior administration had done—and Congress was bound to compensate them.*[183] After John Quincy Adams argued that the House had no right to determine the constitutional powers of the president, his effort to limit it was finally tabled, 96 to 76.[184]

Congress was reluctant to vote that the president had acted unconstitutionally, but it did attempt to control his various independent investigations through the power of the purse. It inserted a proviso in an appropriation bill (H. R. 539) forbidding payment of agents or commissioners appointed by the president to conduct investigations until Congress specifically appropriated the funds for such payments. The bill passed, with Attorney General John Nelson characterizing it as enabling Congress to "paralyze a function which it is not competent to destroy."[185]

Congressional Investigative Authority   The House greatly expanded its power of investigation during this period. For example, when Jackson in his final message to Congress in 1836 described the executive departments in glowing terms, Representative Henry A. Wise (D. Va.) proposed a massive investigation of them. When the various parts of the President's message were being referred to relevant committees, Wise suggested that the condition, ability, and integrity of the executive departments be examined by a select committee of nine members with power to send for persons and papers and with an assignment that corresponded exactly with every claim of "ability and integrity" Jack-

---

*For example, Jackson had appointed a commission to investigate the navy, and Van Buren selected special agents to examine and report on both the land and post offices. Their exercise of this authority, moreover, had not been limited to studying abuses, as when Jackson sent an agent to Texas to gather information, and Van Buren dispatched a man abroad to evaluate European armies, discipline, and armaments. 4 *Congressional Globe* 481, 482.

son made for his administration.[186] Although members such as Dutee Pearce (D. R.I.) suggested that so sweeping an inquiry would violate the search-and-seizure provision of the fourth amendment,[187] few could bring themselves to vote against it. As Edward Hannegan (D. Ind.) asserted, the House had power to investigate fully and freely; "the contents of the Executive departments were literally the property of Congress, by whose act, as the agent of the people, everything they contained could be thrown open, and exposed to public investigation."[188] After an amendment to limit the investigation's scope was pushed aside, the House voted 165 to 9 on 17 January 1837 to form the select committee.[189]

The Florida War Constitutional and political ramifications of investigating an ongoing war developed in the debate that followed a proposal by Representative Wise (Va.) on 19 September 1837 that the House investigate the war in Florida. Wise moved that a select committee examine the causes of the war, the delay and costs of its prosecution, and "the manner of its conduct. . . ." The committee was to have power to send for persons and papers; it was also to sit during recess and report to the next session of Congress. He explained that he "never would hesitate, when a war was raging, to make the necessary appropriations to carry it on" and therefore had supported the administration's request for an additional $1.6 million. But such spending, and the alleged incompetence of Secretary of War Lewis Cass, required a full inquiry.*[190]

Opponents of the inquiry objected that investigation of the conduct of a war closely interfered with the executive's authority. Representative James McKay (D. N.C.) noted that the war was already being investigated by the Committee on Indian Affairs and by presidentially appointed commissioners. General Jessup, moreover, was organizing a new campaign, with which it "would certainly be improper for the House to interfere . . ." before it was implemented. "It would be interfering with the legitimate duties of the Executive to send an investigating committee, with power to send for persons and papers, into Florida. . . ." McKay moved to postpone the motion to the next session.[191] No explicit reply to his argument was recorded, but the motion to investigate seems not to have been adopted.[192]

The desired effect of threatened investigations was apparently

---

*Some members objected to the assumption that the war's length and cost were due to its ineffective conduct, contending that these consequences were the result of having to fight an Indian war in jungle swamps. *Id.* 46, 51.

achieved, for there was no apparent lack of communication to Congress in response to its many requests for information on the Seminole War in the winter of 1837–38.[193]

CONTROL OF FOREIGN RELATIONS

From 1829 to 1845, Congress sought to shape executive conduct of foreign affairs by using the appropriation power and resolutions to influence negotiations.* The purse served both as a restraint on executive conduct of diplomacy and an inducement for the president to negotiate. The president often sought advice, and Congress's cautious responses staved off several threats of war on a variety of fronts. Such conduct was the precursor of a more regularized and energetic sharing of responsibility in foreign and military affairs later in the century.

The Power of the Purse

Congress frequently attempted to withhold funds when the president shifted monies appropriated from one specific object to another, but it usually conceded that the executive's expenses were the result of decisions within his constitutional prerogatives and that the House must respect his exercise of discretion except in an extreme case.[194] The criteria for such an "extreme case," however, remained undefined.†

Congress on its own initiative added funds to an executive budget by appropriating funds for an Austrian minister at the same time as Jackson's Department of State was endeavoring to establish a firm relationship with Austria.[195] Martin Van Buren merely informed Congress on 5 December 1837 that he had corresponded with Austria with a view toward establishment of diplomatic relations "in conformity with the wishes of Congress. . . ."[196] He made no mention of the prior involvement of the executive branch or the constitutional propriety of Con-

---

*Other forms of legislation also served to control executive conduct. Van Buren, for example, indicated that he regarded himself bound by legislation to impose discriminatory duties on Portugal. An Act of May 25, 1832, provided that when the president determined that the Portuguese had imposed discriminatory duties on American vessels, he was to issue a proclamation imposing such duties in retaliation. Although Van Buren doubted the expediency of this measure, he issued the proclamation on 11 October 1837; yet he asked Congress to consider whether additional legislation ought not to be passed to release him from the obligation to retaliate. 6 *Congressional Globe* 3.

†John Quincy Adams and Caleb Cushing agreed that only in an "extreme case" were both houses bound to intervene to disavow a president's creation of foreign missions, as they defended President Tyler's use of funds to establish missions in Sardinia and Naples. 10 *Congressional Globe* 393–95.

gress's "wishes"; and relations were quickly established as Henry A. Muhlenburg of Pennsylvania was commissioned envoy extraordinary and minister plenipotentiary on 8 February 1838.[197]

Congress's Influence upon Negotiations

Members of both houses became more deeply involved in treaty formation during the Jackson era. The House, particularly, broadened its participation by urging the executive to negotiate with Spain over Mexican territory. It also offered to supply an unrequested appropriation if the executive would undertake treaty negotiations to avoid further war with the Cherokees. Senators went further than their traditional role of rejecting or consenting to treaties when they asked President Jackson to undertake negotiations with Central American nations. Some members of the Senate urged colleagues to pressure President Tyler into making a treaty with England that would recognize U.S. title to the Oregon Territory. Others, such as Henry Clay, proclaimed that the Senate might request some form of action in a situation that held the potential for hostilities. During this time, also, Presidents Jackson and Tyler each came to the conclusion that final settlement of diplomatic problems was an executive responsibility, even though Jackson broke forty years of practice by asking Congress for advice on troublesome issues.

The House's Efforts to Influence Treaty Making   On 30 December 1834, Delegate Ambrose Sevier (Wh.) from the Arkansas Territory proposed that the House request the president "to negotiate with Spain for the right and title to the country lying between the Sabine and Red rivers. . . ."[198] Tennessee's James K. Polk (D.) objected on constitutional grounds that the House had "no part of the treaty-making power" and "no right to interfere in so grave and important a subject. . . ." After some discussion,* Sevier withdrew his resolution.

The House thereafter requested the executive for information regarding when the United States planned to carry out the 1835 treaty of removal with the Cherokee nation and, specifically, how Secretary of War Joel Poinsett would accomplish it.†[199] Van Buren's transmittal

---

*John Quincy Adams and William Archer (Va.) complained on the practical ground that the resolution would antagonize Mexico by implicitly recognizing Spain's title. 2 *Congressional Globe* 83.

†Horace Everett (Wh.) of Vermont claimed that the treaty was invalid because it had not been executed by authorized Cherokee agents; but Hopkins Holsey (Un. D. Ga.) replied that since Congress had confirmed it, the executive had a right "to make use of the standing force of the nation to compel its fulfillment." 6 *Congressional Globe* 69.

followed a week later.*[200] The president thereafter voluntarily sent over a letter from Secretary Poinsett enumerating concessions being offered to the Cherokees to induce them to move peacefully west of the Mississippi and expressed the hope that Congress would help him to effect these concessions.[201]

Some senators at first objected to the president's decision to disregard a treaty the Senate had ratified and to offer new terms unilaterally. They demanded strict compliance with original treaty terms, lest the proposed liberality precipitate a war such as that with the Creeks and Seminoles.[202] But eventually both houses voted the funds the president asked.[203]

Senate Influence upon Negotiations   The Senate pressed Jackson, Van Buren, and Tyler to meet certain critical foreign affairs issues energetically. For example, in order to ensure treaty protection for companies or individuals who might build a canal connecting the Atlantic and Pacific, senators requested Jackson to open negotiations with the governments of Central America. Their resolution of 3 March 1835 specified that the treaty should secure "forever . . . the free and equal right of navigating such canal to all such nations, on the payment of such reasonable tolls as may be established, to compensate the capitalists who may engage in such undertaking and complete the work."[204] The president informed senators on 10 January 1837 that the agent he had appointed to look into the matter had reported that no project was sufficiently advanced to justify opening immediate negotiations.[205]

Both houses urged Presidents Van Buren and Tyler to defend U.S. interests in Oregon in ways that had the potential of involving the United States in war. In submitting a bill proposing U.S. takeover of Oregon,[206] Missouri Senator Lewis Linn admonished the administration that U.S. failure to express its claims would result in losing them. Similarly, Massachusetts Congressman Caleb Cushing (Wh.) called for establishment of military posts in Oregon.[207] These proposals were patent violations of the Conventions of 1818 and 1827 that bound Britain and the United States to joint and open occupation of Oregon.[208] Reactions of the two houses to them differed. The Senate felt free to send Linn's bill to a select committee that would study and report on it.† But

---

*The House remained cautious, however, about the scope of its treaty inquiries and the direction that its examination of information should take. For example, Representative Charles Haynes (D. Ga.) successfully argued that the Committee on Indian Affairs be discharged from further consideration of the Cherokee treaty (103 to 76). He opposed further inquiry into the matter because the only jurisdiction that the House had over treaties was to decide whether or not to pass an appropriation related to a treaty's execution. *Id.* 269–70.

†The committee reported, but no further action was taken. *Id.* 411, 432.

House committee members did not report Cushing's bill out of committee, evidently agreeing with Maryland Representative Benjamin Howard that since the House did not share in the treatymaking power, it
could not properly advise the president to terminate a treaty,[209] and
executive caution was understandable in light of the treaty commitments.

Although President Tyler believed that U.S. emigration would eventually bring about recognition of American title to Oregon "in the
natural course of events,"[210] Missouri activists Thomas Hart Benton
and Lewis Linn were unwilling to wait. Linn introduced a bill on 19
December 1842 containing a preamble stating that U.S. title to Oregon
territory was "certain" and would not be "abandoned."[211] Linn's bill
amounted to a Senate vote of no-confidence in the president's negotiations. Despite bare passage in the Senate, 24 to 22, it died unceremoni-
ously in the House after John Quincy Adams reported unfavorably on it
for the Foreign Relations Committee.[212] But Democrats tried different
strategy in the next session. Illinois Senator James Semple maintained
that before the president concluded a treaty, he was just as constitutionally bound to obtain Senate advice as he was to send a concluded treaty
to the Senate for consent or rejection. He therefore introduced a resolution* in January 1844 that requested Tyler to give notice to Britain that
the United States was abrogating the provision in the Convention of
1827 for the joint occupation of Oregon.[213] "Are we to sit here . . . and
wait until a treaty is made, and then reject it?" Semple asked. He
acknowledged that the president was not obliged to follow the advice of
such a resolution but believed it would be persuasive.[214] Semple's
colleagues, however, rejected 28 to 18 this attempt to influence the
executive's negotiating authority by resolution as an intrusion into
presidential power.†[215] Tyler's policies in the Northwest thus remained
untouched by Congress's abortive attempts to influence them.

Tyler's use of treaty power was surprisingly successful despite the
general failure of his domestic program. He submitted fifteen treaties,
only five of which were not accepted. But the Senate defeated a German

---

*Semple's justification for the propriety of this resolution has been called the "con-
stitutionist" theory of the Senate's role in the treaty process. Morgan, *A Whig Embattled*
120–21.

†Even those who favored the resolution did so for another reason. James Buchanan and
Ambrose Sevier (W. Ark.), for example, said the resolution actually *authorized* the
president to abrogate a convention and thus removed an impediment to his negotiating
functions. 13 *Congressional Globe* 191, 353, 370, 417. Sevier's view that the president "has
no power *per se* to abrogate [an] existing convention" had many opponents, as debate over
Oregon revealed during Polk's administration. *See infra* Chapter 2, pp. 126–28. The
matter was not settled by Polk, but accepted current practice is that the President alone
should exercise this power. E. Corwin, *The President, Office and Powers* 435–36 n.75
(1974); *see also* L. Henkin, *Foreign Affairs and the Constitution* 168–71 (1972).

Customs Union Treaty because it proposed to bind Congress for three years to observe tariff schedules negotiated by the executive—and thus, arguably, encroached on Congress's commerce power. The Senate Foreign Relations Committee's unfavorable report on the German treaty categorized "appropriate functions of the Executive" as being

> To follow, not to lead, to fulfill, not to ordain, the law; to carry into effect, by negotiation and compact with foreign Governments, the legislative will, when it has been announced, upon the great subjects of trade and revenue, not to interpose with controlling influence, not to go forward with too ambitious enterprises. . . .[216]

The Senate's vote of 26 to 18 to lay this treaty on the table endorsed the committee's conclusion.[217]

Andrew Jackson initiated a change in the practice of treaty negotiation* on two occasions. In May 1830, he asked Senate advice on a proposed treaty with the Choctaw Indians. "I am fully aware," Jackson wrote, "that in thus resorting to the early practice of the Government, by asking the previous advice of the Senate in the [execution] of this portion of my duties, I am departing from a long, and for many years an unbroken usage in similar cases."[218] However, the reasons for strictly executive handling of negotiations were applicable with less force to Indian treaties than to treaties with foreign nations. He proposed that a treaty should be made, but with changes in the existing draft.[219]

The Senate Committee on Indian Affairs, in a report adopted by the Senate, agreed that the draft provisions were unacceptable. It couched its observations, however, in the most general terms:

> They [the committee] are decidedly of opinion that the terms . . . proposed ought not only to be just but liberal towards the Indians, and in this respect it appears to the committee that if the terms about to be proposed require any alterations they should consist in lessening the considerations to be offered for the lands now occupied by the Choctaws.[220]

The committee then recommended that the Senate take no position on the president's desired changes and requested that it be discharged from further consideration. It wished, particularly, to avoid attempting "to fix in detail the terms and stipulations to be included in a treaty. . . . "[221]

Settlement of the Maine Boundary   In 1832, however, the majority of Senate members accepted Jackson's invitation to advise him on the

---

*Treaty negotiation had been strictly in executive hands since Washington's first term. Sofaer, *Origins* 95–96.

attempted settlement of the boundary controversy between Canada and Maine. The king of the Netherlands had been selected arbiter of the dispute and submitted an opinion, though not to Maine's satisfaction.[222] Although Britain agreed to the king's compromise, Jackson decided not to decide and instead submitted the proposal to the Senate for its consideration.

During the course of debate, Henry Clay dealt at length with the propriety of the president's requesting and the Senate's supplying advice in formulating treaties. He concluded that the complications and inconvenience of President Washington's consulting the Senate "rendered it altogether inexpedient to take the advice and consent of the Senate previous to the conclusion of treaties." Clay inferred from the historical background* and established practice that the Senate could not constitutionally advise the president without a "national compact" in some form before it, and he therefore opposed any resolution "which would imply the right of the Senate to express any opinion on the matter in its present state and condition."[223]

The Senate disregarded Clay's contentions and advised rejection of the king's proposal.[224] This recommendation was unanimous, apparently gaining even Clay's concurrence and thus fully undermining his claim of the Senate's incapacity to act in such contexts.

Maine congressmen later attempted to require the executive to order a survey in accordance with the Treaty of Paris of 1783, although England had rejected this approach. But their two bills failed: other legislators were unwilling to direct the president to take specific acts in a foreign affairs dispute, and resolutions were adopted expressing only Congress's desire that the parties resolve their differences amicably.[225]

Pennsylvania Senator James Buchanan claimed that one of these bills, by Senator Reuel Williams,[226] wrested control from the executive and assumed responsibility for terminating the pending negotiations with Great Britain—an action that probably would lead to war.[227] If Congress passed a bill calling for "absolute determination where the treaty line is ... perpetuated by erection of monuments," Buchanan declared that it must be prepared to authorize the use of the military to execute it. He particularly criticized an alternative suggestion that the president be given discretionary power to run the line as an improper

---

*The fact that early presidents did not have to obtain the Senate's advice in forming treaties did not mean that the president might not seek such advice or that the Senate could not volunteer it. If Clay's argument were valid, the Senate could give advice on foreign policy matters only when the president sought it through a formal request for legislative action or by submission of concluded agreements with foreign powers. Yet early practice amply demonstrated the Senate's capacity to state its position on foreign policy questions. *See, e.g.,* Sofaer, *Origins* 99, 100, 208.

delegation by Congress of the war power, inasmuch as he believed that hostilities would erupt once the president attempted to exercise his authority.[228] Buchanan as chairman of the Foreign Relations Committee then reported two resolutions identical to those in the House that called for tabling of Williams's bill as being "inexpedient . . . until all reasonable means of negotiating a settlement were exhausted."[229] The Senate unanimously passed Buchanan's resolutions on 4 July 1838.[230]

Recognition of Texas   Congressional influence on executive conduct of foreign relations seemed to stop short of direct interference with the negotiation and execution of treaties, but such reticence did not preclude legislative pressure on the president to recognize the political status of new countries in the process of achieving their independence. In the case of the republic of Texas, preliminary reports from the Battle of San Jacinto in 1836 began to confirm that Santa Anna's army had been routed and that the Texans were triumphant. This news was translated by some senators into a mandate for U.S. government recognition of Texas.[231]

Mississippi Senator Robert J. Walker, for example, declared that if Texas had a successful government in operation, the Senate would be violating the law of nations if it did not at once disparage the existence of Mexican authority, since "the Senate has a right to act on this subject, not only as a branch of the Legislature, but as a branch of the executive department, in controlling our foreign relations."[232] Henry Clay, on the other hand, reported on the subject for the Committee on Foreign Relations. He concluded that the Senate alone was not legally competent to recognize the existence of a foreign power. If, however, the president should be tardy in giving recognition, "he may be quickened in the exercise of his power by the expression of the opinion, or by other acts, of one or both branches of Congress. . . ."[233] Clay emphasized that the committee was not saying that President Jackson was dilatory, but its report nonetheless recommended adoption of a resolution calling for U.S. recognition of Texas independence whenever it should be established that successful civil government was in operation. This report was accepted unanimously, 39 to 0.*[234]

President Jackson refused to leap at the opportunity to define the proper moment but bided his time and advised the second session of the Twenty-fourth Congress to do the same.[235] He promised to send the results of confidential inquiries about the Texas government to Congress.[236] His message placed the recognition issue in Congress's hands.

---

*The House carefully tabled a resolution authorizing sending a minister to Texas. 12 *Register* 4499 (John Bell, Wh. Tenn.).

Relying on Jackson's promise to "cheerfully unite with Congress,"[237] the Senate adopted (23 to 19) Robert Walker's resolution that the "independent political existence" of Texas be acknowledged by the government of the United States.[238] The House was less enthusiastic: it was only after lengthy parliamentary maneuvers that it attached an amendment to the civil and diplomatic appropriation bill, providing funds for a "diplomatic agent" for Texas whenever the president received evidence of its independence and determined it "expedient" to make the appointment.[239] John Quincy Adams intervened on behalf of this approach, which the Senate had spurned, because in his judgment recognition "properly belonged" to the executive alone.[240] The issue of which branch might give recognition (and under what circumstances) did not, therefore, appear to have been clarified by the end of Jackson's tenure.

Executive Initiatives

Claims against Mexico   As has been noted, President Jackson sought and obtained advice from the Senate, and congressmen even enacted highly discretionary legislation in an attempt to persuade Van Buren to take an important foreign affairs action having potential military consequences.[241] Nevertheless, both Jackson and Tyler took bold unilateral steps and made strong policy statements that made it clear each felt ultimately responsible for the foreign affairs commitments of the U.S. government. Jackson clearly held the reins, although in two instances he offered Congress the opportunity of sharing with him the shaping of alternative policy on critical issues. He did this not only in the case of recognition of Texas but also as he sought collection of U.S. citizens' claims against Mexico for personal and property damages. Though Jackson urged Congress to give Mexico one more opportunity to fulfill her obligations, he asserted that the United States should be fully prepared to "take immediate satisfaction" if the repeated demand were not met. He recommended that the demand should be made on board a U.S. warship on the Mexican coast.*[242] President Jackson then asked Congress to enact legislation authorizing reprisals if there should be a Mexican refusal to adjust the claims.

The Senate Foreign Relations Committee agreed with the president on two points. First, it accepted the policy of moderation, so that Mexico might be given another opportunity to make redress.[243] It conceded, further, that the method of the demand should be left up to the presi-

---

*A final demand made in this nondiplomatic, potentially explosive setting would have been another instance of critical decisionmaking relegated to officers in the field. *See* Sofaer, *Origins* 202–05, 346–55.

dent.* Significantly, the Senate unanimously (46 to 0) adopted the committee's report, which required that Jackson come back to Congress with evidence of nonsatisfaction so that the next session might recommend either war or reprisals.†[244]

The House Committee on Foreign Affairs agreed that another demand should be made on Mexico; however, it was not prepared to invest the president with reprisal authority while he made the final demand. Like the Senate, it tried to set guidelines for the demand, expressing the opinion that a diplomatic representative of the highest grade should make "the last appeal." The end of the session, however, prevented the report from being considered by the full House.[245]

Martin Van Buren reminded Congress of the unresolved claims in the next session, on 5 December 1837. He noted the previous Congress's "indisposition ... to vest a discretionary authority in the Executive to take redress. ...", but since the demand had been made, he asked for a mode of redress without contingency.[246] Despite lengthy debate, there was no concrete action taken by either house. It was clear that Congress required more aggravation from Mexico before it sanctioned measures that could lead to war.

Mississippi Senator Robert Walker suggested on 11 April 1838 that Congress should authorize sending a squadron to demand redress, which, if not granted, should be followed by blockade of Mexico.[247] His colleague James Buchanan concurred that matters were serious and deserved response, but not from the Senate. Buchanan argued that coercive measures leading to war had historically emanated from the House, whose members as the more immediate representatives of the people were the originators of revenue measures.[248] Senator Clay agreed, counseling against precipitous action in light of the debilitating economic situation** and suggesting that the administration had rashly

---

*There may well have been some fear that the president's "warship" demand might have led to hostilities, even though neither he nor Congress intended reprisals, and thus could produce war. The committee, however, only suggested that the president should rely on Article 34 of the Treaty of Amity, Commerce, and Navigation with Mexico of 5 April 1831 as his format; the absence of mandatory language left the manner of presentation to him.

†Senators obviously shared in Buchanan's questioning the propriety of delegating the congressional war power of reprisal to the president along with the discretion to determine the contingency for its use. "It was always safer and more constitutional," he said, to grant such power after events occurred. 4 *Congressional Globe* 210.

**Secretary of State Forsyth recited examples of Mexican unresponsiveness to U.S. demands, but Congress did not regard them as forming a sufficient basis for reprisals. It was particularly cautious in not responding to a series of events that had occurred during a recess. Mexico's capture of several U.S. merchant vessels led to seizure of the Mexican ship *General Urrea* by the U.S. warship *Natchez*. Mexican authorities authorized a blockade of Texas in retaliation, in violation of the U.S. treaty with her, and imprisoned some Americans on board U.S. merchant vessels that violated the blockade. Mexico later lifted the blockade and released the Americans. 6 *Congressional Globe Appendix* 1.

broken off negotiations following the last demand. Buchanan rejoined that even if the administration's cancellation of negotiations had been precipitate, several other incidents warranted the serious consideration of retributive measures.[249] Walker was unwilling to accept Buchanan's deference to the House, stating that the Senate was at least co-equal in war power and claiming the treatymaking power gave it the additional authority to initiate war measures.[250] Buchanan retorted that if Walker was not satisfied with Senate conduct, he should introduce a resolution instructing the Senate Foreign Relations Committee to report a war measure; but Walker did not do so.

In the House, John Quincy Adams charged that executive acts including the demand for redress, Forsyth's report, and the president's message had been designed to tell Congress it had no alternative but war.[251] Executive initiatives resolved the matter peacefully, however, after Congress refused to enact war measures. Van Buren subsequently announced the conclusion of a treaty to refer the Mexican claims to arbitration,[252] and Congress's participation was no longer required.

The Acquittal of Alexander McLeod and British Accommodation   John Tyler displayed ability to impose foreign policy effectively and unilaterally. His secretary of state, Daniel Webster, successfully handled the *Caroline** affair inherited from Martin Van Buren, even though a tense Congress indicated its desire to vindicate national honor by confronting equally belligerent England. Tyler also had to resolve controversy surrounding the prosecution of a British subject, Alexander McLeod, for the murder of an American citizen during the *Caroline* incident. Webster was convinced that should McLeod be found guilty and hanged for what the British government determined was a public act, there would be enough support in England for war against the United States.[253] Webster defused the inflammatory aspects of the incident by agreeing that under the law of nations, McLeod had committed a public act, for which Great Britain avowed responsibility. Webster then used the

---

*See supra p. 21. On 29 December 1837, a small Canadian force attacked an American steamer, the *Caroline* (which had been used to aid a Canadian rebellion), on the American side of the Niagara River. They wounded some of the crew, killed an American named Amos Durfee, and sent the vessel over the Falls. The United States protested the violation of its territorial sovereignty, but the British countered that the acts were taken in self-defense against piratical raiders. The situation was further complicated by the arrest and indictment for murder in New York State three years later of one Alexander McLeod, a Canadian, who had bragged while in New York that he had killed Durfee. J. Reeves, *American Diplomacy under Tyler and Polk* 17, 18 (1907). Many depositions of participants giving accounts of the occurrence are set forth in 3 *Diplomatic Correspondence of the United States: Canadian Relations 1784–1860,* at 416ff., 647ff. (1943) (hereinafter "*Diplomatic Correspondence (Canadian)*").

British admission as grounds for redress for destruction of the *Caroline*.[254] McLeod was acquitted, and the danger of war completely obviated when Lord Ashburton came to Washington not only to make an official apology but also with full powers to make a definitive settlement on every disputed Anglo-American issue.[255] President Tyler and Secretary Webster then seized this unusual opportunity to compromise the Northeast boundary question.* Webster and Lord Ashburton deliberately chose to conduct open, informal discussions that avoided becoming snagged in the disagreements over geography that had destroyed previous negotiating attempts.[256] Senators Thomas Hart Benton and James Buchanan dissented from this kind of unrecorded give-and-take,[257] charging Webster with bargaining away U.S. territory. Other articles dealing with suppression of the African slave trade were also negotiated and included in the treaty. Benton suspected that articles providing for inspection of each other's vessels had originated with the British and were being imposed on the United States. He proposed a qualified but lengthy resolution requesting information concerning the "history and progress" of these articles, which the Senate accepted.[258] William Archer (Va.), however, argued that the Senate should not send such a request to the president,[259] and Tyler agreed, characterizing Benton's inquiry as "without precedent." Benton, indeed, must have been embarrassed when Tyler, "out of a profound respect," informed the Senate that he had directed that the articles be proposed to the British. The Senate made no comment.[260]

MILITARY AFFAIRS AND AUTHORIZATIONS, 1829–1845

Introduction

The years 1829 to 1845, though not officially war years, were of considerable military importance. The United States engaged in no declared war from 1814 until 1846, when Polk led the nation into a formal war with Mexico. But during the years prior to Polk's presidency, many military initiatives short of war were undertaken, some without legislative authority. These engagements reflect existing understandings concerning the president's authority to use force in the absence of formal war and any other form of legislative authority. They also indicate the increasing capacity of presidents to undertake military initiatives without requesting special legislative support. Finally, some

*The treaty was signed on 9 August 1842 and sent to the Senate two days later. Reeves, *American Diplomacy under Tyler and Polk* 51–57; 5 S. Bemis, *The American Secretaries of State and Their Diplomacy* 41, 42 (1927–29). *See also* H. Jones, *To the Webster-Ashburton Treaty: A Study in Anglo-American Relations, 1783–1843* (1977), *passim*.

of the incidents show how a president may expand his authority to use force simply because he has the initiative to inform Congress about military incidents. He also possesses the opportunity of marshalling his facts in such a way that their recitation underscores the action already taken as being a proper exercise of unilateral presidential authority.

Military Actions Short of War: The Navy

By 1830, the nation was far from the "great naval power" that John Quincy Adams predicted it would become[261] but had a regular naval force sizable enough to make its presence simultaneously felt in several places around the world. Jackson, harkening back to early Republican dogma, favored a small navy. In 1836, the navy possessed only two capital vessels in active service, yet by 1853 "the United States possessed not one vessel that could have stood up against any first-class European warship."[262] Nevertheless, the navy had several squadrons that were capable of protecting American commerce in many of the far-flung areas in which it then thrived. Commanders and captains were required to exercise discretion in implementing broadly phrased orders in novel and unanticipated situations.* Although the protection of commerce was less glamorous militarily than the shoot-outs of 1812–1814, these operations raised constitutional questions far more complex and controversial than actions authorized by a declaration of war.

The constitutional propriety of naval actions short of war appears to have turned on two variables: the party against whom some action seemed required and the form of action taken. The navy dealt with several categories of offending parties, including pirates, natives with whose "governments" no established relations existed, and the vessels and peoples of so-called civilized nations. The most justifiable form of conduct undertaken against any of these parties was defensive measures designed to prevent seizures of U.S. public or private vessels or of U.S. property. Congress had repeatedly approved or authorized such

---

*The necessity of interpreting a general order often involved a knowledge of international law by the naval officer, a knowledge, which it appears, was assumed by the government. Many statesmen in the earlier stages of American history believed that the law of nations governed the president's conduct in the absence of contrary legislative direction. Sofaer, *Origins* 154. The naval officer was often regarded as a "sailor-diplomat"; he was sometimes sent to distant places where no official representative was present; or, sometimes, he acted on his own initiative and even went so far as to make treaties. C. Paullin, *Diplomatic Negotiations of American Naval Officers, 1778–1883,* at 8–9 (1912). *See also* supporting memoranda regarding the origins and development of granting discretionary power to officers, A.B.A. War Powers Study Papers, Rare Book and Manuscript Library, Columbia University (hereinafter "War Powers Papers").

actions prior to 1830, and the propriety of defense measures taken to fend off attacks on American vessels was never questioned.*

Actions against pirates went far beyond defensive measures. Congress had passed Piracy Acts dated 3 March 1819 and 20 December 1822, which conferred general authority to seize and bring pirates to justice.[263] But to the extent these laws failed clearly to confer authority for stopping, searching, and pursuing suspected pirates, the navy appears to have relied, without legislative criticism, on international norms of conduct that made pirates the enemies of all nations.

Reprisals against Natives

Sumatra   The acts of lawless communities, rather than the conduct of certain irresponsible members of a community that condemned, policed, and disciplined piracy, were treated with little formality by naval officers prior to 1829.† The executive undoubtedly assumed it would be pointless to attempt to negotiate formal arrangements with natives whose language could not be understood. This policy was explicitly adopted by President Jackson and the navy in 1831 after a series of attacks on American merchant vessels at Sumatra culminated in one particularly egregious incident.

On 7 February 1831, natives of the Sumatran village of Quallah Battoo attacked the American vessel *Friendship* as it was taking on a cargo of pepper. The mate and two sailors were killed, and the vessel suffered some $40,000 in damages. The vessel's owners protested, and Jackson acted immediately. "[T]he piratical perpetrators," he explained to Congress when it reconvened, "being in such a state of society that the usual course of proceeding between civilized nations could not be pursued, I forthwith despatched a frigate with orders to require immediate satisfaction for the injury, and indemnity to the sufferers."[264] The commander, John Downes, was expected to obtain an indemnity for that "barbarous and piratical injury."[265]

Downes was warned first to determine if a "regular responsible

---

*Piracy actions deriving authority from Acts of March 3, 1819, December 20, 1822, and May 18, 1826 (3 Stat. 510; *id.* 720; 4 Stat. 170, respectively), are described in Sofaer, *Origins* 371–77, *passim*. Statutes such as the Act of April 5, 1826 (4 Stat. 152), addressed the protection of American commerce and served as authority to oppose a Brazilian blockade. Sofaer, *Origins* 277. The right to protect against Indian depredations was seen as authorization for numerous incursions into the territory of foreign powers. *Id.* 341ff. Also, Congress concluded that the 1807 act prohibiting slave importation authorized use of the navy in territorial waters to seize vessels engaged in the slave trade. *Id.* 338–39.

†Depredations committed by natives in places such as Sumatra were analogous to those committed in earlier times by Tripolitan and other Barbary powers. *See id.* 186, 209, 210, 217–21.

government" would make satisfaction. If not, he was to say that the United States would take further measures. In the absence of regular government, the commander was to demand restitution or indemnity for "property plundered" and "immediate punishment of those concerned in the murder of American citizens. . . ." Further details reflected additional official caution.* Yet Downes, upon reaching Quallah Battoo in February 1832, made no effort to ascertain the nature of authority installed there. He made no demand on any government, regular or irregular. He was "satisfied, from what knowledge [he] had already of the character of the people," he later explained, "that no such demand [for restitution] would be answered."[266] Instead, he immediately dispatched 250 men who captured four native forts and burned the village to ashes. The action cost two American lives and seven wounded, in contrast to 150 natives reportedly killed. The remaining natives "expressed the greatest penitence for their misdeeds, sued most humbly for peace, . . . and requested that all hostilities cease."[267]

On 12 July 1832, the House adopted a motion requesting the president to send copies of Downes's instructions and his reports of the attack, "except such parts as may, in his judgment, require secrecy." Jackson sent copies the same day, saying that "the instructions, with the papers annexed, are all that have been given hearing on this subject" and that nothing had been omitted from the originals.[268] The documents clearly showed that Downes had used force without seeking a peaceful settlement.† This might well account for the president's comment in sending the documents to the House—that "in justice to" Downes, the contents of his dispatches "should not be published until he can enjoy a further opportunity of giving more full explanations of all the circumstances under which he conducted."[269] The House deferred to the president's suggestion and discharged the Committee on Foreign Affairs from further consideration of the matter.[270]

---

*Downes was to send any known murderers to the United States for trial as pirates; he was to retake stolen property and destroy boats that participated in the piracy as well as "forts and dwellings near the scene of the aggression used for shelter or defence. . . . " Woodbury to Downes, 9 August 1831, National Archives Microfilm, Department of the Navy, *Letters Sent by the Secretary of the Navy to Officers,* M149, roll 20; *see also* 4 *American State Papers, Naval Affairs,* 150–58.

†The annual report of the secretary of the navy in December 1832 also informed Congress that a "[c]hastisement" had been "inflicted by a frigate *Potomac* on the piratical Malays. . . . " The commander "was to investigate the plunder of the *Friendship,* to demand indemnity, and the punishment of the offenders," he wrote, without explaining that no indemnity had been demanded. "[T]he result of that visit," he added, "has been to silence all exultation and menaces of further violence from those sea robbers," and to draw from them acknowledgments of past errors and promises of future forebearance from like offenses. 9 *Register App.* 15.

Both the president's message and Secretary Woodbury's annual report of December 1832 summarized Downes's orders.[271] But Jackson misstated the instructions and gave an inaccurate view of Downes's conduct:

> An act of atrocious piracy having been committed on one of our trading ships by the inhabitants of a settlement on the west coast of Sumatra, a frigate was dispatched with orders to demand satisfaction for the injury if those who committed it should be found to be members of a regular government, capable of maintaining the usual relations with foreign nations; but if, as it was supposed and as they proved to be, they were a band of lawless pirates, to inflict such a chastisement as would deter them and others from like aggressions. This last was done, and the effect has been an increased respect for our flag in those distant seas and additional security for our commerce.[272]

In addition, Jackson did not mention that Downes had failed to make demand of a government not deemed "regular" and that the punishment he inflicted had exceeded the limits set by his instructions.

There is no record of any debate concerning the Sumatra incident. When Downes later requested reimbursement for "extraordinary" expenses (mainly gifts to natives) incurred on his cruise, the House Committee on Foreign Affairs recorded that he had acted in accordance with his instructions, recommended he be paid $1,080, and stated that in the committee's judgment, "no vessel-of-war has ever . . . performed more valuable services" in the Pacific.[273]

No member of either the executive or legislative branches publicly expressed any doubt about the constitutional propriety of sending an expedition of this kind without legislative approval. In fact, the administration could arguably have included the "caution" in Downes's instructions as a means of utilizing the naval force without prior legislative authorization. Downes's violation of instructions without official executive or legislative reprimand* does not mean Jackson did not consider himself bound to condition the use of force. General Jackson's actions in East Florida had been justified by President Monroe under a similar rationale: Monroe conceded in effect that he could not have ordered Jackson to act against Spanish posts but contended that the commander-on-the-spot could properly conclude that offensive actions against the Spanish were necessary to suppress Indian attacks on Americans.[274]

---

*Downes was privately severely reprimanded. The fury of the president and Secretary Woodbury was matched by the anger expressed in newspapers that questioned the executive's constitutional authority to unilaterally use force to punish. A. Schlesinger, *The Imperial Presidency* 53 (1973).

Fiji Further support for the notion that the president was expected to condition the use of force in authorizing reprisals against natives is found in the manner that instructions were issued by President Van Buren to the Charles Wilkes Expedition in 1836. Section 2 of the naval appropriations bill for that year authorized the president "to send out a surveying and exploring expedition" to the Pacific and other seas, employing ships "as may be necessary and proper to render the said expedition efficient and useful."[275] The terms of this act gave the president considerable discretion in setting up the expedition, but Commodore Wilkes was ordered to engage only in "necessary defense ... against any attempt to disturb [the expedition's] operations by the warlike inhabitants of those islands." The expedition was, Wilkes later wrote, "considered to be entirely divested of all military character."[276]

Wilkes's conduct, however, reinforces the probability that little weight was given to the caution that the executive urged in dealing with natives. When, in 1840, a launch being used by a surveying party from Wilkes's expedition went aground in a squall at Sualib Bay, Fiji, the natives stripped the launch of everything valuable. Wilkes then sent his men ashore, where they burned the entire village of "about sixty huts of flimsy construction ... to the ground."[277] Days later, two American sailors were killed (one of them Wilkes's nephew) and another seriously injured while attempting to barter with the natives. Wilkes ordered Sualib destroyed, as well as a village called Arro, and fifty-seven natives were killed.[278] Both the president and Congress were satisfied, apparently, if actions against natives were prompt and effective. Neither branch seriously questioned the commander's judgment as to the necessity of using force,* even though in most instances no attempt was made to peacefully settle offenses that had been committed.†

Depredations against Commerce The right to authorize reprisals for depredations against commerce was contemporaneously thought to be

---

*Wilkes did face a court martial when he returned from an expedition authorized by a Democratic administration to face Tyler's Whig administration. He was charged with murder, brutality, and tyranny stemming from the "chastisements" of natives, but all these charges were dropped or resulted in acquittals. He was convicted, however, on one charge of excessively punishing a sailor. D. Henderson, *The Hidden Coasts: A Biography of Admiral Charles Wilkes* 156, 201–13 (1953); R. Silverberg, *Stormy Voyager: The Story of Charles Wilkes* 168–72 (1968).

†Similar examples of excessive use of force against natives occurred in 1841 at Drummond Island and Samoa; in the Fiji Islands in 1855 and 1858; and Johanna Island in 1851. H. Ellsworth, *One Hundred Eighty Landings of United States Marines, 1800–1934* 72, 74, 80–82, 106–07, 145–46 (1974); M. Offut, *Protection of Citizens Abroad by the Armed Forces of the United States* 26, 35–36, 40–41 (1928).

derived from the warmaking power of Congress.* Yet the executive department continued through the Tyler administration to authorize reprisals.† For example, when Tyler's secretary of the navy, Abel P. Upshur, instructed Commodore Matthew Perry to protect American commerce and to suppress the slave trade in the Mediterranean,** the only qualification on this order was that Perry use his forces "to protect the rights and interests of [his] countrymen, without violating those of any other people. . . ."[279] Perry clearly felt his primary role was that of defending U.S. citizens' commercial rights, inasmuch as Upshur had called it the chief purpose of the mission and had subordinated even the quashing of the slave trade to it.[280] Upshur also had impressed the president with his view that native chiefs must be taught to fear and respect Americans.[281] From these circumstances, Perry fashioned the outlines of his discretion. He was to punish Africans for their attacks on Americans and their property and impress them with demonstrations of U.S. military might. He quickly discovered that inhabitants of the coastal village of Little Berriby had been responsible for an attack on the U.S. merchant vessel *Mary Carver,* whose captain and crew had been killed.[282] Perry informed both Upshur and Navy Secretary David Henshaw on two separate occasions that he planned severe chastisement of the Berriby natives and did so when there was ample time for there to have been an official countermand.[283] By its silence, Washington approved Perry's plans.

Apparently, Perry tried to fulfil the letter of his instructions, which were to avoid killing and "to fire only in self-defense." He first demanded reparations and requested that those natives who had attacked the *Mary Carver* be tried and executed. At some point during these negotiations, a musket was fired and fighting began. Perry claimed that the "shedding of blood . . . was unpremeditated and accidental."[284] His

---

*The power to regulate commerce and thus to punish for spoliations; the power to issue letters of marque and reprisal; the power to declare war; and the power to define and punish for offenses against the law of nations—all were regarded as sources for a legislative authority over reprisals. For example, *see* W. Duer, *Outlines of the Constitutional Jurisprudence of the United States* 117, 118, 147 (1833); C. Lofgren, "War Making under the Constitution: The Original Understanding," 81 *Yale Law Journal* 672 (1972).

†Jackson asked Congress to provide him with the authority to institute reprisals against such powers as Mexico and France. But in the Falkland Islands incident, he justified his unapproved action by claiming the Falklands contained a *nest of pirates* against whom the executive had statutory authority to act, and were *not a national entity* against whom reprisal authority had to be sought. *Infra* p. 57. The same reasoning was adopted by President Pierce, when to silence congressional claims that he had usurped its authority by bombarding Greytown, he characterized it as a "piratical" community against which he already had power to act. *Infra* Chapter 2, p. 166.

**The African squadron which Perry commanded was established in compliance with Article 8 of the Webster-Ashburton Treaty. This article called for Great Britain and the United States each to maintain a squadron of not less than eighty guns to enforce the laws of the respective countries for suppression of the slave trade. 4 *Treaties* 363–70.

troops continued the "punishment," however, burning four deserted villages that belonged to the tribe from Little Berriby.[285] This village-burning clearly exceeded the scope of Perry's orders and was one of the many nineteenth century examples of an officer in the field unilaterally making and executing military policy with impunity.*

Neither the president nor Congress rebuked Perry. Congress did not reprimand Tyler for unlawful authorization of reprisals. But it could not have done so without the official correspondence, which Tyler withheld from the House.† The fact that retribution was swift, Berriby was no power, and war no threat doubtless made a difference to Congress.

Actions against "Civilized" Nations: The Falkland Islands   No president from Jackson to Tyler explicitly authorized reprisals against any nation with whom the United States had diplomatic relations for violations of commercial rights. The usual procedure in such cases was for the president to demand satisfaction through established diplomatic channels. This was done in several instances and promptly reported to Congress.**

An incident arose early in Jackson's administration that showed how the president's power to characterize interference with American commerce enabled him to treat at least some actions by civilized nations as piratical. Given the differences in the forms of naval action that Jackson was prepared to authorize or subsequently to approve, this power to classify was of great importance in defining the president's capacity to use force short of war. Jackson arbitrarily characterized a regular government under Argentina's authority as "piratical." Thus, he legitimized a reprisal action and created tension between the United States and Argentina that could have produced war.

The Argentine republic had established one Louis Vernet as governor of the Falkland Islands.†† Vernet executed Argentine orders to warn all fishing vessels to cease their activities in the islands, and in 1831, the

See, for example, Chapter 2 *infra,* Edmund Gaines and the invasion of Mexican territory, and Perry's own further activities in the Pacific, pp. 101–103; 112–116.

†It was rare for Tyler to have withheld data that the House requested in the foreign affairs area; also, it was unusual for the House to have unqualified its request of 3 January 1844 for all instructions to commanders of the African squadron. 13 *Congressional Globe* 97; 5 *Messages and Papers* 2173.

**For example, Jackson reported in December 1831 claims against England, France, Spain, Holland, Sweden, Denmark, Naples, and Portugal, who "had all, in a greater or lesser degree, infringed our neutral rights. Demands for reparation were made upon all." 3 *Messages and Papers* 1107, 1109.

††See, for background, J. Goebel, *The Struggle for the Falkland Islands* 434–38 (1927). The Falklands, lying 250 miles off the Argentine coast in the South Atlantic, were also claimed by the British, who did not maintain military presence but preserved their claim by lodging protests with Buenos Aires. *Id.*

U.S. schooner *Harriet,* with other American ships engaged in sealing, was caught in violation of these regulations and escorted to Buenos Aires for trial. When U.S. Consul George Slacum protested, he received an Argentine reply, which he regarded as an avowal of Vernet's seizure action.[286] Slacum also informed U.S. naval commander Silas Duncan, who was under orders to protect U.S. commerce "consistent with the neutral character of our country," [287] that the *Harriet* had been taken. Duncan told Slacum he understood that the seizures had been undertaken by authority of Buenos Aires but felt duty-bound to sail to the Falklands "for the protection of the Citizens and Commerce of the United States. . . ."[288] By the time Slacum informed the Argentine government that Duncan had vowed to sail to the Falklands[289] and had written Secretary of State Edward Livingston that Duncan would proceed against Vernet as a private adventurer,[290] Duncan had spiked Vernet's guns, captured most of the inhabitants of the Falklands, and disarmed them.*

Knowing only about the *Harriet's* capture and not Duncan's plan to raid the Falklands, President Jackson announced to Congress on 6 December 1831 that an American vessel had been seized while engaged in a trade long enjoyed "without molestation" by men pretending to act under Argentine authority and that he had sent an armed vessel "to join our squadron in those seas" to protect U.S. trade. He then requested "authority and means" to defend American fishing and trading.[291]

The armed vessel was the *Enterprise,* whose captain, George Rodgers, was ordered to afford "complete" protection to American interests while ascertaining whether the "aggressions" were authorized by "some regular Government." If he found there was no such authority, Rodgers was to "break up" the pirates' operations and, insofar as possible, get indemnity from them.[292]

Also early in 1832, before President Jackson learned that Duncan had raided the Vernet Settlement in the Falklands, he sent Francis Baylies

---

*Interestingly, Duncan decided to sail to the Falklands early on 9 December without waiting for Anchorena's reply to Slacum's "ultimatum," which expired that day and which might have provided some basis for negotiation and conciliation. Anchorena to Slacum, 9 December 1831, 20 *British and Foreign State Papers* 320–22. It is true that Anchorena's reply in fact would not have persuaded Duncan to remain in Buenos Aires, but this Duncan could not have known for certain in advance. *See* Slacum to Livingston, 20 December 1831, *Diplomatic Correspondence of the United States: Inter-American Affairs, 1831-1860 (Argentina)* 85 (1932) (hereinafter "*Diplomatic Correspondence (Argentina)*"). Duncan released his captives in Montevideo, Uruguay, only after obtaining assurance from Buenos Aires that it assumed authority for their actions against U.S. commerce. Slacum and Duncan had concluded that destroying Vernet's Falkland Island settlement was the lesser of two potentially inflammatory courses of action. It would have been much more difficult militarily to have recaptured the *Harriet* in Buenos Aires harbor than to treat Vernet as a pirate. Moreover, Vernet's destruction would have been less likely to cause a major military confrontation.

as *chargé d'affaires* to Buenos Aires, empowered to claim extensive fishing and landing rights in the region.* Although Secretary of State Livingston had received notice in 1829 that Argentina purported to regulate fishing off the Falklands, he still characterized Vernet's actions as lawless and piratical in orders he gave to Baylies in January 1832.† The *chargé's* instructions tracked those Rodgers had received: if the seizures of the U.S. ships were avowed, Baylies was to ask for redress from Argentina. If disavowed, Baylies was to order the U.S. squadron in the area to break up Vernet's settlement and take him to Buenos Aires for trial.

Francis Baylies demanded restitution** for seizure of the fishing vessels from Argentina's acting foreign minister Don Manuel V. de Maza but did not comment on Duncan's conduct. De Maza retorted that U.S. rights would be protected but not at the expense of Vernet's and Argentina's.[293] De Maza then wrote directly to Secretary Livingston that the trial of the *Harriet* was an internal matter. To Baylies's claim of U.S. fishing rights, the Argentinian replied that the United States had sidestepped the real issue of Duncan's outrageous conduct, for which he demanded full satisfaction.[294]

Baylies clearly expressed the U.S. position as to Duncan in his first negotiation with de Maza:

> [A]lthough Captain Duncan had not received express orders from his Government to break up that establishment, yet, this act was a consequence of the general instructions to all our naval Commanders in whatever part, to *protect American commerce*—he had dislodged Vernet and his followers, who had attacked and committed repeated depredations on our commerce, in just conformity to those instructions. . . . [295]

Since de Maza refused to yield his condition that indemnification for the Duncan raid must precede negotiations, Baylies demanded his passports but conferred with the British minister in Buenos Aires, Henry Fox, before he left. Baylies told Fox that the United States would claim "free fishery" in the Falklands against Britain if it had to and even complained that the British, having already asserted their authority, were obviously tolerating a horde of pirates in the Falklands who

---

*Francis Rawle refers to this instruction as Secretary of State Edward Livingston's "scarcely legal claim to the inshore fisheries on unsettled coasts and bays, arms of the sea, gulfs, and other inlets incapable of fortification." 4 Bemis, *The American Secretaries of State* 254.

†"The lawless and piratical nature of these acts could not permit the President, for a moment, to believe they were authorized by a friendly power." S. Exec. Doc. No. 109 (pt. 2), 32d Cong., 1st Sess. 8, 9 (hereinafter "S. Exec. Doc. No. 109").

**Baylies doubtless learned of Duncan's conduct when he arrived in Buenos Aires. Therefore, instructions authorizing him to order Rodgers to raid the Vernet settlement on a particular contingency were not operative.

were "annoying" U.S. commerce. On the basis of this conversation,* Baylies assumed that Britain would take decisive action in the Falklands, since the Argentinians had sent an armed vessel on the scene with the intent of taking formal possession.[296]

Jackson's request to be clothed with "authority" was a desire for Congress to approve a line of conduct he had already unilaterally undertaken. Had he waited a week before dispatching an armed vessel, Congress would have begun a new session, at which time he could have informed it of his intended action. But Jackson did not submit either the naval or diplomatic instructions to Congress before sending Rodgers and Baylies on their missions.† Had he done so, the instructions would have shown clearly that Jackson ordered diplomats to seek the nature of Vernet's settlement after he had described Vernet's agents as pirates. The president unquestionably approved of the Duncan raid.[297] Duncan himself was uncertain of the legality of his conduct since he omitted to mention the raid in his log[298] and asked assurances from Buenos Aires that persons he had captured during his attack on the Falklands had been acting under its authority.[299] Secretary of State Livingston, however, was satisfied to accept Duncan's and Slacum's original characterization of Vernet and his settlement as piratical,[300] though members of Congress might have been interested in checking on evidence to support such a description if they had had access to correspondence between Slacum and the various Argentine foreign ministers.

The decision to send no information to Congress was conscious and implemented against an express legislative request to be informed. Jackson did not refer to Duncan's raid or his approval of it in his annual

---

*One cannot be sure of Baylies's intentions during his interview with Fox. But he appears to have been inviting Britain to exercise its claim and hoping thereby to secure American fishing interests. At the least, he was suggesting that the United States would do nothing if Britain took the Falklands, despite the Monroe Doctrine. Whatever his intent, the British seem to have taken the hint. Three months after Baylies's interview with Fox, two British warships assumed control of the Falklands. Message of the Government of the House of Representatives of the Province of Buenos Ayres, relative to the occupation of the Malvinas (Falkland Islands) by Great Britain on 24 January 1833, in 20 British and Foreign State Papers 1194. See also correspondence between British and Argentinian Commanders, British and Argentinian ministers, id. 1197ff. Later efforts by the Argentine republic to obtain American help in securing the return of the islands were fruitless, since successive administrations treated title as having vested in Britain prior to the Monroe Doctrine, therefore excluding the Falklands from the Doctrine's application. E.g., Secretary of State Thomas Bayard to Vincente Quesada, 18 March 1886, in 1 J. Moore, ed., A Digest of International Law 889–90 (1906). However, the United States maintained a different position vis-à-vis Great Britain. When an American vessel was seized (but subsequently released) in the Falklands, in 1853, the United States complained, remarking that it did not regard the question of sovereignty as settled. A claim for damages was prepared but never presented. Id. 888.

†Only the instructions to Baylies were ever sent to Congress and then only by President Fillmore on 28 August 1852 in compliance with a Senate resolution requesting information concerning correspondence with Peru. S. Exec. Doc. No. 109, p. 8.

message to the second session of the Twenty-second Congress.[301] He announced simply that he refrained "from making any communication on the subject of our affairs with Buenos Aires because the negotiation communicated to you in my last message was ... still pending, and in a state that would render a publication of the details inexpedient." How communication to Congress of the facts of Duncan's raid would have upset negotiations in Buenos Aires is difficult to explain. Possibly, the material was withheld on the theory that legislative differences with the executive decision to avow Duncan's raid might interfere with negotiations aimed at absolving the United States from all liability.

The administration's attitude was further revealed a few weeks later. By that time, Baylies had returned to the United States, and negotiations with Buenos Aires had been terminated. Representative John Quincy Adams introduced a request for the correspondence between the United States and Buenos Aires resulting in Baylies's return, as well as "instructions to said *Chargé d'Affaires,*" insofar as such a communication may in the president's opinion "comport with the public interest...."[302] Adams explained that the nations seemed to be "in a condition approaching to a state of war" as a result of alleged "outrages" committed by U.S. officers against citizens of the South American republic. On the other hand, William Archer (Va.), chairman of the House Committee on Foreign Affairs, assured the members that there was no reason to fear war with Buenos Aires, since the Argentines had manifested a disposition to renew negotiations in the United States. But the resolution was adopted without opposition, and Archer "presumed there could not be the least objection to a full disclosure of all the resolution called for."[303]

Jackson thought otherwise and refused the information. He told the House that although the *chargé* had "found it necessary to return," the negotiations "are not considered as broken off, but are suspended only until the arrival of a minister who ... will be sent to this country to treat on the subject." Therefore, the president continued, communicating the correspondence and instructions to the House was not "consistent with the public interest ... so long as the negotiation shall be pending."[304] Jackson presented the House with no official announcement of the Argentine government's intentions,* but the House accepted his decision by tabling his message and taking no further action.

---

*Jackson probably did possess, in December 1832, information that Argentina desired to continue negotiating. On 13 October 1832, de Maza had written Livingston that his government would communicate directly with Washington through a minister charged "to ... dispel the errors which may exist with regard to the proceedings of Captain Duncan." It was not until 20 December that de Maza wrote that an Envoy Extraordinary actually had been appointed and was on his way; but, of course, Jackson did not have this latter communication at the time he addressed Congress. *Diplomatic Correspondence (Argentina)* 165–67.

Months after Jackson's message, the minister from Buenos Aires still had not appeared. The Argentines were confronted with more pressing matters by that time, including Britain's seizure of the islands and war against Peru and Bolivia. In the meantime, the U.S. government had sent a new consul to Buenos Aires, who reported that in his opinion Argentina did not intend to send its minister to the United States but that mediation by a "friendly power" would be "received with particular satisfaction."[305] But Jackson did not appear disposed to accept such a settlement, and the suggestion was not acted upon. An Argentine minister, General Don Carlos Maria Alvear, presented a claim in 1838 for the losses caused by Duncan's raid, but Secretary of State Daniel Webster neatly deferred any answer pending settlement of the controversy between Buenos Aires and Britain over which was sovereign.* Great Britain thus took over the Falklands without U.S. interference, and England's claim thereafter blocked Argentina's demand for damages for Commodore Duncan's attack on the Vernet settlement.[306]

The Monterey Incident   President John Tyler, unlike Jackson, did respond to a congressional demand for information on an overt act of war against Mexico, with whom the United States was at peace. He made it clear, however, that he was under no obligation to send forward materials at Congress's request, even if the possibility of war was involved. For, although Commodore Thomas ap Catesby Jones had captured a Mexican fort at Monterey, California, in October 1842, the executive disavowed the act and denied suspicions that the seizure was a design for expansion.

Jones, in command of a small naval squadron off the west coast of South America, had read inaccurate reports and news articles that convinced him that war was imminent between the United States and Mexico.[307] He later acknowledged that he had not received any official correspondence substantiating the reports and other data that influenced him but that nonetheless he had decided that he should take over California to forestall any potential British claims.[308] Jones thereupon

---

*The question of sovereignty received considerable ventilation in U.S. courts. In a case involving application of rights of salvage under the law of nations, a federal District Court denied recovery to a member of Duncan's crew who had pressed a claim, and the Circuit Court affirmed. The Circuit Court pronounced that Vernet's settlement legally fell under the protection of Argentina, and that Duncan's entry had been unwarranted. *Davison v. Seal-Skins*, 7 Fed. Cas. 192 (C.C.D. Conn. 1835). However, in another situation, the U.S. Supreme Court refused to pass upon the sovereignty of the Falklands. In considering whether the master of the *Harriet* acted with discretion in engaging in seal fishing in the Falklands, the Court ruled that he was not bound by law to abandon his voyage under threat of seizure, since the U.S. government had decided that U.S. commerce possessed rights in that region. "[I]n this view it is not material to inquire, nor is it the province of this Court to determine, whether the Executive be right or wrong. It is enough to know that in the exercise of his constitutional functions, he has decided the question." *Williams v. The Suffolk Insurance Co.*, 38 U.S. (13 Pet.) 415, 420, 421 (1839).

demanded the surrender of Monterey "in the name of the United States of America ... to avoid ... the horrors of war."[309] When he suddenly became aware of the true status of U.S.-Mexican relations, Commodore Jones rehoisted and saluted the Mexican flag.[310] Mexican Foreign Minister Bocanegra swiftly received apologies and promise of reparations from U.S. Minister Waddy Thompson,[311] and the matter was declared closed.[312] Despite U.S. official disavowal, Jones was not punished. Secretary of State Daniel Webster remarked that some allowances had to be made for indiscreet judgments reached "in a quarter so remote."[313]

John Quincy Adams, however, was not content to let the matter rest. On 2 February 1843, the House passed his unqualified* resolution requesting the president to release the instructions under which Commodore Jones had acted.[314] Tyler sent over the instructions only because he could foresee no harm from releasing them.[315] But he asserted that neither house could control executive discretion to withhold instructions or similar documentation to field commanders. This discretion proceeded from his duty to protect and to promote "public objects." The president thus unequivocally declared that in foreign affairs he could withhold information concerning warmaking, a matter peculiarly within the province of the legislature.

Adams, unwilling to see in the Monterey seizure anything less than a design for the plunder of Mexico, further conquest, and war with England, denounced Jones's act to Secretary Webster, though Webster denied that there was any administration plot afoot.[316] Yet Adams made an effort to curb presidential adventuring by introducing a resolution that called for further and stricter regulation.† It was only narrowly defeated, 83 to 74.[317]

Military Affairs and Authorizations: The Army

Neither Congress nor the country favored a large standing army during the Jacksonian era. Virtually any speaker, whatever his politi-

---

*Adams explained that he felt qualification would be improper, since Jones's act was "avowedly war," which was exclusively Congress's prerogative to declare. Thus, Congress had a constitutional duty to seek information about what appeared to be a usurpation of its legislative function. 11 John Quincy Adams, *Memoirs* 305, 307 (1874–77).

†In referring to the resolution, the *Globe* states that "Mr. Adams offered a resolution which was understood to be declaratory of some general principles in relation to the capture of Monterey":

> *Resolved,* That the invasion of the territory of a foreign nation at peace with the United States, by any military or naval officer of the United States, is at once an aggravated offence against that foreign nation, against the peace of the world, and against the Constitution and people of the United States, for the signal punishment of which further provision ought to be made by law.

12 *Congressional Globe* 400.

cal persuasion, could gain a willing audience if he alluded to the unhappy results of a permanent military establishment.[318] Yet the defense of the United States could not have been entrusted to state militia service, which was dependent only upon the hazards of local planning. The overall general decline in the standing army* was reflected in cutbacks in appropriations, so that the army under Jackson became the minimum consistent with defense and was usually increased only in order to end hostilities, such as the Seminole War in Florida.†

Executive Initiatives for Defense   Congress nudged the executive to plan for military defense. During 1837, for example, the House and Senate passed resolutions calling on the secretary of war to submit plans for defending the western frontier against Indian aggression.[319] The Senate also called for plans to protect the northern and eastern frontiers.[320] Pointed demands for specifications of the minimum forces required on each frontier tended to force the executive to take concrete positions, which could then be reviewed by Congress.

One possible consequence of the congressional request for plans to protect the frontiers was Van Buren's admission that the western and northern borders were inadequately defended, since entire garrisons had been stripped of regular forces to assemble an army to fight in Florida. Van Buren, therefore, recommended improvements in the militia, expansion of the regular army, construction of a line of forts along the western frontier, and funds to provide a naval squadron to protect commerce on the eastern coast.[321] As a result of various external military threats described in reports of the secretaries of state and war, he succeeded in obtaining a modest increase in the military establishment in 1838, despite strong opposition.[322]

One significant reason for Congress's acquiescence in Van Buren's defense program was the care that the president took to indicate that he had no desire to lead the United States into war.[323] For example, his Neutrality Act of 10 March 1838 was passed despite opponents' charges that he sought expansion of executive power. It authorized civil authorities on the U.S.-Canadian border to seize arms, ammunition, vehicles, and vessels involved in any expedition attempting to enter Canada.[324] Both Congress and British Minister to Canada Henry Fox became certain that Van Buren wanted to avoid war, since the presi-

*In *Soldiers and Civilians: The Martial Spirit in America, 1775–1865,* 184, 185 (1968), Marcus Cunliffe expresses the belief that the reason for the decline was not that citizens opposed universal military training but that a man was not free if he could be taken from his home and subjected to "uncongenial discipline."

†For example, on 14 October 1837, both houses passed a supplemental appropriation of $1.6 million to carry on the Seminole War, in accordance with Secretary of War Joel Poinsett's request. 5 *Congressional Globe* 139, 142, 143.

dent's annual message of December 1838 castigated those "misguided" individuals in the United States who aimed to upset the "peace and order of a neighboring country."[325] General Winfield Scott delivered a personal message from the president to Maine Governor John Fairfield ordering him not to permit his troops to enter the land disputed by Maine and Canada and informing him that in the event of hostilities the president would issue new orders.[326] But Maine's troops failed to disband, and Congress finally authorized President Van Buren to call out 50,000 militia as well as to spend up to $10 million to defend the frontier[327] until further negotiations calmed the situation. General Scott then defused the legislature in Maine by getting New Brunswick to agree to disavow occupation if Maine removed all but a token military presence, an accord that both sides accepted.[328]

Even Van Buren's adroit handling of the Canadian crisis, however, was insufficient to convince Congress to implement Secretary of War Joel Poinsett's radical program to reform the militia. Poinsett, in the wake of the Canadian disturbances and unsettled Maine boundary problem, felt the solution lay in an extraordinary militia increase and universal military training. He advocated enrollment of every male between ages 20 and 45 for instruction under federal supervision, of which the states would then choose 100,000 men to establish an active force. One-fourth per year would retire to reserve status.[329] But the shortcomings of this proposal were several. It left the impression, in an election year, that the president wanted to exercise extensive control over state troops. The bill also appeared to accomplish centralization of military resources, which was precisely the opposite of general administration policy, and became somewhat emblematic of Van Buren's loss of touch with the Democratic electorate that presaged Harrison's victory in 1840.[330]

Although it did not act on this radical executive program, Congress continued to favor substantial, though gradual, defense increases through 1841. For example, it called on the secretary of war to submit plans for whatever works he thought would be necessary to put the northeast frontier in a "permanent state of defense."[331] And after a long debate, both houses passed an important amendment to the army appropriation bill for 1840 that authorized Van Buren to suspend funds to improve certain military installations* if funds to meet other appropriations were insufficient.[332] New Jersey Senator Samuel Southard objected that the proposed amendment transferred Congress's power to the executive and opened the door to unlimited peacetime exercise of presidential discretion to spend for military objectives.[333] Disagreeing,

---

*The authorized improvements included repairs and expansion of facilities at various barracks and armories. 8 *Congressional Globe* 535.

Senator James Buchanan replied that the limitation in the amendment was quite precise in that the Senate had clearly shown the president what it could do without in case of a treasury deficiency: "[W]e chose to exercise this dispensing power ourselves, and not to confer it on the Executive." To Buchanan, the amendment was a rein on executive discretion—a limitation and not an extension.[334] Senator Henry Hubbard (N.H.) also defended the amendment, comparing it to the bill passed in the previous session where "at one sweep" discretion was given the president to raise 50,000 men and $10 million with no comment from Congress that power had been improperly delegated.[335] Southard remained adamant, however, that if the services in question were of low priority and treasury funds were insufficient, Congress alone should strike them—particularly in peacetime—when the exigencies of war did not excuse an improper delegation of power.[336] The amendment's passage was only a modest triumph for Van Buren in terms of the scope of the delegation, but it was a substantial precedent for yielding authority to the executive to alter military appropriations set by Congress.

Dorr's Rebellion: Expansion of Executive Discretion   When President John Tyler took swift defensive action to quash an 1842 rebellion in Rhode Island, his moves raised the issue of the effect of statutory authority on the executive's military powers. Rhode Island Governor Sam King wrote to Tyler in April 1842 that domestic violence would probably erupt after delegates "elected" at meetings organized by one Thomas Dorr had convened and ratified a new liberal state constitution.[337] King asked the president to intervene, and Tyler studied his options. Governor King's call was improper under existing statutes because Rhode Island's legislature was sitting.* But finally, when Tyler became convinced in late June that the Dorrites posed a threat to peace,[338] he sent Secretary of War John Spencer to Rhode Island. Tyler clearly believed overt acts constituting insurrection had been committed and instructed Spencer to call for armed intervention from Massachusetts and Connecticut if he found that there had been rebellion and if proper application was made to the president.† When it

---

*Acts of February 1795 and March 1807 permitted the president to answer the call of a state legislature, or of its governor if the legislature could not be convened, whenever an insurrection occurred. The president might supply militia from other states, or federal armed forces, in such numbers "as he [might] judge sufficient to suppress such insurrection." Act of February 28, 1795, 1 Stat. 424; Act of March 3, 1807, 2 Stat. 442.

†Tyler to Spencer, Instructions, 29 June 1842, in 5 *Messages and Papers* 2160. If Spencer determined there was a case for federal intervention, he was ordered to issue a presidential proclamation demanding that the rebels disperse within twenty-four hours.

became clear that federal intervention was imminent, however, the insurgent effort collapsed.

Congressional Reaction Tyler acknowledged that the Rhode Island matter was the first occasion in which it had become necessary for a president to exercise broad discretion granted under the 1795 and 1807 statutes.[339] Congress apparently experienced doubts about the extent of the discretionary grant: should the president have consulted with Congress regarding whether the contingencies requiring his actions had occurred? Tyler had treated these statutes as self-executing, requiring no further consultation with the legislature. Only the House, however, passed a resolution calling for all papers relating to Tyler's conduct in the Dorr rebellion.*[340] Some members, such as Representative John McClernand (D. Ill.) thought that Congress should first sanction executive interposition and that Tyler thus had transcended his authority in interfering on his own with the private concerns of a state.[341] After Tyler's reply explaining the facts as he saw them, however,[342] the House conducted no substantive debate.

Reaction of the Supreme Court Congress did not attempt definition of the president's authority to use force, but the Supreme Court experienced no such reluctance. In *Luther v. Borden,* 48 U.S. (7 Howard) 1 (1849), the Court upheld Congress's right to vest broad discretionary authority in the president, declaring that under the Acts of 1795 and 1807, the president might judge the existence of a situation that legally bound the government of the United States to act.† Supreme Court Justice Joseph Story, who also sat for the Rhode Island Circuit Court, had written a private letter to Daniel Webster expressing concern that the president would not call up militia and regulars until insurrection was underway. Admitting that the president was limited by statutes, Story urged as legitimate executive power the anticipatory calling up of armed forces in order to protect a state against domestic violence.[343] Such preliminary acts, he argued, would not be unlawful because they were necessary to make the protection effectual.[344]

A year after he had left Tyler's administration, Webster congratulated his former chief for his handling of the Dorr affair: "The case was new, and it was managed with equal discretion and firmness."[345]

---

*The Senate did not take up Ohio Senator William Allen's unqualified demand for all information on which the president was acting in the Dorr case. 11 *Congressional Globe* 430, 431. It could be argued that the Senate by its inaction refused to acknowledge that the president was unauthorized to act.

†The Court had upheld extensive delegations. *E.g., The Aurora v. United States,* 11 U.S. (7 Cranch) 382 (1813); and *The Thomas Gibbons,* 12 U.S. (8 Cranch) 421 (1814). Justice Story sat on the U.S. Supreme Court when *Luther v. Borden* was subsequently appealed, and Webster appeared for the defendants in error. 6 Webster, *Works* 216 (1851).

Yet Webster's flattery was also self-congratulation, since as secretary of state during the Dorr Rebellion, he had been active in advising President Tyler in the disposition of a delicate incident involving the extent of executive discretion.

U.S. Military Actions and the Acquisition of Texas

Jackson and the Texas Boundary   One of the most important U.S. military involvements of the Jacksonian period concerned the diplomatic negotiations that committed the United States to the defense and, ultimately, the acquisition of Texas. These negotiations began ostensibly as settlements of the U.S.-Mexican border.*

But Jackson's territorial aims went far beyond acquiring the disputed territory between the branches of the Sabine River. He wanted Texas and authorized his first minister to Mexico, Joel Poinsett, to offer up to $5 million for it. Mexico adamantly refused to sell,[346] and Poinsett undermined his usefulness by involving himself in domestic political activities within Mexico. His successor, Anthony Butler, quickly demonstrated his willingness to cheat, bribe, or extort to obtain Mexican approval to purchase Texas.[347] Once efforts to buy failed, however, Jackson refused to intervene in the Texas revolution,† and he recognized the independence of Texas only on 3 March 1837, one day before leaving office.[348]

The important military operation that Jackson authorized on the Texas-Louisiana border may have reflected a readiness to take further action if the Texans had failed in their effort for independence. Hostilities began between Texas and Mexico late in 1835, triggered by activities of an increasing flood of American migration. An army of Texans was formed under Sam Houston, Jackson's long-time friend. On receiving news of these events, Jackson through Secretary of War Lewis Cass ordered General Edmund Pendleton Gaines, command officer of the Western Department, to proceed to the Texas border. Gaines was ordered to fulfill the U.S. duty "to remain entirely neutral, and to cause their neutrality to be respected."[349] He was to prevent either of the contesting parties from crossing into the United States and to fulfill

---

*The United States claimed the western boundary of the Louisiana Purchase was the western-most branch of the Sabine River, called the Neches River. Mexico argued that the eastern branch was the true Sabine. American troops were kept outside the territory claimed by Mexico pending a settlement. *See* T. Marshall, *A History of the Western Boundary of the Louisiana Purchase, 1819–1841* (1914).

†On 7 December 1835, just before the outbreak of hostilities between Mexico and Texas, Jackson declared that the United States would remain neutral, but would protect the Texas-American border from any threat. 3 *Congressional Globe* 4.

treaty obligations with Mexico by preventing hostile incursions of Indians into Mexico.

Upon learning of the Alamo's fall, General Gaines proposed a radical expansion in his authority. On 29 March 1836, he suggested to Cass that there was a danger of attacks across the Texas border by both Indians and Mexicans. Unless instructed otherwise, he felt it his duty not only to be ready to defend "our slender frontier, but to anticipate their lawless movements, by crossing our supposed or imaginary national boundary, and meeting the savage marauders wherever to be found in their approach towards our frontier."[350] Gaines was undoubtedly aware that Jackson had used an almost identical rationale for crossing into Florida during the first Seminole War.[351] Without waiting for a reply from Cass,* Gaines then requested the governors of four states to send him each a brigade of volunteers to supplement his own relatively small contingent of 600 men.[†352] Governor White of Louisiana declined for lack of funds, adding he did not believe the force was necessary, while the governors of Alabama and Mississippi did nothing.[353]

After having reviewed the Cass-Gaines correspondence, the House acted promptly, approving on 27 April a bill authorizing the president to accept up to 10,000 volunteers.[354] Representative Lewis Williams (N.C.) had objected to the bill because insufficient information "had been laid before Congress, by which it was shown that so large an extra force was requisite for repelling the Indians; and that it was, to a certain extent,

---

*Secretary Cass replied to Gaines on 25 April. He noted that Gaines anticipated that the contending parties may "approach our frontiers" and may place the lives and property of American citizens in jeopardy. "Should this be the case," he wrote, "the President approves the suggestion you make; and you are authorized to take such position, on either side of the imaginary border line, as may be best for your defensive operations." Cass cautioned Gaines to act only if necessary, to explain fully his instructions to any armed parties he should encounter, and to go no further than old Fort Nacogdoches, "which is within the limits of the United States, as claimed by this government." 6 *American State Papers, Military Affairs* 418–19 (1832–61). Cass wrote again on 4 May, informing Gaines that Jackson expressly sanctioned his request for volunteers from the southwestern states. The War Department had, furthermore, requested the governors of the five states to call up "such militia force as you [Gaines] find necessary in carrying into effect the instructions heretofore given to you. The theatre of operations is so distant from the seat of Government, that much must be intrusted to your discretion." Meanwhile, upon being told on 20 April of the authorization given to Gaines to advance as far as Fort Nacogdoches, the Mexican minister protested that such conduct would be regarded by his government as an unprovoked invasion of Mexican territory and a treaty violation. Gorostiza to Forsyth, 23 April 1836, in W. Weaver, *Examination and Review of Gorostiza's Pamphlet* 59–60 (1838).

†General Gaines's career was marked by similar examples of requisitioning volunteers upon his own authority. In the Seminole War, a Senate investigating committee condemned Generals Jackson and Gaines for exceeding their orders and raising volunteers. Sofaer, *Origins* 363. Gaines also provoked a storm of controversy in the Mexican War, as some legislators argued that such a usurpation by an officer in the field posed a dangerous threat to congressional authority to raise armies. *See* Chapter 2, pp. 100–103.

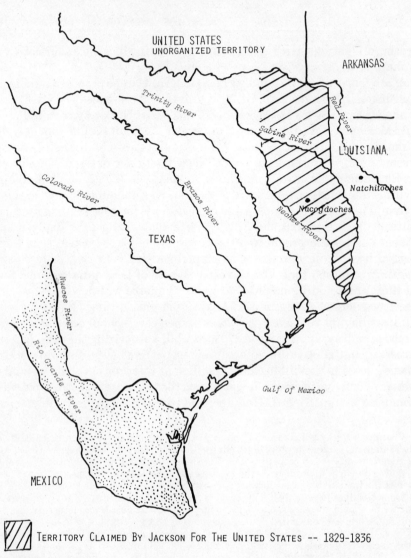

UNITED STATES
UNORGANIZED TERRITORY

ARKANSAS

Trinity River

Sabine River

Red River

LOUISIANA

Colorado River

Brazos River

Natchitoches

Neches River

Nacogdoches

TEXAS

Nueces River

Rio Grande River

Gulf of Mexico

MEXICO

▨ TERRITORY CLAIMED BY JACKSON FOR THE UNITED STATES -- 1829-1836

▦ TERRITORY CLAIMED BY UNITED STATES AS TEXAS -- 1846-1848

Adapted by permission from *The American Heritage Pictorial Atlas of United States History,* c1966, p. 161 and William H. Emory's map of the Texas Republic (Washington: 1844). Emory delineated Texas in his map of 1844, the first scientific mapping of the entire Southwest based on actual observation. His "Map of Texas and the Countries Adjacent" was delivered to the U.S. Senate along with a message from President Tyler, and it figured prominently in Senatorial deliberations on the annexation of Texas. It was the first U.S. government map to acknowledge Texas's own boundary claims as a Republic. (*See* text, pp. 75–77).

authorizing the formation of a new standing army."[355] But Richard M. Johnson (Ky.) saw nothing extraordinary in the power proposed. Existing law, he noted, recognized the president's power to accept volunteers but limited their term of service to three months; the bill would allow volunteers to continue by their own consent.[356] Francis Granger of New York concurred by saying that even if the authority was not given, it "should at all times exist in the President of the United States to call out troops . . . in such an emergency."[357]

Eleazer Ripley (La.) maintained that the United States was well within its rights to enter and occupy the disputed territory under the circumstances Gaines anticipated. "If either the Mexicans or Texans attempt, with an armed force, to occupy one of the branches of the Sabine, to our exclusion, until the line be settled, our forces (notifying both parties) should advance to old Fort Nacogdoches, situated upon the western branch, and hold it until the boundary is ascertained."[358] Even if the disputed territory were considered Mexican, "is there any thing new in the doctrine that a neutral has a right to cross a neighboring line, if, in good faith, it be necessary to save her own citizens and territory from desolation?"[359] He denied John Quincy Adams's claim that the crossing would amount to a declaration of war, reminding him that during the first Seminole War, "in one of the most masterly arguments which has ever emanated from the statesmen of this republic. . . . , in vindication of General Jackson, he [Adams] perfectly established a contrary doctrine, the precise doctrine for which General Gaines contends."[360]

The bill passed the House with John Quincy Adams's amendment placing a $300,000 ceiling on funds available to the president to raise volunteers. After some Senate debate, the bill passed in the upper chamber on 18 May, without a limit on the number of volunteers that could be raised. When the House refused to recede from its version, a conference compromise passed both houses, appropriating $300,000 and authorizing up to 10,000 volunteers.[361]

Meanwhile, Jackson had submitted another bill to the House on 6 May, asking for $1 million for defense of the western frontier.[362] Along with the secretary of war's message, the administration sent both the correspondence with Gaines and Secretary of State Forsyth's memorandum stating that the Mexican minister had been informed that Gaines had been authorized to cross the border. Excluded from the transmittal was the response of Manuel E. Gorostiza, Mexican minister at Washington. It was a vehement protest of Gaines's orders—which the State Department had received on 21 April.[363] The message sought no express approval for the decision to cross the border. Jackson simply assumed that he was within his powers to authorize such conduct unilaterally.

Adams sought to challenge Jackson's assumption. He argued that crossing the border under existing circumstances raised serious constitutional considerations, including whether the president could make war without legislative authorization:

> [A] most extraordinary power had been given to the commanding general to cross the boundary of a foreign State, and take up a position within their territory: in other words, to make war ... [If the Mexican minister has not agreed to this act,] then there is an after consideration of great moment, as to the constitutional power of the President; whether he could authorize a commanding general to march into a foreign country; to commit an act of hostility; to make war, without the consent of Congress.[364]

John Reed (Mass.) complained of the incomplete nature of the information and added that to pass the appropriation would give tacit approval to the president's sanctioning Gaines's letters and "would be taken as a quasi declaration of war."[365] Such arguments led Joseph Underwood (Ky.) to move to amend the bill by inserting a proviso "that the appropriation should not be understood as giving any sanction to an invasion, by the troops of the United States, of the territory of the United Mexican States. ..."[366] But the House apparently was unwilling to deny Jackson the authority he claimed, since Underwood's motion was rejected.

Several representatives complained that the transmittal was incomplete.[367] Even some supporters of the President conceded that Gorostiza's response to Gaines's orders was important to their deliberations.[368] Moreover, Representative Garland, who represented the frontier area of Louisiana, challenged Gaines's facts and said that he had heard nothing about aroused Indians.[369] Furthermore, he argued at length that the boundary in that area had never been disputed by the United States since the treaty with Spain in 1819 and criticized the eagerness of many members of Congress to go to war to assist the Texans in their rebellion.[370]

The pressure to support Jackson, and the popularity of aiding Texas even indirectly, were too great for the House to resist. Approve the funds, argued Tennessee's John Bell, and settle the factual controversies later.*[371] Rejecting all efforts to delay its vote, the House over-

*The *Globe* narrative continued:

> He called upon gentlemen at this stage of the question, to consider whether it would not be most prudent to vote this preliminary appropriation to arm the frontier, and to provide against any possible contingency; and then to discuss the matter or some other proposition which might be brought forward hereafter. Was there a gentleman who would pause at that hour, when there was not only a possibility, but a strong probability of a war upon our frontier, which had no fortifications. ... It seemed to him that they should have a strong explanation of this subject from the executive; but he

whelmingly passed the appropriation 146 to 3; none of those who had spoken in favor of more information voted against the bill.[372] Thereafter, on 10 May, a comprehensive resolution passed calling on Jackson for additional information, and an apparently complete set of correspondence in the War Department files was transmitted to the House on 14 May.*[373]

The appropriation bill fared far less well in the Senate. One reason for this was Senate passage on 23 May of the first bill authorizing volunteers and providing $300,000 for frontier defense. Another was probably the news that Houston and the Texas army had overwhelmed Santa Anna at San Jacinto in late April, which reached Washington on or about 16 May.[374] The Senate sent the $1 million appropriation bill to committee on 9 May, but it never emerged.[375] Before adjourning, however, the Senate unanimously and the House overwhelmingly passed resolutions calling for the recognition of Texas as an independent state as soon as it succeeded in establishing a government capable of performing the duties of a sovereign power.[376]

Gaines went ahead with the administration's plan to occupy the area up to Fort Nacogdoches. On 28 June, he requested regiments from the governors of Kentucky, Tennessee, Mississippi, and Louisiana.[377] He also ordered a U.S. officer to Nacogdoches to restrain any Indian troops or armed forces committing hostilities on U.S. forces—emphasizing that he was to act only on evidence demonstrated by conduct, not threats.†[378] A month later, Gorostiza announced that he had heard Gaines intended to occupy Nacogdoches, using as a pretext the murder of two white men by Indians "sixty or seventy miles beyond the border." He protested and threatened to return to Mexico unless Gaines's authority to cross the border was withdrawn.[379] Jackson was unwilling to withdraw Gaines's authority to cross the border, but he did refuse, on 6 August, to sanction the requisition of Tennessee troops.[380] Gaines had shown no need for more troops, Jackson stated, and a further increase "would warrant the belief that it was done to aid Texas, and not from a desire to prevent an infringement of our territorial or national rights."**

---

would receive those communications hereafter at a time when he could examine them with greater deliberation.

2 *Congressional Globe* 358.

*The noteworthy omission was Gorostiza's letters protesting Gaines's authority to occupy the area up to Nacogdoches.

†Cass meanwhile repeated his instructions that Gaines was to advance to Nacogdoches if the Indians in Texas threatened the frontier and such advance was necessary for protection. 7 *Papers of the Texas Revolution* 420 (J. Jenkins ed. 1973).

**In an earlier draft of this letter, in Jackson's handwriting but written in the third person, the president proposed denying the requisition of Tennessee troops on the ground

Privately, Jackson suggested that Gaines was deliberately attempting to aid Texas and to embarrass the administration.* Gorostiza was pleased at the tone of Jackson's letter but dissatisfied that Gaines's authorization to invade Mexico had not been withdrawn.[381] In fact, on 4 September, Jackson repeated his orders to Gaines that, if Indians who disturbed the peace of the frontier were receiving assistance or shelter within Mexico, he was authorized to pursue and punish them, "wherever they may be found."†[382] But if Gaines found the Indians at peace and the rumors of incitement by the Mexicans untrue, he was to withdraw immediately to within the established boundary.[383]

Gaines had meanwhile crossed the border and occupied Nacogdoches.[384] On 15 October, after repeated failures to obtain assurances that authorization to cross the border would be withdrawn, Gorostiza informed the State Department that Gaines had acted on incomplete information, ended his mission, and left the United States.[385]

In his annual message to Congress in December 1836, Jackson expressed some doubts as to the justification for Gaines's march to Nacogdoches and indicated that he was ordering the troops' conditional withdrawal from Nacogdoches.[386] Yet he hoped that Mexico would take "a more dispassionate and just view of this subject" and not regard a justifiable precaution, made necessary by Mexico's inability to control its frontier, as "an encroachment upon its rights, or a stain upon its honor."[387]

---

that the volunteers' bill had implicitly limited executive authority to call out additional forces. This language was not included in the final draft, however:

> The congress who passed the law authorizing the raising of 10,000 volunteers supposed that number competent for the Defence of our frontier and to put down the little punie Indian war, and unless cases of great emergency should arise before the next meeting of Congress, the Executive cannot sanction the raising of more than that authorized by Congress.

Jackson to Governor Cannon, 3 August 1836 in A. Jackson, 5 *Correspondence* 416–18.
*A letter from Jackson to Postmaster-General Amos Kendall dated 12 August 1836, stated:

> You will discover that the basis on which Genl Gaines made the requisition was the movement of the Mexican troops into Texas, which basis was a violation of that neutrality which we had assumed, and was in fact, an act which Mexico might have viewed an act of war upon her if it had been carried into effect, and I have no doubt was intended by Gaines to get troops there who would have at once went over to the Texan army; but I have stopped it in the bud. And you will find there has been no possible movement by the Indians, and [that] the whole has been projected in New Orleans; however, a full investigation, in due time, will be had. Genl Gaines would do any act to injure and implicate the administration.

Id. 420.
†Jackson added that if Mexico was unwilling or unable to prevent Indians in her territory from committing depredations on U.S. citizens, the law of nations and self-defense authorize that it be done for her. *Id.* 424.

On 22 December, Jackson sent Congress extracts of a report from Henry Morfit, an agent he had appointed to collect information on "the political, military, and civil condition of Texas."*[388] For two months thereafter, legislators exhaustively debated the issue of whether or not to recognize Texas on the basis of the executive's readiness to declare it independent. In the face of Jackson's repeated assertions that he was unwilling to make the decision, the House voted to amend the civil and diplomatic appropriation bill for 1837 to authorize a salary and outfit for a diplomatic officer to be sent to the republic of Texas "whenever the President of the U.S. may receive satisfactory evidence that Texas is an independent power, and shall deem it expedient to appoint such a minister."[389]

The Senate was presented with the choice of leaving this Texas appointment exclusively in the president's discretion or of recognizing Texas on its own. The upper house chose to assert itself and passed a resolution declaring that there was sufficient evidence for the government to acknowledge Texan independence.[390] The next day, it also passed the House bill funding a diplomatic agent.†[391]

Jackson promptly responded to Congress's pronouncements of its judgment. Probably delighted to be able to recognize Texas without accepting the sole responsibility for doing so, he sent the Senate a message on 3 March nominating Alcée La Branche as *chargé d'affaires* to Texas. He reviewed the fact that Congress had provided for a *chargé* to Texas and that the Senate had resolved that Texas had established its independence. "Regarding these proceedings as a virtual decision of the question submitted by me to Congress, I think it my duty to acquiesce therein. . . ."[392] The Senate confirmed the appointment on 6 March.[393]

Jackson probably felt that his unilateral recognition of Texas might have offended Mexico far more than if he acted with legislative support. Furthermore, such action would have complicated presidential candidate Van Buren's task in holding the Democrats together during the election of 1836. Northerners viewed an independent Texas as the first step toward its inclusion in the Union as an additional state permitting slavery—and thereby upsetting the existing balance between North and South. Van Buren's opponents (Clay and Hugh Lawson White) would have welcomed the opportunity of forcing the "Little Wizard" to take a clear position on whether recognition had been properly extended. But Van Buren was far more comfortable supporting the wait-and-see position Jackson adopted. Political factors therefore modified

---

*Since Congress had gone on record in favor of recognizing Texas's independence "whenever satisfactory information should be received," Jackson felt it "proper" that he should "present the considerations" that governed his position. 4 *Congressional Globe* 44.

†The Senate did reject a truncated version of the Houses's funding provision, 16 to 21. *Id.* 214.

the significance of Jackson's unprecedented invitation to Congress to participate with him in deciding whether to take reprisals against Mexico or to recognize Texan independence. Jackson was eager to share responsibility for policies with potential for war, even suggesting that Congress could virtually decide the question of recognition and make it a president's duty to acquiesce. However uncharacteristic of Jackson this behavior may have been, Congress accepted his invitation and established a new level of its own involvement in a fundamental, foreign-affairs decision with potentially far-reaching military consequences.

Tyler and Annexation   The story of diplomatic maneuvers leading to Texas's annexation during the Tyler administration illustrates that Congress believed the president's treatymaking power, if left unchecked, could be a potential cause of war.* The principal concern of the Texas Republic was its vulnerability to attack from Mexico and loss of Britain as an ally if it should begin to negotiate statehood. The United States also risked war with the Mexicans, who were enraged at what they considered deliberate encouragement of the Texas insurrection.†

Texas Minister in Washington Isaac Van Zandt, therefore, sought a guarantee from Secretary of State Abel P. Upshur that the United States would protect Texas during treaty negotiations for annexation and before ratification. Upshur acceded only orally,[394] but the American *chargé* to Texas, W.S. Murphy, agreed in writing with Anson Jones, Texas Minister of Foreign Relations, that the United States would not only guarantee Texan integrity during the negotiations but also Texas's independence, in the event of their failure.[395] A field officer, without executive authorization, thus pledged the United States to employment of force without congressional knowledge or approval, as Texas's Jones sent General Pinckney Henderson to Washington to negotiate a treaty.

Secretary Upshur was accidentally killed in February 1844 and was eventually succeeded by an even more avid enthusiast for Texas, John C. Calhoun.** Before Calhoun took office, however, an interim secretary

*Executive unilateral guarantees of protection to Texas during the delicate negotiating period were criticized by Congress and, arguably, could have involved the United States in war with Mexico earlier than it did occur. Even though Tyler's skillful negotiations were checked by Senate rejection of his treaty (*see* Corwin, *The President* 214, 220), Mexico still smouldered as late as 1843 over the fact that the United States had recognized Texas in 1837. Letter, Juan de Bocanegra to Waddy Thompson, 23 August 1843, in S. Doc. No. 1, 28th Cong., 1st Sess. 26.

†*See* Bocanegra to Webster, 12 May 1843, in 6 Webster, *Works* 442–44.

**Calhoun may have influenced Upshur, as seen in an August 1843 letter outlining Calhoun's belief that British policy in Texas if unchecked would result in abolition of slavery in Texas as well as threaten it throughout the South, thus forcing the formation of a southern confederacy. Calhoun to Upshur, 27 August 1843, in 5 Bemis, *The American Secretaries* 141–44.

of state, John Nelson, repudiated Murphy's promises to Texas as having exceeded the president's constitutional authority. Nelson declared that Tyler had power to concentrate army and naval forces in the southern United States "at a proper time" in the future but that this did not include use of armed force against a nation with whom the U.S. was at peace during treaty negotiations.[396]

Calhoun, in April 1844, granted Van Zandt's more limited request for protection from invasion during the pendency of a negotiated treaty— *i.e.,* from signature to ratification.*[397] He also indicated[398] that deployment orders from the Navy Department had gone out that day—11 April. Yet the treaty with Texas was not signed until 12 April. Thus, orders to protect Texas were given prior to the date Tyler decided to use as the justification for his deployment. The Texas negotiators wrote to their government that Calhoun had assured them verbally that the president had issued orders for commanders in the field to repel any serious demonstrations of Mexican hostile intent, whether by land or water.[399] They were also told that in the event of hostilities, Tyler was also planning to request Congress to adopt defensive measures, while he would "in the meantime consider it his duty to defend Texas . . . and do so. . . ."[400]

The treaty of 12 April 1844 was rejected, 35 to 16,[401] due to northern senators' aggravation at Calhoun's insistence that without Texas in the Union, British abolitionist efforts would jeopardize slavery in the South and thus threaten what he considered to be U.S. national interests.[402] Without knowledge of the treaty rejection, Mexico declared war against Texas, prompting Anson Jones to ask for U.S. military aid.[403] Tilghman Howard, U.S. *chargé* in Texas, turned Jones down,[404] but his refusal did not reflect the highest level interpretation of the obligation that the administration was prepared to assume. Since Tyler was determined to secure annexation by act of Congress† even though the treaty had been defeated, Calhoun instructed Howard that the president planned to defend Texas from attack "pending the question of annexation" by Congress.[405]

Tyler's statements and actions were equivocal. While both he and Calhoun[406] assured Texas of protection and shifted military forces, the president also maintained that the Constitution bestowed upon Congress alone the prerogative to repel a threatened invasion, and Calhoun

---

*The scope of his proposed military aid was uncertain. Calhoun stated that during the guarantee period the president would "use all means placed within his power by the Constitution to protect Texas from all foreign invasion." S. Doc. No. 349, 28th Cong., 1st Sess. 11.

†Early in 1845, Congress passed a joint resolution consenting to annexation of Texas as a state. The Act of March 1, 1845 (5 Stat. 797), gave the president two options. He could select immediate annexation by submitting Congress's resolution to Texas and, upon receiving agreement from the Texan legislature, apply to Congress for its formal ap-

reminded Howard in Texas that the president's powers were circumscribed by the Constitution.[407] No one knew the proposed extent of protection, though a new Texan representative in Washington, C.H. Raymond, believed that the United States would "do rather more for our ... support, if necessary, than they desire should appear. They don't like to leave themselves open to an attack by Congress. ..."[408]

Congressional Reaction After the treaty was rejected, the Senate in secret session asked to know if the executive had made any preparations for war.[409] Tyler replied that while the treaty was pending and under the belief it would be speedily ratified, he had taken military steps in light of Mexico's statement that it would regard annexation of Texas as a declaration of war. He transmitted copies of orders to the armed forces* and called the Senate's attention to his request that field commanders alert him to "hostile design ... with a view the same should promptly be submitted to Congress for its mature deliberations."†[410] Tyler emphasized that he had treated the potential military threat to Texas as if it were an imminent invasion of U.S. territory, which he had unilateral authority under the Constitution to repel.

Several hours before Tyler's response arrived, Senator Thomas Hart Benton reminded his colleagues that the information they sought was critical:

> If military and naval aid was promised before the annexation treaty was signed, then war was made before that treaty was signed. ... [411]

---

proval. Or, he could negotiate a treaty again. House, 25 January 1845 (120 to 98), in 14 *Congressional Globe* 194; Senate, 27 February 1845 (voice vote), *id.* 362; final passage, *id.* 372, 385. Tyler, desiring to be associated with acquisition of Texas, chose to annex by joint resolution and sent Congress's resolution to Texas for legislative acquiescence. President Polk finally approved a joint resolution of Congress admitting Texas as a state in December 1845. Reeves, *American Diplomacy under Tyler and Polk* 185–88.

*If a threat to Texas was believed imminent, General Zachary Taylor was to advance from the town of Natchitoches, in U.S. territory, to the Texas frontier on the Sabine River and await instructions. S. Doc. No. 341, p. 77, 28th Cong., 1st Sess. (*See* map, p. 70.) Commodore David Conner was ordered to show his force at Vera Cruz and "remonstrate" with any commanding officer threatening invasion of Texas. *Id.* 79. Both sets of orders placed officers in positions and in situations likely to result in hostilities, even though their orders were "hedged" with instructions to communicate information to the president and await further orders.

†*Cf.* the Grant administration's argument to justify protection of Santo Domingo, *infra* pp. 312–315. Tyler argued that since there arose an equitable title to Texas by the treaty of annexation, requiring only the action of the Senate to perfect it, any military action against Texas was hostility toward the United States that would justify repulsion by any means at U.S. disposal. 5 *Messages and Papers* 2170. A second, quite similar request for information related to military aid promised to Texas "in the event of an agreement to annex herself to the United States." The president's response was virtually identical, repeating his duty to protect Texas during treaty deliberations. *Id.* 2174.

The Missourian assailed those senators who did not care about the date of the agreement because only a "small war" was involved:

> War is war, whether great or small! and the making of all wars is given to Congress, and no other power dare to make one. The President and Senate cannot—dare not—do it! much less the President and his Secretary of State alone![412]

Benton insisted on discovering when the military aid to Texas had been promised in relation to the 12 April treaty signing.* He was interrupted in a speech by the arrival of the desired information complete to 11 April—the day before the Texas-U.S. treaty was signed. The Senate heard read aloud that Calhoun, by command of the president, had informed General Houston's ministers in writing that "ships and troops would move immediately to the Texian frontier, and the Mexican coast, PREPARED FOR ANY EMERGENCY."[413]

Others in Congress upheld Tyler's decision to deploy military forces as commander-in-chief. Though military officers had been "expressly forbidden to engage in hostilities," Senator Levi Woodbury (D. N.H.) declared that executive use of the army and navy in peacetime to protect "the points which will be most exposed" in the event of hostilities was not a declaration of war or an act in derogation of Congress's authority.[414] Arkansas's Ambrose Sevier believed the president had the right to send military forces into any place in the United States where the interest of the country might require their services.[415] It would have been "downright drivelling" for Tyler to have done less, according to South Carolina Senator George McDuffie. If the use of a "corps of observation" was making war on Mexico, then the United States was at war with

> all the powers in the West Indies, on the Mediterranean, and on the coast of Africa; for we have squadrons of observation in every sea to protect our commerce, and to make war on pirates.[416]

Instead, McDuffie claimed, "if the President had directed these movements with the constitution open before him, and a council of Philadelphia lawyers at his elbow, he could not have plumbed the line of his constitutional power more precisely than he has done." His orders to

---

*Senator Benton characterized as "preposterous" the president's argument "that the treaty was a treaty until *rejected* by the Senate ... instead of being nothing until *ratified!*" *Id.* 498 (emphasis in the original). Such reasoning reversed the power of the Senate, making it necessary for the Senate to undo a treaty sent by the president instead of requiring Senate consent to give it validity.

both army and navy were to watch the threatened Mexican maneuvers and report them so that they might promptly be reported to Congress.[417]

Other legislators asked more subtle questions. Since both Congress and the president had known since 1843 that a treaty of annexation would probably foment war with Mexico,[418] had Tyler usurped Congress's power to declare war by signing the treaty? Were there emergency situations when the president should not exercise his constitutional authority to make treaties? John Quincy Adams offered a resolution flatly repudiating any attempt by the president and Senate to use the treaty power to place the United States in a state of war as "flagrant usurpation" of legislative power.*[419]

Senator Benton insured Senate participation in the constitutional controversy by introducing two resolutions. The first declared that the treatymaking power did not extend to the power of making war, while the second announced that ratification of the Texas treaty would constitute adoption of the Texas war.†[420] Debate on the Benton resolutions extended through 5 June, but discussion was not continued after the treaty was rejected 8 June.[421] On the other hand, Senators McDuffie and Sidney Breese (D. Ill.) supported presidential initiative to make treaties. Breese admitted that perhaps "it would have been respectful to [the Senate], and more satisfactory to the country, if the executive had advised with it." But since in the exercise of his powers the president had not deemed it expedient to do so, "and as, by the practice of the government, he can take the initiative, he is not to be censured for doing so in this instance."[422]

Congress's indignation over Tyler's announcement that troops had been deployed to protect Texas was also expressed in attempts to limit the funds at his disposal. For example, Representative Washington Hunt (Wh. N.Y.) tried to amend the annual appropriation bill in May 1844 so that no more than one-half of it could be used before 1 January 1845, and thus new money would be prevented from going into the executive's hands to let him "consummate . . . the outrage which he had commenced. . . ."[423] The House's eventually overwhelming vote against Hunt's amendment** was probably due to its belief that the Senate

---

*Adams's and a similar resolution of New York Representative Daniel Barnard did not succeed in being formally introduced. 13 *Congressional Globe* 664, 677; 12 Adams, *Memoirs* 531.

†It is interesting to note that the treaty was not adopted and that a negative vote by some senators may have served to register their view that the treaty power had been used to make war.

**At first, the Hunt amendment barely passed in the House (62 to 61, 22 May 1844, in 13 *Congressional Globe* 616), but it was struck down by House members, 111 to 36, on 7 June when the bill was returned from the Senate. *Id.* 651. It was not reinstated by the Conference Committee, which finally resolved the versions of the two houses. *Id.* 692; Act of June 17, 1844, 5 Stat. 699–703.

would reject the annexation treaty the following day, which it did. They also could have reasoned further that rejection would end the president's attempts to protect Texas, which he had described as limited to the pendency of the treaty.

In fact, the failure of the Texas treaty served for a brief period to quiet resolutions of disapproval or affirmation of congressional authority. Political, sectional concerns transcended appeals to constitutional principle, at least until the outbreak of war with Mexico under Polk in 1846.

CONCLUSION

The years before the Mexican War abounded in struggles between president and legislature regarding claims of overlapping or concurrent and implied powers. The executive generally triumphed on the ground of state necessity and the need for flexibility in foreign affairs. But congressmen issued strong challenges to his assertions of independent authority.

By the end of John Tyler's administration, it was still unsettled whether the president might exercise his foreign affairs authority when it had the potential for involving the United States in hostilities abroad. In the modern context, where these powers are concurrent, it has become customary for the executive to take such initiatives.[424]

In the 1830s and 1840s, the executive frequently took initiatives in other areas of concurrent power. When he did, the balance of power was more often than not established in his favor. For example, executive initiatives resulted in the introduction of numerous military bills that dominated the nature of the legislative product. Congressmen also weighed the threat of an executive policy veto as they drafted, debated, and voted on legislation.

By their appointments to important posts, presidents of the Jacksonian period exercised strong influences on sensitive foreign relations that congressmen often contested but rarely defeated by refusals to confirm. In its delegations of authority, Congress usually provided specific guidelines for executive conduct. When faced with the imminent threat of hostilities, such as in the British boundary dispute, it left to the president the determination of that threat and handed him authority to take any military action he felt was necessary, including calling up a large military force. Thus, Congress acknowledged the president's greater capacity to act quickly and effectively in emergencies. The legislature refused, on the other hand, to delegate authority when it believed that its exercise would surely lead to war and where it felt other methods, such as negotiations, could be employed to resolve disputes. It was equally opposed to providing lump sums for discretionary use without specific detailing of the permitted expenditures.

During Jackson's administration, information sharing became highly institutionalized. Lengthy and frequent congressional objections to executive compliance with its requests left no doubt of the unsettled nature of the power to control information concerning the nation's foreign and military affairs. By omitting the public interest reservation or qualification in their requests, congressmen made the statement that they held a co-equal right with the president to judge when the public's interest would be impaired by disclosures. Although legislators debated whether the absence of the qualification did not imply that the president must transmit all information to Congress, they generally accepted the president's decisions concerning what he would send.

Andrew Jackson seized the initiative in information sharing by continuing an earlier practice of simply deleting material without informing Congress that a portion had been stricken. At times, Congress fought back. On one occasion in Tyler's administration when the executive explained his reasons for withholding information, Congress protested his message. At another point, during Jackson's presidency, a frustrated Congress censured his withdrawal of deposits from the Bank of the United States and also attempted unsuccessfully to gain access to a Cabinet discussion. But such vigorous though futile objections and actions were rare.

Both houses attempted to shape foreign policy. They urged the president to settle disputes with foreign nations and to start negotiations over such matters as a Central American canal. The Senate, as an authorized treatymaking partner, exerted more influence than the House, even to the extent of embodying in some of its resolutions the terms a treaty should contain. It stopped short of directing the president to act, however, while he, in turn, expressed his freedom to accept or reject any proffered advice.

Impelled by its perception that the president was not pressing U.S. interests sufficiently in relation to the Oregon territory, Congress developed the thesis that it could urge the abrogation of treaties. Treaty abrogation and an American take-over of Oregon held the potential of war with Britain; but the president refused to act on these policies.

By contrast with Congress's uncertain and limited steps, executive initiatives were not only forceful but also capable of being flexible enough to bring about a satisfactory conclusion. Jackson was thwarted in his effort to obtain the reprisal power to punish for nonpayment of claims. Yet he remained able to negotiate sternly and to drive hard bargains that were still elastic enough to permit negotiations to continue.

In debate over executive power in military affairs, legislators explored the issue of whether the president's commander-in-chief power should end when there is the likelihood that its exercise could alter the status of U.S. relations with a foreign nation from peace to war. Jackson's unilateral ordering of U.S. troops into foreign territory to protect American life and property could easily have plunged the United States into war with Mexico. Congress had difficulty in defining the point of executive usurpation and imposing its will on the president. The problem was not eclipsed by Jackson's invitation to Congress to decide the question of Texan recognition. It surfaced again when John Tyler sought to secure Texas for the United States. Both Jackson and Tyler prevailed, unaffected by controversies over their deployments. Jackson ordered a troop withdrawal from the disputed area only after the Texan revolution had succeeded and the territory had become part of the Texas Republic. There was no testing of his intention to aid the revolution, since his intervention became unnecessary to achieve the goal of freedom for Texas that he always had in view. And there is evidence Tyler's pledge of protection to Texas continued even after the justified interval for the pledge had terminated—that is, after the pending Texas treaty was rejected.

Presidents of the Jackson era predicated their exercise of authority on grants of power contained in the Constitution and upon interpretation of the law of nations. But the fact that they continued to maintain the initiatives in the "twilight zones" of authority became the harbinger of a claim that later chief executives would develop and refine—an inherent right of the president to act decisively when swift decisionmaking could benefit the general welfare.

✳   *Chapter 2*

Consolidating the Continent, 1845–1857

INTRODUCTION

James Knox Polk, dark horse candidate for president in 1844 and successful in upsetting Martin Van Buren for the Democratic nomination, rode to election upon a platform of being his own man. Though he acknowledged the significance of the Jacksonians as advisers and owed to them a spiritual heritage, Polk carved a nearly unique niche in the history of the presidency by his announcement and attainment of four definite goals. A few days after he took the oath of office, he told Secretary of the navy George Bancroft, "There are four great measures which are to be measures of my administration: one, a reduction of the tariff; another, the independent treasury; a third, the settlement of the Oregon boundary question; and lastly, the acquisition of California."[1] It was also during Polk's presidency that diplomat and soldier alike dealt with Mexican intransigence in the face of Yankee acquisitiveness and the U.S. legislature had the first major war on its hands in nearly thirty-five years.

In the conduct of the Mexican War and other significant events of his administration, Polk sought to use more authority as commander-in-chief than any previous chief executive. As the directing force* of U.S.

---

*Polk as a worker and thinker was methodical and industrious, insisting on being the center of his programs. He demanded monthly reports from members of the Cabinet concerning even clerks' performance of duties and paid close attention to estimates from the heads of bureaus within departments. George Bancroft felt that one of the keys to his success lay in the unified sense of direction he was able to give to his Cabinet. 1 J. Polk, *The Diary of James Polk during His Presidency, 1845 to 1849,* xxix 48, 49, 314 (Quaife ed.) (hereinafter "Polk, *Diary* (Quaife ed.)").

foreign relations, his obvious motivation was more than settlement of matters at hand. The president coveted all the land west of the Rio Grande to the Pacific, and though he seemed honestly willing to pay for it, Polk was determined to use other means if negotiators were unwilling to sell. Legislators were ill at ease with executive conduct that appeared to tamper with their prerogatives and voiced dissent over questions of executive appointment, appropriations for both war and peace purposes, and significant instances of withheld information. The politics of slavery often benefitted Polk's efforts at aggrandizement of power, but in significant cases they were just as influential in preventing expansion, as Congress sought to shape and determine the course of foreign policy. The growth of the presidency as both chief of state and head of government thus was importantly forged by Polk's and Congress's interaction over their respective concepts of war powers.

Zachary Taylor, a soldier who earned the sobriquet "Rough and Ready" from his subordinates, was by contrast a man of almost excessive modesty. He was catapulted into the presidency from a fame garnered at Buena Vista and Monterey, yet he appeared surprised to be the Whig nominee for president in 1848, admitting that his completely apolitical background included never having voted in a presidential election.

Though he espoused the fundamental Whig principle—a sparing use of executive power—elevation to the presidency made Taylor a firm nationalist. He vowed in response to British minister Crampton's complaint that he would personally dispatch any expedition necessary to crush a threatened filibuster to annex Canada. His deployment of naval vessels into Cuban waters to intercept an American-based try to overthrow the Spanish dominion of Cuba was denounced in Congress as an unconstitutional usurpation of executive power as well as a violation of international law.

Taylor's skilled diplomatist John Clayton brilliantly filled the chair of secretary of state. In his treaty with Henry Bulwer, Clayton steered through the treacherous shoals of an accord with England in negotiating the concept of a southern waterway open to all nations, free from excessive domination. Taylor died in office, however, before he would have been required to deal with Congress's many concerns over the treaty.

Taylor's vice-president, Millard Fillmore, was a large, handsome, self-educated lawyer—a "safe" Whig who, unlike his predecessor, was thoroughly schooled in party principles. Fillmore as president proved to be less aggressive than Taylor or Polk in dealing with important foreign policy and diplomatic issues such as problems with Canada over fishing rights, but he refused to communicate important information to Congress concerning the Clayton-Bulwer Treaty, rendered firm instructions to Matthew C. Perry to seize the initiative in opening trade with Japan, and emphatically declared that he would uphold federal law in the territory of New Mexico against any unwarranted seizures of land, including dispatching troops if necessary to enforce U.S. law.

Fillmore's successor was both a lawyer and a soldier, as well as a skilled Democratic party leader. Brigadier General Franklin Pierce had survived important tests of leadership* and had the reputation of being a successful administrator.†

Although president and titular chief of a reunited Democratic party in 1853, Pierce unfortunately soon disappointed those who had seen in him a demonstrated executive ability: Most of his Cabinet appointments, with the exception of William L. Marcy and Jefferson Davis as secretaries of state and war, respectively, were men of little or no national consequence.** His first annual message displayed a fundamental lack of creativity and too easy reliance on precedent alone to solve the sectional crisis. Guardedly, Pierce endorsed the concept of a western railroad as far as he felt it could be sustained under the war power but felt that it should be subsidized and undertaken by a private corporation rather than by the U.S. government.[2] Trusting almost entirely to sectional forbearance, Pierce tragically mistook his verbal pronouncements concerning American nationalism as a valid counterbalance to the political and social disintegration that slavery was causing everywhere in the United States. But mere denials could not mask deep-seated rivalries or create a nationalism that the American republic had still not made its own.

It would be an error, however, to join forces with the legion of historians who have simply written off the Pierce administration as virtually the *nadir* of the American presidential experience, for in the

---

*Pierce was made a brigadier general of militia at the outset of the Mexican War and served in several campaigns. At the zenith of his state political power he virtually single-handedly removed a Democratic candidate for New Hampshire governor who Pierce convinced the state's party committee was disloyal. R. Nichols, *Franklin Pierce* 185 (1931).

†Pierce's friend Nathaniel Hawthorne saw scores of men as being brighter but found in Pierce an administrative talent that could "move men about like pawns on a chessboard." *Id.* 217.

**Pierce seemed to derive enormous satisfaction from dealing with a welter of detail, so much so that his chief biographer, Roy F. Nichols, felt that absorption in trivia was a concomitant of Pierce's inability to handle key issues more successfully and at times compensated for his failure to deal with major problems. A feud he seemed unwilling or unable to control between Secretary of War Jefferson Davis and General Winfield Scott was one example of unnecessary antagonism among the members of his administration. Strangely, too, unlike his New Hampshire political experience, he neither tied the political fortunes of national party chieftains to his own nor surrounded himself with them. Thus lacking any factional support whose power depended on his own strength, his presidency was doomed to a single term. *Id.* 300ff.

use of executive war power, Pierce was often far more decisive in the diplomatic arena than in domestic political concerns. While one of his chief biographers, Roy F. Nichols, finds it "curious"* that in order to quell Indian atrocities Pierce received $300,000—with no real difficulty—from a Congress in which he had few friends, Pierce's authority as commander-in-chief or his ability to execute the laws never sank so low that Congress would not accede to the basic needs of defense. Indeed, in an energetic response to what were conceived to be British-backed aggressions in Central America, Pierce approved the virtual demolition of Greytown, Nicaragua,† and in another action recognized the regime of filibusterer William Walker in Nicaragua, defying British minister Crampton while making no preliminary effort to advise Congress that he was even considering doing so.**[3] The Pierce administration was actively neutral, not isolationist, in measuring the effects of European involvement in the Crimean War on the reaction time that U.S. diplomats possessed to gain valuable concessions in Central America and Cuba. For example, Pierce shrewdly guessed he could attempt to acquire Cuba without any substantial European reaction.††

Each president from 1845 to 1857, two Whigs and two Democrats, thus had opportunities that he used to shape and contribute to the growing concept of executive war powers. The congressional response was mainly one of increasing uneasiness with exceptional or unilateral presidential activities, special requests for delegation of powers, or unfilled requests for information. The fear of executive self-aggrandizement intensified after the Mexican War in direct proportion as the sections of the country had also grown to mistrust each other and to question even more than prior generations the specific meaning of war powers claims under the U.S. Constitution. Presidential and congressional use of this power neither fluctuated with political fortunes nor was it irrevocably anchored to the threat of secession that strictured the American consciousness in the last decade before the Civil War. At least in one of the most important examples of the use of war powers in American diplomacy, all four of these administrations exhibited some

*Id. 460.

†Infra p. 164, 166.

**A savage uprising in Kansas, in May 1856, between pro- and antislavery forces focused congressional attention on far more urgent concerns than the possible misuse of executive war powers.

††Thus, Pierce's administration demonstrated fairly accurately that Britain and France did not support Spanish rule in Cuba. See infra p. 122 for discussion of the Ostend Manifesto; also, A. Dowty, The Limits of American Isolation (1971), passim, for the thesis that U.S. diplomatic demands at this time were not always consistent but were nonetheless confident and that with the Crimea pressing Britain, U.S. demands that England withdraw from Central America almost succeeded until the bombardment of Greytown, Nicaragua.

measure of this continuity: Polk's territorial initiatives directed U.S. attention to the need for rapid westward communications, while Taylor negotiated the Clayton-Bulwer Treaty to obtain a swifter westward route, and both Fillmore and Pierce defended it.

EXECUTIVE-CONGRESSIONAL RELATIONS

Power of Appointment and Removal

Appointment: Polk President Polk had a gift for persuasion and routinely called leading congressmen to the White House for conferences on critical administration problems—an art that Richard Neustadt, among others, has termed vital to the functioning of a system characterized by checks and balances.[4]

Early in his administration, Polk overcame Congress's threat to restrict the source or pool from which he should make nominations. Thomas Hart Benton (D. Mo.) led the Senate in rejecting a House attempt to limit the president's choices to the regular line of the army as an unconstitutional limitation on presidential power, just as Monroe had maintained that it was in 1822.*[5] The Senate again defeated a similar restriction on increasing the number of generals† and appeared to favor leaving presidential authority untrammeled in the face of a military crisis.[6]

Although the president obtained two major generals and four brigadiers, an attempt to create the rank of lieutenant general failed.** Congressmen's suspicion of a covert design to achieve a successor "by passing into other hands, the powers of the Chief Magistracy" was the basic reason for their refusal to accede to Polk's request for a commander in the field with virtual plenipotentiary authority.††

Congress lost many other efforts to curb presidential powers of appointment and removal, including suggestions that volunteers elect their own officers, proposals that the president consult the Senate on removal as well as appointment, and attempts to deter Polk's practice of submitting nominations too late for Senate consideration. But legislators did exercise discretion to require the president to appoint field

---

*The Senate rejected Monroe's argument that Congress had no constitutional right to restrain the president's "selection of proper persons from the whole body of his fellow-citizens." 2 *Messages and Papers* 701; 15 *Congressional Globe* 827, 828.

†The bill under consideration was entitled "the bill supplementary to the act providing for the prosecution of the existing war between the United States and Mexico." *Id.* 864.

**It received its first defeat in January 1847 as an amendment to a bill to raise ten regiments and fared no better as a separate bill in the Senate. J. Schroeder, *Mr. Polk's War: American Opposition and Dissent, 1846–1848,* at 65 (1973); 16 *Congressional Globe* 116, 160.

††Remarks of George Badger (W. N.C.). *Id.* 186.

officers only with Senate consent. They designated company officers as "inferior" and thus constitutionally able to be appointed by the president alone, even during a recess,* without diminishing either the president's or the Senate's authority.†[7]

By the tactic of sending occasional nominations to the Senate too late for consideration, Polk avoided the confirmation process and successfully withstood the charge that his actions violated the spirit of the Constitution when a resolution seeking information failed.[8] Although Congress's efforts to control appointments reflected many changes in its attitude toward military officers as instruments of policy, legislators achieved no workable constitutional formula for dampening Polk's use of this power.

Removal: Polk and Taylor   Senators John C. Calhoun (D. S.C.), John Clayton (Wh. Del.), and Daniel Webster (Wh. Mass.) attacked the congressional decision of 1789 that recognized the removal power to reside in the president alone** and argued for a system of officer tenure based on statutory regulation. Webster, particularly, felt it was anomalous for the president not to consult with Congress on removal, which in every constitutional government was "considered part and parcel of the power of appointment." Their attempt to provide permanent tenure for certain officers was defeated, and the spoils system remained firmly ensconced.[9] And even though President Taylor declared in his inaugural that only the lack of "honesty, capacity and fidelity" would dismiss a federal employee, he fired thousands of civil servants†† upon becoming chief executive. When the Senate considered and ultimately defeated a move to request the president to lay before it his reasons for removals,*** senators perceived it sound practice for the executive to

---

*From both the standpoints of historical experience and legal analysis, appointment of so-called inferior officers had successfully been vested in the president with no loss of legislative authority. George Washington was authorized by Congress in 1791 to raise a corps of 2,000 noncommissioned officers, privates, and musicians and "alone to appoint the commissioned officers thereof." On another occasion in 1792, he was permitted to appoint commissioned officers among certain cavalrymen. *Id.* 348, citing Acts of March 5, 1792. Examples from similar acts of Congress tended to show that since the early republic, certain military personnel were considered "inferior," and their appointments not required to be reviewed by Congress.

†The position that the president had no right to fill an original office requiring Senate approval during a recess seemed to have been generally accepted. *See* Sofaer, *Origins* 258–60. But Polk sought and received confirmation of his own opinion that he had authority to make various kinds of recess appointments from not only his Attorney General but also the rest of his Cabinet except Buchanan. *E.g.*, 1 Polk, *Diary* 79 (Quaife ed.).

**See Sofaer, *Origins* 63–65.

††Removals under Taylor certainly exceeded those of his predecessors. In 1849–50, of 17,780 civil servants, 3,400 were removed and 2,800 resigned. H. Hamilton, *Zachary Taylor: Soldier in the White House* ch. XVII, "The Loaves and Fishes," 203–18 (1951).

***James Bradbury (D. Me.) introduced a resolution requesting the reasons for removals and not merely a statement that they had occurred. 19 *Congressional Globe Appendix* 50.

withhold certain confidential documents impossible to separate from other materials, claiming that facts regarding candidates for office would not be written to the executive if correspondents might expose themselves to recrimination.[10] Since abuse of either the appointment or removal power is an impeachable offense, the Senate recognized that it was unreasonable for a president to communicate potentially incriminating evidence.* Inquiry into President Taylor's power to remove was thus finally halted on the basis that reasons for removal might well involve an improper demand for executive documentation.

Planning Legislation

Congress expected to receive executive military measures† and continued as before either to reserve or withhold approval as its principal check on executive power, introducing the right of independent investigation or examination of such proposals as it felt the circumstances demanded.** Of course, Congress did not ignore its duty to make recommendations for national defense. For example, in December 1845 Michigan Senator Lewis Cass introduced resolutions inquiring into the state of national preparedness in the light of possible conflict with England over Oregon. His Ohio colleague William Allen led the fight to pass them unanimously (48 to 0).††[11]

An executive request for a modest two-regiment increase in the military establishment, ostensibly to protect settlers on their way to Oregon, was defeated by amendments early in 1846. But as the likelihood of war with Mexico drew nearer, the climate of opinion changed. The House passed legislation authorizing enlargements of army companies at the president's discretion.[12] In the Senate, the bill was passed on 11 May with amendments that would permit an extraordinary

---

*President Andrew Jackson had refused to furnish Congress with information dealing with a removal on the basis that it could found accusations against him:

I shall resist all such attempts as an invasion of the principles of justice as well as of the Constitution, and I shall esteem it my sacred duty to the people of the United States to resist them as I would the establishment of the Spanish Inquisition. *Id.* 483; H.R. Doc. No. 194, 24th Cong., 2d Sess. 23.

†Sofaer, *Origins* 65–70.

**House members strongly disapproved, however, of the executive's frequent technique during wartime of submitting its proposed legislation to a committee such as the Ways and Means Committee, which in turn sent it directly to the floor for discussion, thus disguising the bill's origin. 17 *Congressional Globe* 71–72, 404, 406.

††Allen countered the opposition of Senator Willie P. Mangum (W. N.C.), who wanted to leave planning for defense strictly up to the president with consultations as necessary with Congress. Allen earnestly importuned Congress to take an active part in determining defense status by initiating inquiries and responding to them by law. 15 *Congressional Globe* 50.

increase per company up to 100 men, and the House concurred. Thus, the president swiftly obtained authority to raise the standing army to about 15,000 men, a potential increase of almost 50 percent, although Senator Benton attempted to allay any fear of a dramatic rise by showing that the executive had also been empowered to reduce the number of men in each company to sixty-four if they were not needed.[13]

By May, when the president was about to send his message to Congress asking Congress to declare war on Mexico, the climate of urgency made increased troop strength more palatable. On 16 July 1846, by the thumping margin of 159 to 4, the House passed a bill* "making appropriations for the support of volunteers and other troops to be employed in the prosecution of the war with Mexico."

The same principle applied to naval expansion. In January 1846, before war was a reality, the administration unsuccessfully endeavored to obtain passage of a bill authorizing the construction of ten new iron steamships as well as to make completions and repairs of other vessels. Discussion went to the heart of presidential discretion to arm before a potential conflict. Though senators believed not enough steps were being taken to protect the United States in case of war with Great Britain, most objected that the bill contained no criterion except the president's own judgment, "and therefore the authority was absolute."[14] The bill was defeated† by those who found absolute exercise of discretion appropriate only as a war measure.[15]

Since there was no war during Fillmore's administration, Congress would not support executive military expenditures until members had debated their right to challenge the accuracy of executive estimates** by independent examination. On a $9 million overall budget request for the army, Congress exercised its prerogative to review and to question, as well as to modify, executive requests. A War Department study had indicated that recently extended frontiers could not be defended at eight-year-old contract prices for subsistence, but Connecticut's Chauncey Cleveland spoke for the majority in a successful bid to cut costs, asserting that it was the people's prerogative through their elected

---

*John Quincy Adams was among the four dissenters. Debate provided members of Congress with the opportunity to argue the constitutionality of the war itself (*id.* 1107), although the bill passed in the Senate without amendment. *Id.* 1113.

†Senator Cass successfully maneuvered aside the naval bill on 10 February (*id.* 350), and no record of further substantive action in either House can be found. *Id.* 377, 572.

**There was perhaps some kind of justice in this treatment of the administration's estimates. In 1841, when Fillmore was chairman of the Ways and Means Committee, he sent numerous multipoint interrogatories to commissioners and department secretaries, seeking detailed explanations for various budget items, and in 1842 he placed various agencies under "strict scrutiny." White, *The Jacksonians* 129–30.

representatives to defend government itself from the claim that estimates from executive departments "through its agents, are to control the action of the people's representatives."[16]

Congress also voted down an amendment delegating discretion to the secretary of war to modify the character and number of troops, so that whatever funds were appropriated could be apportioned as he saw fit. A similar attempt was disapproved that would have permitted the president the discretion to cut the army in half rather than ask him to support 12,000 men on the subsistence for half that number.[17]

When Franklin Pierce asked for $3 million to improve existing armaments and increase U.S. production of small arms, his request posed the previous question of Congress's need to rely on executive assessments of military requirements. Legislators wanted to explore "the drift of the President." Misinterpretation of his motive was always possible, and some feared that improvement of arms would not be understood as merely the desire to keep pace with the European powers but seen in fact as a deliberate challenge to England.[18] The bill was ultimately lost,* but not before Congress decided that the president should have the discretion to transfer appropriated funds among specified objects in order to meet a defense need if it arose.[19] The Senate had in fact conceded that the executive possessed superior information regarding an imminent threat in analyzing Pierce's recommendation for the raising of four volunteer regiments to suppress Indian hostilities and protect routes to Oregon and California.[20] For senators to say there was no need for 3,000 troops to repel Indian attacks was "to come in direct collision with the President" in the performance of his duty to defend the country. Not only did the president get the regulars† that he needed, but Congress saw to it that the president alone was authorized to appoint some commissioned officers during congressional recess. The issue was concluded in the president's favor without the extended acrimonious exchanges that occurred during the Polk administration.[21]

Congress was not willing to relinquish certain defense-related functions entirely to the executive, even though the plans in question represented only readiness for defense. It recognized in 1852 that the key to U.S. military strength was not always the overt buildup of military forces. The potential of the nation to make war could also be

---

*The total bill was reduced to $1,800,000, and while it passed the Senate on 21 July 1856, 25 *Congressional Globe* 1876, it was lost in the House Military Affairs Committee. *Id.* 989.

†The secretary of war had asked for volunteers, recommending that they could be put into the field more rapidly. 24 *Congressional Globe* 442. But the administration was not willing to accept four regiments of regulars because circumstances were favorable for recruiting them. *Id.* 511.

realized indirectly through the radical proposition that private enterprise might participate as a partner with government. Thus Congress
passed a bill subsidizing the conversion of a major steamship line's fleet
to military use. And in an effort to protect emigrants to Oregon, it also
attempted to attract settlers to accept land along the Oregon Trail and
to support themselves but to join the army and defend the route as part
of the bargain.

The British-subsidized Cunard Steam Ship Line had made significant
engineering improvements in order to convert mail steamers almost
overnight to naval use. Congress overcame the objection that such a
project as U.S. subsidy of a similar venture would prompt the government of the United States to "become one vast jobbing concern. . . ."[22]
Strong bipartisan support enabled Congress to increase a subsidy to the
Collins Steamship Lines to keep pace with the British.[23] Instructing the
president on his duty to protect emigrants to Oregon, however, was
another matter.

An 1849 statute provided for Oregon emigrants' protection, but when
congressmen questioned the actual extent of Fillmore's measures to do
so, Representative Thomas Bayly (D. Va.) denied the authority of either
house of Congress "to give any direction in respect to the posting of the
Army" to the commander-in-chief. The withholding of supplies, said
Bayly, was Congress's sole means of control.[24] Opponents who claimed
that Congress possessed summary power expressly to designate troop
movements were reminded by Vermont congressman James Meacham
that Polk had frequently changed U.S. troop positions without Congress's authority before the Mexican War. As a practical matter, it was
generally agreed that the assent of both houses and the approval of the
executive was required to direct the army, not merely the voice of the
House of Representatives alone.*[25]

Senators led by Vice-President William R. King approached the
problem of Oregon defense with a more novel plan than direct provision
of forces. The Senate proposed a large volunteer army to protect the
route and be completely self-supporting, receiving as compensation a
640-acre tract of land of their own selection. Stephen A. Douglas
supported it as a pragmatic solution: A line of permanent military
colonies would be established, and it would save the government enor-

___

*Representative Humphrey Marshall (Wh. Ky.) stated that the House (and probably
the Congress) did not possess the necessary information to make informed judgments
about direction of the troops, in order to actually order the secretary of war to recall troops
from one position and station them elsewhere. Such direction, based on insufficient
knowledge, could cause "unnumbered misfortunes." 21 *Congressional Globe* 517. Informal
consultation, however, with the secretary of war achieved both the desired result and the
supremacy of executive authority, since the secretary of war agreed to station troops along
roads to Oregon. *Id.* 519–20.

mous expense. Not only was the concept new, but senators complained that it had the constitutional impact of turning "Congress into a sort of commander-in-chief of the Army."[26] It met the fate of a $100 million bill espousing emigrant protection that called for the president to contract for building a railroad and telegraph line "connecting the valley of the Mississippi with the Pacific Ocean" and authorizing presidential use of the U.S. Army to support the corporate work of building and expanding communications.* In both instances active consideration of the measures simply ceased.[27] Such a quantum leap in presidential authority and power could not be justified even by unabashed post-Mexican War expansionism.

Congress thus successfully exercised its prerogative not only to review and to modify executive appropriations but also to question the president's sources of data before supporting what members often characterized as an extensive peacetime establishment. Its inquiry into the ways and means of supporting defense activities led congressmen to consider and to implement an economy-minded rationale: they were willing to support subsidies to private entrepreneurs who were expected to perform defense-related functions that Congress was not willing to see relinquished to the authority of the president alone.

Delegation of Discretionary Power

Congress generally delegated broad discretion in areas relating to exercise of the war power. It granted the president authority to increase the army when there was a need to respond to Indian attacks. In foreign affairs, President Fillmore and Congress easily cooperated in investigating a filibustering expedition undertaken by some American citizens against Spanish rule in Cuba; and the Senate authorized the president to investigate injuries to foreign individuals' properties within the United States in order to make restitution. The legislature also decided that peacetime defense policies would be more effectively executed if the president possessed the power to improve ship design and increase seamen's pay. Moreover, Congress accorded the secretary of the navy authority to investigate whether or not new frigates should be built under contract in private shipyards. With one exception, however, in which patronage was the key issue, Congress refused to permit delegation of its prerogative to determine where to place a military installation, saying that the location of a military base had nothing to do with executive power.

---

*The sheer size alone of this appropriation militated against its passage. In addition to military protection, 50 million acres of land and $20 million in 5 percent bonds were requested. 22 *Congressional Globe* 678; 22 *Congressional Globe Appendix* 185.

When Zachary Taylor recommended an increase in troops located in the western Army posts situated on territory ceded by the Mexican treaty, Senator Jefferson Davis championed passage of a bill permitting the president to increase or reduce the rank and file up to half the current establishment at his own discretion.[28] Davis, however, objected to an imprecise amendment that the House attached, and in which the Senate had acquiesced, that also gave the president discretion to "mount" a portion of the infantry. His definition of discretion did not include turning "over the law, half made, to be finished at the discretion of the Executive. We should, if we want cavalry, say so, and how many."[29] But the compelling argument of putting a "stop to the scalping of women and children along the frontier" overcame talk of economy and the proprieties involved in executive discretion.[30]

Congress gave full authority to the president to investigate and settle the claims of foreign citizens that arose as the result of American reaction to the Narciso Lopez affair. Lopez, a Venezuelan adventurer, led hundreds of armed men from New Orleans to Cuba to attempt Cuban liberation from Spain.* When he and many of his supporters were caught and executed, and some imprisoned in Spain, anti-Spanish rioters in New Orleans destroyed the Spanish consulate.[31]

Fillmore's dilemma was how to face up to Spain and to obtain the swiftest release of the captives without arousing France and England who, as colonial powers in the Caribbean, threatened to stop and search U.S. ships in order to guard against attacks on their own possessions. Both powers issued orders to their naval commanders "to prevent by force, if necessary, the landing of adventurers from any nation on the Island of Cuba with hostile intent."[32] As soon as both Fillmore and Congress had made it clear, however, that the Lopez expedition was strictly contrary to both U.S. law and the country's foreign policy of nonintervention, Britain and France responded that their respective military forces had been instructed to exercise "every care" to avoid any hostile interference with normal commercial activity.†[33]

When the president urged Congress to make indemnity, Florida Senator Stephen Mallory introduced a resolution on 29 March 1852 instructing the Senate Foreign Relations Committee "to inquire into the propriety of authorizing the President of the United States" to

---

*This expedition of 3 August 1851 was a virtual repetition of Lopez's abortive expedition of two years previous. Congress was not in session when it occurred, and its details received considerable attention in President Fillmore's state of the union message of 2 December 1851. 21 *Congressional Globe* 16.

†Apprehension aroused by this outburst of filibustering did prompt the British and French governments to approach the United States in April 1852, however, with a proposal of a tripartite convention by which Cuba would be guaranteed to Spain. *See infra* p. 132 n.

investigate the damages and to make prompt restitution to the Spanish government; the Senate agreed.*[34] Fillmore suggested a basis for indemnification, and after pardon and release of the captives, Congress appropriated $25,000 to make indemnity.[35]

Navy Secretary J.G. Dobbin informed the president and Congress that the U.S. fleet was in such decay that there were not forty U.S. vessels that could be pressed into service in ninety-days' time. Dobbin urged construction of at least six "first class steam driven" frigates with screw propellers, the improved propulsion system of Swedish inventor John Ericsson that was more fuel efficient and secure against exposure "to the shot of the enemy" since the blades were submerged.[36] The Senate quickly passed a bill drawn "in exact accordance" with the navy secretary's recommendation,[37] but in the House there was a more cautious approach toward the discretion granted the secretary as to the place and mode of construction and even pay increases to naval personnel manning the ships.

Although there was general concurrence that the improved design was preferable, there was wide divergence on whether or not the frigates should be built in private shipyards at the discretion of the secretary of the navy. Thomas Bocock on 28 March favored granting discretion to the navy secretary, since he "would enjoy, in the investigation of the subject, many advantages which the House did not possess."[38] Several congressmen, however, joined Benton in favoring construction in any one of seven available U.S. navy yards, as the Missouri congressman demanded to know what Congress would "think of a man who possessed seven mills sending his tub of meal to his neighbor for the purpose of having it ground?"[39] The House finally agreed to permit the new construction according discretion as Dobbin suggested,† without a

---

*Congress's right to conduct investigations stems, at least in part, from the constitutional requirement that the president give Congress information from time to time and from Congress's need to obtain information independently in order to legislate effectively and knowledgeably. The right to investigate, firmly established in British parliamentary tradition, was an easy step from the right to request information. As early as 1792, a motion was made requesting that the president institute an inquiry, and although the proper scope of legislative investigation has arisen as an issue from time to time (*see generally* Landis, "Constitutional Limitations on the Congressional Power to Investigate," 40 *Harvard Law Review* 753 (1926); White, *The Jacksonians* 150), the power to delegate authority within certain definable limits appears settled, not having been prohibited by the Constitution. Sofaer, *Origins* 4–5, 79.

†In reply to objections concerning the discretion given the secretary to make pay raises, Bocock indicated that the secretary already possessed legal authority to raise wages to eighteen dollars per month but that the only impediment to his obtaining salary comparability with the merchant marine was "that our friends of the Committee of Ways and Means hold the purse strings a little too tight on him." 23 *Congressional Globe* 809. The bill passed substantially akin to the Senate version, authorizing the secretary to contract for the vessels' construction as he "may think most advisable for the public interest." *Id.* 830, 834, 847; Act of April 6, 1854, 10 Stat. 273.

crippling proviso that would have required him to use already appropriated funds to hire "efficient seamen" for ships then in service.[40]

Congress emphatically refused to delegate authority to the Pierce administration to select the site of a naval base, the final choice for which vacillated for a brief period in 1857 between Brunswick, Georgia, and Amelia Island, Florida. The bill to create the naval station at Brunswick passed the House but languished in the Senate Naval Affairs Committee apparently at the request of Florida Senator Stephen R. Mallory, probably because the Florida legislature had petitioned Congress to permit it to be established at Amelia Island. Most senators preferred the Georgia location, based on strategic advantages and the availability of ship timber.[41] Sufficient indecision remained, however, to prompt an amendment that would have left final site selection to a board of five naval officers to be appointed by the president. Senate rejection of this effort to delegate legislative prerogative was so lopsided, however (14 to 30), that Florida Senator David L. Yulee refrained from offering an alternative, and the Senate finally chose Brunswick, Georgia.[42] This example of legislative withholding of discretion was, therefore, one of the rare examples of friction in a comparatively harmonious decade of accommodation between the branches concerning the delegation of discretionary power. In this case, Congress acted without setting any criteria by which the president or any department head might recommend or even insist on a choice of base location, either because of contemplated military operations or due to special executive knowledge of superior facilities.

Control of Information

Voluntary Transmittals   In Polk's first message to Congress of 5 December 1845,[43] the president stated that he had ordered "a strong squadron" to the coasts of Mexico, concentrated a military force on the western frontier of Texas, and instructed the army to take a position between the Nueces and Del Norte, with orders to repel any invasion of Texan territory attempted by Mexican forces. His remarks produced astonishment in Congress and a flood of requests for detailed information.*[44] Likewise, President Taylor's simple assurance that he had

---

*Polk reported, also, about the status of negotiations with Great Britain concerning the Oregon Territory and his intention to resist any European nation's efforts to maintain a "balance of power" on the North American continent (the "Polk Doctrine"), matters that elicited both protracted debate and requests for information. *See infra* pp. 126–28. Summaries of U.S. relations with other nations similarly produced information queries, *e.g.,* requests for correspondence concerning France and Brazil. 17 *Congressional Globe* 230, 549, 804; *id.* 526, 604, 827 (responses). Requests for documents giving statistical summaries, *id.* 58, 76; *id.* 725, 604 (responses).

taken the "means" to prevent adventurers from seizing Cuba was small comfort to legislators who had not been consulted before they read in the newspapers that the chief executive had sent warships to Cuba. Congress, however, finally tabled disapprobation of Taylor's conduct after it debated the rationale for his unilateral undertaking.

Whether or not information Taylor later sent was sufficient to enable the Senate intelligently to ratify the Clayton-Bulwer Treaty in 1850, by 1853, many congressmen were claiming that the executive department had broken faith with the Senate in failing to supply key details of the preliminaries, and only by a narrow margin did they refuse to reconsider its ratification of this major diplomatic accord. Millard Fillmore and Franklin Pierce also voluntarily offered Congress only the most negligible general information, though they responded somewhat more fully to specific requests. There was, therefore, no comparison among Taylor, Fillmore, and Pierce with the degree of Polk's boldness and apparent willingness to share information voluntarily with Congress so long as he felt there was no compromise of the national interest in doing so.

Legislative Attempts to Obtain Information　The congressional quest for information during the Polk administration centered upon U.S. relations with Mexico and stimulated attacks on Mexican War policy. Even though partisan interests were clearly involved, most political inquiries acknowledged the necessity for executive discretion in response to questions involving foreign relations.* This was not the case when Congress asked for military information relating to expenses, quantities of arms, conduct of officers, or numbers of soldiers. Such business was usually the subject of unqualified requests, probably because Congress recognized the primacy of its constitutional role as "watchdog" over the military.

Voting on information requests usually was strictly partisan, inspired by a coalition of Whigs and Southern Democrats, but final approval of men and supplies for prosecution of war was not. Only the radical Whigs actually took the unpopular, unpatriotic course of voting against supply bills.

In both the Twenty-ninth and Thirtieth Congresses, President Polk acknowledged Congress's right to seek information. At the same time, however, he imposed limitations on his duty to respond, usually

---

*On 13 March 1848, John Cummins (D. Oh.) moved that the House adopt a resolution recognizing Congress's and the president's respective rights concerning information. Though the matter was laid aside, the language of this resolution is an excellent philosophical statement of the balancing principle involved in the right of Congress to request and the executive judiciously to respond. *Id.* 458.

grounded on the danger to the public interest rather than as a threat to the separation of powers. He wrestled with himself and his Cabinet over releasing delicate information regarding Anglo-American relations in Oregon, and stood completely apart from the Cabinet in his desire to transmit to Congress at least some of the correspondence between the secretary of state and the U.S. minister in London.* On the other hand, there is evidence that the executive department was quite willing to manipulate information, doling it out piecemeal either to achieve administration goals or to prevent outright confrontation on issues of secret diplomacy and military maneuvers. Searches for statistics, detailed correspondence, and memoranda from nations other than Mexico received an understandably greater percentage of executive response.

One of the two most significant legislative requests for information overlapped the Taylor, Fillmore, and Pierce administrations and concerned the Clayton-Bulwer Treaty. The other was for data concerning the two Perry missions to Japan. President Pierce's replies to most requests were even more cautious than those of his predecessor Fillmore, since Pierce responded only to approximately half of Congress's inquiries.† However, in the emergency of Spain's seizure of the SS *Black Warrior* in retaliation for Narciso Lopez's adventurism, even though Pierce acted independently to meet the imminent threat, he responded in full to Congress's call for information and voluntarily sent a supplement that was too voluminous for transmission upon the initial request.

General Gaines and Militia Recruits   Major General Edmund Gaines in New Orleans acted illegally in calling up militia without authorization and directly requisitioning the militia without calling on state governors. The Department of War and the president assuredly knew of this practice but acquiesced in it even in light of the imminent outbreak of war between the United States and Mexico** until Congress finally questioned it. Polk almost immediately responded with all of the information at his disposal, fully cognizant of the fact that his prior knowledge and seeming toleration of this conduct could have been viewed as a potentially impeachable offense.

Shortly after the Mexican War began in May 1846, Senator Lewis

---

*This correspondence dealt with England's military and naval preparations for war. In response to Senate and House calls of 29 January and 3 February 1846, respectively, Polk decided to separate out material that could be communicated without endangering the public interest. 1 Polk, *Diary* 209–14, *passim* (Quaife ed.).

†For example, forty qualified Senate and House requests for information on pending issues during the first session of the Pierce administration produced twenty replies. There were only two replies to four unqualified queries.

**Gaines's conduct had commenced in 1845. 15 *Congressional Globe Appendix* 649–50, 654.

Cass (D. Mich) discovered that Gaines had received a copy* of orders from the Department of War to General Taylor indicating that the president contemplated a "contingency" that might render it "proper ... to draw an auxiliary force from some of the United States." Cass alleged Gaines had directly called up 12,000 men for a six-month term without making requests of the governors of states and "without any authority"[45] and demanded an explanation of whether there were emergency circumstances justifying Gaines's conduct without presidential authorization.[46] Cass declared that had the president called up militia without first placing a request with a governor for his requisition, "he would have been liable for impeachment the very next day."[47] After reading Gaines's order, Daniel Webster agreed:

> [T]his is raising an army! ... It is as the Senator [Cass] states, no requisition for militia, but an order to raise an army under the authority of a major general. ... Certainly ... a very extraordinary procedure—a procedure that the President could not authorize.[48]

Several senators felt that a military officer faced with impending calamity possessed emergency powers.[49] Others indicated that Gaines had raised 1,100 men after the Seminole War broke out and marched at their head to render aid to the U.S. Army[50] and that the government had approved of this conduct.†[51] Webster, however, appealed to his colleagues not to set aside all provisions of the Constitution and all enactments of law, "under a loose idea of an overwhelming present necessity."[52] Thereupon, Lewis Cass obtained passage of one request for information on 5 June,[53] and the president answered with "all the information in [his] possession relating to the Senate's request...."[54] Polk's transmittal indicated that he had not ratified or received militiamen who had not been requisitioned through a state governor.**

---

*A copy of the orders had been sent to General Gaines on 25 August 1845. General Taylor was in command of the army of occupation in Texas, and it was feared that a recently reinforced Mexican army might surround U.S. military forces. His orders from Secretary of War Marcy appear in *id.* 657.

†Arguably, only Congress, and not the president, could ratify an illegal act. Apparently, Congress chose not to ratify Gaines's conduct. *See* 15 *Congressional Globe* 964, where on 15 June 1846 a joint resolution was passed authorizing refunding monies expended by governors of states for the "fitting out and preparing ... volunteers or militia to join the army under ... General Taylor...." A proviso was attached stating that the resolution should not be construed as approving General Gaines's calling for volunteers or militia and receiving them into service "without authority of law." Gaines's letter of defense, addressed to the secretary of war, was sent to the Senate on 24 June. *Id.* 1014.

**Secretary of War Marcy's covering letter 8 June 1846 summarized Gaines's conduct

Gaines had, however, recruited two companies through the governor of Louisiana and sent them to Zachary Taylor in Texas where they were inducted into the army. When Secretary of War William L. Marcy immediately informed Gaines that the president had not authorized such a call, he defined the sole exception to the rule requiring express authorization as a situation in which the peril was so great it was obvious that the president would have acted.[55] Gaines replied that he considered instructions to General Taylor tantamount to instructions to subordinate generals, a position that both Cass and Webster found illegal and unjustifiable under the Constitution and that Marcy stated was erroneous.[56] Yet Gaines made no fewer than twelve calls independently of state governors* and clearly without presidential authorization.

The president finally settled the matter informally outside of Congress. He confided to Missouri Senator Thomas Hart Benton that as a consequence of Gaines's violations of orders, he was unable to execute an act of June 1846 providing for militia officers to command the volunteers, since both the officers and their subordinates had been called up illegally. Benton then promised Polk that if Marcy should write Congress stating the problem, Benton "would run a Supplemental Bill through . . . conferring the power on the President to appoint these officers."[57] When Maryland Senator Reverdy Johnson, whose position as of 5 June was that the emergency justified Gaines's conduct,[58] made a call on 29 June for correspondence in the War Department regarding the possible authorization of any individual to raise volunteers, Polk called him in to show him that the requested correspondence detailed, among other matters, a projected military campaign into Upper California by both land and sea. Johnson agreed that publication of this material would be improper and injurious, assuring Polk that Marcy should not respond to the request and that if any reason was demanded, he would explain the circumstances to his colleagues. Johnson limited his own next call for information strictly to whether a court of inquiry had been ordered in the Gaines matter.[59]

The administration subsequently ordered Gaines to be court-martialed. The court found him guilty of violating orders and taking

---

since 1845 and accompanied the executive response to the inquiry for the correspondence between Gaines and the secretary of war. 15 *Congressional Globe Appendix* 649–50.

*Marcy, in a separate memorandum, detailed the nature of these illegal recruitments. He noted that Gaines's twelve calls could have exceeded 12,000 men "besides a regiment of foot from Missouri, which has been accepted by the War Department." *Id.* 654. Thus, the secretary of war clearly disavowed that any calls for troops other than those destined for Texas had been ratified, since the president himself would have lacked the constitutional authority to have performed the very acts that his subordinate Gaines undertook to accomplish.

several illegal actions but only reprimanded him because of his long service to the country. Polk then assigned him to administrative duties in the North.[60]

Correspondence of Polk and His Generals   President Polk customarily, like Thomas Jefferson, conducted his own multilevel correspondence. Some of it was official while the rest was either unofficial or private, and certainly any unofficial correspondence to generals in the field would not normally have been routinely made available to Congress.[61] He did, however, make some documents available more quickly than others.

When Mississippi Congressman Jacob Thompson requested Polk to communicate to the House all unpublished correspondence with General Taylor since the Mexican War began,[62] George Ashmun (Wh. Mass.) accused Thompson of attempting to obtain a background for a censure of Taylor so that Polk could create the rank of lieutenant general to supersede him.* Ashmun believed that the president would send forward only condemnatory correspondence, while Taylor would be prohibited from publishing any justification. Ashmun submitted an amendment to rebut this purported censure effort, but his amendment failed (76 to 99), while Thompson's request for the Taylor correspondence succeeded (101 to 62).[63]

On 27 February, Polk fully complied with the House resolution, stating that since the military operations were well "advanced," undoubtedly the Mexicans had already received "so much information in relation to the intended movements of our army" that any precautionary withholding was unnecessary.[64] Yet House members waited more than six weeks without any reaction to a resolution requesting copies of all correspondence between the secretary of war and Zachary Taylor, Winfield Scott, and Commissioner Nicholas Trist.† When Polk sent certain of these materials, Representative Thomas Clingman (Wh. N.C.) objected that important known documents had been omitted and that in many instances the executive had furnished only extracts of correspondence. He remarked that withholding was doubtless viewed as an honest exercise of power, since the executive must have considered any information lowering the present administration in public esteem as being detrimental to the public interest. On the contrary, the missing information would indicate the administration's "miserable" prosecution of the war, when it revealed General Scott's campaign plan.[65]

---

*It was Thompson who had introduced the lieutenant general measure into the House after the Committee on Military Affairs failed to recommend the president's proposal made in a special message on 4 January. *See supra* p. 89 n. discussion of "Ten Regiment bill."

†The motion had been made by George Houston (D. Ala.) on 7 February 1848, with no response until 20 March. 17 *Congressional Globe* 308.

Clingman demanded that before any of the correspondence was printed, four particular letters of General Scott should be furnished that were known to exist but had not been released.* Representative Thomas Henley (D. Ind.) in a private interview with the secretary of war had been informed that "those letters would have been furnished if it had been supposed that they were called for."[66] Representative Alexander Stephens (D. Ga.) then questioned why it was not "supposed" these letters had been asked for in the House's original demand for "copies of *all* correspondence. . . ."[67] Charging that such treatment was offensive to the "dignity" of the American Congress, Stephens protested the fact that the instructions to John Slidell had been published in newspapers after President Polk had told Congress "that he could not, consistently with the public interest, declare to the freemen of this country—his masters and theirs—what they were. . . ."†[68]

Stephens believed that it would be improper for the House to receive letters or reports from either the secretary of war or the president if they were rendered in any other manner than "under the obligation of their official stations."**[69] He challenged the reading aloud of a "garbled" portion of a letter by General Taylor when the full text showed that General Scott had asked Taylor to put himself in a highly vulnerable position with less than 1,000 regulars to face an army of 20,000.††[70]

Clingman's resolution passed on 17 April[71] retaining the request for the four "informally" offered letters and further designed to obtain all General Scott's correspondence with the secretary of war during October and November 1846. This summons produced a second, and more complete, presidential response on 26 April.[72] The entire transmission,

---

*Representative Robert McLane (D. Md.) contended that the letters that Clingman specified were beyond the scope of the request of 7 February because that call for information asked the president to furnish Scott's correspondence while he was in Mexico. Since Scott had sailed for Mexico on 25 November 1846, McLane reasoned that letters dated previously were not included in the call. Clingman disputed this interpretation. *Id.* 583–84.

†Stephens also charged that Polk had ordered U.S. troops to advance on Corpus Christi on 13 January, before he could possibly have learned of John Slidell's rejection by Mexico, and then had arranged for an administration spokesman, R. Barnwell Rhett (D. S.C.), to inform the House that Rhett had interviewed the secretary of state and had seen an endorsement *dated 12 January* on a communication indicating that Slidell would not be accepted. *Id.* 587.

**Such standards of acceptability varied. When on 25 January 1848 Senator John Crittenden (Ky.) inquired of Lewis Cass (D. Mich.), chairman of the Senate Military Affairs Committee, as to the status of Generals Worth and Scott, Crittenden appeared satisfied when Cass told him that he had obtained the information in informal conversation with the executive and was authorized to give it out. Moreover, Crittenden, who was a committee member, appeared to accept the implication that the choice to impart this information rested with the president. *Id.* 242.

††Congressman Henley apparently had rendered only "garbled portions" of Taylor's letter to Scott dated 15 January 1847, but they were reiterated just as he had obtained them from the secretary of war. *Id.* 587.

including those materials obtained from the second presidential response, was then authorized to be published with one exception: a letter of Secretary of War Marcy written to Major General Scott on 21 April, four days *after* passage of the resolution calling for the president's second response.* This gargantuan forty-nine-page letter was written with knowledge that the legislative branch had demanded significant documents for publication, and, in Clingman's words, contained a "tirade of abuse" against Winfield Scott as "a defence for [the secretary of war] and the Administration ... ," in a position paper clearly manufactured after the fact.† House members questioned its obvious partiality under these circumstances and refused to give it the same credence as documentary evidence produced substantially earlier than the call for it.[73]

The Senate's generally greater success in obtaining documents was partly based on its more confidential relation with the executive, since any response could be transmitted for reception in executive session as soon as prepared. For example, on 17 March 1848, Senator John Clarke (Wh. R.I.) obtained Senate concurrence in a qualified resolution asking the president to communicate to the Senate a dispatch written to Thomas O. Larkin, U.S. consul at Monterey, carried by Marine Captain Archibald Gillespie, but intentionally destroyed by Gillespie before he entered the port of Vera Cruz.**[74] Within one week, Polk's response including the dispatch was transmitted to the Senate in executive session even though the request originated in legislative session. Polk reasoned he could have withheld it since publication was "not compatible with the public interests," but he decided to comply because he was unwilling to withhold from the Senate information deemed "important to that body."[75]

Congressmen realized that their own capacity to keep a secret was often the basis on which the executive decided to release information.

---

*Some members wanted this item suppressed (*id.* 689), and an amendment to this effect offered by Representative Henry Hilliard (Wh. Ala.) was adopted. *Id.* 693.

†Representative Hilliard characterized the document as "a long, labored, well-prepared defence of the Administration, on consultation with his political friends." *Id.* 692. It is H.R. Ex. Doc. No. 59, 30th Cong., 1st Sess., Ser. 518, and in manuscript is to be found in RG233, National Archives, "Original Message from the President," March 24–August 14, 1848, Legislative Records (House).

**The original was sent with Commodore Stockton by way of the Sandwich Islands, but since his voyage around South America would have taken more than six months, the administration decided to choose a speedier mode of delivery through Mexico. The dispatch advised Larkin how to handle both the delicate task of discouraging British and French influence in California and of encouraging the Texas mode of revolution and voluntary annexation. C. Sellers, *James K. Polk, Continentalist, 1843–1846,* at 334 (1957–58); J. Polk, *Polk: Diary of a President, 1845–1849* at 22(1952) (Nevins ed.) (hereinafter "Polk, *Diary* (Nevins ed.)"). *See also* discussion of Fremont in California, *infra* p. 157.

But when the Senate Committee on the Judiciary reported out a bill designed to punish violation of secret proceedings, on 29 May 1848, there was no further action.[76] The Senate as a whole thus was unwilling to decide whether it wished to place sanctions of some kind on members of Congress to discipline them for unauthorized release of information. While Congress apparently considered executive documentation critical to its understanding of an issue, there were still no agreed criteria for the handling and release of sensitive information.*

Reconsideration of Ratification of the Clayton-Bulwer Treaty One of the most important accommodations that took place between England and the United States before the Civil War was the Clayton-Bulwer Treaty. In that agreement, both nations focused on resolving their conflicting interests in Central America, which had consistently prevented harmonious development of an interoceanic transportation route. The treaty was a mutual pledge that neither Britain nor the United States would occupy, fortify, colonize, or assume dominion over any part of Central America. Though ratifications were exchanged in 1850, many senators gave serious thought two years later to reconsidering the Senate's vote to ratify on the ground that Secretary of State John Clayton and the British negotiators had made a secret understanding that certain territory was to be excluded from the ban against British influence in Central America. The Senate, claiming it did not have relevant information at hand at the time the executive sought its consent, demanded to know the reasons for the withholding. On the other hand, by 1853 former Secretary of State John Clayton was in the Senate from Delaware and was ultimately able to convince those who raised the issue to abandon it, since significant information bearing on the issues involved had been placed at least in the hands of the Senate Foreign Relations Committee if not the full Senate.

Background of the Clayton-Bulwer Treaty Several commercial and navigation treaties had been negotiated by representatives of both Polk and Taylor with Costa Rica, Honduras, Nicaragua, Guatemala, and San Salvador in 1848 and 1849. One that was negotiated by Elijah Hise, contrary to instructions, guaranteed Nicaraguan security in return for a ship canal right-of-way but was never submitted for ratification.† A second Nicaraguan commercial treaty, obtained by Ephraim Squier, did

---

*Both Representatives Hall and Schenck, during the debate on the Slidell instructions, touched on the difficulty of maintaining confidentiality in Congress. 17 *Globe* 207 (Hall); *id.* 167, 168 (Schenck). See discussion *infra* p. 118, where Schenck described the method provided by the House to insure secrecy.

†The release of this treaty, dated 21 June 1849, came only after Taylor's death in the summer of 1850. *See infra* p. 109.

not guarantee Nicaraguan independence but provided for a U.S. right–of–way.[77]

President Taylor promised Congress that five treaties negotiated with Central American countries* would be "laid before the Senate,"[78] but both houses became impatient and issued information requests concerning the president's actions. The House passed Representative John Savage's (Tenn.) qualified request for information about (1) treaties, (2) rumors of British interference in Central America— "alleged extraordinary proceedings"—amounting to the forcible seizure and occupation of the island of Tigre on the Pacific coast of Nicaragua,† and (3) any executive knowledge of attempted or actual seizure or occupation of "any port, river, town, territory, or island belonging to or claimed by any of the States of Central America."[79] The Department of State, however, did not want Britain to know U.S. plans regarding a proposed canal or to promote any undue friction between Britain and the United States over the seizure of Tigre. Taylor, therefore, did not communicate the information requested by the House** but said that he would do so as soon as the public interest permitted.[80] He also withheld from the Senate the earlier treaties and copies of communications between the Department of State and the various Central American states. His response to the Senate constituted an example of withholding of information because the upper chamber had specified that it would receive the information in executive session if transmittal in open

---

*President Taylor had two treaties on his desk: one with Nicaragua, granting U.S. rights to construct and control a canal or railroad (June 1849); the other with Honduras, ceding to the U.S. (temporarily) the island of Tigre, which would probably be the Pacific terminus of a Nicaraguan route (September 1849). Taylor apparently believed ratification of either treaty would lead to collision with England. Since both nations appeared to favor compromise, negotiations were underway that would produce, in April 1850, the Clayton-Bulwer Treaty. S. Bemis, *A Diplomatic History of the United States* 247–49 (hereinafter "Bemis, *A Diplomatic History*"); *Diplomatic Correspondence of the United States, Inter-American Affairs. 1831-1860: 3 Central America, 1831–1850* (1933) (hereinafter "*Diplomatic Correspondence (Central America)*"); M. Williams, *Anglo-American Isthmian Diplomacy, 1815–1915* at 60–66 (1916).

†Savage mistakenly thought Tigre belonged to Nicaragua. British minister Frederick Chatfield, who was negotiating in Nicaragua to secure control of a canal route for Great Britain, had authorized a British naval officer to seize Tigre on the pretext that the island would serve as security for British claims against Honduras. Since the island had already been ceded to the United States (albeit in a treaty yet to be ratified), this action created potential for conflict between the two countries. The seizure was disavowed shortly thereafter, after formal protest by the U.S. Williams, *Anglo-American Isthmian Diplomacy* 64–66; Bemis, *A Diplomatic History* 249.

**Is the president under an obligation to forward to the Senate all signed treaties? President Jefferson withheld from the Senate a treaty negotiated with England by Minister James Monroe. Since he was determined not to accept it even if the Senate "advised," he reasoned, "why call the Senate together?" Aside from Jefferson's pragmatic attitude, some Federalists acknowledged that the president had acted constitutionally. Sofaer *Origins* 197.

session appeared inconsistent with the public interest.[81] Taylor's refusal was not only to prevent legislative ventilation of the whole matter of Tigre* but also to avoid discussion of the British "protectorate" over Nicaragua's Mosquito Coast, its occupation of Greytown (San Juan), and Britain's "intrigues" in Costa Rica—all of which Taylor feared would prove unfavorable to settlement of the heated situation in Central America.†[82]

Meanwhile, the canal right-of-way that Squier had obtained from Nicaragua was being discussed confidentially during negotiations in both London and Washington. Because news reports of multinational interest in a Nicaraguan canal began to excite congressional interest, Secretary Clayton feared that Anglo-American correspondence would have to be released, though the matter was still too delicate for an open forum. He turned, therefore, to Sir Henry Bulwer, British minister in Washington, to continue discussions that then ripened into an understanding that the Squier treaty would not be submitted to Congress.** Both Clayton and Bulwer acted without instructions, agreeing that "if their Governments should fail to approve it, [their treaty] should be considered 'as having never been made.'"[83] But their effort was approved, signed, and accepted in Congress after only a day's discussion.††[84]

Lord Palmerston found the treaty's use of geographical references such as "Central America" vague, and instructed Bulwer to inform Clayton that the British would not apply the terms of the treaty to British Honduras (Belize).[85] Before ratifications were exchanged, Secre-

---

*Taylor, to preserve a climate conducive to the Clayton-Bulwer negotiations, wanted to suppress Squier's Honduras treaty giving the United States an interest in Tigre, since the British seizure of Tigre in December was in direct conflict with that interest and would inflame Congress. 5 *Treaties* 738–39 (Miller ed.). But Taylor expected Britain's cooperation. Clayton, on 26 December 1849, wrote U.S. Ambassador Lawrence that Britain must withdraw from Tigre, disavow the seizure, and make explanations; otherwise, the Honduras treaty would be submitted to the Senate. *Id.*

†To what extent was the president obliged to inform Congress of what historian Samuel Flagg Bemis has termed a "crisis" in Anglo-American relations? Was it misleading, under the circumstances of the ongoing delicate negotiations, for Taylor to characterize these relations in his message as being "of the most friendly character"? The Tigre documentation was transmitted by President Fillmore only after talks in London had defused the situation and Clayton and Bulwer had negotiated their understanding. No evidence appears in the *Congressional Globe* that would indicate that Congress was aware of the reasons for the delicately timed withholding and release of the Tigre information.

**In the wake of uncertain British government reaction to the Clayton-Bulwer project and a discouraging note from Lord Palmerston straddling the Tigre question by reserving Britain's right to seize territory as a claims indemnity, Squier's earlier effort was used as a policy alternative and finally sent to the Senate without Bulwer's knowledge on 19 March 1850; but no action was taken on it. *Id.* 757.

††The resolution of advice and consent was passed on 22 May, and the treaty was ratified by the United States on 23 May and by Britain on 11 June. *Id.* 671.

tary of State Clayton carefully declined to affirm or deny British title to Belize and its island dependencies, assuring himself that since the chairman of the Senate Foreign Relations Committee understood Palmerston's reservation over Belize, the full Senate would just as well.[86]

Four days after the treaty took effect, Zachary Taylor died without deciding whether to communicate documentation promised both in his December 1849 message and in his responses to information requests in February 1850. But on 18 July 1850, Millard Fillmore partially complied with the House request by sending it information concerning the seizure and occupation of Tigre Island[87] plus a copy of Elijah Hise's early canal treaty,* which Taylor had refused to transmit. He also sent the Clayton-Bulwer Treaty[88] but asserted that the other treaties negotiated with Central American states would not be forwarded until they had been acted upon by the Senate, which was considering them at that time. However, Fillmore did *not* send Bulwer's declaration of 29 June and Clayton's notes of 4 July, even though Congress did not adjourn until 30 September 1850.

Pressure for Reconsideration of Senate Ratification After newspaper accounts announced that the islands off the coast of British Honduras would constitute a British colony, Whig Senator Lewis Cass introduced two requests for information in December 1852 that precipitated months of intense controversy over the meaning of the Clayton-Bulwer Treaty. The president replied on 4 January 1853 with correspondence relating to the treaty that had not been in the hands of the Senate at the time of its consent. Senator Cass and others then declared that had they known the full story† of the negotiations, particularly the exchange of notes between Bulwer and Clayton in June and July 1850, they never would have voted to ratify the treaty. They insisted that Clayton's construction, given *after* the Senate's approval, could not be binding.[89] Others felt that the objectives of the treaty—to prevent further British expansion—were consistent with the new information before the Senate.[90] The issues of executive-congressional relations that emerged thus included not only (1) the executive's failure to communicate information but also (2) the validity of ratification if qualifications have been attached to a treaty after Senate consent and (3) the apparent refusal of President Taylor to transmit the earlier Hise treaty to the Senate.

Cass was furious when he discovered that in their correspondence Clayton and Bulwer had apparently eliminated the application of the treaty's first article to British Honduras and that Chairman William King, Foreign Relations Committee, had assured Clayton that the

---

See supra p. 107.
†S. Exec. Doc. No. 12, 32d Cong., 2d Sess. (ser. 660).

Senate "perfectly understood" the exemption:

> [W]hen I voted for the ratification of that treaty, I had not the slightest
> doubt that it prevented the British Government from establishing any
> colonial dependency in that part of the country. . . . I distinctly stated that
> my object in voting for that treaty was to sweep away all British claims to
> Central America.[91]

Other senators, however, such as Maryland's James Pearce, argued that
they had understood the object of the treaty at the time.[92] Pearce
concluded that the purpose of the treaty of 1850 was to prevent British
expansion beyond Greytown and to neutralize the line of communication from the Atlantic to the Pacific. He added that the correspondence
between Clayton and Bulwer was known not only to Senator King but
also to the president and the Cabinet.

Requests for more information elicited further data. The president
duly sent to the Senate on 21 January all relevant correspondence,
including an eighty-five-page letter from U.S. minister Lawrence to
Secretary of State Clayton dated 9 April 1850 that reviewed the entire
matter, though he refused to respond to a monumental unqualified
request from Senator Stephen A. Douglas for the entire diplomatic bag
between Elijah Hise and the Department of State.[93]

Newly elected Senator John Clayton, with a virtually unmatched
knowledge of all relevant executive documents, answered Senator
Douglas's charge in March 1853 that Clayton as secretary of state had
suppressed the Hise treaty. Clayton stated that President Taylor had
informed the Senate he would refuse to send a treaty negotiated outside
of an agent's powers, particularly because this treaty's guarantee of
Nicaraguan security created a political relationship that would have
brought the United States into collision, and eventually war, with other
nations.*[94]

Senator Cass, however, pointedly† objected to the British legal construction of the treaty, which he had requested and obtained from
President Pierce.**[95] He complained that "executive interference" by
"peremptory concession" of the secretary of state could make private

---

*Clayton recalled that Hise's treaty even if transmitted to and approved by the Senate
could never have become law, since it had been disapproved by the Nicaraguan government. 22 *Congressional Globe Appendix* 253.

†Clayton got to the heart of Douglas's objection when they agreed that the issue
between them was the extent to which the United States had the exclusive privilege of
controlling communication between the oceans or should do so in partnership with
another power and thus be forced to abandon any project of annexing Central America. *Id.*
257, 261, 268.

**Pierce's reply included secret British official reviews of Clayton's remarks on the
Senate floor, which Clayton felt placed him in the position of being "met here upon the
floor by Lord Clarendon and Mr. Hardinge, the Queen's advocate," without an opportunity
to face them "in fair, manly argument upon this whole question." 23 *Congressional Globe*

understandings of negotiations more significant than treaties themselves. Cass felt that it was highly improper for Clayton to have asked Senator William King's sole opinion as to whether Central America included British Honduras.

Clayton challenged Cass to define "Central America," which no one had ever agreed consisted of more than the five states of Costa Rica, Nicaragua, San Salvador, Honduras, and Guatemala.* Moreover, he explained that he exchanged ratifications after receiving Sir Henry Bulwer's declaration on the ground that "I might be justly censured if I broke up this treaty between the two Governments" because of excessive caution.[96] Clayton explained that Bulwer thoroughly understood no alteration in the treaty was made by his declaration nor by Clayton's reply. "I also denied his authority or power even to propose any alteration; and he made no attempt to assert that he had such a power."†[97] Moreover, Clayton felt as a practical matter that he had every right to rely on the assurances of Senator King as chairman of the Senate Foreign Relations Committee, simply because he could not have consulted all sixty-two senators.[98] Clayton's latitude in dealing with the post-ratification correspondence, as well as the gradual release of information concerning the many Central American treaties and correspondence supporting them, met with eventual legislative acceptance—but not before Congress had squarely placed a serious challenge at the feet of the executive in the course of its dealing with a highly sensitive diplomatic initiative.

Executive Initiatives to Open Japan   Legislators were not generally interested enough to know why the United States felt it was necessary to send visitors to Japan in 1852.** Thus they did not ask for information

---

108. He claimed that the manner in which the speech of a member of Congress was reviewed by the British cabinet and then transmitted back to Congress was a fundamental abridgement of congressmen's essential rights to be free of questions concerning their debates "in any other place" than the legislature. *Id.* 108. *See* U.S. Const. art. I, §6, cl. 1.

*This was the complete definition according to the Central American Federation Treaty of 1825.

†In the case of the Mexican treaty protocol of 1848, Senator Clayton asserted that the power explicitly possessed by the U.S. commissioners sent to exchange treaty ratifications also included the authority "to make explanations in regard to the amendments of the Senate" without such explanations being considered legal interpretations. Inasmuch as the protocol was not a diplomatic convention—having never been submitted to the Senate and the Mexican government's having been forewarned of the fact—the United States was absolved from any responsibility to construe the Treaty of Guadalupe Hidalgo by anything contained in it "... and the Congress of the United States sustained Mr. Polk, in the ground which he took, that the protocol was absolutely and utterly void." 23 *Congressional Globe Appendix* 91. *See infra* p. 125–28.

**Some congressmen envisioned that a mission could result in a war that the legislature would be required to finance (21 *Congressional Globe* 942, 943), and President Fillmore

on the purposes of Matthew Calbraith Perry's voyages there until long after completion of his second mission in 1854, partly from sheer lack of suspicion on the part of either house that Perry would act as boldly as he did. Yet evidence exists of the president's almost complete advance investiture of discretion in Perry without Congress's knowledge.

Few were concerned,* because Perry returned triumphantly. It was not until early 1855, when Perry's report was disseminated and President Pierce's reply to the Senate with nearly complete documentation was communicated, that Congress received arguably "enough" information upon which to act. Because Perry was eventually successful, none refused to accept the benefits of the Treaty of Yokohama (1854) that he extracted from the emperor of Japan; but both before he went on his missions and during their course, neither branch of government seriously attempted to restrain him by recourse to its own war powers. Commodore Perry did not hesitate to fill the void.

On 24 November 1852, Matthew Perry had steamed out of Norfolk harbor with an impressive armada of ten ships.[99] Under orders from President Fillmore, his purpose was ostensibly to provide for the safety of shipwrecked American seamen, to supply U.S. vessels in Japanese ports, and to open one or more ports for trading.† Superiors instructed Perry that if the Japanese refused to negotiate a treaty, he was emphatically to insist on humane treatment for U.S. seamen and vessels and to state that any future incidents would be "severely chastised," although not during his own visit.[100]

Secretary of State Webster was in poor health and suggested that Perry write the instructions for his own mission, which he did.[101] The

responded to the one qualified request seeking documentation of the "existing relations" between the United States and Japan. *Id.* 966–67, 1044.

*The Senate's resolution of 6 December 1854 for complete documentation of Perry's instructions and treaty negotiations (24 *Congressional Globe* 15) was more comprehensive than the House request simply for the secretary of the navy to transmit Commodore Perry's report so that its full text and accompanying illustrations might be printed. *Id.* 400, 732. The president replied to the Senate on 30 January 1855, while the Navy Department delayed only long enough to complete its report. *Id.* 732.

It is hardly surprising that Perry's "opening wedge" received scant congressional attention because of the comparatively limited general publicity each of his trips to Japan had obtained. T. Bailey, *A Diplomatic History of the American People* 311 (1958). President Pierce's second annual message in December 1854 gave it scarcely two sentences in a total of twenty printed pages, merely concluding that the mission had been successfully and "skillfully" terminated by treaty. 7 *Messages and Papers* 2812.

†U.S. economic interests had been expressed in a diplomatic effort to obtain a Nicaraguan canal and in consolidation of the vast territories won from Mexico; the potential of Far Eastern commerce was only a logical next step. President Fillmore himself laid the groundwork in his third annual message by saying that ". . . an attempt should be made to open the opposite regions of Asia tó mutually beneficial intercourse. It is obvious that this attempt could be made by no power to so great advantage as by the United States. . . ." 6 *Messages and Papers* 2703.

Department of State redrafted these orders, which, as attached to directives from the Department of the Navy, invested him with such discretionary powers "that any departure from usage or any error of judgment he may commit will be viewed with indulgence."*[102] For instance, Navy Secretary John Kennedy ordered Perry to use force only in self-defense since the president had no power to declare war. He could, however, "resent an act of personal violence offered to himself or one of his officers."[103]

The executive minimized the extent of Congress's prior notice of planning for the Japanese expedition. Apparently Fillmore was dedicated to quashing the fervor for overseas expansion, and at the risk of imperiling his future candidacy, he could not with consistency squelch aggression against Cuba† while ordering incursion against Japan. Leading newspapers had reported it, and there was no element of secrecy involved. In fact, the opposition press had severely criticized the upcoming expedition, and some foreign papers agreed: the London *Times* asked whether the emperor of Japan would receive Perry with "most indignation or most contempt."[104]

Congressman Orin Fowler (Wh. Mass.) remarked on the House floor with evident concern on 31 March 1852:

> [T]he public prints affirm (and hitherto I have seen no official contradiction) that this squadron is to establish commercial relations with Japan *at all hazards*—by which, I suppose, is meant, peaceably if they can, forcibly if they must. . . . [I]f such be its objects, I enter my protest against its movements. . . .[105]

The executive responded punctiliously to senatorial requests for information, at least one of which predated the official announcement of the expedition and even Perry's orders.** Though Congress may have possessed little knowledge of the force that Perry contemplated using before he embarked, the Senate unquestionably became aware of the size of his fleet after a naval coal contract dispute that occurred during

---

*The Department of State instructions were contained in a letter attached to Secretary of the Navy Kennedy's orders, which Kennedy declared were to be an integral part of the orders for the mission. S. Exec. Doc. No. 34, at 2.

†Fillmore signed orders to stop U.S. citizens from fomenting an insurrection in Cuba. 6 *Messages and Papers* 2647. And in his first annual message of December 1850 the president had proclaimed, "We instigate no revolutions, nor suffer any hostile military expeditions to be fitted out in the United States to invade the territory or provinces of a friendly nation." *Id.* 2614.

**Executive messages were sent on 8 April 1852, plus 31 March and 12 July 1854. *Id.* 2685; 7 *Messages and Papers* 2769, 2776. One message contained the details of the treatment of shipwrecked sailors and the lack of success of previous, nonaggressive expeditions. S. Exec. Doc. No. 59, 32d Cong., 1st Sess. 2–87 *passim*.

the mission.[106] A debate of 17 March 1853, in its concern that coal merchants supply Perry without fail, expressed more than one senator's approbation of a mission that "might be entirely prostrated, or at least paralyzed, if the coal was not put in such a condition as to be obtained when wanted."[107]

Perry's conduct indicated that he considered the unhindered command of his entire force as being indispensably necessary to success. After occupying the Lew Chews Islands for several months, he received cautious permission to establish a temporary base there for rendezvous and refuge if he could do so peacefully.[108] Even though no force was involved, Perry's superiors had in fact authorized an act of war. Perry refrained from occupying the Bonin Islands only when he failed to receive a reply from Washington to his suggestion that he take possession of them "in the name of the United States."[109]

Commodore Perry went on to Japan itself in the summer of 1853 but was stymied by the Japanese refusal to negotiate.* Withdrawing temporarily, he then pressed Washington for outright acquisition of the Lew Chews,[110] convinced that he could not return to Japan without some show of force. Perry rationalized his plan to take Grand Lew Chew Island (Okinawa) "under the surveillance of the American Flag upon the ground of reclamation for insults and injuries committed upon American citizens ... until the decision of my government shall be known," whether to avow or disavow my acts."†[111] Before he received the executive response bluntly stating that his idea was "embarrassing" and unacceptable to the president, "who ... is disinclined, without the authority of Congress, to take and retain possession of an island in that distant country, ..."[112] Perry had raised the U.S. flag over the Lew Chews on 5 February 1854. The delay in the executive reply permitted sufficient time for Perry to influence the sluggish negotiations.

Determined to succeed, he rearrived in Japan with ten ships, 134 guns, and over 2,000 men. He informed Japanese officials that if his proposals were rejected, he was prepared to make war at once and that in the event of war, he "could summon a command of one hundred ships

---

*Despite orders to the contrary, authorizing him to deliver his letters of introduction to representatives of the emperor, Perry threatened force unless permitted to confer with the emperor or the foreign secretary. In further violation of his orders he threatened force "whatever the consequences might be" if he was not permitted to land. Acting Secretary of State Conrad to Secretary of the Navy Kennedy, 5 November 1852, in S. Exec. Doc. No. 34, 33d Cong., 2d Sess. 4, 6; notes referring to events preceding Perry's negotiations with authorities of Japan, id. 45, 47.

†Perry had received a letter from Secretary of the Navy Dobbin in response to Perry's ingenuous description of the threats he had been employing, telling Perry that the president wanted him to succeed, but "without wrong to Japan." Id. 57, 58 (letter of secretary of the navy to Perry, 14 November 1853).

After Commodore Matthew C. Perry's "opening" of Japan (*see* pp. 114–16), Japanese visitors to the U.S. warship *Powhatan,* seated amid powerful cannon, must have been made conscious of U.S. military strength in relation to their own. (L.C.)

within twenty days."[113] Perry reportedly minced no words:

> If your country becomes an enemy, we will exhaust our resources if necessary to wage war, we are fully prepared to engage in a struggle for victory. Our country has just had a war with a neighboring country, Mexico, and even attacked and captured its capital. Circumstances may lead your country also into a similar plight.[114]

When he concluded the Treaty of Yokohama on 31 March 1854, in which the Japanese conceded Fillmore's proposals, Perry reportedly told his interpreter, "[W]e will be prepared at any time to help you in every way possible with warships and guns should you engage in war along your coast with any foreign country."[115] No official instructions contained authority to make such an undefined military commitment, nor is there reference to this commitment in Perry's own reports or in executive responses to congressional requests for information. Commodore Perry's threats to the Japanese probably were unknown to the executive. By the time enough was known about the mission for there to have been serious inquiry as to whether there had been overly broad executive delegation of discretion, popular approbation had made any postmission congressional objection impossible.* The entire incident also illustrates a mode of conduct used by former presidents to gain the benefit of an unlawful act without seeming to authorize it.[116]

Executive Withholding

Abrogation of the Anglo-American Treaty of 1818   Both the House and Senate submitted requests for information dealing with abrogation of the Anglo-American Treaty concerning the Oregon territory. Although some members doubted they had been fully informed, a carefully phrased executive response contended that the president's transmittal containing no documents was indeed complete, when in fact it was not.

The Convention of 1818 governing Anglo-American relations in Oregon had been amended in 1827 to provide that each party had the right to abrogate the agreement by giving twelve months' notice to the other that thereafter it would not abide by the convention's terms. A critical provision, which abrogation would eliminate, stated that regardless of the parties' disputed claims, the territory, together with its harbors, bays, and rivers, would be free and open to the vessels and citizens of the two powers.[117]

The president in his annual message of 2 December 1845[118] had recommended that Congress adopt measures for giving the required notice and protecting the rights of Americans in the period to follow. However, both Houses, expressing concern that they lacked vital information, launched qualified requests† to secure the facts that they considered necessary to critical decisionmaking.** Identical information sent to each house indicated that Britain was not undertaking preparation for war, nor was the U.S. government interested in referring the Oregon dispute with England to binding arbitration.[119]

After reading the president's transmittal, Senator Webster was unimpressed. Speaking on 30 March to support John M. Clayton's (Wh. Del.) resolution for more information,[120] Webster criticized the policy of

---

*Congress itself was in no mood for strict inquiry and in time approved all Perry accomplished. On 15 July 1854, the Senate ratified the Treaty of Yokohama, which Perry had negotiated with the Japanese. The Senate Committee on Foreign Relations recommended special compensation for him, and Congress, as a whole, approved a $20,000 bonus. 24 *Congressional Globe* 742, 1094.

†15 *Globe* 275 (Senate, 29 January 1845); *id.* 303–304 (House, 3 February 1846).

**The Whigs had been prepared to go along with the president's demand for notice, believing that such a move might lead to a compromise of the issues; but having been informed by an administration spokesman (Lewis Cass) that if England did not yield a large part of her claim, war would ensue one year after notice, the Whigs balked. Sellers, *James K. Polk, Continentalist, 1843–1846*, at 362.

abrogating a treaty and putting the United States on a war footing without exhausting the possibilities of negotiation.*

Opponents of the resolution concluded "probing" implied "distrust." On the contrary, John Clayton found that the reposing of discretion implied "the highest confidence."[121]

The Senate's second qualified resolution was passed on 11 April (27 to 17).[122] Polk stated two days later that there had been no additional correspondence relating to Oregon since the last submission he had made to Congress.[123] Senator Webster appeared surprised, since he believed there had been a more recent correspondence between Louis McLane, U.S. minister at London, and the State Department; but Senator Clayton pointed out that this correspondence was not comprised in the call for information.[124]

Webster was correct. But Polk was unsuccessful in swaying his Cabinet to reveal the fact that England had been preparing for war in case the Oregon negotiations broke down. A majority of the Cabinet wanted all correspondence withheld between Secretary of State Buchanan and U.S. minister at London Louis McLane concerning British military and naval preparedness for war. Polk had vacillated and at length sent only a portion of it in response to the first qualified request.[125] Since the legislators had submitted qualified requests, however, their claim of unjustified withholding was not appropriate. But Congress was left with only a partial estimate of the critical circumstances under which it labored to resolve the Oregon matter—a view, incidentally, that helped to forge Polk's "hard line" policy on Oregon, since the legislature was unaware how close war might be.

The Slidell Mission to Mexico An "excited discussion"† took place in the House in January 1848 when Representative William Goggin (Wh. Va.) moved, without reservation, to obtain instructions issued in 1845 to John Slidell, minister plenipotentiary to Mexico, in addition to orders regarding the return of Santa Anna to Mexico.[126] Polk firmly refused to transmit either set of instructions to the House[127] on the ground that even though the possibility of reviving negotiations had been abruptly concluded by the outbreak of war, Goggin's unconditional resolution sought information whose release would have been extremely impolitic.

The president used George Washington's refusal of a 1796 House summons as a standard by which to evaluate the request but reasoned that his own justification for noncompliance was even stronger, since

---

*Webster and other Whigs were part of a "peace coalition" that was engaging in a delaying action on the notice issue. *Id.* 362ff.; 15 *Globe* 567.

†Polk, *Diary* (Nevins ed.) 295, 296.

negotiations had not been terminated in the usual official sense.*[128] Congressman Isaac Holmes (D. S.C.) fully concurred that the surrender of executive power to withhold sensitive information would have withdrawn one of the surest means of restoring peace, which was the freedom to deal with the top echelon of the Mexican government.[129] Polk's other supporters argued that he could be impeached if release was later found to be improper and that virtually all resolutions seeking such information and passed by both houses had been qualified.[130]

On the other hand, John Quincy Adams found that Polk had denied the constitutional power of the House to call for documents,† which it had gone on record in its own *Journal* as having the right to obtain.**[131] Congressman Robert Schenck (Wh. Ohio) added that President Washington's refusal to release was based on the desired evidence's irrelevance to a House function. Here, Schenck argued, the data were directly relevant. Secrecy might be maintained by clearing the House of all but its members and officers "while they took up the subject of the information . . . necessary for their . . . action in time of war."††

Polk did make the effort to approach Senators Cass and Sevier to determine whether he should send the instructions to the Senate confidentially, in executive session. After reading them, however, both senators said that they should not be sent on the ground that publicity could adversely affect the public's interest if and when the information went to Mexico.[132]

Slidell's instructions were sensitive, and their release even as late as they were requested could have damaged U.S. ambitions in Mexico. Before Slidell left, the president and his Cabinet had weighed authorizing General Zachary Taylor to treat a Mexican crossing of the Del Norte as an act of war. If he judged it advisable, Taylor was to assault Mexico

---

See Sofaer, *Origins* 85–93. Polk did not, in his own words, "[deem] it to be necessary . . . to examine . . . other reasons" for withholding the instructions; and thus, he did not invoke the principle upon which Washington had mainly relied: that since the papers were relevant to no House function, the House had no right to request them.

†Adams was probably referring to that part of Polk's message in which he said that "[t]o admit . . . a right in the House of Representatives *to demand,* and to have, as a matter of course, all the papers respecting a negotiation with a foreign power, would be to establish a dangerous precedent." 17 *Congressional Globe* 167.

**Adams recalled that the House really disapproved of Washington's refusal to communicate needed materials. The record of debate concerning its request for John Jay's instructions clearly sets forth that the House affirmed, following Washington's refusal, its own discretionary role in the area of foreign relations. 5 *Annals of Congress* 782–83.

††17 *Congressional Globe* 167, 168. Schenck advocated establishment of a select committee to determine in this case what should be done "to guard and vindicate the rights of the House and of the people." Said Congressman Patrick Tompkins (Wh. Miss.), Congress simply wanted to know "what was to be accomplished . . . and how . . ." with relation to the Mexican War. *Id.* 204. After Polk's declining to send the Slidell instructions to the House, however, the issue was finally dropped. *Id.*

before he was attacked and to pursue but not penetrate any great distance into Mexican territory. Upon hearing of the outbreak of war, Commodore David Conner, commander of the Gulf Squadron, was to blockade and seize Mexican ports.[133] On 16 September 1845, however, Polk received word that General Paredes would not march to Texas*[134] and that Mexico would receive a minister. So Polk obtained his Cabinet's unanimous consent to send Slidell on a mission of "profound" secrecy aimed at adjusting a permanent boundary between the United States and Mexico and purchasing Upper California and New Mexico for up to $40 million.†[135]

Polk also sent an official, confidential letter to Slidell on the same day[136] urging him if possible to acquire both California and New Mexico for up to $15 million. Before he could have received a reply, the president sent an unofficial second letter mentioning the projected acquisition only as the "object" mentioned in his first letter, lest the second letter be intercepted.[137] Polk delegated even further discretion to Slidell, stating that he was "ready to take the whole responsibility" for it: should Slidell find the funds inadequate he was to propose any "reasonable additional sum" enabling him to succeed and was authorized to include a stipulation for payment of it in the treaty. Polk also desired Slidell to obtain Mexican ratification so that it would be ready to accompany the treaty to the Senate. The Mexican government, however, rebuffed Slidell, and Polk then ordered General Taylor to proceed to the Rio Grande.

Slidell had also been instructed to claim territory near the mouth of the Rio Grande for the United States: land that was "indisputably" Mexican and had never been claimed a part of Texas.** After the war, Polk extended U.S. military rule over territory east of the Rio Grande, claiming that the area was disputed and that boundaries could not have been concluded in wartime.[138] Thereupon, he sent a special message to Congress to create *civil* territorial governments in the newly acquired lands, including Oregon, without obtaining Congress's opinion of the status of the disputed Texan boundary. Although Congress finally

---

*The fact that Paredes was not sent to Texas was due to threat of internal strife in Mexico, according to confidential agent William Parrott. 1 Polk, *Diary* 33 (Quaife ed.).

†The secrecy was paramount to prevent Britain or France from defeating the objects of the mission. Slidell's instructions were dispatched to him on 10 November 1845. *Id.* 93. *See* National Archives Microfilm, Department of State, Diplomatic Instructions (Mexico), M77, roll 112, pp. 1–23.

**Although Secretary of State Buchanan acknowledged that this land, like the rest of New Mexico west of Del Norte, had historically been Mexican, its inclusion might help preclude future boundary disputes. Incorporation of all of New Mexico, he felt, was even more desirable, and Slidell was instructed that the United States would pay $5 million for the whole territory. 6 Buchanan, *Works* 294, 295, 300, 302, 303.

acquiesced,* some legislators indicated that Polk's earlier statements about claiming only the "true" boundary of Texas had been deceptive† and that if the land had ever been Texan or even disputed there would have been no need for civil government of it.[139] Clearly, the withholding of Slidell's instructions at the time was an absolute necessity from the executive viewpoint, in order to shield Polk's aims of territorial conquest from disclosure rather than merely to protect stalled negotiations.

Polk also refused to forward full documentation regarding exiled Santa Anna's return to Mexico. Instead, he merely referred a January 1848 House inquiry to his annual message of 8 December 1846. In that message, Polk had stated that in May 1846 he had requested Commander David Conner to permit Santa Anna to return to Mexico unobstructed and that these orders were given on the belief that Santa Anna's restoration to power could encourage peace.**[140] Most significantly, the president assured Congress that Conner's orders went forward without any "direct or indirect" understandings having been concluded with Santa Anna or anyone else.[141]

In fact, however, Polk had conferred in February 1846 with Santa Anna's agent, Colonel Alexander Atocha, who assured the president that Santa Anna favored a treaty with the United States that would not only adjust the boundary with the Del Norte as the western Texas line but also would cede parts of California "for a pecuniary consideration. . . ."[142] Atocha had said such an agreement could materialize only if it appeared Mexico was forced to agree; therefore, he advised that the U.S. Army "should be marched at once from Corpus Christi to the Del Norte, and a strong naval force assembled at Vera Cruz. . . ."[143] Polk indicated in his diary that he made no promises to Atocha, although subsequent events, including the instructions of 13 May 1846 to Conner, bore unmistakable influence of their conversation. Arguably, Polk could not have been criticized had he sent whatever documents he chose to transmit pertaining to the Santa Anna inquiry. But by asserting in January 1848 that he had had no understanding with any person prior to issuing Conner's orders, Polk deliberately chose to ignore mention of the Atocha interview. Polk had even further confirmed his understanding with Atocha by sending his special mes-

---

*House members agreed finally to take up legislation to provide government for the disputed area (17 Congressional Globe 992), while Senate concern over the extension of slavery caused its acquiescence in a House version to deal with the territories and their governments separately.

†Representative Alexander Stephens (D. Ga.) noticed that the Slidell instructions had been "slipped in with other papers" along with the president's message, and he called attention to Buchanan's description of the eastern portion of land at the mouth of the Rio Grande as historically Mexican. Id. 911, 990.

**These orders had been issued immediately upon the outbreak of war between the United States and Mexico.

senger, Alexander Slidell MacKenzie, to Santa Anna in Mexico in June 1846. MacKenzie reported to the president that Santa Anna had agreed to make all of the necessary concessions. Thus, when Polk and his Cabinet decided[144] in January 1848 not to send MacKenzie's report to Congress, it was because of the complete devastation that this report and the Atocha meeting would have made of his claim that there had been no prior agreement or understanding between the Mexican general and the American president.*

Executive Response: The *Black Warrior* Incident

Franklin Pierce's unabashed response to an information request in early 1854 revealed the strong position he took with Spain over seizure of a U.S. vessel—somewhat startling in a period usually associated with presidential caution.

When a private merchant vessel, the *Black Warrior*, was seized by Cuban authorities in Havana on 28 February 1854 in retaliation for the Lopez incidents,† President Pierce rebuked Spain for permitting Cuba to exercise improper authority, barely stopping short of denominating it an act of war. His message was inflammatory, but Spain managed to tone down U.S. minister to Spain Pierre Soulé's intemperate demands before an accord was achieved.**

Congress requested information about the vessel's detention and her officers' capture,[145] and President Pierce fully complied.[146] The president indicated that he had requested indemnity as well as informed the Spanish government of the fact that unfriendly acts near the U.S. coast could not "long consist with peaceful relations."††[147]

Many Northern members suggested that the president was really

---

*Polk evidently considered the whole MacKenzie incident so sensitive that he never wrote of it in his diary until the January 1848 entry.

†*See infra* p. 133. At the time of the *Black Warrior*'s seizure, it was known by Spanish authorities that another Cuban filibuster was being planned. Pierce ultimately realized that if negotiations with Spain were to succeed, he would have to issue a proclamation specifically prohibiting these activities, which he did on 31 May 1854. 7 *Messages and Papers* 2805–06.

**The *Black Warrior* regularly plied a course between U.S. ports and Havana. The practice arose of exempting her from declaring a cargo manifest, but suddenly Cuban port authorities demanded a manifest and would permit no time for its preparation and presentation. They seized and fined the ship $6,000 for violation of customs regulations, only releasing her two weeks later after protest by the United States. Spain, finally, made satisfactory amends. Bemis, *A Diplomatic History of the United States* 321 n.1; Bailey, *A Diplomatic History of the American People* 314 n.23.

††The executive threat of unilateral action implied in this language appeared qualified by Pierce's subsequent assurance that if amicable measures for adjustment failed, he would apply to Congress for "authority and means . . . to insure an observance of our just rights. . . ." 23 *Congressional Globe* 637. The president also asked that Congress adopt "such provisional measures" as might seem proper in anticipation of the "contingency" that "amicable adjustment" might fail. *Id.*

laying the groundwork for involving the United States in a war with Spain in order to acquire Cuba and prevent the emancipation of her slaves.[148] There was a certain amount of justification for these contentions. Statesmen since Jefferson had maintained that the United States should obtain Cuba at the earliest possible opportunity; and Secretary of State Buchanan marshaled arguments that the U.S. minister to Spain might use to purchase it in 1848.* Flamboyant Pierre Soulé was appointed U.S. minister to Spain in 1853. His earliest instructions were explicit that no Cuban purchase proposal be made to Spain.[149] By early April 1854, however, Secretary of State William Marcy directed Soulé to await a suitable opportunity to buy Cuba for even as much as $130 million. If he was unsuccessful in purchasing it for a reasonable sum, Soulé was to attempt "to detach that island from the Spanish dominion. . . ."† The key reason prompting the policy change was Spain's preparation to introduce an agricultural apprentice-labor system into Cuba that would "Africanize" the island** and, with its promise of slave freedom, pose a serious threat to U.S. political unity.

In the meantime, Marcy had authorized Soulé to demand a $300,000 indemnity for the *Black Warrior* seizure. Soulé, however, insisted on not only the indemnity but also dismissal of all persons responsible for the seizure, and demanded that a reply be made within forty-eight hours. Fortunately, Spain ignored Soulé's warlike posturing and paid damages to the vessel's owners.[150]

Congress failed to give Pierce funds to send a special commission to Spain to deal with outstanding problems.[151] Instead, the president appointed U.S. ministers James Buchanan, at London, John Mason, at Paris, and Soulé to recommend measures that would facilitate negotiations at Madrid. The result was the unambiguous recommendation to "wrest" Cuba from Spain contained in the Ostend Manifesto,†† a confi-

---

*Buchanan told Romulus Saunders that he might suggest to Spanish authorities that they could lose Cuba by revolution or seizure by another nation such as Britain (which the United States would not tolerate). He authorized Saunders to offer $100 million for Cuba. 8 Buchanan, *Works* 89, 102, *passim.*

†Contemporary or subsequent published versions of these instructions do not contain the phrase "to detach," although it is clearly to be found in the manuscript letter of instructions in the files of the Department of State. 6 Bemis, *The American Secretaries of State and Their Diplomacy* 193. Perhaps the term influenced the language of the Ostend Manifesto, which postulated that if Spain refused to sell Cuba to the United States, "we should be justified in wresting it from Spain. . . ." H.R. Exec. Doc. No. 93, at 129, 131, 33d Cong. 2d Sess. (American ministers to Marcy, 18 October 1854).

**Marcy apprised Soulé of this development in his instructions of 3 April 1854. The labor program meant Negro freedom in Cuba and a challenge to the internal political solidarity of the United States. Nichols, *Franklin Pierce* 328.

††The conference commenced at Ostend, Belgium; but fearful of spies, the three men removed to Aix-la-Chappelle, where the dispatch was signed 18 October 1854.

dential dispatch to Marcy but later repudiated by him after its publication "shocked the world."[152]

Congressional Response

Some congressmen expressed curiosity about the Ostend conference and the status of the *Black Warrior* affair,* but Pierce's annual message was silent on it.[153] On 5 December 1854, the House adopted Representative Augustus Sollers's (Wh. Md.) qualified resolution aimed at discovering whether or not the Ostend conference came about in obedience to the secretary of state's instructions.†[154] Congress seemed to find no substantive misconduct or evidence of impropriety serious enough to call Pierce or the Department of State to task, although legislators knew nothing of Soulé's instructions to "detach" Cuba, as later expressed in the Ostend Manifesto. The House merely ordered the president's transmittal to be printed, while in the Senate there occurred only a general discussion of Cuban policy that did not focus on the Ostend conference.[155]

THE CONDUCT OF FOREIGN AFFAIRS

The epoch 1845–57 in American diplomacy was highly significant in the history of emerging American nationalism. During this period no president completely relinquished his control of foreign policy, although Congress exercised initiative to control foreign policy after Polk. President Polk did not spurn Secretary of State Buchanan to the same extent Franklin Pierce ignored Lewis Cass, but in most cases Polk acted as his own secretary of state and clearly manifested his belief that a tight personal rein on foreign affairs would be the only style with which he would feel fully comfortable.

---

*Although Spain had paid damages to the private owners of the vessel, she steadily refused to indemnify the United States, denying there had been any insult to the American flag. 6 Bemis, *The American Secretaries of State and Their Diplomacy* 197. U.S. minister Horatio J. Perry, in May 1855, finally negotiated settlement of the affair. Janes, "The *Black Warrior* Affair," 12 *American Historical Association Review* 289 n.4 (1907).

†Representative Thomas Bayly (S.R.D. Va.) considered that disclosure would be premature and moved that Sollers's resolution be referred instead to the Committee on Foreign Affairs. 24 *Congressional Globe* 9; concurring, John Wentworth (D. Ill.), *id.* 9. Representative Benjamin Grey of Kentucky (Wh.), on the other hand, could perceive no reason to direct the resolution to the committee since the president's response would be discretionary and no injury could be done by the request no matter how delicate the subject matter. *Id.* 9, 10; concurring, Israel Washburne (Wh. Me.), *id.* 10. The Ostend resolution was placed before the House and adopted on 23 February (*id.* 905), and the president's response of 2 March (*id.* 1158) was ordered printed, becoming the Report on the Ostend Conference. H.R. Exec. Doc. No. 93, 33d Cong., 2d Sess.

Though he coveted and eventually won California, Polk's concept of U.S. interests was worldwide.* In order to shape a foreign policy to suit his needs as well as the expansionist urges within the United States, he boldly adapted the primarily defensive declaration that James Monroe had issued over two decades earlier to a policy of national security based on "advance."[156]

Polk's dramatic announcement in his annual message of 2 December 1845—that future U.S. policy would be based upon the principle of resistance to any European interference "in the political arrangements of this continent"[157]—inspired an attempt to enlist Congress's active partnership in implementing the "Polk Doctrine," since many legislators felt that "the precise character of the interference" was a fit subject for Senate deliberation and decision.†[158] Congress, however, was not fully ready to act with the executive to shape an effective policy,**[159] and efforts failed to express a resolve to cooperate in the executive's policy. Senator Calhoun more accurately expressed Congress's perception that such a major commitment would require the United States to

---

*Edward Everett was sent to China and Anthony Ten Eyck to Hawaii as reminders of the U.S. presence and active interest in discouraging other powers' influence in those distant places. 6 Buchanan, *Works* 141, 256. Polk employed many confidential agents, as had others before him. Charles Wycliffe was told to proceed to Texas to counteract foreign intriguing (*id.* 130), while W.S. Parrott went to Mexico after Secretary Buchanan severely rebuked his predecessor, Wilson Shannon, for deliberately and unilaterally assuming the high responsibility of severing diplomatic relations. *Id.* 134–35. Polk illustrated that he was a consummate diplomat in his earliest policy toward Mexico, which he proclaimed to be "firmness of action accompanied by moderation of language." *Id.* Buchanan also had to disabuse Henry Wise, U.S. minister to Brazil, of the notion that he could forcibly detain Brazilian subjects on board the American brig *Porpoise* and read him a lesson from international law that every country possessed independent jurisdiction over merchant vessels of other nations in its harbors. *Id.* 267–68. Edward Hopkins also exceeded his authority as a special agent to Paraguay, which was merely to obtain information to enable the president and Congress to decide whether the United States should recognize Paraguayan independence. Instead, Hopkins informed Paraguay's president that he was invested with diplomatic character, committed Polk to recognition of Paraguayan independence, and offered U.S. mediation in a dispute between Paraguay and Buenos Aires. Buchanan peremptorily ordered him to return to the United States. *Id.* 447–49.

†To achieve this objective, Senator William Allen (D. Oh.) asked Congress to declare its intention to resist any European effort to "intermeddle" in the affairs of American states. 15 *Congressional Globe* 197. Allen told the Senate that it was proper for him to seek such a declaration of purpose and that they had a "duty to respond"; he reminded them that Daniel Webster, in 1824, sought aid for Greece, even when U.S. territory and integrity were not threatened in words having modern relevance: "What is all [this] to us? . . . We are one of the nations. . . . The age we live in, and our own active character, have connected us with all the nations of the world. . . ." *Id.* 244. It does not appear that Allen's resolution of congressional intention was ever reported out of the Committee on Foreign Relations. *Id.* 248.

**Michigan Senator Lewis Cass pointed out that since Polk's principle of European noninterference was limited strictly to North America, it was even more cautious than James Monroe's. *Id.* 240–41.

"become a great military government"—a role that would impose the burden of raising a powerful revenue.*[160] Congressmen thus eagerly vied for an opportunity to comment on Polk's foreign policy as well as to influence it. This personal ease in meeting the demands of diplomacy while managing to permit the legislature just enough information to keep it at bay enabled President Polk to manage foreign policy and direct to a great extent the reactions of each House to his proposals.

Executive Initiatives

Protocol to the Treaty of Guadalupe Hidalgo   Several initiatives undertaken during Polk's administration illustrated his firmness in dealing with both Congress and foreign powers. Polk followed the Trist Treaty of Guadalupe Hidalgo of 1848† with a protocol that had not been submitted to the Senate either for ratification or information, yet purported to explain certain Senate amendments. Congress was alarmed by news of this protocol, and the House in February 1849 demanded to know its substance as well as whether Polk was aware of its existence at the time that he proclaimed final ratification on 4 July 1848.[161] At least one of the purported "interpretations" of an article dealing with recognition of Texas land titles almost directly contradicted Senate amendment.**[162] When the House's unqualified request for information passed overwhelmingly,[163] the president quickly replied, stating that he had not included the protocol with the ratified treaty because he deemed it was important. Its execution had changed nothing, since the commissioners had adhered to his careful instructions that

> [n]one of the amendments adopted by the Senate can be rejected or modified, except by the authority of that body. . . . Your mission is confined to procuring a ratification from the Mexican Government of the treaty as it

---

*Calhoun also observed that the principle of the resolution was unlimited—it called upon the United States to interfere whenever a European nation, "right or wrong," engaged in conflict with another nation on this continent. *Id.* 245. Allen's resolve, on the other hand, reflected the position many legislators held twenty years after Monroe had heightened fears of the Holy Alliance in his declaration: European powers could still, theoretically, implement their balance of power by carving up the world among themselves.

†The treaty was signed in Mexico on 2 February 1848 and transmitted to the Senate on 23 February. The Senate passed a resolution of advice and consent (38 to 14) on 10 March 1848, and ratifications were exchanged by the respective governments on 30 March. 5 *Treaties* 207 (Miller ed.).

**This was Article 10, which recognized the validity of Mexican grants of land in ceded territories but was stricken from the treaty. Yet the protocol contained language guaranteeing "conformably to the law of the United States" those titles that were legitimate under Mexican law. 18 *Congressional Globe* 449.

came from the Senate, and does not extend to the slightest modification in any of its provisions.[164]

Polk then set forth each of the explanations contained in the protocol and defended them, reviewing at length their limited operation.* Acknowledging that if any of the protocol's explanations varied the treaty terms they would have been invalid, Polk explained that he would have felt duty bound to make this fact clear to the Mexican government if he had felt there was any possibility of a misunderstanding.[165]

Contrary to Polk's disaffirmations, the Mexican government had relied upon the protocol as a basis for its ratification.† Secretary Buchanan affirmed the president's determination to execute the treaty in good faith and responded to Mexican minister Luis de la Rosa that if the Mexican government believed that the treaty would not be executed in accordance with the president's review of the protocol's clauses, Mexico would receive a satisfactory answer upon relaying "the points of supposed difficulty."[166] Polk's Cabinet ignored Mexican protestations.** Since Mexico took part payment of the $15 million that it was ultimately to receive for the cession of New Mexico and Upper California,†† President Taylor's secretary of state, John Clayton, later declared to the Mexican minister that Mexico's receipt of an installment payment for ceded territory was an acknowledgement of the treaty exactly as it came from the Senate.

Acquisition of Oregon Territory   Polk had exercised decisive leadership in wielding the clever parliamentary stroke*** by which Texas was annexed in December 1845 and thus obviated the need of a two-thirds

---

*The president, for example, asserted that the protocol's explanation as to why the third article of the Louisiana treaty was substituted for the original ninth article was that the Louisiana treaty's third article already guaranteed civil, political, and religious rights to Mexican inhabitants in the ceded territories. The ninth article as adopted by the Senate was "more comprehensive in its terms . . . explicit in its meaning, and it clearly embraces, in comparatively few words, all the guarantees inserted in the original article." 18 *Globe* 487; 5 *Treaties* 381 (Miller ed.) (protocol text).

†Discussion of the point in correspondence involved Luis de la Rosa, then Mexican minister at Washington, who had himself signed the protocol, and the secretary of state (James Buchanan until 7 March 1849 and John Clayton thereafter). *Id.* 383.

**De la Rosa's inquiries seeking assurance that the United States would abide by the protocol fared no better during the Taylor administration.

††Article 12 provided for payment of $15 million to Mexico for the ceded territory, $3 million immediately after ratification, and the remainder in annual installments of $3 million. *Id.* 222.

***Tyler had already preempted Polk by selecting joint resolution as the mode of annexing Texas. Polk had the option of reversing Tyler but, reportedly pledged to the treaty alternative, failed to act and thus acquiesced in Tyler's choice. E. McCormac, *James K. Polk: A Political Biography* 314–18 (1922); Reeves, *Diplomacy under Tyler and Polk* 188–89.

majority that would have been required in the Senate if the United States and the Republic of Texas had entered into treaty negotiation.* When Britain rejected Polk's compromise of the 49th parallel in Oregon,† the president just as firmly asserted title to the whole territory and recommended in December 1845 that Congress determine whether it should exercise the option contained in the Convention of 1827 to give a year's notice to abrogate the Anglo-American Treaty of 1818.**

Despite the opposition of congressmen who insisted that no one could negotiate away territory to which the United States had title, Senators Cass, Haywood, Reverdy Johnson, and Calhoun concluded that Polk could and should compromise. On 4 March, Maryland Senator Johnson insisted that Polk represented the nation and must deal with Britain again even though three times previously 49 degrees had been refused. There was no need to think that the United State should "go for 54° 40' or a fight."[167] On 16 April, a resolution passed authorizing the president to give notice at his discretion†† and encouraging negotiation unequivocally.***[168]

When the question of "notice" came before the House, Kentucky Representative Garrett Davis††† doubted whether the House might "be

---

*See supra Chapter 1, pp. 77–78 n. (discussion of constitutional issues involved in the adoption, in March 1845, of a joint resolution consenting to Texas's application for statehood). The resolution admitting Texas passed 31 to 14 in the Senate and 141 to 56 in the House. 15 Congressional Globe 65, 92.

†For a brief description of U.S.-British negotiations regarding Oregon, see James Buchanan's letter to Louis McLane, U.S. minister to Great Britain, in 6 Buchanan, *Works* 186–93.

**Polk discussed particularly the operation of the Third Article of the Convention between Britain and the United States providing for a ten-year free and open period of occupation and navigation of territory west of the Rocky Mountains claimed by both nations. 15 Congressional Globe 6. This was the critical article, providing for a kind of joint occupation that would be terminated by abrogation. See Bemis, *A Diplomatic History of the United States* 276–79; (2 Sellers, *James K. Polk, Continentalist* 360). However, certain members of Congress did not want participation, either because of political expediency (abrogation of the treaty appeared to be a call to war); or because of constitutional objections.

††Senator Ambrose Sevier (D. Ark.) charged that his colleagues were handing the president "power to make war" by giving him the discretion to act on a notice resolution. But he also criticized those senators who would add the expressions of desire to settle the question by compromise and negotiation—the Constitution already conferred this power on him, and "[i]t would set a dangerous example of tampering with the functions of the Executive, and perhaps ultimately lead to inroads on the Constitution." 15 Globe 42–48.

***The resolution urged the governments of both countries to "earnestly and immediately" direct renewed efforts to the "amicable settlement of all their differences" in respect to Oregon.

†††Garrett Davis, who (along with Representatives Truman Smith and Caleb Smith) submitted the minority report on whether the legislature should instruct the president to give notice of abrogation, revealed talent for cogent constitutional reasoning throughout a long state and federal legislative career. See *Biographical Directory of the American Congress 1774–1971*, at 831.

properly united with the President and the Senate" in the act of giving notice.[169] Davis thought that since the House was excluded from treaty-making, only through its power to declare war could it constitutionally end treaties. Ohio Congressman Allen Thurman disagreed, finding Congress's authority broad enough under the "common defense" clause to rid the United States of a foreign jurisdiction. Furthermore, occupation of U.S. territory by British subjects interfered with U.S. "commerce" and "trade with the Indian tribes." Congress had exercised concurrent jurisdiction many times with the executive—such as in the annulment of the commercial treaties of 1778 with France and the recognition of the independence of several governments carved out of the territories of other powers. Therefore, it should not abstain from its prerogative and leave it to Polk to annul the law of the land at his discretion.[170] Those who denied that the House possessed the legislative power to abrogate the 1827 convention found neither "bad faith" by Great Britain nor a "transcendent" event demanding that elemental governmental power be used to end any unfavorable treaty stipulations. They also recognized that Congress had the right to advise the president and that if notice was given, the president had power to compromise the entire matter.[171] On 9 February, the House voted unanimously requiring the executive to give notice, asserting that the resolution was not intended to interfere with amicable settlement.*[172] And the final Senate-House compromise was anything but warlike.[173]

Aid to Yucatan   Efforts to define a U.S. obligation to assist Yucatan† during an Indian uprising exacerbated tensions between the executive and Congress. Although Congress wished to limit U.S. involvement only to military aid as the result of a specific request, Polk tried to preempt the legislature by sending a naval force. The navy was utilized only to a limited extent, inasmuch as Yucatan settled its own internal problems.

After a Cabinet session in which he agreed that he would seek Congress's authority,[174] Polk on 29 April 1848 asked Congress to

---

*On 10 June 1846, Polk submitted to the Senate a proposition received from Britain that the Senate advised should be accepted as a basis for an Oregon territory. 1 Polk, *Diary* 455 (Quaife ed.). Within weeks, Secretary of State James Buchanan and Richard Pakenham, representing Her Majesty's government, signed a treaty recognizing the forty-ninth parallel as the westward boundary between the United States and Great Britain. 15 *Congressional Globe* 1199–1200.

†Situated in the Gulf of Mexico and in the vicinity of the Florida capes, New Orleans, and the entire southwestern coast, the Yucatan peninsula occupied a commanding strategic position that in 1823 President Monroe had denominated as becoming potentially "dangerous" to U.S. "peace and safety" if it should fall into the hands of any European power. *See* Sofaer, *Origins* 255, 255*, 256, 264†.

consider a request to the executive from Yucatan* for help in putting down an insurrection threatening "white extermination." Senate Foreign Relations Committee chairman Edward Hannegan reported a bill on 4 May enabling Polk temporarily to occupy Yucatan and to arm "the white population" against Indian rebels.[175] He claimed that British agents were supplying the Indians with muskets bearing the stamp of the Tower of London.† New York Senator John Dix attempted to amend Hannegan's bill so that the United States would in no case occupy the country but would render military aid only in case Yucatan asked for it.[176] Before a vote could be taken on Dix's amendment, however, Hannegan asked for a delay on the proposed bill in light of a treaty reportedly concluded between the government of Yucatan and the Indians. He reasoned that the delay could not be harmful since the United States was still at war with Mexico and no foreign vessel would attempt to enter Yucatanese ports. Besides, Hannegan felt that a force of 400 marines ordered to Laguna would "suffice under the circumstances."

While Congress called for additional information, Calhoun remarked that Polk probably regarded himself authorized to act unilaterally since Yucatan was a part of Mexico.[177] The president sent Congress texts of orders that the Navy Department had issued on 8 March and 12 May 1848 to Commodore Matthew Perry,** directing him to allow gunpowder to be landed at Sisal (assuming it would not be used against the United States) and ordering the entire force of the marines at Alvarado to be sent to Laguna, with instructions to repel the Indians.[178] The orders indicated that confrontation with another power was considered possi-

*Though Yucatan was a Mexican state, it had declared its neutrality in the Mexican War. 3 Polk, *Diary* (Quaife ed.) 434. Both chairmen of the House and Senate Foreign Relations Committees were invited to read the draft and approved the president's message seeking intervention on the ground that it would be "dangerous" and a violation of settled U.S. policy "to permit Great Britain or Spain to interfere." *Id.* 434, 437–38. For additional views of the executive on Yucatan, *see* Buchanan to Henry Hilliard, chairman (*pro tem*) of the House Committee on Foreign Affairs, 3 May 1848, in 8 Buchanan, *Works* 56–59.

†The opposition minimized the British threat, characterizing supplying arms to the Indians as a trade transaction, since the other side had also been offered arms by the British. Additionally, Polk's support of Yucatan's cause was seen as a desire to wreck the pending Treaty of Guadalupe Hidalgo with Mexico, probably because it was believed Polk desired more territory than the Mexicans had ceded. 17 *Congressional Globe* 729, 765; 17 *Congressional Globe Appendix* 599, 600.

**Perry informed Navy Secretary Mason that he never received his orders dated 12 May 1848 (S. Exec. Doc. No. 45, 30th Cong., 1st Sess. 3–4), despite the fact that he read them in the newspapers. Perry to Mason, 5 June 1848, in National Archives Microfilm, Area Collection, M625, reel 203 (area 8). He acted by sending some additional marines to Laguna, even though Mason had suggested dispatching the entire marine force. In a letter of 12 June to one of his officers, Perry indicated his instructions were to use full-scale efforts to "tranquilize" Yucatan without compromising the peace treaty with Mexico, as well as to become a listening post regarding European intentions *vis-à-vis* Yucatan. *Id.*

ble and informed senators that Perry had been instructed to communicate the presence of any other nation so that "the President may take such measures as his constitutional duty will require. . . ."[179] Polk, however, had already noted the threat, the availability of a limited force, and the basis of his authority to employ it in his message of 29 April 1848.[180]

Legislative Attempts to Influence Diplomacy

Congress attempted not only to exercise much stronger influence on executive conduct of foreign affairs but also to inaugurate certain policies of its own. After Austria's subjugation of Hungary, legislators expressed a unilateral desire to suspend diplomatic relations with Austria and extend a warm welcome to Louis Kossuth. There was no consensus on a policy toward Cuba, and they vacillated between purchasing the island, discouraging other powers from taking it, or adopting a "wait and see" approach. Certain congressmen, however, vehemently declared that the executive was not doing all in its power to counter the upsurge of European colonization in the Americas. For example, the Senate demanded that Mexico reconsider mortgaging a right-of-way across Tehuantepec in southern Mexico to a British concern and wanted to counter with force the ouster of U.S. engineering personnel in Tehuantepec. Congress also severely criticized the president for his alleged failure to deal aggressively with the fisheries disputes that had for years beclouded U.S.-Canadian relations. Most important was the increasing congressional pressure to have a hand in the conduct of treaty formation and dissolution. The House reintroduced its periodic threat to withhold appropriations unless it was allowed more of an opportunity to shape foreign affairs. For instance, Congress tried to prescribe the precise terms that should be included in two treaties—one with the Chippewa Indians and the other with Indonesia—without citing any precedent. The House claimed that it should have a role in abrogating a treaty with Denmark that had specified that the executive alone could give notice of abrogation, since Denmark and the United States might become involved in a war in which the House of Representatives would definitely have an interest. The Gadsden purchase treaty, in addition, raised the issue of how the House could properly perform its role of appropriating funds to acquire territory without knowing why the land was necessary and thus allegedly deprived House members of exercising a valid sanction that they possessed over treaty approval.

Efforts to Curtail Diplomatic Relations with Austria   Members of both houses earnestly debated Congress's authority to suspend U.S. diplomatic relations with another country. When Michigan Senator Lewis

Cass introduced a resolution that the Foreign Relations Committee "inquire into the expediency of suspending diplomatic relations with Austria"[181] to express its repulsion over Austria's war of oppression against Hungary,*[182] Whig Senator Truman Smith (Ct.) not only denied that Congress could lawfully terminate diplomatic relations with any government but also maintained that refusal to appropriate for a mission was the only method by which Congress could act upon the subject.[183] Cass's move to strike an appropriation of $4,500 for outfitting the *chargé d'affaires* to Austria, already approved in the House,†[184] was defeated 17 to 28.[185] Apparently, although the Senate was unhappy about Austria's oppressive government, it was not ready to tamper with executive control over diplomatic agents. And President Taylor regarded *de facto* recognition of Hungary as an executive prerogative.[186]

Louis Kossuth, the leader of the Hungarian revolution, came to the United States on board the U.S. frigate *Mississippi,*** and President Fillmore asked Congress to consider how to receive him.††[187] Controversy over the welcome illustrated Congress's struggle to use the joint resolution as a tool for participating in the shaping of foreign policy. Both houses debated whether official reception would imply U.S. government support and possible eventual involvement in a European war. A majority of House members, particularly, was not willing to turn the floor of Congress "into a lecture room ... where American statesmen may receive their lessons in political wisdom ... from a foreigner who has not been yet thirty days upon our shores."[188] Both the Senate and the House finally introduced him, but he did not speak, and receptions were then given in his honor.*** No formal policy statement favoring

---

*President Taylor had announced in his annual message of 24 December 1849 that he had stood ready to welcome Hungary as a fledgling independent nation if it had successfully won its fight to be free from Austria. 19 *Congressional Globe* 67, 70; 6 *Messages and Papers* 2550.

†Cass's original proposition was postponed and never was taken up again. 19 *Congressional Globe* 293.

**On 3 March 1851, both houses passed a resolution requesting the president to authorize the use of a government vessel to bring Kossuth and his companions to the United States. This is an excellent example of the melding of powers of both branches to effect a foreign policy objective. 21 *Congressional Globe* 16.

††It is likely that president and Congress possess concurrent authority to issue asylum, but the president, in this instance, appeared ready to encourage Congress to preempt the field of action.

***The Kossuth affair had wider political meanings than are evident from the congressional debates—its implications pertained to Secretary of State Daniel Webster's presidential ambitions. The Austrian minister J.G. Hulsemann "believed that he had oral assurances from Webster that Kossuth would be received not as a political leader but as a private person" (I. Bartlett, *Daniel Webster* 261 (1978)), but Webster reneged on these when Kossuth's popularity made it clear that his reception could be politically useful. "Webster had always been more interested in what Hungary could do for him than in what America could do for Hungary." *Id.* 263. Kossuth returned to Europe, empty-handed, in the summer of 1852.

either freedom for Hungary or nonintervention was issued from either house, even though before and after the dispute over Kossuth's reception, Congress thoroughly ventilated its unwillingness for the United States to be indifferent to acts of injustice.[189] While acknowledging the wisdom of Washington's nonintervention policy in a world of sixty years earlier, Senator Cass condemned those whose indifference "to the conditions of the human race" would not permit them to make at least a statement that despotic powers should not aid each other in time of revolution.[190] Congress, however, was not prepared to issue a resolution of any kind on the point.

Attempt to Counter Foreign Presence in Cuba   Though President Polk had secretly offered to buy Cuba* in an earlier effort to keep it from falling into foreign hands,[191] Millard Fillmore informed Congress that he would "regard its incorporation into the Union at the present time as fraught with serious peril."† But Senate Foreign Relations Committee chairman James M. Mason deplored the fact that Fillmore's apparent opposition to Cuban annexation should delay U.S. acquisition.** Like most southern expansionists, he believed that the moment would come when "the fruit will ripen, and fall from the parent stem, [and] when that time shall come, its political coalition with this continent is inevitable ... the combined power of Europe cannot prevent it."[192]

Senator Cass (D. Mich.), on 4 January 1853, introduced a joint resolution that tracked the language of the Monroe Doctrine of 2 December 1823, characterizing any efforts "to procure possession ... of that Island" as unfriendly acts directed against the government of the United States, "to be resisted by all the means in their power."[193] Cass noted a *New York Times* report of a French citizen's plan to colonize northern Mexico "as the only means of checking the rapid and formidable growth of the United States, and preventing forever the acquisition of a railroad from the Mississippi to the Pacific Ocean."††[194]

William H. Seward (N.Y.) declared that the subject was being aired at

---

*An offer of up to $100 million was made despite a deeply divided Cabinet, 3 Polk *Diary* 483 (Quaife ed.), but failed when Spanish foreign minister Pedro Pidal told Polk's emissary Romulus Saunders that Spain "would prefer seeing [Cuba] sunk in the ocean" than transferred to any power. H.R. Exec. Doc. No. 121, at 57–59, 32d Cong., 1st Sess. (Ser. 648).

†Third Annual Message, 6 December 1852. 6 *Messages and Papers* 2699, 2701.

**Privy only to Fillmore's declaration that he would not give reasons for opposing annexation, other than exacerbation of sectional tensions, Mason's reaction was understandable. He "deeply regretted" Fillmore's transmittal to the House of correspondence with Spain regarding Cuba, supplied in response to a request of 2 February 1852. 21 *Congressional Globe* 442.

††Spain was too weak to be any problem, but French and British interests in the area posed a definite threat. Lewis Cass's concern about British activities in Belize and in the Bay of Islands, which stimulated his challenge of the Clayton-Bulwer Treaty, should be carefully noted in this context.

an inappropriate moment, inasmuch as President Pierce was to take office within one month and a president should have the initiative in foreign policy.[195]

Undoubtedly, Pierce's stern warning to Spain that its seizure of the *Black Warrior* was an unfriendly and even warlike act was the prelude to his own initiatives to acquire Cuba. Congress neither rebuked the Pierce administration for its boldness toward Spain in view of the sentiments of many who supported the Ostend Manifesto, nor did it feel itself ready to advocate purchase or conquest of Cuba, though most members wished to see no one else but innocuous Spain own it.

Effort to Address the Fisheries Dispute Newspapers reported in 1852 that U.S. fishing boats were being seized by British naval vessels off the coast of Labrador and Newfoundland because of alleged violations of the Convention of 1818.*[196] In practice, this convention had been unenforced, but reports of a nineteen-vessel British fleet having been dispatched to Canada heightened the belief that tensions would culminate in "a blaze of war."[197] Congressional resolutions to learn everything possible about U.S. fishing rights, actions taken to protect them, and moves by British and Canadian cruisers passed in both houses with no debate.[198]

The president informed Congress that the steam frigate *Mississippi*, commanded by Commodore Matthew Perry, had been sent to the critical area to protect "the rights of American fishermen under the Convention of 1818."[199] Perry intended to warn his countrymen against encroaching upon the limits prescribed by the convention, and his mission was thus a "diplomatic voyage" with amicable intent. But he also maintained that he would protect American vessels from visitation or interference at ports where American interpretations of their treaty rights were being challenged.[200]

Though the real British motivation was unclear,† the public demanded that the navy be sent to the area. Upon receiving the requested

---

*American fishing rights on the Grand Banks of Nova Scotia had long been established. These rights had been acknowledged initially by Britain in the Treaty of 1783 on the basis of accustomed usage but were more sharply limited by terms of the Convention of 1818. This convention, among other provisions, granted U.S. citizens the "liberty" to fish "forever" outside a three-mile limit on the west coast of Newfoundland and to dry and cure their catch along the coast of Labrador and certain areas of Newfoundland, so long as those parts remained unsettled. 6 Bemis, *The American Secretaries of State and Their Diplomacy* 109–10.

†It was suggested that the British intended to use the leverage of force to induce the United States to negotiate favorably new trading and fishing rights in the Chesapeake Bay area. 21 *Congressional Globe* 1893; Bailey, *A Diplomatic History of the American People* 297. It appeared, however, that the real reason for British intervention was to put pressure on the United States to sign a reciprocal trade agreement with the Canadian colonies and not a desire to exclude U.S. fishermen from Canadian fisheries. 21 *Congressional Globe Appendix* 898.

information from the executive, Congress criticized the president for his failure to deal aggressively with the fisheries issue,[201] but in fact itself had failed to do so when requested by the president or its own members. Senator Seward pointed out that President Fillmore had invited Congress to consider reciprocal trade legislation less than a year before and had even volunteered information to Congress detailing the measures Great Britain might adopt* "if some arrangement upon [the] subject shall not be made."[202] When the British minister informed the president on 5 July that a naval force was being stationed off Nova Scotia, Prince Edward Island, and in the Gulf of St. Lawrence, Seward said that it was with the reservation that there would be no interference with U.S. vessels' activities unless they were in the act of violating the treaty† and that British commanders would avoid giving "complaint by the adoption of harsh or unnecessary proceedings when circumstances compel their arrest or seizure."[203] Moreover, Fillmore had not felt that there were sufficient grounds for war, since some U.S. vessels had been seized for treaty violations every year since 1818. Congress possessed enough relevant information to have modified commercial regulations,** a matter properly its province and not an executive concern to be accomplished by treaty.[204]

Although President Pierce sent a fleet to the fishing area with orders to use force if necessary to prevent interference with vessels' rights,[205] he described the situation in the fishing waters in relatively tame language as he announced the opening of negotiations with Britain that had "a fair prospect of a favorable result."[206] The fisheries question was, indeed, settled by treaty even though it involved complex reciprocity provisions. In 1854, a special British mission headed by Lord Elgin arrived in Washington. A spirit of compromise was in the air, and no senator appeared to object to the removal of revenue modifications from congressional prerogatives. Although there is negligible mention of the treaty in published debates in Congress, Lord Elgin's secretary recorded that British entertainments were not wasted upon influential U.S.

---

*Seward reminded senators that the British minister had communicated definite willingness to make much greater concessions to U.S. fishermen "'on certain conditions and with certain reservations'" (Id. 914–15), but Congress did not respond.

†Webster had issued a "proclamation" on 6 July 1852, setting forth information that he had informally obtained. Id. 915. He admonished U.S. fishermen about the difficulties they might face in Canadian waters and cited precedents for this type of warning in Jefferson's conduct while secretary of state under Washington. Webster admitted in his announcement that the Convention of 1818 could be technically construed to accord with Britain's contentions but that the United States dissented from such a construction. 21 Congressional Globe 915.

**Some senators attempted to address the issue during the following session by seeking enactment of reciprocal trade legislation, but their efforts were of no avail. E.g., 22 Congressional Globe 582, 953–75 passim.

diplomats and that the treaty had been "floated through on champagne." The treaty was signed 5 June 1854.[207]

Ratification appeared assured. Southern senators approved New England's fishing rights in a gesture of conciliation* and favored reciprocal tariff privileges for Canadians in order to quell their restlessness to merge with the Union and thus increase "free" territory. But to make doubly certain of a favorable response in both the U.S. Congress and the provincial legislatures of Canada, the Department of State employed an experienced lobbyist, Israel D. Andrews, at a cost of over $200,000, to smooth the reception of the treaty both in Congress and in the Maritime Provinces.[208]

Prescription to the Executive of Terms on Which Treaties Should Be Negotiated: The Chippewa Indians and Indonesia   During President Pierce's administration, each house of Congress attempted to augment its own role in the treatymaking process. In 1854, South Carolina Congressman James Orr urged adoption of provisions specifying the terms on which treaties should be negotiated† with the Chippewa Indians.[209] Arkansas Senator William K. Sebastian suggested that Congress had formerly taken the initiative regarding Indian treaties by referring to an 1830 act "by which the President was empowered to negotiate ... treaties ... which were to embrace particular features"[210] and said that the purpose of the legislation had been to introduce uniformity into such treatymaking.** But opponents delayed and thereby defeated Orr's measure on the ground that they could not see how President Pierce would possibly approve "the introduction of the House of Representatives into the treaty-making power," which was no less than a "direct encroachment" on authority granted exclusively to the executive by the Constitution.[211]

Massachusetts Senator Henry Wilson thereafter, in 1857, managed to have the Senate Foreign Relations Committee inquire into the expediency of sending a commissioner to the East Indian Archipelago (Indonesia)[212] with full powers to investigate Dutch claims to

---

*1854 was a year conducive to rapprochement between Northern and Southern partisans because of passage of the Kansas-Nebraska Act.

†Abundant evidence points to the Framers' rejection of the House of Representatives as a participant in treatymaking. *Records of the Federal Convention of 1787*, 392–94 (Farrand ed. 1937). Careful rationales were also composed in *The Federalist* by John Jay in No. 64, 400–06, and by Alexander Hamilton in No. 75, 468–69 (Lodge ed. 1888).

**Sebastian maintained that all such treaties should contain prescribed, uniform conditions, such as the establishment of inalienable proprietary reservations, and that addition of these terms would not thereby "take from the Executive the power to introduce any other provision which he may, in his discretion, deem proper to adopt." 23 *Congressional Globe* 1403.

sovereignty and to enter into treaties with any sufficiently important states or tribes. Wilson's constituents were concerned over Dutch claims that could be injurious to New England merchants' trade in the Far East.* The House Committee on Foreign Relations recommended that such a commission be created, but members' objections defeated it, and opposition by the secretary of state ended Senate consideration.[213] The concept of an East Indian commercial treaty was undoubtedly an idea prompted and considered by Congress on its own initiative, since President Pierce made no such recommendations to Congress at any time in the session.

The Effort to Enlarge House Participation in Treaty Practice: The Sound Dues Treaty with Denmark and the Gadsden Purchase Treaty   Other important examples of strong pressure to control treaty formation and dissolution were the congressional attempts to involve both houses actively in the abrogation of a treaty with Denmark and a treaty for the purchase of a substantial portion of New Mexico. The United States and Denmark concluded a treaty on 14 April 1826 requiring U.S. vessels to pay for the privilege of passing through a Danish-owned sound. Mechanically similar to the Convention of August 1827 with Great Britain regarding Oregon, the Sound Dues Treaty could be abrogated by the government of either party one year after notification of intent to do so. On 3 March 1855,[214] President Pierce alone received authority from the Senate to give the notice,† and he announced in his annual message for 1855 that he had done so on 14 April.

Believing that the full will of the legislature should have been involved, Massachusetts senator Charles Sumner on 6 March 1856 pronounced the president's action an unconstitutional assumption of a foreign relations power. He argued that all of Congress should be involved in dissolving treaties,[215] stating that notice of abrogation of the Convention of 1827 had not been accomplished by the president with the advice of the Senate in secret session but by a joint resolution of Congress.[216] Moreover, since Article VI of the Constitution states that

---

*In a contemporary incident, the Dutch had arrested Captain Walter M. Gibson, a merchant ship captain, who had attempted to send a message to an independent tribal prince: the Dutch asserting that they, and not the prince, were the legal rulers of the area involved. 26 *Congressional Globe* 498.

†In addition to the Senate resolution of 3 March 1855, which authorized the president to terminate the Danish dues treaty, the House, during the previous session, had passed a joint resolution authorizing the president to give the requisite notice to terminate U.S. reciprocity treaties with states that, in his opinion, manifested "illiberality" in commercial intercourse with the United States. The Senate did not act on this resolution but passed the 3 March resolution in lieu of it. Thus, although each House, arguably, had acted separately on the subject, there was nothing that could clearly and legally be regarded as congressional action. 24 *Congressional Globe* 414; 25 *Congressional Globe* 1148.

"all treaties made ... shall be the supreme law of the land," Sumner asserted the authority of both houses of Congress was as necessary to dissolve treaties as it was to abrogate all existing laws.*

Others saw no problem with the Senate and president acting together as "the Government" to end a treaty, since insofar as foreign relations were concerned, these two organs were the government.† Senators passed Sumner's resolution** but deleted language suggesting the president had acted unconstitutionally.[217]

On 7 April, the Senate Foreign Relations Committee resolved that Pierce's notice had been "sufficient. ...." But several members continued to declare, as New Hampshire's John Hale did, that "[T]he power of abrogation ... can only be exercised in ... that capacity in which it makes war."[218] Senator Judah P. Benjamin agreed that the president and two-thirds of the Senate were undisputed agents of "the United States" for treaty formation but called it "heresy in law and in politics" to pretend that because one is vested with the power to contract, he has the power to annul.[219]

Pierce unilaterally extended the Sound Dues Treaty for sixty days in response to a request from the Danish government.[220] Senator John Crittenden proposed that the president should give the notice but communicate the fact that it had been done to the Senate, so that its members might still have the opportunity to reject or ratify by a two-thirds concurrence.

Senator James Mason responded for the administration that since Denmark was in conference with other powers on the subject of Sound dues and its government might be embarrassed by precipitate enforcement, President Pierce had extended the treaty in order to accommodate Denmark, "with the distinct intimation that, in the opinion of the President [and in] the judgment of the country ... the treaty expired by limitation on the 14th of April, but that the Executive would take no steps until the 14th of June."[221] Congressional consideration of the Sound dues matter came to a halt after the treaty expired.

When a House bill to finance the $10 million Gadsden purchase was debated in June 1854, legislators broadened discussion of their author-

---

*In 1829, the Supreme Court held that since the Constitution declares a treaty to be the law of the land, it is regarded as equivalent to an act of the legislature. *Foster v. Neilson*, 27 U.S. (2 Peters) 254, 314 (1829), cited in 25 *Congressional Globe* 600.

†Senator William Seward (R. N.Y.) denied, however, that the term "Government of the United States" as used in the treaty with Denmark could have such a special meaning. The president, being simply the executive arm, under principles of republican government, could act for the nation only by authority of his whole legislature. *Id.* 601–02.

**The Sumner resolution called upon the Committee on Foreign Relations to consider appropriate legislation legally to accomplish the abrogation by taking into account "the function of the House of Representatives in the abrogation of all existing laws." *Id.* 528, 607.

Missouri Senator Thomas Hart Benton declared that Congress's power to make war was a "form without substance," and that instead the President's power "to make a quarrel with any nation" constituted the war power of the United States. (*See* p. 139.) (L.C.)

ity to request information regarding the treaty of purchase[222] into an analysis of the power of the House in treatymaking, similar to the 1796 debate over Jay's treaty.* Some House members felt that the House had no right to have "anything to do with documents shaping the background of this treaty,"[223] but others desired to know why there was need for more territory[224] and insisted the House had the right to call for "the papers in the case."[225] Thomas Hart Benton vigorously denied that the House was required to support treaties negotiated by the Senate and executive.† He cited the acquisition of Louisiana, the Floridas, and California** as three parallel instances in which Congress gave its free assent upon "full consideration of the negotiation and treaty."[226] Any other construction yielded the traditional power of the purse. On the other hand, Benton seemed ruefully disposed to admit that whatever power Congress might have seemed to possess over warmaking had become essentially nonexistent, if, in fact, it had ever existed at all:

> The war power—the power to make war—is, as a grant to Congress, a mere illusion—a form without substance. To be sure, Congress is called upon to issue the declaration, as it is now called upon to pass this bill; but the real power of making the war resides elsewhere—resides in the Executive Government alone—which, in its power to conduct our foreign relations, has power to make a quarrel with any nation that it pleases; and when the quarrel is got up, our people will fight. This is what I was accustomed to hear aged men say when I first came to the public councils; and my own observations since I have been in them have confirmed their opinion. I consider the war power now as being substantially in the hands of the President, and that it depends upon him to make war, or not, when he pleases.[227]

No congressman's argument responded directly to Benton's sagacious observation that an important ingredient of the war power resided in the executive branch, which possessed in its foreign relations outreach

---

*Sofaer, *Origins* 85–93. Permission to introduce the information request was defeated. 23 *Congressional Globe* 541–42.

†Neither Benton nor Thomas Bayly (S.R.D. Va.) felt that the 1796 argument for House support of treaties promulgated during discussion of the Jay treaty had any validity in the current debate. But Bayly still held a limited view of the scope of the House's discretion, which he said should be exercised only if a treaty "palpably" subverted the best interests of the people, in which case Congress had the duty to withhold the appropriation. 23 *Congressional Globe Appendix* 1042, 1043. He found no such subversion in the Gadsden purchase, however, and expressed the desire to vote for it.

**A fourth, the treaty for the incorporation of Texas, was rejected by the Senate, and annexation legislatively accomplished by joint resolution. But Indian treaties for the extinction of land titles, Benton indicated, were *preceded* by appropriations authorizing them and were further confirmation of the principle that prevailed in the acquisitions of Louisiana, Florida, and California. *Id.* 1033.

the true power to make a quarrel. The appropriation for the Gadsden purchase passed as expected, 103 to 62, on 28 June 1854.[228]

Executive Response

The executive vigorously curtailed virtually every congressional initiative undertaken during this period. In only one significant instance, in which the presidentially appointed Mexican Boundary Commission altered a portion of the boundary agreed upon in the Treaty of Guadalupe Hidalgo, did Congress refuse to accept the executive's surrender of nearly thirty miles of land acquired by treaty even though the treaty delineation was in error and the presidential commission was technically correct.*

Zachary Taylor terminated diplomatic relations with Austria, while Franklin Pierce successfully concluded a reciprocity treaty with Canada that quieted the fisheries dispute without any congressional pressure to take warlike acts or interference in the complex tariff provisions Congress might normally have felt were its prerogative. Pierce also parried a House threat to withhold an appropriation to purchase territory and a Senate resolve to question his unilateral issue of notice to terminate the Danish Sound Dues Treaty. Fillmore's public opposition to Cuban annexation was succeeded by Pierce's more warlike posture; yet in neither administration did the congressional adherents of Cuban acquisition consummate a program that was opposed to the executive position. In no case did Congress's desire to spell out treaty terms supersede executive initiative to deal with either Indians or foreign nations. Congress did not prevail on Fillmore to go to war over the failure of the Mexican right-of-way westward. In the majority of foreign policy questions, therefore, the executive retained control. One

---

*Texas senator Thomas Rusk sought to prevent Congress from sanctioning a boundary not provided for in the 1848 treaty. 21 *Congressional Globe* 1404–05. Rusk informed his colleagues that J.B. Bartlett, the chief Mexican boundary commissioner, had performed an actual survey of the boundary, in contrast to the map attached to the treaty known as the Disturnell map, which had been compiled without investigation of the territory. Bartlett recommended that the initial point of the boundary be established thirty miles north of the description given in Disturnell's map. *Id.* 1405. The practical effect of Bartlett's action would have been formal U.S. agreement to surrender to Mexico up to thirty miles of territory without Congress's concurrence. Regardless of his correctness, some senators construed Bartlett's act as derogation of the Senate's prerogative to consent to treaties. *Id.* 1628. After consideration of a Department of the Interior report of the incident, the Senate Foreign Relations Committee resolved that no power or authority had been given to the boundary commissioners to disregard the treaty and to establish a parallel "determined by astronomical observations." *Id.* 2271. Congress finally agreed not to use an $80,000 appropriation for running the boundary unless the southern boundary of New Mexico was established no farther north of the town of Paso "than the same is laid down in Disturnell's map" attached to the treaty. *Id.* 2407.

interesting example of presidential retention of authority to negotiate occurred when a group of private investors approached Pierce to join with them and the British government in subsidizing the Atlantic cable. The submarine cable was an invention whose potential of instantaneous communication had significant bearing on the war powers of the president. Senator William H. Seward introduced a bill granting the secretary of state discretion to contract for a cable between Newfoundland and Ireland "on such terms and conditions as shall seem to the President just and reasonable."[229] When Seward was asked to explain what the U.S. position would be if war erupted between the United States and Britain, since both telegraph terminals were in British dominions,* Seward clarified why he considered the cable bill a "war" issue. The endeavor to accomplish speedier diplomatic exchange was in itself an implementation of foreign policy, although, indeed, war was possible— ". . . whenever such a connection as this shall be made, we diminish the chances of war."

The Seward bill, unamended, passed the Senate on 22 January 1857,[230] and after brief House consideration, passed 101 to 82.[231] Congress thus attempted to curtail, but the president preserved a significant initiative to control an important modern tool of diplomacy: the power of immediate communication.

THE CONTROL OF MILITARY AFFAIRS

Polk, Taylor, Fillmore, and Pierce dealt with an increasingly severe problem: the political and diplomatic control of the southern hemisphere in light of the impulse of U.S. citizens to own and occupy western land. Every significant military imbroglio during each of these administrations tested the earlier policy of nonintervention in Latin America that James Monroe had announced in 1823 but by 1845 included the rich temptation of easy western conquest to both Europe and the United States. Spain was weak, as was her offspring Mexico. The Caribbean jewel of Cuba, rich concessions for western communication arteries and land for development of an entirely new civilization, heightened many countries' appetite for conquest.

The Mexican War (1846–48) was the first substantial conflict with a foreign power that the United States had experienced since the War of

---

*The terminals were to be located in Ireland and Newfoundland because it was not geographically practicable otherwise, and at that moment it was even undetermined whether wire would "carry the [electric] fluid with sufficient strength to communicate" across those 1,700 miles. 26 *Congressional Globe* 395. The cable laid in 1857 malfunctioned, and subsequent cable laid in 1858 had but a brief success. The Atlantic cable became practical only after the Civil War.

1812. It involved the use of both volunteer armies and militia organizations as supplements to the regular army, partly because of fear of presidential recess appointments to increase patronage and augment the commander-in-chief's authority over too many troops. Yet after a mighty struggle, the executive finally controlled the extent and type of force at its disposal, even as Congress attempted to shape the size of the army and navy. Despite its talk of the injustice of the Mexican War, Congress was actually much less willing to abridge the established military might of the United States than it had been in the War of 1812.[232]

There were fewer inquiries regarding military affairs than for information regarding foreign relations and for infrequent replies regarding ongoing military operations.[233] Congress authorized almost no military operations before they were actually begun. The deployment of troops to the Rio Grande, John C. Fremont's operations in California, the dispatch of federal troops in response to a threat by Texas state militia to take over New Mexico, the freeing of Hungarian refugee Martin Koszta, and U.S. bombardment of Greytown, Nicaragua, all occurred as a result of executive policy and in response to direct orders from the chief executive. Congress, as it had done before in time of crisis, chose to place the implementation of military policy in executive hands.

All four presidents recognized that there existed limits upon their authority to wage or cause war and did not merely give lip service to their constitutional obligations. Polk's positioning of troops along the Texas border in 1845 was arguably a lawful defensive act, since Texas was a legitimate object of U.S. concern once it accepted the terms of the joint resolution of annexation. Polk made it clear to Texas authorities that he expected Texan troops to augment the 3,000 federal troops he had stationed along the Texas border in May 1845 in case of a Mexican invasion.[234] Commentators have not ceased to assert that Polk was looking for a pretext to order Taylor to the Del Norte. Yet there is evidence of protracted efforts to initiate negotiations. Polk had instructed Secretary of State Buchanan to order John Slidell, if rebuffed in Mexico, to try to be received again and then, if still refused, to remain in Mexico to observe and even to attempt to contact a successor government should one be created.[235] Thus, even though Polk undertook a substantive military buildup on land and sea, he at least expressed a clear desire to exhaust possibilities for negotiation before he authorized military activity. Precedent for Polk's military readiness can be found in President Madison's message to Congress of December 1810, in which Madison explained that he had unilaterally ordered military takeover in West Florida because the subversion of Spanish authority in West Florida exposed the United States to "ulterior events which might essentially affect the rights and welfare of the Union."[236] There was severe divergence in the Polk Cabinet over the issue of declaring war: both Polk and Secretary of State Buchanan felt that the imminent danger of aggression gave the president the leverage to seek a declaration of war, while Navy Secretary Bancroft looked for a hostile act[237] as evidence of the need. Hostilities then occurred before Polk deliberated and requested Congress* to declare war.

The importance and constant use of individual officers and agents in the field, as was the case in prior administrations, cannot be overemphasized. Executive instructions gave latitude and inspired initiative and were tolerated and understood by legislators as being often necessarily imprecise or appearing to vacillate. For example, there was certainly no question that the executive wanted John C. Fremont to succeed in implementing the "Polk Doctrine"—specifically, that California was not to fall into the hands of a foreign power.[238] Congress reviewed the fact that Fremont, though uninstructed to do so, arguably fomented an act of war in California prior to the outbreak of the Mexican War by raising a U.S. flag over Mexican territory. Although this point has remained controversial, legislators' affirmation of his activities once he arrived in California after the Mexican War had been declared constituted retroactive approval of military action taken by an officer of the U.S. Army without prior express executive authorization. During these years, therefore, the executive arm of the U.S. government never relinquished control of military affairs, even though its prerogatives and methods were often questioned.

The Mexican War, 1846–1848

The Authority to Involve the Nation in War   Study of the orders given General Taylor, the course of the Slidell mission, decisions made in Cabinet conferences, and relevant private correspondences reveal that President Polk's view of his authority to order troops into disputed territory was far from absolute. His concepts were strongly influenced by contemporary judgments of what constituted the president's constitutional prerogative to act in the national interest.

Polk maintained until his death that the Mexican War was the result of years of aggravated and unredressed wrongs by Mexico against the

---

*During the earliest period of the war, President Polk informally shared with Congress his plan for a campaign against the Northern Provinces. Senator Thomas Hart Benton approved it. 1 Polk, *Diary* 404. (Quaife ed.) On 15 May, he conferred with members of Congress to indicate how many volunteers would be requisitioned from each state. *Id.* 401. All during the conduct of the war, Polk consulted at length with his Cabinet about policy objectives as well as strategy (*e.g.*, whether to take Vera Cruz and Tampico, as well as whether General Taylor should hold and fortify positions as he advanced). *Id.* 198.

United States. The U.S. entry into war was officially in response to a Mexican army attack upon General Zachary Taylor's forces on the banks of the Rio Grande in 1846. But the seeds of conflict had been sown years earlier with the advent of Mexican independence from Spain and the seizure and spoliation of U.S. citizens' property.

President Polk ordered the armed protection of Texas by dispatching U.S. army and naval forces* immediately upon the Texas Republic's acceptance of the terms of President John Tyler's overtures for state-hood.† These overtures Polk reiterated six days after he became president:

> The moment the terms of annexation offered by the United States were accepted by Texas, the latter became so far a part of our country as to make it our duty to afford such protection and defense.[239]

Polk, however, followed this description of the deployment of forces with a statement that he lacked congressional authority to deal with a host of abuses and hostile acts, other than to be prepared to defend against Mexican oppression. He did not request such authority in December because he had taken steps in September 1845 to find out whether Mexico planned to invade Texas, declare war, or undertake the settlement of differences; and in November, after careful discussion with his Cabinet and members of Congress, he sent John Slidell to Mexico as envoy extraordinary and minister plenipotentiary to adjust and to settle all pending differences.[240]

On 11 May 1846, Polk announced that the defensive posture he had taken to avoid invasion of Texas by Mexican armies had been breached by Mexican hostilities on 24 April. The president then asked Congress for a declaration that would recognize the existence of war and called for authority to raise "a large body of volunteers to serve for not less than six or twelve months...."[241] Congress plunged into a brief but intense debate on the issue of whether war legally exists before Congress makes a formal declaration and on the meaning to both president and Congress of either legal situation.

John C. Calhoun distinguished between "hostilities" (or invasion that may be repelled by the president without Congress) and "war" (which

---

*Polk, in his own records, ordered a strong squadron to the coasts of Mexico. He concentrated a military force on the western frontier of Texas and instructed the army to take a position between the Nueces and Del Norte and to repel any invasion of Texan territory attempted by Mexican forces. 15 *Congressional Globe* 4, 5.

†The congressional joint resolution endorsing statehood for Texas had been passed at the close of Tyler's administration and dispatched by him to Texas for consent by the Texan Congress and adoption of a constitution. Reeves, *American Diplomacy under Tyler and Polk* 184–85.

requires a solemn declaration). Congress must not respond precipitately to a momentous act. Many Senate colleagues agreed that their lack of more exact information could involve the country in war merely at the pleasure of "the officers and men on the Rio Grande."[242] Others wanted to put the matter before the Senate Foreign Relations Committee since it concerned U.S. diplomacy.[243] Senator James Morehead declared that legislative measures short of a declaration of war had effectively repelled aggression in the quasi-war with France in 1798,[244] while Delaware's John Clayton claimed that war existed but that Polk had acted unconstitutionally when he ordered the army into the position it occupied just before the outbreak of hostilities.[245] Both Clayton and Kentucky's John Crittenden agreed, however, that "there was but one course to pursue" after hostilities had begun.[246]

In the House, Ohio Representative Jacob Brinkerhoff introduced a resolution claiming that Mexico began a "state of war" with the United States, which the president was authorized to prosecute "to a successful termination. . . ."[247] Florida's William Brockenbrough agreed that the Congress of the United States should provide the president with means to conduct an offensive action "if we mean to avoid what the Duke of Wellington had called the greatest of evils—a small war by a great country."[248]

Some congressmen, however, were reluctant to bring on bloodshed. Isaac Holmes (D. S.C.) denied that the collision of forces automatically created war, any more than it was produced by the British capture of the U.S. frigate *Chesapeake* in 1807. He urged Congress to refrain from declaring war. Garrett Davis (Wh. Ky.) denominated the bill's preamble a "falsehood" for stating that Mexico started the conflict, because it was under Polk's orders that General Taylor not only moved into the west bank of the Nueces but also blockaded the port of Matamoros, ordered off English and U.S. vessels, directed capture of a Spanish schooner, and trained a battery of cannon within 300 yards of the Matamoros public square.[249]

The bill that passed 11 May by the overwhelming vote of 174 to 14 affirmed that a state of war existed by act of Mexico, called for speedy prosecution of the war, and authorized funds and forces to that end.[250] Perhaps the sense of congressmen who had spoken out strongly in disfavor accorded with Thomas Bayly (S.R.D. Va.) who finally voted for passage:

I am unwilling . . . under the circumstances, to vote for a declaration of war. I do not think such a declaration necessary to meet the emergency. On the other hand, I am anxious to vote such supplies of men and money as will afford succor to our army, and repel the invasion.[251]

Senators Calhoun and Clayton agreed that the title and preamble of the House bill calling for prosecution of an "existing war" caused "by the act of the Republic of Mexico" conferred unbridled discretion on the executive.[252] Clayton was astounded that the House should decide a policy of war or peace before the Senate had seen in print a single one of the "mass" of documents that the president had sent over. The House version authorized $10 million for prosecution of the war, which Clayton held was an action "not . . . in conformity with the Constitution" in that it stated no specific amounts to be used for the army, navy, or provisions.[253] To Clayton's knowledge, no treatise on the law of nations stated that purely defensive measures constituted war;* and Calhoun asked his colleagues to think what would happen if the Senate declared war while the Mexican government disavowed that war existed.[254]

Virginia senator Isaac Pennybacker, however, argued that the overriding reason for a declaration of war was for the sake of predictability:

> that the people might all know their position; that neutral nations might conduct themselves suitably; and that there might be an open and palpable occasion shown for the voting of the supplies necessary to its energetic prosecution.[255]

He was supported by James Westcott (D. Fla.), who believed that events would be better served if Congress made an unequivocal, independent, and affirmative declaration of war that would assist the executive in prosecuting the necessary hostilities efficiently and successfully. A declaration would strengthen the executive's hand in the United States, abroad in Mexico, and in Congress. Without the express authority of Congress, he could not commission privateers, issue letters of marque and reprisal,† blockade Mexican ports, or authorize capture of Mexican

---

*Lewis Cass (D. Mich.) defined war as "a fact created by an effort made by one nation to injure another" and remarked, "One party may make a war, though it requires two parties to make a peace." Cass said that the War of 1812, for example, was declared on 18 June, but the manifesto of the Prince Regent declaring war against the United States was not issued until 10 January 1813. In the meantime, U.S. borders "had been penetrated in many directions, an army had been subdued and captured, and the whole territory of Michigan had been overrun and seized." 15 *Congressional Globe* 800. Senator John Berrien (Wh. Ga.) concurred that a formal declaration was unrequired on the ground that recognition of a state of war would end treaties and "the accumulated claims of our citizens would be obliterated." *Id.* 801.

†On 7 August 1846, the Senate passed a bill authorizing Polk to issue letters of marque and reprisal against Mexico in light of executive information concerning a similar measure before the Mexican Congress proposing that it publish letters of marque and reprisal against the United States. *Id.* 1206. There was no House passage because on 8 August a bill passed that provided funds requested by the president to settle difficulties with Mexico, signaling to many members that peace was imminent. *Id.* 1211, 1213–18 *passim.*

vessels on the high seas as prizes of war.* Shipments of armaments might be sent to Mexico by foreign nations and, if captured, be unable to be forfeited as "contraband of war." Mexican soldiers could not be held by executive authority as prisoners of war. Treason in aiding Mexican troops might even go unpunished. Above all, the duty of neutrality, the principal obligation of other countries toward the United States, could not be properly enforced.[256]

Although the bill's form was challenged by several amendments and a motion to strike the preamble, it was impossible to halt the groundswell of opinion that had overtaken Congress in favor of giving some evidence of recognition that a war existed, in however imprecise language that war resolution might be framed.† Despite sporadic protests concerning the preamble, the House bill passed the Senate on 12 May, 40 to 2,[257] and the House concurred in minor Senate amendments on the same evening.[258]

Efforts to Declare the War Unconstitutional and to Define Objectives
Congress long deliberated whether its appropriations were to be considered ratification of the war. But to the administration's taunts that if Congress doubted the justice of the war effort it should not finance it, Abraham Lincoln and others replied that approval of needed supplies should never furnish an excuse for the conflict.

On 3 January 1848, Representative John Houston (Wh. Del.) introduced a joint resolution of thanks to Major General Zachary Taylor and the regular army and volunteers under his command for their valor in a major battle that resulted in the surrender of Monterey. Congressman Alexander Evans (Wh. Md.) submitted an amendment that the capitulation of Monterey met with the Congress's entire approbation, which George Ashmun (Wh. Mass.) moved to amend by adding the words, "in a war unnecessarily and unconstitutionally begun by the President of the United States." Ashmun's amendment was thereupon narrowly adopted, 85 to 81.[259] An attempt to expunge it was laid on the table on 14 February by a vote of 105 to 94,[260] but the main resolution of

---

*For another view of the president's right to issue letters of marque and reprisal after congressional authorization, in circumstances not involving declaration of war, *see* Lofgren, "War-Making under the Constitution: The Original Understanding," p. 672.

†A continuing debate on the issue of whether war may exist before formal declaration carried on into the following week during consideration of an army appropriation bill, which passed the House unanimously on 19 May. 15 *Congressional Globe* 839–43. Both the House and the Senate on 16 and 17 June, respectively, passed a Supplemental War Act, reported out by a conference committee, "providing for the prosecution of the war between the United States and the Republic of Mexico." House passage was accomplished, 94 to 54, and the Senate approved, 32 to 19. *Id.* 984, 985.

3 January and the Ashmun amendment did not come up for consideration again.*

Representative Abraham Lincoln (Wh. Ill.), who voted for the Ashmun amendment, had initially believed that he should stay clear of the issue of Polk's causation of the war until hostilities terminated. But the president had tried to convey an impression that Congress's silent approval of supplies was approbation of his conduct both in the commencement and in the prosecution of the war; therefore, Lincoln said, members were compelled to prevent this misrepresentation.[261]

Because the Mexican War seemed to many to be a war of conquest and not one of defense against an aggressor, it was continually denounced. Senator Calhoun wanted to control the conduct of the war by limiting its objectives, but his fellow South Carolinian Robert B. Rhett in the House argued that the executive must have freedom to prosecute the war successfully. There was, however, no final congressional limitation placed upon the president's control of the direction of the war.

The administration's territorial objectives became a source of growing concern in Congress late in 1847. Senator John C. Calhoun (D. S.C.), troubled that there were signs that the war to establish the Texas boundary was becoming a war of conquest,† submitted a series of resolutions declaring that conquest was neither the avowed aim of the war nor in harmony with the U.S. government's "free and popular institutions."[262]

As it became abundantly clear throughout 1847 that the United States was likely to continue to be victorious, other policy resolutions continued to surface in each House.** But Calhoun pressed for consideration of his own first, suggesting that the current "cloudy, drifting" condition of war whose outer limits no one understood could have been avoided by a *declaration* of war as differentiated from the mere *recognition* of it. Until it was clearly stated it was not the intent of the U.S. government to conquer Mexico, there could be no decision upon how

---

*Another vote of thanks to General Taylor, introduced by Representative Alexander Stephens (D. Ga.) passed effortlessly, 181 to 1, on 7 February without amendment (17 *Congressional Globe* 304), and Senate consideration of the Stephens resolutions was virtually unanimously favorable: the vote was 47 to 1. *Id.* 368. The joint resolution of thanks was returned to the House from the Senate on 4 May 1848, with minor verbal amendments, and was concurred in by the House. *Id.* 725.

†The president's declaration that any treaty must include ample indemnity for the expenses of war represented, to many congressmen, a virtual declaration that the goals had come to include dismemberment of Mexico. *Id.* 5.

**As an example, on 15 December 1847, Congressman Isaac Holmes (D. S.C.) attempted to introduce a resolution that the United States "recede" all territory taken from Mexico, conditioned upon free ingress and egress of all U.S. citizens into New Mexico and upper California. *Id.* 38. Congressman Daniel Dickenson (D. N.Y.) submitted several administration-sponsored resolutions on 20 December 1847, proposing free and unhindered addition of such "contiguous territory" as could be "justly obtained" and leaving all domestic policy questions to popularly chosen legislatures. *Id.* 54.

many supplies, men, and money to authorize, or, indeed, whether there should be an end to the war.* But when Calhoun's resolutions finally came before the Senate on 4 January 1848,[263] a motion to lay them on the table was tantamount to extinguishing their further consideration.

At the same time as Calhoun's resolutions in the Senate, the House discussed the authority of Congress to conduct war and presidential authority to initiate hostilities without congressional action. Congressman Robert B. Rhett (D. S.C.), like his fellow South Carolinian Calhoun, argued that there was a critical difference between "declaring" and "making" war, but Rhett came to a much different conclusion from Calhoun: the power to make or conduct war "was an Executive function." He did not contend, however, that Congress lacked significant powers under the Constitution to *control* the course of war by being "omnipotent over supplies" and the funds to obtain them or to prescribe any conditions regarding their use. "The President, I suppose," he continued, "does not exactly realize the Roman's definition of a rich man—one who can support an army." Thus, the cooperation of Congress and the chief executive was indispensable to continuation of any war. Rhett concluded, however, that since the warmaking power was not in Congress, the legislature did not possess the right to prescribe, limit, and determine the objects of a war nor even to receive all information at the president's disposal. Although he stated there was a risk of his being considered a "monarchist," Rhett declared that he was in favor of executive power in government:

> [A]nd, if I was not, I would be in favor of no government at all; for government cannot exist without being operative, and, to be operative, must be enforced by an Executive.[264]

Therefore, Polk could mobilize the army and navy, short of ordering actual hostilities.

Others objected to Rhett's mandate for the president to place the nation "without aid of Congress" in a state of hostilities as distinct from a state of war,[265] thereby enabling the chief executive "insidiously" to adopt a course that would inevitably result in hostilities.[266] Abraham Lincoln had gone even further with a resolution on 22 December 1847, seeking first, to clarify whether the conflict leading to the Mexican War had actually taken place on U.S. soil as Polk had said and, second, whether it had involved U.S. citizens or U.S. soldiers, a critical distinc-

---

*Calhoun preferred Congress's recapture of control over policy-shaping by discussing the whole affairs of the nation on the Senate floor openly rather than being limited to piecemeal presentation from committees. The "good old practice" in the early republic, he said, was to ventilate whole affairs of the nation in the same way that it was done in the British Parliament and the French Chamber of Deputies; but his remarks produced no recorded reaction. *Id.* 55.

tion going to the issue of Polk's credibility.[267] No measures of executive control resulted from these debates, but there was far from unanimity even in the minds of the party in power as to how much authority James K. Polk might use, even as there was little doubt that the reservoir of authority from which he could draw as president was large and not susceptible of easy definition.

The executive often escaped from congressional limitations by creating fiscal deficiencies and then asking for additional money to meet a moral if not legal obligation. Congress was thus placed in an awkward position: failure to appropriate could mean "the credit of the country [would] be dishonored,"[268] while acquiescence might indicate sacrificing a valued prerogative. The dilemma, of course, could be expected to be more pronounced in wartime. Consequently, in the winter of 1848, when Congress addressed the question of a military deficiency, a bill appropriating the requested amount passed in both houses without amendment and virtually without discussion.*

The president did not always receive the funds for which he asked. For example, a requested loan of $18,500,000 prompted additional debate over the extent of the U.S. involvement in the Mexican War. Representative David Fisher (Wh. Oh.) believed that when the executive sought additional funds to prosecute the war, Congress should enlarge its investigation of the nature of commitment to a conflict in which there was

> not the least evidence that Mexico ever struck the first blow, or any blow, until after aggressions had been made by troops of these United States.††[269]

His colleague, George Marsh (Wh. Vt.) also denied that the appropriation of funds constituted automatic ratification of the cause of the war. He concluded that the supply bill of 1846 had been hastily voted in the belief that U.S. forces were in peril** and that the decision to supply funds could be reexamined.††[270]

---

*A bill making a $1 million deficiency appropriation for the year ending 30 June 1848 passed both houses. *Id.* 65, 75.

†Fisher further discussed the objects of the war and the peacemaking process. He denied that Polk had the right to make war to obtain indemnities for spoliations: the proper course would have been to appoint commissioners to deal directly with the Mexican government. Any progress toward peace such as the president claimed, Fisher asserted, should have been communicated to Congress. *Id.* 324.

**The meaning to be given appropriation of funds was the subject of debate during the Vietnam War. Recognition that Congress cannot abandon U.S. troops abroad nor merely supply funds enough for withdrawal in the middle of a campaign resulted in the insertion of a clause in the 1973 War Powers Resolution providing that appropriations shall not be deemed ratification. War Powers Resolution §8(a)(1), 87 Stat. 555 (1973).

††Marsh stated that he did not believe Polk had "wantonly" sought the conflict. But he felt there was strong justification for the belief that the president had goaded Mexico into hostile acts from which it was an easy step for him to request funds for a larger military

Representative Alexander Sims (D. S.C.) responded for the administration by asking why the Twenty-ninth Congress continued to vote funds to carry on the war. If the war was unjust and unnecessary "... it became gentlemen who entertained that view to refuse all future supplies. ..."[271] Congressman John Hale (N.H.) then attempted to prohibit use of monies authorized under this act for war expenses, but his amendment lost by an overwhelming margin, 23 to 118.[272] The bill finally was successfully amended to authorize a loan not to exceed $16 million[273] and passed 192 to 14.[274] In the Senate, the House loan bill was passed, 34 to 2, on 28 March without debate.[275]

Initiatives to End the War   President Polk asked Congress* for $2 million for negotiation and settlement of outstanding boundary disputes between Mexico and the United States. Polk needed the money because on 27 July 1846 he had already secretly authorized Commodore David Conner to tender a peace overture to the Mexicans.[276] The $2 million was to be applied to the total of any sum actually appropriated to settle outstanding problems and was intended as an inducement to be paid after a treaty had been signed and ratifications exchanged.[277] James McKay (D. N.C.) sponsored a bill calling for the president to receive the funds "for ... defraying any extraordinary expenses which may be incurred in the intercourse between the United States and foreign nations" and to account for them later.

Many congressmen thought that the fund was intended as a bribe to induce Mexican authorities to sue for peace and thus covertly to pressure them into ceding California.[278] Garrett Davis (Wh. Ky.) frankly wanted to see the United States get California by "honest, old fashioned" purchase rather than some kind of subterfuge[279] and felt that the president might use the appropriation as an authorization to continue the war "until Mexico is whipped into its cession."[280]

Others, though they had opposed either Texas annexation or the war itself, were nevertheless prepared to support the new appropriation. Alexander Sims (D. S.C.) did not find the objectives of the fund mysterious but claimed that Polk's opponents would never agree with his approach, whether he wanted either war or peace. Robert Owen (D. Ind.) emphasized that the House was constitutionally not privy to the treaty-making process,†[281] while John Quincy Adams favored a somewhat

---

force, "and a proportionate augmentation of Executive patronage." 17 *Congressional Globe* 331.

*The request was made 8 August 1846 and was debated the same day in the House. 15 *Congressional Globe* 1211.

†In all probability, certain House members did know the reason for the appropriation. Polk sent a confidential message to the Senate on 28 July 1846, explaining his plan to meet with Mexico and advance money to induce the agreement. The Senate approved the president's plan on 8 August. Senators expected a similar confidential message would go

middle ground: passage of the McKay bill with an amendment clearly specifying that the $2 million was to be used for negotiating a peace with Mexico.*

Intense pressure forced McKay to submit a substitute bill incorporating the specific purpose for the requested funds. The new bill announced that executive assurances had been given to the Mexican government that all questions between the United States and the Republic of Mexico would be settled "on the most liberal and satisfactory terms." It requested an appropriation of $30,000 for entry upon negotiations and $2 million to enable the president to conclude a treaty of peace. By indicating that presidential overtures toward settlement were underway, McKay's revised bill intimated facts that had not previously been brought to Congress's attention. Although it finally passed in the House on 8 August by a vote of 87 to 64,[282] it was defeated in the Senate on 10 August by a filibuster—a loss keenly disappointing to Polk, who had believed Senate victory was assured owing to the favorable resolution passed in executive session.[283]

The president decided, however, to try the same maneuver again. On 18 January 1847, he secretly renewed his offer to Mexican authorities, who demanded that U.S. armed forces withdraw as a precondition to negotiation. Polk refused but informed Mexican foreign minister Monasterio that Nicholas Trist had been sent to U.S. Army headquarters and was merely awaiting the opportunity to deal whenever Mexico dropped this precondition.[284] The president, however, then saw fit to insert his own qualifications, such as delineation of the western boundary of Texas as the east bank of Del Norte and the openness of Mexico to U.S. acquisition of California and New Mexico.[285] This time the president was ultimately successful in raising the funds he desired in order to press the initiative already in progress.

In early February 1847, Senator Ambrose Sevier (D. Ark.) introduced an administration bill requesting a $3 million appropriation to defray "any extraordinary expenses" undertaken to end the war.†[286] The "Three Million bill" was vociferously attacked as a possible grant of too much discretionary authority to the President.**

---

to the House, but Polk, fearing secrecy would not be maintained, said he would explain the reason for the appropriation to a "few leading members of the House." Polk, *Diary* (Nevins ed.) 135–36.

*The form of the McKay bill stated only that the funds were to be used for negotiation with foreign powers, while the president's message had requested it for the purpose of making peace with Mexico. 15 *Congressional Globe* 1215, 1216.

†In his state of the union message of 8 December 1846, the president had alluded to the two occasions when the same amount was granted President Jefferson for costs of territorial acquisitions (Louisiana and West Florida). *Id.* 9.

**The discretionary language read:

Be it enacted, &c., That a sum of money not exceeding three millions of dollars, be, and the same is hereby, appropriated, for the purpose of defraying any extraordinary

Senator John Berrien (Wh. Ga.), on 5 February, proposed amending the bill to state that it was not Congress's intent in making a $3 million appropriation to prosecute the war in order to acquire Mexican territory. Lewis Cass (D. Mich.) argued, however, that Congress's intent in making the appropriation* was to obtain a reasonable indemnity from Mexico, the nature and extent of which were "proper subjects" for "executive consideration, when negotiations for peace may be opened. . . ."[287]

Berrien replied that he wanted the Senate actively to superintend the prosecution of war. The president merely carried into execution the act declaring war—the public will as declared by Congress and not his own. In this light, Congress had both the right and the duty from time to time to specify "the objects, the motives, the principles, on which it is to be conducted. . . ."†[288] Maryland's Reverdy Johnson speculated upon the dangerous course of events that could occur if a war had to continue until a president sent the Senate a treaty for ratification.[289] Did Congress possess no control over an unreasonable president who refused to listen to compromise or reason "until he gets tired with his triumphs or his defeats"?

Cass defended Polk's efforts to negotiate a treaty with adequate funds at his disposal as just and in strict accordance with the usage of nations. President Polk's object was clear:

> It is to have the money ready, and if a satisfactory treaty is signed and ratified, then to make a payment into the treasury of Mexico, which will be disposed of by the Government of that country, agreeably as to its own laws.[290]

---

expenses which may be incurred in order to bring the existing war with Mexico to a speedy and honorable conclusion, to be paid out of any money in the treasury not otherwise appropriated, and to be applied under the direction of the President of the United States, who shall cause an account of the expenditure thereof to be laid before Congress. . . .

Id. 305.

*Senator Jacob Miller (Wh. N.J.) complained that while the object of the bill was to make peace, it should have been a resolution advising the president to settle differences by adjustment of the original causes of the war. *Id.* 308. Although Miller acknowledged that conduct of the war and peacemaking were matters within executive control, it appeared proper for the Senate to "interfere" when the president had assumed the responsibility for making war without the knowledge or consent of Congress. Even if the executive did *not* seek advice, Miller believed that it was the Senate's duty to define the objects of further prosecution of the war and advise as to the manner of bringing it to "speedy termination." Precedent for such consultation between the executive and legislature was an executive conference with the Senate concerning the "terms and conditions" for settling the Oregon boundary dispute at a time when there was danger of war with Great Britain. 16 *Congressional Globe Appendix* 277.

†As evidence of Congress's participation in war making, Berrien relied on the fact that during the War of 1812, a war of about two and one-half years' duration, Congress was in session nearly two years of that time, by its own provision. 16 *Congressional Globe* 327.

Berrien's amendment was eventually rejected.[291] On 1 March 1847, after debate lasting nearly one month, the Senate passed the $3 million bill by a vote of 29 to 24,[292] and in the House the bill was pushed through on the last day of the session and passed without amendment, 115 to 81.[293]

Executive Creation of Civil Government in Mexico   President Polk exercised temporary civil authority in Mexico prior to receiving legislative authorization. He reported creation of civilian governments in his state of the union message of 8 December 1846 and asked Congress for appropriations to erect fortifications and defray the expenses of maintaining authority in the area.* Dissension erupted in the Senate regarding continuation of this authority. Senator James Westcott opposed the president's continued exercise of power in the territories, which was implemented by army and navy commanders under his instructions, and proposed to substitute congressional control.[294]

In their stricter construction of executive power, many House Whigs denounced Polk's "usurpation" of power from the outset of the war and distinguished the commander-in-chief of a wartime army from a president who approved or vetoed bills, received ambassadors, or nominated judges—mingling of the two roles was unconstitutional. A victorious nation's sovereignty over conquered territory should be exercised by the legislature,[295] not by its "indefinite extension of power to the President." Ohio's Joseph Root gleefully satirized those worthy gentlemen who knew presidential power just had to be "somewhere" in the Constitution:

> The learned gentlemen's search for Executive power to set up civil governments reminded [Root] of a sort of game he had once seen played with thimbles and balls—he forgot now how it was played exactly or what it was called. [A voice: 'Thimblerig.' A laugh.] Yes; it was likely that was it. It was played with three thimbles and a ball, and the ball was sometimes found under one, and sometimes under another—but it was there somewhere. The thing was, to tell under which thimble. [Much laughter.] Nothing but the governing habit of the abstractionist school could have produced such a reading of the Constitution.[296]

---

*One possible source of the funds, somewhat ironic in view of the similar tax that had been imposed by England in 1773 against British subjects in America, was Polk's proposal on 13 February 1847 to place a special revenue duty on tea and coffee for the duration of the war with Mexico. *Id.* 417. Congress, however, did not give Polk this authority. Initially, the president had proposed this revenue measure in his annual message of 8 December 1846, as part of a package to defray the various costs of conducting the war, including establishment of military government in Mexico (*see supra* p. 152 n.) and the $2 million to secure peace with Mexico. *Id.* 9.

Democratic supporters held that the president, under his power as commander-in-chief, could prescribe legal regulations for conquered provinces. For example, Representative Thomas Bayly (S.R.D. Fla.) carefully reasoned that the president had both the right and duty to establish a "quasi"-civil government in a conquered nation, civil in form and proceeding but military in origin:

> [I]f [Congress] declare war or recognize its existence without any such legislation, I . . . inquire whether they do not thereby require the Commander-in-Chief to follow and obey the usages of civilized nations. By the very act of providing for carrying on the war you impliedly require this of him. . . . The President is sworn to execute the laws of nations. . . . *[297]

In 1848, senators debated increasing the army†[298] in light of the fact that Polk had unilaterally imposed excise taxes and imposts on Mexico and anticipated the need of troops to collect them. Senator Calhoun found no authority for the provision of troops to collect duties and imposts.** Powers related to the commander-in-chief power arose from exigencies immediately connected with the army or its safety but did not include exercising power over conquered territory[299] or increasing the president's own authority to secure funds that could enable him to make war on neighboring countries.[300] Polk's chief opponent in the House was Virginia's Congressman John Botts, who challenged Polk's claim that as president he possessed authority to assess a tariff in conquered territory on the theory that international law gave all nations such power.[301] Polk responded that his authority as commander-in-

---

*Bayly's remarks of 23 December echoed the president's response of the previous day to an information request by the House on 15 December for orders or instructions to officers of the government relating to establishment of civil government in any portion of Mexico taken possession of by the army or navy of the United States. The president noted that the orders and instructions were given to regulate the exercise of the rights of belligerents over conquered territory, as recognized by the laws of nations. *Id.* 67–68.

†In January 1848, Lewis Cass introduced a second "Ten Regiments" bill (*supra* p. 89 n.), which prompted sharp debate over presidential conduct of the war and three possible contingency plans for future prosecution of the war as submitted by the secretary of war before "the constitutional depository of the war-making power" proceeded to increase the army. 17 *Congressional Globe* 79.

**Other congressmen were of the same opinion. Motions for information were submitted in both houses in early 1848 (January 31, House; February 1, Senate). Only the Senate's unqualified request passed, asking that the president inform the Senate whether he had laid duties and by what authority such levy had been made. *Id.* 269, 284. The president responded on 11 February 1848. *Id.* 339–40. He stated that he had already informed Congress in his annual message (7 December 1847) that orders had been given to military and naval commanders to levy contributions upon the enemy to support the army. Such a policy, averred Polk, stemmed from the right of conquest: "The right to levy these contributions is essential to the successful prosecution of war in an enemy's country and the practice of nations has been in accordance with this principle."

chief and his power to see that laws be "faithfully executed" were the bases of his actions. Moreover, since the Constitution prescribed no methods for carrying on a war, the president was free to use modes employed by other nations, which included levying contributions from the enemy.[302]

Congressman Samuel Vinton (Wh. Oh.) hotly disputed Polk's interpretation and supported Robert Toombs (S.R.D. Ga.), who moved that Polk's message be referred to a select committee because it involved "assumptions ... dangerous to this form of government."[303] Vinton pointed out that even conceding Polk's authority to order the military to plunder the enemy, he had levied the tariff on U.S. and neutral commerce. Of what avail would be the two-year Constitutional limitation upon Congress's power to grant supplies, "evidently intended as a restriction upon the Executive," if a president possessed the unilaterally derived means to conduct a war despite the will of Congress or the people?[304]

Executive Response

Polk had sought advice concerning his authority to levy the tariff and thus extend the civil authority of the executive into Mexico. Thomas Hart Benton informed the president that he had the power to establish such regulations under the laws of war as part of international law defining the rights of a conqueror.[305] Attorney General Nathan Clifford concurred, as did Secretary of State James Buchanan;[306] and Treasury Secretary Robert Walker was instructed to issue the orders in accordance with the Mexican tariff system.

Both Lewis Cass and Jefferson Davis believed that the president as commander-in-chief could impose duties as powers necessarily pertaining to a state of war. Legislative rights would follow when Congress took possession of the conquered territory, but "[u]p to that point nothing but the power of the Executive department flows in."*[307] Congress found no persuasive argument that would deny to the president the authority to govern and administer conquered properties, nor did the president in the least appear unwilling to relinquish control over them once peace was assured and a duly constituted representative government chosen.

---

*Davis also challenged Calhoun's argument that the president had no right, on his own initiative, to order troops into disputed territory. He argued it could not be expected that the executive should stand by powerless while a foreign power seized disputed territory, thus gaining command over determination of that dispute. Further, such a limitation on the executive's authority to respond would invite boundary disputes; every nation that was physically adjacent to the United States could with impunity trifle with national borders. *Id.* 498.

John C. Fremont's Initiatives in California

Major John Charles Fremont was originally sent to California as an explorer but arguably committed a warlike act by raising the U.S. flag over Mexican territory before the outbreak of the Mexican War. The Senate reviewed Fremont's 1845–46 activities in March 1848, during its consideration of the claims arising out of the capture and military occupation of California, and according to Senator Thomas Hart Benton, it was unanimous in recommending their payment, since the United States had reaped the benefits of the "revolutionary movement" that brought about acquisition of an enormous territory. The committee also ventured an opinion that the action of conquest was taken without either government sanction or knowledge by the participants that Mexico and the United States were at war. By its retrospective approval of these claims, the Senate sanctioned aggressive military action taken by an officer of the U.S. Army without prior express executive authorization.

Benton, who was Fremont's father-in-law and ardent supporter, gave Congress a useful factual account of Fremont's involvement despite an understandably favorable bias. In May 1845, on Fremont's third scientific exploration to the far West, he had to pass through Mexican territory to reach the Pacific Ocean. Cognizant of outstanding political and diplomatic differences between the United States and Mexico, Fremont traveled alone to Monterey to make it clear to Mexican authorities that he came to California solely as an explorer. His request to spend the winter of 1845–46 was at first granted but subsequently revoked on the pretext that his mission was not scientific but political. Mexican troops were raised and marched to attack him. Their lives endangered, Fremont and sixty supporters erected a log fort and raised the U.S. flag at Hawk's Peak, California, determined to defend themselves;* but after no attack came, they withdrew and set out for Oregon to give no further cause for complaint by staying in California.

While in Oregon in May 1846, he was informed by an advance guard that dispatches from Washington were underway. Fremont then rode

*The fact that Fremont acted defensively has been cited by commentators as proof that it is unlikely that he had received instructions from the administration, prior to setting forth on this expedition, to foment revolution in California. Local American settlers offered assistance to Fremont if he were attacked, but Fremont refused their assistance, even though, together with Fremont's men, they would have comprised an effective fighting force. It can be reasoned, therefore, that if Fremont had been under secret orders, American offers of aid would have been used as an opportunity to commence their execution. Letter from Fremont to James Clyman, 19 December 1845, J. Fremont, *Papers* ("Notebook of Journey to Oregon 1844–46," narrated by J. Clyman to Ivan Petroff, 1878). If genuine, this letter must have been written in March 1846 when the Hawk's Peak incident took place.

sixty miles to meet Marine Lieutenant Archibald H. Gillespie, who possessed communications from the Department of State. Gillespie's verbal instructions, said to have been memorized to prevent their being discovered by Mexican authorities, have been the subject of much controversy;* but later evidence showed that Fremont had received orders by way of Gillespie to counteract any "foreign schemes" in California and to "conciliate" the good will of the residents of California toward the United States.†[308] His orders arguably permitted Fremont to support and defend American settlers but not to foment war.

Fremont, years later, concluded that his sense of his orders from Gillespie "absolved me from my duty as an explorer," leaving him to his responsibility as an officer of the U.S. Army, "with the further authoritative knowledge" that the U.S. government intended to take California:

> [I]t had been made known to me now on the authority of the Secretary of the Navy, that to obtain possession of California was the chief object of the President.**

Fremont arrived in the Sacramento Valley at a time when war had already broken out with Mexico. The news had not reached California for certain, though Lieutenant Gillespie probably believed that hos-

---

*E.g., 5 H. Bancroft, History of California 25–26 (1884–90). Even this historian, severely critical of Fremont, maintained that there were no secret instructions to foment revolution. "How far he was actually responsible for fomenting that revolt," wrote R. Cleland, "is one of those disputed points upon which there is no possibility of agreement." R. Cleland, History of California: The American Period 200 (1922).

†The Senate later wanted proof that a certain letter of 17 October 1845, from Secretary of State Buchanan to U.S. consul at Monterey Thomas O. Larkin, did not contain the same instructions alleged to have been sent to Fremont through Gillespie to instigate a rebellion in California before the Mexican War began. 17 Congressional Globe 483. Polk stated that publication of the letter would prove the falsehood of the inference (3 Polk, Diary 395 (Quaife ed.)), and he sent it to the Senate in executive session within a week, even though the resolution requesting it was passed in legislative session. Id. 395; 6 Messages and Papers 2428. The letter instructed Larkin to discover and to defeat any foreign government's attempts to seize control in California. Then Buchanan related what has since been called the "Polk Doctrine": that though the United States could take no part in a contest between Mexico and California, it could not "view with indifference" the transfer of California to Great Britain or any other European power. 6 Buchanan, Works 275–76. Polk had reiterated the same "doctrine" in discussion with Benton on 24 October 1845. 1 Polk, Diary, 69–71 (Quaife ed.).

**Quoted in Fremont, Papers (W. Swasey, "Obituary for Fremont" 25 (1891)). This information was sent to Fremont by George Bancroft in a memorandum dated 3 September 1886, which Fremont subsequently paraphrased. Fremont, Papers. William Swasey was consular secretary to Larkin. He claimed that Gillespie's oral instructions for Fremont did order Fremont's return to California to "hold himself in readiness to cooperate in any movement" that would forward the "conquest" of California. Id. (Swasey, "Obituary" 21–22; Swasey, "California 1845–1846," 9).

tilities were close.* General José Castro was said to be marching against the Americans in that valley; there were reports of Indians who could be influenced to attack American families.[309] British Vice-Consul James A. Forbes was working with a party of pro-British sympathizers in California to engineer a new English protectorate there and to transfer large grants of the public domain to British subjects. Thus, the political climate was ripe for conflict, as the explorer party under Fremont arrived to find lives and property interests severely threatened.†[310]

Commodore John D. Sloat, commanding officer of the U.S. naval forces in the Pacific, had held standing orders from Secretary of the Navy George Bancroft for nearly a year to take San Francisco—and other ports, assuming his forces permitted—upon the beginning of hostilities by Mexico.** Sloat learned of the outbreak of war no later than 18 May, a little more than a week after hostilities occurred at the Rio Grande,†† but he failed to sail from Mazatlan to Upper California until 8 June, arriving in Monterey on 1 July.*** His delay was possibly owing to U.S. consul Thomas O. Larkin's importuning Sloat to delay until there was a clear expression of American acquiescence in the change of government.††† Nonetheless, on 7 July the U.S. flag was raised over the *alcaldia* of Monterey, and Sloat issued a proclamation claiming California for the United States.§

Sloat's action in taking Monterey on 7 July was based on his belief that Fremont's aid to American settlers in the capture of Sonoma, the chief stronghold of Californians north of the Bay region, had been

---

*War formally commenced on 12 May 1846, two days after Fremont and Gillespie began their return to California. 15 *Congressional Globe* 804.

†Benton explained in his narration to the Senate that establishment of the protectorate and the property transfers were done in anticipation of war, in order to shelter California from the reclamations of the United States. 17 *Congressional Globe* 606. Buchanan warned Polk that if he made an announcement that California was a U.S. war aim, then Britain and France would join Mexico against the United States. He appeared to want Polk to disclaim any ambition to acquire California. Polk, however, would not budge and said that any foreign inquiry into the matter was an insult. He instructed the U.S. minister to Britain not to answer and would not pledge to others the terms of a U.S. peace. 1 Polk, *Diary* 398 (Quaife ed.). Buchanan then said that England's attitude over California would prevent an Oregon settlement and there still would be war. *Id.* 396–97.

**Fremont, *Papers* (orders, Bancroft to Sloat, 24 June 1845, noted in memorandum by Bancroft, 2 September 1886). These orders were repeated in August and October 1845 and in February 1846. *Id.*

††5 T. Larkin, *Papers* 58–59 (letter of 20 June 1846, Larkin to Commander J.B. Montgomery, aboard the *Portsmouth*).

***5 Larkin, *Papers* 126–27 (letter of 20 June 1846, Larkin to Buchanan). Sloat was later rebuked for this delay and relieved of his Pacific command. S. Exec. Doc. No. 33, 30th Cong., 1st Sess. (1848) (order from Bancroft to Sloat, 12 July 1846, "Transcript of Fremont Court-martial" 59–60).

†††R. Kelsey, *The United States Consulate in California* 78 (1910).

§5 Larkin, *Papers* 108–09.

authorized by the U.S. government.*[311] Whether Fremont in fact had
played an active role in the taking of Sonoma and raising of the Bear
Flag on 14 June 1846, his presence unquestionably helped precipitate
the takeover.† Fremont had also committed an act of war when, upon
hearing that José Castro was forming a battalion to march north and
quell American influence, he ordered the capture of seventy horses
being driven to San Jose to supply Castro's troops.** On 13 January 1849,
Colonel Fremont and General Andres Pico signed a treaty at Cahuenga
Rancho, formally concluding hostilities (which had actually ended three
days previously with the raising of the American flag over Los
Angeles).[312] The result was significantly due to the strong influence of
Fremont in shaping the course of military and diplomatic events. It was
these activities taken together that gave rise to the question of fact as to
whether Fremont had been authorized to take offensive action to secure
California for the United States after the Mexican War began.

Sloat was succeeded in the Pacific command by Robert F. Stockton,
who commissioned Fremont a major in the U.S. Army. Fremont, ill advisedly, sided with Stockton in a power struggle with Stephen Kearney,
general of the army appointed by the president to secure the takeover of
California. For refusing to obey Kearney's orders, Fremont was court-
martialed for insubordination and convicted. Although his sentence
was commuted by President Polk, Fremont resigned from the army.††

Senator Benton's statement of the facts was aptly supplemented by
Senator James Mason's (D. Va.) framing the issue as to whether or not
Congress would give retroactive tacit approval of Fremont's activities
prior to the declaration of war by paying off the debt he incurred, known
thereafter as the California Claims.[313]

On 3 March 1848 Senator Lewis Cass (D. Mich.) reported a bill out of the
Committee on Military Affairs appropriating $700,000 to satisfy these
claims. In addition, the bill proposed the creation of a board under Fremont's chairmanship to determine their validity.[314] Senator Thomas
Rusk (D. Tex.) concurred with Benton's evaluation that all of Fremont's

---

*Both Fremont and Gillespie described Sloat's surprise and disturbance when he
learned that the authority upon which he based his operations had not been given.
Testimony before the Senate Committee on Military Affairs, S. Rep. No. 75, 30th Cong.,
1st Sess. 12, 32.

†17 Globe 607; Fremont, Papers 519, 522 (J. Bidwell, "Fremont in the Conquest of
California"). See also id. (T.S. Martin, "Narrative of John C. Fremont Expedition to
California in 1845–46," at 23–24). Some settlers, and even a member of Fremont's party,
attributed a more active role to Fremont. 17 Globe 607; S. Rep. No. 75, 30th Cong., 1st
Sess. (transcript of hearing before the Senate Committee on Military Affairs 34, 38).

**Fremont, Papers (letter of 14 June 1846, Larkin to Castro, in S. Dunbar, "Transcript of
Fort Sutter Papers").

††Transcript of Fremont court-martial 59–60, S. Exec. Doc. No. 33, 30th Cong., 1st Sess.

activities were addressed to thwarting a British takeover of California and thus occurred with U.S. government sanction. Senator Samuel Phelps (Wh. Vt.) stated that though the claims originated in an irregular manner, "they are such as we would have directed if we had been acquainted with the circumstances, and it is necessary and proper that we should legalize them."[315] On 17 April, the Senate voted to return the bill to committee; and when reported out the next day, the major point of debate became whether Fremont himself could be an impartial arbiter of the claims. Its major opposition mollified, the bill was passed in amended version as reported by the Committee on Military Affairs, on 28 April 1848.*[316] By accepting responsibility for paying the debts he incurred, the Senate admitted the value of Fremont's operations and thus vindicated him. The final chapter of this affair was not written, however, until 31 August 1852, with passage of Section 6 of the Army Appropriations Act, which provided for the payment of Fremont and the other California claimants.†

By endorsing the conduct of an officer in the field ostensibly doing no more than protecting the lives of U.S. citizens, Congress ratified investing the military arm of the executive with considerable power. It approved expenses incurred by secret operatives carrying out word-of-mouth instructions that could not, in all practicality, be revoked. The Fremont expedition, whatever the truth of its real mission, was a stunning success, possibly surprising no one quite so much as John C. Fremont himself. Had the expedition been a failure, the same questions as to authority and even sponsorship would have remained, but probably there would have been no congressional effort to legitimize the venture. Instead, in this instance at least, Congress accepted and endorsed a pattern of executive initiative aimed at obtaining an objective deliberately vague in its definition and long deferred in its achievement.

Executive Intervention to Prevent the Use of Military Force in New Mexico and Texas

Both the Taylor and Fillmore administrations exercised civil and military authority over California and New Mexico prior to their statehood. When Texas attempted to broaden its borders to include that portion of the New Mexico territory east of the Rio Grande, Congress addressed the question of whether the president alone could employ

---

*Some amendments were proposed in the House, including a provision to establish a board to liquidate the claims, which did not pass. Upon its return to the Senate there was no immediate further action. 17 *Congressional Globe* 1064.

†S. Exec. Doc. No. 49, 33d Cong., 1st Sess.

military force to prevent a state from extending its jurisdiction into disputed territory.

On its face, the query appeared to be concerned with a purely domestic issue rather than foreign policy. Contemporary examples (in which presidential authority to use armed force in disputed territory would be analogous) have involved instances of foreign governments' threats to use troops or their actual movement of arms into areas that the United States has deemed to be related to its security.

Both James K. Polk and Secretary of War William Marcy recognized the New Mexico territory east of the Rio Grande as lawfully within Texas, and Polk had informed the House of his position.[317] Receiving no objection, Polk prepared instructions to federal officers at Santa Fe to respect Texan authority.[318] Senators during Taylor's administration then demanded to know if Taylor had ordered military officers "to hold possession" of Santa Fe "against the authority of Texas."*[319] On 17 June, the president replied that no such orders had been given.[320] Congress, however, took no steps to settle the boundary or to define the permissible extent of executive military action.

In one of his strongest messages to Congress, President Fillmore on 6 August 1850 addressed the executive's right to authorize unilateral force in disputed territory. Informed that the governor of Texas had dispatched a commissioner to extend civil jurisdiction over certain New Mexico counties that Texas claimed, Fillmore announced that U.S. "military officers, stationed at Santa Fe, [had] interposed adversely, with the inhabitants, to the fulfillment of his [the Commissioner's] object. . . ."[321]

Fillmore invoked federal law as the basis for his assertion of authority to repel Texas forces. Since U.S. "title by conquest" had been confirmed by the Treaty of Guadalupe Hidalgo, the territory was to be governed by federal law "until it shall be displaced or superseded by other legal provisions."[322] Fillmore informed Congress, therefore, that any Texas forces entering New Mexico would be dealt with as aggressors or trespassers. He also strongly hinted that if legislators would establish a boundary between the two, disturbances or collisions might be avoided,

---

*In 1836, the rebellious province of Texas had signed a treaty of peace with Mexico by whose terms boundaries were "not to extend beyond the Rio Grande." This vague provision laid the basis for subsequent claims by the Lone Star Republic for territory as far west as the Rio Grande. Since Santa Fe, capital of New Mexico, was *east* of the Rio Grande, it was apparent the boundaries of the new republic were beyond those of the former province. Claim to the additional territory was evidently based on rights gained by conquest, the Mexican army having withdrawn beyond the Rio Grande. 1 G. Rives, *The United States and Mexico, 1812–1848*, at 357, 358, 390 (1913; 1969 repr.). Moreover, the Polk administration had based a claim to New Mexican territory east of the Rio Grande on the practical consideration of avoiding boundary disputes with Mexico by using the river as a natural boundary. *See* Slidell instructions, *supra* at p. 117.

and he urged Congress to make a high priority of establishing a boundary line.[323]

The president's stand evoked a furor. Tennessee Congressman John Savage abhorred the president's use of armed forces and a military officer to "aid" inhabitants of New Mexico in establishing a civil government of their own.[324] Others such as future chief executive Andrew Johnson (D. Tenn.) foresaw unwelcome governmental consolidation. "The danger," he exclaimed, "arises from the probability there is of making the centripetal power of the Government greater than the centrifugal."[325] Espousing the theory that the U.S. government was not "titled" in the territory of New Mexico but only an "umpire" in a boundary dispute between Texas and Mexico, Johnson demanded that Fillmore withdraw U.S. troops from Texas's borders.[326] Virginia Congressman Thomas Bayly maintained that the executive had merely been authorized to send troops to assist process in the courts or repel invasion but that without further legislative enactment, Fillmore's contemplated actions might constitute "an act of war—of civil war, ... commenced without authority of law."[327]

Congress, however, acted rapidly on the president's recommendation. On 9 September it approved an act "proposing to the State of Texas the establishment of her northern and western boundaries," relinquishment of all territory claimed by the state beyond these boundaries, and establishment of a territorial government in New Mexico. The Texas state legislature on 25 November accepted these propositions; and in his comments in a message to Congress, President Fillmore gratefully acknowledged its cooperation in bringing about conciliation regarding the "difficulties felt, and the dangers apprehended, from the vast acquisitions of territory under the late treaty with Mexico. ..."[328]

Koszta Incident in Turkey and the Destruction of Greytown, Nicaragua

Congress supported Franklin Pierce's unilateral military actions without requiring nearly as full explanations for the reasons that those actions had been undertaken as they had demanded from his predecessors. In one instance, a Hungarian refugee, Martin Koszta, was freed from an Austrian brig by intervention of U.S. diplomatic and military officials who later received the approbation of both Congress and the president.* Pierce, in ratifying the acts that precipitated Koszta's

*A native Hungarian, Martin Koszta had resided in the United States for two years and declared his intent to become a U.S. citizen. When he visited Turkey in 1853, Austrian authorities seized him at Smyrna for violation of a prohibition against return of Hungarian refugees. Initial efforts of U.S. consular personnel to secure his release from an Austrian brig failed; he was not freed until the U.S. *chargé d'affaires* John P. Brown at

release, concluded that Koszta had been wrongfully seized and detained and that at the time of his arrest he was "clothed with the nationality of the United States" by virtue of a declaration that he wished to become a citizen.*[329]

Congress was unconcerned that a *chargé*, without prior presidential or congressional consultation, authorized a use of force that could have resulted in hostilities between the United States and Austria. On the contrary, Representative John Perkins (D. La.) glowingly cited Captain Duncan Ingraham for "the propriety and gallantry of his conduct in the rescue of Martin Koszta."†[330]

A second and potentially more serious incident was Pierce's reprisal action against officials of San Juan del Norte (Greytown), Nicaragua, for injuries to U.S. citizens' property. Former Secretary of State Daniel Webster had received reports in February 1853[331] that Greytown officials ordered the American-owned Accessory Transit Company to leave Greytown and had punctuated efforts to enforce its order with scattered acts of violence.** Secretary Webster then announced that all British or U.S. property would be protected "peaceably if we can, forcibly if we must."[332]

Navy Captain George N. Hollins of the S.S. *Cyane,* who was cruising in the vicinity under orders from the Fillmore administration, on 14 March 1853 posted an ultimatum in the city of Greytown promising that the American navy would protect U.S. citizens from "future molestation."[333] When British Captain Wilson of HBM *Geyser* questioned Hollins's authority for such a proclamation, Hollins claimed that his

---

Smyrna ordered a U.S. ship captain, Duncan Ingraham, to use his own initiative to secure Koszta's release either by verbal request or else by force. S. Exec. Doc. No. 40, 33d Cong., 1st Sess. 2–11.

Ingraham delivered an ultimatum to the Austrian brig commander to release Koszta. Before what seemed certain to have become a violent confrontation, U.S. consul Edward Offley arranged with his Austrian counterpart to bring up Koszta, who emerged from the hold of the brig in chains; and he was handed over to the French Consul General at Smyrna. *Id.* 20–25. By 14 October 1853, Koszta was on his way to Boston (S. Exec. Doc. No. 52, 33d Cong., 1st Sess. 31), and Austrian protests were waved aside.

*Pierce remarked, "The acts of our officers ... were justifiable, and their conduct ... fully approved by me. ..." Secretary of State Marcy's approval had been given on 31 August 1853. S. Exec. Doc. No. 53, 33d Cong., 1st Sess. 9. Referring to the correspondence between the Austrian *chargé d'affaires* and the secretary of state, he stated, "The principles and policy therein maintained on the part of the United States will, whenever a proper occasion occurs, be applied and enforced." 6 *Messages and Papers* 2732.

†In fact, Congress awarded the "doughty captain" a gold medal. 23 *Congressional Globe* Appendix 84. *See* Schlesinger, *The Imperial Presidency* 55.

**Greytown had declared independence from Nicaragua in 1852. A private U.S. corporation chartered by Nicaragua, the Accessory Transit Company, was ordered out of Greytown by the new government; yet, despite affirmation of the order by Greytown's Supreme Court and actions by the City Council and Marshal, Greytown seemed powerless to eject the company, and U.S. military officers in the vicinity became increasingly unable to protect property from destruction. S. Exec. Doc. No. 8, 33d Cong., 1st Sess. 5, 25.

orders emanated from former Secretary of State Webster's policy. In the meantime, Pierce's Secretary of State William Marcy had received several citizen complaints and had instructed Secretary of the Navy James Dobbin to order the commander of the home squadron to make occasional visits to Greytown.[334] On 30 March 1853, Hollins reported to Dobbin that he had stepped in to protect American citizens from assault, ejectment, and other outrages. Dobbin assured Captain Hollins that he had full power and approval to do what he had done,*[335] since Greytown's *de facto* government had not been recognized by the United States. Despite the fact that the United States did not formally recognize the independence of Greytown,† U.S. commercial agents remained there until mid-1854. One of these agents, Joseph Fabens, complained in early 1854 that Accessory Transit Company and private U.S. citizens were being subjected to continued harassment, and on 9 June 1854, Marcy replied that Captain Hollins was steaming directly to Greytown to demand an apology.[336] After three weeks' incessant demands were ignored, however, Hollins acted on his understanding of his orders of 10 June** and issued an ultimatum on 12 July demanding payment within twenty-four hours or he would start a bombardment of the town. Failing to receive any response, he opened fire on 13 July and leveled most of Greytown without loss of life.[337] Though destruction was almost total, Hollins penned a justification to Marcy:

> [I]t was thought best to make the punishment of such a character as to inculcate a lesson never to be forgotten by those who have for so long a time set at defiance all the warnings and satisfy the whole world that the United States have the power and determination to enforce that reparation and respect due them as a government in whatever quarter the outrages may be committed.††[338]

---

*Hollins was informed that in the future he would be acting to protect American interests at Greytown, which were lodged chiefly in the Accessory Transit Co. Under his former Whig instructions, Hollins had been implementing Clayton-Bulwer Treaty provisions requiring joint protection by United States and Britain of interoceanic communications interests. *Id.* 7.

†In 1852, Secretary of State Webster had instructed the commander of the home squadron of the navy to recognize Greytown but also authorized the naval commanders to exercise "full power to correct abuses and settle all difficulties." *Id.* 33.

**Hollins was ordered to consult Fabens to get the facts regarding theft and destruction of property. Dobbin informed Hollins it was "desirable" that Greytown officials know that the United States was determined to "check" the outrages but that he hoped that Hollins could do so without resort to violence, destruction of property, and loss of life. Dobbin felt that the mere presence of Hollins's vessel would prove useful. The momentum of events was such, however, that Hollins felt he had to take the step that the Navy Department hoped could be avoided. S. Doc. No. 85, 33d Cong., 1st Sess. at 21.

††Secretary of State Marcy was not certain what position to take. He wrote to James Buchanan at the Court of St. James that perhaps Hollins was "too severe" but that Marcy would have no opinion until both Fabens and Hollins returned to the United States. Marcy

On 28 July Senator James Pierce (Wh. Md.) and Representative Joseph Chandler (Wh. Pa.) each submitted resolutions, requesting any orders sent to Hollins.[339] Three days later, on 31 July, Pierce sent to Congress all communications on the incident; and in his second state of the union address on 4 December 1853, related his own account. The president reported that orders to Captain Hollins were not intended to give him great leeway in the use of force if it could have been avoided but implied that Hollins possessed clear authority to resort to violence, since "the people themselves, by their extraordinary conduct in the affair, frustrated all the possible mild measures for obtaining satisfaction." He reminded congressmen that their own estimate of Greytown's importance as the conduit of North American enterprise westward through Nicaragua had led them to provide at the previous session "a temporary force . . . at considerable expense to the United States" to protect citizens' lives and property.[340]

Hollins's orders did not, indeed, authorize him to conduct a military reprisal.[341] But President Pierce eventually completely ratified his conduct. Although there was evidence of de facto U.S. recognition of Greytown, Pierce defended its destruction by characterizing the community as "a piratical resort of outlaws or savages,"[342] believing that such a classification clothed him with the power to engage in actions not otherwise open to him under the Constitution or the law of nations.*[343]

Only two Representatives† rebuked Pierce shortly after the convening of the second session. In particular, Congressman Rufus W. Peckham (D. N.Y.) believed that the power vested in Congress "to grant letters of marque and reprisal"—a remedy employed among nations to enforce payment of debt or performance of some duty—was intended "carefully to avoid conferring upon the Executive, under any circumstances without the consent of Congress, power to involve the country in war."[344] Peckham asked what would prevent the president from making war on Cuba:[345]

---

reassured Buchanan that the incident should not trouble the British since Greytown claimed independent and even sovereign status—a surprising affirmation considering Marcy's earlier and later characterizations of Greytown. National Archives Microfilm, Department of State, *Diplomatic Instructions,* M77, roll 75 (letter of 8 August 1854). Some commentators have reported that Buchanan even disavowed Hollins's act to the British government. Schlesinger, *The Imperial Presidency* 56.

*Pierce had the precedent of Jackson's ratification of an unauthorized action taken against the Falkland Islands, which Jackson described as piratical, although in fact it was a community operating under color of law. *See* Chapter 1, p. 57.

†One congressman, Leander M. Cox (Wh. Ky.) disputed the constitutionality of the entire executive response to the Greytown episode and demanded to know under what clause of the Constitution the power was found to enable the president to judge the case, pass sentence, and execute it himself? 24 *Congressional Globe Appendix* 70.

What is the limit to his power? What but his own will shall prevent him involving the country in war at any time?[346]

Although Congress's discussion of the Greytown incident ceased, the judiciary took a broad view of the president's constitutional powers to rescue and protect American citizens and their property abroad. In *Durand v. Hollins,** 8 F. Cas. 111 (No. 4186) (C.C.S.D.N.Y. 1860), the court held that the president is the legitimate organ of government to deal with foreign nations in matters concerning the interests of its citizens abroad and asserted that it was to him that citizens abroad must look for protection. To this end, the court viewed the president as possessor of the "whole executive power of the country" under the Constitution and the laws passed under it. The different departments of government provide the means to execute this power, "whether by negotiation or by force—a department of state and a department of the navy." Since the response to violence usually must be prompt to afford effective protection, the duty must "of necessity," rest in the discretion of the president.†

CONCLUSION

The years of the Mexican War (1846–48) and the decade immediately following were a time of substantial change in the balance of the war powers of Congress and the executive. There were a few challenges to the president's power of appointment, in which the commander-in-chief did not obtain all of the generals he requested and was refused his desire that a supernumerary commanding general should be elevated from the pool of generals in the field. Aside from these attempts to curb military appointments, however, Congress failed to hinder the executive prerogative to appoint or remove, even during a legislative recess. During

---

*The plaintiff, Calvin Durand, brought an action in trespass against George Hollins personally for losses sustained in the bombardment and burning of Greytown. In holding for the defendant, Justice Nelson made it clear that "in all cases where a public act or order rests in executive discretion neither [the president] nor his authorized agent is personally civilly liable for the consequences." Adverting to language of Chief Justice Marshall in *Marbury v. Madison,* 5 U.S. (1 Cranch) 165 (1803), Nelson stated that whether it was the duty of the president to interpose for protection of citizens at Greytown against an "irresponsible and marauding community that had established itself there, was a public political question which belonged to the Executive to determine. . . ." *Durand v. Hollins,* 8 F. Cas. 111, 112 (No. 4186) (C.C.S.D. N.Y.).

†Justice Nelson saw Greytown through much the same eyes as Pierce—as a marauding and even piratical community. But his decision was applied to a particular fact situation in which reported acts of violence were a daily occurrence. It has been cited by certain attorneys and commentators since as justification for unlimited presidential action against a lawless community regardless of the nature of the activities or the legitimacy of the government allegedly performing them. *See* Schlesinger, *The Imperial Presidency* 56.

Polk's administration Congress backed away from demanding reasons for removals. Under Zachary Taylor, George Washington's concept that it was constitutionally permissible for the chief executive to remove an officer without consultation with Congress was expanded further than the first president had ever dreamed, while congressmen under both Polk and Taylor yielded to the power that the executive might acquire in both appointments and removals.

Congress took a more fundamental role in determining the course and commitment of funds and armaments and the policy behind their use than at any previous point. In applying for money to meet a military deficiency, Polk received $2 million less than he requested, and a bill to upgrade the U.S. fleet was diverted. The Senate felt no reservation in offering bills for national defense, and troop increases were, as expected, approved in wartime. The House, however, extensively questioned funds and interjected that a peacetime request of President Pierce for improved arms could pose a threat of war with England.

Generally, broad discretion similar to that given by Congress to Polk was also granted to Presidents Fillmore and Pierce. There was no serious objection of impropriety or expression of constitutional danger inasmuch as the objects for which delegation was sought were well delineated. Congress did flatly refuse to permit Franklin Pierce to select the final site for a naval depot but did so purely for partisan and patronage reasons that were unrelated to executive prerogatives.

Information control had become quite sophisticated by the mid-nineteenth century. Complex qualified requests outnumbered unqualified four or five times to one. Almost the only queries concerning ongoing military affairs were partisan, and they were seldom answered. Little presidential information was volunteered outside of annual messages except to make points regarding needed arms or supplies. The Polk administration both volunteered and withheld more information than succeeding administrations in the post-Mexican War decade. Of the four chief executives, 1845–57, Polk was by far the most skillful manipulator of information, concealing the avidity of his interest in acquiring California, the real war posture of Britain respecting Oregon, and his real desire personally to intervene in foreign politics; but Congress clearly saw through Secretary of War Marcy's letter written after the fact that was intended to damage Zachary Taylor's political chances in the election of 1848. The House insinuated misbehavior but did not charge Polk with abuse of his powers.

Chief executives were generally reluctant to inform Congress concerning the details of treatymaking. President Taylor did not regard it as his constitutional duty to send to Congress a signed but "unacceptable" treaty, even as Thomas Jefferson had refused to do. Presidents

Fillmore and Pierce tended to be exceedingly cautious in replying to requests, and in only one significant instance, the *Black Warrior* seizure, did Pierce volunteer more than he was asked.

Congress could have probed deeper, though it was usually vigilant in seeking information. The Perry mission's size and character were not unknown, and Congress's careful attention even to what information was transmitted would have uncovered his deliberate disobedience of orders if not his imperious behavior toward the Japanese. The Senate qualified its requests for documents relevant to the abrogation of the Anglo-American Treaty of 1818, and Polk withheld information that England had been preparing for war in case Oregon boundary negotiations broke down.

Many House members felt comfortable with the understanding that there was some reason to withhold certain information, and the distinction was even voiced that the House was less trustworthy than the Senate; but no senator ventured to suggest penalties in his own house for premature release of information. Information was thus either released or not on the basis of the kind of decision the executive had to make. If Congress did not need to be informed in order to supply a need, an executive generally used what funds he had available and acted through private emissaries. Release of much of the executive's private correspondence with his agents would not only have proved politically embarrassing but also, in more than one instance, could have endangered the lives of American citizens and exposed the diplomatic positions of the U.S. government.

Polk clearly directed his foreign policy with a network of agents and a conviction that national security depended on the widest possible outreach. As much as possible, he aligned Congress on the side of reinterpreting Monroe's message of 1823, so that resistance to European interference in the Western Hemisphere meant the president of the United States might interfere in the affairs of other nations. He won Congress over to his position that an explanation of the Treaty of Guadalupe Hidalgo was not an interpretation of it and denied that Mexico had a legal right to rely on an executive explanation of treaty terms. He asked Congress's guidance in formulating policy toward Oregon, but most of the Senate concluded that the president could and should compromise, and the House found no "transcendent event" that required its power to be used to end unfavorable treaty stipulations. Thus, Congress responded favorably to Polk's requests to lead the nation in case of a threat to the peace and safety of the United States or to any announced policy or doctrine.

Congress occasionally expressed its view of executive policy by failing to enact certain programs. At the invitation of President Fillmore, it turned down the opportunity to become involved in foreign policy formulation by refusing to assume its proper constitutional role in legislating reciprocity provisions. Franklin Pierce, instead, pressed through Congress a treaty of his own. Only once did Congress refuse an executive request to change a law that was itself the result of executive bargaining—the Treaty of Guadalupe Hidalgo—when it declined to roll back the boundary between the United States and Mexico solemnly agreed upon by those two nations.

Even at the lowest point of Pierce's domestic political influence, the executive war power was not only firmly exercised but also survived some attacks upon its authority. When the House voiced its ancient argument that it possessed authority to block treaties by refusing to appropriate funds to implement them, Congressman Thomas Hart Benton resented the fact that congressional power could no longer be relied upon as a viable threat to executive war power, which was the momentous power to quarrel. The notion of withholding funds to implement treaties was for all intents and purposes a dead letter, only to be resuscitated if a treaty palpably subverted the best interests of the United States.

Presidents during this period used a variety of justifications for their authority to take military action. Certain acts, such as Polk's deployment of troops in the disputed area of Texas, were only grudgingly and painfully acknowledged as a *fait accompli* by legislation. Others, such as Fremont's expedition that helped bring California into possession of the United States, were justified by implication and ratified by both Congress and the executive. Additional acts unknown at the time of their execution were ratified, as in the case of Martin Koszta's release and Captain Hollins's bombardment of Greytown, Nicaragua.

In significant debates on military affairs, Congress affirmed the policies of each chief executive. Though lawmakers were initially reluctant to declare war against Mexico without more justification, the Senate felt a declaration was mandated because the executive could not otherwise use the express war power authority of Congress. On the other hand, the Mexican War never quite overcame the stigma of being an undefined war of conquest, symbolizing the antithesis of the promise of liberty and freedom from oppression that was the heritage of the United States. One must contrast Abraham Lincoln's and others' assertions that a House appropriation was no justification of military action, with the careful appropriation of funds for the use of vessels in John Quincy Adams's and earlier administrations as being justified for clearly defined purposes such as fighting Indians, enforcing treaties, and suppressing piracy.

The key question was what the president perceived to be his authority in military matters during this time frame. All four presidents recognized that there were limits to their authority, and none acted without seeking advice. Their principal reliance was upon powers to defend against invasion and the power to preserve and protect the laws as comprehended by the fact that the United States was a member of the community of nations and entitled to the protection of international law.

Each president clearly demonstrated at least one example of his prerogative to protect and defend when he felt himself to be on firm ground. Polk claimed that the citizens' rights to security and protection justified his gathering of forces in Texas and sending embassies to Mexico in advance of conflict and his directing the course of military operations while Congress debated what support it was to give. Millard Fillmore used the same authority as well as the defense of natural territorial integrity to claim that Texas was a trespasser when it threatened the New Mexico territory and to assure the local governments involved that he would not hesitate to use federal authorities to put down a threat to territorial and thus federal law. Pierce was concerned about the protection of persons and property as he took steps to protest the seizure of the *Black Warrior* and to defend the pecuniary interests of U.S. citizens in Greytown, Nicaragua. President Polk also found a constitutional executive prerogative to seek indemnity for the past wrongs of a nation against U.S. citizens; and Congress backed him in his institution of civil law and the laying of a tariff in Mexico so long as he relinquished the power to assess taxes within a reasonable time. Congress did not, therefore, see any threat to its own hegemony in such a limited "caretaker" government by the executive.

If a president is committed to a military policy of territorial aggrandizement, as certainly President Polk was, the constitutional prerogative to assure the safety and protection of the nation may well become an artificial rationale for acts taken without consultation with Congress. Polk and Pierce opened up the potential of confrontations with European powers. Particularly, Polk's belief in the importance of territorial advance exposed American citizens in an affected area to the potential of injury and even death. There are many examples of presidential willingness to risk potential confrontation with foreign powers, with comparatively minimal congressional consultation or advice. By accepting and endorsing such executive conduct, Congress extended its definition of the type of acts that a president can take short of obtaining a declaration of war. Polk did not advise Congress that Britain was preparing for war over Oregon as he invited lawmakers to abrogate the

Treaty of 1818. Taylor and Fillmore did not inform Congress that Britain really meant to preserve for itself concessions in Central America, despite the Clayton-Bulwer Treaty. Polk landed marines and military supplies in Yucatan without advising Congress he was doing so. Polk knew, also, that jealous European interests with powerful navies coveted California as much as he, when naval commanders on the spot in California were ordered to reduce it to U.S. possession the moment war broke out between the United States and Mexico. Even prior to war they were encouraged to do all in their power to bring about U.S. acquisition short of military coercion. Congress agreed that John C. Fremont's activities helped thwart the British and thus were in the service of the U.S. government. It legitimized the venture and encouraged the executive to embark on military initiatives with the knowledge that success might bring forth its approval.

These presidents designated personal agents as executives had done in the past, with virtually unlimited discretion to act and to accept the favorable results of their endeavor. No evidence suggests that their delegates executed various missions with any thought of carrying out some constitutionally impermissible act. For example, no agent appears to have had secret orders to foment war before using diplomacy. The mode of instructing an agent expected to be 10,000 miles from Washington with no prospect of quick communication was firmness tempered with discretion. A host of actions known only to the heads of executive departments, such as Matthew Perry's brash behavior with the sensitive Japanese, were generally tolerated if they supported U.S. influence abroad and quietly but firmly rebuked if they did not. Congress had begun to recognize the president's emerging authority to act as the principal even though not the sole organ of American foreign relations. Thus, Congress assented retroactively to unilateral executive actions undertaken without its knowledge or consent, so long as the activities themselves were successful and did not involve fundamental abrogation of constitutional principle.

❈   *Chapter 3*

National Policy in Domestic Crisis, 1857–1869

EXECUTIVE-CONGRESSIONAL RELATIONS:
INTRODUCTION

During the presidencies of James Buchanan, Abraham Lincoln, and
Andrew Johnson, slavery and secession had an unmistakable impact on
each governmental branch's perception of its own war powers. As the
nation experienced bitter fratricidal conflicts in Kansas, it prepared for
a larger-level confrontation that would bring about not only unprecedented social disintegration but also a fundamental realignment of the
powers of government branches during wartime.

In 1856, the Democratic party nominated for the presidency James
Buchanan, a robust lawyer with a political philosophy of seeking to
avoid any possible confrontation with Congress over the extent of his
power as chief executive. His strict construction of presidential power
was tested to the utmost over the threat of secession, but he refused to
take military action against any state without Congress's approval.
Buchanan attempted to get prior authorization from Congress to use
force in the Caribbean and Central America, but he resolutely maintained that Congress was the sole constitutional source of executive war
power.

The candidate whom Democrats could least afford to see occupy the
White House was Abraham Lincoln, whose election in 1860 contributed
to the secession of seven states. He opposed Buchanan's apparent
passivity in the face of disunion and pursued an aggressive war policy
whose momentum, influenced by contemporary industrial and social

changes, increased in strength and intensity after his assassination and the cessation of rebellion.

The political reins then suddenly fell into the hands of Andrew Johnson, a tailor who had become a legislator of marked probity and intelligence but who was, unfortunately, ineffective as chief executive. Johnson expressed an abhorrence of military government but was never able to stem the energy with which extreme Republican party politicians sought legislative vengeance for Southern rebellion.

Between 1861 and 1865, there occurred a fundamental shift in the administration and exercise of the war power. In 1861, the president's bipartisan supporters voted daily to support full military action initiated by the executive and were virtually unchallenged. In 1865, after Lee's surrender, Radical Republicans ignored executive provisional governments in the South and imposed army rule. Thus, the military arm of the executive was made accountable to congressional leadership.

Congress focused its energies during the first session of the Thirty-seventh Congress on secession and the four-month-old Civil War. Its most extensive debate concerned the president's right to have acted unilaterally. In this respect, the thrust of the session closely paralleled that of the Twenty-ninth Congress under Polk. Legislators regulated many of the actions Lincoln had already undertaken,* since Congress provided the forces required. Although they enacted broad delegations of discretionary authority, lawmakers clearly intended to follow a traditional pattern of making executive performance as responsible to their wishes as possible.

Power of Appointment and Removal

Attempts to Curtail Executive Power   In 1864, Congress reestablished the special office of lieutenant general (formerly held only by Washington and Winfield Scott, hero of the Mexican War) with Ulysses S. Grant pointedly in mind. Underlying the move were Grant's decisive victories in the Mississippi Valley theater, which occurred at the same time as the Army of the Potomac was making virtually no military progress.

The House bill that passed 96 to 41 stopped short of requiring Lincoln to name Grant. The Senate finally agreed to the idea of creating a commander of the armies, 31 to 6, but rejected the House recommendation that named the officer, since the Senate would have to pass judgment later upon the merits of the president's selection.[1]

---

*These included, among other acts, imposing a naval blockade against the Confederacy, suspending the writ of *habeus corpus,* calling out 75,000 volunteers on his own initiative, and increasing forces in the army and navy.

While some argued that there was no precise precedent for the office being created for Grant, New Hampshire Republican Senator Hale decried the literalism that might have required the president to send "for some pettifogging lawyer to hunt authorities and find out . . . what a President of the United States might do" in an emergency such as the fast-paced series of event that led Abraham Lincoln to call out 75,000 men to defend the Union, instead of waiting for Congress to convene. ". . . [H]e did it without law; but he did not do it without law. There was a law higher than any Congress had made or could make, and that was 'the safety of the Republic.' . . ."[2]

But tension between the branches resulted from the proposals, counterproposals, and compromises regarding appointment of brigadier and major generals. Senators, in particular, discussed whether they should rely merely on the president's perceptions or explore the nation's war needs on their own.[3] An example was the Senate Committee on Finance's amendment to an appropriation bill (H.R. 450) that would have restricted the number of presidentially appointed major and brigadier

Earliest known photograph of the interior of the Capitol building, showing the old House of Representatives chamber as it appeared about 1861. Brady photo. (L.C.)

generals.[4] Senator Lyman Trumbull (R. Ill.) felt that Congress could ill afford to surrender to the executive the power to define the size of an army.[5] Opponents, however, supported New Hampshire's John Hale, who succeeded in erasing a ceiling of 750,000 on the number of volunteers.[6] After much haggling, another authorization increasing brigadier and major generals was compromised at thirty majors and seventy-five brigadiers.[7]

Predictably, a struggle developed at the end of the war to curtail executive removal authority over the military. Some legislators claimed that the president already possessed the whole removal power under the Constitution. Others such as Ohio Congressman Robert Schenck supported repeal of an 1862 act* that provided for presidential dismissal of officers without intervention of a court-martial. Schenck argued that the purpose for this summary power was over. A conference committee proposed a substitute, which was enacted. The president could dismiss but was required to order a trial if the officer made an application for one.[8] Although this compromise qualified presidential removal power to a limited extent, Lincoln retained authority to muster out general officers from the service. Congress agreed that justice and the public interest could best be served by careful executive administration of that responsibility and that no inflexible rule expressed in legislation could meet the need so well.[9] This accord, however, was short-lived and came to an end in 1867.

Resurgence of the Removal Controversy   Congress finally achieved for a time limitations over presidential appointment and removal practice, which it had sought for many decades, by effectively terminating Andrew Johnson's civilian and military powers of removal. The perennial issue of executive removal of persons appointed with Senate advice and consent came to a head in 1867 with Congress's passage of both the Tenure of Office Act (S. 453),† and the Stevens Reconstruction bill (H.R. 1143), which divided the South into military districts and imposed army rule upon them.[10] The Tenure of Office Act's chief opponent, Charles Buckalew (D. Pa.) argued that while the Constitution did not expressly

---

*Act of July 17, 1862. Whether or not this section was an effective delegation of authority became complicated by an opinion issued by the army's judge advocate general that asserted that the president had always summarily dismissed officers, a power that "seems to inhere in him under the Constitution as Commander-in-Chief of the Army and Navy." The power, he concluded, had not been derived from the 1862 act, which was only declaratory of a presidential right exercised since "earliest history." 35 *Congressional Globe* 1399, 1412–13.

†This act required that all civil officers appointed by the executive, after receiving Senate confirmation, should hold office until their successors were appointed and confirmed; department heads, on the other hand, could be directly removed by the executive, subject to advice and consent of the Senate. Act of March 2, 1867, 14 Stat. 430.

confer this power on the president, all branches of government had acquiesced that the power resided with him. Buckalew claimed that the First Congress had fully discussed the matter and had decided that the president should have the power to remove, a principle President Washington had fully endorsed.*

Buckalew recalled that during Jackson's presidency, the concern had been whether or not the president should indicate to the Senate his reasons for removing an incumbent.[11] He thus conceived the real issue to be political: "to put a bit into [Johnson's] mouth to curb ... him to prevent him from exercising a power which has been exercised almost unquestioned by all his predecessors."[12] Maryland's Reverdy Johnson then questioned whether Andrew Jackson would have had the full power to see that the laws were faithfully executed, without the authority to remove Treasury Secretary William Duane, who refused to withdraw federal deposits from the Bank of the United States.[13] Other senators such as California's James McDougall attacked the bill as an abuse of the principle of the separation of powers,[14] but it passed the Senate by a wide margin (29 to 9). No one in the House spoke in its favor, and only one against—Ohio Representative William Finck, who expressed doubt that abuses of power to remove would be any less likely if the Senate had a share of it.[15] The House passed it overwhelmingly (111 to 38).[16]

President Johnson's primary reason for vetoing the Tenure bill was that in eliminating the president's power of removal, it unconstitutionally denied an authority indispensable to his full exercise of the war power and the executive authority of the nation.[17] Citing the fact that Lincoln's removal of Confederate sympathizers and abettors in every department of government was a critical aspect of his ability to govern during the Civil War, Johnson expressed confidence that the executive's removal power would continue to be an indispensable part of "the legitimate actions of this Government."†[18]

The passage of the Stevens Reconstruction bill** over Johnson's veto was particularly bitter, since Congress also enacted an enabling amendment to an army appropriation bill that placed Lieutenant General

---

*Analysis of the debates of the First Federal Congress leaves unclear the theory upon which an exclusive executive removal power was accepted. *Annals of Congress* 387–92; 473–77, 607–08. James Madison, himself a participant in the debate and proponent of the executive power, wrote in June of the same year that the doctrine was subject to modification. Madison to Edmund Pendleton, 5 J. Madison, *The Writings of James Madison* 405–06 (Hunt ed. 1900–10).

†On 2 March 1867, the veto was overturned in both the House and the Senate. 37 *Congressional Globe* 1739, 1966.

**Act of July 19, 1867, 15 Stat. 14, 15.

Ulysses Grant in command of the military district troops and prohibited the president from removing him.[19]

Delegations of Discretionary Power

Defeat of Buchanan's Quest for Authority to Use Force in Mexico   President Buchanan's strict construction of the powers of the presidency encouraged him to request Congress to delegate broad authority to act, which the legislature permitted in certain military affairs and in delicate foreign relations involving the possible commitment of armed forces to defend U.S. interests abroad.

The administration failed, however, to counter European attempts to make a protectorate of Mexico. Foreign powers had striven to see which of them would be first to take advantage of a full-scale civil war that had plagued Mexico for several years. Without State Department sanction, Mexican foreign minister Tejada and U.S. minister John Forsyth managed to negotiate a series of commercial and claims treaties and to work out a loan to Mexico earmarked to retire a debt to England that stood as "the last and greatest lever of British political influence with this Govt."[20] Despite Forsyth's arguments, Franklin Pierce did not act on the treaty, and James Buchanan preferred to consider other alternatives.

Buchanan wanted to establish a temporary protectorate at least over northern Mexico to defy British ambitions, even though mounting sectionalism effectively insured a moratorium on permanent acquisitions that would fuel the slavery debate.[21] He desired also to protect the lives and property of American citizens under constant threat due to the Mexican civil war.[22] The president's position was based on an avalanche of correspondence from responsible diplomats urging the executive to extend political control in Mexico.[23] He voiced particular concern in his 1858 annual message, in which he asserted that the treaty of Guadalupe Hidalgo was being ignored:

> No American citizen can now visit Mexico on lawful business, without imminent danger to his person and property. There is no adequate protection to either; and in this respect our treaty with that Republic is almost a dead letter.[24]

If the constitutional faction within Mexico did not prevail, he wanted Congress to delegate the power

> to take possession of a sufficient portion of the remote and unsettled territory of Mexico, to be held in pledge until our injuries shall be redressed

and our just demands be satisfied. We have already exhausted every milder means of obtaining justice. In such a case, this remedy of reprisals is recognized by the law of nations not only as just in itself, but as a means of preventing actual war.[25]

Although Buchanan did not regard occupation of Mexican territory as an act of war, he would not act to seize foreign land on his own authority, since reprisal was a war power expressly granted to Congress under the Constitution.

Congressman Thomas Anderson (Amer. Mo.) favored the delegation and advocated the executive stance on the advantages of American involvement in Mexico. Since Congress possessed the war powers, it alone, Anderson argued, could provide the president with " 'the sinews of war.' "[26] Although Anderson did not urge a congressional declaration of war, he recommended authorizing the president to occupy portions of Mexico along the Arizona territorial border in order to protect it "from lawless Mexicans and wandering tribes of thieving savages." Such occupation he did not deem to be an act of war but rather an indemnification "for injuries unredressed, and demands unsatisfied."[27]

No action was taken, however, on the president's recommendation. Potential danger to Mexican independence and to the Monroe Doctrine represented by a sudden foreign invasion remained unabated.

Only upon the change of U.S. administrations did there occur an alteration in the executive's blatant, though ineffectual, spirit of "manifest destiny." Secretary of State William H. Seward, himself an expansionist of 1856 regarding Mexico,[28] made it abundantly clear in 1861 that President Lincoln was willing to give the Juarez regime time to establish itself. His instructions to U.S. minister Corwin thus declared that the United States had no designs for a protectorate over Mexico, nor would it look favorably upon one conceived by any foreign nation.[29]

Grant of Lincoln's Bid for Emergency Powers President Lincoln received virtually full discretion to take military action according to his perception of need, with the exception of certain authority to defend the United States which could have involved the Union in conflict with foreign powers. In cases where war might become a reality, Congress saw a danger in wide executive discretion to initiate certain defense measures and acted swiftly and positively to curb presidential naval activities.

Secretary of the Navy Gideon Welles received broad discretion to build up to twenty ironclad steamships in either private or public shipyards, and Congress appropriated $10 million to construct them.[30] The House joined in passing Senate Bill No. 36, providing Welles with discretion to appoint three "skilful" officers to investigate specifications for new ironclads and floating batteries and, on the basis of their report, to decide whether or not to approve one or more armored ships or batteries, up to a cost of $1.5 million.[31]

Many congressmen would have acceded in having Lincoln take over railroad and telegraph lines by virtue of his own war power, without legislation. Maine Senator William Fessenden described presidential authority to act as a necessary concomitant of prosecuting the war: "dangerous," to be sure, "but as a matter of law, in my judgment, this power is incident to the carrying on of war always."[32] Some members felt that the authority was concurrent,[33] requiring a delegation Congress ought to award lest the executive seize it out of "necessity." The bill passed 23 to 12, on 28 January. But Fessenden called upon his colleagues to avoid the "confusion" of legislating on war powers matters

> because the line is so very indistinct that it is difficult to tell on which side is the right and on which side is the wrong. Let us ... leave the war power ... to be wielded by ... the President of the United States. ... [34]

Both houses in July 1861 gave their overwhelming approval to Lincoln's discretionary use of force, with no further consultation, in the collection of duties and prevention of any revenue vessel's capture.[35] He was authorized to forbid commerce between any state and the federal government if he first declared the inhabitants of that state to be rebels.[36] Congress also had no difficulty in enacting an appropriation bill that included a provision delegating to the president the discretion to abrogate all treaties with any Indian tribe "in actual hostility to the United States."[37]

Congress refused, however, to delegate unspecified authority to spend for defense. Unquestionably, augmented defenses were necessary in view of both the Civil War and possible foreign incursion. Yet when the Senate considered a House-passed bill (H.R. 156) that provided for increased fortification,[38] there was little unanimity on the issue of broad executive discretion to use the appropriation. Senator John Sherman (R. Oh.) sought to amend the House bill's enumerated appropriations to permit the president to use the total appropriations for defense as he saw fit, with no specification from Congress. Others, such as William Fessenden (R. Me.) and John Ten Eyck (R. N.J.), feared that unbridled executive wartime expenditures could bring the United States into direct confrontation with foreign powers. Fessenden alluded inferentially to the *Trent* affair* and warned that the bill should state precisely

*Charles Wilkes, commanding the S.S. *San Jacinto,* captured Confederate diplomatic agents James Mason and John Slidell in November 1861 and removed them from the British mail packet *Trent.* Eventually, both Britain and the United States found ways to

how U.S. fortifications were proposed to be strengthened. Though the bill passed the Senate on 12 February 1862 (28 to 10), it rejected Sherman's amendment proposing presidential discretionary use of $2 million for defense of the northern coast and frontier.[39]

Senators also evaluated and, at first, refused to delegate authority to issue letters of marque and reprisal.*[40] Since Southern commerce had been severely restricted by the Union blockade, the risk of hostilities from erroneous capture of neutrals appeared to outweigh any real gains that delegation of authority to issue the letters might have otherwise produced.† The Senate finally passed a bill on 17 February 1863, conferring authority upon the president to issue letters of marque and reprisal "in all domestic and foreign wars" for a three-year period.**[41]

Toward war's end, the Senate Committee on Finance sought to give the president wide discretion to use a $1.5 million appropriation for fortifications aimed at protecting the United States from possible war with Great Britain and France.[42] Senate debate emphasized Congress's feeling that while it was wise to prepare for future war,[43] it had a certain uneasiness about lodging discretion with the president over a decision that rested with Congress,††[44] and the House concurred.[45]

Congress's delegation of much of its power over conscription automatically enlarged Lincoln's war power by expanding the immediacy of his authority. Lawmakers questioned more the extent of the delegation rather than whether it could be made. For example, Delaware Senator James Bayard criticized the terms of a conscription bill (S. 511), calling

---

back away from war gracefully. See *Papers Relating to the Foreign Relations of the United States 1861–1931,* 14–17. *See also* discussion *infra* p. 209 describing in detail the executive-congressional handling of this matter.

*Issue of letters of marque and reprisal was considered at least the equivalent of an onset of imperfect war. By the time of the Civil War, some senators considered the practice outmoded. 32 *Congressional Globe* 3325. *See* Lofgren, "War Making under the Constitution," p. 672.

†*See* Sofaer, *Origins* 163, 270–72. *See also* discussion of marque and reprisal during the Jackson administration, *supra* Chapter 1, p. 56 n.

**The original bill had been revised by the Senate Committee on Naval Affairs, and what Senator Sumner termed the most obnoxious part of the bill, entrusting to the president "the power to declare war," was cut out. 33 *Congressional Globe* 221. However, when a version similar to the original was revived and passed, Charles Sumner only managed to limit it to a three-year life. *Id.* 1026.

††It was not until April 1866 that legislation was enacted authorizing the president to transfer a gunboat to Liberia and the secretary of the navy to negotiate a contract for payment (36 *Congressional Globe* 1730, 1796, 1817), thus asserting congressional power to withhold consent from possible executive attempts to intervene in the affairs of other states. In 1981, Congress exercised its authority to control executive foreign policy objectives when committees in both houses voted to impose restrictions on military aid to El Salvador. Despite President Reagan's disapproval, Congress's restrictions specifically required the executive to certify as a condition of transfer of materials that the Salvadorean government was willing to negotiate a political settlement with its opposition. *The New York Times,* 13 May 1981, at A–8.

the right to fix the number of men to be called out a matter of "high discretion" beyond Congress's power to delegate.[46] Most members agreed that if Congress possessed the power to raise and support armies, it also had the authority to judge and devise the *manner* in which they were raised,[47] and the bill passed both houses rather easily.[48] When it was proposed, however, that the president alone be empowered to set regulations for enrolling and drafting state militia and to fix their terms of military service,[49] Senators James Bayard and Virginia's John Carlile (Un.) condemned it* for ignoring the constitutionally-prescribed relation of state militia to federal troops.[50] Bayard claimed that Congress's ultimate regulatory authority was endangered if the president received absolute "power to make your rules and articles of war. . . . "[51] Ohio's John Sherman, on the other hand, asked his colleagues to cease "wrangling," let the president have what he needed to wage war, and leave questions of constitutionality to the judicial process.†[52] A successful motion to recommit the bill to the Committee on Military Affairs for further study resulted in its virtual withdrawal from further consideration in either house.[53]

Failure of Johnson's Attempt to Acquire Reprisal Authority   After the Civil War, President Johnson's administration become concerned with reports of European claims of sovereignty over naturalized American citizens traveling abroad. Alleged British abuses of U.S. citizens came as the result of attempts to control Fenian (Irish Republican) secret society unrest. Yet Irish-Americans who had never been Fenians were imprisoned without charges or trial or acquitted but still kept incarcerated.[54] For several months, the American public remonstrated continuously against these practices, deluging Congress with memorials from thousands of residents of major cities and several state legislatures.[55]

Legislation introduced in 1868 contained provisions for the executive to take extraordinary steps. A revised House bill (H.R. 768) sanctioned a sharply defined addition to presidential authority by allowing the chief executive to suspend commercial relations with an offending nation and permitting him to arrest foreign nationals within the jurisdiction of the United States. It passed in the House on 20 April 1868 (104 to 4).[56] The Senate then substituted a new section that simply allowed the president to use means short of war to effect release of any imprisoned or detained U.S. citizens in violation of U.S. law.[57] Significantly, the chief executive

*S. 493, considered in February 1863.
†By the end of the Civil War, debate on draft-related measures usually related to procedural concerns. *E.g.*, provisions relating to persons refusing to enroll or to state quotas. 35 *Congressional Globe* 974ff., 1155.

was to communicate to Congress any such incidents and efforts made on American citizens' behalf.

The bill's reprisal provision drew criticism. New Hampshire Senator James Patterson believed that empowering the president to make reprisal emulated the worst in British conduct.[58] Charles Sumner of Massachusetts agreed that seizure of innocent foreign nationals was "barbarous" and a degradation of the U.S. position, as well as a flagrant violation of the Constitution by conferring powers on the president tantamount to a declaration of war.* Some critics, such as George Williams (R. Ore.), felt the bill did not go far enough—that it should require the president to use whatever means were necessary to secure a citizen's release rather than rely upon his discretionary authority.[59]

Proponents of delegation of the reprisal authority, however, such as California's John Conness, dismissed fears of war. Conness, a naturalized Irish emigrant, stated that the statute was intended only to provide protection for U.S. citizens and was not a war proposal.[60] Neither Conness nor Nevada Senator William Stewart believed that war could come if the president was firm,[61] though they felt that no conflict would be more justifiable than one resulting from reprisals taken on behalf of U.S. citizens.[62] However, the Senate amendment passed without inclusion of the reprisal authority or power to suspend commercial relations, on 25 July 1868 (39 to 5),[63] and the House voted to concur on the same day.[64] The vague language that made it the president's "duty" to use "such means not amounting to acts of war" thus appeared to accommodate both the bold and the fearful.

Control of Information

Challenge to Executive Responses   When Congress made information requests, it often sought to avoid confrontation by adding the qualification that the president should transmit whatever he could, compatible with the public interest. On 17 December 1857, Senator William H. Seward (R. N.Y.) requested documents supporting claims by subjects of France and Great Britain for damages alleged to have been sustained at the bombardment of Greytown.†[65] President Buchanan quickly satisfied this request plus several unqualified resolutions regarding the affairs of the Kansas Territory, and there was no complaint that any important document had been withheld.[66] But Buchanan's recommendation for Kansas statehood on the basis of the Lecompton Con-

---

*Sumner also indicated that the British Foreign Ministry showed indications of willingness to accept the U.S. position on naturalization in order to eliminate all misunderstanding. 39 *Congressional Globe* 4205.

†*See supra* p. 165.

stitution[67] provoked a bitter review of his role in the Kansas ordeal. The president was accused by Massachusetts Representative Henry L. Dawes of having attempted to force an unwanted proslavery constitution on the citizens "at the point of the bayonet."[68] George W. Palmer (R. N.Y.) recommended impeachment for an executive who covered messages to Congress with "sophistry" and "perversion of fact" while suppressing the truth of actual conditions. Specifically, he accused Buchanan of misrepresenting communications from the former governors of Kansas and of concealing information by selecting extracts from letters of Governors Walker and Stanton written at a time, "as they themselves say, when they were ill-informed of the condition of affairs," while he "studiously" suppressed "their later communications, made at a period immediately connected with the history of the Lecompton constitution."[69] Palmer did not divulge the nature of the purported omissions and suppressions, and Congress dropped the subject.

President Lincoln was rarely accused of being deliberately and unwarrantedly evasive. On 2 December 1861, however, New York Congressman Roscoe Conkling obtained passage of a resolution requesting the secretary of war to report to the House* whether "any, and if any, what measures have been taken to ascertain" who was responsible for a "disastrous" battle at Ball's Bluff.†[70] Conkling included no inference that any kind of investigation was intended; nevertheless, the War Department replied that this inquiry would "at this time be injurious to the public service."[71] Conkling complained on 6 January 1862 that the response from the secretary of war** was "wholly evasive and nonresponsive to the resolution." He explained that his request demanded no specifics and was a simple device to learn what, if any, internal investigations were being undertaken to discover the reasons for the Union's severe defeat. He succeeded in obtaining House passage of a second resolution demanding a more responsive answer,[72] but this resolution elicited stiff debate. Kentucky's John Crittenden felt that the

---

*Representative Clement Vallandingham (D. Okla.) was opposed to this and to Conkling's subsequent request, on the ground that by requesting instead of demanding the desired information from an executive department, Conkling impliedly had compromised a principle that the House had established by an 1820 rule that heads of departments were to be peremptorily ordered to furnish information. Vallandingham stated that the earlier House rule was based on the belief that "the Executive Departments, being created by Congress, and so far its creatures, are therefore subject to its supervision and control." 32 *Congressional Globe* 194.

†In October 1861, Union troops were defeated at this engagement along the Potomac near Washington, D.C. Charges of mismanagement leveled at General McClellan had far-reaching effects: a Committee on the Conduct of the War was created and "[a] fatal hesitation took possession of McClellan." W. Andrews, ed., *Concise Dictionary of American History* 81 (1962).

**Secretary of War Simon Cameron's reply of 12 December 1861 transmitted a report from the adjutant general that purported to respond to the request of 2 December. 32 *Congressional Globe* 191.

executive and not Congress had the immediate duty to investigate mismanagement of war, and that if the president failed in this duty, the country and not Congress would hold him responsible.[73] Conkling reiterated that Congress had the right to know simply if something was being done about the military affairs of the nation, and the House concurred by adopting the second resolution, 79 to 54. This time, the secretary of war replied that while measures had been undertaken to ascertain responsibility for the defeat, it was not deemed compatible with the public interest to reveal them.[74]

There was no significant withholding of information in the Johnson administration. Whether qualified or unqualified,* important questions regarding U.S. foreign relations received swift answers.

On one occasion, Johnson boldly replied to a Senate request to be informed whether the president had established any new military department since 1 August 1867.[75] He stated that he had established a military department of Alaska and a military division of the Atlantic. The president claimed that his authority for such action was long-established usage under the president's power as commander-in-chief, in addition to the unchallenged custom adhered to by his predecessors.[76] This response was referred to the Committee on Military Affairs and was not further discussed during Johnson's term of office.[77]

Attempts to Systematize the Search for Information   Congress took an exceptionally meticulous interest in the details of the Civil War hostilities.[78] Lawmakers made far fewer inquiries into foreign affairs, however, than at any other wartime period in the nation's history.[79] For example, of approximately thirty-five important requests during the Thirty-seventh Congress relating to both foreign affairs and military operations, only nine bore upon foreign relations.†

Foreign relations requests and queries relating to actual conduct of the war were nearly always qualified,[80] while inquiries of purely routine nature were not** because the information was not expected to be sensitive.[81] Many of the more significant House inquiries related to

*An index of growing congressional discontent with Andrew Johnson was the number of unqualified requests for information—a far greater percentage than in any prior administration. In the Fortieth Congress, there were 118 requests, of which 89 were unqualified (75 percent).

†Congressmen were neither ignorant of foreign relations nor reluctant to be well informed. They knew the disaster that foreign intervention could well have posed to the Union cause. The relative paucity of these inquiries is misleading: their broad nature was still specific enough to indicate substantive familiarity with international concerns. Winning the domestic conflict was, however, the obvious goal; thus, Congress acquiesced in the executive administration of foreign relations during the severest testing of domestic military control that the United States had ever experienced.

**The procedure of including or excluding a reservation in the public interest was similar to the pattern followed by the Polk administration (*See* pp. 99ff.).

executive communications with foreign powers regarding the Civil War. Lincoln availed himself of the reservation in the public interest by refusing to provide New York Representative Erastus Corning with information that the president had received from abroad concerning the Civil War. Similarly, he rebuffed Ohio Congressman Samuel S. Cox's request for all correspondence since 1853 regarding U.S. maritime rights.*[82] On the other hand, Wisconsin Senator Timothy Howe asked for instructions concerning the rebellion issued by the executive to foreign ministers;[83] and the president transmitted a report of the secretary of state.[84] He also replied to a House request for information dealing with the intentions of European powers to establish a monarchy in Mexico[85] and then forwarded the same data to the Senate.

Senators made more demands than representatives upon the administration, which responded to some, though not all, important qualified requests. Lincoln communicated more substantive information voluntarily in one congressional session† than had any previous executive. All but three voluntary transmittals concerned the *Trent* affair.[86] One such release of information consisted of correspondences between the secretaries of state and war and the governor of Maine[87] concerning the status of northern defenses. Another dealt with the seizure of the Spanish barque *Providencia* by a federal blockading vessel.**[88] Lincoln, however, refused to send over the correspondence of certain army officers.[89] He did not reply either to Senator Charles Sumner's request for State Department correspondence on the subject of neutral rights since the Congress of Paris (1856)[90] or to a demand for orders of the executive to General George McClellan to advance to Richmond.

Lincoln, as did others preceding him, was willing to respond in executive session as a means of insuring secrecy during ongoing negotiations.†† A single unqualified resolution relating to U.S.-Paraguayan relations was passed in executive session, to which the president replied in the same manner.[91] Since queries for sensitive information almost

---

*The United States had abrogated the Reciprocity Treaty of 1854 with England, ending certain U.S. fishing privileges. *Infra* p. 210 n. Bailey, *A Diplomatic History of the American People* 383. Lincoln announced to Congress on 19 July 1861 that the British minister in Washington had proposed a joint commission to inquire into the development and preservation of Canadian fisheries and requested Congress to permit executive appointment of a commission to represent the United States (31 *Congressional Globe* 215), but further diplomatic complexities arising between England and the United States during the Civil War period were to postpone any material attempt to deal with the fisheries question.

†37th Cong., 1st Sess.

**Hostilities were averted by the passage of legislation awarding compensation to the owners of the *Providencia* for her wrongful seizure and detention. 32 *Congressional Globe* 1230, 1967.

††*See* Sofaer, *Origins* 246–48, for discussion of executive and congressional efforts to devise a system for dealing with confidentiality.

invariably contained the public interest reservation, he did not have to ignore a request in order to withhold data he felt should not be divulged. Thus, whether consciously or not, Congress generally did not press Lincoln into a position from which he could not extricate himself gracefully.*

Congress has consistently manifested concern when the executive has withheld information either because he has claimed that the legislature was not entitled to ask for it or when he has maintained executive privilege. Its usual practice during Lincoln's tenure was to attempt to obtain compliance by making a second request. Follow-up requests were also made occasionally when an initial reply was regarded as inadequate.†

Partial responses tended to suggest that the president was manipulating the reply. When Senator Benjamin Wade (R. Oh.) requested correspondence between the secretary of state and the Mexican minister regarding suspected trade in contraband between the United States and France while France was at war with Mexico,[92] his colleagues received only "a partial report" from the secretary of state. Only Charles Sumner saw the documents, as chairman of the Senate Foreign Relations Committee. The administration's aim seemed to be to delay or to shelve publication at the same time as it appeared to satisfy the request by supplying information only to the committee's chairman. Further discussion on the papers' disposition elicited Wade's comment that no committee had the sole "right to investigate these public documents that are called out by a Senator, and at their election suppress them altogether" or to use the plea that economy prevented them from being printed and disseminated.[93]

Efforts to Investigate the Executive Congress attempted to use its investigative process to control the executive departments as well as in order to elicit information relating to warfare and foreign affairs. One of

---

*There were a few exceptions. On 18 February 1863, the Senate made an unqualified request for a copy of Major General John Pope's report on operations of the Army of Virginia—obviously sensitive material—which was not supplied. 33 *Congressional Globe* 1066 (no reply). Similarly, an unqualified request for all correspondence regarding the Army of the Potomac—an enormous quantity of documentation—brought no response. *Id.* 16. He did bow to two Senate demands for complex financial information to be delivered within three weeks of the request, and the Secretary of the Treasury replied in four days. 35 *Congressional Globe* 360–61 (requests of 23 January 1865 sponsored by Henry Winston (R. Mass.) concerning internal revenue collections and deposits in national banks, answered 27 January).

†Senator Lyman Trumbull complained about the increase in second resolutions resulting from departmental "disregard" of the first calls for information, even when requests were based on statutes making the supply of such information mandatory. *Id.* 269–70. Examples of follow-up requests included unqualified demands for names and numbers of brigadier generals. 33 *Congressional Globe* 16; *id.* 465 (reply); *id.* 466; *id.* 607 (reply).

the most important examples of conflict over this process occurred
during Buchanan's administration. Congressman John Covode* (R.
Pa.) introduced a resolution on 5 March 1860 alleging that President
Buchanan had used improper influence to obtain passage of a Kansas
statehood bill.†94

Several congressmen accused the president of using both patronage
and money to help enact Representative William English's bill** upholding the Lecompton constitution.95 John Hickman (D. Pa.) stated that
Buchanan tried to "purchase" him by "offering more than I am worth"
but that he had "refused to sell . . ."†† Similarly, John Haskin (D. N.Y.)
and Garnett Adrain (D. N.J.) each alleged that he was approached with
promises and threats intended to win favor for the administration.96
Buchanan flatly denied that any corrupt proposition had emanated
from him "to any human being."97 Nonetheless, the House adopted
Covode's vaguely worded resolution, calling for both examination of
executive influence "for or against the passage of any law appertaining
to the rights of any State or Territory" as well as an inquiry into
"whether the President has failed or refused to compel the execution of
any law . . ."98

Buchanan strongly believed that impeachment was the sole process
for dealing with cognizable wrongs of a president. Consequently, he
objected to formation of the Covode Committee, which was not an
impeachment organ, and to the accusatorial, as opposed to the remedial,
portions of the resolutions. Investigations for the purpose of remedying
public agencies' abuses were remedial and, therefore, permissible:

> The House of Representatives possess no power under the Constitution over
> the first or accusatory portion of the resolution, except as an impeaching
> body; whilst over the last, in common with the Senate, their authority as a
> legislative body is . . . admitted.99

Citing the impeachment of Judge Peck*** as a valuable precedent,
Buchanan contended that certain procedural safeguards employed in

*The Covode Committee was initiated mainly by House Republicans in 1860 in order to
investigate alleged misconduct practiced by the executive branch.
†See supra p. 183.
**William H. English (D. Ind.) played a leading part in producing a compromise on the
issue of Kansas's admission that passed Congress but eventually proved unacceptable to
the Kansas voters. His bill in effect offered the people of Kansas a bribe of public land
amounting to five million acres if they would ratify the proslavery Lecompton constitution.
††Hickman was alluding to the fact that executive power in the form of denunciations
and denial of patronage were used to procure his adherence to administration measures
and undermine his support for anti-Lecompton policies. 29 Congressional Globe 119.
***James Hawkins Peck, a Missouri federal district judge, was impeached but finally
acquitted for punishing an attorney who published a criticism of one of Peck's opinions.
James Buchanan, as a member of the House, prosecuted Judge Peck before the Senate in a

that case were completely lacking in the proposed investigation. He objected specifically to the presence of one of his accusers on the committee and the vagueness of the charges.[100] Although procedural due process was imprecisely framed in the U.S. Constitution, Buchanan considered that it was guaranteed at least to some degree in an impeachment proceeding. He espoused as being equally applicable to the chief executive as to any accused, both the rights to know and to answer the specific charges against him in order to prepare an adequate defense and also to establish a fair mode of procedure.[101] Moreover, if House committees could engage in multifarious investigations of the executive, thus involving themselves intimately in the direction of both foreign and domestic affairs, Buchanan feared the undermining of executive independence.[102]

John Sherman (D. Oh.) objected to Buchanan's claim of immunity from the proposed broad investigation.[103] He questioned how it was possible to impeach an officer without at first having preliminary proof of the fact that he had violated his duties. Taking of testimony was the only way to get an insight into the gravity of what could be involved, although, as Burton Craige (D. N.C.) subsequently indicated, Buchanan was concerned with the mode of this particular investigation and not with the act of inquiry itself.[104]

The matter was submitted to the House Committee on the Judiciary,[105] which dissented from Buchanan's message of 28 March, saying that "the extent of power contemplated in the adoption of the resolution of inquiry is necessary to the proper discharge of the constitutional duties devolved on Congress" and that law, custom, and former presidents' opinions sanctioned its exercise as well as Congress's continued need to supervise executive power.[106] The whole House by a vote of 88 to 40 affirmed the Judiciary Committee's fear that an undue "concentration of power in the hands of the President was dangerous to the rights of a free people."[107]

The Covode Committee then reported on 16 June, submitting both majority and minority reports,[108] but there was neither any discussion of them nor further debate on the substantial issues that had prompted the investigation. Buchanan, in a message on 22 June 1860, claimed a victory, since Covode's Committee had failed either to censure him or to recommend impeachment. The president asserted that his vindication was more complete, in that the committee had not even reported so much as a resolution indicating any departmental abuses that required

---

trial lasting six weeks in 1830–31, losing the case to former Attorney General William Wirt. According to Buchanan, the case established lasting practices aimed at protecting procedural rights and immunities belonging to the executive as well as private individuals. *Id.* 1435.

legislative correction.[109] The fact that the investigation did proceed, however, indicated that Buchanan incorrectly assumed that Congress's sole remedy against suspected presidential wrongdoing was impeachment.

Certain Civil War military disasters[110] inspired several of Roscoe Conkling's colleagues in the House, as well as Senators Henry Wilson (R. Mass.), William Fessenden (R. Me.), and John Sherman (R. Oh.) to call for a joint committee of inquiry into the conduct of the war.[111] This committee was to consist of three senators and four congressmen, who were to sit during sessions of either house and to have the power to send for persons and papers.[112] Wilson expected such a commission to bring "out the facts, pinning responsibility on those deserving of it, and teach the civil and military authorities that they are expected not to make mistakes." Fessenden's and Sherman's position was less pragmatic. Both envisioned Congress as the people's agent, whose function reached a "high duty" of inquiry, not only into the disasters but also the general conduct of the war.[113] In addition, the Senate passed a resolution requesting its Committee on the Conduct of the War to inquire into whether disloyal persons had been employed in the executive branch, but Maryland's Reverdy Johnson helped defeat further consideration of this proposed inquest by saying that the committee's conclusions and recommendations would have no legally binding effect on the executive.

Late in the war, a proposed bill would have required certain Cabinet officers to attend the House and provide information to questions.[114] Representative George Pendleton (Oh.) justified the measure by arguing that Congress as the creator of the departments had power to impose duties upon them.*[115] The bill's sponsor, James A. Garfield (R. Oh.), explained that one reason that members of the Cabinet should attend Congress on a regular basis was that although the executive had promised to have the secretary of war send a report with accompanying documents to update army campaigns since Lincoln's last annual message, five weeks after the close of the session Congress still had not heard from Stanton.[116] If Congress had a right to information, it had the right to institute a process to get it from offices that were dependent on congressional statutes and whose conduct was subject to congressional investigations.[117] The bill was laid aside without action, however, at the close of the session, on 3 March 1865.

---

*Pendleton cited in support that the law organizing the Department of the Treasury in 1789 asserted that by simple resolution the secretary of the treasury could be required to come upon the floor to explain measures he recommended. Similarly, the laws organizing each department required their secretaries to report directly to Congress. He also relied on the implied powers clause of Article I. 35 *Congressional Globe Appendix* 103, 105.

THE CONTROL OF FOREIGN RELATIONS

Executive Initiatives

James Buchanan's restricted view of the executive grants of power under the Constitution resulted in cautious diplomacy. He did not act unilaterally to force events and then later expect Congress to ratify his deeds. Instead, Buchanan preferred to have Congress's prospective authorizations serve not only as a prerequisite to executive action but also as the means of acquiring broad authority derived from his own liberal interpretation of such measures. Using this approach, Buchanan augmented his power with limited success in his administration's foreign affairs initiatives.*

Endeavor to Secure Cuba   Sectional antagonisms and differing interpretations of the allocation of the war powers combined to defeat Buchanan's attempt to secure $30 million† to negotiate with Spain for Cuba. The president disclaimed any intention of annexing Cuba except by treaty but still insisted upon a $30 million appropriation. In his annual message of 6 December 1858, he impliedly acknowledged his partial bypassing of the Senate with this request:

> [T]he large appropriation . . . is especially necessary, as it may become indispensable to success, that I should be entrusted with the means of making an advance to the Spanish Government immediately after the signing of the treaty, without awaiting the ratification of it by the Senate.[118]

Citing the prior appropriation for the Louisiana purchase as a precedent, Buchanan justified his proposal on the ground that it was a defense measure.

> With that island under the dominion of a distant foreign Power, this trade [from the Mississippi] of vital importance to these States, is exposed to the danger of being destroyed in time of war, and it has hitherto been subject to perpetual injury and annoyance in time of peace.[119]

Thus, the president's request seemed to be grounded upon the right to

---

*Despite Buchanan's own estimate that his conduct of foreign relations met "with great and uncommon success," there were no truly noteworthy diplomatic accomplishments during his administration. 12 Buchanan, *Works* 236ff.

†Sponsored by John Slidell (S.R.D. La.), S. 497 was introduced on 10 January 1859. 28 *Congressional Globe* 277.

take necessary steps to avoid war, an emergency measure that was at least an adjunct to the more conventional treatymaking procedures.

Initially, the bill received a favorable review from the reporting committees. It merely provided for "making an appropriation for the acquisition of the Island of Cuba by negotiation."[120] The House Foreign Affairs Committee reported a similar bill.[121] Neither the House nor Senate version mentioned any possible conflicts with the treatymaking power. Ostensibly, they represented the committee's decisions to ignore constitutional objections and maintain a peaceful* attitude toward Spain.

Legislators soon debated the constitutional merits of these bills. In favoring the appropriation measure, Senator Robert Toombs (S.R.D. Ga.) emphasized that the bill avoided the twin problems of prospectively ratifying a treaty and thereby unconstitutionally delegating the whole treatymaking power to the president. He urged the Senate only to consider whether

> the amount is so great ... that we are unwilling to ... risk ... the loss of $30,000,000, rather than enable the President, in the use of his constitutional power (for he alone can address foreign nations), to inaugurate a system of negotiation by which he hopes to acquire Cuba.[122]
> ... The Executive believes ... that to have a portion of the price in hand ... will be advantageous to the happy termination of a treaty. ... If this be so, I will consent to let him have it.[123]

Reports in both Houses† suggested that this bill lay within the shadowy constitutional area where Congress could not refuse to act:

> He [the President] takes occasion to repeat what he said in his annual message, that it is highly important, if not indispensable to the success of any negotiation for the purchase, that the measure should receive the previous sanction of Congress.
> This emphatic reiteration of his previous recommendation throws upon

---

*Representative Anderson's (Mo.) more belligerent measure was not incorporated into the committee's version. *Id.* 297. But perhaps the most bellicose of all was Senator Jefferson Davis's ultimatum (expressed in a resolution of 22 December 1858 that was not adopted) calling upon the president to take possession of Cuba within six months unless satisfaction of $128,635 in U.S. citizens' claims and appropriate apologies for injuries suffered were rendered to the government of the United States. *Id.* 185.

†The Senate committee report strongly suggested that Congress had an obligation to defer to the president in foreign affairs when neither war nor the immediate ratification of a treaty was involved. Even if this duty derived only from politics, it displayed a contemporaneous notion of the proper allocation of power between the two branches. The reports gave the president the primary role in determining foreign policy, with Congress obliged to facilitate the executive's plans. The House report appears at 28 *Congressional Globe Appendix* 96–100.

Congress the responsibility of failure if withheld. Indeed, the inference is sufficiently clear that, without some expression of opinion by Congress, the President will not feel justified in renewing negotiations.[124]

Supporters of the bill cited historical precedents. The Senate Committee report referred to the purchase of Louisiana and Florida and the conclusion of the Mexican War:

[W]e have three different acts upon the statute book, placing large sums of money at the disposition of the President for the purpose of aiding him in negotiations for the acquisition of territory.[125]

Opponents, however, analyzed the extent to which it was mandated by an emergency or other extraordinary situation. Due to Louisiana's proximity and England's historical threat to seize it, Congressman H.E. Royce (R. Vt.) and Senator John J. Crittenden (Un. Ky.) argued that the welfare of the United States had required the acquisition of Louisiana, while annexation of Cuba was less critical to national security.[126] Crittenden, fearing that an appropriation of $30 million would serve as a precedent for large appropriations in unexceptional circumstances, expressed his unwillingness to allow the president to dominate foreign policy, particularly in areas in which Congress has legitimate authority to act.*[127]

Some legislators were concerned that if the Senate voted for the bill, but subsequently desired to disapprove of the treaty, rejection could prove difficult after such a large outlay during negotiations. Buchanan might attempt to coerce the Senate into ratifying it by pointing to the encouragement that he had received to embark upon the negotiation and the monies already expended. Thus, the principle of checks and balances so integral to the American system would be scrapped, and the bill could threaten the Senate's role in conducting foreign affairs.

Senator William H. Seward was among those dissatisfied with a shift in power to the executive in the treatymaking† as well as the appropria-

---

*Senator John Bell (Wh. Tenn.), Congressman Royce, and Senator Crittenden made a distinction between Buchanan's request and those of Polk and Jefferson. Although Jefferson received $2 million to negotiate the Louisiana purchase, the funds were appropriated secretly. The sum of $3 million to enable Polk to effect a peace with Mexico was voted during a war. 28 *Congressional Globe* 1342. Much of Bell's objection reflected his conviction that Cuba was not worth acquiring; but he also spoke vehemently against the proposal of both the president and the Senate Foreign Relations Committee to "surrender . . . the war-making power to the President." *Id.* 1345.

†Seward's argument that a congressional appropriation enabling the president to acquire land by treaty constituted an abandonment by the Senate of its treatymaking power found no acceptance in Toombs, for whom earlier historical examples of acquiring a country by purchase were a "conceded point in our public policy" and had not been

tions arenas. If the president could justify a request for money to conduct foreign relations as unrefusable, Congress's power over the purse was correspondingly decreased. Moreover, this measure was one of a series of legislative requests which promised to erode congressional power. Seward remarked:

> One ... proposes that Congress shall authorize the President to move the Army and the Navy ... into ... Mexico and establish a protectorate there. Another asks our consent to invest the President ... with the power to make war in his own discretion ... against ... nearly all ... the Spanish-American States on this continent.[128]

Since Spain long had opposed ceding Cuba, some legislators viewed encouragement of negotiations to purchase Cuba as tantamount to giving Buchanan discretion to initiate hostilities. Although Congress might intend only peaceful negotiations for the purchase of Cuba, Senator James Dixon (R. Conn.) suggested that Buchanan could utilize the money to involve the nation in an undeclared war:

> [H]e says he will avenge the wrongs which he claims are constantly committed against citizens of this country, whether the power is given to him by Congress or not. ... I should not dare to trust the President ... with the power of using $30,000,000 in this manner. Taking his own language, I should expect him to involve the country in war.*[129]

Attempt to Abrogate the Clayton-Bulwer Treaty   Anxious to substitute American for European influence in Central America, Buchanan embarked on a vigorous foreign policy in the Southern Hemisphere. Despite his diplomatic experience as minister to Russia and Great Britain and secretary of state under Polk, Buchanan failed in these initiatives, but a mediocre treaty record did not terminate his involvement in Central American affairs. What he failed to achieve through negotiation, he sought to obtain by threats of reprisals to avenge attacks on American lives and property. Unwilling to effectuate his plans only on his own authority, he requested prior congressional authorization. Despite some strong support in Congress, however, Buchanan failed

---

accomplished in derogation of any of the Senate's rights. *Id.* 541. Senator Trusten Polk (D. Mo.) also cited the acquisition of Louisiana, Florida, and some Mexican territory as precedents for the appropriation of funds to negotiate the purchase by the United States of foreign lands, contending that these activities violated "no provision of the Constitution." *Id.* 1085, 1086.

*Buchanan could have engineered a war, however, without maneuvering any congressional appropriation. Dixon's position did not receive substantial support in Congress and seems to represent more a partisan attack than a valid constitutional objection.

largely because of fears of the expansion of slavery and of an unconstitutional delegation of Congress's power to declare war.

President Buchanan and many legislators believed the abrogation of the Clayton-Bulwer treaty* would establish and maintain U.S. rights-of-way across the Central American isthmus. Such rights were to be guaranteed, if necessary, by U.S. troops. Yet Congress was unwilling to initiate overtly hostile legislation because of its belief that the decision to abrogate a treaty vested in the president† as part of his foreign affairs power, as well as owing to a fear of retarding the negotiations and initiating a war. Congressional debates focused upon the proper role for Congress to assume in the administration's decision to abrogate a treaty.

House resolutions proposing that the president take steps to terminate the treaty[130] were attacked as interfering with the treatymaking power vested in the president and Senate. In May 1858, Representative Henry W. Davis (Natl. Am. Md.) construed treaty abrogation by Congress as containing an implied "declaration of war."[131] His colleague, Daniel E. Sickles (D. N.Y.) concurred, denying to the House any role in deciding to terminate a treaty, unless it was grounded upon one of Congress's own powers.

Not all congressmen agreed with a limited conception of the House's power. John A. Quitman (D. Miss.) construed the resolution as expressing the sense of the House on a matter of foreign affairs. By this interpretation, he virtually could include any consideration of a treaty's operation as falling within the House's power to mold foreign policy:

> [T]his House has as much right under the Constitution, in shaping the great foreign policy of this country, to express its views, as any other department of the Government.[132]

But the effort to abrogate was defeated.**[133]

Search for Authorization to Use Force in Central America and the Caribbean Having failed to obtain treaties that would have given the United States more of a political and economic foothold in Central

---

*See supra pp. 109–11.

†Buchanan suggested abrogation to avoid friction. Letter, Buchanan to Lord Clarendon (3 April 1859), 10 Buchanan, *Works* 316. Although he brought the problem to Congress's attention, Buchanan privately assured Lord Napier, the British minister at Washington, that he merely wanted official assurance that the British government would settle Central American questions in accordance with U.S. construction of the Treaty. 6 Bemis, The *American Secretaries of State and Their Diplomacy* 308.

**Ultimately, the controversy was settled amicably when Britain and the two Central American states negotiated treaties embracing the spirit of the U.S. construction of the Clayton-Bulwer treaty. *Id.*

America,* President Buchanan during 1858 and 1859 sought congressional authorization to use force in order to redress U.S. "grievances." In a message of December 1858 to Congress, he justified including prior military authorizations in the Nicaraguan treaty as a deterrent to so-called hostile parties who theoretically could commit aggression along the transit route. But President Buchanan realistically judged that actual U.S. military intervention would probably never occur.[134]

Buchanan's statements reveal his narrow concept of the scope of presidential war powers. While he acknowledged that he could not constitutionally implement the treaty provision obligating use of U.S. troops to employ force in Nicaragua, he conceded that should an exigency develop, he would be obliged to employ force. To avoid possible abuse of his power or even impeachment, Buchanan urged Congress to grant him a large degree of discretion† in resorting to force, accompanied by such restrictions as it felt were necessary:

> The executive goverment ... is limited to the employment of diplomacy alone. ... It cannot legitimately resort to force, without the direct authority of Congress except in resisting and repelling hostile attacks. It would have no authority to enter ... Nicaragua, even to prevent the destruction of the transit, and protect the lives and property of our own citizens on their passage. It is true, that on a sudden emergency of this character, the President would direct any armed force in the vicinity to march to their relief; but in doing this he would act upon his responsibility.[135]

Buchanan believed that the president could use force only prophylactically. Thus, he considered deployment of the navy in the Gulf of Mexico only in order to deter British attacks to be the fullest exercise of his constitutional powers. Although presidential use of the military to protect U.S. citizens could be construed as an action short of war, Buchanan thought that legislative authorization of executive action constituted a proper exercise of congressional war powers:

> The Executive Governments of ... other countries, possessing the warmaking power, can promptly employ the necessary means to enforce immediate redress for similar outrages upon their subjects. Not so the

---

*As an example, in the fall of 1857, President Buchanan had presented to the Senate the Cass-Yrissari treaty with Nicaragua—an executive version of constructive abrogation—which maintained U.S. rights-of-way across the Central American Isthmus to be guaranteed by armed forces. The Senate defeated this treaty, finding that its authorization of U.S. forces' occupation was in sharp conflict with Clayton-Bulwer's prohibition against any such occupation. This was a greater blow to Buchanan than the House failure to pass a resolution favoring abrogation, since it thwarted his attempt to gain a route across the Isthmus.

†He repeated this request on 18 February 1859. 28 *Congressional Globe* 1118.

Buchanan's Secretary of State Lewis Cass's policies in Mexico and Cuba were
frustrated (pp. 178, 194). But he did secure from Great Britain abandonment of
all claims to a right of visit and search of American vessels. (L.C.)

Executive Government of the United States. . . . He cannot, without transcending his constitutional power, direct a gun to be fired into a port, or land a seaman or marine, to protect the lives of our countrymen on shore or to obtain redress for a recent outrage on their property.[136]

Buchanan explained that he sought authority merely to conduct limited hostility, not war, whereas Congress's war power was much more general and could even include ordering the president to seize a citizen's illegally captured vessel:

[C]an Congress act only after the fact . . . ? . . . To confer this authority to meet future cases, under circumstances strictly specified, is as clearly within the war-declaring power . . . as such an authority conferred upon the President by act of Congress after the deed has been done.*[137]

Controversy began over two bills introduced in 1858.† Stephen A. Douglas (D. Ill.) sponsored a bill authorizing the president to use force without consulting Congress "under circumstances requiring prompt redress."[138] A Committee on Foreign Relations' substitute applied solely to certain Central American countries.[139] Douglas, however, clearly aimed his bill at Great Britain and "cases of flagrant violations of the law of nations, under circumstances admitting of no delay."[140] The more encompassing committee version authorized a preventative utilization of force as well as the repulsion of future attacks. It reflected a belief that if such an enactment applied to Great Britain, war might result, while weaker Central American countries would not so easily undertake a hostile response. By applying to nonemergency situations, the committee bill also gave the president a greater latitude to use force.

Both Douglas and the Committee on Foreign Relations denied that their bills delegated or exercised the power to declare war.[141] But opponents of the Douglas resolution argued that its possible application to European nations constituted an excessive delegation of Congress's power to declare war. Like the president, they characterized the Douglas bill as a "war measure." For example, Senator Lyman Trumbull asserted that Congress could only exercise its warmaking power after the provocative event occurred. "[I]f, when we investigate our difficulties with England, there is a cause for war, let us declare it. . . ."[142]

---

*Although Buchanan asserted that Congress previously had granted several prior authorizations, he chose a precedent from his own administration, the Paraguayan resolution (*infra* p. 231) to illustrate the point.

†A third version of the prospective authorization bill was introduced by Senator James S. Green (D. Mo.). He distinguished between perfect and imperfect wars, suggesting that Congress could allow the president to wage only the latter prospectively since it was "a thing not contemplated under the Constitution. . . ." 27 *Congressional Globe* 2748.

Neither bill came to a vote, in spite of its supporters' eloquence.[143] The Paraguayan incident* probably contributed to Congress's refusal to accede to Buchanan's request, since it had demonstrated that Congress could lose control over future military events:

> [I]t was said . . . that it [the Paraguayan resolution] really amounted to nothing: that all the President desired was to send a single vessel. . . . [W]e know now . . . that . . . an expedition has been sent out for the purpose of bringing Paraguay to terms, consisting of some twenty vessels, . . . of which we really know nothing as to what are its ultimate intentions.[144]

Maine Senator Fessenden perceived that a prospective authorization, while perhaps permitting the president to act more effectively, increased the possibility that he would present the Congress with an unanticipated *fait accompli:* "We are the power to judge when the contingency arises, and whether there shall be war or not."[145]

Senator Jefferson Davis's (D. Miss.) opposition signaled the ultimate failure of Buchanan's policy. The resolutions, for Davis, emasculated Congress and centralized too much power in one individual:

> Every step the Congress takes in renunciation of the power vested in them by the Constitution, and lodging it in the hands, and subject to the discretion of any man, is a step taken in the road to despotism.[146]

Davis was nominally a strong administration supporter, but a northern Republican could easily have made the same statement. It summarized many legislators' suspicions of Buchanan's motives in Central America and denoted the prematurity of certain of his requests. Yet aside from Republican animadversions to Buchanan that in part rendered his domestic program ineffective, Congress was at least willing to consider prior authorization as a means of allocating the war powers between the two branches. It heralded the distributive shift that would be attempted and exercised in the future.

Seward's Plan for Reunion   President Lincoln and Secretary of State William H. Seward used executive power to direct foreign affairs by initiating events that could have led to a foreign war without the knowledge of the Cabinet or Congress. Only a few days before the outbreak of the Civil War, Seward planned a final attempt to reunite the nation by proposing to draw attention to Spanish government

---

Infra p. 229. An unprovoked Paraguayan attack on the SS *Water Witch* as it was performing scientific experiments on the La Plata River culminated in the passage of a resolution prospectively authorizing the president to use force to attack an aggressor.

activities in the Caribbean. He had been notified by the U.S. consul general at Havana that Spain had sent a war vessel to take over Santo Domingo and that additional support troops from Spain and Cuba were underway. Secretary Seward interpreted this Santo Domingo expedition as part of a larger plan for Spanish acquisition of Mexico. Believing that the South would support a Caribbean war in their drive to expand southward,[147] Seward presented a plan to Lincoln that emphasized strengthening the Gulf forts. Lincoln responded affirmatively: "The news ... in regard to Santo Domingo certainly brings a new item within the range of our foreign policy."[148] Lincoln ordered Seward to give the plan to General Winfield Scott: "Tell him that I wish this thing done, and not to let it fail. ..."[149]

Orders were drafted for the president to sign on 1 April 1861, without the knowledge of the secretaries of the navy and war.* They directed the commandant of the navy yard at New York to fit out the warship *Powhatan* for Lieutenant David Porter to command on a secret service mission that "you will under no circumstance communicate to the Navy Department."[150] Another order summarily removed Captain Mercer from command of the *Powhatan*. General Winfield Scott and Seward immediately conferred on the exact nature of instructions to be given,[151] and orders quickly followed designed to strengthen the Gulf forts.† Lincoln also directed Seward to furnish Captain Meigs $10,000 from the secret-service fund.[152]

Seward lost no time warning the Spanish minister at Washington, Gabriel Garcia Tassara, that the United States regarded Spain's expedition to Santo Domingo "as a first step in a policy of armed intervention ... in the American countries which once constituted Spanish America. ..." He added that any further prosecution of the enterprise in regard to the Dominican Republic, or any part of the American continent, would be met with "prompt, persistent, and, if possible, effective resistance."[153] The secretary of state hoped that the series of events that would unfold would bring a direct confrontation with Spain, but he recognized that there was no way to require the Home Squadron

---

*Captain M.C. Meigs and Lieutenant David Porter drafted the orders. Besides Meigs and Porter, only General Winfield Scott, his military secretary, Colonel E.D. Keyes, and, of course, Seward and Lincoln knew about them. 3 J. Nicolay and J. Hay, *Abraham Lincoln: A History* 436 (1890).

†Porter was ordered to proceed to Pensacola harbor and prevent "any expedition from the mainland reaching Fort Pickens or Santa Rosa." Scott then obtained Lincoln's approval of an order directing Captain Harvey Brown of the army to take command of the expedition. Brown was to secure Fort Pickens from attack as well as to make Fort Jefferson in the Dry Tortugas his principal base of operations. The "fortresses in the Florida Reef" were "deemed of even greater importance than Fort Pickens." 4 Naval Records Office, *Official Records of the Union and Confederate Navies in the War of the Rebellion* 107, 108 (1896).

to remain at Vera Cruz or return to it without Secretary of the Navy Gideon Welles's knowledge.

Seward also got Lincoln to sign a confidential instruction sent on 1 April to Secretary Welles ordering him to despatch Captain G.J. Pendergrast to Vera Cruz* with the Home Squadron.[154] Welles's own recitation of the exact language of the order was that he was instructed to have Pendergrast "remain in observation at Vera Cruz."[155] Only Welles knew that Pendergrast was actually at Norfolk, Virginia, for repairs,[156] whereas the draftsmen of the order, as well as perhaps even Lincoln, believed Pendergrast's squadron still to be in the Gulf of Mexico. Welles swiftly confronted the president and reportedly protested that he needed Pendergrast for other duties.†[157] Lincoln immediately backed down and informed him that he could disregard the order.[158] But Lincoln did not tell Welles that he had sent other instructions to the commandant of the New York navy yard that same day. Ignorant of the president's intended use of the *Powhatan* and dismissal of Captain Mercer as its commander, four days later Welles ordered the *Powhatan* under Mercer to proceed to Charleston harbor to reinforce Fort Sumter. Welles subsequently related that he had read aloud to Lincoln the instructions he prepared concerning Mercer and the *Powhatan* and that the president had approved them.[159] When the conflicting instructions required clarification, however, both Seward and Welles went to an embarrassed Lincoln, who then ordered Seward to restore the *Powhatan* to Mercer, so that "on no account . . . the Sumter expedition [should] fail or be interfered with."[160] Seward reluctantly obeyed, but when he sent the new instructions, Lieutenant Porter refused to acknowledge Seward's authority or obey the countermand, stating he was operating under presidential orders. Porter then proceeded in accordance with his original instructions to strengthen Fort Pickens, one of the Gulf forts.[161]

Seward underestimated the determination of the secessionist movement and was misled by his own belief that Lincoln was incapable of leadership. His plan thus failed. It was abandoned on 5 April 1861 and did not surface again after the outbreak of the Civil War.[162] Historians

---

*Benito Juarez's government in Mexico had its headquarters in Vera Cruz, and the State Department had information that Spain would commence its military operations in Mexico against Juarez. 7 Bemis, *The American Secretaries of State and Their Diplomacy* 33.

†Welles made no mention of requiring Pendergrast's presence elsewhere in his *Diary*. Professor Bemis cites as his authority an article in *Galaxy* magazine of November 1870. *Id.* 33. The underlying reason for Welles's obvious dismay at administration tactics was Lincoln's circumventing his secretary of the navy and using subordinate officers to draft orders, many of which, according to Welles, Lincoln admitted he did not read before signing.

have ventured the suggestion that Lincoln did not share his secretary of state's singleminded purpose to create a foreign war in order to unite North and South but saw it as a venture in foreign affairs clearly secondary in importance to the strengthening of Fort Sumter. Thus, Welles's declaration that other duties required Commodore Pendergrast's attention appeared to bear equal weight with the Santo Domingo expedition in the president's final decision.[163] Seward's biographer Frederick Bancroft believed that Lincoln signed his orders without taking time to consider their meaning but subsequently was led to repudiate whatever interfered with the Fort Sumter expedition.[164] The record clearly indicates Lincoln's acute embarrassment at being caught in an apparent effort to undermine his own Cabinet. Another ship might easily have replaced the *Powhatan* in the Sumter mission, but Lincoln obviously chose not to do so and risk further detailing his unorthodox behavior. Only the pressing circumstances of national self-defense kept Abraham Lincoln from provoking a major diplomatic incident on his responsibility, with potentially serious military and political consequences for the U.S. government.

Shaping of Wartime Diplomacy   Lincoln and Seward agreed after May 1861 to avoid any foreign diplomatic rupture in order to promote the neutrality that was critical to American foreign policy. A series of bold U.S. diplomatic initiatives implemented by Charles Francis Adams, U.S. minister at London, warned the British government against conducting relations of any kind with the "domestic enemies" of the United States, including plans to offer mediation that would probably lead to recognition of the Confederacy as an independent state.[165] Britain was highly conciliatory, and France also ultimately abandoned the proposal to recognize Confederate independence.[166]

Congress's enacting legislation giving Lincoln the authority to issue letters of marque and reprisal alarmed Britain into fulfillment of her obligations as a neutral. The U.S. government insisted that it rested with England to take measures that would arrest the president's order.[167] Lord Russell's government finally seized the ironclad "Laird rams"* in October 1863, inspiring other European nations' complete observance of neutral obligations.

At the same time as significant executive initiatives were underway, members of the House of Representatives wanted to be included in the peacemaking process. For example, Thaddeus Stevens (R. Pa.) urged

---

*British steamships made for the Confederacy were equipped with a projection below the water line that could pierce the wooden hulls of U.S. warships maintaining the blockade.

colleagues to resolve not to accept mediation of any foreign nation in the rebellion.* On 10 February 1863, Connecticut Senator Lafayette Foster requested executive information regarding French mediation attempts.[168] Lincoln's response then prompted the Committee on Foreign Relations to draft resolutions that repudiated any attempts at foreign intervention as unfriendly acts[169] and to request Lincoln to transmit these resolutions to foreign nations. Delaware's senator, Willard Saulsbury, however, denounced them as infringements on executive authority. Since management of foreign relations was "immediately entrusted" to the chief executive, who had not asked for Senate advice, there was "no propriety" in their gratuitous recommendations to him.[170] Senator John Carlile of Virginia agreed that the Senate could not possibly act as well advised as the State Department, inasmuch as omitted information did not give the Senate sufficient data upon which to legislate.[171] But both houses passed the resolutions by wide margins on the same day.[172]

Much later in the course of the war, Representative Samuel S. Cox declared that Congress could urge the executive to make peace. His resolution of 16 January 1865 called on Lincoln to receive or send agents with a view to ending hostilities. Although the resolution was laid on the table, it was only because it seemed bad policy, since the Confederacy had spurned peace overtures, and not because Congressman Cox's view of the allocation of authority appeared mistaken.[173]

Legislative Initiatives

Control of Expenditures   Congress continued to maintain its influence upon foreign affairs by using its power of the purse, resolutions, and treaty powers. A vivid illustration of such control occurred in the handling of a delicate aspect of U.S.-Spanish relations that President Buchanan raised in his annual message of 19 December 1859. Buchanan declared that certain Spanish claims had remained unpaid since the Tyler administration and recommended that Congress appropriate funds to be paid to Spain to be distributed among claimants in the *Amistad* case.†[174]

---

*Earlier, House members almost uniformly had felt that foreign recognition of the Confederacy would have been an act hostile to the Union; but they considered the matter to be an executive prerogative and refused to debate a resolution proposed on 13 July 1861 calling for immediate suspension of diplomatic relations with any foreign power if that nation should recognize Confederate independence. 31 *Congressional Globe* 115–16.

†Articles 8, 9, and 10 of the Treaty of 27 October 1795 (Pinckney Treaty) with Spain provided for the protection of merchandise of the United States and Spain in each other's ports, as well as the restoration of any properties rescued on the high seas, under due proof of ownership. 2 *Treaties* 318, 324–26 (Miller ed.). These treaty terms provided the basis for

In 1839, the *Amistad*, a Spanish ship laden with blacks kidnapped from Africa sailed into Havana in violation of Spanish law and was later detained in U.S. waters. Two Spaniards, José Ruis and Pedro Montez, claimed that the cargo and slaves should be delivered to them under the provisions of the Pinckney Treaty of 1795, but a Federal District Court awarded the Spaniards only the cargo, not the blacks. The Supreme Court upheld the decisions of the lower federal courts and declared the blacks free—they need not be returned either to Africa or to Spain.

Ruis and Montez then petitioned their own government to press the claim against the United States, but to no avail. Senator James Dixon (R. Conn.) concluded that Buchanan's urging of an appropriation to remunerate the two Spaniards was a misconstruction of treaty terms and was ill-founded,* since federal courts had already adjudicated against the claims.[175]

Congress balked at giving any further consideration to Buchanan's plea, and the president vented his unconcealed frustration in his next annual message on 3 December 1860.[176] Since the Senate had refused to "advise and consent" to the convention's ratification, relations with Spain had been placed "in an awkward and embarrassing position." He ruefully concluded that the final disposition of the *Amistad* claim would devolve upon his successor.[177]

Buchanan's defeat was undoubtedly bitter, since it undermined his attempt to improve relations with Spain in order to create a climate in favor of the acquisition of Cuba. Furthermore, though two of his predecessors had also recommended payment,† it was not until Buchanan's administration that Congress had given public recognition to the supremacy of judicial findings in the *Amistad* matter, a position that brought a corresponding limitation on the executive.

Bills for army appropriations provided congressmen the opportunity to ventilate other constitutional issues. Representative John Sherman (R. Oh.) felt that the executive could easily evade if not "virtually overthrow" the constitutional power of the House because of its marked propensity

---

the claims arising out of the *Amistad* incident. *See* Samuel F. Bemis's comprehensive treatment in *Pinckney's Treaty: America's Advantage from Europe's Distress* (1960).

*The Pinckney Treaty provided for remuneration of owners of stolen "merchandise," but that term did not include enslaved foreigners. Moreover, by Spanish law the slave trade had been abolished nineteen years before the *Amistad* incident, thus invalidating any claim that the Negroes were slaves and could be regarded as anyone's merchandise. 29 *Congressional Globe* 376.

†Although Tyler seemed to maintain on September 1841 that the claim was unfounded (6 *Messages and Papers* 2720), both Polk (*id.* 2401) and Pierce (*id.* 2742) recommended payment, and Fillmore had asked Congress to study the matter and appropriate funds if it found the claim just. *Id.* 2720.

to transfer appropriations made for one purpose, to any other purpose in the same Department, thus defeating all checks. Without law they use money appropriated specifically for the service of one fiscal year, to pay for the service of another fiscal year.[178]

He complained that Buchanan's habit of making contracts in advance of appropriations compelled Congress "either to sanction them or violate the public faith."[179] Sherman feared that the president would continue to extend his powers by construction into areas belonging to the House by creating the necessity for expenditures that left the House no alternative but compliance.[180]

The House passed the army appropriations bill, 102 to 81.[181] The Senate then evaluated an amendment questioning whether a Seminole Indian attack in Florida constituted such an emergency as justified presidential use of volunteers costing $385,000.[182] Florida Senator David Yulee (D.) claimed that since the president was the sole judge of an emergency, Congress had to appropriate any just debt incurred.[183] Supporters of the amendment to pay the Florida volunteers did not quibble over the executive's exercise of war powers without prior congressional action. They held that Buchanan had acted according to a statute so that his behavior was legal. The Senate handily passed both the amendment and the entire bill,[184] to which the House eventually acquiesced.[185]

During still other debates over appropriations, there occurred specific examination of war powers issues posed in the cases of the Utah "war" and the Kansas "insurrection." Since deployment of forces in both of these instances came about as a result of President Buchanan's unilateral decisionmaking and action, these discussions illuminate congressional interest in and legislative response to executive use of the war powers.

Buchanan went to Congress for funds to support federal troops he had sent into Utah and Kansas.[186] His deficiency bill to defray the costs of these operations produced controversy over the executive's right to incur expenses in excess of appropriations already made for military purposes. Opponents concurred that only an extreme emergency such as an actual invasion could justify such discretionary action.[187]

The bill's supporters, such as Representative John Quitman (D. Minn.), stated that emergency conditions in Utah justified passage of a deficiency bill, particularly since Buchanan had not made any "extravagant" contract for supplies for troops deployed in the mountains of Utah.[188] The House eventually passed the bill, 111 to 96.[189]

Senator Judah P. Benjamin (D. La.) maintained that negotiation of supply contracts was an intrinsically executive function, concomitant to the president's duty to see that the laws were faithfully executed. The bill passed easily in the Senate, 29 to 19,[190] primarily because of reluctance to eliminate supply lines to troops in the field. But the Senate did add a restrictive amendment, in which the House concurred, that contained reporting requirements and prohibited execution of supply contracts "except in cases of pressing exigency."[191] Faced with an executive *fait accompli*, Congress thus deferred to the executive in his request for additional funds.

In June 1858, Buchanan's request for support of his expedition into Kansas produced far more vehement discussion than the Utah debates because it focused on the slavery issue rather than on the president's right to use funds on his own authority. The administration bill failed in the Senate, 16 to 35,[192] although no attempts were made to withhold support from already committed troops.[193]

Buchanan also requested an appropriation for the construction of a Pacific railroad as a means of repelling invasion, relying upon Congress's warmaking powers as a source of authority for the measure:

> I consider it clear that under the war-making power, Congress may appropriate money for the construction of a military road through the Territories of the United States, when this is absolutely necessary for the defense of any of the States against foreign invasion.[194]

Representative George W. Jones (D. Tenn.) completely disagreed with the president's use of a war powers rationale:

> [T]here is no such power as he [Buchanan] claims delegated to Congress, either under the war-making power or any other power, to make roads or canals by this Government.[195]

Jones argued that if the defense forces must be bolstered, an increase in the army comprised the only proper and constitutional method. John Covode (R. Pa.) found a military justification in the Mormon uprising and a possible danger of an invasion of California.[196] But John S. Millson (D. Va.) contended that a Pacific railroad could not be grounded in the warmaking power because then every road in the United States could become a military highway.[197]

Although several bills aimed at federal assistance for a Pacific railroad were introduced during the next four sessions, none succeeded in hurdling the principal constitutional objection that Congress possessed no general war power to legislate for the common defense from which any authority regarding railroads could be derived.[198]

Shaping Foreign Policy by Resolutions President Lincoln's report on foreign relations in his 1861 annual message set a tone of restraint* adhered to throughout his administration, although his presidency was filled with repeated foreign attempts to intervene in U.S. domestic affairs. While he comprehended their natural resentment against such intervention, Lincoln chided the legislators' "unwise" complaints against foreign influence.[199] Nevertheless, reacting to foreign pressures, Congress itself attempted on several occasions to influence and direct the course of U.S. diplomacy during the Civil War.

For example, administration critics Senator James A. McDougall (D. Calif.) and Congressman H.H. Winter Davis (D. Md.) led many others in disapprobation of French occupation of Mexico. The House passed H.R. 58, which declared essentially that Congress was unwilling to sit silent while a monarchical government under European auspices was "erected on the ruins of any republican Government in America. . . ."†[200] The Senate Committee on Foreign Relations, however, refused to report it out,[201] and Congressman Rufus Spalding complained that the unanimous vote of the House had been "treated lightly."**[202] Yet McDougall and Davis tried in vain to elicit firm policy statements from their respective houses.[203] Each man introduced strong resolutions—Davis's, in particular, sought executive recognition of a congressional right to shape foreign policy.[204]

Secretary of State Seward ultimately repudiated the House joint resolution (H.R. 58) by asking U.S. representatives in France to

---

*Lincoln asked for "adequate and ample" defenses on every U.S. frontier in light of the fact that foreign dangers necessarily attend domestic difficulties. He alluded to the commercial treaties that had been negotiated and would be submitted to the Senate. His inclusion of correspondence regarding the erroneous detention of the British ship *Perthshire* in June 1861 reflected the restraint of the U.S. government in dealing with breaches of the federal blockade. The president also sought Congress's approval for recognition of Haiti and Liberia and asked for funds to maintain a *chargé* in each country. 32 *Congressional Globe Appendix* 1 (message of 3 December 1861).

†H.R. 58 passed 109 to 0 after an attempt by Ohio Representative Cox to make it more threatening to the Maximilian government. 34 *Congressional Globe* 1402, 1408–09. Modern efforts by House members to be heard in foreign affairs include a letter signed by sixty-seven House members and sent on 7 July 1981 to Argentine president Roberto Viola urging that his government prohibit denial of the civil and political rights of Jews in Argentina. Released by Representative Charles E. Schumer (D. N.Y.), the declaration stemmed from reports by a former newspaper publisher, Jacobo Timerman, who was jailed and tortured by Argentine authorities.

**France's official newspaper, *Le Moniteur,* stated that Napoleon was satisfied with an executive explanation, including the Senate's indefinite postponement of the question, "to which," it editorialized, "the executive power would not have given its sanction." H. Winter Davis thereupon introduced a qualified resolution requesting the president to communicate any executive explanations made to France regarding the "sense and bearing" of the unanimous House resolution. Lincoln's reply substantially confirmed *Le Moniteur*'s representation of the administration position. *Id.* 2475.

apologize to the French government.[205] Congressman Davis thereupon demanded that the executive respect Congress's constitutional right to an "authoritative" role in "declaring and prescribing foreign policy . . . not less in diplomatic negotiations than in the use of the national force when authorized by law. . . ." This resolution repeated one he had unsuccessfully submitted during the prior session,[206] but this time it passed, 118 to 8, on 19 December 1864.[207] The resolution also asserted that the propriety of any foreign policy declaration was established by the vote pronouncing it and that any such proposition was not a fit topic for diplomatic discussion with a foreign power while it was pending.[208]

During 1865 and 1866, sporadic congressional efforts were made to direct executive policy on Austrian influence in Mexico. Representative Kellian Whaley (Wh. W. Va.) urged President Johnson to seek alliances with all of the republics of the continent and "use all means at their command" to block establishment of European power in the Americas.*[209] By 1867, when Maximilian was overthrown, many members of the House introduced resolutions in support of the Mexican Republic,[210] while New York congressman Lewis Selye obtained passage of a resolution on 18 July 1867 requesting the president to issue a proclamation if he was satisfied that armed groups in the United States reportedly were about to invade Mexico in violation of U.S. neutrality. Such an order required all U.S. officers to prevent such an invasion and to warn participants that their actions would result in forfeiture of the right to U.S. protection.[211] Although the House enacted this request, President Johnson did not act on it.

Administration Control of the Trent *Affair*   The *Trent* was the most highly charged foreign policy issue to arise between Britain and the United States since the Clayton-Bulwer treaty,[212] but a full discussion of it was carefully discouraged at the same time as the executive satisfied Congress's appetite for information with voluntary transmittals and diplomats of both nations contemporaneously worked to defuse a potential explosion.[213] The Lincoln administration thus isolated Congress from its confidences as a policy decision was made to avoid a foreign war, as Washington had done in 1793 when he issued the Neutrality Proclamation.

The popular and political climate was sharply belligerent. Secretary Seward, who had been convinced in March 1861 that a foreign war could

---

*Several House resolutions proposed to lend the Republic of Mexico varying amounts up to $50 million to stave off its overthrow by a European monarchy. 36 *Congressional Globe* 3217–18; 37 *Congressional Globe* 170.

reunite the country, realized later that year that not only was all hope of reunion gone but also that war on any more than the home front would pose a possibly insuperable problem for the Union forces. On 19 December 1861, the British issued an ultimatum for the release of Confederate diplomats James Mason and John Slidell, captured on board the *Trent* November 8.[214] Seward invited Senator Charles Sumner to attend a Cabinet meeting on 25 December in order to try to influence Lincoln against giving in to bellicose Cabinet members who wanted to refuse to release the diplomats. Sumner informed the Cabinet and the president about serious British military preparations underway against the United States in Canada. Unlike Seward and Postmaster General Montgomery Blair, Sumner was willing to work gradually toward arbitration that would eventually include release of the men.[215] But he had a difficult task during the ensuing week to mollify his jingoistic colleagues.

Even temperate debate on such a volatile issue could have strongly influenced the Senate against compromise. John Hale of New Hampshire, hoping for Senate hostility, requested all dispatches between Great Britain and the United States relating to the seizure. Sumner, however, challenged Hale's claim that the British had arrogantly demanded the *Trent*'s passengers James Mason and John Slidell. He reassured the Senate that the administration would not surrender the Confederate emissaries. On the same day, however, Secretary Seward acknowledged to Britain that Captain Charles Wilkes had seized Mason and Slidell in error and conceded that they should be released. When, ten days later, the executive voluntarily informed both houses the captives had been freed,[216] Sumner moved quickly to refer the message to the Foreign Relations Committee. The matter did not arise again in either house.*

The possibility of British official support of the Confederacy realistically was *de minimis* after the battle of Gettysburg, but rebel foreign relations policy never assumed that serious friction could not still be provoked between England and the United States. Senator Sumner and others conceived of the St. Albans invasion† as a deliberate attempt to embroil the United States and Great Britain in conflict; but no mention

---

*Word that the Confederates were to be freed was buried in the House Committee on Foreign Affairs shortly after some members condemned the action. 32 *Congressional Globe* 207–10. On 27 January, when the House was on the verge of considering French interposition in the *Trent* affair, the issue was shunted to the same committee, where it did not resurface. *Id.* 494.

†A raid conducted by Confederate soldiers, dressed in plain clothes, against St. Albans, Vermont, in October 1864. Bailey, *A Diplomatic History of the American People* 373.

occurred in debate as to whether the president could have deployed troops to the border without congressional authority, and Congress took no conclusive action.[217]

Defining the House's Role in Treatymaking   The House of Representatives continued its struggle to achieve a larger role in determining the effect of treaties on national policy. During Lincoln's administration, there occurred acknowledgment of the House's role in the treaty abrogation process,* as well as the right of Congress to participate in treaty negotiation. Debate over execution of the Alaska treaty during the Johnson administration also appeared likely to expand the House's role.

In discussing whether Congress could impose the requirement to regulate duties on the executive, Congressman Rufus Spalding (D. Oh.) argued that the grant to Congress of power to regulate commerce with foreign nations could not be delegated to the president in the course of his exercise of the treaty power, even with Senate consent. But there was no final resolution of this issue. Although the House delayed consideration of the committee resolution requiring the president to give notice of abrogation,[218] the final version that passed both houses† included the unequivocal demand that notice "be given" and "charged" the president to communicate it.**[219] The House thus made its point that it should be assumed to be a partner in treaty abrogation.

---

*Early in 1864, the House attempted to require the executive to give the notice of termination and to enter into diplomatic negotiations when the 1854 Canadian reciprocity treaty with Britain (*see* Chapter 2, p. 186) became subject to termination. Legislators sought to end this treaty because certain Canadian provinces had imposed tariffs inconsistent with its spirit, and Vermont representative Justin Morrill introduced H.R. 56, which sought to authorize the president to give the required one-year notice prior to termination. 34 *Congressional Globe* 9, 377. Because the bill involved tariffs rather than international law, it went to the House Commerce Committee, which reported out a more strongly worded version that "authorized and required" the president to give notice of termination and convey to Britain the U.S. desire to negotiate.

†Before the final passage of H.R. 265 in January 1865, senators debated the legal effect of the Constitutional provisions for treaty formation on the House's treatymaking role. If a treaty purported to regulate duties, Senator Jacob Collamer (Vt.) complained that it violated the Constitutional requirement that revenue bills originate in the House of Representatives. 35 *Congressional Globe* 208–09. In disagreement, Wisconsin's Timothy Howe argued that the right to originate revenue was a prerogative no more authoritative than the power given to the president and Senate to make treaties. If it were otherwise, said Howe, "I do not know when or where a treaty can be made without consulting the House of Representatives." *Id.* 211. Inasmuch as this treaty was not aimed at raising revenue but at regulating trade, Howe could see no other way to avoid perpetual confrontation of the branches than for the House to accept and to absorb a theoretical invasion of its prerogatives.

**The Senate also eliminated the words expressive of Congress's desire that the parties negotiate another treaty, which appeared in the House version. *Id.* 96.

While Congress was out of session, Lincoln alone on 23 November 1864 gave Britain notice that the Rush-Bagot disarmament treaty of 1817 would be terminated. Without the anxious debate over the termination of earlier treaties, both houses eventually ratified this notice "as if the same had been authorized by Congress."[220] The theory behind Senator Charles Sumner's pressure to approve a new approach was elegant in its simplicity. Great Britain believed Lincoln's notice was valid, since he was chief of state, and protocol forbade one sovereign's challenge of another's authority. Even though some senators were ready to admit that Lincoln had exceeded his authority, Sumner and others reasoned that ratification could operate to cure the defect. Subsequent legislation would place the president's action precisely on the same footing as if he had been authorized in advance.*[221]

Indian Peace Negotiation by Congressional Commission Congress traditionally had regarded Indian peace negotiations as more amenable to congressional intervention than similar undertakings with "civilized nations."[222] A bill (S. 136) proposing that a legislative commission should negotiate Indian treaties instead of the president passed both houses without significant constitutional objection.[223] As introduced,† the bill created a commission of military and civilian personnel to negotiate peace with the Plains Indians (Sioux, Arapahoes, and Apaches). This commission was to be under "Executive direction" but was to use its own discretion in making treaties and to report all its activities to the president. Most senators agreed that the Plains conflict had escalated into war, despite some arguments that neither the president nor the general of the army had so informed Congress, nor had the secretary of war replied to a congressional query as to whether war existed.[224] For example, Senator John B. Henderson (D. Mo.) remarked that the conflict had to be taken seriously, since the Indians at close range were defeating the U.S. cavalry and the cost of the conflict at up to $250,000 per day might become tens of millions of dollars in six months.[225] There was only limited objection that this bill proposed to take away the president's power to make treaties, just before it passed overwhelmingly.[226]

---

*Though Seward did give Britain formal notice of intent to terminate the disarmament treaty, he rescinded his actions in March 1865, when the stir over the St. Albans raid (*see supra* p. 209 n.) had quieted down. Bailey, *A Diplomatic History of the American People* 373.

†The bill was amended to include on the commission the chairmen of both the House and Senate Committees on Indian Affairs.

House Efforts to Define Treatymaking Prerogatives: Alaska   During the debate over whether the United States should acquire "Russian America," some representatives decided to base their evaluation of the treaty of purchase on whether they believed that the addition would enhance the American economy, and others merely took Russian gold to assure their approval.[227] Most legislators, however, carefully studied the issue of whether the House might consider withholding an appropriation for a treaty whose merits it questioned. Those who urged a larger voice for the House in treatymaking argued that when enabling legislation such as appropriations was required, a treaty was imperfect in law and became the supreme law of the land only after both houses approved it.[228] According to Pennsylvania Congressman Thomas Williams, the House Foreign Affairs Committee took the position that its members could decide whether a particular treaty was within the scope of the treatymaking power and whether refusal of an appropriation might be in the nation's best interest.[229] On the other hand, proponents of the Alaska treaty, such as New York's John Pruyn (D.), denied that the House could debate the treaty once it had been ratified. Pruyn maintained the House could always inquire whether there had been fraud or misrepresentation during negotiations. If, on the other hand, the House examined a treaty from the standpoint of whether a price was fair or purchase desirable, it might diminish the Constitutional power of the president and Senate. [230] Others who later voted funds to execute the purchase maintained that the House acted as a necessary restraint on the treatymaking power. They perceived that the people's representatives should evaluate whether the treaty contravened the established principles and interests of government and concluded that the House possessed unquestioned right to consider the subject matter of a treaty before or after it was negotiated or at any time the national interest dictated. [231] It was recognized that a foreign power could interpret House refusal to execute a treaty as hostility; but some members argued that even with the threat of war, they should possess the ultimate right to judge whether a treaty appeared to jeopardize the best interests of the American people.[232]

Ultimately, many congressmen submerged their respective interpretations of the House's treatymaking role in order to vote for the appropriation. Commercial advantage, good faith, and national honor convinced them to put aside their carefully articulated declarations of the House's prerogatives.[233] The treaty passed both houses in July 1868*.

---

*Opponents tacked on an amendment stating that the House possessed the right to debate treaties and that any lands acquired by treaty were not to be taken before the

MILITARY AFFAIRS AND AUTHORIZATIONS

Executive Policy in Wartime

Perceptions of Executive Emergency Powers: Buchanan and Congress Two presidents had to face one of nineteenth century America's most important military questions. How could the chief executive execute federal constitutional law against states formerly swearing allegiance to the federal union but which, by 1860, had chosen to establish themselves as a foreign nation? Both men were required to evaluate the question of commitment of force against the Confederacy, yet the responses that James Buchanan and Abraham Lincoln gave to this question were as different as their concepts of U.S. constitutionalism. Buchanan's Democratic party was rooted in the compact theory of the Constitution, while Lincoln rejected the belief that states could break the federal bond that had joined them after 1787. Democratic party theory chose not to disturb or interfere with a state that felt moved to abrogate federal law. Republican Lincoln pronounced secession as apostasy: an aberration in the orderly flow of law and government that had been the heritage of John Marshall's nationalism and of which Lincoln was a firm disciple.

The vision of what lay ahead militarily was not obscured from the seasoned veteran, General Winfield Scott. As general-in-chief of the U.S. Army, Scott advised President Buchanan in a letter of 29 October 1860 that should Lincoln be elected, some of the southern states would secede. He wrote of the danger that secession would signify to federal forts that were undermanned and would be the instant target of revolutionaries. Since there were insufficient troops in the federal army, Scott urged Buchanan to prepare a call-up of volunteers. Strategically, he felt that it made sense for Buchanan to let any coastal state from the Potomac to the Gulf of Mexico including Texas secede if it wished, but to invade any interior state whose absence from the Union would leave a void between the North and the U.S. coastline.[234]

Buchanan personally considered secession unconstitutional but determined to pursue a policy of inaction before Lincoln's election, seeking every possible means to avoid giving secessionists excuses to leave the Union. He had insufficient troops to garrison federal fortifications in the

---

House made specific appropriation for them. However, after the House passed the Alaska appropriations bill with this amendment, 113 to 44 (39 *Congressional Globe* 4055), the Senate deleted it and the House concurred in the conference committee's version which sustained the deletion. *Id.* 4159, 4394, 4404 (H.R. 1096, approved 27 July 1868).

South and refused to consider raising volunteers on his own initiative. Unsure of his proper course, he asked his attorney general, Jeremiah S. Black, for information, and together they hammered out five interrogatories:

1. In case of a conflict between the authorities of any state and those of the United States, can there be any doubt that the laws of the Federal Government, if constitutionally passed, are supreme?
2. What is the extent of my official power to collect the duties on imports at a port where the revenue laws are resisted by a force which drives the collector from the custom house?
3. What right have I to defend the public property (for instance, a fort, arsenal, and navy yard), in case it should be assaulted?
4. What are the legal means at my disposal for executing those laws of the United States which are usually administered through the courts and their officers?
5. Can a military force be used for any purpose whatever under the Acts of 1795 and 1807, within the limits of a state where there are no judges, marshals, or other civil officers?[235]

Three days afterward, Black submitted his opinion. Under the Constitution, he wrote, the president had the duty to see the laws faithfully executed; and to assist him in this mandate, he had been designated commander-in-chief of the army and navy. But the duty was not absolute, since the president "cannot accomplish a legal purpose by illegal means"[236] and could only execute the laws "in the manner prescribed by the legislative department."[237] The law did not comprehend presidential execution of laws in rebellious states and addressed only military assistance to ordinary judicial process. The executive could "execute to the extent of the defensive means placed in [his] hands. . . ."[238] As a result, federal troops might be increased to a larger and stronger marshal's *posse comitatus*. Realistically, however, southern federal officials would place state loyalties paramount and refuse to enforce federal law. The United States could not invade state territory to execute the law where no civil service existed to implement it. While the president could use force to defend public property and could recapture it if seized, Buchanan could take no other affirmative act without legislative authority, since "to send military force into any state with orders to act against the people would be simply making war upon them."[239] Thus, if war against a rebellious state was not legislatively authorized, there was no executive war power to sanction such hostilities.

Buchanan incorporated the opinion in his annual message of 3 December 1860 and a second presidential speech of 8 January 1861.*[240] Black, however, began to alter his views as his experience with the secession movement turned sour. As secretary of state, he advised Buchanan that troops at Fort Sumter should be augmented, by force if necessary,[241] and that the city of Washington should be garrisoned for protection. His later view reflected the concerns of one whose new position guided him into weighing his former written legal opinions on a scale with extraordinary and unforeseen circumstances.

For several weeks, a Select Committee of Five appointed by the members of the House of Representatives investigated the legalities involved in secession† and wrestled with the "constitutional remedy" of secession itself that its proponents claimed to be a national panacea.[242]

This committee concluded in its report of 28 February that there was no legal basis for secession[243] and that force could be employed against the states, whose right to revolution (not secession) implied the corresponding right of the thirty-three remaining states to resist it by their combined power.[244] It was implied that the president could act only after being enabled to do so by congressional authorization. Nowhere in this remarkable document was there any allusion to the president's acting on his own authority, either to respond to or to initiate hostilities.

Debates in Congress during January 1861 pounded away at the enigma of Buchanan's near-isolationist stance on the impending civil war. Buchanan's greatest dread in facing the legislature in former years had been his fear of impeachment if he exceeded his constitutional powers, but secure in the knowledge that Abraham Lincoln would become president in scarcely eight weeks, he became immobile,** taking a posture that could only delay the inevitable dramatic exercise of some form of executive authority.†† His supporters withstood Senator James

---

*Jeremiah Black drafted the text of this second message. J. Black, *Papers.* Until the end of his administration, the president generally kept intact his policy against ruffling the South. At one point, Buchanan insisted Governor Pickens of South Carolina be informed that any assault on Fort Sumter would be regarded as an attack by a foreign country. But Pickens backed down before Buchanan's strong words ever left his desk. 8 Buchanan, *Works* 71–72 and n. 1.

†Especially, as referred to in President Buchanan's special message of 8 January 1861, in which Buchanan asserted that the only constitutional power he possessed was "to use military force defensively against those who resisted the Federal officers in the execution of their legal functions, and against those who assail the property of the Federal Government. . . ." 7 *Messages and Papers* 3186, 3187; 30 *Congressional Globe* 294–95.

**The report of the House Committee of Five, which suggested Buchanan could take aggressive action, did not serve as encouragement, since it was not the voice of Congress nor was there evidence that it had been accepted by the whole House.

††Congress was equally indecisive. During a debate on an army appropriation bill, Buchanan's opponent Representative Samuel Cox questioned the ultimate use of defensive war power as a device to protect federal property and assure revenue collection, when it was sure to be opposed with a large aggressive force, but he could not say for himself or

Mason's (D. Va.) unqualified demand of 5 January for copies of all orders from the Department of War or the commander-in-chief of the army since 1 November 1860 and all recommendations or plans for increase of federal forces in virtually every state south of the District of Columbia.[245] This monumental request foundered on 14 January as discussion focused on whether the inquiry should be directed to the president or the secretary of war. Administration supporters objected to an unqualified request seeking a wealth of military detail as an improper interference into the exclusively executive matters of military proceedings.[246]

Congress considered but rejected bills granting the president authority to reorganize the Washington, D.C., militia and order it to suppress insurrection and repel invasion.[247] These efforts to strengthen the force and use of the militia* were unwelcome to southern legislators who saw in them little more than a license to the chief executive to crush secession.

Federal troops were continuously in evidence in the capital city, and Representative Lawrence Branch (D. N.C.) proposed that they be removed. His resolution was tabled after Philip Fouke (D. Ill.) came to Buchanan's defense to urge that as commander-in-chief the president had a right to quarter troops wherever necessary.[248] The president himself underscored that position in a message dated 1 March, submitting that the sole purpose for federal troops was "to act as a *posse comitatus* in strict subordination to the civil authority, for the purpose of preserving peace and order in the city of Washington should this be necessary before or at the period of the inauguration of the President elect."[249] But this show of force was also, he said, in response to what appeared to be the obvious duty of a chief executive, in a capital city alive with whispers of incipient revolution, to act to safeguard "the immense amount of public property in this city" as well as "the archives of the Government, in which all the States, and especially the new States, in which the public lands are situated, have a deep interest."[250] Congress offered no further objection to this show of strength, and Lincoln was soon safely delivered to Washington without incident in time to take the oath to defend a constitutional regime that was in the gravest need of defending in its seventy-four-year history.

Lincoln and Congress   Upon the outbreak of war in April, with lightning-like rapidity Lincoln called volunteers into service, suspended the

---

Congress what should be done in case "a certain result follows the performance of present duty."

*In earlier debate upon proposed Constitutional amendments, Judah P. Benjamin (D. La.) emphasized that the power of the president, or Congress, to call out the militia and use the army and navy to prevent insurrection did not mean that he might do so of his own volition without the intervention of a civil power, such as the courts, a marshal, or attorney, to declare that the law had been violated before it could be lawfully enforced. *Id.* 216–17.

writ of *habeas corpus,* increased the navy and regular army, and blockaded southern ports. His exercise of emergency powers during Congress's adjournment was the subject of intense debate in July and August 1861, though Congress eventually approved most of his actions as if they had been executed at its direction.

The president's suspension of *habeas corpus* created an opportunity for both the executive and Congress to explore what emergency powers might be derived from the war power. A few congressmen expressed the belief that democratic government in wartime included the paradoxical necessity of curbing civil liberties as a means of preserving them.[251] They maintained that the necessity to preserve the civil government also tended to sanction any power not clearly illegal as a means of dealing with the emergency. On the whole, however, congressmen expressed gravest doubts concerning the legitimacy of executive war powers when they included arbitrary arrest and imprisonment.

Lincoln did not rescind his orders after Chief Justice Taney's decision in *Ex parte Merryman,** and so theoretically, at least, authority to suspend *habeas corpus* remained available to officers impeded or troubled by the civilian populace, until Congress defined the situation. He asked Attorney General Edward Bates for his opinion of the powers of the president during a military emergency and received a lengthy answer stating that exceptional times called for the use of extraordinary powers.[252] Bates found in the last clause of the president's oath of office the implied power to perform any act of guardianship necessary to "preserve, protect, and defend" the Constitution, as distinct from the oath of other officers who are required only to swear "to support this Constitution." Unlike Attorney General Black, Bates found mandated in the Acts of 1795 and 1807 only the *means* that the executive was authorized to use to put down insurrection. There was no discussion of *method;* consequently, the discretion as to how to meet exigencies rested fully with the chief executive and had been admitted by the Supreme Court in *Martin v. Mott.*† Furthermore, the executive's duty to take care that the laws be faithfully executed was a constitutional obligation that the president undertook in his civil capacity, but he could permissibly link it with his role as commander-in-chief when he employed the army

---

*Mr. Justice Roger B. Taney in *Luther v. Borden,* 48 U.S. (7 Howard) 44 (1842), had said that U.S. officers under presidential authority could arrest a man to suppress a rebellion against a state government and that thus the president could commit armed forces to detain an "abettor" of rebellion without judicial process or congressional intervention. On the other hand, in the much expanded arena of national conflict, he put his foot down firmly as Chief Justice in *Ex parte Merryman,* 17 F. Cas. 144 (No. 9487) (C.C.D. Md. 1861), holding that individual civil liberties could not be suspended by the executive in time of war.

†25 U.S. (12 Wheaton) 19 (1827). The Court held that the president possessed under these acts unreviewable discretion to judge when the delegated powers, such as the calling up of militia or federal troops, might be used.

to perform his duties.* Bates admitted that this great emergency power had often been denied because it could be abused; but the peace and safety of the nation demanded that it be exercised from time to time. Suspension of *habeas corpus* thus could be considered an emergency method of executing the presidential war power.

Congress, on the other hand, laid claim to the suspension power. Some members debated whether Congress could delegate the specifically enumerated power to suspend the writ of *habeas corpus* merely on the president's plea that public safety demanded it.[253] Though it appeared impossible for Congress to ratify the president's acts by delegating a specifically enumerated power, there was no general agreement either that Congress alone possessed the right to suspend the writ or that it could not be considered a prerogative of the president during hostilities.†[254] A bill permitting executive suspension of *habeas corpus* under certain circumstances** hurdled Senate opposition on 23 February 1863, 24 to 13[255] and finally passed both houses. It not only authorized the suspension of *habeas corpus* but also constituted the president's proclamation of suspension as a complete defense against any prosecution for search, seizure, arrest, or imprisonment.[256]

President Lincoln defended the call for 75,000 militia after the assault on Fort Sumter as necessitated by military and public demand. Legislative confirmation of these acts was the first order of business in the new session, and Congress's consideration of Senate Joint Resolution 1[257] inspired extensive debate of the proposition that congressional ratification could validate all of the extraordinary steps Lincoln had taken as if "issued and done under the previous express authority and direction of the Congress of the United States." Missouri Senator Trusten Polk denounced Lincoln for calling out the militia in every case but the defense of Washington, D.C., on the ground that the Act of 1795,

---

*Bates's analysis led him to the perception that Congress had accorded recognition to this inherent right in the Act of March 3, 1807 (2 Stat. 445). Fusion of authority to use the army to execute the laws with discretion to choose the method to accomplish it vested enormous power in the executive.

†Representative Samuel Shellabarger (R. Oh.) expressed the view that suspension of *habeas corpus* was "wisely accorded" to the president as a power "essential to the existence of every government." 32 *Congressional Globe* 2074. On 8 July 1862, the House passed a bill containing a provision giving the president discretionary power to suspend the privilege of the writ (*id.* 3183–84), but the Senate at that time refused to pass it, apparently unready to say definitively that the president lacked power to suspend *habeas corpus* as a grant from the Constitution. For a narrow view of Lincoln's power in this area, see Corwin, *The President: Office and Powers, 1787–1957*, 141–42; 229–32.

**The statute (H.R. 591) was highly discretionary, and its scope sweeping. 33 *Congressional Globe* 1205; 33 *Congressional Globe Appendix* 217. Some legal commentators have regarded its language, "the President . . . is authorized," to mean that Congress was uncommitted, as to how or by whom authorized. *E.g.*, Corwin, *The President: Office and Powers, 1787–1957*, 145, 230.

while permitting the president to utilize the militia on basis of his judgment alone, was not intended for the purpose of making war on the sovereign states.[258] Claiming that it had been the policy of the previous Congress to refuse to pass bills calculated to carry on a war, Polk said that Lincoln had taken it on his own authority to increase both the army and navy and to deploy them to initiate war.[259] Polk also contested the president's right to institute blockades of U.S. ports, since he contended that blockade was a war measure and might not be proclaimed by a president until Congress had declared war.[260] In agreement, Kentucky's John C. Breckinridge insisted there was no way Congress could validate the violation of the Constitution by another branch of government without declaring that Congress had the power to alter the Constitution.[261] He argued eloquently:

> The Constitution declares that Congress alone shall have power 'to declare war.' The President has made war. Congress alone shall have power 'to raise and support armies.' The President has raised and supported armies on his own authority. Congress shall have power 'to provide and maintain a navy.' The President has provided an immense Navy, and maintains it without authority of law. The Constitution declares that no money shall be taken from the Treasury except in pursuance of appropriations made by law. The President has taken money from the Treasury without appropriations made by law for the purpose of carrying out the preceding unconstitutional acts.[262]

Tennessee Senator Andrew Johnson defended the ratifying resolution, stating that Lincoln's call for militia occurred during an exigency comprehended in Mr. Justice Story's definition of a proper occasion for the exercise of presidential military command.* Additions to the army and navy were reactions to "the great law of necessity" basic to a government's right to maintain itself.[263] Blockade of southern ports had come only in response to the "practical acts of war" then in progress.[264] And Vermont Senator Justin Morrill held that so long as Lincoln acted within the constitutional scope of the government, Congress could ratify acts he performed in absence of its prior consent. Ratification was in fact unnecessary since President Lincoln's measures were "necessarily and logically deducible from the powers conferred upon [him] in the U.S. Constitution."†[265]

---

*"The power itself is to be exercised upon sudden emergencies, upon great occasions of state, and under circumstances which may be vital to the existence of the Union." *Martin v. Mott*, 25 U.S. (12 Wheaton) 19 (1827).

†If the authority for these executive actions was implied from expressly granted power, then Morrill's perception of the power Lincoln relied upon was akin to the implied powers of Congress granted in the "sweeping" clause of the Constitution. Art. I, cl. 18.

Voting was postponed until, on 5 and 6 August, the substantive provisions of the resolution were attached to a military pay bill (S. 69) and passed by both houses.[266] All orders, proclamations, and acts of the president after 4 March 1861 regarding the army, navy, and volunteers, as well as the calling out of state militia,* were approved.

Conduct of the War

Provision of Forces   Congress turned to the work of providing forces to win the war. It swiftly passed S. 1, a bill authorizing the use of volunteers to enforce the laws and to protect public property and also providing for the recruitment of up to 500,000 men for no more than a three-year enlistment, "as [the president] may deem necessary."† Another volunteer bill that passed in July 1861 provided for wide exercise of presidential appointment power by authorizing the executive to appoint as many major and brigadier generals as he felt were required.[267]

The president's temporary increase of the navy during the "emergency" was also approved,[268] including giving unlimited discretion to the navy secretary to charter or buy twelve side wheel steamers.[269] Increases in funds to buy arms**[270] were accompanied by authorizations to increase the standing army.[271] With all of these augmentations in men and materiel, however, Congress was not committed to permanent maintenance of a large standing army even at the moment of making its authorizations. Its S. 2[272] provided for the reduction of the standing army to 25,000 men at the end of the war without further legislation.[273] In passing this bill, Congress specifically limited the armed forces of the United States in time of war.

Late in the war, Lincoln agreed to honor an appeal from five northwestern governors to raise "100-day" troops for routine duty so that

---

*An attempt in the House to strike the ratifying language of S. 69 was defeated, and the bill passed. 31 *Congressional Globe* 448–49.

†The bill passed in the Senate on 12 July, 35–4 (*id.* 50, 54, 80, 82), and after House passage (*id.* 144, 147) the Conference Committee struck the three-year provision. *Id.* 194, 205, 219. Another nearly identical bill (H.R. 28) contained an administration request for 400,000 men that the House Committee on Military Affairs raised on its own initiative to 500,000; and this effort survived attempts to amend the number downward. *Id.* 94–102. The House resolved 121 to 5 on 16 July to vote any amount of money and men to suppress the rebellion. *Id.* 131. H.R. 15, which provided payment for militia and volunteers that Lincoln called into service, was an additional form of ratification of the president's unauthorized acts, and it passed both houses. *Id.* 31, 62, 77, 92; *see also infra* p. 221 (passage of H.R. 69 expressing approval).

**Congress appropriated $10 million to buy arms for regular and volunteer troops in July 1861. Funds were also placed at the discretion of the secretary of war to repair and construct fortifications as necessary, and neither house disputed such a broad delegation to the executive. *Id.* 369, 430 (passage in Senate, 1 August, and House, 3 August 1861).

seasoned men could be released for the summer campaign. Lincoln issued the call in the spring of 1864, and the House passed H.R. 69, appropriating $20 million to cover expenses involved in the proposed replacement maneuver even though Congress had admonished the administration to spend cautiously. Staunch Senate Republicans voiced their doubts about presidential authority to raise additional troops in circumstances that did not satisfy the prescribed requirements set forth in the Acts of 1795 and 1862. Maryland Senator Reverdy Johnson concluded that the call was invalid since it had been made when Congress was in session and also since Lincoln had violated the Act of July 12, 1862, requiring him to specify a term of service for those called.[274]

New Hampshire's John Hale agreed with Johnson and others that this call constituted usurpation of Congress's authority to raise troops. John Carlile (Un. Va.) disapproved of several governors' asking the president to bring men into service and Lincoln's sanction of their plan without consulting Congress. Disagreeing, Maine Senator William P. Fessenden retorted that he was no military man but that his duty was to furnish the means for carrying on the war—the legislature could scrutinize executive conduct as much as it desired in time of peace. Although Senator Hale expressed his distaste for the bill, he indicated that he would vote in favor of it lest his opposition blunt the war effort, as did many others at the last moment. H.R. 69 finally passed the Senate, 23 to 14,[275] and Lincoln approved it on 10 May 1864.*[276]

The Emancipation Proclamation: An Expression of Executive War Power

One of the most dramatic of Lincoln's military appeals to end the war was his effort to obtain congressional support for an official declaration, under the authority of the war powers of the president, that blacks in the seceded states were free. Late in 1861, Massachusetts Representative Thomas Eliot first proposed that emancipation be used "to weaken the power of the rebels in arms." Eliot argued that Lincoln as commander-in-chief had power to bring about the end of the war and that emancipation was an incident of the war power.[277] Eliot and Thaddeus Stevens introduced similar resolutions to that effect in the House and Senate, respectively, but they were postponed. Lincoln himself, in March 1862, then submitted a joint resolution proposing financial aid to states

---

*There was a precedent in 1863 when both houses agreed to a measure (H.R. 137) empowering Kentucky's governor Beriah Magoffin to act as the president's agent to raise and organize up to 20,000 volunteers at the direction of the president whenever he judged there was a need for them. 33 *Congressional Globe* 274, 276; *id.* 725.

abolishing slavery and urged its adoption as a significant means of ending the war. This resolution was barely defeated in the House, 74 to 78.[278]

Several lawmakers argued that Congress had the authority to free the slaves under the war power.* In debate on H.R. 471, finally passed by both houses, Senator Charles Sumner declared that the Constitution's grant of power to make rules regarding captures[279] and the laws of war under international law enabled Congress to confiscate slave property.[280] Illinois's Orville Browning disagreed, claiming that the bill evaded the "plain constitutional provision" that left the question of slavery to the states. Browning further regarded the seizure of enemy property as a matter of military necessity that belonged to the commander-in-chief. Lyman Trumbull replied that neither the law of nations† nor the Constitution granted to the president powers from which he could derive authority to confiscate property:

> [H]e is Commander-in-Chief to act according to the regulations pre-
> scribed by Congress; and he has the same powers and none others than if he
> were appointed Commander-in-Chief by act of Congress. . . . [281]

President Lincoln published his intention to emancipate slaves in rebel states "as a fit and necessary war measure for suppressing said rebellion" by issuing a proclamation on 1 January 1863.[282] To encourage those states to return to the Union and avoid the loss of their slaves, Lincoln stated that he would announce in January 1863 which states were in rebellion. Lincoln also visualized that he would attract rebel states into the Union by promising financial aid for any states voluntarily freeing their slaves, at the same time as emancipation would deprive the South of its economic basis for continuing the war.**

---

*Constitutional elimination of slavery was a major topic of legislative discussion in 1862. A bill to confiscate rebel property raised the question whether Constitutional safeguards applied to seceded states to protect their property in slaves. 32 *Congressional Globe* 334, 461, 463 (S. 151). A bill (H.R. 224) to increase the number of cadets at West Point was used to debate whether a war powers argument could justify confiscation and emancipation of slaves. *Id.* 503, 643. An act of approving their confiscation was signed by the president during the final day of the session after Congress successfully implemented its war power, by enacting a confiscation of property act, which would deprive the states in insurrection of their slave-power. *Id.* 2360–61, 3006. The Senate emphasized the enabling authority when it retitled the House's confiscation of property act, an act to suppress insurrection, etc. *See Congressional Globe Appendix* 412–13 (Act of July 17, 1862).

†Trumbull was unimpressed with international law as a source for U.S. war powers, since no such law could prevail if it violated the Constitution. 32 *Congressional Globe* 2960–61.

**This was the second emancipation plan that emerged in 1862. It was formally reiterated in his state of the union message on 1 December 1862. 33 *Congressional Globe Appendix* 3. Lincoln sought a constitutional amendment to implement his plan for financial aid to the states, and Congress unsuccessfully attempted to legislate the aid, basing its authority on the war power.

At first, most House members found some Constitutional validity in the executive approach. On 15 December, the House alone adopted* (78 to 51) Representative Samuel Fessenden's (R. Me.) resolutions stating that the proclamation was a constitutional exercise of the war power in that it was "well adapted" to hasten the restoration of peace and was a war measure that exercised power with a proper regard for the rights of the states and of free government.[283]

Administration opponents such as Kentucky Congressmen Charles Wickliffe, George Yeaman, and John Menzies, however, argued in December 1862 that an executive proclamation freeing the slaves in the rebel states would be unconstitutional as either a war measure or for restoration of peace. In 1861, Kentucky's John Crittenden had led a resolution to passage stating simply that the Union's purpose was to put down disorder.[284] Menzies claimed, therefore, that the Republican Party's support of the proclamation violated the spirit of Crittenden's resolution,[285] while Wickliffe challenged Lincoln's authority to countermand state law under the guise of implementing the war power, which was defined as "anything which he supposes will best subdue the enemy."[286]

Many bills proposing compensated emancipation were introduced.[287] The administration in the meantime suggested various legislative approaches to encourage voluntary emancipation. One (H.R. 634) proposed to give financial compensation to Missouri once it enacted a law for either immediate or gradual emancipation.[288] Senator David Turpie (D. Ind.), however, termed the bill a federal bribe offered to Missouri for her property rights, under the guise of war powers:

> This war power is a most singular article. India rubber has had some reputation heretofore for being elastic; gold and silver for being malleable and ductile; but sir, they must yield to this war power in all those qualities. Why sir, it 'Lives through all life, extends through all extent, spreads undivided, operates unspent.'[289]

Others such as Illinois Senator William Richardson (D.) and Kentucky's Garrett Davis criticized endless expansion of the war power. Not "one iota of the war power is vested in the President," Davis exclaimed. Only Congress could adopt war policy; and whether or not Lincoln wished it, Congress could end the war "tomorrow, if it chooses to do so ... "[290] The bill passed the Senate on 12 February 1863 (23 to 18), but it was killed in a House Committee, and the House's own version expired at the close of the session.†

---

*Senate consideration of a resolution favoring Lincoln's proclamation was tabled early in the session. *Congressional Globe* 6.

†When it went to the House, the Senate bill was recommitted to the Select Committee

Garrett Davis (Wh. Ky.) often contributed skillful legal analyses of the respective powers of the branches to debates in the House. (*See* p. 223.) Mathew Brady photo, Library of Congress.

The Lincoln administration declared that since military necessity created the need for emancipation, the power of the War Department would continue to be required to be invoked for the order, organization, protection, and respect that were needed to implement the purpose of the proclamation. Moreover, since liberated slaves were wartime captives, Congress had the power to "make rules concerning captures on land." After their liberation, slaves would become full citizens, whose protection would proceed from legislation.[291] On the other hand, opponents such as Ohio's S.S. Cox objected that the welfare of former slaves should not involve the executive war power. Nor was it a function of Congress's war power since the Confederacy was not a foreign sovereignty. It was not until the Johnson administration that Congress exercised its authority to guarantee republican government as the constitutional rationale for enacting Reconstruction legislation as a peace, and not a war, power.

Reconstruction Debates as Sources of War Powers Principles

Congress's reconstruction enactments* during the Johnson administration were politically conceived, but they were also the legislature's attempt to resolve its conflicts with the executive over allocation of authority to commit forces to hostilities. The leading war powers issue, after General Lee's surrender, was which branch of government should decide when the Civil War was over and then, after hostilities had ceased, which branch was empowered to order reestablishment of normal civil legal institutions.

During discussion of reports by Generals Ulysses Grant and Carl Schurz on the condition of the rebel states,[292] Senator James Doolittle (D. Wisc.) declared that Congress had authorized the president to judge when the war had ended by its Act of July 22, 1861, authorizing Lincoln

---

on Emancipation by a vote of 81 to 51 (*id.* 1056), but it never emerged from the committee. The House Select Committee effectively maneuvered the demise of the Senate's version, but its own also died when the session expired. *Id.* 1294–95, 1545.

*The structure and procedures finally imposed on the South were embodied in four statutes passed between March 1867 and February 1868: (1) H.R. 1143, enacted 2 March 1867, established five military districts over the former Confederacy (37 *Congressional Globe Appendix* 197–98); (2) H.R. 33, 23 March 1867, provided an orderly method of electing delegates to state conventions to draft constitutions and establish civil governments for the seceded States (38 *Congressional Globe Appendix* 39–40); (3) S. 131, passed 19 July 1867, empowered commanders of districts named in H.R. 1143 to remove civilian officials and replace them with military ones, regulate voting procedures and qualify voters (*id.* 43–44); (4) H.R. 214 of 25 February 1868, the final major piece of Reconstruction legislation, established among other matters certain regulations for citizens' voting to ratify a State constitution (39 *Congressional Globe Appendix* 500).

to accept 500,000 volunteers and to disband them "at the end of the war." It was a power, he said, "imposed upon him by Congress as a duty."[293] Congress thus had required the president ". . . to make war; and . . . to stop making war after its end is reached; in other words, to make peace. . . ."[294] In addition to asserting that presidential authority to make peace was derived from Congress, Doolittle sweepingly likened the power of the president in his capacity as commander-in-chief to that of a "temporary dictator."[295]

Doolittle's opponents had no constitutional difficulty with the principle that the president drew upon his own powers as commander-in-chief to establish provisional governments that restored order after the rebellion was put down.[296] Other proponents of presidential authority appealed to necessity as a source of executive power. As James Hubbell (R. Oh.) expressed it, "A restoration of order and civil government out of the chaos and confusion that prevailed in those States, would necessarily encounter technical irregularity, whether conducted by the legislative or the executive department. . . ."[297]

Those lawmakers who believed the president's peacemaking authority emanated from Congress were not satisfied that he had exercised the delegated authority Doolittle described or would in fact do so.* It was therefore not unexpected that a radical Republican Congress, fresh from its triumphs at the polls in 1866, would conclude that Andrew Johnson was not exercising the kind of leadership that the party was determined to have. But like Polk's Congress during the interval between the final U.S. victories in Mexico and the Treaty of Guadalupe Hidalgo,[298] the post-Civil War Congress faced a dilemma. It possessed, along with the arguable authority to make peace, the constitutional duty to make regulations for the territories (should the conquered South be deemed a territory), and if the South should be regarded as part of the United States, Congress had the responsibility to guarantee a republican form of government to every state. Yet the president had the absolute authority to direct all U.S. military activities in the field, and since there had as yet been no declaration from either branch that peace had been fully restored, conflict between the two branches could reasonably be expected.

While the executive wielded the absolute military power that held the South under Union authority, Pennsylvania Congressman Thomas Williams expressed the will of a majority of his colleagues when he

---

*Representative George Anderson (Rad. R. Mo.) echoed his party's sentiment that even the president thought that the war was continuing. *Habeas corpus,* he said, was still in suspension; and since there had been no "invasion" to cause it to be suspended, Anderson concluded that President Johnson evidently believed the rebellion was still in progress. 36 *Congressional Globe* 1478.

stated that Congress had to relieve the president of this function. Williams perceived that the commander-in-chief power could be supplanted by congressional action.[299]

Connecticut's Henry Deming (R.) and Illinois' Samuel Moulton (D.) also believed that Congress could restore peace and order, but each emphasized that the South was a vanquished people whose status could only be determined by both the legislative and the executive branches of the government.[300] Thus, they envisioned that the commander-in-chief and the legislature should cooperate at least to some extent.

Opponents of the first Reconstruction enactment (H.R. 1143) could not find within the war power any express or implied authority granted either to the president or Congress to institute what amounted to martial law in the South.[301] Others disapproved of the provision that appointment of the various officers to head military districts was to be made by the general of the army, not by the president who, as commander-in-chief, possessed the constitutional power of appointment.[302] Although it passed the bill, Congress first eliminated this section that tampered with presidential authority and thus refused temporarily to seize the appointment power.[303]

Johnson, in his first of four vetoes of the Reconstruction Acts, objected to the military rule established by the legislature. He perceived it as being despotic,[304] since hostilities had ended and a state of peace existed: "There is not in any one of the States . . . either war or insurrection."[305] Johnson argued that the bill was unconstitutional because Congress was asserting in peace time a power that it possessed only in time of war; i.e., establishment of martial law.[306] But both houses passed the bill over the president's veto.[307]

Radical Republicans continued to try to give General Grant effective control over the military districts and eventually succeeded in passing the Command of the Army Act,[308] which provided Grant with authority to execute the Reconstruction Acts. Among other provisions, the second section of this bill[309] required that any issue of orders in violation of its terms was to be considered a misdemeanor in office,* a provision that some congressmen felt would guarantee the president's impeachment.

Opponents of the bill, such as Representative William E. Niblack (D. Ind.), found it mysterious and extraordinary that it had been introduced into an appropriation bill (H.R. 1126). Niblack described the entire section as "revolutionary" and further characterized its effects as "wholly nugatory" in terms of the Constitution.[310] Representative Ed-

---

*Representative Francis Le Blond termed it a paradox for the president to have to face possible impeachment for fulfilling his duties as commander-in-chief under the Constitution. 37 *Congressional Globe* 1353–54.

win Wright (D. N.J.) similarly warned his colleagues not to override the Constitution by this "ill-advised scheme," a proposition "outside of any appropriation, except it may be appropriation of the powers of the President."[311] But attempts to amend or eliminate the section were defeated, and the bill passed in the House, 90 to 32.[312]

Senate opponents objected to Congress's attempt to absorb the commander-in-chief's powers, but they were no more successful than their colleagues in the House,* and the bill passed.[313] General Grant was therefore empowered to issue instructions to subordinates that conformed more closely to congressional policy than to the executive's, without fear of removal or any other interference from the president. The passage of the Reconstruction Acts and their auxiliaries (the Command of the Army and Tenure of Office Acts) thus created the anomaly of a major legislative program being carried forward over presidential opposition.

When Andrew Johnson had asked the Cabinet for individual opinions about the Tenure of Office Act, every member denounced it.[314] But when he sought advice about the second section of the Army Appropriation Act, he received differing opinions. Orville Browning, secretary of the interior, prepared a veto message, but Edwin M. Stanton and William H. Seward disapproved of transmitting it to Congress. Both pointed out that if Johnson vetoed the bill, the army would be thrown into disarray at a critical time. The president followed their advice as he signed the bill, but insisted on accompanying his approval with a protest, prepared by Attorney General Henry Stanbery, which asserted that the act's second section "virtually deprives the President of his constitutional functions as Commander-in-Chief of the Army. . . ."[315]

President Johnson, however, was unaware that Stanton had drafted the rider. While the bill was pending and shortly thereafter, only Senator Fessenden and Representatives George Boutwell (R. Mass.), Thaddeus Stevens (R. Pa.), and Speaker of the House Schuyler Colfax (R. Ind.) knew that Secretary Stanton was the author of Section 2.[316]

Subsequent discussions of Reconstruction policy expressed concerns about the branches' respective powers to determine that war had ceased and to exercise peacemaking functions. The legislative majority was unwilling to accept Andrew Johnson's assertion that war had ceased, and like Thomas Eliot (R. Mass.) insisted that " . . . the rights and powers of Congress were such as a condition of war created. . . ."[317] The majority agreed that Congress's rights had not ceased upon Lee's

---

*The only substantial Senate amendment to Section 2 of H.R. 1126 succeeded in permitting the president to assign the general of the army outside Washington if the general of the army requested it. *Id.* 1847. This amendment was concurred in by the House and survived conference discussions. *Id.* 1705, 1949–50, 1978, 14 Stat. 485, 486–87.

surrender but would continue until it had secured governments in the rebel states that would unite in harmonious political relationship with the general government.[318]

Implicit in many lawmakers' arguments was the idea that Congress was the supreme power in national government, particularly in time of war or national emergency.[319] During debate on H.R. 439,* Representative William Loughridge (R. Iowa) cited John C. Calhoun as having stated that the legislative branch was strongest and that Congress "possesses besides, by an express provision of the Constitution, all the discretionary powers vested in the Government, whether the same appertain to the legislative, executive, or judicial departments."[320] Legislators thus maintained that Congress had the supreme power to make regulations for the armed forces despite the fact that the president is commander-in-chief.[321] The majority, therefore, asserted that Congress's authority to regulate the use of military power and its right to assign troops in conquered areas was more justifiable when a war was over and the Constitutional prerogatives of the commander-in-chief were not necessary in order to direct the work of rebuilding shattered governments.

Since Johnson had either deliberately or unwittingly ignored Congress in his program for reestablishment of those governments, legislators perceived that their own exercise of military power constitutionally overrode any exercise of the commander-in-chief power that the president had exercised. Moreover, the legislation appeared to be justified as a temporary measure until the states had made the transition from a state of disorganization to one of subordination to the Constitution.

Executive Use of Prospective Authorizations

The Water Witch *Incident*   Congress did permit President Buchanan to retaliate in case of unredressed aggression abroad but did not favor increasing his power to protect the individual states from insurrection.†

---

*This bill provided that the provisional governments of the former rebel states were illegal and authorized the general of the army to establish republican governments in these states, including the power to remove former civil officers. But legislation that authorized the president to instruct or remove military commanders in the military departments was repealed. 39 *Congressional Globe* 476.

†It was far from clear before the Civil War whether the president alone possessed authority to preserve peace between two or more states within the federal system by use of anything more than persuasion. The Acts of 1795 and 1807 did not confer such power. *See supra* pp. 217–18. Congress did not respond favorably to a resolution proposed by Illinois Senator Stephen Douglas urging that Congress pass a statute conferring plenary power on the president to repel invasion from outside the United States and defend a state of the Union from attack by another state. 29 *Congressional Globe* 448. The chief executive

Legislators discussed the full extent of force they believed the president could use short of war, as well as the criteria by which they felt such military strength might be brought to bear, but did not grant fuller offensive and defensive authority prospectively.

Congress authorized Buchanan to retaliate for unredressed aggression against a U.S. naval vessel in a resolution of 2 June 1858, which also implied the authority to charter an unspecified number of military vessels for an expedition to Paraguay.* Buchanan's reasons for requesting authority to use force against Paraguay included personal dislike of Paraguay's President Lopez, although the official cause was the *Water Witch* incident.

In 1853, a small river steamer, the SS *Water Witch,* was dispatched to the La Plata River to ascertain the fitness of the river and its tributaries for navigation. Ostensibly engaged in a scientific experiment, she was unmolested until February 1855 when, while cruising up the La Plata's main tributary, the Parana River, the *Water Witch* was fired upon by a Paraguayan fort. The helmsman was killed, three men were wounded, and several other shots pierced her hull, while return fire was ineffective since the ship was not equipped with the arms of a warship.[322]

Buchanan informed Congress that the pretext on which the attack occurred was an 1854 decree of Paraguayan President Lopez prohibiting foreign war vessels from navigating Paraguay's rivers. But President Buchanan denied that the ship could possibly have been considered a war vessel.† Moreover, since Paraguay owned only one bank of the Parana River while a number of the Argentine confederation had title to the rest, he asserted that the government of Paraguay could not reasonably have expected that Lopez's decree would be honored.[323]

President Lopez had offered to negotiate a treaty** "acknowledging

---

was not expected to delay using federal troops "until the invading army shall have been organized and drilled and placed in march. . . ." *Id.* 553. Most legislators agreed that Congress possessed power to legislate upon the subject but tabled Douglas's resolution on the ground that the president might use the military to search for conspiracies. *Id.* 591.

*Since no trial of force developed, however, the significance of this particular prior authorization can only be approximated by references to congressional debates and Buchanan's remarks.

†Although Buchanan characterized the *Water Witch*'s mission as scientific, he knew at the time of his annual message of 1857 to Congress that more was involved. Commander Thomas Page wrote to Secretary of State Marcy in 1854 that Paraguay's prohibition against all foreign men-of-war ascending the La Plata River had been issued "in consequence of the part taken by the *Water Witch* under my command" to remove certain American citizens from Paraguay. The U.S. commander noted that President Lopez considered Page's acts hostile because the citizens removed were entrepreneurs who were abandoning companies in debt to Paraguay. S. Rep. No. 60 (Letters of 17 October and 5 November 1854, "Difficulties with Paraguay"), 35th Cong., 1st Sess. 43, 45; *id.* 54 (Minister of Foreign Relations Nicholas Vasquez to Special Commissioner Richard Fitzpatrick, 8 November 1856).

**This offer had initially been extended in 1855 to an American agent who possessed no negotiating authority. A treaty that had been negotiated between the United States and

the wrong inflicted" on the U.S. vessel, but[324] the U.S. government had given neither formal notice of the grievance nor requirement for redress. Thus, some senators found it objectionable that the initial U.S. demand on Paraguay should be backed by force.[325] Buchanan maintained that acquiescence to U.S. demands would be more likely if military force could be used to reinforce them[326] and hoped for congressional authorization to "use such force as in his judgment may be necessary, in the event of a refusal of just satisfaction. . . ."[327]

In a letter to Navy Secretary Isaac Toucey written after passage of the resolution, Buchanan termed Lopez too ambitious and tyrannical,[328] and though he did not discuss the purpose of the intended expedition, he alluded to the possibility of inciting the Chaco Indians to overthrow him. Buchanan held firm that the threat of force would alone suffice to topple Lopez:

> If our expedition be of such character as to render our victory certain
> . . . Lopez will yield without a fight, but not otherwise.[329]

Buchanan was apparently unconcerned that Paraguay would regard incitement of the Chaco Indians as an act of war. Had conflict erupted as a result, his actions would have usurped Congress's power. Even if Congress had intended by its resolution to urge on an Indian revolt, such an authorization likely would have exceeded constitutional limits on the delegability of the war powers.

The Senate Foreign Relations Committee's report was accompanied by a resolution that authorized the president to use force if negotiations between the United States and Paraguay failed.[330] Vermont's Jacob Collamer sought unsuccessfully to amend* the resolution by deleting the discretion to use force, but the Senate passed it and[331] thus tendered to Buchanan the potential for wide discretion. House consideration was swift: though some members argued that the resolution transferred the authority to declare war to the president, others rebutted that whatever force the president used would be authorized by Congress under defined circumstances. The House passed the resolution without revision, 115 to 79.[332]

Paraguay in 1853 lay undelivered at Buenos Aires. Lopez preferred a new treaty that would include reclamations for all issues pending between the two countries. 27 *Congressional Globe* 1704, 1782.

*Collamer's proposed amendment was defeated, 15 to 25. 19 *Congressional Globe* 1963. He had pointed out that the president had traditionally been regarded as competent to employ force against "barbarous and uncivilized" people to obtain redress of grievances for outrages committed against Americans (*e.g.*, in the Fiji Islands and at Greytown), but never was it regarded as proper to clothe him with discretion "to commence a forcible war" upon "a civilized people" with whom the United States reciprocated diplomatic relations. 27 *Congressional Globe* 1727.

Similar constitutional problems arose over an executive proposal to increase the navy in order to deal with the Paraguayan imbroglio. President Buchanan requested additional funds to pay for previously contracted vessels and to purchase or hire new ones for his expedition to Central America. Congress then scrutinized Buchanan's activities in relation to deployment of and contracting for ships and considered Secretary of the Navy Isaac Toucey's report that

> Congress having authorized the President to use force to obtain redress from the Government of Paraguay, it was deemed expedient to send a powerful fleet into that neighborhood to be employed, if necessary for that purpose.
>
> In fitting out this expedition it became necessary, in consequence of a deficiency in the Navy of vessels ... to charter a number of steamers. . . . [333]

Representative Thomas S. Bocock (D. Va.) felt the request was proper and would prevent loss of time in final settlement:

> The commissioner proposes his terms ... and when the Government of Paraguay hears them, with a distinct knowledge that, if it refuses to accede to them, there is a fleet to back him, then it will be more apt to assent to the terms. [334]

Bocock's advocacy of this appropriation implied that executive deployment of ships was constitutional even if the resolution that underpinned it was not. Another broad construction by Congressman John Phelps (Missouri) envisioned no problem with Toucey's chartering of ships required to supply the naval deficiency. [335] But Representative H. Winter Davis (R. Md.) sharply challenged Buchanan's *"unlimited* power," conferred by an "improvident resolution." He urged an argument strongly reminiscent of contemporary opposition to the acquisition of Cuba: Executive contracts followed by requests for their support in the form of deficiency appropriations constituted unwarranted and illegal delegation of the power of the purse [336] that enabled the president "to create out of funds which we did not give him, a fleet ... and with that instrument of his own creation, to wage the war which we authorized him, in an unguarded moment of warlike enthusiasm, to wage." [337] Congressman Horace Clark (D. N.Y.) believed that even if the Paraguay expedition had not been intended as a peace measure, its purpose was to permit the president to use the already existing army and navy, and was not meant to be authority to "purchase ... a new navy." [338] In spite of these protestations, the administration again emerged successful. After defeating several restrictive substitute amendments, a majority enacted the bill (House, 83 to 77; Senate, 28 to 8). Although it ostensibly restricted the secretary of the navy to chartering vessels, it allowed him to purchase them if he felt it necessary and appropriated the requested $289,000 for the purpose.[339]

Faced with a vigorous foreign policy, Congress once more acceded to Buchanan's requests although they might have appeared to decrease legislative control in foreign affairs. The Paraguay incident thus stands as an example of congressional deference to the executive, although involving a military exigency demonstrably less imperative than earlier instances of foreign challenge. It also illustrates Buchanan's apparent belief that his foreign exploits required legislative authorizations, as well as his penchant for drafting them in the most general language possible.

In his annual message to Congress of 19 December 1854, Buchanan relished the thought that the mere threat of force had produced a favorable treaty of friendship, commerce, and navigation in three weeks without a battle:

> The appearance of so large a force ... had a happy effect in favor of our country throughout all that remote portion of the world.[340]

Buchanan did not give cause for alarm by actually ordering U.S. warships to initiate hostilities. It was likely that the administration's success in obtaining passage of measures calculated to permit presidential use of military force was in no small measure due to Buchanan's own consistent record of care in refusing to exceed the bounds of Congress's authority, or at least in appearing to be willing to ascertain it whenever he was in doubt.

British Maritime Aggression In May 1858, Congress debated additional criteria by which the legislature might constitutionally delegate a quantum of authority—short of war—that would permit the executive to defend U.S. vessels under actual threat of attack. Thus, theoretically, both the prospective and actual possibilities of the use of force might be joined to constitute the full power that the executive could exercise lawfully without a declaration of war.

Numerous American merchant vessels on the high seas had been stopped and questioned, while others had been fired upon by British armed cruisers in the Gulf of Mexico and the West Indies. Though the British claimed that their conduct was justified in order to help suppress the slave trade, the United States unqualifiedly refused to recognize either the right of visitation or search in time of peace, and the matter became the subject of diplomatic negotiation. President Buchanan deployed a naval force with orders "to protect all vessels of the United States on the high seas from search or detention. . . ." The Senate Foreign Relations Committee reported that it felt that legislation was not required, judging that Buchanan's "preventive and temporary" exercise of "the full extent of the Executive power in the absence of legislative provision," had momentarily arrested the aggression.[341] The committee did, however, recommend approval of Buchanan's deploy-ment,* evidencing its belief that the president could take some steps short of war on his own authority. Although the report did not enumer-ate permissible actions, it implied that the president had the power to direct the navy to an area where a threat of hostilities existed.† The committee recommended that the president should be enabled to take more vigorous action if required. Its reluctance to see Buchanan take more serious immediate action reflects not only approval of his conduct but also fear of involving the United States in a war with Great Britain at a time when both countries were engaged in discussions that eventu-ally resolved the problem.** Apparently, the committee did not want to jeopardize the opportunities to settle international differences.††

A distinction arose between two theoretical positions dealing with presidential power to use force on the high seas. The president was considered competent to resist a search but not empowered to take the offensive to prevent aggression.[342] While some legislators strictly be-lieved that any executive military act had to receive prior authorization from Congress, others, such as Illinois' Stephen A. Douglas, agreed with the committee that the commander-in-chief power should extend not to ordering ships into combat but to their deployment into a troubled area. Douglas sought to enable the executive to "instantly avenge the wrong on the spot" by arresting and bringing the offenders into port.[343] He denied that such legislation delegated the warmaking power, and insisted it conferred a right to use more limited force:

> It is not the war-making power which I propose to confer. I propose only to authorize the President to repel and punish aggressions in certain extreme cases, which do not admit of delay. . . .[344]

---

*The report was based on a transmittal of documents from the president in response to a Senate resolution of 14 May. *Id.* 2122, 2238, 2451. The Senate sought additional informa-tion after the British seized the American vessel *Panchita* on the coast of Africa. *Id.* 2297.

†The committee also recommended that the two countries finally dispose of the issue so as to preclude recurrence of such aggressions. *Id.* 2452.

**England finally agreed by July 1858 to discontinue the practice of visitation and search as to the United States and to engage in a "search" for a solution through diplomacy. 6 Bemis, *The American Secretaries of State and Their Diplomacy* 316–23.

††House members resisted attempts to submit authorizing legislation recommended by the House's Committee on Foreign Affairs, 27 *Congressional Globe* 3015–18 *passim.*

Mentioning no offending nation, Douglas introduced a bill "to clothe" the executive with the power to take "instant action" to redress any outrages committed against U.S. citizens.*[345] The Senate Foreign Relations Committee, however, reported a substitute bill on June 1 that addressed outrages occurring solely in Mexico, Nicaragua, Costa Rica, and New Granada. Both Douglas's and the committee's† bills provided for full reports to Congress of the facts of each case as early as practicable after presidential action, together with executive justification of the steps taken.

William H. Seward objected to the substitute bill on constitutional grounds as "giving the President . . . power to make war against even one nation, much more half a dozen, or all together."[346] But Douglas complained that the Committee's bill did not apply specifically to Great Britain:

> I had introduced a bill to authorize the President, in cases of flagrant violations of the law of nations, under circumstances admitting of no delay, to repel and punish the aggression. The Senator from Virginia [Mason] takes the provisions of that bill and indorses them as to four feeble crippled Powers, and omits the very country [Great Britain] that is now committing outrages upon our flag and our shipping.**[347]

Further discussion of naval appropriations brought about another unsuccessful attempt to confer a prospective authorization of power. On 7 June 1858, Senator James S. Green (D. Mo.) proposed an amendment that would give authority to the president to issue letters of marque after "the flagrant commission of outrages on our citizens by other Powers . . . and . . . then inform Congress of all the facts that induced his action. . . ."[348] His criteria for calling this extraordinary remedy into play exhibited reluctance to invest the president with "dangerous power":

> [I]t must be a case of flagrant wrong, it must be upon the commerce of the United States . . . it must be foreign . . . it must be imminent . . . and

---

*Douglas implied that while he proposed the bill because others did not believe that the president possessed sufficient power, he did not consider prior authorization necessary:

> It seems to be understood, although I am not prepared to concur in the opinion, that his [the President's] power extends simply to the point of preventing a search while the act is being done.

Id. 2496. *See* discussion of Douglas bill, *supra* p. 229 n.

†The Foreign Relations Committee's bill, however, authorized the use of these extraordinary powers only until January 1860, or for a period of approximately six months.

**Senator Mason defended the substitute by maintaining that the use of force against England would be the equivalent of plunging the country into "unpardonable" war. 27 *Congressional Globe* 2744.

redress must be required for the protection of rights. . . . And yet, lest there be danger of an abuse of the power [to issue letters of marque], this section says it shall only continue until the next meeting of Congress, leaving it for Congress then to continue it or not. . . .[349]

Senator Lyman Trumbull (R. Ill.) denied

that we have any authority to surrender the war-making power to the President. . . . He is not vested with it by the Constitution; and we have no right to divest ourselves of that power which the Constitution vests in us. I trust, therefore, that this measure and all like measures will be voted down; and if, when we investigate our difficulties with England, there is a cause for war, let us declare it; if there is a cause for reprisals, let us direct them to be made.[350]

Green responded that he was authorizing the president to wage imperfect war, "a thing not contemplated under the Constitution of the United States."[351]

I . . . presume everybody knows that the power to declare war is lodged in Congress alone; yet Congress has a right, in anticipation, to arm the Executive with authority to do certain acts of a warlike character.[352]

Green's amendment was defeated by a vote of 6 to 40,[353] as Congress persisted in its refusal to define the elements of an emergency that would permit the executive on his own to act in defense of the interests of the United States.

Unilateral Executive Actions

William Walker's Nicaraguan Expedition   There were no major U.S. military engagements except the Civil War itself during the period 1857–69. Several unilateral executive actions with potential military consequences provided the focus for intense discussions of the allocation of military power between the branches both before and after the Civil War, but there was no substantial ratification of presidential initiatives to undertake hostilities in pursuit of U.S. interests in the territories and in foreign nations.

Fully intending to establish a colony in troubled Nicaragua, the slightly built but monumentally ambitious filibusterer William Walker sailed to Central America with a group of armed men in 1857. After Commodore Hiram Paulding arrested Walker in a Nicaraguan harbor, President Buchanan asked Congress for legislation to restrain citizens such as Walker from "committing such outrages."[354] Neither house,

Attorney and constitutional scholar Lyman Trumbull of Illinois was unwilling for his Senate colleagues to delegate unrestricted power to President Lincoln during war time (p. 236). Mathew Brady photo, Library of Congress.

however, adopted a position. In a message of 7 January 1858, Buchanan claimed that Paulding had acted "in grave error" but that as president he already possessed the authority to arrest nationals thought to be embarking on an invasion of a foreign power outside American territorial waters. Legislators, however, debated whether there was any legal authority for the capture, which took place on Nicaraguan soil.

Many congressmen wondered whether Paulding believed that he was authorized to land in a foreign jurisdiction in order to arrest Walker.* If the landing had official sanction, Congress could well have felt that the executive was not coming before it in good faith.[355] Those who conceived of Central America as a fertile ground for the expansion of slavery approved of Walker's expedition to establish a quasi-American domain there and censured Paulding. Opponents of slavery praised him. Behind this general alignment were congressmen who feared that any acknowledgement of unilateral presidential authority to use force outside the United States could serve as a precedent to increase executive war powers, by analogizing authority to use force in "uncivilized" Nicaragua to the deployment of troops in the territories.†

Buchanan emphatically disavowed any executive approval of the capture.[356] He faulted Paulding for

> exceeding his instructions, and landing his sailors and marines in Nicaragua, whether with or without her consent, for the purpose of making war upon any military force. . . . This power certainly did not belong to him. Obedience to law and conformity to instructions are the best and safest guides for all officers. . . . [357]

He contended that such expeditions constituted "usurpation of the warmaking power, which belongs alone to Congress. . . . "[358] But the president suggested that Paulding, if so instructed, would have been justified in arresting Walker on the high seas,[359] inasmuch as he justified his own authority by interpreting the Neutrality Act of 1818** as a "collection of

---

*A similar incident serves as a useful comparison. James Buchanan ratified the conduct of Captain Pickett who acted to protect the lives and property of U.S. citizens on San Juan Island off the coast of Vancouver. In the wake of a clash that had occurred between American settlers who claimed the island and agents of Hudson's Bay Company, Pickett established a protective defense force on it, despite the absence of orders from the president. The incident of San Juan Island illustrates Buchanan's concept of legitimate use of force, suggesting the propriety of emergency unilateral activity by military subordinates to protect American lives and property, even in a jurisdiction whose ownership is in dispute. *See* 10 Buchanan, *Works* 350–52; P. Klein, *President James Buchanan, A Biography* (1962).

†*See supra* p. 205.

**Act of April 20, 1818 (3 Stat. 447). *See* the account of the genesis of the Neutrality Act (1 Stat. 381) in the administration of George Washington. Sofaer, *Origins* 103–16. Buchanan clearly suggested that additional legislation would be needed to authorize capture of filibusterers in a foreign jurisdiction. 27 *Congressional Globe Appendix* 4.

pre-existing laws" giving authority to the executive to make an arrest on the high seas without prior, specific congressional approval.[360]

His suggestion promoted a vigorous discussion of the allocation of the warmaking powers. Senator Jefferson Davis (D. Miss.), who usually advocated a strong presidential role in military affairs, contended that not even a treaty could have legitimized the arrest and insisted upon a prior authorization from Congress before the executive attempted to place "the Army and Navy ... at foreign ports and arrest persons suspected of a misdemeanor."[361] Davis and his colleague, George Pugh (D. Oh.) denied that the president possessed any statutory or constitutional authority to use the navy as a police force to cruise the oceans for wrongdoers, unless he could point to a law defining some offense on the high seas other than piracy.[362] Similarly, Senator Robert Toombs (D. Ga.) maintained that the executive could employ troops only *within* American territory. Use of troops to enforce laws outside of the United States would require direct congressional authorization.[363]

Representatives Thomas Clingman (D. N.C.) and Sydenham Moore (D. Ala.) regarded Paulding's action as an unconstitutional transfer of power from the legislative to the executive branch, which, in Moore's words, appeared as " ... the first dawning of an attempt on the part of one branch of the Government to invade the powers delegated to another."*[364] Others contended that authority for any presidentially approved arrest in a foreign country must lie in the executive's power as commander-in-chief but that this power was too narrow to accommodate authority to punish, since U.S. courts lacked jurisdiction over crimes committed on foreign soil. Senator Albert Brown (D. Miss.) argued that even if a host country consented to American military intervention, there arose an opportunity for war once the military became enmeshed with a foreign government. Any such possibility mandated prior approval by Congress for the deployment of troops.[365]

Proponents of the administration position sometimes outstripped the president's claims of authority as they alluded to his role as chief architect of foreign policy and to his exceptional power to act in emergencies without prior consultation with Congress. Several legislators discerned a viable source of executive power in natural law and

---

*Moore believed that another dangerous delegation of legislative power occurred in the Martin Koszta case (*see* Chapter 2, *supra* p. 163), an abuse that Congress had not seen fit to correct. On the other hand, William Kellogg (R. Ill.) cited the Koszta incident as a parallel: "Without the knowledge of the Executive, without an order from the Government, Ingraham went aboard an Austrian vessel of war, and took therefrom Koszta, who had only declared his intention to become an American citizen." Both Ingraham and Paulding acted lawfully, said Kellogg; no express instruction was required since the navy is the ministerial power in the hands of the executive by which international laws are enforced: "Where American rights are invaded, no legal order issues—nothing but the general order of the Executive—to enforce our rights and redress our grievances." 27 *Congressional Globe* 256.

the law of nations rather than the Constitution,* believing that the law of nations enabled the chief executive to order an arrest outside of the United States and to take other steps to avoid war:

> [U]nder the law of nations ... Paulding had a right not only to land and prevent this man from abusing the privileges which he had obtained from our flag, but ... to follow him to any portion of Nicaragua, to prevent the abuse of these privileges, and to prevent our being precipitated into war by the criminal acts of this marauder.[366]

Representative Daniel Sickles (D. N.Y.) found simply in the president's power to conduct foreign affairs the only support that he required. By characterizing the capture as a means to promote foreign amity and intercourse, Sickles emphasized Paulding's act as a measure designed to prevent rather than to encourage hostilities between the two countries. Such a peaceful purpose could best be attained, he contended, by giving the president the dominant role in foreign policy decisions and according full validity to them until clearly convincing evidence rebutted the strong presumption in his favor.[367]

Exploring whether Paulding had actually received instructions to make the arrest on foreign soil, Representative Samuel Curtis (R. Iowa) noted that one of Paulding's subordinates had applied to the secretary of the navy for more explicit instructions, which, although ambiguous,† apparently gave Paulding discretion to act in a foreign port.**[368]

The report and resolutions of the Senate Committee on Foreign Relations represented a political compromise containing ambivalent constitutional attitudes. Despite the narrow construction of the Neutrality Act of 1818 by such southern congressmen as Representative John Quitman†† (D. Miss.), the committee concluded that

---

*The natural law concept in this context was espoused primarily by Representatives John Thompson (R. N.Y.) (*id.* 259–60) and William Montgomery (D. Pa.) (*id.* 282–83), both northern Republicans, and may be regarded as a precursor of Justice Sutherland's view, expressed in *Curtiss-Wright,* that the executive's foreign affairs power is derived from a source outside the Constitution. *U.S. v. Curtiss-Wright Exporting Co.,* 299 U.S. 304, 315–18 (1936). *Cf.* Levitan, "The Foreign Relations Power: An Analysis of Mr. Justice Sutherland's Theory," 55 *Yale Law Journal* 467, 478 (1946).

†*Cf.* the controversy between Monroe and Jackson over Jackson's capture of Spanish forts in Florida. This is arguably another example of an administration official drafting purposely vague orders to induce his agent in the field to do something the executive wanted done because the president doubted his own authority to assume responsibility for the undertaking. *See* Sofaer, *Origins* 342–55.

**The texts of the orders are set forth in 28 *Congressional Globe* 689, 690, 691.

††Quitman contended that Congress had legislated to the fullest extent of its power. Any greater authorization would have to come from a treaty with the foreign country involved or, presumably, a declaration of war. 27 *Congressional Globe* 195. Since the Senate report did not accept Buchanan's suggestion that additional legislation be enacted to stop the filibustering by authorizing landing on foreign soil, it agreed to this extent with Quitman's limited application of the Neutrality Act to U.S. territory.

no further provisions of law are necessary to confer authority on the President to cause arrests and seizures to be made on the high seas, for offenses committed against the act [of 1818] . . .

That the place where William Walker and his followers were arrested, being without the jurisdiction of the United States, their arrest was without warrant of law. But, in view of the circumstances attending it, and its results . . . it may not call for further censure than as it might hereafter be drawn into precedent, if suffered to pass without remark.[369]

The committee was willing to legitimize Paulding's action. But since Paulding actually had received the gratitude of the Nicaraguan government, it would have been awkward for the United States to have censured him. As if to maintain some degree of independence, the Senate asserted that Congress had not authorized the arrest. Undoubtedly, Buchanan's public chiding of Paulding contributed to the Senate committee's failure to criticize the executive directly. Buchanan had successfully shifted the responsibilities for unlawful behavior to an agent, and neither house took a position on the president's authority to act to prevent or to initiate an action abroad that carried with it potential military consequences.*

Proposed Intervention in Mexico President Buchanan periodically reviewed the virtual chaos in Mexico, torn by revolution, and assessed its effect on American lives and property. He asked Congress for authority to place a temporary protectorate over northern portions of Mexico and establish military posts to discourage incursions by hostile Indians into U.S. territories, but the legislature refused.† Buchanan attempted again to intervene with American armed force.[370] He told Congress that he wanted to aid Mexico not only because of a continuous frontier of nearly a thousand miles but also because of U.S. opposition to intervention by European powers.[371] Buchanan recommended that Congress

---

*Members of both houses, however, did discuss the issue of constructive executive consent. In a subsequent resolution of thanks to Paulding, Vermont Senator Solomon Foot squarely blamed the administration for issuing vague and general instructions to its subordinates. While he avoided charging Buchanan with duplicity, there was no doubt that he believed that the executive planned unilaterally to break up filibustering expeditions and, when the deed was done, shifted the responsibility for taking any action "under the subterfuge or pretext that it was done without orders. . . ." 32 *Congressional Globe* 691–92.

†Since Congress possessed the war powers, only Congress could arm the executive with "the sinews of war," said Representative Thomas Anderson (Amer. Mo.), one of the few legislators making any relevant response to Buchanan's call for a Mexican program. He urged Congress to authorize the president to take certain steps short of war, such as taking possession of sufficient Mexican territory to provide indemnification for unredressed injuries. 29 *Congressional Globe* 297, 298. Senator Sam Houston (D. Tex.) also introduced a resolution to implement Buchanan's suggestion to establish a protectorate, but this was tabled. 27 *Congressional Globe* 1680, 1892.

authorize the president, "under such conditions as they might deem expedient, to employ a sufficient military force to enter Mexico for the purpose of obtaining indemnity for the past and security for the future." He also asked once more for authority to establish military posts.[372]

Buchanan again was denied his wish. Antislavery Senator Lafayette Foster (R. Conn.) declared that an authorization of the president to raise and use an army "to attack a foreign Government," at his discretion, was an unconstitutional delegation of Congress's war power.[373] Although he had voted for the president's authority to undertake the Paraguay expedition, "it was the exercise of a very doubtful power," and he would not again vote the same way "unless under very extraordinary circumstances." Foster believed that international law directed all nations to stay out of others' internal affairs no matter how much the intervening power might feel such affairs "need reformation." He termed prohibition against armed intervention one of the chief reasons for the Framers' separation of the war power from the American executive in 1787, even though it was inextricably woven into the fabric of executive prerogatives in other nations.[374] On the other hand, Samuel S. Cox (D. Oh.) called intervention the only true security of commerce and saw no impediment to a sweeping use of presidential authority to intervene and to annex:

What is the empty crown of royalty, without the head to plan or the arm to execute. Mexico has the right, but not the power; *we furnish the last.*[375]

He stated that Jefferson, John Quincy Adams, Polk, and Pierce had envisioned large-scale interventionist plans in their respective tenures as chief executive. But no such action was possible under Buchanan; by 1860 any notion of unleashing a Democratic president with a war party at his disposal into nearly helpless Mexico was preordained to defeat in Congress.

The Schofield Mission   There was no executive confrontation with Congress over proposed use of troops in Johnson's administration. But in one case, General of the Armies U.S. Grant unilaterally embarked on a mission to eliminate French intervention in Mexico, which he termed "a direct act of war against the United States."[376] Without even qualified permission from the president,* Grant ordered 52,000 men under

---

*When he had attended Cabinet sessions and urged President Johnson to warn the French either to leave Mexico or face U.S. intervention, Johnson and his Cabinet rejected both of Grant's suggestions that the U.S. intervene or that the government send rifles to Mexican agents. 2 F. Bancroft, *The Life of William H. Seward* (1900) 434; 2 G. Welles, *Diary* 317 (Beale ed. 1960)(entry of 16 June 1865). Secretary Stanton, on the other hand, did favor the mission. D. Perkins, *The Monroe Doctrine, 1826–67,* 471, 473, 475 (1965).

General Philip Sheridan to the Mexican frontier. Officially expected to root out and subdue Confederates still in the area, Sheridan's unofficial mission was to spread U.S. soldiers and munitions along the Rio Grande and thus to menace imperial troops in Mexico.[*377]

Grant then met with Matias Romero, Mexican minister at Washington, and found that Mexican liberals wanted to recruit U.S. troops led by a prominent northern general in a war against enemies of the Mexican Republic. Grant and Romero chose General John Schofield to lead the enterprise.[378] The proposed army was to be organized in Mexican territory under commissions from the Mexican government, thus avoiding the necessity of any action under the auspices of the United States.[†379] Schofield met with the president, Seward, Stanton, Grant, and Romero in June 1865, and there is some evidence that plans were approved to place Schofield on leave and put him in charge of the proposed effort to remove the French from Mexico. He recalled that "not much was said between me and the President or either of the secretaries at that time about the means to be employed; but it appeared to be understood by all that force would probably be necessary. . . ."[**380]

Secretary of State Seward thought that the proposed mission would probably involve the United States in an unnecessary war with France, and opposed it. During a Cabinet meeting on 16 June 1865, Seward declared that the entire French imperial episode in Mexico would collapse within six months. The consensus was to leave matters in Seward's hands,[381] and he did not delay. Since Romero had appealed directly to President Johnson, Secretary Seward issued a circular "requesting" foreign diplomats to conduct their business through the State Department.[382] Then he convinced General Schofield to go to France to ask Napoleon to withdraw his army from Mexico.[383] Schofield's role in France was kept insignificant, since Seward sent him no instructions for more than three months. In the meantime, Seward conducted independent diplomacy with Napoleon that resulted in an agreement for the withdrawal of French forces.[384]

*Some commentators have charged that Grant intended to use the troops affirmatively to provoke hostilities and make war inevitable. H.M. McCulloch, *Men and Measures of Half a Century* 387 (1888); J. Callaghan, *American Foreign Policy in Mexican Relations* 305 (1932).

†Mexican authorities were to pay the troops and provide funds for the costs of military operations, and a loan was to be negotiated in the United States. J.M. Schofield, *Forty-Six Years in the Army* 380 (1897); Bancroft, *The Life of William H. Seward* 434.

**One biographer doubts executive authorization, since Johnson appeared to support Seward's efforts to negotiate a peaceful settlement. L. Stryker, *Andrew Johnson: A Study in Courage* 390 (1929). Two other commentators believe that Johnson gave his approval to the Romero plan. Perkins, *The Monroe Doctrine, 1826–1907*, 473 (1965); J. Rippy, *The United States and Mexico* 269 (1941). But Schofield himself was not absolutely certain Grant had given more than informal approval to the program he and Romero had designed. Schofield 381.

Although Grant's enterprise lacked formal official authorization, the momentum generated by high-level discussion and tacit approval had brought about the serious possibility of U.S. armed intervention in a foreign nation without prior congressional approval. Congress did not discuss the plan, though Seward's opposition to it helped to defeat a bill providing for a U.S. guarantee of Mexican bonds being sold in the United States to finance the expedition. Even adherents of Mexican liberation were forced to consider Seward's argument that a U.S.-guaranteed loan enabling a more vigorous Mexican response to French forces would have comprised a breach of neutrality; and numerous attempts to press such bills through failed.[385]

Conclusion

Both before and after the Civil War, Congress and the president exercised their respective perceptions of broad-based constitutional prerogatives regarding the possible commitment of American troops to hostilities on not only foreign soil but also in the states and territories. Numerous previous conflicts involving the U.S. military had been fought primarily with foreign powers. When the North and South made war, it was on home ground, yet many of the arguments used to augment either congressional or executive influence over military and diplomatic affairs in foreign wars were employed to maneuver for control of the prerogative to conduct war and peace at home. Thus, whether the land surface sought to be controlled was the property of a foreign nation, eleven states in the southern federal system, or unsettled territories such as Kansas and Utah, they were either potentially or actually subject to the deployment or engagement of U.S. troops. Congress and the president themselves created the analogy between domestic and foreign warmaking, during their frequent discussions on allocation of the war powers.

Lincoln's concept that the power of the commander-in-chief was a tool to be used in the exercise of his executive authority was significant later in constitutional history, as was Buchanan's belief that authorizations prospectively granted could be broadly interpreted by the executive. But the executive uses of power when measured against the actions of Congress reveal that Congress's increasing dominance after Polk had developed into supremacy over the executive by 1860. Lincoln's exercise of broad powers as commander-in-chief and chief executive was usually linked to a delegation and ratification of authority from Congress and was not claimed as a Constitutional grant to the executive. The augmented influence of Congress was not the work of a moment nor the result of pressures by a single party. It resulted in part from the impact of increased American importance in foreign affairs and the awakening of Congress to its world responsibility. Congress controlled successfully what it considered to be executive excesses—as when it refused Buchanan's requests to use force in Mexico, the Caribbean, and Central America, and denied Johnson's petition to employ reprisal authority. The delegation of authority to Buchanan to use force against Paraguay stands alone as an aberration, followed by numerous refusals of similar requests for authority. At no time did Congress agree on criteria defining an emergency that would permit the unilateral executive use of military force. Instead, it continuously used the device of the congressional resolution to express its sense and will.

Congress's resolutions stating its position were bolstered by well reasoned debates and cast a long shadow over foreign affairs. Though Lincoln tended to ignore congressional advice to take a strong stand with France and Austria over Mexico, resolutions have continued to be a precedent for Congress's position on contemporary events such as American participation in the Vietnam War.

Lincoln's liberal treatment by Congress constituted a response to emergency and recognition of a *fait accompli* and was not a reallocation of authority under the Constitution. Congress's ratification of executive steps taken while it was not in session was a statement of its legislative retention of authority and not release of power to the president. Although Lincoln's attorney general found an expansive executive power to act in an emergency—an authority that presumably would not require subsequent congressional action—Lincoln did not rely on Attorney General Bates's opinion and did not seek Congress's approval of it.

Congress was, at times, jealous of bestowing authority on the executive, particularly where there was doubt as to which branch possessed the power to act. During the discussion of the William Walker incident and British maritime aggression, Congress not only refused to grant the executive's request for authority but also commented unfavorably on Buchanan's claims that he already possessed the authority to act but wanted legislative acknowledgment in order to avoid future controversy.

There was a brief period during the Civil War when Congress spoke of its participation in decisionmaking regarding conduct of the war as the exercise of a concurrent authority with the executive. By early 1863, moderates of each party visualized the war power as a joint exercise of both civilian and military authority by the president and Congress and not a tug-of-war between a frustrated legislature bent on saving its prerogatives and a president committed to expand the war at the cost of balanced government. Strict Democratic party theory that the South had rebelled within the Constitutional system was overruled by the

Union's need to defeat a stubborn enemy not entitled to Constitutional protection. Thus, while Congress rejected what it termed executive meddling in state law, both branches became committed to reinstatement of republican government in the seceded states. During 1863–64, the war power of the Lincoln administration and the Republican Congress developed into a peace power aimed at bringing an end to conflict by both military subjugation and the reestablishment of legal norms. By 1867, through Reconstruction, Congress demonstrated its capability of characterizing the civil conflict as ended and enacting laws that would supplant the commander-in-chief power.

For many years, Congress had attempted to acquire broader control over the personnel who carried out executive policy—failing in its efforts as much as it succeeded—but in the process expressing a philosophical basis for substantive review of the uses of appropriations for both appointments of personnel and execution of treaties. In the vacuum of authority after Lincoln's death, Congress seized the government from Andrew Johnson and, among other acts, denied the president any but the most severely restricted power to appoint any officer, military or civilian. By 1867, Congress could ignore the executive's complaint that to strip him of a constitutional power was in effect to blunt his capacity to function as commander-in-chief. It curtailed his power to remove and placed Lieutenant General Grant in such a position of authority that he could virtually dictate American foreign policy in Mexico to President Johnson. Grant was foiled only by executive diplomatic intercession—not by the exercise of presidential war power—which had collapsed in effectiveness though it did not, of course, cease to exist. The executive war power depended for its successful implementation upon the will of Congress, which had simply made the political decision not to have Andrew Johnson exercise it. Congress's action in this particular case was so blatantly political and reflected so little Constitutional principle that its success had scant precedential value for successive administrations. But in general, Congress exercised military supremacy after the war on the theory that the executive possessed power subject to the law of the land. Thus, Congress could assign special duties to military officers as it had done since 1789 and could insist on accountability by exercising removal power. In holding to this principle, the legislative branch was effectively reversing the decision it had made early in the Washington administration to delegate to executive officers the task of planning government policy in foreign, military, and economic affairs.

Chapter 4

The Executive Challenge to Congressional Supremacy, 1869–1901

INTRODUCTION

Five lawyers, a teacher, James Garfield, and a general occupied the White House during the final three decades of the nineteenth century. Analysis of the period from the Civil War through the death of William McKinley has traditionally placed greater emphasis upon the Republican Congress's political accomplishments than on the various chief executives' application of the commander-in-chief and other Article Two powers of the Constitution. During this period, however, there was full testing and development of executive prerogatives, as well as legislative responses to them.

Even as Congress struggled to impose its will on Andrew Johnson's successor, General Ulysses Grant frequently declared his stance in favor of a strong presidency and felt impelled to exercise full control over foreign affairs through Secretary of State Hamilton Fish.

Each president thereafter jealously guarded both his foreign affairs prerogatives and domestic authority. Rutherford Hayes's wide reputation as a wise administrator in governing Ohio helped to pacify the South, even as it helped him develop a national approach to the emergencies he faced seemingly all at once during the year 1877. James Abram Garfield stood firmly on his belief in the independence of the presidency until an assassin's bullet cut short the presidential career of one long trained in the art of dealing with Congress. Chester Alan Arthur proclaimed his determination that foreign affairs was the province of the president. Mistrusted by his party, the distinguished Arthur was not renominated and was followed by Buffalo attorney Grover

Cleveland. Cleveland's wooden defense of his position in domestic political issues was matched by a correlative application of virtually intractable "morality" in international relations that nearly provoked war with England in 1895. Benjamin Harrison's administration, traditionally viewed as that of a middle-course politician, came between Cleveland's two periods in office and was replete with assertions of executive supremacy in foreign affairs. Finally, William McKinley bridged the nineteenth and twentieth centuries, demonstrating the diplomatic mastery of Chester Arthur and the tenacity of Lincoln. McKinley sought and vigorously executed congressional delegations of authority, instituted his own program for military victory in an unauthorized and undeclared war, and established his own regulations for governing conquered territory. Congress finally had to rescind McKinley's rules in order to replace them with its own.

Executive power was more fully implemented during these three decades than historians have previously emphasized, though neither branch shaped a matrix for future shared responsibility in conducting military and foreign affairs. Most presidents and Congresses discussed in this chapter, however, dealt with issues concerning the authority either to commit or to prevent the deployment of troops to hostilities. Several administrations confronted issues that polarized the branches regarding information Congress felt it lacked on actions already taken. Finally, many debates concentrated upon incidents strikingly analogous to circumstances that have arisen in the late twentieth century.

EXECUTIVE-CONGRESSIONAL RELATIONS

Delegation of Discretionary Authority

Throughout the late nineteenth century, Congress legislated discretionary authority to the president, permitting him far more latitude to deal with national and international circumstances containing potential for hostile involvement than it had before. In only a few cases from 1869 to 1900 was the president actually denied congressional authority to act when he requested it. On the other hand, he generally triumphed over attempts to take away previously granted authority.

"Peace at the Polls"   In the 1870s the executive battled with Congress to retain a delegation involving the use of U.S. forces in the South, as the government dealt with the threat of civilian violence at polling places. Presidential claims of constitutional authority to handle civilian disturbances rested on thinking that harked back to Lincoln's invoking of the war powers of the president as though he were repulsing a foreign invader. Such claims were also based on an Act of February 25, 1865,[1] that generally prohibited executive use of the army to maintain do-

mestic order but contained a conspicuous exception allowing presidential use of military force at the polls.

Democratic congressmen took the position that Congress's exclusive authority to supervise its own elections and the use of the war power for this purpose were available to the executive only to the extent that Congress authorized it.[2] Therefore, they sponsored an amendment known as Section 6 of the army appropriation bill (H.R. 1), which would delete "peace at the polls" authority from the Act of 1865.*[3]

Republicans, however, argued that besides the commander-in-chief power, the president's position as chief executive officer justified his use of troops to keep domestic order. They also maintained that Congress had always authorized such intervention by statute.[4]

The House examined the effect of Section 6 on the president's war powers but came to no conclusion as to whether authority to keep peace at the polls was already a function of executive responsibility to protect the states against domestic violence.† The bill was finally pushed through by the Democratic majority, 148 to 122, with the president's authority intact.[5] The Senate passed the bill 41 to 30 on 25 April in the form reported from the House, but President Hayes vetoed it.**[6]

When the House failed to override the veto, Democrats introduced a bill that included a new Section 6, which explicitly refused to appropriate funds for the use of the army "as a police force to keep peace at the polls" (H.R. 2175).†† The bill passed in the House 172 to 31[7] but

---

*Both sides clashed over the extent to which Congress and the president might use coercive tactics during the appropriations process—namely, by adding riders such as the one under discussion. Republicans claimed that riders were generally disapproved in English legislative doctrine, while Democrats cited the fact that Parliament had used the power of the purse to make policy. 9 *Congressional Record* 211, 724, 725. Senator James Beck (D. Ky.) listed some of the more important precedents for use of riders by Congress, including bills admitting California as a state, excluding slavery from territory acquired during the Mexican War, and providing terms of congressional intervention in Kansas. *Id.* 475, 666.

†If the president's authority to keep the peace at the polls under federal law was a function of his responsibility under Article IV, section 4, it was unnecessary to include it in positive legislation, or, as in this case, it could be eliminated from an existing statute. Alexander Stephens (D. Ga.), on the other hand, said that Article IV, section 4, required statutory implementation, which was inferrable from the process of legislation in the Act of 1865. *Id.* 107, 108, 113. An amendment offered by Indiana Democrat Jeptha D. New was passed providing that section 6 of H.R. 1 would not infringe upon the president's power to act under section 4 of Article IV. *Id.* 252, 253, 258. This statement implied that no qualification of the Act of 1865 would affect any residual power that the president might have.

**Hayes criticized Congress for abusing the "power of the purse." By its threat to stop the government, Congress was attaching to appropriations legislation a provision that would not receive support as an independent bill. 10 *Messages and Papers* 4475, 4479–80, 4481–84.

††The clause that would remove "peace at the polls" language from the statute was separated and introduced as a separate measure, H.R. 1382. 9 *Congressional Record* 1049, 1092–95.

succeeded in the Senate 32 to 19 (20 June 1879) only after vitriolic debate[8] according to strict party lines. Hayes approved it on 23 June 1879 without indicating further whether he felt the statute tended to hamper existing executive authority. In this form, however, the bill did not achieve its larger objective of removing presidential authority to use the military to keep the peace. Subsequently, the House passed H.R. 1382, which did repeal the exception in the Act of 1865 but allowed the president to use troops "to repel the armed enemies of the United States" or under authority arising from Article IV, section 4, and its statutes.[9]

During Senate consideration of H.R. 1382, John Morgan (D. Ala.) denied the president's claim to legislative power and declared that it was therefore improper for him either to base the veto upon the form of the legislation (*i.e.,* use of the rider) or to question the motives of Congress.[10] Morgan replied to the president's argument that the repeal interfered with his implementation of the laws by pointing out that earlier statutes had controlled the president's use of regular troops for domestic intervention.[11]

Republicans such as Senator George Edmunds (R. Vt.) argued in opposition that a certain kind of police power, which he called "peace of the United States," emanated from such constitutional provisions as the guarantee of a republican form of government and the executive's obligation to see that the laws were faithfully executed. Edmunds asserted that the exercise of this power through the president "from the fathers to this day" had been recognized as a necessary predicate of a government's need for self-preservation* and that the delegation of power to keep peace at the polls was purely an implementation of this indispensable authority.[12]

The Senate finally passed the bill on 9 May, but Hayes vetoed it,[13] claiming that H.R. 1382 posed serious impairment of executive power. The president argued that the broader delegation was required to enforce the law, and he observed that "military force may properly and constitutionally be used at the place of elections, when such use is necessary to enforce the Constitution and the laws."[14] Since the House was unable to override the veto,[15] the effort to withdraw the delegation of authority failed.

Authority to Deal with Domestic Emergencies   Congress, on the other hand, did grant the president emergency powers discretion in several instances. In response to President Grant's message to Congress of 23

---

*Analogous arguments have been modelled on this reasoning to justify executive use of troops abroad. *See, e.g.,* a contemporary discussion of the war power in Note, "Congress, the President and the Power to Commit Forces to Combat," 81 *Harvard Law Review* 1771 (1968).

March 1871[16] that had protested Ku Klux Klan outrages, Congress considered a bill (H.R. 320) that not only permitted the president to call out militia, land, and naval forces to prevent domestic violence but also to suspend *habeas corpus* and to declare martial law in prescribed emergency situations. Though the martial law provision was finally dropped in the version that passed both houses, there was enough retained to give broad discretion to the president. Samuel Shellabarger (Nonpart. Oh.), apparently aware of the extent of the grant, emphasized the particularity of the guidelines for executive action. Upon introducing the bill, he took care to detail the criteria necessary before the president could act: A state had to be unable, fail, or refuse to protect a citizen. It must neglect to apply for aid, and the violence must deprive citizens of the privileges and immunities inherent in American citizenship.[17]

The spirit impelling these proposed delegations, though they involved authority to quell domestic violence,[18] was similar to other grants of power to chief executives facing duress from a foreign threat. Whether aggression had been measured as an attack on U.S. citizens' property,[19] as the imprisonment or trial without due process of law of naturalized Americans,[20] or as the threat of loss of newly won or claimed territory,[21] the common denominator that inspired Congress to accord this delegation and to deputize the president to act with the voice of American government was defense—a need for quick action to preserve liberty and prevent the loss of U.S. life and property in any case of emergency and without which the constitutional rights of citizens would stand in imminent jeopardy.

The president's enormous discretion drew the most fire. Indiana's Michael C. Kerr objected that the president's judgment on any question apparently was final, whether correct, hasty, reckless, dishonest, or wise. "No tribunal can review it or stay his hand."[22] He lamented that the president alone could determine when a domestic upheaval had proceeded so far that he could use any means necessary to quash it.[23] Proponents, however, agreed with Illinois Representative John B. Howley's distinction between unwarranted interference in the execution of state laws and H.R. 320, dealing only with state conditions that were contrary to federal law. In the latter case intervention by the federal government had always been allowed.*[24]

---

*Congressman Howley recited several examples of earlier statutes granting federal intervention. They included: the Act of May 2, 1792, which gave discretion to a federal judge to determine when conditions warranted national forces to put down rebellion; the Act of November 29, 1794, which authorized the president to use militia to crush rebellion in four counties of a state; the Act of February 28, 1795, which gave the president discretion to call out militia to crush rebellion; the Act of March 3, 1807, which gave the

Many of the bill's supporters would not have voted for it without Congressman Samuel Shellabarger's agreement to drop the provision permitting the executive to proclaim martial law in an affected area.[25] All Democrats responding to the roll call in both houses voted against the bill, while the vast majority of Republicans approved it.[26]

Authority to Deal with Foreign Emergencies   On 19 December 1894, the Senate took up a bill authorizing private financing of a Nicaraguan Canal through bonds guaranteed by the United States (S. 1481).[27] Among its provisions was a grant of discretion to President Cleveland to ascertain costs and feasibility of the Nicaraguan route. Senator John Morgan favored broad discretionary authority and emphasized the ever-present power of Congress to overrule the executive's conduct. He opposed an effort by David Turpie of Indiana to curtail executive discretion;[28] the president, declared Morgan, should have enough discretion to negotiate in any kind of emergency. But, Morgan added, this kind of flexibility had limitations; it was intended purely to give the president power, without the agreement of any other government, to order proper supervision of the work on the canal as it progressed and to stop the supply of money for building it whenever, in his judgment, sufficient reason existed for such a course. Morgan concluded that the check on such broad executive authority was Congress's power to overrule the president's action.[29] The bill passed in the Senate[30] but was never voted on in the House after it was reported out of committee.[31]

Later delegation of authority became virtually unanimous before the United States declared war on Spain in 1898. After suspicions had been thrown on Spain concerning the sinking of the *Maine* in Havana harbor, President McKinley requested and received a $50 million "contingency" appropriation for any possible military action arising from the incident: a sum that the president might use until January 1899 (H.R. 8927). The House and Senate unanimously passed this largest such authorization in history,[32] while several House members cautioned that the delegation, passed under circumstances that constituted an emergency, would be improper in normal times.[33]

McKinley's requests for military discretion, although granted for the most part,* were quite carefully examined. In one instance, a House

---

president authority to call out regular army and navy; and finally Lincoln's proclamation of April 15, 1861, which rested on the law of 1795. 44 *Congressional Globe* 380–81. Lionel A. Sheldon (R. La.) agreed that it would not be meddling for the federal government to step in, should a state refuse to protect its citizens. *Id.* 368.

*McKinley sought and received discretion in affairs ranging from organizing a Signal Corps (31 *Congressional Record* 4862) to enlisting volunteer Cubans in the army of the United States. *Id.* 4727. In a volunteer army bill, he received the traditional right to appoint staff and general officers. *Id.* 4114. Despite objection that future chief executives

resolution to permit the secretary of war to erect temporary forts without the approval of a host state, when that state's legislature was not in session, was finally compromised with Senate states' rights advocates who insisted that it must be the president alone who determined there was an emergency[34] before the requirement of consent could be lifted. This substitute passed both houses with only minor opposition.[35]

Control of Information

After 1870, information-sharing by the president and methods of data-gathering by Congress varied somewhat from that of previous Congresses. With the possible exception of Presidents Grant and Cleveland, presidents down to the turn of the twentieth century began more frequently to withhold information, while the House during Hayes's tenure made a rare declaration that it possessed a withholding privilege. There was also during this time an increasing tendency to ask for facts regarding foreign affairs without the traditional qualification.[36] Answers to congressional inquiries during this time were sometimes complicated by departments' assertions of a need to withhold information; yet Congress generally acquiesced to the transmittals supplied by the executive branch.

Impact of Partisanship   Partisanship, with its tendency toward harassment, generated its own share of information requests. President Grant's transmittals were often aimed at deflecting purely partisan requests.* Rutherford Hayes received a virtual barrage of requests for executive information, particularly in the second Congress of his administration. Yet the political opposition to Hayes appeared to be even-handed, since unqualified requests came equally from both parties. More than sixty-five out of eighty routine requests during that session were unqualified; and of the less than a dozen that deferred to presidential judgment about the national interest, nearly all were related to foreign affairs. Neither Hayes nor Grover Cleveland† tended to withhold information, even though both of their administrations were

---

might abuse a grant to raise a volunteer army at their will, McKinley succeeded in obtaining this discretion. *Id.* 4120–21, 4413–35, 4154–63. And during House debate on the establishment of an auxiliary naval force, despite protest over giving the president power to fix the number of men and the duration of the organization (*id.* 4867), amendments granting such discretion were tailored to meet these obligations. *Id.* 4872, 5159.

*In Grant's second administration, the Democratic House was responsible for thirty-one of the forty-four information requests passed.

†The administrations of Hayes and Cleveland offer, however, a few instances of information control worthy of note. *See supra* p. 205; pp. 258, 275.

targets for heavy Republican criticism regarding domestic programs. For example, Cleveland was not close-fisted with official information about potentially inflammatory conditions affecting U.S. citizens in Haiti and Samoa.[37] Only William McKinley of the late nineteenth century presidents drew attack from members of both parties for his attempts to strain out data that might increase Congress's determination to seek war in 1898.[38]

Congress's Approach Congress sometimes preferred to embark on information-gathering unilaterally by exercising its investigative authority. During Hayes's administration, senators agreed to the proposal of Roscoe Conkling of New York that they appoint a select committee of seven members for the purpose of investigating U.S.-Mexican relations and making recommendations to promote commerce, and "to establish a just and peaceful condition of affairs" on the border.*[39] This committee† was given subpoena powers as well as authority "to confer with the executive branch,"[40] though there is no record of its having had such a conference.

Senators believed that Hayes was singlehandedly contributing to the decay of U.S.-Mexican relations because he refused to recognize the new government of General Porfirio Diaz. Hayes, in his first annual message, had admitted that it was customary to recognize a *de facto* government as soon as it had popular approval[41] but departed from tradition because of the "depredations" on American property at the Rio Grande border. He conditioned official recognition upon the Mexican government's control of border disorders, which, he asserted, Diaz had the power to exert.[42]

House members attempted committee action first in preference to approaching the president directly. New York's Abram S. Hewitt introduced a motion to direct the House Foreign Affairs Committee to make recommendations[43] on Mexican-American relations as they affected commerce, but on the advice of Ohio Congressman James Garfield, Hewitt agreed to strike from his motion a controversial clause that would have enabled the committee to make any recommendations concerning treaties.[44]

In another situation in which the House was attempting to exercise

---

*In the next session of the Forty-fifth Congress, Hayes volunteered that negotiations had progressed quite satisfactorily with Mexico, which seemed to be taking better care to secure its borders. The president promised diplomatic recognition at the "earliest opportunity consistent with this plain duty to protect lives and property of our citizens." 8 *Congressional Record* 4 (annual message of December 1878).

†Named to the committee on 14 December 1877 were Senators Roscoe Conkling, Hannibal Hamlin, Timothy Howe, John Jones, James Cameron, William Eaton, and Samuel Maxey. 7 *Congressional Record* 208.

initiative to obtain foreign affairs information, Robert Hitt of Illinois sought all correspondence of the U.S. government with Great Britain concerning the dispute over seal hunting in the Bering Sea.[45] William Breckinridge (D. Ky.) felt that the foreign affairs situation should be momentous to justify the House taking the first step, since it was the president's right to introduce the subject to Congress whenever he thought proper:

> [F]rom any facts known to the committee or its chairman, is there any such gravity in the situation of affairs in the Behring Sea as to justify this House in taking the initiative, and thereby making proclamation that matters have gone to such an extent that it is the duty of the House to obtain possession of the facts without waiting for the President to take the initiative?[46]

Breckinridge acknowledged the Senate's right to initiate requests related to foreign affairs but saw the House's role, ordinarily, as limited to making appropriations as an aid to resolving U.S. differences with other nations or, in the extreme, to the expressly granted authority of declaring war.[47] Hitt fitted his reply to his colleague's theories; he pointed out that England was serious: British torpedo boats were being held "in convenient readiness" in case the seal fisheries question was not settled. Despite Breckinridge's opposition, Hitt's resolution of inquiry was passed, and Harrison responded not only with the requested correspondence[48] but also, in the next session, with voluntary documentation.[49]

Senator Morgan, a few years later, reconsidered the information prerogatives of Congress in a grave situation. When the U.S. vessel *The Competitor* was seized by Spanish forces, and U.S. citizens on board were taken into custody, Morgan and other senators considered Cleveland's pursuit of diplomatic remedies inadequate.* As chairman of the Senate Committee on Foreign Relations, Morgan on 14 December 1896 obtained passage of a qualified request for information on conditions in Cuba as well as details of *The Competitor* incident.[50] He criticized

---

*Cleveland reported to Congress in his annual message of December 1896 that the Spanish coast guard had captured, off the Cuban coast, an American schooner carrying men and supplies to aid the Cuban insurrection. The prisoners, among them several American citizens, were given a summary military trial, which did not conform with the essential safeguards of procedures stipulated by earlier conventions between the United States and Spain. Cleveland reported that the U.S. government had intervened and secured for its citizens all the rights to which they were entitled, including an appeal from a death sentence. As a result, an appeals tribunal at Madrid set aside the convictions and remanded the cases for trial. 29 *Congressional Record* 166. Morgan asserted that the president's intervention had been inadequate because under U.S. treaties with Spain no summary military trial in peace time had the right to condemn a U.S. citizen to death. *Id.*

Cleveland's policy of "patient waiting" and claimed that Congress had a responsibility to alter the normal course of permitting the executive to retain charge when the "disproof" of facts Cleveland had asserted was "overpowering."[51] Morgan also claimed that in any case in which hostilities threatened the safety and well-being of U.S. citizens, the president was obligated by statute[52] to communicate to Congress all facts and proceedings under which U.S. citizens were unjustly deprived of their liberty by a foreign government. In effect, Morgan argued, the law required the president to give the information to Congress and Congress to act.*[53] But the president had not replied, and the Senate could not relieve the president of his statutory duty to reply. Time was precious: Congress could not wait until publication of the Department of State's *Foreign Relations* volume in order for it to act "advisedly."†[54]

Withholding of Information

House Withholding   In an unusual twist, at one point during the last quarter of the nineteenth century, the House declared that it could not be required to respond to an information query. Congressmen maintained that they alone might exercise final authority concerning dissemination of information under House control.

The incident arose in the case of a subpoena served on a House file

---

*Morgan reminded his colleagues that only "common rumor" had kept the Senate advised of the facts in *The Competitor* situation: the president, in the first session of the Fifty-fourth Congress, had refused to transmit all the documents specifically requested by a qualified resolution. 28 *Congressional Record* 5277; *id.* 5603. Undaunted, Morgan had submitted on 3 June 1896 a second resolution, this time unqualified, asking for all information about the capture and imprisonment of U.S. citizens taken from *The Competitor* and citing in support the aforementioned statute which created a duty that the president inform Congress concerning such situations. 15 Stat. 223, 224 (Act of July 27, 1868). Morgan told the senators that since Washington's time, the construction placed upon the president's constitutional privileges was that he was required to send to Congress information it needed about the state of the union, subject to the courtesy extended him of withholding matters relating to pending negotiations. He then concluded his remarks with a vigorous statement about executive-legislative control of foreign affairs:

[A]fter all, the action of the President in his Constitutional function is not independent of the Congress of the United States; even in matters that may be called strictly diplomatic.

28 *Congressional Record* 6140, 6269. This resolution was never voted on, since the session ended on 10 June.

†President Cleveland's response of 22 January 1897, asserting that he was sending only information "which I deem it not incompatible with the public interests to communicate," implied that he was omitting information. His withholding in the public interest denied Morgan's claim that Congress possessed an absolute right to such information under the 1868 statute and maintained an executive right to exercise independent judgment regarding a course of action even when that action was mandated by statute. 14 *Messages and Papers* 6180.

clerk in 1879,* requiring him to appear before a New York state court martial and to bring with him the record of certain testimony given before the House Committee on Military Affairs in 1872. The House Judiciary Committee urged noncompliance; and the entire chamber concluded that the House was entitled to judge for itself whether production or inspection of its papers would be injurious to the public interest.†[55] The committee explained that it had reasoned from the rule of disclosure applied to the executive branch:

> [I]t is a principle well understood that the President, the governor of a State, or the head of a department is not bound to produce papers or disclose information communicated to him when in his own judgment the disclosure would, on consideration of public policy, be improper or inexpedient, and by parity or reason the House of Representatives having the exclusive custody and absolute control of the papers belonging to its own archives, should judge for itself whether the production or inspection of these papers would be injurious to the public interests or not, and refuse or permit such production or inspection according as its own judgment might dictate.**[56]

Executive Withholding: Grant and Cleveland President Grant willingly shared information with Congress,[57] refusing it only when he perceived that the request infringed upon the independence of the executive department. In one case, he rejected a House inquiry concerning the executive acts and duties he had performed away from Washington.[58] Grant told the House that he considered its inquiry an encroachment upon the executive department as a coordinate branch of government and reminded members what he considered to be the House's rights to information:

> What the House ... may require as a right in its demand upon the

---

*That same year, the House also approved a procedural device that tended to encourage and speed executive responses. A bipartisan majority, in May 1879, changed House Rule 130 so that resolutions were required to be introduced on Monday and were then immediately referred to the appropriate committee, which had to recommend action within a week. 9 *Congressional Record* 1018–19. Proponents urged that the change would reduce duplication and encourage a prompt response from the executive. It might also tend to avoid introduction of individual requests by "a skillful minority," desiring "to prevent the views of the majority from being shaped into legislation." *Id.* 1018.

†To the present day, the House exercises far more jealous prerogative over study and dissemination of its records than the Senate. It is still necessary before consulting House records of the earliest Congresses in the National Archives to obtain permission to inspect them from the clerk of the House. Such permission is not required to examine Senate records.

**In this instance, the committee recommended a compromise that affirmed the House's authority to control its papers and agents but provided access to the records so that the parties concerned might obtain certified copies—and this recommendation was approved. *Id.* 535, 679, 681.

Executive for information is limited to what is necessary for the proper discharge of its powers of legislation or of impeachment.[59]

President Cleveland's sweeping claims of right to withhold are noteworthy as precedent, even though one controversy arose outside the area of foreign affairs. When Cleveland, in July 1885, removed President Arthur's appointee as district attorney for the Southern District of Alabama in order to make room for his own, he refused to give certain information to the Senate's Judiciary Committee. The Senate passed a resolution directing Attorney General Augustus Garland to forward all papers relating to the conduct of Arthur's appointee.* Garland refused on the ground that the president had "directed" him to say it would not be in the public interest to comply.[60] A majority of the Judiciary Committee then announced that the Senate would refuse advice and consent to proposed removals if in such cases it demanded papers referring to purported "official or personal misconduct by the Executive" and was refused access to them.[61]

Cleveland explained to the Senate on 1 March 1886 that he had told Garland not to forward the papers because he regarded the incoming correspondence relating to the two men as "purely unofficial and private, not infrequently confidential, and having reference to the performance of a duty exclusively mine ... I suppose if I desired to take them into my custody I might do so with entire propriety, and if I saw fit to destroy them no one could complain. ..."[62] Cleveland limited the application of his broad claim to letters addressed to him by private citizens who had written voluntarily "without any official invitation or subject to any official control." Letters of this kind, said the president, were given little or no weight by the executive in determining the questions to which they were supposed to relate.[63]

By a narrow margin, 32 to 25, the Senate censured the attorney general's refusal to send the required documents as a violation of his official duty and subversive of principles of good government and declined by one vote (30 to 29) to advise and consent to Cleveland's nominee.[64] But later presidents would have cause to be grateful for Cleveland's "stubborn defense of his power."[65]

Dual Reporting of Information   President Harrison's secretary of state, John W. Foster, wanted to make his own preliminary classification of information that could properly be transmitted to Congress, even before

---

*It had been the committee's practice since passage of the 1867 Tenure of Office Act to address a note to the attorney general asking for all papers relating to the conduct of the person to be removed and the character and conduct of the person to be appointed. 17 *Congressional Record* 1585.

A view of the Senate chamber in the early 1880s. (L.C.)

any requests were received. In a confidential letter, Secretary Foster instructed U.S. minister to Hawaii John Stevens to write two classes of dispatches, one which gave a narrative of public affairs "in their open, historical aspect"; the other "commenting upon matters of personal intrigue and the like. . . ." Stevens had tended to combine the two kinds of reports, which made publication, "in event of a call by Congress, inexpedient, and, indeed, impracticable without extended omission."[66] On the other hand, Foster's order, even though it may have reflected a practice not unknown in diplomacy of other periods, tended to create problems in information-sharing, since there is no evidence that Congress was aware of the dual reporting practice being carried on in the Harrison administration. Congress's customary qualified request acknowledged the executive need to withhold certain foreign affairs information "in the public interest." And the State Department's usual method of excising sensitive matter put Congress on notice that certain data had not been transmitted or were to be sent later. Therefore, if Congress received reports with no omissions, it could have assumed only that all relevant information had been transmitted in response to a qualified request and would have been lulled into a false belief that the executive had withheld nothing.

Withholding of the Sources of Information   The most significant example of refusal to communicate information, in an administration almost distinguished by the *punctilio* of its responses to Congress, was President McKinley's refusal to give the names of the U.S. consuls in Cuba supplying information on the exact status of the Cuban insurrection.* Senator Morgan, on 19 May 1897, told his colleagues that in offering to release information about events in Cuba,† the president had agreed to give the consuls' names only to Morgan and two other senators on the Foreign Relations Committee—Joseph Foraker (R. Oh.) and Eugene Hale (R. Me.). He had forbidden their transmittal to the other senators. Although the president had agreed to full communication of the *substance* of the reports, Morgan refused the offer, saying he would never accept information that he was not permitted to share freely with his colleagues "as a Senator should."**[67] Morgan charged that the president's tactics†† were a ploy to delay or even prevent passage of S.R. 26,

---

*All congressional requests concerning the Cuban insurrection contained the usual reservation, and the refusal by McKinley to name and locate those individual consuls in Cuba who were providing reports on the insurrection was the only outright denial occurring in the first session of the Fifty-fifth Congress. The president was using his power over information to prevent passage of S.R. 26, which proposed a joint declaration of Cuba's belligerent rights in her struggle with Spain, as well as U.S. neutrality (*See infra* at p. 261). Probably of equal importance to the president as the policy the resolution declared was the fact that it assumed Congress's right to recognize these international facts and set the foreign policy of the United States.

†The unpublished consular reports had been requested on 29 April in a resolution that contained the usual qualification and passed without debate. 30 *Congressional Record* 847. While Morgan did not mention the discretionary style of the request, it may be assumed his colleagues knew about it; the Senate, therefore, had expressed in advance its agreement to the president's withholding of information in the public interest.

**Intelligence briefings by the State Department and acceptance of their classified nature have become more generally palatable. This was indicated recently, for example, when the State Department conducted such a briefing of twenty-six prominent officials of past Republican and Democratic administrations on the need for military aid in El Salvador. This method seems to promote two objectives while satisfying the exigencies of secrecy: (1) giving Congress information it needs in order to legislate knowledgeably and (2) securing for the executive the legislation that it wants by "pushing" convincing information to a chosen few. *Washington Post*, 11 March 1982, at A–1.

††The Department of State had insisted that the consular despatches be edited before they were transmitted to the three-man delegation from the Foreign Relations Committee, consisting of Morgan, Hale, and Foraker, who had journeyed to the department to be briefed on them. The three were finally verbally briefed about the material, with the injunction that they not reveal the consuls' names and their locations, information that

which would recognize Cuba as a belligerent and accord it the appropriate rights under international law.*[68]

Although Morgan was dissatisfied with the executive explanation that a consular massacre could result from release of unedited dispatches, Foraker claimed that what was later termed "executive privilege" had been exercised since the earliest days of the Republic.[69] Its exercise in this instance was perfectly reasonable, given the potential of danger to the informants and fear that disclosure would cut short the State Department's sources of information. George Hoar of Massachusetts added that once the consuls were identified, Spain would demand their recall and that this was one of the reasons for attachment of the qualification to foreign affairs requests. On the other hand, Missouri's George Vest called for release of all information, arguing that the limitations affected the sources' credibility and authority when it was not possible to check them. He said that warships should be sent to protect endangered U.S. consuls as part of the government's duty to shield them in performance of their functions.[70] This controversy over McKinley's control of information occurred the day before the resolution on Cuban belligerent status (S.R. 26) was passed in the Senate, indicating that the withholding was a delaying tactic to block Senate recognition of Cuban belligerency.† Significantly, the episode reveals how aggressive the Senate Foreign Relations Committee could be in its demands upon an equally tenacious executive. None of the several other important congressional requests for specific information met with this kind of impediment or outright denial of access.[71]

Withholding for Reasons of Policy   Congress also expressed its disposition for war with Spain by its tendency to suspect that McKinley's desire to avoid war led him to withhold information of Spanish aggressions against the United States. Although these suspicions were translated into charges of executive withholding, no resolutions seeking information were adopted. In fact, resolutions of inquiry stopped entirely once

---

the department apparently intended to delete before sending the despatches to the full Senate. 30 *Congressional Record* 1147–49.

*Most of the Congress desired war with Spain and used information requests as only one of a variety of means to pressure McKinley into taking acts which could lead to U.S. military involvement over Cuba. Others included the use of petitions, resolutions regarding incidents in Cuba, and debate calling for ships to protect U.S. rights in Cuba. *E.g., id.* 119, 575, 576, 580; *id.* 758, 463, 2753. *See generally* debate on S.R. 26, *infra* p. 279.

†After the State Department presented its conditions and conducted discussions with the senators, thus causing controversy and delay, it receded from its initial position. Foraker's statements under questioning by Senator Stephen White (D. Calif.) indicated that the final version being prepared for the Senate would contain the consuls' names, but the documents were to be considered only in executive session. *Id.* 1149. Foraker's knowledge was based upon an evening visit to the secretary of state's house, which Morgan had refused to attend. *Id.*

the president requested authorization for military measures.* For example, in the period after the exploding of the *Maine* but before McKinley had spoken to Congress about actions he had taken and proposed to take,†[72] McKinley was charged with withholding relevant information in order to prevent Congress from authorizing a military response to various incidents.**[73]

The war itself bred more inquiries, most of which were unqualified.†† Three of these represented varying degrees of success and failure attending Congress's efforts to obtain information about the president's war and peace policies. On 16 January 1900, Massachusetts Senator George Hoar submitted a qualified resolution that, among a host of related questions, pressed the executive for both versions of a proclamation directed to the Filipinos regarding their status and U.S. intentions respecting the Philippine Islands. The version sent by McKinley to the Philippines apparently differed in some particulars from the one actually proclaimed by the U.S. General in Command, Elwell Otis. The Senate wanted to know whether McKinley or the War Department had authorized the changes.[74] The president transmitted documents responsive to the queries of the resolution on three different dates,*** and senators did not indicate any displeasure with the executive response.†††[75]

---

*On 8 March 1891, at the president's request, the two houses placed at his disposal $50 million, to be used in his discretion "for the national defense and every purpose connected therewith." 31 *Congressional Record* 3969.

†McKinley announced that the Navy Department was investigating the *Maine* incident. But some senators contended that it would be of value to conduct an independent congressional investigation, and a resolution calling for one was passed. *Id.* 1873–74, 1877, 1879, 1958. Nonetheless, the Senate's inquiry team chose to take no action until the navy's own investigation was completed, and legislation passed giving the navy power to compel testimony. *Id.* 2758.

**Senator George Turner (Fus. Wash.) accused McKinley of delay and subterfuge in seeking a complete investigation of the *Maine* explosion; Senator Joseph Rawlins (D. Utah) charged that the president retained information on the mistreatment of American citizens in Cuba in order to prevent war from being declared; and Representative Joseph Bailey (D. Tex.) expressed a similar concern when he contended that McKinley was withholding information on the administration's negotiations with Spain. *Id.* 3500, 3514, 3822.

††Only one-third of the forty-eight requests in the first session of the Fifty-sixth Congress (1899–1900) contained the public interest reservation.

***In his 5 March response, the president said that he had sent the proclamation and instructions to General Otis for his promulgation and had later approved Otis's revised version. The president enclosed Otis's version and his own letter of instructions, dated 21 December 1898, which McKinley apparently intended to serve also as a proclamation. 33 *Congressional Record* 2523–24; S. Doc. No. 208, 56th Cong., 1st Sess. (1900) (Ser. 3854).

†††Later Senate debate, in January 1901, brought forward that Otis had changed the president's language because he feared that the president's references to U.S. sovereignty over the Philippines and immediate occupation of the islands would cause an uprising. While those senators who requested the documents did not comment on the president's

Departmental Responses   The problem of how to elicit from department heads the information that legislators desired was considered first during Washington's administration, when congressmen discussed having the chief officers in the executive departments attend Congress and participate in debates.*[76] Ohio's Senator George Pendleton raised the proposal once more in 1881, supported by James G. Blaine, but was as unsuccessful as he had been in the House in 1864 when he and James A. Garfield failed to convince Congress that it was necessary or desirable to have Cabinet officials join in legislative deliberations.[77]

Congress generally did not press department heads to make full disclosures. More vigorous demands only arguably would have resulted in increased responsiveness. During Grant's first term, for example, Congressman James Beck (D. Ky.) made an unsuccessful effort to require independent information-gathering by congressional committees rather than rely on transmittals from the executive departments. During debate on a military appropriations bill,[78] Beck prodded his associates to require legislative committees to work independently to collect more information than they were being given by the departments and not to pass laws unless the information Congress put together sustained executive recommendations.[79] "Everything that is accessible to the head of any Department is equally accessible to the committees of this House."[80] William Niblack (R. Ind.), on the other hand, represented the majority, which favored appropriating whatever was called for in an executive estimate of military appropriations.[81]

On another occasion, Attorney General Richard Olney withheld critical information from President Cleveland that would have influenced the president's decision regarding the actual need for federal troops to intervene in the 1894 Pullman strike in Chicago. Cleveland had refused at first to treat the strike as more than a local problem until Olney proved that it posed an insurmountable obstacle to delivery of the

---

assertions of right and occupation of territory not yet ceded to the United States (treaty ratification was some seven weeks away on 21 December 1898), this fact was not lost on others in 1901, some of whom characterized the December document as a declaration of war on supporters of the Filipino Republic. 34 *Congressional Record* 1548, 1549; 15 *Messages and Papers* 6581. More extensive treatment of the controversy over presidential conduct in the interim between the treaty's signing and ratification appears *infra* at p. 318.

*Far from raising any constitutional difficulties, E.S. Corwin characterized the idea of Cabinet or agency head consultation as having "the countenance of early practice under the Constitution." *The President: Office and Powers, 1787–1957*, at 296. Justice Story placed his imprimatur on it by declaring that the president would consequently have to appoint strong men to Cabinet positions who could justify administration policies and thus foster openness and responsibility in government. The Confederate Constitution had authorized its Congress to grant to the head of each department a seat upon the floor of either house with the privilege of speaking about measures pertaining to his department. *See* Schlesinger, *The Imperial Presidency* 390.

U.S. mail, interference with which was a federal offense.[82] When Cleveland refused his urging to send troops, Olney, who had been a railroad counsel and remained sympathetic to railroad interests, arranged for the Chicago district attorney to obtain an injunction against the strikers. Olney kept these facts from the president. Federal judges not only granted the restraining order but even assisted in drafting it.[83] Cleveland then assented to the dispatch of troops. When strikers reacted by blockading tracks, burning freight cars, and stopping passenger trains, the president asserted that if it took the whole army or navy to deliver a post card, the whole army or navy would be used.[84]

Populist Senator William V. Allen (Neb.) requested all relevant information on the strike and related litigation directly from Olney on 26 July 1894. Allen's resolution passed but was recalled without his knowledge on the following day. Allen did not learn about its sudden withdrawal from Olney's office until months later, on 5 December.[85] James Pugh had obtained the recall on the ground that the Justice Department could not release information on criminal trials in progress. But Allen maintained that Attorney General Olney had pressured senators to take this highly irregular action. Allen insisted that legislators had every right to see the correspondence between the office of the attorney general and the railway "to the end that [we] may be informed and ... prevent recurrence of an affair of that kind."[86] Although the Senate agreed to reconsider the Allen resolution, no vote was taken. President Cleveland voluntarily,* on 10 December 1894, sent Congress a report of the Strike Commission appointed in July 1894.[87] The obvious gap between the information that Cleveland himself obtained and that available in the Justice Department for dissemination underscored the fact that Congress from time to time perceived the necessity to question the quality and the amount of information that it was receiving from the executive. Although unsuccessful in obtaining it, the legislative branch was at least voicing its right to know the relevant facts in matters critical to the national interest.

---

*Cleveland, however, did not escape an attempt by House members to condemn his military intervention. Although his resolution attacking Cleveland for dispatching troops when Illinois Governor Altgeld had declined to accept or to call for the U.S. army failed, George Fithian (D. Ill.) concluded that if President Cleveland's actions in Chicago had been taken by a Republican, "he would not have escaped having articles of impeachment preferred against him by this Democratic Congress." 27 Congressional Record 2799, 2801–03. The Supreme Court in In Re Debs, 158 U.S. 564 (1894), asserted that Cleveland's action was lawful and continued, by way of dictum, to expand the basis for use of national force by the executive to include enforcement of all domestic law and security of all rights. Id. 582. The apparent meaning that the president could employ federal troops at his discretion, in the absence of restrictive legislation, reversed the assumption of the Act of 1807 "that such employment ... must first be authorized by Congress." See Corwin, The President: Office and Powers 134.

As already indicated, Congress's attempts to improve information-gathering from departments were not consistently successful even when the information sought was routine and integral to legislative oversight. In January 1894, eight Cabinet members were asked why they had not responded to an earlier request for data regarding their respective departments' implementation of the civil-service law. Representative Charles Grosvenor (R. Oh.) explained that the requests were not qualified because Congress had no intention of permitting heads of departments the latitude of evaluating the disclosure of information according to their interpretation of what best served the public interest: these men were statutory officers and were required to respond to Congress's demands.[88] Although the secretaries of state and of the treasury responded with the data sought, claiming that it had been omitted from earlier reports through inadvertence,[89] other department chiefs did not reply, and no action was taken or protest recorded. Congress thus failed to require department heads to respond to it.

Congressional attempts to gain some degree of authority over the departments' withholding of information were, therefore, remarkable for their lack of success, particularly in a period not characterized by executive dominance. The majority of department heads regarded information requests as a form of harassment and failed to communicate any sense of pressure to the president. Many of Congress's failures to impose its will were procedural, such as resolutions lost in committee; others stemmed from a passive acceptance of the executive department's refusal to respond. The instances of confrontation with executive claims to withhold, such as the ones reported here, were relatively rare. But members did make the effort, as their predecessors had done, to keep alive the concept that Congress had a right to information and would struggle to obtain it.

Executive Responses   While President Arthur gave brief replies to inquiries during the first session of the Forty-seventh Congress, he seldom replied at all in the second session. Congress, rather surprisingly, tended not to follow up on this executive silence. Arthur's ignoring of even qualified requests,* accompanied by seeming legislative indifference, would appear on the surface to indicate a lack of concern for

*There was an attempt in the House to alter the pattern of qualifying foreign affairs requests by adoption of a subtle variation. An unqualified request for foreign relations information assured President Arthur that if he deemed publication of the information incompatible with the public interest, it would be considered in secret session. But the resolution was referred to and lost in the Committee on Foreign Affairs. 13 *Congressional Record* 146. Some earlier presidents, however, had employed the device of sending sensitive information for consideration in executive (Senate) or secret session. *See supra* p. 105.

international politics on the part of both branches. There is evidence to the contrary, however, that shows Arthur to have been master of the flow of information and Congress to have been most interested in receiving it. For example, the president made frequent voluntary transmittals to Congress in the first session,[90] and in many cases, follow-up materials were generous as well.[91] Arthur's state-of-the-union messages often contained detailed information about subjects requiring Congress's legislative consideration. His final message, for example, presented Congress with comprehensive programs to promote and extend foreign trade and guide military and diplomatic affairs—all examples of extensive planning.[92]

It might appear that Congress lacked a compelling interest in foreign affairs during Arthur's tenure, since only thirty-five of the sixty-five information requests passed by the Forty-eighth Congress related to diplomacy. Confidence that foreign affairs are well in hand may often produce a lack of concern or defuse a partisan attack. On the other hand, legislators made variously successful efforts to obtain more data when they considered President Arthur's transmissions inadequate.* Moreover, a gauge of the level of interest is the depth of commitment of U.S. government policy in a given region.† For example, Congress was quick to ask for information on the vital issue of construction of a Central American canal, particularly whether Navy Secretary William Chandler had dispatched a survey team to Nicaragua to study the proposed canal route and, if so, "under what authority of law such orders were issued. . . ."**[93] The Senate was concerned about the executive's usurpation of authority, since the expedition had been ordered immediately after a U.S.-Nicaraguan treaty was submitted to the Senate for its consent. Senators who believed that executive authority to dispatch an expedition could come only from a ratified treaty regarded the president's action as unauthorized. But Secretary Chandler based executive authority to send out the expedition on a broadly construed commander-

---

*Congress prodded Arthur and got supplemental data in the case of materials relating to a Franco-American claims commission. 16 *Congressional Record* 581 (second resolution, unqualified, 9 January 1885; president's reply, 19 February 1885). The House also asked for and subsequently received more information than the president had promised when transmitting a preliminary report on the Congo Conference in response to an earlier House resolution. *Id.* 1164 (2 February 1885; president's reply, 19 February 1885).

†Senator John Miller's (R. Calif.) request directed the secretary of state to send copies of all treaties entered into and ratified by the United States, as well as notes concerning them. The Senate immediately approved the resolution, and staff at the Department of State began a completion which had not been undertaken for the preceding decade. *Id.* 269 (unqualified, 16 December 1884; reply, 24 January 1885). Such a resolve came perhaps from an uninformed but not from an uninterested Congress.

**The unqualified resolution, proposed by Senator George Vest (D. Mo.) directed the navy secretary to answer the Senate's inquiry. It was agreed to immediately. *Id.* 231.

in-chief power. He informed the Senate that orders for the expedition had been given "in the exercise of the general power of this Department, under the President, to issue such orders to all officers of the Navy as may be deemed for the public interest."[94] The matter rested there after some further discussion.*

Grover Cleveland responded fully to Congress's inquiry about warships he had sent to Haiti. There is no record of Congress's prior or subsequent approval, but the Senate apparently was undisturbed. Senate concern dwelt more upon the fact that the Haitian Republic had been seized by revolutionaries rather than that naval strength had been deployed.†

In the meantime, the U.S. government was determined to prevent German domination of Samoan independence,** and two warships—the *Nipsic* and the *Trenton*—were ordered to Samoa to protect American interests.[95] In his state-of-the union address of 3 December 1888,[96] Cleveland had promised to supply Congress with full correspondence concerning Samoan problems. Later, he sent no less than five sets of correspondence dealing with these events, stating that "the subject in its present stage is submitted to the wider discretion conferred by the Constitution upon the legislative branch of the Government."[97] There is no reason to believe that there was any withholding of information. Congress did not protest the sending of these ships to Samoa; instead,

---

*Senator Vest, concerned about Chandler's reply, asserted that he wanted to discuss "the proposition advanced . . . by the Secretary of the Navy that the right rests in any Department of the Government to order such an expedition without any action on the part of Congress." On 18 December, he introduced a joint resolution (S.R. 106) declaring the action of the secretary illegal. The resolution directed the secretary to discontinue the arrangements and not enforce any orders already made until definite and final action had been taken by Congress on the resolution. *Id.* 299, 326. The next day the senator amended the resolution to remove any mention of illegality; instead, he characterized the expedition as "not expedient." *Id.* 362.

The question of considering Vest's resolution was dealt with in executive session for some three and one-half hours; no further action was taken. *Id.* 389.

†The unrest caused by revolutions in 1888 prompted Department of State officials John Thompson, minister resident to Haiti, and Stanislaus Houtier, U.S. consul at Cape Haytien, to press for an American presence. Thompson got Secretary of State Bayard's consent to the placement of a warship, ordered to Haiti by Secretary of the Navy Whitney. When this ship departed and further violence occurred, Bayard denied Thompson's second request on the ground that demands for warships were unseemly for a diplomat. Thompson and Houtier made many other similar demands for a military presence, however, some of which were granted. There was no discussion of the Haitian domestic uproar. A Senate request of the president resulted in transmission of the correspondence comprising S. Exec. Doc. No. 69, received in the Senate on 16 January 1889. 20 *Congressional Record* 830. S. Exec. Doc. No. 69, 50th Cong., 2d Sess. (1889), is a 264-page executive document representing full compliance with the request and giving details about the ordering of U.S. ships to Haiti. It was ordered printed without debate.

**See Bailey, *A Diplomatic History of the American People* 421–27; Bemis, *A Diplomatic History of the United States* 453–59; R. Logan, *The Diplomatic Relations of the United States with Haiti, 1776–1891* at 397 (1941).

both houses were interested in expanding executive authority to deal with Samoan unrest in the event of an unfavorable turn of events. An appropriation for protection of U.S. interests in Samoa passed in early 1889.[98] This legislation amounted to a virtual U.S. guarantee of Samoan independence and indicated that Congress was willing to delegate considerable discretion to the president to take military action, if necessary, without further consultation. Despite Texas Senator John Reagan's belief that the appropriation for Samoa was insufficient by itself to increase presidential authority to deal with the crisis, the majority agreed with John Sherman that it amounted to a grant of additional authority as well as increased funds.[99]

CONTROL OF FOREIGN RELATIONS

Portions of the post-Civil War era in American diplomacy have been termed the "awkward years"* because it was during the three decades before the turn of the twentieth century that the United States emerged into full maturity in foreign relations after making enormous territorial gains in the second quarter of the nineteenth century. As it added more territory and caught the fever of imperialism, the U.S. government carved out stable international relationships envied by the rest of the world.

New patterns for the conduct of foreign affairs emerged. Some European nations, for example, received foreign policy initiatives from both the president and Congress. From time to time, secretaries of state, such as presidential aspirant James G. Blaine, stressed programs that displaced or eclipsed the landmark efforts in Central America of earlier secretaries, such as William H. Seward. Though the executive and legislative branches sometimes clashed over which would provide leadership in foreign affairs, Congress increasingly shared with the executive more of its claimed prerogatives. For example, while Congress at midcentury had been unwilling to have James K. Polk declare his own regulations for governance of conquered Mexican territory, it accepted, although reluctantly, William McKinley's program for ruling the Philippines and Hawaii in 1898.

Executive Foreign Policy Initiatives

The president multiplied his opportunities to act as chief diplomat of the United States, with or without congressional acquiescence, even though executive activities tended to absorb areas of concern in foreign

---

*D. Pletcher, *The Awkward Years: American Foreign Relations under Cleveland and Arthur* (1962).

affairs that earlier Congresses had clearly designated as being at least a joint responsibility of the branches. For example, James Garfield's policy of bringing about peace and cultivating trade relations with all American states in both the northern and southern hemispheres, though hammered out by Secretary of State James G. Blaine,[100] was altered by President Arthur* without any substantial interference from Congress.† Arthur used diplomats as it suited him to attend conferences.** He announced to Congress in April 1882 that he had invited the independent countries of North and South America to attend a general congress in Washington in November 1883 and asserted that the constitutional provision authorizing him to make treaties also conferred on him the power "to take all requisite measures to initiate them." To further this objective, he planned to have this general congress "freely confer" with one or several commissioners or delegates from other nations.[101] Arthur's invitation to Congress to express its views and his statement that he would suit his actions to the legislative consensus reflected more an intent to cooperate with Congress than acknowledgment of its legislative authority.[102] Congress did not take up the president's invitation for advice.††

The president often sought the delegation of more authority to act for

---

*Arthur's secretary of state, Frederick Frelinghuysen, tried to temper the inflammatory policies of his predecessor Blaine toward Chile. Blaine had ordered his special envoy to Chile, William Trescott, to suspend diplomatic relations with Chile if it removed pro-U.S. Francisco Calderon from the Chilean presidency. *Papers Relating to the Foreign Relations of the United States* 142–43 (1881). Freylinghuysen altered these orders with new instructions. *See* Bastert, "Diplomatic Reversal: Frelinghuysen's Opposition to Blaine's Pan American Policy in 1882," 42 *Mississippi Valley Historical Review* 653–71 (1956).

†The plan to convene a Pan-American Congress in Washington, conceived during the Garfield administration, was unilaterally implemented by President Arthur, who issued invitations in November 1881. Although the president abandoned the undertaking, it was not because of congressional objections. 11 *Messages and Papers* 4684. Congress's relative passivity on the issue (13 *Congressional Record* 1284) was a dramatic reversal from the impassioned debate that occurred when President John Quincy Adams proposed to send ministers to the Panama Congress of 1825. Both houses at that time insisted that it was their right and duty to make a determination about the wisdom of attending as well as the propriety of creating the office of minister to the conference. Sofaer, *Origins* 262.

**Arthur accepted Bismarck's invitation to attend the Berlin Congo Conference of 1884 before his unilateral decision to participate was made known to Congress. Congress did not disapprove since the conference was for discussion and not the shaping of final decisions. 8 Bemis, *The Secretaries of State and Their Diplomacy* 32, 33.

††Since Arthur did not mention that a convening of the republics had been planned when he submitted his annual message of 6 December 1881 (10 *Messages and Papers* 4624–29; 11 *Messages and Papers* 4685–86), a qualified resolution seeking information was passed in the Senate on 1 February 1882. 13 *Congressional Record* 781. Arthur declared firmly that authority over the matter resided with the executive. He apparently considered it important to define his authority for Congress even though he had decided by the end of January 1882 to cancel the general congress. *Papers Relating to the Foreign Relations of the United States* 57–58 (1882).

the United States,* and in some cases he obtained it. During the Hayes administration, Congress passed Representative Samuel Cox's (D. Oh.) resolution giving the president authority to intervene in a manner "short of war" to influence the British to release an American citizen imprisoned for the alleged rescue of two Irish nationalists.† Hayes also pressured Congress to authorize him to take action to secure U.S. interests in the Isthmus of Panama. After one failure to convince Congress to assist the executive in securing "adequate naval stations and harbors" in Central America,** he finally obtained the authority that would permit him quite a broad spectrum of naval activity.

Hayes's supporters in Congress made their bid for increased presidential authority in February 1881. The president had informed Congress in his annual message of December 1880 that in order to meet the requirements of commercial relations with Latin America, the secretary of the navy would be establishing coaling stations on the east side of the isthmus at Chiriqui Lagoon in the Caribbean Sea and also in the Pacific at the Bay of Golfito, less than a hundred miles away.††[103] On 25 February 1881, John Goode (D. Va.) offered an amendment to the regular appropriation bill to provide $200,000 to enable the navy secretary to establish naval stations at the Isthmus of Panama and coal supplies for "steamships of war."[104] Since the president already had the power to establish coal depots, the amendment's significance was its authorization of the naval stations[105] and implementation of broader policies in the Isthmus.*** The Senate was probably aware that the

---

*Earlier presidents did not generally believe that they possessed a plenary foreign affairs power. While some scholars have found inherent in sovereignty itself an extensive foreign affairs authority for the executive, this view has many dissenters. For discussion of these varying points of view, see, e.g., Levitan, "The Foreign Relations Power," p. 467; Story, Commentaries on the Constitution of the United States 148; Henkin, "Some Reflections on Current Constitutional Controversy," 109 University of Pennsylvania Law Review, 637, 645–46 (1961); Henkin, Foreign Affairs and the Constitution, Chs. II and III passim.

†The president was already authorized by statute to intervene in a foreign nation short of war to enforce U.S. legal rights under the law of nations. Cox's resolution was passed in the House and Senate on 13 and 14 June 1878, respectively (17 Congressional Record 4569, 4571, 4591), enabling the president to intervene short of war "as he may think necessary and proper."

**S. 127, which would have authorized the secretary of the navy to obtain appropriate stations, did not pass at the end of the second session of the Forty-sixth Congress, 10 Congressional Record 4508, 4610. Other proposals, based on U.S. rights under the Monroe Doctrine, which would have given Hayes authority to deal with the canal issue, were likewise unsuccessful. See, e.g., id. 128, 133, 1392, 1699, 1775, 1777.

††Hayes doubtless found authority for this action in an Act of March 3, 1847, 9 Stat. 169, which was construed to empower the naval secretary to establish "suitable depots of coal, and other fuel," as well as in the Act of April 30, 1798, 1 Stat. 553, which authorized him to do whatever may be necessary and useful to promote the Navy Department. See also 11 Congressional Record 2099, 2100.

***According to some congressmen, "naval stations" connoted a broader delegation than "coal depots," since they claimed that the president had inherent power to build depots and

funds would also be used to purchase or lease land on the Isthmus,[106] since the United States had contracted to purchase land on the Atlantic side at the end of Buchanan's administration.[107] Goode's amendment passed, becoming law with the appropriations bill.[108]

Unilateral Diplomatic Conduct Possibly Leading to Hostilities— Korea   The administrations of Presidents Arthur, Cleveland, and Harrison provide examples of unilateral diplomatic conduct of either the executive or an executive officer, having the potential of leading to hostilities. After Chester Arthur learned that his emissary, Robert Shufeldt, had exceeded his authority to negotiate a treaty for the opening of Korea, the president ratified his agent's actions. Arthur told Congress that the resulting commitment*[109] was an expression of the Koreans' confidence in this Republic and bound the United States so that it could "not regard with indifference any encroachment on their [Korean] rights."†[110] The president failed to inform Congress that both China and Japan claimed Korea as a dependency. Nonetheless, he urged the interpretation that the United States was a guarantor of Korean independence, without giving Congress this information.[111]

Chile   Benjamin Harrison expanded a relatively minor foreign relations dispute into a major controversy when he issued an ultimatum to Chile. The USS *Baltimore*, commanded by Captain W.S. Schley, was anchored in Valpariso harbor** when a Chilean mob killed two of her

---

that the secretary of the navy possessed literal authority (under earlier statutes, *supra* p. 270) to establish coaling stations. 11 *Congressional Record* 2100. Tennessee Congressman Washington Whitthorne (D.) affirmed the interpretation of the amendment as he commented on the Isthmus from an historical perspective: "If contemplated improvements are to be made it is to become in the future a naval theater equal to the Bosphoros in the past." *Id.* 2101.

*The treaty ratified in May 1882 exceeded Frelinghuysen's instructions: Schufeldt's mission was restricted to securing a treaty for protection of shipwrecked sailors (National Archives and Department of State, *Diplomatic Instructions*, [RG59], M77, roll 40), (instructions to U.S. minister to China, for Robert Shufeldt, 6 January 1882), but the instrument signed provided for fixed tariffs, extraterritorial privileges, and a pledge to mediate and conciliate. 1 *Treaties, Conventions, International Acts, Protocols, and Agreements between the United States and Other Powers, 1776–1909*, at 334–40 (Malloy ed. 1910) (hereinafter "*Treaties, Conventions* (Malloy ed.)"; 8 Bemis, *The American Secretaries of State and Their Diplomacy* ch. 1.

Correspondence between Shufeldt and Chester Holcombe, U.S. representative at the legation in Peking, reflects the pressures on officers in the field to make unilateral decisions to act beyond their instructions. R. Shufeldt, *Papers, Subject File* (Korea), Box 24, Manuscript Division, Library of Congress (Holcombe to Shufeldt, letters of 3 and 31 Jan. 1882).

†Arthur's description of the U.S. commitment appears to be based on Article I of the treaty, which pledged the United States to act as mediator in any conflict between Korea and another country. 8 Bemis, *The American Secretaries of State and Their Diplomacy* 35–39; 1 *Treaties, Conventions* (Malloy ed.) 334–35.

**Details of the *Baltimore* incident are found in A. Tyler, *The Foreign Policy of James G. Blaine* (1965), and W. Sherman, *The Diplomatic and Commercial Relations of the United*

crew and wounded many others during shore leave on 16 October 1891.
Because U.S. seamen were unpopular in Chile after the *Itata* affair,[112]
officials in Washington decided that the assault was actually an offense
for which the United States could seek reparations. Secretary of State
Blaine felt that the incident was no more than a street brawl,* but the
president became impatient when the Chilean provisional government
delayed in making amends† and concluded his account to Congress on a
threatening note:

> If these just expectations should be disappointed or further needless
> delay intervene, I will by special message bring this matter again to the
> attention of Congress for such action as may be necessary.[113]

Harrison was further aggravated after reading the dispatches from
U.S. minister to Chile Patrick Egan. Egan reported that political
refugees in the American legation had been molested and U.S. property
damaged but that no aid had been forthcoming from the Chilean foreign
office.[114] The tension increased even after a new ministry** had been
formed. Egan suspended diplomatic relations, and Chilean police interference at the U.S. legation increased to such an extent that there was
practically a state of siege.[115] Blaine received some conciliatory gestures
in early January†† but then learned that Chile's government refused to
guarantee the security of U.S. refugees if they left the naval vessel
Yorktown for a merchant ship.[116] Chile's representative in Washington
then asked that Egan be replaced by a minister who might cultivate

States and Chile, 1820–1914 (1926). Harrison's report is included in his message of 25
January 1892, along with accompanying documents in H.R. Exec. Doc. No. 91, 52d Cong.,
1st Sess. (1892) (hereinafter "H.R. Exec. Doc. No. 91").

*A biographer who was an intimate friend of the family wrote that Blaine thought
consideration should be shown Chile as a country emerging from civil war and urged the
broad view that the Chilean dispatches were "temperate," perceiving in them "a disposition . . . to apologize." G. Hamilton (Dodge), *The Biography of James G. Blaine* 675–
76 (1895).

†Harrison told Congress in his annual message, on 9 December 1891, that he was
awaiting the result of the investigation conducted by the Council Court of Valpariso and
that he hoped for an "adequate and satisfactory" response to the State Department's note
of 23 October calling the Chilean government's attention to the attack. 13 *Messages and
Papers* 5621.

**Chilean foreign minister Matta telegraphed Washington on 11 December 1891 just
before he was replaced by Luis Pereira. He claimed that Navy Secretary Benjamin Tracy's
report and Harrison's message to Congress, blaming the incident on hatred for the U.S.
uniform and aimed at the U.S. government, were in error. H.R. Exec. Doc. 91, 179–80.
After Chile's elections, a conciliatory attitude did not ripen due to the hard position taken
by both governments. *Id.* 190–91.

††Blaine received a summary of the judicial proceedings in the *Baltimore* affair, along
with an official statement that the Chilean government regretted and deplored the
unfortunate events of 16 October and would do all in its power to secure trial and
punishment of the guilty parties. *Id.* 226, 228 (letters of 4 and 8 January 1892).

cordial relations.[117] The following day, 21 January, Harrison ordered Blaine not to recall Egan, and Blaine drafted a stern but conciliatory letter that repudiated the Chilean foreign ministry's statements that U.S. reports of the *Baltimore* incident were untrue and insincere.

Blaine submitted his draft note to the president, but Harrison instead sent one that he had personally prepared.* Harrison's ultimatum required Egan to ask for reparations for injury suffered by the government of the United States in the *Baltimore* affair, plus a suitable apology for the incident, as well as withdrawal, with apology, of the Matta note.[118] Diplomatic relations were to be severed if these conditions were not met. Moreover, there would be no response to the request for Egan's withdrawal until Chile replied to Harrison's dispatch.[119]

Before he received an answer from Valparaiso, Harrison transmitted the entire correspondence on the incident to Congress and stated he felt there should be no further delay in bringing these matters to Congress's attention "for such action as may be decreed appropriate."[120] Harrison's impatience for war apparently outstripped his eagerness for congressional action. Navy Secretary Tracy reported that as soon as the ultimatum went forward, immediate plans were laid for war.[121] Senate and House committees conferred with the secretary of the navy; coal was purchased; action plans drawn up; and commanding officers designated.[122]

Chile yielded on every point,[123] yet Harrison delayed in sending the Chilean note to Congress. He knew his ultimatum was under consideration, and he commented in transmitting Chile's response that the turn in the affair was "very gratifying." An agreement in the summer of 1892 whereby Chile paid $75,000 indemnity formally concluded the dispute.[124]

Harrison had put a war message† before Congress, and Congress reacted cautiously, requesting information on 26 January about Harrison's ultimatum to Chile.[125] It had not exercised initiative to obtain information when the incident was first known, and conferences might have altered the course of events. Harrison arguably went further than some of his contemporaries by planning events in a way that preempted Congress's authority to declare for peace or war. By informing Congress of the ultimatum, the president placed before Congress events already

---

*On the margin of Blaine's draft, Harrison wrote, "This prepared by State Department—but my note was substituted." B. Harrison, *Papers,* mf. ser. 1, roll 34, Manuscript Division, Library of Congress (Blaine to Egan (unsigned) 21 January 1892), (hereinafter "Harrison Papers").

†Congressman William C. Breckinridge so described the president's message, and no member objected: "Under the Constitution the power is granted to Congress alone to declare war. The President has put upon us the duty of determining that question. We must face it. . . ." 23 *Congressional Record* 550.

shaped for war and thus curtailed congressional power as decisively as if he had unilaterally committed troops in the field.

Use of Executive Agents

Presidential use of agents to accomplish foreign policy objectives aroused congressional concern during Grover Cleveland's second administration, although the subject usually did not excite legislative interest. No definitive principle regarding the use of executive agents emerged. Congress had not yet reached the point of perceiving extensive use of executive agents as isolating the legislative branch from shared control over foreign commitments.

The Blount Mission to Hawaii   In 1893, Cleveland sent James Blount as a special commissioner to restore the Hawaiian monarchy and oppose American takeover* but met with a phalanx of political opposition. The power to appoint Blount without Senate confirmation was treated as the substantive issue, although the president's Hawaiian policy probably motivated the criticism.

George Hoar (R. Mass.) led senators who were concerned that persons unauthorized by the Senate might bind the United States in negotiations. Hoar wondered whether power had been given Blount to make determinations about the landing and withdrawal of U.S. naval forces in Hawaii. On the other hand, Missouri's George Vest saw no problem in Blount's status† and recounted precedents of chief executives who had sent agents abroad for a variety of purposes.[126]

The Senate Foreign Relations Committee's** majority report essentially upheld Cleveland. It cited the practice of similar appointments, although four Republican dissenters claimed that Blount's appointment was unconstitutional.[127] Consequently, the practice was not discouraged, and President McKinley even asked three senators to act as his agents to negotiate peace with Spain in 1898.[128]

The Venezuelan Boundary Dispute   Cleveland's Hawaiian venture was not a political victory.[129] But his initiative with England over a boun-

---

*See discussion of Hawaiian intervention by Harrison and Cleveland, *infra* pp. 306–08.

†Extracts of Secretary of State Walter Gresham's instructions to Blount appear in Vest's discussion at 26 *Congressional Record* 197. Blount was granted "full discretion and power," in accordance with the commander of the U.S. naval forces at Hawaii, to determine the landing and withdrawal of these forces.

**The House attempt to send to the Judiciary Committee the general question of the president's power to appoint diplomatic agents without senatorial consent and the Blount matter in particular, was unsuccessful. *Id.* 519.

dary dispute with Venezuela was in every respect an enhancement of his office. His belligerence toward Britain provoked no congressional opposition.* Owing to substantial anglophobia in the United States,† Congress was amenable to authorizing the president's complete control over any decision regarding military commitments that he might consider necessary in order to enforce a U.S. boundary commission's determinations.

The administration regarded Britain's and Venezuela's bitter dispute over the drawing of British Guiana's western boundary as tantamount to interference in affairs of the New World and, therefore, a violation of the Monroe Doctrine.** In an extremely strong note that Cleveland labeled Secretary of State Richard Olney's "twenty inch gun," Olney asked Britain to declare before Congress reconvened†† whether it would submit the dispute to arbitration. Britain, however, did not reply until four months later. The British denied the applicability of the Monroe Doctrine and concluded that since the United States was not involved, it could not compel arbitration.[130]

When Congress reconvened, Cleveland told congressmen only that an American note had been sent to Britain and that the British had not yet replied. The president did not send forward Olney's dispatch.[131] In fact, his note was a well-kept secret—no one in the Venezuelan government nor most of the State Department knew it existed.[132] Unlike Olney's note, the president's message did not invoke the Monroe Doctrine but expressed the view that the matter could be settled by friendly arbitration. When Cleveland received Britain's uncooperative reply in December 1895, he was apparently unwilling to proceed unilaterally on a potentially hostile course. After requesting an appropriation for an executive commission to investigate and report upon the merits of the dispute, the president made a bold pronouncement on December 17:***

---

*That the pronouncements of Cleveland and his secretary of state did not lead to war was as much due to British reasonableness as to their involvement in other foreign affairs. *See generally,* Perkins, *The Monroe Doctrine 1867–1907,* at 201–05 (1937); R. Tugwell, *Grover Cleveland* 248 (1968).

†28 *Congressional Record* 261–62; Bailey, *A Diplomatic History of the American People* 436ff; Perkins, *The Monroe Doctrine 1867–1907,* at 146.

**The Olney note asserted the novel concept (the Olney Corollary) that a boundary dispute over land long claimed by a European power was to be considered colonization. Bailey, *A Diplomatic History of the American People* 440–41; Tugwell, *Grover Cleveland* 247–48.

††In a startling burst of rhetoric, Olney asserted that the United States was sovereign on this continent because its "infinite resources . . . render it master of the situation and practically invulnerable as against any or all other powers." Quoted in Bailey, *A Diplomatic History of the American People* 441.

***Cleveland transmitted the Olney note with this message, apparently ready to share with Congress, at this point, the initiative he had hoped would head off an almost certain "field day on foreign affairs" in the Congress. Blake, "The Background of Cleveland's

When such a report is made *and accepted*, it will, in my opinion, be the duty of the United States to resist by every means in its power, as a willful aggression upon its rights and interests, the appropriation by Great Britain of any lands or the exercise of governmental jurisdiction over any territory which *after investigation* we have determined of right belongs to Venezuela. In making these recommendations I am fully alive to the responsibility incurred and keenly realize all the consequences that may follow.[133]

While he clearly intended to use force in the event of British "appropriation" of Venezuelan territory, it is not clear whether Cleveland believed that he had to come again to Congress for authority to use the force contemplated in the message. Nor did Congress clarify this point as it speedily and unanimously authorized an imposed determination of the dispute by a commission appointed solely by the executive.*[134] Most of the nation rose to the president's support, and for a moment during a grinding depression, many citizens applauded the chief executive's decisive use of his authority.[135] The quarreling parties cooperated with the commission, and a treaty was signed in February 1897.[136]

Congress's Attempt to Control Foreign Policy

The Use of Resolutions to Affect Treaties and Diplomatic Negotiations
Congress did not always succeed in its efforts to shape American foreign policy. But its mechanisms for accomplishing its aims included joint resolutions to bring certain foreign policy matters to the attention of another country;† attempts to call for the complete execution of treaties;** directions to the secretary of state to institute or to abrogate reciprocity treaties;†† and requests that the president open diplomatic negotiations with foreign powers.

Venezuelan Policy," 47 *American Historical Review* 270 (1942); Young, "Intervention under the Monroe Doctrine: The Olney Corollary," 57 *Political Science Quarterly* 247 (1942).

*Although the House pushed through H.R. 2137 without permitting discussion of its scope (28 *Congressional Record* 235), debate arose in the Senate over giving the president power to appoint the commissioners alone. A Senate majority rejected the claim that this feature would diminish its war powers by weakening control over commissioners whose findings could precipitate war. *Id.* 244, 260–61.

†Both houses passed a joint resolution requesting the president to negotiate a reciprocal trade agreement with Mexico. 13 *Congressional Record* 2401, 2599. The belief held by some legislators that revenue raising provisions of such treaties diminished House prerogative to originate revenue bills did not deter passage of this resolution.

**For example, the resolution calling for complete execution on April 9 of the Adams-Onis Treaty of 1819 requiring satisfaction of Spanish claims for injuries due to operation of the American Army in the Floridas prior to 1819. *See* Sofaer, *Origins* 306–17, 343ff.; 3 *Treaties*, 10, 12 (Miller ed.); 13 *Congressional Record* 212, 978, 6968.

††There was no action taken on a resolution directing the secretary of state to institute a reciprocity treaty between the United States and Central and South America. *Id.* 978.

Venezuelan Claims Lawmakers frequently debated whether a congressional resolution could properly be used to influence foreign policy. For example, after President Arthur asked Congress to look into the matter of U.S.-Venezuela claims, Congressman William Rice offered a resolution that the president be "requested" to open negotiations with Venezuela.[137] Its opponents insisted that notwithstanding the president's request, Congress's function should be purely advisory and that Rice's detailed resolution usurped executive power.[138] A majority of both houses passed the Rice resolution.*[139] Congress also tried to fashion a policy for an interoceanic canal. This program was expressed in a joint resolution (S. 122) that would have required President Cleveland to inform European powers of congressional policy in Central America. Alabama Senator John Morgan protested what he termed the "inopportune and premature" assumption of an executive function. Ohio's John Sherman answered that it was Congress's right to declare public policy because Congress expressed the people's will, to which the president was bound to conform.[140] The resolution was passed in the Senate[141] but was never voted on in the House.[142]

Isthmian Policy Several times, Congress attempted to shape isthmian policy in order to achieve U.S. *de facto* control over the various proposed canal projects. This was a perilous program, since most legislators also wanted to avoid the overt breach of the Clayton-Bulwer treaty and an adverse British military reaction. The Supreme Court had announced in *Whitney v. Robertson,* 124 U.S. 190, 194 (1888),[143] that a treaty and legislation were on equal footing, permitting the conclusion that legislation inconsistent with a treaty could lawfully be enacted so far as domestic legislation was concerned. Many senators, however, were reluctant to threaten a breach of treaty obligations. Thus, when it was proposed during Harrison's administration that the original charter of the Maritime Canal Company of Nicaragua† be amended to enable the

---

Equally unsuccessful were attempts to abrogate various treaties. *See* 14 *Congressional Record* 18 (resolution giving notice of intention to terminate treaty of 22 February 1868 with North German Confederation; referred to House Committee on Foreign Affairs); *id.* 1003, 1005, 3322 (resolution to terminate reciprocity treaty of 1875 with Hawaii; referred to Finance Committee in House and Foreign Relations Committee in the Senate).

*Representative William Rice's (R. Mass.) first resolution requesting the president to open negotiations with Venezuela to revive the Treaty of 1866 was unsuccessful. 13 *Congressional Record* 978.

†This company, which subsequently received a concession from the Nicaraguan government for construction of a canal, was granted a charter from Congress during Cleveland's first tenure in February 1889 (S. 1305) despite serious objections. Congressman James Cobb (D. Ala.) wondered how the government could bestow upon a corporation authority that Congress itself did not have, to acquire land outside the United States. 20 *Congressional Record* 91. Representative Hilary Herbert (D. Ala.) asked if the government was prepared to spend $50 to $100 million every year to set up naval stations at each

U.S. government to purchase 70 percent of the stock (S. 4827),[144] opposing senators invoked the Clayton-Bulwer Treaty. They argued that such a measure violated the requirement that Britain and the United States jointly undertake all Central American canal projects. The bill was laid aside and not called up again.[145]

Again, early in 1893, fears that breach of Clayton-Bulwer would lead to war were enough to defeat S. 1218,* a bill its supporters described as "ensuring to the United States the absolute political and business control of this canal forever."[146] During debate, Senator Morgan defended U.S. guarantee of the canal's company's bonds in return for a majority of its stock.† The civilized world, he asserted, wanted the United States to control an isthmian canal so long as it was available to all nations.[147]

Cuba   The two most important debates of the Cleveland and McKinley administrations involving Congress's role in foreign relations dealt with Cuban insurgency. The Fifty-fourth Congress struggled with the question of which branch had the power to recognize *de facto* independence. Cleveland's somewhat ambiguous position tended toward sympathy for the strife-torn Cuban people,** but many senators found his stance too mild. They wanted an "emphatic" and "positive" expression of "true American continental policy" that would establish the United States as an innovator in "the code of international statutes."[148]

Although Congress did not declare that it possessed power to recognize another nation's independence, it seriously questioned whether the executive might do so alone. Senator George Vest (D. Mo.) termed it "astounding . . . that while the warmaking power was given to Congress, the president could bring about a war by exercising the high prerogative of declaring whether a people struggling to achieve their independence were entitled to recognition. . . ."[149] Florida's Augustus Bacon (D.) introduced a resolution declaring that recognition of inde-

---

end of the canal or, in lieu of that, to acquire all the territory between the United States and Nicaragua in order to march armies there. *Id.* 94.

*House consideration of the subject continued with appointment of a special committee of five to investigate money spent by the Panama Canal Company to prevent opposition to the canal in the United States. The committee reported at the end of the session. 24 *Congressional Record* 905, 2579.

†Four years later, in 1897, senators again tried to legislate the plan that Morgan had envisioned but were defeated by claims that authorization of the U.S. government as the majority shareholder would have an adverse impact on relations with Nicaragua. 29 *Congressional Record* 1052–62.

**Cleveland had declared in his annual message of December 1896 (14 *Messages and Papers* 6146, 6154) that the situation in Cuba could develop to the point that the U.S. obligations to Spain would be superseded by "higher obligations which we can hardly hesitate to recognize and discharge."

pendence was the sole prerogative of Congress and belonged to the president only to the same extent that he might exercise a veto over an act of Congress.[150] He reasoned that since recognition often created legal relations and obligations having force of law, it was legislative in effect even though it might not be statutory in form.[151]

Senator Roger Mills (D. Tex.) concurred that the executive role should be only to conclude, either recognition or nonrecognition, whichever was Congress's wish.*[152]

Senate Foreign Relations Committee chairman John Morgan joined in the attempt to place Congress in charge of setting U.S. policy over recognition of foreign states. He assumed that Congress had authority over all subjects that related not only to war but also to the existence of war in a foreign country.†[153] Therefore, Morgan introduced a joint resolution (S. 26), which declared the neutrality of the United States in the struggle between Spain and the Cuban people and aimed to achieve belligerent status for *both* sides. He knew that McKinley believed that passage of the resolution would break U.S. diplomatic relations with Spain.**

A moderate group of Morgan's supporters raised the possibility that Congress and the president should legally share the power to shape recognition policy. Fighting the administration's desire to bury the resolution in committee, they defined recognition as a power to be exercised jointly, with the executive taking the initiative and Congress giving advice in case the president wanted to act.[154] For example, John Thurston of Nebraska (R.) called recognition one of the "quasi-executive-legislative actions" that could be taken properly either by the president or Congress.[155] On the other hand, Virginia's John Daniel, the most sweeping advocate of congressional recognition, claimed that because the declaration pertained to a situation involving commerce, Congress could make it alone; the president did indeed share in the

---

*Mills reminded his colleagues that only Lincoln had asserted an "exclusive" presidential right to deal with recognition. President Lincoln had dismissed House opposition to recognition of the Mexican monarchy as mere expression of sentiment on a "purely executive question," which he was not required to adopt. Seward to Dayton, 7 April 1864, in H.R. Exec. Doc. No. 92, reproduced in 29 *Congressional Record* 658; *see also* Chapter 3, p. 207. The House characterized the president's claim as "novel" and "inadmissible," continued Mills, and passed another resolution asserting its powers. *Id.* 653.

†David Turpie (D. Ind.) pointed out that President Monroe had recognized the belligerency of the South American colonies in their revolt from Spain and had received congressional concurrence in the form of an appropriation. But Morgan characterized Monroe's proclamation as an imitation of the process; only Congress, he claimed, had the "ultimate power of making the declaration good." 30 *Congressional Record* 620–21.

**Morgan also knew that the president might veto the resolution, and he wondered, as he had in the earlier recognition debates (28 *Congressional Record* 2058), whether the president had the veto power over this kind of joint resolution. 30 *Congressional Record* 615.

power, but only as a part of his executive function. Congress's share was superior, Daniel added, because while the president executed the law, Congress determined what the law was.*[156]

After Morgan and his supporters defeated the referral motion, the resolution passed in the Senate (41 to 14).†[157] But McKinley rallied House Republicans with the aid of Speaker Thomas Reed, who would not permit a vote to be taken, though Democrats attempted to raise the Cuban issue in any form for debate or a vote. Many resolutions regarding Cuban policy were lost because parliamentary maneuvers prevented appointment of members of the House Committee on Foreign Affairs until the final half hour of the first session of the Fifty-fifth Congress.[158] Thus, the executive successfully prevented the House from acting on the Senate's resolution in particular and the Cuban issue in general.

Another House attempt to compel the president to recognize Cuban belligerent status was ruled out of order during the following session.[159] The chair decided that recognition of belligerency could not be added as an amendment to a diplomatic appropriation bill.[160] After President McKinley sought authority to intervene in Cuba, however, the House overwhelmingly approved a resolution that recognized the independence of the Cuban people.[161] Both the House and Senate then were

---

*Though in the twentieth century, Congress has acknowledged that the president possesses exclusive authority over recognition, Henkin, *Foreign Affairs and the Constitution* 47 and note, Congress expressed the belief on earlier occasions that it possessed at least the concurrent power to extend recognition to foreign nations. For example, both houses of Congress passed a joint resolution unqualifiedly recognizing Brazil's 1890 regime as a "lawful and rightful Government and ordering the President to notify Brazil of Congress's enactment of recognition." 21 *Congressional Record* 216, 1229. The Senate approved the resolution (54 to 0) on 11 February 1890 on the ground that it had already confirmed sending an envoy extraordinary to Brazil and it would be appropriate that Congress's declaration of recognition accompany him. *Id.* 1229. President Benjamin Harrison signed it into law before his own cautious program of waiting for the Brazilians' assent to the new government could go into effect. *Id.* 1577. Senator John Morgan maintained that the government's *declaration* of recognition should be swift, while the president could either open diplomatic relations with the provisional government or postpone further *acts* of recognition until satisfied that the new government was permanent. *Id.* 313. Morgan did not propose to deny such power to the president but only to assert that it should be exercised concurrently, with perhaps an edge in favor of Congress should the president be slow to act.

†Joint Resolution S.J. Res. 26, as passed, read:

Resolved by the Senate and House of Representatives, ... that a condition of public war exists between the Government of Spain and the government proclaimed and for some time maintained by force of arms by the people of Cuba, and that the United States of America shall maintain a strict neutrality between the contending powers, according to each all the right of belligerents in the ports and territory of the United States.

30 *Congressional Record* 1186.

House Speaker Thomas B. Reed (R. Me.) as he appeared in 1897. Reed tenaciously opposed intervention in Cuba (*see* p. 280) and Hawaiian annexation, resigning as speaker in 1899 following the war with Spain. (L.C.)

willing to alter their positions and join in a simple affirmation that the "people of the island of Cuba" were free and independent,[162] thus preserving administration policy on recognition of nation states.[163]

Congressional Modification of Treaties   During the late nineteenth century, Congress frequently tested the constitutional issue of whether it might modify a treaty by statute. For example, in 1879,* a bill limiting the number of Chinese who could be imported on a given vessel (H.R. 2423) directly contravened several articles of the Anson Burlingame Treaty with China[164] but passed in the House 155 to 72, largely because of its emotional appeal. Some senators, however, denied that Congress could repeal a treaty provision by statute.†[165] Most appeared concerned with how to achieve the statute's goals without insulting the Chinese government, and the bill passed on 15 January 1879 with only minor amendment.[166] President Hayes in a veto message[167] declared that while Congress possessed unquestionable authority to terminate a treaty, it was not "competent" to modify an existing treaty, since modification belonged to the treatymaking power. This executive position defined Congress's role at the time,** since the House vote (110 to 96) was not sufficient to override the veto. Though legislators may not have been aware of the distinction Hayes drew between abrogation and modification, it was clear to the president that Congress could not legislate piecemeal changes—a process that belonged to the shared treatymaking power between the Senate and the president.

During Grover Cleveland's first term, two of twelve bills proposing to limit or totally to exclude Chinese immigration were passed and signed into law against a background of claims that they proposed to abrogate

---

*During the Grant administration no occasion arose to deal with the legal status of a treaty compared with that of a statute. However, a proposal on 3 April 1876 that the president open negotiations with the Chinese about commercial treaties did not succeed because many members doubted that it was "fit that the Senate of the United States should in advance undertake to point out to the President what sort of a treaty he ought to make with a particular power." 4 *Congressional Record* 2158 (George Edmunds, R. Vt.). No suggested modification was passed because no legislator resolved the constitutional objection that Senate prerogative did not include directing executive treaty negotiations. *Id.* 4420.

†Abrogation of a treaty was viewed differently; senators pointed out that a nation might abrogate a treaty, under natural law, on the ground of self-preservation. 8 *Congressional Record* 1304, 1305.

**In 1888, however, the legal consequence of an act of Congress inconsistent with a treaty was settled by the Supreme Court in *Whitney v. Robertson*, 124 U.S. 190, 194 (1888). The Court held that a treaty would be treated like a statute: When the two relate to the same subject, the court will always endeavor to construe them so as to give effect to both without violating the language of either; but where inconsistency is found, the one last in date will control. *See also The Chinese Exclusion Case*, 130 U.S. 581, 600 (1889).

or to modify treaties. In one instance, Nevada Senator William Stewart (R.) suggested a method of bypassing Hayes's objection that proved successful. Stewart requested President Cleveland to negotiate a new treaty with the emperor of China that would "get out of our way those treaty restrictions which prevent us from legislating to prohibit Chinese laborers from immigrating to this country."[168] Cleveland did so, the Senate approved, and Congress moved to execute its provisions by enacting legislation (S. 3304) prohibiting entry of Chinese laborers.*[169]

The principle that Congress has the power to enact legislation "even if it be against a treaty" was regarded as judicially settled by Cleveland's second term.[170] Thus, Congress had succeeded in its two-decade campaign to take charge of Sino-American affairs. The legislation controlling Chinese immigration (the Chinese Exclusion Act) was constitutional and operated to modify the policies and objectives achieved by the executive through the treaty power.[171]

Public opinion exerted a powerful influence on Congress's shaping of foreign policy. Citizens' pressures on the legislature usually took the form of petitions. For example, many petitions were used, especially in the House, to bring the question of Cuba before Congress and publicize alleged Spanish atrocities.[172] And while anti-administration forces in Congress generally failed to remove prohibitions against public debate in order to gain popular support for their programs dealing with foreign affairs, such efforts were occasionally successful.† For example, many senators wanted to take the "unprecedented" step of making public the debate that had defined the deteriorating understanding of Canada and the United States over fishing rights. Virginia Congressman Harrison Riddleberger (Readj.) finally succeeded in removing the injunction of secrecy on discussion of the fisheries treaty of 1887 that Grover Cleveland and Secretary of State Bayard had negotiated.[173]

---

*The House passed a bill (H.R. 11336) with provisions similar to S. 3304 to ensure exclusion in the event the Chinese government failed to ratify the new treaty. 19 *Congressional Record* 8227. After the Senate learned, on 7 September 1888, that the treaty had been postponed for deliberation, it went ahead with passage of H.R. 11336 (*id.* 8309), known as the Scott (Exclusion) Act of 1888. The act's constitutionality was upheld in *The Chinese Exclusion Case.*

†Open treaty debate had been rejected during Grant's presidency, when Senator Thomas Ferry proposed an amendment to the Senate secrecy rule to permit discussion in open session of any treaty whose ratification would result in U.S. acquisition of foreign territory. The Santo Domingo treaty was being widely discussed in newspapers, and Ferry wanted it to be publicly understood that if a takeover was planned, "it may be necessary to defend that position by force of arms." The Foreign Relations Committee was unprepared to accept this argument, however, and the amendment was indefinitely postponed. 42 *Congressional Record* 4131. Newspapers alluded to President Grant's withdrawal of a large sum from the Treasury without any sanction of law to "acquire the consent of the executive authority of a foreign government to the occupation of a portion of the territory of that Government by the United States." *Id.*

Congress Initiates Foreign Policy   Congress was more active than at any point in former history in undertaking initiatives having the potential of involving the government in serious escalation of diplomatic differences leading to war. For example, the Senate adopted joint resolutions in January 1896 expressing concern that Turkish massacres of Armenian Christians threatened the rights of Christians everywhere. Legislators called upon President Cleveland to communicate Congress's hope to the signatories* of the Treaty of Berlin (1878) that "decisive measures" would be taken to stop the violence to Christians in Turkey and secure them the rights provided by the treaty. The resolutions promised House-Senate support of the president "in the most vigorous action he may take for protection of U.S. citizens in Turkey...."[174]

A few senators thought the resolutions did not go far enough.[175] Williamson Call (D. Fla.) characterized them as signifying nothing: "nations . . . will look upon it as an empty and unmeaning declaration of sympathy."[176] His concurrent resolution, lost in the Foreign Relations Committee, asserted that human and religious principles demanded that civilized governments prevent the massacres, by force if necessary.[177] George Hoar, on the other hand, complained that the resolutions infringed upon the executive's diplomatic function; the Senate should have withheld its expression of indignation until the diplomacy was concluded.[178]

The House adopted the Senate resolutions, although some members had presented less "irritating" substitutes,[179] all of which were summarily rejected. A few congressmen, like William Hepburn (R. Iowa), favored the strongest expression of all—a direction to the president to dismiss the Turkish minister. Hepburn's amendment was rejected (19 to 121) because it exceeded the limits of congressional power.[180] The House in its passage of the Senate's resolutions also registered its acceptance of the theory that though the U.S. government was not a signatory of the 1878 treaty, it could still take an active interest in Armenia.

Both houses continued to press the president to exercise this authority to negotiate. And in one case of executive acquiescence in a legislative initiative, Benjamin Harrison's compliance with Congress's direction to monitor and execute U.S. claims in the Bering Sea brought the United States close to war with England. Shortly before Grover Cleveland left office, he signed a bill asserting the dominance of the United States in the Bering Sea. The statute made it the duty of the

---

*The resolutions pointedly named the signatory powers—the Ottoman Empire, Britain, Germany, Austria, France, Italy, and Russia. 28 *Congressional Record* 959.

president to issue an annual proclamation against violation of U.S. laws for the protection of the fisheries and called for the placement of American ships to cruise in the disputed waters and make arrests.[181] On 21 March 1889, President Harrison issued the proclamation that forbade the killing of fur-bearing animals in Alaskan waters.[182] Then, within two days, Secretary of the Treasury William Windom ordered Captain L.G. Shepard of the revenue steamer *Rush* to "diligently cruise" the Bering Sea and seize any vessels violating U.S. law.[183] On 15 March 1890, the proclamation went into effect for another year, and additional orders went to the *Rush*.[184] But when Secretary Blaine received warning in June 1890 that four British cruisers were heading for the Bering Sea with instructions indicating "apprehension" of war,[185] Blaine undertook a course of correspondence with British minister Sir Julian Pauncefote that culminated in eventual American retreat from the closed sea principle.*[186]

Some senators, such as Oregon's Joseph Dolph, complained that the president had not exercised the discretionary authority Congress delegated to him to retaliate against Canadian goods and fishing vessels in the event American fishermen were refused entry into Canadian waters.†[187] Dolph called upon Congress to demand indemnification from England if the president failed to implement the statute's provisions for retaliation.[188] Instead, Cleveland had conducted negotiations with Canada to resolve the differences and sent the resulting treaty to the Senate on 21 February 1888. Had the Act of 1887 in effect forbidden the president to enter into negotiations? If not, could Cleveland be expected to implement a statute that had the effect of undoing his ongoing negotiations?

Many senators, like Ephraim Wilson (D. Md.), considered it "absurd" to say that Congress's grant of discretionary power would suspend or modify the president's constitutional "power as an independent branch of the Government" to deal with a problem as he felt necessary. Eli Saulsbury (D.) of Delaware challenged "Congress if it desires to try belligerent measures [to] assume the responsibility and enact a law, the

---

*Pacified by Blaine's dropping the principle of *mare clausum,* or "closed sea," which they had regarded as a nonnegotiable obstacle to an agreement, the British consented to arbitration. An international agreement was concluded in 1911. J. Callahan, *American Foreign Policy in Canadian Relations* 524–25 (1937). During Cleveland's second administration Congress approved $75,000 as settlement of British claims for seizure of cruisers in the Bering Sea. 28 *Congressional Record* 4560, 5019.

†Whenever Canada denied U.S. fishing vessels most favored nation status, the president was authorized under the retaliatory act to issue a proclamation prohibiting Canadian vessels from entering U.S. waters and the importation of Canadian goods. 19 *Congressional Record* 7904.

responsibility for which will rest upon the Congress, and not in the discretion of the President."[189] John Morgan also chastised disgruntled colleagues:

> We have no more right to instruct the President of the United States that he shall cease negotiations than we have a right to require him to resign his office, not a bit, and whenever in the course of affairs his judgment recommends to him the exercise of the treaty making power, it is his right and his duty to exercise it, and send his work here for ratification or rejection or amendment by the Senate.[190]

When the Senate refused to ratify Cleveland's "work," the president then asked both houses to pass retaliatory legislation that would empower him to carry out the purposes of the Act of 1887.[191] Representative Thomas Wilson (D. Minn.) obliged by introducing H.R. 11257, which permitted the president means of retaliating against discriminatory Canadian practices.*[192] Senator Morgan described the bill as a necessary supplement to the Act of March 3, 1887, but did not acknowledge that Cleveland was bound to retaliate. That would be a war measure, and Morgan believed that Congress intended its retaliatory law as pressure on the president to make a treaty.[193] Wilson's bill passed the House[194] but was not voted on in the Senate.†

Congressional pressure to shape U.S. foreign policy reached a crescendo over recognition of Cuba.[195] Despite both houses' passage of a joint resolution in April 1896 proposing that Cleveland assist Spain in negotiating peace with an independent Cuba, the president refused to budge. The Senate appeared unwilling to bring on war without executive concurrence, yet seemed equally insistent upon Congress's right to recognize Cuban independence regardless of executive wishes or inclinations.[196] Congressmen used various means to influence the president's policy. McKinley was pressured to take diplomatic action, such as to protest the capture and imprisonment of U.S. citizens**[197] and to insist on the treatment of prisoners according to international law. Congressional protest also influenced suspension of the death sentence

---

*The president received authority to prohibit transportation across U.S. territory without payment of duty on goods imported or exported from any foreign country and bound for Canada. *Id.* 7901.

†Several senators, such as George Edmunds (R. Vt.), George Hoar (R. Mass.), and John Sherman (R. Oh.), believed that the president possessed sufficient authority under the Act of March 3, 1887, without additional legislation. *Id.* 7903, 7905–96, 7915–19.

**Debate had propaganda value for the president. After vigorous Senate debate on S.R. 25 requesting relief for U.S. citizens in Cuba, Cleveland submitted his own legislation. Congress quickly granted the president's request for $50,000 for food and medicine for the relief of U.S. citizens caught in Spanish General Weyler's reconcentration policy in Cuba. 30 *Congressional Record* 1081, 1196–1203.

for Ruiz Rivera, a Cuban rebel leader captured by Spain.* Additionally, McKinley was persistently badgered throughout the first session of the Fifty-fifth Congress to send warships to Havana.

Congressmen generally agreed that the president possessed control over deployment of warships under the Constitution. They disagreed, however, on the propriety of Congress's urging the president to deploy warships for national purposes.† Senator John Morgan, on 6 April 1897, called on the president to dispatch ships to protect U.S. life and property, such as a mature nation like Great Britain would do.[198] Senators John Thurston (R. Neb.) and Arthur Gorman (D. Md.) similarly indicated that executive deployment of military might under the circumstances was a solemn duty.[199] But Morgan's resolution did not pass, and President McKinley never relinquished his control over deployment. He sent the *Maine* into Havana only after the U.S. commissioners he had dispatched earlier to Cuba returned unsuccessful from their mission. Nonetheless, much executive decisionmaking regarding foreign affairs was inextricably involved with legislative initiatives in a blend that bespoke more of cooperation than contention. Each branch thus complemented the war powers of the other in a way not previously seen in the country's history.

Foreign Policy as a Joint Endeavor of the Branches

Both the executive and Congress after 1895 began to act as if they believed that neither might speak as the voice of government in isolation from the other. For example, Delaware Senator George Gray represented the majority position of "joint endeavor" by declaring that the enumerated war powers could only be properly exercised by the legislative process, which included the president. Gray reasoned that the president had to receive and act upon a declaration by Congress in

---

*Nebraska Senator William V. Allen moved that the U.S. government protest the drumhead court martial and possible execution of Rivera, while administration supporters like George Hoar said he opposed the affront to a friendly power that such a protest could cause. *Id.* 563. Allen's resolution passed on 5 April (*id.* 580), and on 13 April John Morgan reported that Rivera's death sentence had been suspended. Spanish ambassador Depuy de Lome had been quoted as having said Rivera's punishment largely depended on the conduct of Cuban sympathizers in the United States and that Rivera was thus held hostage for U.S. good conduct. *Id.* 691.

†After the Hawaiian "revolution," Henry Cabot Lodge (R. Mass.) introduced what he admitted was an irregular resolution stating as the Senate's opinion that a man-of-war should be maintained at Honolulu to prevent counterrevolution. He argued that despite the fact that ordering such a ship to be sent went beyond Congress's power, in the case of "great interests" Congress had a place in making such a decision. 27 *Congressional Record* 623. John Morgan (D. Ala.) and George Gray (D. Del.) objected to the resolution as an infringement on the independence of a coordinate department of government. *Id.* 624, 627–30. The resolution did not come to a vote. *Id.* 1167.

order for the expression of the war power to be complete.[200] However, as in the case of legislation based on any other enumerated power, if the president rejected the declaration, Congress might still opt for war by repassage over the executive veto.*

John Morgan took a completely opposite stand, claiming that Congress's power over war was not subject to exercise of the other enumerated powers. Therefore, Congress might say whether or not war existed in Cuba, "without the aid, or assistance, or participation of the Executive."†[201] Congress had even "the right to command the Commander-in-Chief of the Army and Navy to go on the field . . . in person to see to the execution of that order."[202]

Each branch tested its conception of its powers during the heated boundary dispute between England and Venezuela.** Cleveland asked for and got authority from Congress to finance a commission to investigate and report on the merits of the two nations' claims. Congress knew that the president was prepared to resist a British takeover of Venezuelan territory in defiance of the commission's recommendations, "by every means" within U.S. power. Despite the fact that nothing less than the power to make war or peace was involved, legislators debated the problem only briefly and then collaborated with Cleveland by providing $100,000 to carry out his program of ascertaining the proper boundary. The president believed that U.S. right of intervention rested on the Monroe Doctrine; Shelby Cullom (R. Ill.) therefore proposed that the Monroe Doctrine be proclaimed by joint resolution as the "recognized rightful policy of the United States"—in effect, "a fixed and permanent ordinance."[203] Other legislators hastened to propose similar resolutions, but none was adopted.[204]

The brilliant, unconventional senior senator from Alabama, John Morgan, probably spoke for more than himself when in justifying the annexation of Hawaii by joint resolution, he referred to this form of annexation as a joint venture, completely constitutional and an expression of the war power. The president's war power, Morgan claimed, allowed him to seize any territory by force, and thereupon Congress could ratify such action by a simple resolution.††[205] Not a single critic

---

*California Senator Stephen White agreed with Gray, concluding that Congress lacked the power apart from the president to declare belligerency. He doubted further that a joint resolution unsigned by the president amounted to more than an expression of Congress's opinion. 28 *Congressional Record* 2164.

†This was an extreme position for Morgan who, in another and more accommodating mood, admitted that the president could initiate a declaration of belligerency, even as Congress had the power to make such a declaration "good." 30 *Congressional Record* 620–21.

**See supra* at pp. 275–76.

††The joint resolution passed (31 *Congressional Record* 6019, 6712), giving the House a vote equal to the Senate in an important foreign policy decision. Congress thus affirmed

challenged this startling declaration that the executive possessed the unilateral power of seizure. Populist Senator William V. Allen (Nebraska) claimed only that such exercise of executive war power did not affect the Senate's prerogatives in treatymaking;[206] only in case the president concluded an obviously unsatisfactory or illegal arrangement would it seem justified for Congress to seize the upper hand by refusing to ratify his acts.[207]

Congress has historically exercised a right to appraise both the constitutional implications of territorial acquisition and the military implications of conquest, including the right of Congress to declare what role it should play. In the case of the Philippines,* the only senator who defended keeping the islands on constitutional grounds was Colorado's Henry Teller, who said that it was unthinkable that the United States, because it was a republic, should be barred from acquiring distant territory. Teller saw no legal reason that sovereignty over such territory would not be consonant with American traditions, since the Filipinos could still be given self-government and independence.†[208] His opponent, Augustus Bacon (D. Ga.), declared that there could be no such thing as an "imperial republic" and charged that McKinley's recommended standing army of 100,000 men was a revolutionary concept that could involve the nation in disastrous future wars.[209] Donelson Caffery (D. La.) maintained that the United States was constitutionally prohibited from waging any war of conquest and from retaining as a result of war any territory whose people had a germ of nationality, unless their consent had been given to American sovereignty.[210]

McKinley's policy of territorial acquisition by lowering the requisite number of votes from two-thirds to a simple majority. *Compare* the annexation of Texas, *supra* Chapter 2, pp. 161–63.

*There was substantial disagreement in Congress in 1899 as to whether Emilio Aguinaldo had achieved a substantive rebel victory over Spain in Manila before Dewey. Washington's George Turner, South Carolina's Ben Tillman, and South Dakota's Richard F. Pettigrew accused the U.S. government of bad faith toward Aguinaldo, alleging that U.S. policy had led the Filipinos to believe they would attain their independence if they fought Spain. 33 *Congressional Record* 1038–43, 1256, 6525. Senator James Williams (D. Ill.) showed that rebels had assembled an army of 30,000, had taken thousands of prisoners, had driven Spanish forces into Manila, and ended Spanish sovereignty in the hundreds of Philippine island dependencies. *Id.* 6718. On the other hand, Henry Cabot Lodge claimed that Dewey had conferred with Aguinaldo, who was expected to aid the U.S. Army but instead installed himself as Filipino dictator. *Id.* 2622, 2624. And Alabama's John Morgan, with John McLaurin (D. S.C.), concurred that only Spain had had lawful title to the islands in order to be able to surrender them. *Id.* 6018, 2382.

†Teller, however, was concerned that Republican policy included governing islands under imperial power. *Id.* 6510–11. Advocates of the peace with Spain signed on 10 December 1898, such as Orville Platt, argued that war or peace power was not the only vehicle for acquiring territory. The very fact of sovereignty itself included the right to acquire and the right to govern what was acquired; and though a people could become capable of being self-governed, there was no obligation to confer citizenship or statehood upon unoccupied territory. 32 *Congressional Record* 287–97 *passim*.

The ultimate stewardship concept that evolved reflected the reasoning of Henry Cabot Lodge, who proposed to vest all civilian, military, and judicial power in a person designated by the president, until Congress provided otherwise. However, he added that continued exercise of the war power by the president at the end of hostilities would erode Congress's authority.[211] McKinley acknowledged Lodge's view that Congress properly should provide for the Philippine government but still asserted his authority as commander-in-chief to provide a temporary government until Congress assumed control.[212]

The president did not rely completely upon the doctrine of emergency but made laws for the Philippines under claim of right.[213] McKinley could have sought legislative ratification of his action as did Zachary Taylor for the acts of the military government of California.[214] The fact that this executive stewardship was not challenged meant only that Congress acquiesced, since through its subsequent acts Congress made it clear that such executive government could have been superseded at any time by legislation, as it ultimately was in the Philippines. By the end of the century, therefore, each branch perceived that it had a substantive role in forging American foreign policy. The foremost representative of U.S. foreign affairs was the executive, but the legislature had succeeded in shaping and modifying the tone of executive formulations. The net result was that the executive did not realistically expect to conclude any foreign policy endeavor having military overtones without at least some contribution of Congress's thinking and experience.

MILITARY AFFAIRS AND AUTHORIZATIONS

The Struggle over the Size and Deployment of Military Force

The late nineteenth century defense program of the U.S. government resulted in the evolution of a modern navy and tended to deemphasize for a time the importance of the U.S. Army. Though for more than a decade after the conflict of *Monitor* and *Merrimac* many U.S. naval authorities and congressmen were content to armor-plate antique American fighting ships unchanged in design for a half-century,* this policy soon began to change.

The president and Congress often bargained for the prerogative to define the nature and direction of U.S. defenses, devoting particular

---

*Harold and Margaret Sprout, in *The Rise of American Naval Power* 180 (1939), point out that the Grant administration inherited a worthless collection of antiquated ships, whose renovation was enriching shipbuilding contractors.

attention to construction of new ships and ports. During the Grant administration, a few congressmen* began to stir their colleagues to consider upgrading the navy, helping to precipitate a legislative movement in the direction of improvements that would last well into the 1890s.

In successive administrations, a modern peacetime navy gradually became a reality. At the same time, executive requests for army increases received much less enthusiastic response, primarily because of fears that the army might be used to suppress popular domestic uprisings such as labor unrest.† Typical of Congress's diminished interest in the army was its refusal to consider President Hayes's request in 1880 for an increase in the size of the army to its maximum allowable limit of 30,000 men and its refusal to provide the funds the president claimed were needed to upgrade fortifications and artillery.[215] This reluctance was in sharp contrast to Congress's passage of the naval appropriations bill (H.R. 6969), with the eloquent comment by chairman of the House Naval Affairs Committee W.C. Whitthorne, "We have no navy and ought to commence from the bottom and build it up." The bill passed unanimously, 215 to 0, in the House, and the Senate even increased the appropriations voted in the lower chamber.**[216]

Despite some lagging in naval improvements during Arthur's tenure,†† a four-year plan for modernization involving building new ships became law during Cleveland's first administration (H.R. 6664).***[217]

---

*In 1870, Cadwallader Washburne (R. Wis.) warned his colleagues that the House Committee on Appropriations would not consider devoting large sums to repair virtually useless wooden warships or cruisers. Washburne advocated, instead, appropriations for construction of "swift subsidized iron merchant ships," which the committee foresaw could be converted into cruisers and used to prey on enemy commerce in wartime as Britain had done. 42 *Congressional Globe* 2882, 2883. Opponents leveled charges that in sixteen months, $37 million had failed to repair naval deficiencies. Many objections, however, were directed not at policy but at executive conduct that exceeded its lawful bounds: for example, the Navy's consistent pattern of outrunning its appropriations, showing no regard for Congress's will. Concern was also expressed at the president's appointment of an admiral into the department, thereby violating the legislative intention that the Department operate under a civil administration. *See* 42 *Congressional Globe Appendix* 106–13, 122–25. (Speeches of Samuel Cox (D. N.Y.), Aaron F. Stevens (R. N.H.), Henry Dawes (R. Mass.), C.W. Morgan (D. Ohio), and James Beck (D. Ky.)).

†*See* discussion of the Pullman strike, *supra* pp. 263–64.

**A bill to provide the secretary of the navy with a permanent construction fund (to come from appropriated monies and proceeds from sale of old ships), from which the secretary of the navy could spend up to $1 million annually without Congress's consent, ran aground in the Senate, where it was objected that the bill gave the secretary of the navy and his board of review too much authority. 11 *Congressional Record* 2115, 2196, 2205.

††Arthur's slight progress in rebuilding the navy came to an almost complete halt despite the building programs that he asked Congress to legislate in December 1883 and March 1884 as that body awaited the result of the presidential election of 1884.

***During the first Cleveland administration (50th Cong., 2d Sess., February 1889), the House achieved virtually complete control over warship design. The Naval Bill for 1890

The fiscal 1886 appropriation bill stirred some controversy over its provision to create a board to report to Congress on what measures should be taken to equip and defend the U.S. coastline. Three of this board's five members were to be presidentially appointed, while the remaining two were to be designated one each by the speaker of the House and president of the Senate. Opponents called the proposal an unconstitutional encroachment on the executive's appointment authority, since acceptance of the principle could result in later legislation giving those congressional officials power to appoint all of the members. The executive would thus be deprived not only of authority to appoint his own commission but also of the work of handling U.S. defense. But Clifton Breckinridge (D. Ark.) argued, as evidence of the bill's constitutionality, that the Senate and House jointly chose other officers of the U.S. government. And John Reagan (D. Tex.) maintained that the board was intended to aid the president, not to sap his power.[218] The bill passed, with the provision intact, in July 1886.[219]

At times, Congress halted the executive department's push for naval modernization, fearing that the existence of a large navy would encourage its use for war. For example, during President Harrison's term, an amendment to the naval appropriations bill (H.R. 7093) pledging expansion of naval capability was defeated on the ground that a large navy might tend to invite conflict.*[220] However, succeeding administrations up to the Spanish-American war gradually fulfilled the dream of attaining at least respectability in terms of size, if not parity, with the fleets of other large nations. Thus, during Cleveland's second administration, only a minority in the House was opposed to building huge battleships to compete with foreign navies. When future House speaker Joseph Cannon pressed for an "urgent" naval deficiency appropriation, New York Congressman Amos Cummings asked if the repairs Cannon spoke of were not necessary so that the navy could be kept practically on a "war footing."[221] Cannon's careful reply undoubtedly helped obtain the bill's

---

(H.R. 12329) provided authority for one steel cruiser to be built "according to plans and specifications to be furnished to the Navy Department by Hon. John R. Thomas of Illinois, to be approved by the Secretary of the Navy." Thomas had submitted to the House's Naval Affairs Committee certain plans drafted by a number of naval officers. 20 *Congressional Record* 1747–48. Despite strong opposition in both houses, the bill passed with an amendment giving the executive only token discretion over the cruiser design by mandating the use of Thomas's plans without his name, and providing for their approval by a naval board. *Id.* 1769, 1770. The only design that the board might approve was the one that had been legislatively authorized; therefore, it lacked true discretion.

*Benjamin Harrison did achieve some of his goals for the navy. Earlier authorizations resulting from Congress's willingness to legislate an expanded naval capacity were already being implemented. Harrison noted in his state of the union message on 6 December 1892 that $35 million in contracts had been let for new vessels. 13 *Messages and Papers* 5759.

passage: "[T]o keep it upon a proper footing in peace and efficient if war comes."[222]

At the same time as comprehensive naval defense programs were being implemented, legislators debated executive use of the army, both in defense of U.S. citizens and in the execution of the laws, and weighed the two branches' power over troop deployment. Congress also examined the president's use of the army in several instances of domestic crises, with implications for the international uses of the war power.

President Hayes's request for funds to pay the army* in fiscal 1878 sparked a debate on control of the army with important implications for executive use of military power. The final Congress of Grant's second administration had adjourned without appropriating funds for the army, which had served many months without pay by the time Hayes took office. The new army appropriations bill (H.R. 902) was therefore critical.

Democrats had wanted troops removed from the South, and, true to a prearranged formula, Hayes recalled most federal soldiers stationed in the southern states upon his assumption of the presidency.† Nonetheless, southern congressmen demanded a statutory guarantee that federal troops would be kept out of the South. Others, because of unrest on the Mexican frontier, wanted to direct the president to station troops on the Texas border. Westerners desired soldiers to be sent to the Indian frontier to reinforce skeleton regiments left after raids had taken heavy casualties and thus opposed southern congressmen's pressures to diminish the total number of troops. As pressure escalated to pass a bill so that the army could be paid, both houses vigorously debated the issue of whether Congress or the president would control army deployment.[223]

The House responded to a provision in the army bill proposing that the executive deploy a "sufficient force" of cavalry to defend the Mexican and Indian frontiers.**[224] Michigan Representative Omar Conger (R.) objected that without some form of limitation on troop number the president could escalate a tense military situation and involve the country in war; and the House agreed to limit the force to be used to four cavalry regiments of up to 100 men in each company.[225] Several con-

---

*The president had recommended (6 *Congressional Record* 6) that the appropriation be based on the army's maximum legal number of 25,000 men, whereas it was claimed that the appropriation should be related to the actual number of men in the standing army, which had fallen to 22,000. *Id.* 287 (statement by John Atkins, 8 November 1877). A figure as low as 20,000 was also mentioned.

†The story is convincingly and thoroughly told in C. Vann Woodward, *Reunion and Reaction* (1956).

**The question of whether Congress can direct the president to station troops at a particular site had been resolved in favor of the executive in the Polk and Lincoln administrations. *See supra* Chapters 2, 3, pp. 100–03; 216–20.

gressmen objected to this restriction as usurpation of the president's commander-in-chief power to direct the army, not only because of the restriction as to size but also because of the requirement that "certain troops shall be stationed for a certain purpose in a certain place. . . ."[226] The Senate agreed with the dissenters on this point, modifying the bill in order to require the executive to deploy the simple but ambiguous number—a "sufficient force." During the Senate debate James Beck commented that it was strictly "the duty of the Commander-in-Chief of the Army to be governed by the exigencies of the service and that it is not the business of Congress to instruct him in that regard."[227] After some limited debate in the House, the Senate amendments and the whole bill were passed by the bare margin of five votes, 134 to 129.[228] Arguably, it was the sense of Congress that the best judgment of the executive based upon his own superior knowledge of changing times and events would have to be the "sufficient" guide for Congress to permit the president to deploy a force of the size he might require.

During the bill's passage the issue arose whether to authorize recruitment of enough men to bring the army up to its maximum statutory strength of 25,000 troops. Congressmen Gustave Schleicher (D. Tex.) and William Calkins (R. Ind.) strove for a force sufficient to punish "the Indians and our Mexican robber neighbors"[229] and were answered by James Blount's (D. Ga.) denunciation of congressmen or military men who "always regard the country as in a state of war."[230] Others, such as John Luttrell (D. Calif.), were worried that a large standing army might be used by an overzealous executive to put down domestic problems such as labor strikes.[231] But those arguing in favor of greater military strength achieved victory.[232]

During Hayes's tenure, Congress persevered in its attempt to circumscribe the exercise of executive authority over the armed forces. It provided criminal penalties of fine, imprisonment, or both in the army bill for fiscal 1879 (H.R. 4867) against "any person" violating the act if the army was used except as provided for in the Constitution or by statute.* Both houses also enacted legislation that enjoined the use of the army as a *posse comitatus* to execute the laws without the express authority of Congress or the Constitution.†[233] Congress thus controlled

---

*This provision aimed to place "command of the Army into the hands of Congress" by imposing a new penalty. While some Senate members indicated that the president as commander-in-chief would be subject to the penalty (7 *Congressional Record* 7241–42), the major thrust of debate, particularly in the House, demonstrated intent to reach only army officers who either authorized funds for the illegal activity or gave the orders. *Id.* 3845.

†The law of 1807 authorized use of federal troops in the same contingencies that the president was empowered to call up the militia. Thus, the president, under proper circumstances, could send regulars to quell insurrection in the states, where these troops would aid the federal marshal in a manner resembling the sheriff summoning to his assistance to keep the peace a body of citizens called the *posse comitatus*.

presidential power by claiming power to permit or to prohibit the army to be used in situations of local insurrection.*[234] Apparently, the majority of legislators perceived in this action no prejudice of the president's constitutional responsibility to execute the laws or to act as commander-in-chief.†[235]

Hayes sought to reopen the question,[236] and Senator Algernon Paddock (R. Neb.) introduced S. 1492 to eliminate the requirement of prior congressional authorization of army operations in any place "subject to Indian incursion."[237] Although passed by the Senate, it was not acted on in the House.**[238] Instead, the Democratic majority in both houses successfully passed a new bill[239] that skirted some of the constitutional issues by prohibiting spending of funds for use of the army as a peace force in elections.[240] When this restrictive measure (the Sparks amendment)†† came up for repassage,[241] Republicans rebutted that the Supreme Court in *Ex Parte Siebold*, 100 U.S. 371 (1879), had held not only that there was a "peace of the United States"[242] that could be implemented by statute but that the federal government might as a sovereign do anything necessary to its self-preservation.[243] Ohio Representative J. Warren Keifer (R.) remarked that after *Siebold*, no congressional regulation could enjoin the president's performance of his duty to execute the law and, if necessary, his "right to use physical power" to enforce it.

Despite objection, the Sparks amendment passed in both houses and

---

In adopting such harsh measures, legislators may have had in mind numerous instances during the previous administration in which President Grant used the army as a militia force. *See supra* pp. 250–51; *see also* the extensive debate on Grant's efforts to use a federal marshal in Utah to call out the U.S. Army to execute federal law. 46 *Congressional Globe* 634, 635, 638, 1813–1814.

*In conference, language was added that the punishable act had to be willful, but language requiring Congress's authorization to be express was retained. 7 *Congressional Record* 4295, 4304, 4648, 4686.

†Left unresolved was the question of whether the president had a residual power "to employ the Army for any purpose not authorized by law." *Id.* 3849.

**Representative Abram Hewitt (D. N.Y.) opposed the Paddock amendment. His remarks crystallized the central idea that the *"posse comitatus"* clause represented for its supporters:

> I repelled then, and I repel now, the idea that the President of the United States has any control as Commander-in-Chief of the Army except that which is in accordance with the statutes which Congress may adopt. He is the organ through which the orders of the people, expressed by Congress, are to be given to the Army; and to surrender the power of regulating and controlling the use of the Army would be to convert this Government into a centralized despotism.

8 *Congressional Record* 898 (remarks during House debate on an army reorganization bill).

††This rider to the 1879 army appropriation bill, H.R. 5523, specifically curtailed use of any money for "subsistence, equipment, transportation, or compensation" of the army if used at the polls within any state as a police force. 10 *Congressional Record* 2340. This amendment passed both houses and was signed by the president. *Id.* 2360, 2364, 2637, 2639, 2641–42, 2648.

Hayes approved the bill that incorporated it.[244] It was plain that by the device of amendments to appropriation bills, Congress claimed a significant share both in formulating national defense policy and in curtailing the president's use of the army to implement such policy.

Executive Authority to Deploy Military Force

Congress was concerned with defining the criteria for the constitutional use of available military strength by the executive in various crisis situations. In May 1879, Senator Joseph E. McDonald (D. Ind.) unsuccessfully proposed a bill (S. 621) designed to replace statutes that had been accumulating since 1792 concerning emergency use of militia and federal troops by the president.[245] While McDonald's bill gave the president general authority to use troops to suppress violence, whether domestic or foreign, the bill retained the limitations of the *posse comitatus* clause of 1878. There was some debate, but no vote was ever taken.[246]

Other congressmen during the same session sought to limit presidential authority with a bill that allowed use of force in only two specific instances: to repel armed enemies and to protect the states against violence or invasion.[247] Senator Morgan (D. Ala.) supported this limitation, arguing that in all of U.S. history, the chief executive had possessed unconditional authority to use both regular troops and militia only immediately after the Civil War.[248] His opponent, George F. Edmunds (R. Vt.) remarked, however, that it had always been constitutional for a president to use the army for any legitimate federal objective. Edmunds deduced from the president's duty to execute the laws (Article II, section 3) that there was a "peace of the United States," which the president had a duty to protect as a necessary part of a government's right to self-preservation.[249]

The House and Senate each passed this limitation upon presidential use of the army by wide margins,[250] but President Hayes vetoed it on the ground that not only had other statutes sustained the right of the president to use force if required to uphold the law but that this bill's two exceptions were unacceptably narrow: thus, the statute would "seriously impair the efficiency of the executive department."[251] The House failed to override the veto, 128 to 97.[252]

Congress did not seriously question President Arthur's effort to implement the reforms in naval defenses called for in his first annual message,[253] and the first all-steel U.S. warships were launched in his administration. The American executive no longer lacked the means to execute policy by force, whereas lack of coercive power had often compelled earlier presidents to adopt programs of action that were less expansive than their views of presidential authority.* While Arthur possessed a greater command of *materiel*, he still believed that his authority for the use of force had to be strictly construed. For example, when the governor of Arizona territory sought aid from Arthur to defend against "armed bands of desperadoes, known as cowboys," the president turned to Congress for authority to use the army to aid local officials.[254] However, Senator Edmunds reported that the Judiciary Committee believed that the statutes and Constitution gave Arthur all the power he needed to use the army to enforce the laws, and the committee recommended no additional legislation.[255]

Arthur's secretary of the navy, William Chandler, asserted commander-in-chief power to deploy naval personnel perhaps bolder than that claimed by any previous executive. Chandler anticipated that Secretary of State Frelinghuysen's 1884 treaty with Nicaragua creating a jointly owned isthmian canal was about to be ratified by the Senate and ordered a surveying party to Nicaragua to plan a route.[256] Senator George Vest, who claimed there was danger in such an assumption of power, sought to enjoin Chandler while Congress studied the suitability of the proposed expedition. But the Senate failed to pass his resolution aimed at blocking the expedition and thus missed an opportunity to challenge the executive's extravagant claim of power. The surveyors departed,† and the secretary of the navy continued to follow a unilateral course of action. On 9 January 1885, Ensign Washington Chambers wrote to Secretary Chandler concerning his observations of the work done by the canal company in Panama, noting that he was operating under "confidential" instructions from the secretary.[257]

Legislators in 1898 came closer than at any time in history** to making war on their own terms as they dealt with a president who did not favor war with Spain. President McKinley requested Congress to authorize him to take all necessary diplomatic and military measures to end the war between the Cuban people and Spain and achieve stable government.[258] But Congress insisted on language in the war resolution that ordered the president to pursue certain diplomatic options with Spain, and then it directed him to use force if Spain did not comply. Congress's joint resolution of 20 April, first, recognized the independence of Cuban people; second, declared that it was the U.S. government's duty to

---

*President Washington, for example, had demonstrated a highly expansive view of his authority, restricted, however, by the lack of naval and army strength. *See* Sofaer, *Origins* 116–17.

†The work and conclusions of the survey expedition are set forth in K. Hagan, *American Gunboat Diplomacy and the Old Navy, 1877–1889*, at 158–59 (1973).

**Congress did declare war against Mexico in 1846 but only after President Polk had moved U.S. troops across the border. *Supra* Chapter 2, pp. 143–47.

demand that Spain relinquish its authority and withdraw its military forces in Cuba; and, third, *directed* the president to use necessary force to carry these demands into effect.* This resolution passed in the Senate, 42 to 35, and the House, 311 to 6.

Implicit in the requirement that Spain withdraw from Cuba was Congress's acknowledgement that the president himself would present this demand to Spain; but should the president decide when Spain had finally refused Congress's ultimatum? And if the Spanish refused, should McKinley have the option of implementing military force or be required to lay the exchange before Congress for its appraisal and await a declaration of war?†

Senator Edward Pettus (D. Ala.) firmly maintained that the president could not constitutionally be given the directive to determine the extent of an undeclared military action. Joseph Foraker (R. Oh.) then expanded on Pettus's theme by denying that the president could be given authority in advance to use military force if negotiations failed.[259] But Henry Cabot Lodge (R. Mass.) answered that the president alone possessed all diplomatic functions under the Constitution and should determine when negotiations had failed; Congress had authority to clothe the president with the war power and "should not attempt to shrink from what it means. . . ."[260]

As in the Quasi-War with France in 1798, the hostilities that Congress directed** the president to enter into by its resolution of 20 April 1898 were to constitute an "imperfect war," without a formal declaration. Several senators believed that Congress should determine when the conditions of the resolution were fulfilled and force could be used.[261] Senator Pettus also argued that Congress must "direct" and not "authorize" a president to intervene. With Jeter Pritchard (R. N.C.), he

---

*When, subsequently, Spain effectively refused these demands, McKinley severed diplomatic relations, asked Congress to declare war and obtained its compliance. 31 *Congressional Record* 4244, 4252.

†This latter issue evolved from the changes Congress made in McKinley's proposal that resulted in a resolution affirming the independence of the Cuban people and the withdrawal of Spain instead of adhering to McKinley's neutral objectives of terminating hostilities and securing a stable government.

**The language of *direction* to the executive does not occur in prior legislative resolutions, such as for information or the purpose of delegating authority. Nearly always, congressional resolution authorized or requested a president to act. Therefore, the 20 April 1898 resolution constitutes an unusual expression of congressional delegation of power, framed virtually as a legal agency, in which the president was expected to act as the agent of Congress to accomplish a particular purpose. Implicit, however, in that order may be seen the expectation that the president keep Congress apprised of circumstances arising in the course of business in which he was engaged. Though Pettus and Pritchard did not articulate a reporting requirement, it is inferrable, from such a direction, that Congress might have expected the president to respond to any legislative questions regarding hostilities that resulted from implementation of the 20 April resolution.

maintained that Congress must set the criteria by which either a general or limited war was carried on, and determine when the power may be exercised. By any form of declaration of war, however, Congress would assume, in Pritchard's words, full jurisdiction over the "entire subject."[262]

The final Senate version, in which the House concurred, did not require Congress's determination that conditions had been satisfied. McKinley was simply directed to enforce the resolution by military means "to such extent as may be necessary. . . ."[263]

The second part of the debate focused on McKinley's proposition that he be authorized to secure a stable government in Cuba. McKinley had counselled legislators for over a year prior to war not to recognize the independence of Cuba because of uncertainty whether the regime that triumphed would be a friendly or even stable one.[264] Some such as Senator Marion Butler (Pop. N.C.) thought that recognition of Cuba's independence would prevent the president from enforcing a pacification program.[265] The resulting declaration recognized the freedom of the people of Cuba but not the existence of a Cuban republic. The House approved, forcing the executive to accept compromise language calling for independence but substantially preserving his interpretation of the diplomatic and political consequences of nonrecognition. The legislation that authorized war in 1898 thus was shaped cautiously to avoid the implication that it was intended to confer any power on the executive other than the execution of the will of Congress.*

Unilateral Executive Military Actions and Congress's Response

Executive Initiatives   Presidents from Ulysses Grant through William McKinley frequently sought to limit Congress's influence in warmaking by presenting a case of action or intervention to the legislature as a *fait accompli*. They warned that even vocal opposition tending to upset executive planning would not inure to the nation's benefit. One of the most sensational such incidents in the history of U.S. foreign policy involved the November 1873 seizure and execution of many of the American crew of the *Virginius*, a vessel with fraudulent U.S. registry actually owned by Cubans. Spain was in the process of suppressing a

---

*In order to resolve any doubts about his right to conduct a war against Spain, President McKinley sought the legal imprimatur of a "perfect" war. On 25 April, he reported to Congress that since Spain had refused U.S. demands, he had imposed a blockade and called for volunteers—all in accordance with Congress's authorization of 20 April. In response to McKinley's request, Congress immediately declared that a state of war existed. 24 *Messages and Papers* 6296, 6297.

Cuban insurrection; and although it seized the *Virginius* on the high seas, the Spanish government meted out as swift punishment to the suspected rebels as if they had been captured in Cuban waters.

Congress was not in session, but Grant boldly ordered that the navy be placed on a war footing. The president did not inform Congress what specific steps had been taken without its authorization, but in requesting special funds, Secretary George Robeson told Congress that he was already outfitting every ship for duty and enlisting 1,500 to 2,000 more men beyond the legally authorized number.[266] Even though the president had not transmitted all correspondence relating to the incident,* Congress immediately set about dealing with this *fait accompli.*[267]

Representative Glenni Scofield (R. Pa.) on 10 December 1873, reported H.R. 480 providing for an increase of naval enlistees by 1,500 men, the approximate number that the secretary had already started to enroll. James A. Garfield proposed an amendment providing that the increase be only temporary[268] and was joined by others who wanted Congress to retain control of all such increases.[269] The House voted overwhelmingly for Garfield's amendment, 134 to 26, and the bill passed.[270] But soon afterward it became clear that the executive, with the help of House committee chairmen, such as Glenni Scofield, the chairman of the Committee on Naval Affairs, had misled Congress into providing more military support than would have been forthcoming had all the facts become known. When Representative Garfield introduced H.R. 481 to fund the extraordinary expenses Robeson had incurred, several House members balked† at a proviso allowing the president to transfer appropriations from one bureau to another "in case of emergency."[271] Since some congressmen felt that the provision might be applied in future emergencies,[272] two changes were suggested. One amendment limited the transfers to expenses that had already been incurred. The second instructed the president to inform Congress of all transfers "whenever the good of the public service will permit." After House passage,[273] the Senate removed the transfer provision from the funding bill, regarding it as a dangerous departure from the ordinary rules governing appropriations.[274] It then passed H.R. 481 to cover the expenses Robeson had unilaterally incurred[275] but never voted on the bill to approve the increase in naval enlistees (H.R. 480).

In debate over the naval appropriations bill (H.R. 1013) for the

---

*As he had promised in his December message, however, Grant sent Congress another message on 5 January 1874 summarizing what was then known about the *Virginius* affair. 2 *Congressional Record* 368.

†Representative Samuel S. Cox (D. N.Y.), for example, deplored Congress's deferential attitude in the face of information that left the legislature completely "in the dark as to our recent diplomacy." *Id.* 181.

succeeding fiscal year, it was discovered that the Navy Department had diverted over $5 million appropriated for naval pay to recompense these arguably unauthorized men. Congressman James Beck charged that he had not known that sailors had been paid prior to the authorization of their recruitment. He also assailed Scofield for concealing the fact that the crisis had ended.[276]

Scofield admitted that at the time the authorization and funding bills were debated and passed in the House, he knew there would be no war with Spain since the order had been given for delivery of the *Virginius* back to the United States. Yet he reported out the bill for additional enlistees because his committee believed in an augmented force even without "this Cuba-Spanish craze."[277] James Garfield came to Scofield's defense by saying that Secretary of the Navy George Robeson had asked for the bill to be brought in to ratify his unauthorized increase of the Navy in an emergency. Congressman Beck, however, angrily contended that the actual meaning of H.R. 480 was to pardon the Secretary of the Navy for wrongdoing in enlisting sailors without legislative authorization. Garfield replied, "It was not regarded as 'wrong,' it was a violation of law; but not wrong."[278] Beck then reminded committee members that they worked for Congress and not the President:

> [W]e deny the right of any Secretary, or of the President himself, to put his hands into the Treasury of the United States and take out what he pleases without authority of law, or to increase the Army or Navy at his pleasure; and we demand of all our committees, whenever they may have any private information from a Secretary, or any other official ... that they should state what they know, whether it militates against their own views or sustains them.[279]

Garfield vigorously responded that Congress knew Secretary Robeson planned to "put every available iron and wooden ship of our Navy in condition for immediate duty" and that he at that moment was "enlisting men to supply and fill up the crews of all our vessels." Garfield stated that Congress, on 13 December 1873, had appropriated funds to pay those who manned the ships. There was nothing underhanded or secret in this, and the fact that the secretary acted during a recess gave his acts no clandestine character.[280]

Allan Nevins says Grant himself "expressed amazement" at the "lamblike" conduct of Congress during the *Virginius* affair, attributing this meekness as much to the panic and industrial depression then gripping the United States as a desire for friendliness with the new republican government of Spain.[281] The brief tension that did surface can at least be regarded as reflecting a minority's thinking on the proper extent of executive authority during an emergency.

Another example of comparatively passive congressional reaction to executive unilateral conduct occurred during the Hayes administration. Throughout 1876 and 1877, constant attacks upon U.S. citizens by Mexican Indian marauders* had brought forth resolutions such as H.R. 96 of 12 July 1876, authorizing the president to station cavalry and infantry units on the border and to order them to cross into Mexico "when in hot pursuit of the robbers," if in his judgment it became necessary to protect American rights.[282] Though Congress failed to authorize sending troops into Mexico,† President Hayes acted without benefit of legislative approval. On 1 June 1877, Secretary of War George McCrary wrote to General of the Army William Sherman that border raids should no longer be endured. The government of Mexico was to be invited to join in preventing them, but even if it neglected this duty, the U.S. Army was ordered to suppress these outrages, even if quelling them meant crossing the Mexican border in hot pursuit.[283] Mexico responded by sending troops to the border, and a confrontation occurred which nearly resulted in an outbreak of hostilities. U.S. minister Foster wrote Secretary of State William Evarts, in October 1877, that Mexican troops had pursued American troops on Mexican soil and that the Americans had turned and faced the Mexicans in battle lines. After the forces faced each other for some time, the Americans turned and retreated across the Rio Grande.**[284]

*Texas border problems during the decade of the 1870s threatened war between the United States and Mexico. American troops entered Mexican territory numerous times without Mexican authorization. The executive had sought but had been refused permission to pursue the marauders and had, as a result, told the Mexican government "unofficially" that it was considering pursuit anyway. A raid was made on a Kickapoo village in 1873. It was protested by the Mexican government and defended by the U.S. secretary of state as an action within the limits of international law. Another U.S. raid in 1875, which resulted in a skirmish with regular Mexican troops, caused President Grant to bring the condition to Congress's attention; and investigation of the border troubles by a House special committee led to proposal of joint resolution H.R. 96. H.R. Exec. Doc. No. 1, pt. I (Ser. 1594), 43rd Cong., 1st Sess. 607, 610, 634, 644, 655, 708–09; H.R. Misc. Doc. No. 64 (Ser. 1820), 45th Cong., 2d Sess. 1, 89, 105–06, 138–39, 142–43, 148–50, 187–88, 213–16; H.R. Rep. No. 343, pt. XVI (Ser. 1709), 44th Cong., 1st Sess. 87–98; 10 Messages and Papers 4295 (Grant's seventh annual message, 7 December 1875); 4 Congressional Record 297, 800, 1066, 1366.
†When the resolution finally came to a vote in the House on 20 July 1876, the impression predominated that its second branch gave the president too much power and might even lead to war with Mexico. It was defeated 89 to 96. The first section, providing simply for the stationing of troops along the border, passed (id. 4753, 4755) and was routinely passed in the Senate. Id.
**House members' careful probing of the Texas border controversy revealed aspects of military conduct probably unknown fully even to the executive. The House asked for information about conditions on the Mexican frontier and ultimately conducted inquiries into the border situation, but the result was inconclusive so far as Hayes's order of June 1st was concerned. 6 Congressional Record 211; H.R. Exec. Doc. No. 13, 45th Cong., 1st Sess. 4–5. Late in November 1877, the House Committee on Military Affairs began to hear testimony from Secretary of War McCrary, General Sherman, General Ord, Lieutenant-

Implicit in the order was its justification by necessity, but whatever its rationale, Congress neither directly attacked the president's right to issue it, nor did it affirm his action. The power to order deployment of troops in hot pursuit onto the soil of a friendly neighbor took on some aspects of a power concurrent with Congress as an action short of war permitted to the president.

President Hayes's first annual message to Congress alluded to the Mexican border imbroglio as having a potential of "mischances of action ... unfavorable to complete amity."[285] New York Congressman Abram S. Hewitt (D.) was disturbed by Hayes's statement:

> This passage looks ... either toward peace or toward war. And if by any possibility we should be plunged into hostilities with our neighbor it will be alleged that Congress had due notice and should have taken action in the premises. . . . The danger is that, if this Congress should adjourn without devising some peaceful solution we may find ourselves ... compelled to vote upon questions of supply for military operations, which we cannot refuse to make without imputation upon our own patriotism and public spirit.[286]

When Hewitt proposed that the House Committee on Foreign Affairs study and report on the problem, the committee favored retention of a U.S. military presence on the Texas border. But the House refused to adopt the committee's joint resolution,* and Congress was thus precluded from a vote that would have directly affirmed or rejected Hayes's conduct.

Hayes's diplomacy during the summer of 1878 provided a solution to the border problems and thus ended the tension over the executive's

---

Colonel Shafter, and many other American military and diplomatic officials. As the inquiry moved up the chain of command, there occurred an astonishing disintegration of information. While Lieutenant-Colonel Shafter reported routine scouting expeditions into Mexican territory, General Ord admitted to crossing the Rio Grande "about a dozen times or oftener," and General Sherman finally confirmed crossing "four or five times at any rate." H.R. Misc. Doc. No. 64, 45th Cong., 2d Sess. 23, 88, 158–59. Sherman then maintained that the War Department had issued orders for troops to enter Mexico. Ord said that he gave his own orders six months before the 1 June 1877 presidential directive and communicated them to the administration, which did not disapprove—a fact that Ord regarded as tacit approval. Shafter claimed that field commanders took the responsibility among themselves for the initial invasion of Mexican soil, when they crossed "without any orders." *Id.* 33, 103, 176.

*After promulgating a report (H.R. Rep. No. 701, at pp. 1–173) the House Committee on Foreign Affairs urged adoption of a joint resolution (H.R. 167) that recognized the necessity of maintaining an "adequate" force on the Texas border and that characterized Hayes's 1 June orders as "necessary" to protect the lives and property of American citizens. The committee also recommended that the president's orders should remain in force until a treaty between the United States and Mexico embodied assurances of citizens' safety. But the resolution was tabled and a motion to reconsider it was defeated.

claims to power in this area. U.S. minister Foster reported that the Mexican Senate had secretly conferred on its executive the power to enter into a convention regarding the pursuit of Indians;[287] and while no formal agreements were ever consummated, Hayes's annual message of 2 December 1878 reflected the official executive desire on the part of both governments to wind down the crisis.*[288]

Although President Grant had asked for limited authority to recruit volunteers to fight Indians,[289] Hayes responded differently as he faced not only Nez Perce Indian uprisings but also labor strikes† and the Mexican border problem in 1877.

The president addressed the three-pronged military crisis at a time when Congress had adjourned without making an appropriation for the army. He did not call a special session to meet these emergencies, but between 1 July and 15 November 1877, he recruited over 1,000 volunteer soldiers for the army without Congress's knowledge or prior authorization. Hayes was well aware that no funds existed to pay wages of those in the service, let alone recruit additional forces.[290] Moreover, he did not exercise the option of explaining the troop situation to Congress once it did convene in October 1877. Despite token outbursts of disfavor, however, Congress did not formally dissent, tolerating arguably severe inroads on its constitutional prerogative to raise armies simply because most legislators must have been convinced there was no satisfactory alternative.

Hayes's Cabinet was in session in mid-July when it received word from Washington territory about an increase in the forces of Nez Perce Chief Joseph. After brief consultation, the Cabinet apparently recommended, and the executive approved, raising 200 volunteers from either Washington or Oregon, with the option to recruit up to 500 men if the commanding general felt it necessary.[291] As it did in the Mexican border crisis, the House investigated Department of War reports, particularly concentrating upon the alleged numbers of enlisted men. Secretary of War George McCrary, in response to its request, wrote the House Committee on Appropriations that there were 21,363 men in the armed forces of the United States as of 15 October 1877.[292] The adjutant general and commanding general, however, informed the committee that

---

*No formal agreements were consummated by the two governments, but the foreign ministers continued their efforts. Congressmen remarked that President Diaz desired peace; Foster wrote Secretary Evarts to the same effect; and the president responded by revoking the order of 1 June 1877. H.R. Exec. Doc. No. 1, pt. I, 45th Cong., 3d Sess. 608; 9 *Congressional Record* 2463; H.R. Exec. Doc. No. 1, pt. I, 46th Cong., 3d Sess. 726–27, 744, 781.

†These involved railway labor disputes in six states and the District of Columbia. H.R. Exec. Doc. No. 1, pt. 2, 45th Cong., 2d Sess. iv–vi, xii–xiii (1877) (Report, Secretary of War McCrary to President Hayes, 19 November 1877).

the correct number was much larger—21,902.[293] When the committee again asked for the total in November, the adjutant general affirmed that the precise count indeed was 21,902, "an increase, since the communication from the Secretary of October 30, of 539." This statement caused an uproar, since it gave the impression 539 men had been recruited while the appropriation bill was being considered, "without authority of law and without one dollar of appropriation. . . ."[294] The discrepancy sparked House curiosity. Why was it difficult for the army to agree on a number?

The adjutant general informed the House, on 12 November 1877, that since 1 July, 1,023 men had been recruited.[295] Secretary of War McCrary also on 12 November claimed existing law permitted such recruiting and stated that "the temporary failure of the Army appropriation bill" did not "take away the power of the President, expressly conferred, to keep the Army in existence and up to a given standard by recruiting."[296] The secretary then admitted, however, that General McDowell had appealed for recruits to fight Indians on the Pacific coast during the summer and that authority to recruit had been granted.[297]

Outraged Congressmen John Atkins (D. Tenn.) and Abram Hewitt (D. N.Y.) denounced the secretary of war, the president, and the adjutant general, not only for the illegal enlistments but also for lying by stating to the committee that recruitment had been halted for lack of funds.[298] They doubtless suspected that the army's clumsy performance was aimed at keeping secret an activity that might be beyond its constitutional power. Atkins, for example, denied that the president had any conferred power to recruit except what was given to him by an annual appropriation:

> The claim of Charles I was that he not only had the right to maintain the Army, but the right to go outside of the votes of supply and raise money for its support . . . and the patriots of that time . . . brought his head to the scaffold in consequence of this violation of law.[299]

Representative Garfield championed the innovative argument that the executive had the power as commander-in-chief to ensure U.S. defense and thus to accept the offer of endangered citizens to protect themselves from Indian attack. These individuals, he said, had gone to several army posts and enlisted, although they had been warned that the army was unable to pay anything for their services. "This recruitment did not cost this Government one cent, because the endangered people came and tendered their services without solicitation."[300] But in reply to Garfield's suggestion that the army might not exist for failure of an appropriation, Hewitt replied that the executive's simple remedy to any imminent danger of dissolution would be to call an extra session of Congress and make statutory provision to assure that U.S. defenses remained intact.

Instead, Hayes's conduct gave Congress no chance to perform its constitutional role. He did not even request ratification for what might have been considered emergency measures, as Lincoln had done.[301] If the War Department had approved the troop increase without Hayes's knowledge, the secretary of war would have been subject to severe admonition from the executive. President Hayes, however, was content to stand behind the War Department and let its justification* constitute his own. The furor subsided, no steps were taken to protest the executive action, and H.R. 902, after a month's delay, was consented to by both houses on 17 November 1877.[302]

Congressional Failure to Respond to Executive Military Action

Hawaii   On several separate occasions during the early 1890s, presidential military action caused almost no congressional reaction. In fact, in the case of American involvement in the Hawaiian revolution of 1893, Congress objected to U.S. military action only when Benjamin Harrison's successor, Grover Cleveland, decided to *withdraw* American forces from Honolulu—not because Harrison had put them there.

For the better part of two decades, the United States had sought and obtained commercial hegemony† in the Hawaiian Islands. Several civil disturbances in the late 1880s resulting from the instability of the Hawaiian government[303] impressed American officials with the need to maintain a ship at Honolulu at all times to protect U.S. lives and property.**

The climate within the Harrison administration seemed receptive to

---

*Secretary George McCrary, among other points, argued by analogy that the president is constitutionally empowered to appoint judges upon failure of salary appropriations and thus that the failure of the army's appropriation did not prevent the president from keeping an army in existence and up to a given standard. 6 *Congressional Record* 347–48 (Letter, McCrary to Garfield, 12 November 1877).

†The 1876 reciprocity treaty between the Hawaiian monarchy and the United States granted significant trade and territorial privileges to the United States that were not enjoyed by any other country. 1 *Treaties, Conventions* (Malloy ed.) 915–19.

**E.g., on 2 August 1889, U.S. Minister George Merrill telegraphed the Department of State that troops had been landed from the USS *Adams* to protect lives and property during an attempt on 30 July "to subvert the existing government of the Hawaiian Islands." Acting Secretary Moore's reply on 12 August indicated a broad view of what constituted appropriate protection when he expressed the U.S. government's "satisfaction" that the "insurrection was suppressed. ..." National Archives Microfilm, Department of State, *Diplomatic Instructions*, M77, roll 100 (Moore to Merrill, 12 August 1889, no. 136).

acquisition of the islands in June 1889 when John Stevens, protégé of Secretary of State Blaine, became Minister to Hawaii. The new minister was a fervent annexationist. The free rein Washington permitted him* culminated in Stevens's intervention in Hawaiian affairs to an extent that surpassed his predecessor George Merrill.

Stevens wrote to Blaine and Blaine's successor, John W. Foster, explaining to both secretaries of state his belief that political turmoil in the islands could enable England to gain a foothold ahead of the United States unless "decisive" steps were taken.[304] In neither case was there a specific reply. Stevens more directly asked Blaine what the minister and the naval commander should do if the Hawaiian government were overthrown,[305] but the records of the U.S. legation in Hawaii do not contain a response. Under similar circumstances, General Andrew Jackson had written to President Monroe asking for instructions to take the Floridas during the Seminole War and received no answer. In each instance, a subordinate executive officer sought permission to exceed his instructions before an event that catapulted the officer into a position of accomplishing what the chief executive hoped would happen but would not authorize.[306]

John Stevens was quickly placed in such a position when, on 14 January 1893, Queen Liliuokalani announced she would promulgate a constitution for the islands that in effect would disenfranchise nearly all property owners. Americans such as Sanford Dole, who had encouraged previous uprisings that had chipped away Hawaiian monarchical power, decided to wrest all control from the queen.[307] Dole's "Committee of Safety" asked both Stevens and Captain George Wiltse of the SS *Boston* to cooperate with their pledge to resist Liliuokalani. Stevens insisted twice in his replies that if the committee showed some kind of evidence that it exerted political control, he would recognize a new government, despite the fact that he possessed no explicit authority to do so.[308] Stevens then asked Wiltse to land marines and sailors to protect the U.S. legation and consulate and to secure the safety of American life and property,[309] and 164 U.S. servicemen were duly bivouacked in a hall near the palace and government buildings. Dole then accepted the position of head of Hawaii's provisional government, and the queen abdicated when she learned that Stevens had recognized the provisional government.[310]

*Blaine wrote Stevens a brief note in June 1889 stating that he was enclosing his commission as minister to Hawaii and his "printed instructions." At the end of the note the enclosures are again cited, but they do not appear in the State Department's files. National Archives Records Service, *Records of the State Department*, RG59 (instructions to U.S. Legations, Hawaii). Julius Pratt comments on the absence of these official instructions in *Expansionists of 1898; The Acquisition of Hawaii and the Spanish Islands* 50 (1936).

President Harrison approved of Stevens's conduct. One of Secretary Foster's dispatches to Stevens dated 28 January 1893 commended him for "recognizing an unopposed *de facto* Government." In a second, on 11 February, Foster authorized Stevens to arrange with Captain Wiltse for the continued on-shore presence of as large a marine force as necessary to secure American lives and property.* Stevens was instructed to use his own judgment as to when it was necessary to repress any lawlessness and public disturbances. Given his predilections, events detrimental to U.S. security could have included efforts of the queen to regain power.[311]

President Harrison reinforced the acts of his subordinates. Within a month of the *coup d'état,* emissaries of the provisional government brought a treaty of annexation to Washington, which the president signed and then transmitted to the Senate with a message asserting that the overthrow of Liliuokalani was not in any way being promoted by the U.S. government.[312] Other official supporting papers not only gave no indication that the use of force in Hawaii had influenced the outcome of the takeover but also maintained that the Marines had had no effect whatsoever upon the course of events.[313]

Though most senators favored annexation, action on the treaty was delayed because President-elect Grover Cleveland desired the opportunity to study the question, and upon becoming president, Cleveland swiftly withdrew the treaty from the Senate.[314] Cleveland thus prevented annexation, but Congress would not help restore the monarchy.[315]

Brazil An outstanding example of congressional acquiescence in presidential exercise of military power abroad was the general acclaim for U.S. Rear Admiral Andrew Benham's unneutral and unauthorized interposition in defense of U.S. merchant ships at Rio de Janeiro in 1894. U.S. policy decidedly favored dictator Floriano Peixoto's government, which, though imperial in tone, was opposed by royalist sympathizers such as Admiral Saldanha Da Gama, who wanted Brazil to return to a European-style monarchy. Insurgents led by Da Gama had established control of Rio Harbor, and Da Gama had announced his intention to obstruct all neutral commerce with the established govern-

---

*However, Foster's 11 February letter did include a specific disavowal of Stevens's unauthorized action in declaring an American protectorate in Hawaii, a declaration that the minister had issued at the provisional government's request two weeks after its takeover of the island. The limited rebuke, on the one hand, joined with ratification of Stevens's other course of conduct and reaffirmation of his discretionary authority under the original instructions, amounted, said the Democratic newspaper the *St. Louis Republic*, to a verdict of "Guilty, but go on doing it." Quoted in W. Russ, *The Hawaiian Revolution, 1893–1894*, 134–35 (1959), as clipped from the *New York Post* of 23 February 1893.

ment. Even before this announcement, however, merchants had had to risk persistent fire between the combatants in order to load and unload their cargoes.[316]

Benham responded to pleas of American merchant captains for protection as they sought to unload goods at the wharves, even though Admiral Da Gama had not replied to Benham's request that he cease all molestation of neutral—and particularly American—shipping.[317] Benham later emphasized that he alone decided to take the provocative step of convoying the merchant vessels:

> Having failed to receive assurance from ... da Gama that American vessels would not be interfered with, and three ... being desirous of going ... to discharge cargo, I decided to place them in their berths by force.[318]

He thereupon gave orders not only to convoy but also to return any insurgent fire.* When Benham's squadron (two American merchant vessels) passed by, the two sides traded several shots. The insurgents fired blank shells, but the U.S. warships discharged live ammunition, striking one Brazilian vessel with a musket shot. The battle ended when several Brazilian tugboats pulled alongside the U.S. merchantmen, offering to unload their cargoes.[319] Neither Secretary of State Walter Gresham nor Navy Secretary Hillary Herbert had given Benham explicit orders to use force, but when they learned of his action, both cabled approval of his conduct and proclaimed it was within his instructions.†[320]

By November 1893, Gresham had yielded to Minister Thompson's urging and approved the use of force by U.S. naval vessels to protect unloading of American goods so long as the vessels being unloaded did not cross the insurgents' "line of fire."[321] But Gresham's ambiguous phrase induced Commander Picking to withdraw protection from the

---

*Before the convoy set out, U.S. minister Thompson informed Secretary Gresham that an engagement with insurgent forces was likely. *Papers Relating to the Foreign Relations of the United States* (29 January 1894).

†The early instructions by Secretary Gresham to U.S. minister to Brazil Thomas Thompson included the phrase that he was to "exert himself in favor of innocent trade of American vessels." *Id.* (Gresham to Thompson, 11 October 1893). Gresham cautioned Thompson against intervention, instructing him to "observe the attitude of an indifferent spectator" and to "espouse the cause of neither side." *Id.* (Gresham to Thompson, 25 October 1893). But Thompson had taken it upon himself to adopt a more aggressive policy. When the USS *Charleston* arrived at Rio on 26 September 1893, Thompson ordered its commander, Henry F. Picking, to protect American goods in barges from seizure by insurgents and "to use force if necessary" (*id.* Thompson to Gresham, 28 September), in contrast to Picking's mild instructions from the State Department to prevent bloodshed "by exertion of all the moral force of the government ... by protest and otherwise. ...." *Id.* (Acting Secretary of State Strobel to Thompson, 29 September).

merchant vessels when the insurgents announced their blockade, since Picking believed that Thompson's demands constituted abandonment of strict neutrality.[322] Secretary Gresham provided no new light on the controversy when he cabled Thompson on 11 January 1894 that the insurgents' interference with neutral shipping by random firing was both "illegitimate and intolerable."[323] On the other hand, Benham justified unhesitating defense of the ships as consistent with the rights of neutrals and claimed that the vessels should be free from search and seizure even if they carried contraband.* Undoubtedly, Benham's forceful action dashed insurgents' hopes of achieving military victory by blockading Rio harbor. Other foreign commanders swiftly followed Benham's lead and protected their merchant fleets.[324]

Admiral Benham's unilateral reversal of a more cautious interpretation of U.S. neutrality was ratified by the administration. A policy of interposition, involving use of force sufficient to protect life and property without favoring any combatant, was stretched until it became intervention—a use of force capable of influencing the outcome of a civil war. Moreover, the force was being used not only to protect lives and property but also American trade.†

Cleveland provided Congress with only a cryptic reference to the Brazilian revolt in his annual message of December 1893, as he stated that the United States was following a "fixed policy of ... neutrality."[325] But in the annual message of 1894, Cleveland described Benham's "neutral" action in glowing terms, characterizing the incident as a precedent that would have a potentially "wholesome influence" on future "like circumstances."[326] The administration even used the incident as an argument** for increased expenditure for the construction of three new battleships and twelve torpedo boats.[327]

Congress throughout the course of events in Brazil was content to leave U.S. policy entirely within executive control. No substantive

---

*Legal scholar John Bassett Moore observed that breach of a blockade by a neutral was contrary to international law. 2 Moore ed., *A Digest of International Law* 1119. Arguably, however, a blockade instituted by insurgents who had not been recognized as a nation state might have been legally breached by neutral shipping.

†Grover Cleveland had used force to protect U.S. trade in Samoa in the wake of civil war and the threat of European powers to obtain spheres of influence. In late December 1888, the president dispatched the USS *Trenton* to join the *Nipsic*, already in Samoa, in defense of U.S. lives and property. Cleveland did not inform Congress of this action until 15 January 1889. But both houses approved an amendment to the diplomatic and consular bill that provided up to $500,000 for executive disposal to protect U.S. interests under its treaty of 1878 with Samoa. 20 *Congressional Record* 1371, 1381, 1984.

**The president's argument, moreover, contributed to the House's defeat (67 to 202) of an effort to recommit the naval appropriations bill of 1895 to committee for the purpose of deleting the provisions authorizing the new ships. 27 *Congressional Record* 2231–38, 2262, 2468–69.

discussions took place concerning the Benham incident.* Congressional apathy stood in stark contrast to pervasive, repeated discussions in the House of Commons on British policy in the Rio crisis of 1893.[328] Members of Parliament queried British ministers, who expressed profound concern that strict neutrality be preserved in a volatile international setting.†

Chile President Harrison did not inform legislators of the orders he had given the navy in the spring of 1891 to pursue the Chilean armed transport *Itata*, which during Chile's civil war had violated U.S. neutrality by receiving arms and munitions in American waters** and escaping to Chile.[329] The Cabinet had been divided over the legality of pursuit. The majority was uncertain whether U.S. warships had the right to capture the *Itata* beyond U.S. territorial limits.[330] Harrison, however, was "indignant" at *Itata*'s escape, which he saw as a serious affront to the United States and sided with Attorney General William Miller and Secretary of the Navy Benjamin Tracy who favored her recapture.[331] Secretary Tracy therefore ordered the *Charleston* and the *Omaha* to pursue and seize both the *Itata* and a convoy with her:

> If demand refused, enforce it if your force is clearly sufficient; if not
> ... follow *Itata* till you fall in with Admiral Brown ... who has been
> ordered to intercept her.††[332]

Charleston did not intercept *Itata*, but arrived at Iquique on 3 June 1891, a day before *Itata* arrived and was turned over to U.S. au-

---

*A resolution praising Benham's "prompt and energetic" action was introduced in the House and favorably reported out of committee but failed to come to a vote. 26 *Congressional Record* 1825; H.R. Rep. No. 391, 53rd Cong., 2d Sess.

†British discussions confirmed that Benham had acted counter to his superior's orders when he used force to land the cargo of U.S. merchant vessels. Policy developed in consultation with other powers including the United States indicated that great efforts would be made to protest and land cargo consistent with the principle of strict neutrality but that this would not include giving protection in a firing zone while combatants were engaged. When Admiral de Mello threatened to bomb Rio, all but Germany decided to inform him that force would be used if necessary to prevent the bombing. *Hansard's Parliamentary Debates* 656 (2 January 1894), 1347 (11 January 1894), 388 (13 February 1894), and 1134 (1 March 1894) (reprint 1969).

**While Alice Felt Tyler claims in chapter 6 of *The Foreign Policy of James G. Blaine* that the transfer of arms from an American schooner to the *Itata* took place on the high seas, John Bassett Moore, assistant secretary of state at the time, denied it. 2 Moore, ed., *A Digest of International Law* 985–86. Chilean insurgents, when informed of the *Itata*'s escape from American custody, gave written assurance to U.S. Admiral Brown on 13 May 1891 that they would deliver the *Itata* with her arms cargo to U.S. naval forces in Chilean waters. H.R. Exec. Doc. No. 91, 52d Cong., 1st Sess. 253–54 (reprinted in 1891 *Papers Relating to the Foreign Relations of the United States* 314ff.).

††The *Charleston* was also ordered "under no circumstances to permit a transfer of arms or munitions of war from the *Itata*," if the vessel had "sufficient force to prevent it." *Id.* 257.

thorities.[333] Harrison thus swept aside doubt as to his authority. He chose a broad application of powers to take care that the law be faithfully executed. Like Lincoln, Harrison allied the "take care" authority with the commander-in-chief function and acted to vindicate the nation's honor. His instructions had the potential of involving the United States in hostilities, had a nation state been involved. Undoubtedly, it was the knowledge that he dealt with a political entity less than a recognized nation that Harrison relied on to justify his orders to use force. He did not mention these instructions to Congress when it convened in December 1891 and ambiguously referred to his insistence that the *Itata* be returned to San Diego as the only possible conclusion that would comport with the national honor.*

Presidential Triumph over Congressional Opposition

Santo Domingo   Unilateral executive military action encountered stiff legislative objections in several major instances. In one case, President Grant's deployment of a naval force to Santo Domingo evoked a firmly negative response. Grant had negotiated a treaty guaranteeing the Dominican Republic protection from foreign "intervention" and "interposition" during the time required for its ratification.† But after the Senate declined to advise and consent to the treaty with Santo Domingo, Grant did not withdraw the naval force he had ordered to implement the guarantee.

Congress eventually questioned not only the original deployment but also Grant's failure to withdraw.** It learned, for example, that Grant's special agent for negotiations of the treaty, General Orville Babcock, had been instructed to order military action that would implement the guarantee provisions before he returned to the United States in December 1869 with the treaty. Babcock had confidentially informed Lieutenant Commander Bunce of USS *Nantasket* to "use all your force to carry

---

*Harrison did not submit any documents concerning the *Itata* with his message, and Congress did not request any information. 23 *Congressional Record* 10; 13 *Messages and Papers* 5618–19.

†The text of the proposed treaty of annexation and convention to lease Samana Bay are set forth at 17 *Senate Executive Journal* 83–86, 41st Cong., 3d Sess. The Senate rejected the treaty 28 to 28 on 30 June 1870 and did not vote on the convention. *Id.* 501–03. *See also* W. Holt, *Treaties Defeated by the Senate* 127, 129 (1933), for analysis of the tie vote. C. Tansill, *The United States and Santo Domingo, 1798–1873: A Chapter in Caribbean Diplomacy* (1938), contains a general discussion of the treaty negotiations and surrounding political circumstances.

**Congress adjourned after the treaty was rejected without questioning President Grant's authority to deploy naval force for purposes other than defense. But executive "protection" did not end with the rejection; there were numerous subsequent actions taken by the U.S. Navy to support the Dominican President. S. Exec. Doc. 34, 41st Cong., 3d Sess. 22–33.

out, to the letter, the guarantees given in the treaties . . ."[334] and left two U.S. naval vessels on guard in the waters of Santo Domingo.*

Grant had sought and obtained authority and an appropriation for a commission to report on the feasibility of annexation,[335] and in March 1871, the Senate debated the issue once more. Anticipating a report favoring annexation, Charles Sumner of Massachusetts introduced a series of resolutions condemning Grant's military actions.[336] In a three-hour speech, Sumner paraded evidence before his colleagues that the navy, under orders from Washington, had engaged in intervention, "being war without the authority of Congress." Not only had Grant's original use of the navy violated the Constitution, charged Sumner, but its continued use after the defeat of the treaty in the Senate had compounded the offense. Grant, concluded the senator, "had seized the war powers carefully guarded by the Constitution."[337] Claiming that war could exist without battles, Sumner chastised Grant for doing indirectly what he could not do directly, utilizing the excuse of protecting treaty negotiation as the rationale for a far more serious act of military occupation.[338] Wisconsin's Carl Schurz agreed, believing that the president's power to use force on his own initiative was limited to attacks made on the United States. Thus, the president lacked discretionary power to define a contingency for use of arms to commit a belligerent act, and his decision to defend the inchoate interests he had created by negotiating the treaty usurped Congress's right to determine questions of war or peace.[339]

The opposition responded that no guns had been fired or violence used,[340] so that the allegations amounted to a mere "war of words."[341] Wisconsin Republican Timothy Howe† distinguished an act of war from a declaration of war (the latter being a congressional power),[342] and Senator James Harlan cited precedents supporting his belief that a president could initiate acts of war in absence of formal declaration.**[343]

---

*Additional orders went out in January 1870 to Admiral C.M. Poor, who was instructed to inform Haitian authorities that the United States intended to use "all its power" to protect the Dominican government and that he was to use his force to protect the republic "against any power attempting to interfere with it." *Id.* 11.

†Senator Howe also argued that the Senate had notice of the guarantee and by failing to take positive action had acquiesced in the president's conduct. 44 *Congressional Globe Appendix* 40–46.

**These precedents included Indian wars, military forces arrayed in the Northeast when that boundary was in dispute, bombardment of Greytown by the navy (*see supra* p. 163), bombardment of Japanese ports by the United States, France, and England, and a naval engagement in Chinese waters. The administration's strongest argument was that Haiti's invasion of Santo Domingo during negotiations would be an act of war against both the Dominican Republic and the United States by reason of the inchoate right the United States acquired in Santo Domingo through the negotiated treaty. 44 *Congressional Globe Appendix* 64–65.

Senator Charles Sumner (R. Mass.) defused the Mason and Slidell affair (p. 208), and by defeating resolutions that would inevitably have drawn the United States into war with France and England, greatly aided the Union cause in the Civil War. Unfortunately for Sumner, his opposition to President Grant's acquisition of Santo Domingo (p. 313) and to official attempts to settle U.S. claims against England brought on his removal as Chairman of the Senate Foreign Relations Committee. Mathew Brady photo, Library of Congress.

Indiana Senator Oliver P. Morton endorsed the "inchoate interests" theory. He insisted that Grant had acted similarly to John Tyler who, in 1844, informed Mexico that U.S. honor and its citizens' safety and welfare would not permit Texas's annexation to be defeated by an invasion "while the question is pending."[344] Morton said that Secretary of War John C. Calhoun had promised the Texas government, during and after the pending annexation agreement, that President Tyler would use all of the power he held under the Constitution to protect Texas from foreign invasion.[345] But the precedent was not compelling: There was no way for Morton to prove Tyler would not have felt obliged to confer with Congress before ordering the actual commission of hostilities in Texas's defense any more than Grant's opponent, Senator Carl Schurz, could disprove that Tyler intended to order unilaterally the use of force in case Texas needed immediate protection.*[346] Senator Harlan, after three days' debate of the resolutions, moved that they be tabled. The motion passed 39 to 16, and thus the resolution died.[347]

President Grant did not seek theoretical justification in the commander-in-chief power. The use of force under the "inchoate interests" theory appeared to derive from the president's role as chief diplomat of the United States. But since the president's right to act to protect an inchoate treaty ceased when the treaty was rejected, his continued use of force after 30 June 1870 was clearly unconstitutional and bordered on flagrant disregard of the Senate's expressed will, if not open defiance. Only the fact that no European power was concerned (and war between the Dominican Republic and Haiti was unlikely) minimized the pragmatic consequences. The Senate did not assert positive controls, such as censure or disavowal, that could have been implemented through passage of Sumner's resolutions. But this bitter debate indicated that even during a period of old guard Republican ascendancy, a Republican Senate would not tolerate what both friends and enemies of President Grant denounced as unjustified exercise of executive power.

Cuba President William McKinley emerged from frequent confrontations with Congress as one of the preeminent diplomatic and political strategists of the nineteenth century. For example, although Congress successfully imposed on the president its authority both to initiate war in Cuba and direct the conduct on terms it defined, he scored a political victory by influencing terms and conditions that were finally adopted. Moreover, McKinley's action in the Philippines was a victory of execu-

---

*Senator Frelinghuysen concurred generally with Morton that the president could constitutionally defend the inchoate interests arising from negotiations. This right proceeded from the executive duty to care for the nation's dignity, and Frelinghuysen argued that if war resulted from such action, it would be lawful. *Id.* 315.

tive power. He initiated the military action there, fought it on his own terms, and led Congress into a three-year conflict over who would control the Philippine Islands.

McKinley and his predecessor, Grover Cleveland, shared a common abhorrence of being drawn into the Spanish-Cuban conflict. Yet despite Cleveland's announced policy of strict neutrality, seventy-one filibustering expeditions were prepared against Spain from February 1895 until April 1898, forty-six of which occurred during Cleveland's administration and twenty-five in McKinley's. In all of the total of forty-four successful missions, Americans acknowledged their responsibility for thirty-three.[348] Spain's complaints were largely dismissed: only in 1898 did a federal judge rule that one who knowingly aided or took part in a filibustering expedition bound for Cuba, no matter how badly organized, violated U.S. neutrality legislation.[349] Many of the U.S. citizens arrested and confined during the Cuban rebellion were naturalized Cubans; and pro-insurgent congressional pressure did not lessen the tension.[350] Congress recognized that the time had come to intervene in some form in Cuba and formulated some resolutions. At the same time, McKinley's preliminarily cool handling of the Cuban crisis finally escalated into conviction that intervention would be required.

Like McKinley, Republican leaders such as Mark Hanna, Stephen Elkins, and Nelson Aldrich had chosen intervention only as the last resort but were dumbfounded by McKinley's refusal to include a request for a resolution proclaiming Cuban independence. Allied, however, with House Speaker Thomas B. Reed, the president threatened to veto any joint resolution that recognized the insurgents, since by refusing immediate recognition, the United States could maintain the option to retain military control and thus define future Cuban relations. McKinley built majorities in both houses and created uneasiness among party members, lest they refuse to go along.[351] But the president did not oppose the self-denying Teller Amendment* to the joint resolution, since it was not his purpose to conquer and annex Cuba.[352] Inclusion of this disclaimer of annexation served to assuage the anti-imperialists but never lessened McKinley's resolve to thwart any congressional attempt to recognize Cuban independence.† Moreover, the Teller Amendment suited McKinley's concept of refusing to give official U.S. imprimatur to an unknown Cuban government; meanwhile, it per-

---

*The Teller Amendment disclaimed U.S. intent to annex Cuba and was the final section of the four-part joint resolution of 19 April 1898. 31 *Congressional Record* 4062–64.

†Others have made the point that the United States refused to claim any hegemony whatsoever by the Teller Amendment but may have neglected "the self-assertive implications of non-recognition." *See* C. Vahle, "Congress, the President, and Overseas Expansion, 1897–1901" (1967).

President William McKinley dictating to one of his secretaries in his White House office in 1897. Library of Congress.

mitted McKinley to set his own timetable for withdrawal after military involvement was completed.*

When McKinley delivered his annual message of December 1898, he continued the U.S. position on Cuban independence that the resolution of April 1898 had crystallized.[353] He stated simply that until Congress legislated otherwise, American military government would remain on the island after complete possession and pacification had occurred, though he promised that "aid and direction" would be given the Cubans to form their own government.[354]

Some options were open to McKinley regarding how he might remove U.S. military presence from Cuba once peace was established. "Pacification" allowed some room to maneuver around the imperative of the Teller Amendment. At the same time, the administration did not wish to risk Cuban rebellion in the face of indefinite occupation. McKinley finally accepted Secretary of War Elihu Root's proposals for military evacuation (which later became the Platt Amendment)† as the condi-

---

*Whitelaw Reid, on the other hand, considered it "singularly unfortunate" that this amendment had been passed and felt sure the commitment would "long plague us." J. Wilson, *Papers* (Reid to James H. Wilson, 13 February 1900).

†The Platt Amendment to the army appropriation bill of 2 March 1901 contained among other provisions the demand that Cuba not permit any foreign power to obtain a

tion for withdrawal, thus assuring that only the United States would determine Cuba's future. Cuba objected that the U.S. government was keeping a right to intervene at will in its affairs; Root, however, assured Cubans that the amendment would not be a vehicle for meddling but a formalization of the obligations for preserving Cuban independence imposed by the Treaty of Paris.[355] Nevertheless, under Theodore Roosevelt, Cuba became a quasi-protectorate of the United States, due to fears that a major power might secure a foothold there and jeopardize the U.S. coast as well as damage valuable commercial interests. Not until 1909 were U.S. troops finally withdrawn.[356]

The Philippines   The administration's decision to evacuate the military from Cuba after certain guarantees had been met was determined by its fear that a declared intention to occupy and dominate Cuba after the Peace of Paris in 1898 would involve the United States in prolonged guerrilla warfare. However, McKinley did not avoid such a war in the Philippines. The president's decision to take control of the Philippines resulted in an extensive and bloody conflict, which was unresolved until the United States decided to withdraw after three years' intense struggle.

The decision to annex the Philippines was gradual, reinforced by a summer's lobbying for guidance from both legislators and the people of the United States. The shape of McKinley's own delegation to the Paris talks in August 1898 was clearly defined, since four of the five commissioners clearly favored annexing the Philippines. But some members raised the question whether senatorial delegates William Frye (Maine), Cushman Davis (Minn.), and George Gray (Del.)* had been unconstitutionally designated as executive agents.†[357] When McKinley finally

---

foothold in the island and that the United States be allowed to intervene for the purpose of preserving order and maintaining Cuban independence. 34 *Congressional Record* 3151–52; *see id.* 2966, 3106, 3126, 3132, 3141, 3145–46 (debate). An illuminating tale of the formulation of the Platt Amendment is presented in Senator William Chandler's "memo for the record" of 21 April 1906, which relates how Republican members of the Senate Committee on Cuban Relations, chaired by Senator Platt, met at Chandler's home to discuss the whole question. W. Chandler, *Papers.* The terms of the Platt Amendment were embodied both in a treaty and in the Cuban constitution. 1 *Treaties, Conventions* 362–64, (Malloy ed.)

*Senator George Gray (D. Del.) was the sole member of the delegation who opposed annexation of the Philippines. An avowed antiexpansionist who fought Hawaii's annexation, he did not favor taking anything at all. Pratt, *Expansionists of 1898: The Acquisition of Hawaii and the Spanish Islands* 337. Secretary of State William Day and Whitelaw Reid, editor of the *New York Tribune*, completed the commission and favored taking the Philippines, although Day represented a moderate viewpoint. *Id.* 332.

†Senator William E. Chandler objected vehemently to McKinley's use of senators as executive agents, calling the dispatch of Frye, Davis, and Gray an unconstitutional commingling of the powers of the branches, and a number of senators joined the fray. *New*

George F. Hoar (R. Mass.) vigorously opposed the McKinley administration's Philippine policy (p. 320 n.), thus courting political disaster in his home state. Yet he was reelected to his Senate post in 1901 by a large majority. (L.C.)

agreed to pay "a reasonable sum" as compensation for the proposed annexation,[358] it was upon the basis that a stunning victory had been achieved, and Spain reluctantly accepted $20 million to end negotiation on U.S. terms. The Treaty of Paris, however, soon was to become the peace that caused a war.

The Philippines annexation provisions raised some Senate opposition. A few senators, such as George Hoar (R. Mass.) and Augustus Bacon (D. Ga.), foresaw problems arising from forcible annexation of a people, in Bacon's words, "without consent or subjugation."*[359] But Populist Senator William Allen of Nebraska focused directly on the exercise of the war power in the Philippines. Allen submitted a resolution that bypassed the question of territorial acquisition and challenged the constitutional authority of the president to conduct a war against the Filipinos† without consent of Congress. In his words, "Any aggressive action by Army or Navy on the part of the United States against the Filipinos would be an act of war unwarranted on the part of the President and the exercise of constitutional power vested exclusively in Congress."[360] He reasoned that U.S. sovereignty had to come from the treaty that the Senate must first ratify. Moreover, any authority to conduct a war in the Philippines would have to proceed from Congress. Allen also considered the issue of jurisdiction. Recalling that the Filipinos had an organized government recognized by a popular majority and had successfully defied Spanish authority, he argued that Dewey's Manila victory may have given the United States control over the islands but had not removed jurisdiction from the Filipinos.[361]

Allen's resolution did not come to a vote before the outbreak of conflict between U.S. and Filipino forces. Before war mooted congressional efforts to define how power would be exercised in the Philippines by the executive and Congress, Senator Bacon introduced an anti-annexation resolution that called for the United States to give the Filipinos the rights secured from Spain, whenever a stable government was established in the Philippines, and included a Teller-like disclaimer of U.S.

York Tribune, 8 December 1898; 17 W. McKinley, Papers (Chandler to McKinley, 17 August 1898). However, McKinley personally conferred with Chandler and admitted that the senator was constitutionally correct, but urged him to abandon his opposition in view of the inconvenience and delay that Chandler's stand might incur. Chandler complied, and a minor constitutional crisis was averted. 1 C. Olcott, The Life of William McKinley 339 (1916).

*Hoar also considered the territorial acquisition to be unconstitutional because annexation would not promote the general welfare, common defense, or a more perfect union. 32 Congressional Record 496.

†Between the conclusion of negotiations and ratification of the Treaty of Paris, Filipinos had refused to give control of Iloilo city to American forces reportedly moving against them, and it seemed likely that fighting would occur.

intention to exercise sovereignty.*[362] This resolution was defeated by the vice president's casting of a tie-breaking (29 to 29) vote against it. Thus, the purpose of the adminstration became clear, and the dominant mood in Congress made a parallel shift from conciliation to coercion.

War broke out in Manila on 4 February 1899, two days before the treaty with Spain was ratified. Could the president use force to suppress the Philippines without congressional authorization? Were the Philippines a foreign nation, entitled to belligerent rights, whose sovereignty could not be ceded by treaty? Senators also grappled with more immediate constitutional issues. Henry Cabot Lodge, although a recognized spokesman for the president, made the surprising argument that rejection of the treaty could lead to McKinley's exercise of unchecked power, whereas the treaty committed the islands to Congress's later disposition and to ways and practices of peace. If the treaty failed in the Senate, the Philippines would be left in the sole power of the president, who would rule them "armed with the war power, which he can use unchecked as Commander and Chief of the Army and Navy."[363] At the same time, Lodge assured his colleagues that treaty passage did not commit his colleagues to permanent annexation. Mississippi Senator Hernando Money, however, objected to ratification followed by Congress's adjournment without legislating on the subject, thereby handing over to the president not only a legislative prerogative but also its constitutional duty to establish Philippine policy and details of government.†[364]

Few senators were similarly concerned, and the treaty passed without amendment, 57 to 27, on 6 February 1899.[365] As Money had feared, annexation was accomplished without any formal declaration of policy, even one on eventual emancipation. The president had committed himself to a military solution without sufficient manpower.** Since he

---

*Bacon's effort would still have left to the United States government broad discretion to decide when the Filipinos could exercise their independence. *Id.* 1846.

†Attempts to formulate policy were defeated during the ratification process. For example, an amendment that declared that the United States would assume only temporary control until the Filipinos formed a government "suitable to their condition," was defeated 30 to 53. 31 *Journal of the Executive Proceedings of the Senate* 1283. In the House, no provisions regarding policy were attached to the bill appropriating the funds to pay Spain the $20 million required by the treaty, and a Senate resolution declaring the intent of Congress to prepare the Filipinos for self-government did not come to House vote. 32 *Congressional Record* 1138, 1177, 1093, 1102, 1131, 1185, 1479.

**The Army Reorganization Bill called for enlargement of the permanent army to a strength of 100,000. The bill passed the House but was stopped in the Senate. A watered-down bill, maintaining the regular army at its wartime strength of 65,000 and authorizing the president to enlist 35,000 volunteers, passed the Senate on February 27. *Id.* 2434, 2413 (55 to 13).

General Elwell S. Otis commanding U.S. troops in the streets of Manila on 4 February 1899, the first day of armed conflict between American and Filipino forces. (L.C.)

had no guidance from Congress* regarding either the kind of government that should be established in the Philippines or the conduct of the war, he therefore created his own policies† and shaped the information he wanted released concerning them. From the outset, the legislature was led to believe that the start of military action in the Philippines was purely defensive. For example, a report was widely circulated that two

---

*Responsibility for failure to shape a policy is divisible between the branches. McKinley did indicate that he would be amenable to congressional direction concerning the Philippines if Congress saw fit to declare itself on the issue. W. McKinley, *Speeches and Addresses* 185 (1900) (Speech at the dinner of the Home Market Club, Boston, 16 February 1899). However, on 5 December 1899, the president in his message said that it was not desirable at that time to recommend a specific and final form of government until the insurrection was crushed and peace restored. 14 *Messages and Papers* 6356, 6398.

†Representative Jacob Bromwell (R. Oh.) assured the House that McKinley would have the authority only "to attach his signature in approval or disapproval" of a bill expressing congressional policy. 32 *Congressional Record* 1102. Exactly the opposite occurred, and the president moved to fill the legislative vacuum. Full military enforcement eventually demanded the deployment of tens of thousands of troops many thousands of miles from the U.S. mainland. *See generally*, ch. 9, "The Campaign of 1900," in M. Storey and M. Lichauco, *Commentaries on the Constitution of the United States* (1891). *See also* the president's account in 14 *Messages and Papers* 6392–99.

days before treaty ratification, an American guard had defended the newly occupied sector of Manila by challenging and shooting a Filipino who came into it and that vigorous Filipino firing against American positions had then ensued.[366] The administration's account misled Senator Allen, for example, who backed away from his earlier concerns and immediately upheld executive authority to repel the Filipinos' "attack" until they respected "the dignity . . . sovereignty and the flag of this nation."[367] Delaware's George Gray agreed: "I am not in favor of making any concessions to them while they are shooting down on their own soil Americans who have stood by them and have given them the hope for this great boon of liberty and of decent, orderly government there."[368] However, when General Elwell S. Otis later made a report of the first large-scale engagement on the island to the War Department, he alleged it was an operation "strictly defensive on the part of the insurgents and one of vigorous attack by our forces," in which the United States killed 3,000 Filipinos.[369] Instead, the administration misinformed the public. McKinley took the initiative by declaring that "the first blow was struck by the inhabitants," asserting that there would be "no useless parley" with them.[370] Elihu Root declared in another speech at Youngstown, Ohio, in October 1900, that instead of an American sentry shooting a Filipino who refused to halt in a newly declared American zone of Manila,

[an] army of Tagalogs, a tribe inhabiting the central part of Luzon, under the leadership of Aguinaldo, a Chinese half-breed, attacked in vastly superior numbers our little army in possession of Manila, and after a desperate and bloody fight was repulsed in every direction.[371]

The secretary of war took care not to reveal the facts of Filipino resistance to the voting public until at least after the election of 1900 but closely cooperated with military commanders who requested reinforcements.[372]

The administration also established press censorship in Manila, effectively drawing a veil of secrecy over events there. Staff correspondents of leading U.S. newspapers united in a statement: ". . . [O]wing to official dispatches from Manila made public in Washington, the people of the United States have not received a correct impression of the situation in the Philippines. . . . The censorship has compelled us to participate in these misrepresentations by excising or altering uncontroverted statements of fact on the plea, as General Otis stated it, 'that they would alarm the people at home,' or 'have the people of the United States by the ears.'"[373] A censor was quoted as having informed one correspondent, "My instructions are to shut off everything that could hurt McKinley's administration."[374] The president did not respond to a qualified resolution of inquiry, unanimously passed by the Senate, that asked the president whether cables prior to 4 February 1899 (the insurrection's outbreak) were subject to censorship.[375]

An aggressive reconcentration policy began under the direction of General Jacob Smith, whose orders resulted in the killing of thousands of natives.[376] An official inquiry was undertaken years later; as a result General Smith was court martialed and convicted of orders to "burn" and to "kill everybody capable of bearing arms," but he was sentenced merely "to be admonished."*

Though many constitutional and international law questions had been raised early in the conflict, they engaged Congress's attention only at the height of the war. Senator Pettigrew's resolution, seeking to discover what transpired in the 5 February 1899 meeting between General Isidoro Torres, staff officer of Filipino "president" Emilio Aguinaldo, and General Otis, was adopted on 18 April 1900. The resolution asserted Aguinaldo had reportedly declared the fighting had begun accidentally, that he had wanted it stopped, and that he had asked for establishment of a wide neutral zone while peace negotiations went on. It raised several queries. Did Otis reply that once the fighting had begun it must go on until one side was vanquished? Had the secretary of war authorized such a reply?[377] The president responded on 19 May 1900.[378] He stated that General Otis had not been directed by the secretary of war to make the answer set forth in the resolution; Otis had been granted discretion to operate according to his own judgment based on "his superior knowledge of the conditions. . . ." The president, referring to documents he was transmitting, said the 8 February dispatch from Otis had been called "misleading" by the General, and so far as the president could determine, there had not been an "application" to cease fighting.[379]

A few legislators were concerned with the Filipinos' legal status in light of the fact that war broke out between them and the United States two days before the Treaty of Paris was ratified. Senator Charles Towne (R. Minn.), for example,† believed that the president had in effect made

*Secretary of War Elihu Root, as well as army representatives, were apparently satisfied with the sentence, and there was no opposition expressed in Congress. Storey and Lichauco, *Commentaries on the Constitution of the United States* 143; 36 *Congressional Record* 2967. *See* readings taken from testimony before the Senate Committee on the Philippines in 1902 in H. Graff, ed., *American Imperialism and the Philippine Insurrection, passim* (1969).

†Another Senator, Benjamin Tillman (D. S.C.), declared that the Filipinos had become belligerents when fired on by U.S. troops before title had passed. Later, Tillman asserted, the United States inherited only Spain's residuary title in the islands, subject to the rights of natives who had been struggling for freedom before the U.S. went to war with Spain. 32 *Congressional Record* 1530.

war on the Filipinos without consulting Congress by ordering that military government was to be extended into the whole of the ceded territory before the treaty was in force.* By such conduct, charged Towne, McKinley had proceeded against the Philippines as though the United States already had acquired Spain's title and with it the executive's right to suppress insurrection in a territory without further authorization. Towne wondered what had become of the war powers of Congress.[380]

Most of Congress, however, chose to believe that the American military action taken only two days before ratification was solely defensive. Legislators did not concentrate their attention on whether the treaty applied prospectively† and thus authorized the president's actions against the Filipinos or had retrospective application and ratified his conduct.

The Supreme Court in 1901 quieted any lingering doubts that the United States had taken only residual or even no title. The Court held that by virtue of the treaty, the Philippines had been granted and delivered to the United States by their former master and were no longer under the sovereignty of a foreign nation; they had become a U.S. territory over which civil government could be established.**[381]

In 1900, over 70,000 American soldiers barely held a vigorous enemy in check. Finally, in the spring of 1901, Emilio Aguinaldo was captured. He was forced to take an oath of allegiance to the United States and signed a proclamation recommending abandonment of any further resistance. But other Filipinos fought on, and McKinley had to commit an even greater complement of U.S. troops; the final subjugation required the expenditure of millions of dollars and the ultimate presence of 120,000 U.S. servicemen by the spring of 1902, when the fighting ceased.

During this period, the president of the United States was the final legal authority in the Philippines. He placed military and executive authority in the hands of a military governor, while legislative power

---

*On 21 December 1898, McKinley informed the secretary of war that with the treaty signed between the United States and Spain on 10 December, "future control" of the Philippines was ceded to the United States. The president asserted that actual occupation was "immediately necessary" and ordered military government extended to the whole of the ceded territory. 15 *Messages and Papers* 6581.

†The principle of prospective application of a treaty right is similar, if not identical, to the "inchoate rights" theory President Grant's supporters put forth to justify his unilateral conduct in the waters of Santo Domingo. *See supra* pp. 312–15.

**An American soldier who had been on Philippine duty brought back to the United States fourteen diamond rings, which he had acquired in the Islands. He refused to pay duty on them because he alleged that by force of the treaty, the islands had ceased to be foreign territory. The Court upheld his contention in a 5 to 4 decision. *Fourteen Diamond Rings, Pepke v. United States*, 183 U.S. 176 (1901)

was exercised by a commission that he appointed. McKinley outlined the duties of this commission and the general policy toward the Philippines in elaborate instructions that came to be considered the "organic act of the Philippines." The commission "by the authority of the President of the United States" enacted more than 400 laws, subject to the approval of the secretary of war. On 2 March 1901, however, Congress vested authority in the president to govern the Philippines only "until otherwise provided by Congress."[382] From that moment, the president derived his authority from Congress and was no longer acting under his "war powers."[383]

CONCLUSION

Historians have traditionally examined the period 1869–1901 from the standpoint of relative political weakness in the American presidency and the correlative ascendancy of congressional power. Unquestionably, the Republicans controlled Congress and were the dominant party in the White House. But party hegemony alone did not determine or control the constitutional tensions that developed between the branches, and by no means did it relegate the executive to subservience to Congress. On the contrary, during the final years of the nineteenth century, presidents such as Rutherford B. Hayes, Benjamin Harrison, and William McKinley challenged powerful members of their own party as well as the tradition of military supremacy impressed by Congress upon the nation during the administration of Andrew Johnson. They did so through creative interpretation of the Constitution to derive the authority to act in cases of emergency. One such derivation not previously articulated in constitutional history was the "peace of the United States," springing from the guarantee of a republican form of government. It was successfully employed by administration supporters in Congress to defend chief executives from charges of "excessive" actions, as well as to defeat statutory attempts to strip presidents of constitutional authority. But members of Congress did not strictly limit the application of this concept to either potential or actual unrest within the borders of the United States. It was, at times, more broadly analogized as applicable in cases of any violent threat to the harmony and tranquillity of the country from aggressive behavior of any kind. After the experience of protracted debates over delegation of important powers to the president in the Civil War emergency, Ulysses Grant much more easily obtained broad discretion to call out militia and naval forces to prevent and overcome domestic violence. Discretion was accorded to Benjamin Harrison many times to meet international problems containing more than a hint of war. But there were limitations. Even the virtually unanimous congressional mandate to William McKinley to conduct war against Spain was accompanied with an explicit assumption that permission to use force to accomplish a particular purpose could be withdrawn if Congress was unsatisfied with the use of the power. Other such delegations contained at least an implicit assumption that the delegation could be swiftly taken back if necessary.

The president's choice of subordinates to administer grants of power had been greatly circumscribed by the Tenure of Office Act of 1867, and it was not until Grover Cleveland's administration that these burdensome restrictions were completely removed. However, even during the interval of expanded Senate influence, the presidents of this period— particularly Garfield, Arthur, and Cleveland—served as the bellwether for a strengthened executive position. Their assertions of authority not only stopped the erosion of executive power but also opened the way for executive leadership in foreign affairs. For example, though Congress abolished forty consulates and thus drastically limited Ulysses Grant's appointments, he refused, as he signed the bill, to admit "a right in the legislative branch to direct the closing or discontinuing of any of the diplomatic or consular offices of the Government."[384] Succeeding presidents vigorously resisted any general legislative right to control their choices of appointees. President James Garfield stood firm on his choice for collector of the New York Custom House against a mighty opponent, Roscoe Conkling of New York. Garfield asserted that he would maintain the constitutional rights and dignities of his office and that executive discretion over appointments would be preserved—the president was not to become the mere "registering clerk" of the Senate.[385]

Grover Cleveland's resistance to Senate practice was equally bold: He refused to submit certain information concerning his nominee for district attorney in Alabama and the officer whom he proposed to remove. Cleveland's explanation that his position was based on separation of powers principles no doubt offered guidance and resolve to his successors. While the Senate refused by one vote (30 to 29) to consent to the president's nominee, this contest over executive authority was more fueled than settled by the incident.[386]

Presidents Harrison and Arthur also opposed congressional encroachment by vetoing bills that provided for Congress's designation of appointees to office.[387] President McKinley's adherents in Congress fought back suggestions that legislation should be passed that would permit department heads to appoint their subordinates instead of the president.[388] Much of the branches' tension over prerogatives to appoint and remove, however, was relieved by civil service reform. Garfield articulated a desire for improvements in the system in his Inaugural

Address, and the beginning of such reform was realized in the Pendleton Act after his death.[389]

The period marks the zenith in the nineteenth century of executive mastery of the flow of information to Congress. Chester Arthur judiciously forwarded his lawyer-like messages that repeatedly conveyed no more than he wanted known. William McKinley's White House placed such careful control on cables from the Philippine war front that neither the press nor the elected representatives of the people were certain of the military steps that had been undertaken in an undeclared conflict half-way around the world. There is clear evidence that President Harrison at least tolerated, if he did not personally encourage, a dual system of recording diplomatic activities so that there might always appear to be such full reportage of executive actions to Congress as would discourage charges that the administration was withholding information. Such accusations were infrequent: so much information was generally transmitted that Congress digested it slowly. Volunteered data concerning Cleveland's use of force abroad did not prompt concern. Instead, Cleveland's voluntary supply of information regarding a potential outbreak of force over a series of inflammatory events in Samoa led to legislation permitting the president to take military action if necessary without further consultation.

On the other hand, it appears that Congress sensed a shift away from full executive responsiveness, as Congress made more of an effort than ever to elicit information directly from department heads without limit or qualification. To some members of Congress the imposition of the traditional qualification privilege would be to admit that a statutory officer was the best judge of what served the public interest. This kind of an attempted information raid on the bureaus themselves met with little success, and rather than rely on executive transmittals, Congress began the practice of more frequent independent fact-finding. The tight-fistedness of the departments was epitomized by Attorney General Olney's behavior in the matter of the Pullman strike, when details were not even transmitted to President Cleveland.

Congress did curtail executive discretion where it feared diminution of its critical power of the purse. It therefore required congressional approval of executive tariff negotiations before they could go into effect. The president generally functioned as chief diplomat. Where the risk of conflict with a strong adversary was minimal, Congress made no move to limit presidential efforts to blend U.S. trade with the world economy or to interfere in executive actions short of war with non-European countries. Cleveland and Harrison undertook unilateral diplomatic actions with a potential for war but only in sectors of the world where it was believed there would be little or no international repercussions.

Harrison personally drafted critical diplomatic notes and supervised the important diplomatic actions of his subordinates. He emerges significantly as having been capable of forcefully seizing the initiative, while diminishing Congress's legislative impact on foreign affairs.

Congress exercised its most successful influence over American foreign relations by modifying and abrogating treaties. It was not so successful in passing joint resolutions aimed at wielding control. The legislature's primary efforts at treaty modification dealt with agreements concerning Chinese immigration as a threat to U.S. enterprise—efforts that also enjoyed administration political support—while the technique of joint resolution was attempted in key policy debates over Cuba. The legislature unsuccessfully claimed a joint power with the executive to recognize foreign nations, but it did make an impact on presidential authority by bringing almost ceaseless pressure to bear in favor of active intervention in Cuba and deployment of a military presence there before the declaration of war against Spain.

Although by the end of the century both the executive and the legislative branches had spokesmen who talked in terms of the unilateral power of each branch in the war powers arena, in practice only the president seriously contemplated placing the United States in a combined military-diplomatic commitment involving the potential use of military force, without consulting Congress. With no authorization or consultation, President McKinley deployed troops to the Philippines, involved U.S. troops in an undeclared war there, and instituted executive government until Congress assumed control. On the other hand, despite Congress's earnest desire to begin hostilities with Spain over Cuba, it did so only after McKinley acquiesced that war was necessary and inevitable.

Legislators encouraged the rise in U.S. naval power that occurred after 1870 but were concerned about the potential of executive power to make war that a new navy represented. And Congress firmly pressured for a part in deciding troop deployment, agreeing, only after a protracted debate threatened the subsistence of the army itself, to allow the president to judge the size of the force sent to guard the U.S.-Mexican border. Congress forbade the use of army regulars as a federal militia except as provided by law, over Hayes's objections. Lawmakers also tried to define criteria by which the executive should have authority to use military might in an emergency when they limited presidential use of the army to cases of armed invasion or violence in the states. But Hayes vetoed what he considered to be an illegal limitation on a much broader presidential prerogative.

U.S. military power by the mid-1880s was outstanding by comparison to the Civil War. Yet President Arthur was reluctant to use force to execute official policy, even though his own secretary of the navy once did so and escaped congressional censure for it. However, when a reluctant William McKinley did not desire to use American might against Spain, Congress came the closest in history to making war on its own and to defining how the executive should become involved. It directed him to make war if diplomacy failed, using language of initiation that does not occur in prior legislative resolutions. Once committed in Cuba, McKinley crafted the terms of his military victory and almost simultaneously with the peace effort initiated a commitment of military force in the Philippines. Only one senator raised the war power issue of the president's having taken hostile action without the authority of Congress, in contrast to the many who complained on the ground that to take the Philippines represented naked imperialism. Without a legislative policy on Philippine civil government, McKinley, moreover, was free to formulate one and executed his own regulations for a considerable period.

When presidents did take unilateral military action in the late nineteenth century, Congress did little to stop them. No congressional reprimand resulted from the the heated debate over U.S. Grant's actions in the Dominican Republic when he continued a U.S. military presence there after the rejection of his plan to acquire Santo Domingo. He later succeeded in enlisting servicemen without authorization, despite certain knowledge that a dispute with Spain would not end in war. President Hayes sent men across the Mexican border in hot pursuit of bandits and was excused on the ground of "necessity." When he enlisted 1,000 troops to repel Indian attack without either appropriation to pay them or authorization to obtain them, congressmen did not exercise their prerogative to interfere, probably because they were satisfied there was no other alternative. On other occasions, there was no legislative reaction, due to Congress's perception that there would be minimal pragmatic consequences. For example, Benjamin Harrison approved U.S. minister John Stevens's conduct recognizing an American-backed *coup d'état* in Hawaii without the authority to give such recognition. Cleveland approved Admiral Benham's interposition of his naval force between combatants to the point at which it became an actual intervention, whereupon Congress approved the action as justified protection of the U.S. merchant fleet. And President Harrison broadly interpreted his authority to execute the laws as he pursued the *Itata* into her own Chilean waters.

All of these incidents of congressional-executive confrontation on the constitutional issue of the prerogative to create or to defuse a hostile international climate, or to deploy force to meet a threat of war, serve to point the researcher into the tremendous vitality of the debate upon the subject of legal acts of the branches in pursuit of war or peace. This was no period of congressional disinterest in foreign relations, or of presidential impotence. Each branch found the necessary tools to strike a healthy balance of legislative and executive powers. The relatively infrequent examples of real tension that occurred were generally resolved on the following basis: each branch increasingly recognized that actions critical to national security and well-being should not be taken by either without at least a well informed reaction from the other.

Notes

INTRODUCTION

1. E. Corwin, *The President: Office and Powers, 1787–1957* 171 (4th ed. 1957).

2. A. Sofaer, *War, Foreign Affairs and Constitutional Power: The Origins* (1976) (hereinafter "Sofaer, *Origins*").

3. *See* C. Rossiter, *Constitutional Dictatorship: Crisis Government in the Modern Democracies* (1948).

4. 6 *Messages and Papers of the Presidents, 1789–1897* 78 (Richardson ed. 1897) (hereinafter "*Messages and Papers*").

5. Rossiter, *Constitutional Dictatorship: Crisis Government in the Modern Democracies.*

6. L. Cutler, "To Form a Government," 59 *Foreign Affairs* 126 (1980).

7. C. Friedrich, *Constitutional Reason of State: Survival of the Constitutional Order* 4–5 (1957).

8. J. Locke, *The Second Treatise of Civil Government,* par. 160 (Gough ed. 1966).

9. The principal case is *Chadha v. Immigration and Naturalization Service,* 634 F.2d. 408 (9th Cir. 1980);—U.S.—(1983). *See generally* Watson, "Congress Steps Out: A Look at Congressional Control of the Executive," 63 *California Law Review* 983 (1975).

10. Authored by John Jay, James Madison, and Alexander Hamilton to help get the Constitution of 1787 ratified by the states.

11. Among many examples, see the *Prize Cases,* 67 U.S. (2 Black) 635 (1863) (sustaining Lincoln's blockade of Southern ports); *Korematsu v. United States,* 320 U.S. 81 (1944) (upholding internment of Japanese-Americans in World War II on grounds of military necessity).

12. A. Schlesinger, Jr., *The Vital Center* 254 (1949).
13. Quoted in Spaeth, "Book Review," 1 *Stanford Law Review* 178, 179 (1948).

CHAPTER 1: INTRODUCTION

1. 11 *Congressional Globe, Containing the Debates and Procedures, 1833–1873* 482 (hereinafter "*Congressional Globe*").
2. 4 *Congressional Globe* 127–28 (emphasis in original).
3. 2 *Messages and Papers* 321–22, 342.
4. 2 *Records of the Federal Convention of 1787* 318–319 (Farrand ed. 1911–1937).
5. 2 W. Goldsmith, *The Growth of Presidential Power* 714 (1974); R. Morgan, *A Whig Embattled: The Presidency under Tyler* 188–89 (1954).
6. 2 *Messages and Papers* 449.
7. 6 *Register of Debates in Congress, 1824–1837* 558–59 (1825–1837) (hereinafter "*Register*"); *see also* 9 *Register* 769, 772 (a similar debate and result in the Senate over the Guatemalan mission).
8. 7 *Register Appendix* iii; 8 J.Q. Adams, *Memoirs* 6 (C.F. Adams ed. 1874–1877).
9. 7 *Register* 222, 226.
10. *Id.* 213.
11. *Id.* 219–20.
12. Levi Woodbury, *id.* 240–41.
13. *Id.* 248.
14. *Id.* 240.
15. *Id.* 250–51.
16. L. White, *The Jacksonians: A Study in Administrative History, 1829–1861* 115–24 (1954) (hereinafter "White, *The Jacksonians*").
17. *Id.* 33.
18. 6 *Register* 458.
19. *Id.* 460.
20. *Id.* 461.
21. *Id.* 263.
22. *Id.*
23. S. Doc. 109, 23d Cong., 2d Sess. (9 February 1835); 2 *Congressional Globe* 239, 243.
24. *Id.* 243.
25. 11 *Register* 553–63 (Calhoun); *id.* 514–23 (Clay); *id.* 483–91 (White); *id.* 440–47 (Ewing).
26. *See also* Leonard White's comprehensive account of this debate in *The Jacksonians* 33–44.
27. 2 *Congressional Globe* 251.
28. *Id.* 276.
29. *Id.* 278.
30. White, *The Jacksonians* 310–11.

31. 10 *Congressional Globe* 29.

32. *Id.* 42 (accord, Clement Clay (D. Ala.)).

33. *Id.* 42.

34. *Id.* 42–43 (accord, William Archer (Wh. Va.)).

35. 9 *Register Appendix, Laws,* 12 (the "Force" bill).

36. 4 *Messages and Papers* 1606–07.

37. 5 *Messages and Papers* 1901–03.

38. Morgan, *A Whig Embattled* 27; White, *The Jacksonians* 22.

39. Morgan, *A Whig Embattled* 157–58.

40. A. Schlesinger, Jr., *The Age of Jackson* 323–29, 485–87 (Supreme Court) (1945); 3 and 4 *Messages and Papers* (veto messages, generally); 3 *Messages and Papers* 1203 (Nullification Proclamation).

41. "Taney's Letters to Van Buren in 1860," 10 *Maryland Historical Magazine* 23 (1915).

42. Jefferson to Judge Spencer Roane, 19 September 1819, in 15 T. Jefferson, *The Writings of Thomas Jefferson* 214 (Lipscomb and Bergh eds., memorial ed. 1903–1904).

43. 5 *Messages and Papers* 2036, 2037.

44. *Id.*

45. 11 *Congressional Globe* 873–75 (10 August 1842); *id.* 894 (16 August 1842); *id.* 907 (17 August 1842).

46. *Id.* 907 (17 August 1842, Adams); *id.* 164 (24 January 1842, Clay).

47. 12 *Congressional Globe* 157–59, 163.

48. 2 *Official Opinions of the Attorneys General of the United States* (1833) 574 (Lott and Finch eds. 1932) (hereinafter *"Official Opinions of the Attorneys General"*).

49. *Id.* 574–75.

50. *Id.* 284.

51. *Id.*

52. *Id.* 284–85.

53. *Id.* 536–37 (1833).

54. 12 *Register* 2138–44, 2180.

55. 2 *Congressional Globe* 4; 3 *Messages and Papers* 1316, 1319, 1325.

56. 2 *Congressional Globe* 22–23 (emphasis in original).

57. *Id.* 21.

58. *Id.* 23.

59. *Id.* 25 (James Wayne (D. Ga.) and Richard Johnson (D. Ky.)).

60. *Id.* 26.

61. 2 *Congressional Globe* 95.

62. *Id.* 182.

63. *Id.* 212–13.

64. *Id.* 213, 214.

65. *Id.* 214; *id.* 212–13 (letters set forth).

66. *Id.* 216–20 *passim.*

67. 2 *Congressional Globe* 301–02; *id.* 309–14; *id.* 318–23 (resolutions unanimously adopted, 2 March 1835).

68. *Id.* 328 (110 to 77).

69. *Id.* 326.

70. *Id.* 330–32.

71. *E.g.,* 12 *Register* 131, 149–63 (Senate).

72. *Id.* 307; 1 Stat. 345.

73. 12 *Register* 307; 2 Stat. 349–50.

74. 12 *Register* 422–24.

75. *Id.* 258, 262.

76. *Id.* 2402; *see* other House debate, *id.* 2263–314, 2360–438.

77. *Id.* 390–91. On February 22, he announced that the dispute had been settled, but renewed the call for fortifications. *Id.* 580–81.

78. 4 *Messages and Papers* 1446 (message of 10 May 1836).

79. 12 *Register* 1592, 4349, Act of July 2, 1836, 5 Stat. 77.

80. 5 Stat. 78–79.

81. *See* "Foreign Relations," *supra* p. 64.

82. 4 *Messages and Papers* 1616.

83. 6 *Congressional Globe* 79.

84. *Id.* (John Norvell (Mich.)).

85. *Id.* 119.

86. 6 *Congressional Globe Appendix* 144, 6, 205.

87. 6 *Congressional Globe* 214, 215, 216; *id.* 230 (8 March 1838, Senate passage); *id.* 231 (9 March 1838, House passage); Act of March 10, 1838, 5 Stat. 212.

88. 7 *Congressional Globe* 232–33; *Appendix,* 226–33.

89. Act of March 3, 1839, 5 Stat. 355, §1.

90. *Id.* §3.

91. *Id.* §4.

92. 7 *Messages and Papers* 3217.

93. Chapter 3 *supra* p. 216.

94. Act of February 23, 1844, 5 Stat. 651.

95. Contrast Jefferson's use of the navy with Washington's circumspect use of force; Sofaer, *Origins* chs. 1 and 3 (1976).

96. Act of March 3, 1843, 5 Stat. 624; 12 *Congressional Globe* 195, 323.

97. Chapter 2 *supra* p. 112.

98. White, *The Jacksonians* 145–46.

99. 12 *Register* 290–91.

100. 12 *Register Appendix,* Laws, ii, v (sets forth the bills passed).

101. 4 *Congressional Globe* 94, 105.

102. *See* Sofaer, *Origins* 77–93.

103. 6 *Congressional Globe* 20.

104. 4 *Messages and Papers* 1590, 1594–96.

105. 3 *id.* 1154, 1158.

106. 9 *Register* 900, 901.

107. *Id.* 926.

108. *See supra* p. 50.

109. 5 *Congressional Globe* 21, 24, 26.

110. *Id.* 24; *id.* 25 *accord* (Grennell).

111. *Id.* 24.

112. *Id.* 25 (Jesse A. Bynum (D. N.C.)). *See also id.* 26 (Halsey).

113. *Id.* 26.

114. *Id.* 99.

115. 8 *Register* 108–09.

116. *Id.* 1388–90; 3 *Messages and Papers* 1126.

117. *Id.* 1316, 1319–24, 1325.

118. 2 *Congressional Globe* 71. Replies: *Id.* 78 (to House); *id.* 81 (to Senate); *see also* 3 *Messages and Papers* 1345.

119. 2 *Congressional Globe* 182 (qualified); *id.* 212 (reply); 3 *Messages and Papers* 1348–51.

120. *Id.* 1354–61; 4 *id.* 1362–64.

121. Livingston to Count de Rigny, minister of foreign affairs, 29 January 1835, in 4 *Messages and Papers* 1421ff.

122. Forsyth to Livingston, 30 June 1835, in *id.* 1404.

123. R. McLemore, *Franco-American Diplomatic Relations, 1816–1836* 167–68 (1941).

124. 4 *Messages and Papers* 1420.

125. Pageot to Forsyth (1 December 1835), *id.* 1417–18; Forsyth to Pageot (3 December 1835), *id.* 1418–19; Pageot to Forsyth (5 December 1835), *id.* 1419–20.

126. 12 *Register* 103.

127. *Id.*

128. *Id.* 104, 106.

129. 4 *Messages and Papers* 1407, 1408–09 (special message, 15 January 1836; documents set forth).

130. McLemore, *Franco-American Diplomatic Relations* 198–99.

131. 4 *Messages and Papers* 1427ff.

132. 9 *Register* 377.

133. *Id.* 405.

134. *Id.* 406.

135. *Id.* 431.

136. *Id.* 433.

137. 9 *Register Appendix* 197.

138. 5 *Congressional Globe* 101.

139. *Id.*

140. *Supra* p. 64.

141. 8 *Congressional Globe* 126, 127.

142. *Id.*

143. *Id.* 134, 138; *id.* 311; *id.* 337 (response).

144. 11 *Congressional Globe* 579 (unqualified).

145. *Id.* 579.

146. *Id.* 579–80.

147. *Id.* 580, 581.

148. *Id.*

149. *Id.*

150. *Id.* 888, 889.

151. *Id.* 2075.

152. 2 *Messages and Papers* 847.
153. 5 *Messages and Papers* 2076.
154. H.R. Rep. No. 271, 27th Cong., 3d Sess. 10 (1843).
155. 1 *Congressional Globe* 311.
156. 9 *Register* 1936.
157. 3 *Messages and Papers* 8.
158. Schlesinger, *The Age of Jackson* 101.
159. *Id.* 101, 106.
160. 1 *Congressional Globe* 19.
161. *Id.; id.* 59–62 (paper reproduced).
162. *Id.* 20, 21.
163. *Id.* 21.
164. *Id.*
165. *Id.* 21.
166. *Id.* 23.
167. 3 *Messages and Papers* 36.
168. 1 *Congressional Globe* 23.
169. *Id.*
170. 10 *Register Appendix* 98–101.
171. 1 *Congressional Globe* 54.
172. *Id.* 272.
173. *Id.* 368 (adopted 25 to 17, Calhoun); *id.* 369 (adopted 28 to 16, Webster).
174. 4 *Congressional Globe Appendix* 109.
175. *See* comments by Senators Felix Grundy and John Clayton concerning investigating causes of removal from office, in 7 *Register* 86, 119, 154.
176. 11 *Congressional Globe* 214.
177. 5 *Messages and Papers* 1952.
178. 11 *Congressional Globe* 457–58.
179. *Id.* 456.
180. *Id.* 458; *id.* 461.
181. 5 *Messages and Papers* 2005.
182. 11 *Congressional Globe* 476.
183. *Id.* 482.
184. *Id.* 600.
185. 4 *Official Opinions of the Attorneys General* 238. *See* Act of August 26, 1842, 5 Stat. 523, 524, 526.
186. 4 *Congressional Globe* 26.
187. *Id.* 27.
188. 4 *Congressional Globe Appendix* 99.
189. 4 *Congressional Globe* 104.
190. 5 *id.* 42, 46.
191. *Id.* 126.
192. *Id.* 133, 140.
193. 6 *id.* 15, 62, 147, 67, 193, 85, 138, 251, 211, 235, 248, 297.
194. 6 *Register* 557–59.
195. Act of March 3, 1837, 5 Stat. 163; 4 *Congressional Globe* 213 (floor discussion indicating executive assent).

196. 5 *Congressional Globe* 3.

197. 1874 *Register of the Department of State* 60.

198. 2 *Congressional Globe* 82.

199. 6 *Congressional Globe* 68.

200. *Id.* 69, 86.

201. *Id.* 401, 402.

202. *Id.* 403.

203. *Id.* 427, 443.

204. S. Jour., 23d Cong., 2d Sess. 238.

205. 4 *Congressional Globe* 80.

206. 6 *Congressional Globe* 168–69.

207. 6 *Congressional Globe Appendix* 567, 568, 570.

208. 6 *Congressional Globe* 168–69; 6 *Congressional Globe Appendix* 570; 2 *Treaties and Other International Acts of the United States of America. 1776–1863* 658 (Miller ed. 1931–1948) (hereinafter "*Treaties* (Miller ed.)"); 3 *id.* 309.

209. 6 *Congressional Globe Appendix* 567, 568, 570.

210. J. Reeves, *American Diplomacy under Tyler and Polk* 242 (1907).

211. 12 *Congressional Globe* 61–62, 99.

212. *Id.* 212 (John Berrien's pro-administration argument); *id.* 240, 252 (Senate vote); *id.* 297 (House action).

213. 13 *Congressional Globe* 116.

214. *Id.* 186. President Washington had discarded the practice of seeking senatorial advice on treaty negotiations before it had become established usage. *See* Sofaer, *Origins* 95–96.

215. 13 *Congressional Globe* 418.

216. S. Jour., 28th Cong., 1st Sess. 445–56.

217. *Id.* 456.

218. 4 *Senate Executive Journal* 98.

219. *Id.*

220. *Id.* 112.

221. *Id.* 111–12, 119.

222. *See supra* pp. 65–66.

223. 8 *Register* 1413.

224. *Id.* 1393.

225. 6 *Congressional Globe* 168 (bill of George Evans); *id.* 502 (resolutions reported, no further action); 6 *Congressional Globe Appendix* 324 (bill of Reuel Williams); *id.* 330.

226. *Id.*

227. *Id.* 382–83.

228. *Id.* 386.

229. 6 *Congressional Globe* 496.

230. *Id.* 497.

231. 12 *Register* 1415, 1526.

232. *Id.* 1534.

233. *Id.* 1848.

234. *Id.* 1848, 1928.

235. *See supra* pp. 68–76.

236. 4 *Messages and Papers* 1455, 1456–57 (message of 5 December 1836).
237. 4 *Congressional Globe* 44, 45.
238. *Id.* 214.
239. *Id.* 213 (121 to 76).
240. *Id.*
241. *Supra* pp. 64–65.
242. 4 *Congressional Globe* 163; 4 *Messages and Papers* 1497.
243. 4 *Congressional Globe* 194, 210.
244. *Id.*
245. *Id.* 202, 203.
246. 6 *Congressional Globe* 4.
247. *Id.* 299.
248. *Id.*
249. *Id.* 299, 300.
250. *Id.* 299.
251. *Id.* 93.
252. 4 *Messages and Papers* 1702.
253. Louis Cass to Webster, 5 March and 15 March 1841, in 2 G. Curtis, *The Life of Daniel Webster* 62, 64 (1870); Henry S. Fox to Webster, 12 March 1841, in 6 D. Webster, *The Works of Daniel Webster* 247, 249, 250 (9th ed. 1851) (hereinafter "Webster, *Works* "); Andrew Stevenson to Webster, 9 March and 18 March 1841, in 3 *Diplomatic Correspondence of the United States: Canadian Relations, 1784–1860* 614–15, 618–20 (Manning ed. 1943) (hereinafter *"Diplomatic Correspondence (Canada)"*).
254. Webster to Fox, 24 April 1841, in 6 Webster, *Works* 153–54; Webster to Attorney-General Crittenden, 15 March 1841, in *id.* 262–66 (instructions sending him to New York State to confer on the McLeod matter).
255. Reeves, *American Diplomacy* 39.
256. H.M. Jones, *To the Webster-Ashburton Treaty, A Study in Anglo-American Relations, 1783–1843,* at 121–22 (1977).
257. 12 *Congressional Globe* 88.
258. *Id.*
259. *Id.* 85.
260. *Id.* 92–93.
261. 2 *Messages and Papers* 916 (second annual message, 5 December 1826); 3 *id.* 928.
262. White, *The Jacksonians* 214.
263. 3 Stat. 510; *id.* 720.
264. 8 *Register Appendix* 4.
265. *Id.* 20.
266. 4 *American State Papers: Documents, Legislative and Executive, Naval Affairs* 156 (Laurie and Clarke eds. 1832–61) (hereinafter *"American State Papers (Naval Affairs)"*).
267. H. Ellsworth, *One Hundred Eighty Landings of United States Marines, 1800–1934,* at 151–53 (1974) (hereinafter "Ellsworth, *One Hundred Eighty Landings"*).
268. *American State Papers (Naval Affairs)* 150.

269. *Id.*

270. 8 *Register* 3914.

271. 9 *Register Appendix* 3, 15.

272. 9 *id.* 3; 3 *Messages and Papers* 1154, 1159.

273. *American State Papers* (*Naval Affairs*) 716–17.

274. Sofaer, *Origins* 341–65.

275. Act of May 14, 1836, 5 Stat. 61.

276. 1 C. Wilkes, *Narrative of the United States Exploring Expedition during the Years 1838–1842,* at 353 (1844–1874) (hereinafter "Wilkes, *Narrative*").

277. Ellsworth, *One Hundred Eighty Landings* 77–78; 3 Wilkes, *Narrative* 240–43.

278. Ellsworth, *One Hundred Eighty Landings* 78–79; 3 Wilkes, *Narrative* 265–86; M. Offut, *Protection of Citizens Abroad by the Armed Forces of the United States* 25 (1928).

279. H.R. Exec. Doc. No. 104, 35th Cong., 2d Sess. (instructions of 30 March 1843).

280. *Id.*

281. H. Soulsby, *The Right of Search and the Slave Trade in Anglo-American Relations, 1814–1862,* at 121 (1933).

282. *See* H.R. Doc. No. 244, 28th Cong., 1st Sess. 31ff.

283. Letter, Perry to Upshur, 3 August 1843, in S. Doc. No. 150, 28th Cong., 2d Sess. 8; to Henshaw, 22 November 1834, *id.* 20.

284. C. Paullin, *Diplomatic Negotiations of American Naval Officers, 1778–1883,* at 360 (1912); H.R. Exec. Doc. No. 244, 28th Cong., 1st Sess. 4; S. Doc. No. 150, 28th Cong., 2d Sess. 26.

285. H.R. Exec. Doc. No. 244, p. 32. Perry and his colleagues had decided *before* landing at Berriby to destroy its five villages unless presented with "exculpatory evidence." *Id.* 31.

286. Slacum to Anchorena, 21 November 1831, in 20 *British and Foreign State Papers,* 1812-1919, 313 (1841-1923); Anchorena to Slacum, No. 25, 1831, *id.* 314; Slacum to Anchorena, 26 November 1831, *id.* 314–16; Anchorena to Slacum, 3 December 1831, *id.* 316–17.

287. Secretary of Navy Levi Woodbury to Silas Duncan, 10 June 1831, in National Archives Microfilm, Department of the Navy, *Letters,* M149, roll 19; Commodore Benjamin Cooper on SS *Warren,* Rio de Janeiro, to Master Commodore Silas Duncan, SS *Lexington,* 1 November 1831, *id.* M25, roll 164.

288. Slacum to Duncan, 30 November 1831, in 1 *Diplomatic Correspondence of the United States: Inter-American Affairs, 1831–1860 (Argentina)* 76 n.3 (Manning ed. 1932) (hereinafter, *"Diplomatic Correspondence (Argentina)";* Duncan to Slacum, 1 December 1831, *id.* 77 n.1.

289. Slacum to Anchorena, 6 December 1831, in 20 *British and Foreign State Papers* 318–19; Duncan to Anchorena, 7 December 1831, *id.* 319–20.

290. Slacum to Livingston, 23 November 1831, in 1 *Diplomatic Correspondence (Argentina)* 66; same, 9 December 1831, *id.* 75, 77.

291. 3 *Messages and Papers* 544, 553.

292. Secretary of the Navy Levi Woodbury to Rodgers, 29 November 1831, in National Archives Microfilm; Department of the Navy, *Letters,* M149, roll 20;

Rodgers to Secretary Woodbury, 29 December 1831, *id.* M125, roll 165. (Woodbury made a short reference for a possible response to Rodgers' letter: "Destroy establishment used in aggression Demand indemnity.") Confidential, Woodbury to Rodgers, 4 January 1832, *id.* M149, roll 20.

293. Baylies to de Maza, 20 June 1832, in 20 *British and Foreign State Papers* 330–36; de Maza to Baylies, 25 June 1832, *id.* 336; Baylies to de Maza, 26 June 1832, *id.* 336, 337.

294. Baylies to de Maza, 10 July 1832, *id.* 338–55, and 6 August 1832, *id.* 356–58; de Maza to Livingston, 8 August 1832, *id.* 358–60; de Maza to Baylies, 14 August 1832, *id.* 364, 365–67, 369–436.

295. Minute of a conference between Manuel Vicente de Maza, acting minister of foreign affairs of Argentina, and Francis Baylies, United States *chargé d'affaires* at Buenos Aires, 27 August 1832, in 1 *Diplomatic Correspondence (Argentina)* 155, 157. The Argentine version of the minute is in 20 *British and Foreign State Papers* 437.

296. Baylies to Livingston, 26 September 1832, in 1 *Diplomatic Correspondence (Argentina)* 161, 164.

297. Woodbury to Duncan, 4 April 1832, National Archives Microfilm, Department of the Navy, *Letters,* M149, roll 21, Doc. No. 109, 16 (letters sent by Sec'y. of Navy to Officers).

298. J. Goebel, Jr., *The Struggle for the Falkland Islands* 444 (1927).

299. Duncan to Slacum, February 11, 1832; Garcia to Slacum, February 15, 1832, in 20 *British and Foreign State Papers* 328.

300. S. Doc. No. 109, 23d Cong., 2d Sess. 15–16.

301. 9 *Register Appendix* 2, 3.

302. 9 *Register* 900.

303. *Id.* 900–01.

304. *Id.* 926.

305. Eben R. Dorr, U.S. consul at Buenos Aires, to Secretary of State John Forsyth, 17 January 1835, in 1 *Diplomatic Correspondence (Argentina)* 187–88.

306. *See* Goebel, *The Struggle for the Falkland Islands* 462.

307. John Parrott, U.S. consul at Mazatlan, wrote to Jones that diplomatic relations might be ended. *See* Parrott to Jones, H.R. Doc. No. 166, 27th Cong., 3d Sess. 86.

308. Jones to Upshur, 13 September 1842, *id.* 68.

309. Jones to the Governor of Monterey, 19 October 1842, *id.* 22.

310. G. Rives, 1 *The United States and Mexico, 1821–1848,* at 519 (1913).

311. H.R. Doc. No. 166, 27th Cong., 3d Sess. 12.

312. Translation, Mexican *Diario del Gobierno, id.* 16.

313. Webster to Mexican Minister General Juan Almonte, 30 January 1843, *id.* 5; *see also* 6 Webster, *Works* 460–62.

314. 12 *Congressional Globe* 234–35.

315. 5 *Messages and Papers* 2081.

316. 11 Adams, *Memoirs* 346, 374. Adams described Webster as "falter[ing]" and uncertain whether he could answer Adams's questions about California "consistent with his official duty."

317. 12 *Congressional Globe* 400.

318. M. Cunliffe, *Soldiers and Civilians: The Martial Spirit in America, 1775–1865,* at 101ff. (1968).

319. 5 *Congressional Globe* 126, 138.

320. *Id.* 137.

321. 6 *id.* 6–7.

322. 6 *Congressional Globe Appendix* 1, 3, 5; Act of July 2, 1838, 5 Stat. 256.

323. J. Curtis, *The Fox at Bay* 175 (1970).

324. *Supra* p. 65.

325. 4 *Messages and Papers* 1700, 1703.

326. H.R. Doc. No. 169, 26th Cong., 1st Sess. 2 (Joel Poinsett to Winfield Scott, 28 February 1839).

327. 7 *Congressional Globe* 217–19, 224–29; Act of March 3, 1837, 5 Stat. 355–56 (1839).

328. H.R. Doc. No. 169, 26th Cong., 1st Sess. 17.

329. H.R. Doc. No. 153, 26th Cong., 1st Sess. 1–17; Curtis, *The Fox at Bay* 199ff.

330. *Id.*

331. *Id.* 311–13.

332. 8 *Congressional Globe* 536 (Senate passage); *id.* 544 (House passage).

333. *Id.* 535.

334. *Id.* 536.

335. *Id.; see supra* p. 65.

336. 8 *Congressional Globe* 535.

337. Morgan, *A Whig Embattled* 97, 98.

338. 5 *Messages and Papers* 2139ff.

339. Tyler to Governor Sam King, 11 April 1842, in 5 *Messages and Papers* 2144.

340. 13 *Congressional Globe* 426, 28th Cong., 1st Sess.

341. *Id.* 407.

342. 9 April 1842, in 5 *Messages and Papers* 2136.

343. U.S. Const. art. IV, §4.

344. Story to Webster (26 April 1842), D. Webster, *Papers,* reel 17 (Wiltse ed. microfilm 1974).

345. 2 J. Tyler, *The Letters and Times of the Tylers* 199 (L. Tyler ed. 1884–1896).

346. 1 Rives, *The United States and Mexico* 237–38.

347. Butler to Jackson (21 June 1832) in 4 A. Jackson, *Correspondence of Andrew Jackson* 450 (Bassett and Jameson eds. 1926–1935) (hereinafter "Jackson, *Correspondence*"); 18 July 1832, *id.* at 463–64; 28 October 1833 in 5 Jackson, *Correspondence* 219–20.

348. 4 *Messages and Papers* 1500, 1501; *see supra* p. 75.

349. 6 *American State Papers (Military Affairs)* 416, 417.

350. *Id.* 418.

351. Sofaer, *Origins* 345–46; *see also* 347–60.

352. Gaines to governors of Louisiana, Mississippi, Alabama, and Tennessee (8 April 1836), in 6 *American State Papers (Military Affairs)* 420.

353. 1 Rives, *The United States and Mexico* 375.

354. 12 *Register* 3375.

355. *Id.* 3330.

356. *Id.* 3324.

357. *Id.* 3341.

358. *Id.* 3343.

359. *Id.*

360. *Id.* 3343–44.

361. *Id.* 1458, 3820 (Act of May 23, 1836, 5 Stat. 32).

362. 3 *Congressional Globe* 354.

363. 12 *Register* 3511–18.

364. *Id.* 3519.

365. 3 *Congressional Globe* 358.

366. 12 *Register* 3543.

367. *Id.* 3518, 3519, 3528, 3529.

368. *E.g.*, Churchill Cambreling of New York, who had presented the president's bill, in 3 *Congressional Globe* 357.

369. 12 *Register* 3539.

370. *Id.* 3531–38, 3540.

371. 3 *Congressional Globe* 358.

372. *Id.* 359.

373. *Id.* 362–63, 374–78.

374. 12 *Register* 1455–56, 3724.

375. 3 *Congressional Globe* 359.

376. 12 *Register* 1846, 1847, 1848, 4621–22 (Senate, 39 to 0; House, 28 to 20).

377. Gaines to General Bradford, 7 *Papers of the Texas Revolution* 301 (Jenkins ed. 1973).

378. *Id.* 413–15.

379. Gorostiza to Secretary Forsyth, 27 July 1836, 8 *Papers of the Texas Revolution* 50.

380. Jackson to Acting Secretary Dickins, 5 Jackson, *Correspondence* 421.

381. Gorostiza to Forsyth, 2 September 1836, 8 *Papers of the Texas Revolution* 371–73.

382. Jackson to Gaines, 4 September 1836, 5 Jackson, *Correspondence* 424.

383. *Id.*

384. Memorandum of Forsyth's interview with Gorostiza, 23 September 1836, 8 *Papers of the Texas Revolution* 517–518.

385. Gorostiza to Dickins, 15 October 1836, 9 *Papers of the Texas Revolution* 92–98; J. Callahan, *American Foreign Policy in Canadian Relations* 86 (1932); 1 Rives, *The United States and Mexico* 380.

386. 4 *Congressional Globe* 2.

387. *Id.*

388. *Id.* 44.

389. *Id.* 211, 213. (The vote was 121 to 76.)

390. *Id.* 83, 214.

391. *Id.* 216.

392. 4 *Senate Executive Journal* 631.

393. Callahan, *American Foreign Policy in Canadian Relations* 90.

394. Van Zandt to Upshur, 17 January 1844, in S. Doc. No. 271, 28th Cong., 1st Sess. 89; Van Zandt to Anson Jones, 20 January 1844, in 2 *Texas Diplomatic Correspondence* 242.

395. Jones to Murphy, 14 February 1844, in H.R. Exec. Doc. 271, 28th Cong., 1st Sess. 89; Murphy to Jones, 14 February 1844, *id.* 91.

396. *Id.* 95.

397. Calhoun to Van Zandt, 11 April 1844, in S. Doc. No. 349, 28th Cong., 1st Sess. 11.

398. *Id.*

399. 2 Rives, *The United States and Mexico* 608–09.

400. *Id.*

401. 13 *Congressional Globe* 652.

402. 5 S. Bemis, ed., *The American Secretaries of State and Their Diplomacy* 145–60 (1927–29); T. Reeves, *Gentleman Boss: The Life of Chester Alan Arthur* 154–56 (1967).

403. S. Doc. No. 1, 28th Cong., 2d Sess. 26–27.

404. Howard to Jones, 6 August 1844, *id.* 28–29.

405. Calhoun to Howard, *id.* 38–39.

406. 5 J. Calhoun, *Works* 368–69 (Cralle ed. 1853).

407. S. Doc. No. 1, 28th Cong., 2d Sess. 38–39.

408. Raymond to Jones, 13 September 1844, in *Memoranda and Official Correspondence Relating to the Republic of Texas, Its History and Annexation* 383 (Jones ed. 1859).

409. 5 *Messages and Papers* 2169; S. Doc. No. 341, 28th Cong., 1st Sess. 76–81; *see also* H.R. Doc 271, 28th Cong., 1st Sess. 77ff.

410. 5 *Messages and Papers* 2169, 2170.

411. 13 *Congressional Globe Appendix* 497 (Senate, secret session, 1 June 1844).

412. *Id.* 499.

413. *Id.* (emphasis in original).

414. *Id.* 768.

415. 13 *Congressional Globe* 558. *See also* argument of Representative James Belser (D. Ala.), *id.* 520.

416. 13 *Congressional Globe Appendix* 531 (in secret session).

417. *Id.*

418. Bocanegra to Thompson, 23 August 1843, in S. Doc. No. 341, 28th Cong., 1st Sess. 89, 90.

419. 13 *Congressional Globe* 664.

420. 13 *Congressional Globe Appendix* 537; accord, Spencer Jarnagin (D. Tenn.).

421. 6 *Senate Executive Journal* 279, 308, 312.

422. McDuffie, in 13 *Congressional Globe Appendix* 529; Breese, *id.* 540.

423. 13 *Congressional Globe* 612.

424. L. Henkin, *Foreign Affairs and the Constitution* 105 (1972).

CHAPTER 2: CONSOLIDATING THE CONTINENT, 1845–57

1. W. Andrews, ed., *Concise Dictionary of American Biography* 808 (1964).
2. R. Nichols, *The Disruption of American Democracy* 299 (1948).
3. *Id.* 461–62.
4. 1 J.K. Polk, *The Diary of James K. Polk during His Presidency, 1845 to 1849*, at 306 (Quaife ed. 1910) (hereinafter "Polk, *Diary* (Quaife ed.)"); 1 *id.* 282; 1 *id.* 303; R. Neustadt, *Presidential Power: The Politics of Leadership* 10 (1960).
5. 15 *Congressional Globe* 657, 658, 789, 830.
6. *Id.* 865.
7. 16 *Congressional Globe* 375, 377, 347–49.
8. 17 *Congressional Globe* 744, 745.
9. 15 *Congressional Globe* 819, 820, 834.
10. 19 *Congressional Globe App.* 482, 483.
11. 15 *Congressional Globe* 45, 49, 60.
12. *Id.* 534–37, 552.
13. *Id.* 788–89, 795.
14. *Id.* 263.
15. *Id.* 182, 220, 251, 254.
16. 20 *Congressional Globe* 703, 725, 728, 733.
17. *Id.* 735.
18. 25 *Congressional Globe* 512, 523-26.
19. *Id.* 634.
20. 24 *Congressional Globe* 463.
21. *Id.* 1164, 1175.
22. 21 *Congressional Globe* 1243.
23. *Id.* 1494, 1746.
24. *Id.* 509.
25. *Id.* 517, 523.
26. *Id.* 1684.
27. *Id.* 1890, 1914; 22 *Congressional Globe* 489, 742.
28. 19 *Congressional Globe* 1045.
29. *Id.* 1181.
30. *Id.* 1180.
31. 21 *Congressional Globe* 16.
32. *Id.* 15.
33. 21 *Congressional Globe Appendix* 40–42.
34. 21 *Congressional Globe* 903. On 10 May, Mallory introduced a similar resolution on behalf of Spanish subjects in Louisiana. *Id.* 1301.
35. *Id.* 1574, 1789.
36. 23 *Congressional Globe Appendix* 16.
37. 23 *Congressional Globe* 465–66.
38. *Id.* 772.
39. *Id.* 803.
40. *Id.* 808, 809.

41. 26 *Congressional Globe* 469 (remarks of William Seward (R. N.Y.), 19 January 1857).
42. *Id.* 473–74.
43. 5 *Messages and Papers* 2235.
44. *See supra* p. 101.
45. 15 *Congressional Globe* 9271.
46. *Id.* 927, 928, 932.
47. *Id.* 927.
48. *Id.*
49. *Id.* 928–30.
50. *Id.* 929.
51. *See* Sofaer, *Origins* 363.
52. 15 *Congressional Globe* 931.
53. *Id.* 932.
54. 6 *Messages and Papers* 2298–99; 15 *Congressional Globe* 938, Appendix 649–68.
55. *Id.* 649–50, 657–58.
56. *Id.* 657, 658.
57. 1 Polk, *Diary* 480–81 (Quaife ed.)
58. 15 *Congressional Globe* 931.
59. 2 Polk, *Diary* 13–14 (Quaife ed.); 15 *Congressional Globe* 1040, 1128.
60. 2 C. Sellers, *James K. Polk, Continentalist, 1843–1846, at* 438–39 (1957–58); A. Nevins, *Hamilton Fish: The Inner History of the Grant Administration* 139–40 (1934).
61. 2 Polk *Diary* (Quaife ed.) 204–05.
62. 16 *Congressional Globe* 296.
63. *Id.* 303.
64. *Id.* 539–40.
65. 17 *Congressional Globe* 515.
66. *Id.* 586.
67. *Id.*
68. *Id.*
69. *Id.* 587.
70. *Id.* 589.
71. *Id.* 638.
72. *Id.* 679.
73. *Id.* 685–93.
74. *Id.* 483.
75. 5 *Messages and Papers* 2428.
76. 17 *Congressional Globe* 793.
77. 5 *Treaties* (Miller ed.) 662–63.
78. 19 *Congressional Globe* 69, 70.
79. *Id.* 221-22.
80. *Id.* 347.
81. *Id.* 233.
82. 5 *Treaties* (Miller ed.) 747.
83. 6 Bemis, *The American Secretaries of State and Their Diplomacy* 54.

84. 5 *Treaties* (Miller ed.) 680, 769.

85. 6 Bemis, *American Secretaries of State and Their Diplomacy* 64–65.

86. Clayton's note of reply, 4 July 1850, in 5 *Treaties* (Miller ed.) 682; correspondence of Clayton and William R. King, *id.* 683–84.

87. 6 *Messages and Papers* 2601.

88. 19 *Congressional Globe* 1424, 1425.

89. 22 *Congressional Globe* 238.

90. *Id.* 247.

91. *Id.* 237.

92. *Id.* 247.

93. *Id.* 527.

94. 22 *Congressional Globe Appendix* 253.

95. 23 *Congressional Globe* 28, 107–10; 7 *Messages and Papers* 2760.

96. 22 *Congressional Globe* 91.

97. 23 *Congressional Globe Appendix* 91.

98. *Id.* 94.

99. A. Walworth, *Black Ships Off Japan: The Story of Commodore Perry's Expedition* 43 (1966).

100. Instructions from Secretary of Navy John Kennedy and Acting Secretary of State Conrad, in S. Exec. Doc. No. 34, 33d Cong., 2d Sess. 6–8 (1855).

101. W. Griffis, *Matthew Calbraith Perry* 303–04 (1887); R. Leopold, *The Growth of American Foreign Policy: A History* 64 (1966).

102. S. Exec. Doc. No. 34, 33d Cong., 2d Sess. 8 (1855).

103. *Id.* at 8 (letter of Secretary of Navy Kennedy to Perry, 13 November 1852).

104. Walworth, *Black Ships Off Japan: The Story of Commodore Perry's Expedition* 28.

105. 21 *Congressional Globe Appendix* 398.

106. 22 *Congressional Globe Appendix* 279–80 (1853).

107. Remarks of Senator James A. Pearce (Wh. Md.), 17 March 1853, *id.* 280.

108. S. Exec. Doc. No. 34, at 13 (Perry to the secretary of the navy, 14 December 1852; Secretary of State Everett to Perry, 15 February 1853).

109. *Id.* 30 (letter of Perry to the secretary of the navy, 25 June 1853).

110. *Id.* 80–81 (letter of Perry to the secretary of the navy, 24 December 1853).

111. *Id.* 109–10 (letter of Perry to the secretary of the navy, 25 January 1854).

112. *Id.* 112 (letter of secretary of the navy to Perry, 30 May 1854).

113. Hayaski-Daigaku, "Diary of an Official of the *Bakufu*" 101 (1930).

114. *Id.* 104.

115. *Id.* 115.

116. Sofaer, *Origins* 378–79.

117. S. Bemis, *A Diplomatic History of the United States* 273–76 (1946).

118. 15 *Congressional Globe* 4, 7.

119. 5 *Messages and Papers* 2272; 15 *Congressional Globe* 332–34; *id.* 336.

120. *Id.* 449.

121. *Id.* 626, 627.

122. *Id.* 656.

123. 5 *Messages and Papers* 2279.

124. 15 *Congressional Globe* 660.

125. 1 Polk, *Diary* (Quaife ed.) 209–14 *passim* (4–7 February 1846).

126. 17 *Congressional Globe* 57, 103.

127. *Id.* 166–67.

128. *Id.* 167.

129. *Id.*

130. *See id.* 104 (Thomas Bayly (D. Va.)); *id.* 169 (Charles Ingersoll (D. Pa.)); *id.* 207 (Willard Hale (D. Mo.)).

131. *Id.* 167.

132. 3 Polk, *Diary* (Quaife ed.) 310.

133. 1 Polk, *Diary* (Quaife ed.) 9–10.

134. *Id.* 33.

135. *Id.* 34.

136. Polk to Slidell, 10 November 1845 (confidential), Polk, *Papers* 125, Ser. 4, folder 2.

137. Polk to Slidell, 17 December 1845 (private and unofficial), *id.* 198, Ser. 4, folder 3.

138. 17 *Congressional Globe* 990.

139. *Id.* 911.

140. 6 *Messages and Papers* 2415–17; *id.* 2341–42.

141. *Id.* 2415–17.

142. 1 Polk, *Diary* (Quaife ed.) 232–25.

143. *Id.* 228–30.

144. 3 Polk, *Diary* (Quaife ed.) 290–91.

145. 23 *Congressional Globe* 601.

146. *Id.* 636, 857.

147. *Id.* 636–37.

148. *Id.* 647.

149. 6 Bemis, *The American Secretaries of State and Their Diplomacy* 185; H.R. Exec. Doc. No. 93, 33d Cong., 2d Sess.; H.R. Exec. Doc. No. 76, 33d Cong., 1st Sess.

150. H.R. Exec. Docs. Nos. 93 and 76.

151. A. Ettinger, *The Mission to Spain of Pierre Soulé, 1853–1855,* at 341 (1932).

152. *See* Nichols, in T. Bailey, *A Diplomatic History of the American People* (6th ed. 1958); Bemis, 6 *The American Secretaries of State and Their Diplomacy;* H.R. Docs. Nos. 93 and 76.

153. 24 *Congressional Globe Appendix* 1, 2.

154. *Id.* 9, 905.

155. *Id.* 826ff., 832ff.

156. *See generally* F. Merk, *The Monroe Doctrine and American Expansionism, 1843–1849* (1966).

157. 15 *Congressional Globe* 4, 7–8.

158. *Id.* 197, 198.

159. *Id.* 240–41.

160. *Id.* 198, 245, 248.

161. 18 *Congressional Globe* 438.
162. *Id.* 449.
163. *Id.* 454.
164. *Id.* 485, 486.
165. *Id.* 487.
166. Letter of 15 February 1849, in *Treaties* (Miller ed.) 384.
167. 15 *Congressional Globe* 436, 456, 483, 502.
168. *Id.* 683.
169. *Id.* 138.
170. *Id.* 273.
171. *Id.* 231.
172. *Id.* 350.
173. *Id.* 720.
174. 3 Polk, *Diary* (Quaife ed.) 434.
175. 17 *Congressional Globe* 727.
176. *Id.* 771, 777.
177. *Id.* 738.
178. S. Exec. Doc. No. 45, 30th Cong., 1st Sess. 2–4.
179. 17 *Congressional Globe* 769.
180. *Id.* 709.
181. 19 *Congressional Globe* 75.
182. 19 *Congressional Globe Appendix 54, 55.*
183. *Id.* 89.
184. *Id.* 588.
185. *Id.* 746.
186. *Id.* 630 (message dated 28 March 1850 and presented 3 April 1850).
187. 21 *Congressional Globe* 16.
188. *Id.* 160, 164.
189. *Id.* 298 (resolution of William Seward).
190. 21 *Congressional Globe Appendix* 162.
191. 3 Polk, *Diary* (Quaife ed.) 469, 478.
192. 22 *Congressional Globe* 139.
193. *Id.* 199.
194. 22 *Congressional Globe Appendix* 92.
195. 22 *Congressional Globe* 126.
196. 21 *Congressional Globe* 902.
197. *Id.* 1892.
198. *Id.* 1883, 1890, 1897.
199. 6 *Messages and Papers* 269 (president's messages of 2 and 9 August 1852).
200. Griffis, *Matthew Calbraith Perry* 298–301 *passim.*
201. 21 *Congressional Globe Appendix* 898ff.
202. *Id.* 914.
203. *Id.* 914–15.
204. *Id.* 917.
205. *See* S. Exec. Doc. No. 22, at 444–45, 32d Cong., 2d Sess.
206. 23 *Congressional Globe* 8.

207. Bailey, *A Diplomatic History of the American People,* 279.
208. *Id.* 280.
209. 23 *Congressional Globe* 1032.
210. *Id.* 1403.
211. *Id.* 1404.
212. 26 *Congressional Globe* 498.
213. *Id.* 573, 1068.
214. 7 *Messages and Papers* 2867.
215. 25 *Congressional Globe* 600.
216. 9 Stat. 108.
217. 25 *Congressional Globe* 528, 601.
218. *Id.* 1152.
219. *Id.* 1156.
220. *Id.* 1203.
221. *Id.*
222. 23 *Congressional Globe* 1519.
223. 23 *Congressional Globe Appendix* 1015.
224. 23 *Congressional Globe* 1542.
225. *Id.* 1564.
226. 23 *Congressional Globe Appendix* 1033.
227. *Id.* 1031.
228. 23 *Congressional Globe* 1565.
229. 26 *Congressional Globe* 393.
230. *Id.* 425.
231. *Id.* 741.
232. Sofaer, *Origins* 269.
233. *E.g.,* requests for correspondence concerning France and Brazil, in 17 *Congressional Globe* 230, 549, 804; responses, *id.* 526, 604, 827. Requests for documents giving statistical summaries, in 17 *Congressional Globe* 58, 76; responses, *id.* 725, 604.
234. 6 J. Buchanan, *Works* 159, 171–72 (Moore ed. 1908–1911).
235. *Id.* 360, 361.
236. 3 *American State Papers (Foreign Relations)* 337.
237. 1 Polk, *Diary* (Quaife ed.) 384.
238. *Id.* 69–71 *passim.*
239. 15 *Congressional Globe* 4, 5.
240. *Id.* 6.
241. *Id.* 782–83.
242. Remarks of William Archer (Wh. Va.), *id.* 784.
243. *Id.* 784–85.
244. *Id.* 785.
245. *Id.* 787.
246. *Id.* 787–88.
247. *Id.* 791.
248. *Id.* 792.
249. *Id.* 794.
250. *Id.* 795.

251. *Id.*
252. *Id.* 795–97.
253. *Id.* 797.
254. *Id.*
255. *Id.* 799.
256. *Id.* 802.
257. *Id.* 804.
258. *Id.* 810.
259. 17 *Congressional Globe* 95.
260. *Id.* 343–44.
261. *Id.* 154.
262. *Id.* 26.
263. *Id.* 97, 98.
264. 17 *Congressional Globe Appendix* 242.
265. 17 *Congressional Globe* 276.
266. *Id.* 192.
267. *Id.* 64.
268. *Id.* 65 (Representative Samuel Vinton (Wh. Oh.)).
269. *Id.* 323–24.
270. *Id.* 331, 333.
271. *Id.* 348.
272. *Id.* 363.
273. *Id.* 363, 373.
274. *Id.* 374.
275. *Id.* 549.
276. 7 Buchanan, *Works* 38–40.
277. *Id.* 49.
278. 15 *Congressional Globe* 1211–14.
279. *Id.* 1215.
280. *Id.*
281. *Id.* 1214–15, 1216.
282. *Id.* 1218.
283. *Id.* 1221.
284. 7 Buchanan, *Works* 267–68.
285. 2 Polk, *Diary* (Quaife ed.) 323–42 *passim*.
286. 16 *Congressional Globe* 305.
287. *Id.* 325–26.
288. *Id.* 326, 327.
289. *Id.* 337.
290. *Id.* 368.
291. *Id.* 545.
292. *Id.* 556.
293. *Id.* 573; 9 Stat. 174 (3 March 1847).
294. 16 *Congressional Globe* 9, 42.
295. *Id.* 27, 65, 66.
296. *Id.* 85.
297. 17 *Congressional Globe* 75–76.

298. *Id.* 79.
299. *Id.* 479.
300. *Id.*
301. *Id.* 269; 18 *Congressional Globe* 57.
302. *Id.* 148.
303. *Id.* 149.
304. *Id.* 150.
305. 1 Polk, *Diary* (Quaife ed.) 416, 420.
306. *Id.* 422, 424.
307. 18 *Congressional Globe* 487–88, 498.
308. 17 *Congressional Globe* 605 (answers to questions by the Senate Committee on Military Affairs). A. Gillespie, *Papers* (Special Collections Library, University of California at Los Angeles)
309. 17 *Congressional Globe* 606; Gillespie, *Papers* (answers to questions by the Senate Committee on Military Affairs).
310. Gillespie, *Papers* (answers to questions by the Senate Committee on Military Affairs).
311. 17 *Congressional Globe* 606.
312. Andrews, ed., *Concise Dictionary of American History* 132.
313. 17 *Congressional Globe Appendix* 563.
314. 17 *Congressional Globe* 423.
315. *Id.* 568.
316. *Id.* 708.
317. 6 *Messages and Papers* 2444 (24 July 1848, responding to House resolution of 10 July 1848).
318. 4 Polk, *Diary* (Quaife ed.) 150–51.
319. 19 *Congressional Globe* 179.
320. *Id.* 1235.
321. *Id.* 1525.
322. *Id.*
323. *Id.* 1526.
324. 19 *Congressional Globe Appendix* 1032–34.
325. *Id.* 1049.
326. *Id.* 1050, 1051.
327. 19 *Congressional Globe* 1589.
328. 20 *Congressional Globe* 49.
329. 6 *Messages and Papers* 2743.
330. 23 *Congressional Globe Appendix* 79.
331. S. Exec. Doc. No. 8, 33d Cong., 1st Sess. 24–26.
332. *Id.* 33, 34.
333. *Id.* at 10–12, 32.
334. *Id.* at 6, 7; *see also* S. Doc. No. 85, 33d Cong., 1st Sess. 21.
335. S. Exec. Doc. No. 8, 33d Cong., 1st Sess. 7.
336. S. Exec. Doc. No. 85, 33d Cong., 1st Sess. 9–11.
337. *Id.* 28–30.
338. *Id.* 21.
339. 23 *Congressional Globe* 1984, 1988.

340. 7 *Messages and Papers* 2815, 2817.
341. S. Doc. No. 85, 33d Cong., 1st Sess. 21.
342. 7 *Messages and Papers* 2815.
343. *See* Sofaer, *Origins* 365ff., for a discussion of presidential authority to suppress piracy.
344. 24 *Congressional Globe* 951.
345. *Id.*
346. *Id.*

CHAPTER 3: NATIONAL POLICY IN DOMESTIC CRISIS, 1857–69

1. 34 *Congressional Globe* 842.
2. *Id.* 333, 586, 594, 427, 431, 435, 842, 771–72, 850–51, 874, 881.
3. 32 *Congressional Globe* 1936, 1941–44.
4. *Id.* 3039.
5. *Id.* 3042.
6. *Id.* 3039.
7. 33 *Congressional Globe* 914, 1335.
8. 35 *Congressional Globe* 1413.
9. *Id.* 128, 135–36.
10. 37 *Congressional Globe* 1739, 1966; *id.* 1933, 1976.
11. *Id.* 463.
12. *Id.* 467.
13. *Id.* 387.
14. *Id.* 518.
15. *Id.* 936–37.
16. *Id.* 970.
17. *Id.* 1738.
18. *Id.*
19. M. Josephson, *The Politicos* 37 (1963); 14 Stat. 485, 486–87.
20. Forsyth to secretary of state, No. 23 (2 February 1857), National Archives Manuscripts, Records of the Department of State, RG 59, *Despatches Mexico*.
21. J. Musser, *The Establishment of Maximilian's Empire in Mexico* 19 (1918).
22. 6 Bemis, *The American Secretaries of State and Their Diplomacy* 332–42, *passim.*
23. P. Adams, "The American Struggle for a Pre-eminent Position in Mexico," p. 147 (unpublished dissertation, Ohio State University, 1950).
24. 28 *Congressional Globe Appendix* 4.
25. *Id.*
26. 28 *Congressional Globe* 298.
27. *Id.*
28. 5 W. Seward, *The Life and Works of William H. Seward* 33 (Baker ed. 1883–84).

29. Seward to Corwin, No. 2 (6 April 1861), in National Archives Manuscripts, Records of the Department of State, RG 59, *Instructions, Mexico.*

30. 32 *Congressional Globe* 123, 140, 697.

31. 31 *Congressional Globe* 217–18, 236, 256, 347, 363–64, 384–85, 426.

32. 32 *Congressional Globe* 512.

33. *Id.* 515 (John Sherman (R. Oh.)); *id.* 517 (Edgar Cowan (R. Pa.)).

34. *Id.* 513.

35. 31 *Congressional Globe* 56 (House, 136–10); *id.* 84 (Senate, 36–6).

36. *Id.* 54, 55.

37. 32 *Congressional Globe* 2162.

38. *Id.* 3841.

39. *Id.* 747–48, 761.

40. *Id.* 3325.

41. 33 *Congressional Globe* 1023–28 (Senate); *id.* 1489 (2 March 1863, House).

42. 35 *Congressional Globe* 1056–57.

43. *Id.* 1050–51.

44. *Id.* 1052.

45. *Id.* 1125, 1147.

46. 33 *Congressional Globe* 1365.

47. Remarks of Abraham Olin (R. N.Y.), *id.* 1234.

48. *Id.* 1002 (Senate); *id.* 1293 (House).

49. *Id.* 705.

50. *Id.* 708, 711–12.

51. *Id.* 712.

52. *Id.* 735.

53. *Id.* 737–39.

54. 39 *Congressional Globe* 4, 5, 316–17.

55. *Id.* 120, 128, 152, 264, 268, 316–17, 388, 476, 638, 687, 781, 934–35, 1104–05, 1127, 1296, 1334, 2165, 2176, 3364.

56. *Id.* 2317–18.

57. *Id.* 4359.

58. *Id.* 4232.

59. *Id.*

60. *Id.* 4207.

61. *Id.* 4209, 4236.

62. *Id.* 4207, 4238.

63. *Id.* 4446.

64. *Id.* 4474.

65. 37 *Congressional Globe* 61.

66. 27 *Congressional Globe* 165.

67. *Id.* 533.

68. *Id.* 999.

69. *Id.* 1382, 1384.

70. 32 *Congressional Globe* 6.

71. *Id.* 189.

72. *Id.* 191.

73. *Id.* 192–93.

74. *Id.* 264.

75. 39 *Congressional Globe* 2176 (unqualified, 28 March 1868).

76. *Id.* 2331.

77. *Id.* 233.

78. *E.g.*, 33 *Congressional Globe* 16 (8 December 1862, name and number of certain generals); *id.* 17 (8 December 1862, number of aides-de-camp on active duty); *id.* 118 (18 December 1862, information regarding the chartering of certain vessels); *id.* 138 (19 December 1862, information regarding the appointment of rear admirals); *id.* 155 (22 December 1862, information concerning the increase of naval officers).

79. *E.g., id.* 15 (5 December 1862, information on conditions in Mexico); *id.* 837 (10 February 1863, correspondence with the French government regarding a mediation role directed to ending the war).

80. *E.g.*, communications between Great Britain and the United States concerning captured British shipping carrying contraband, *id.* 292, 525; correspondence between the President and General McClellan, *id.* 94.

81. *E.g.*, number of aides-de-camp on duty, *id.* 17.

82. 31 *Congressional Globe* 298 (replies of 25 July 1861).

83. *Id.* 253.

84. 8 *Messages and Papers* 3234.

85. 32 *Congressional Globe* 1040.

86. *See supra* p. 208.

87. 32 *Congressional Globe* 153.

88. *Id.* 488.

89. *Id.* 110, 178 (qualified).

90. *Id.* 182 (2 January 1862, qualified).

91. 12 Senate Executive Journal 330 (4 June 1862); 8 *Messages and Papers* 3281.

92. Resolution passed 31 May 1864, in 35 *Congressional Globe* 2586.

93. *Id.* 3340, 3359–60.

94. 29 *Congressional Globe* 997.

95. Nichols, *The Disruption of American Democracy* 331.

96. 29 *Congressional Globe* 112, 119, 133.

97. *Id.* 1435 (message, 28 March 1860).

98. *Id.* 997.

99. 10 Buchanan, *Works* 399–400; 29 *Congressional Globe* 1434 (message, 28 March 1860).

100. 10 Buchanan, *Works* 402; 29 *Congressional Globe* 1435.

101. 10 Buchanan, *Works* 403; 29 *Congressional Globe* 1435.

102. 10 Buchanan, *Works* 404–05; 29 *Congressional Globe* 1435.

103. 29 *Congressional Globe* 1435.

104. *Id.* 1436.

105. *Id.* 1441.

106. *Id.* 2774.
107. *Id.* 2775.
108. *Id.* 3071.
109. 10 Buchanan, *Works* 442; 7 *Messages and Papers* 3150, 3155.
110. 32 *Congressional Globe* 29.
111. *Id.* 32, 40.
112. *Id.*
113. *Id.* 30, 31.
114. 35 *Congressional Globe* 1398.
115. 35 *Congressional Globe Appendix* 103.
116. *Id.* 444.
117. *Id.* 444–45.
118. 28 *Congressional Globe Appendix* 4.
119. *Id.*
120. 28 *Congressional Globe* 538.
121. *Id.* 747.
122. *Id.* 541.
123. *Id.* 542.
124. 28 *Congressional Globe Appendix* 94 (report of the Senate Committee on Foreign Relations).
125. *Id.* 92.
126. *Id.* 113, 158.
127. *Id.* 159.
128. *Id.* 538.
129. *Id.* 1335.
130. *E.g., id.* 9.
131. 27 *Congressional Globe* 2066.
132. *Id.* 2064.
133. *Id.* 2862–63.
134. 28 *Congressional Globe Appendix* 5.
135. *Id.* 5.
136. 28 *Congressional Globe* 1118.
137. 10 Buchanan, *Works* 361. *Also, Congressional Globe Appendix* 5 (third annual message, 19 December 1859).
138. 27 *Congressional Globe* 2564.
139. *Id.*
140. *Id.* 2744.
141. *Id.*
142. *Id.* 2748.
143. *Id.* 2565; 28 *Congressional Globe* 1141.
144. *Id.* 1120 (Senator William Fessenden (D. Me.)).
145. *Id.* 1121.
146. *Id.* 1123.
147. 7 Bemis, *The American Secretaries of State and Their Diplomacy* 29–31; 2 F. Bancroft, *The Life of William H. Seward* 137 (1900) (hereinafter, "Bancroft, *Seward*").

148. Lincoln to Seward, 1 April 1861, A. Lincoln, *The Papers of Abraham Lincoln*, mf. reel 19, no. 8612, Library of Congress (hereinafter "Lincoln, *Papers*").

149. 3 J. Nicolay and J. Hay, *Abraham Lincoln: A History* 436 (1890).

150. 4 Naval Records Office, *Official Records of the Union and Confederate Navies in the War of the Rebellion* 109 (1896) (hereinafter, "Naval Records Office, *Official Records of the Rebellion*").

151. Scott to Seward, 1 April 1861, in Lincoln, *Papers*, reel 19, no. 8658.

152. 6 A. Lincoln, *Complete Works of Abraham Lincoln* 239 (Nicolay and Hay eds. 1905) (hereinafter "Lincoln, *Works* (Nicolay and Hay eds.)").

153. Seward to Tassara, 2 April 1861, in 7 Bemis, *The American Secretaries of State and Their Diplomacy* 31.

154. *Id.* 33.

155. 1 G. Welles, *Diary of Gideon Welles, Secretary of the Navy under Lincoln and Johnson* 16 (1911) (hereinafter, "Welles, *Diary*").

156. 4 Naval Records Office, *Official Records of the Rebellion* 266–68.

157. 7 Bemis, *The American Secretaries of State and Their Diplomacy* 33.

158. 1 Welles, *Diary* 16–18, 21. *See also* Welles's remarks upon the memorial address of Charles Francis Adams on the late W.H. Seward in G. Welles, *Lincoln and Seward* 60–62 (1874; reprint, 1969).

159. 1 Welles, *Diary* 22–23.

160. *Id.* 24.

161. *Id.* 23–25; 4 Naval Records Office, *Official Records of the Rebellion* 112, 250.

162. *See* the appraisal of Seward's fiasco in G. Van Deusen, *William Henry Seward* 287 (1967).

163. 7 Bemis, *The American Secretaries of State and Their Diplomacy* 34.

164. 2 Bancroft, *Seward* 130 n.5; 1 Welles, *Diary* 17–18.

165. Russell to Palmerston, 17 September 1862, in 7 Bemis, *The American Secretaries of State and Their Diplomacy* 87–88.

166. *Id.* 88–89.

167. Lyons to Russell, 24 February 1863 and 10 March 1863, in 2 E. Adams, *Great Britain and the American Civil War* 126 (1925).

168. 33 *Congressional Globe* 887.

169. *Id.* 1359–60.

170. *Id.* 1497–98.

171. *Id.* 1498.

172. Senate, 31 to 5; House, 103 to 28, 5 March 1863, *id.* 1498, 1541.

173. 35 *Congressional Globe* 275–76.

174. 29 *Congressional Globe Appendix* 1, 3. *United States v. Amistad*, 40 U.S. (15 Peters) 518 (1840).

175. 29 *Congressional Globe* 376.

176. 30 *Congressional Globe Appendix* 4–5.

177. *Id.* 5.

178. 27 *Congressional Globe* 2432.

179. *Id.*

180. *Id.* 2433.

181. *Id.* 2472.
182. *Id.* 2786.
183. *Id.* 2787.
184. *Id.* 2787, 2804.
185. *Id.* 2729.
186. *See supra* p. 183.
187. 27 *Congressional Globe* 1504–05.
188. *Id.* 1524.
189. *Id.* 1550.
190. *Id.* 1779.
191. *Id.* 1811.
192. *Id.* 876.
193. *See also* 7 *Messages and Papers* 3012; 27 *Congressional Globe* 522, 532–35, 821, 1293.
194. 27 *Congressional Globe Appendix* 6.
195. 27 *Congressional Globe* 302.
196. *Id.* 303.
197. *Id.* 351.
198. *Id.* 352–53, 1435, 1535; 28 *Congressional Globe* 448, 627, 634, 1034; 30 *Congressional Globe* 638, 880, 908–09.
199. 33 *Congressional Globe Appendix* 1.
200. 34 *Congressional Globe* 1408.
201. *Id.* 1900.
202. *Id.* 2481.
203. *Id.* 2542, 2741, 2776.
204. McDougall, 14 June 1864, *id.* 2931, 3157–58; Davis, 27 June 1864, *id.* 3309.
205. 35 *Congressional Globe* 48.
206. *Supra* p. 207.
207. 35 *Congressional Globe* 67.
208. *Id.* 66, 67.
209. 36 *Congressional Globe* 811.
210. 38 *Congressional Globe* 509, 511, 600–01.
211. *Id.* 696, 720.
212. Chapter 2, pp. 106–11.
213. Bailey, *A Diplomatic History of the American People* 330.
214. Cohen, "Charles Sumner and the *Trent* Affair," 22 *Journal of Southern History* 205, 207 (1956).
215. *Id.* 207–11.
216. 32 *Congressional Globe* 186, 207–10.
217. 35 *Congressional Globe* 36, 57.
218. 34 *Congressional Globe* 9, 19, 1387, 2298, 2333, 2338, 2364, 2371, 2452–53, 2456, 2476, 2484, 2502, 2509.
219. 35 *Congressional Globe* 32, 96.
220. *Id.* 311, 315, 596.
221. *Id.* 314.
222. Chapter 2, p. 135.

223. 38 *Congressional Globe* 710, 715, 756–57, 761.
224. *Id.* 667, 669, 687.
225. *Id.* 667–69.
226. Remarks of Iowa Senator James Harlan, *id.* 678.
227. Golder, "The Purchase of Alaska," 25 *American History Review* 424 (1920).
228. Cadwalader Washburn, in 39 *Congressional Globe Appendix* 393; Jehu Baker (R. Ill.), 39 *Congressional Globe* 607.
229. 39 *Congressional Globe Appendix* 486.
230. 39 *Congressional Globe* 382–83.
231. Representative Nathaniel Banks (R. Mass.), *id.* 385; Representative Leonard Myers, *id.* 3661.
232. Representative William Higby (R. Cal.), *id.* 3805.
233. *Id.* 3805, 3813; 39 *Congressional Globe Appendix* 377.
234. 2 Curtis, *Life of James Buchanan* 297ff (1883).
235. Klein, *President James Buchanan* 358–59 (1962).
236. 9 *Opinions of the Attorney General* 518, 20 November 1860.
237. *Id.*
238. *Id.* 524.
239. *Id.* 523.
240. 7 *Messages and Papers* 3157, 3186.
241. Black to Buchanan, 18 January 1861, Black Manuscripts, Library of Congress.
242. 30 *Congressional Globe* 295, 296.
243. 30 *Congressional Globe* 1293–94.
244. *Id.*
245. 30 *Congressional Globe* 249.
246. *Id.* 354.
247. *Id.* 366, 889, 891.
248. *Id.* 917.
249. Message, 1 March 1861, 30 *Congressional Globe* 1414.
250. *Id.*
251. Benjamin P. Thomas, *Abraham Lincoln, A Biography* 378 (1952).
252. Bates to Lincoln, 5 July 1861, Papers of Abraham Lincoln, Series 1, Reel 23, Manuscript Division, LC.
253. Art. I, §9, cl. 2.
254. 32 *Congressional Globe* 3183–84.
255. 33 *Congressional Globe* 1208.
256. 33 *Congressional Globe Appendix* 217.
257. 31 *Congressional Globe* 40.
258. *Id.* 67.
259. *Id.* 47–48.
260. *Id.* 67.
261. *Id.* 138.
262. *Id.* 139.
263. *Id.* 290.
264. *Id.* 293–95.

265. *Id.* 392.
266. *Id.* 442, 449.
267. *Id.* 221, 227, 244. *Compare* debates over Polk's appointment powers, Chapter 2, *supra,* pp. 89–90.
268. 31 *Congressional Globe* 156, 209.
269. *Id.* 351, 391, 430.
270. *Id.* 313, 331.
271. *Id.* 72, 77.
272. *Id.* 205, 221.
273. *Id.* 273.
274. 34 *Congressional Globe* 2025–26.
275. *Id.* 2054–55.
276. *Id.* 2207.
277. 32 *Congressional Globe* 5, 6.
278. *Id.* 1102, 2363.
279. § 8, paragraph 11.
280. 32 *Congressional Globe* 2918ff.
281. *Id.* 2972.
282. 8 *Messages and Papers* 3297–99.
283. 33 *Congressional Globe* 92.
284. 31 *Congressional Globe* 222–23.
285. 33 *Congressional Globe* 80–81.
286. 33 *Congressional Globe Appendix* 89, 90.
287. *E.g.,* S. 460, 33 *Congressional Globe* 245, 269, 1501; S. 434, *id.* 52, 138, 302.
288. *Id.* 351.
289. *Id.* 785.
290. *Id.* 796.
291. 34 *Congressional Globe* 572.
292. 36 *Congressional Globe* 78, 331.
293. *Id.* 271.
294. *Id.*
295. *Id.* 272–73.
296. *Id.* 871–72 (Rep. Joseph Defrees (R. Ind.)).
297. *Id.* 661.
298. *See* Chapter 2, p. 154.
299. 36 *Congressional Globe* 786.
300. *Id.* 331, 1617.
301. 37 *Congressional Globe* 1440, 1453 (Senator Doolittle, Senator Willard Saulsbury).
302. *E.g., id.* 1078 (Rep. Francis Le Blond (D. Oh.)).
303. *Id.* 1467, 1469, 1315–16, 1319–20, 1356, 1399–1400.
304. *See* Veto Message, 2 March 1867, 8 *Messages and Papers* 3696, 3698.
305. *Id.* 3702.
306. *Id.* 3703.
307. 37 *Congressional Globe Appendix* 197–98; Act of March 2, 1867, 14 Stat. 428.
308. 14 Stat. 485.

309. H.R. 1126, 37 *Congressional Globe* 1351–52.

310. *Id.* 1354.

311. *Id.* 1355.

312. *Id.* 1404.

313. *Id.* 1855, 14 Stat. 485, 486–87.

314. 3 Welles, *Diary* 8–11.

315. 2 *The Diary of Orville Hickman Browning* 34 (T.C. Pease and J.G. Randall, eds., Springfield, Ill.: 1925–33); 3 Welles, *Diary* 58; Edward McPherson, *Political History of the United States during the Period of Reconstruction* 178 (text of protest) (1864).

316. 2 G. Boutwell, *Reminiscences of Sixty Years in Public Affairs* 107–08 (1902).

317. 39 *Congressional Globe* 572.

318. *Id.*

319. *Id.* 512, 571–72, 585, 709.

320. *Id.* 574.

321. *Id.* 549–50 (John Farnsworth (R. Ill.)); 577 (William Loughridge (R. Ia.)).

322. 27 *Congressional Globe* 1704.

323. 7 *Messages and Papers of the Presidents* 2980 (1897 ed.).

324. 27 *Congressional Globe* 1704.

325. *Id.* 1782, 1929.

326. 7 *Messages and Papers* 2980.

327. 27 *Congressional Globe* 1704.

328. Buchanan to Toucey, 5 August 1858, 10 *The Works of James Buchanan* 226–27 (J. Moore, ed.).

329. *Id.*

330. 27 *Congressional Globe* 624, 1704.

331. *Id.* 1963.

332. *Id.* 2546.

333. 28 *Congressional Globe Appendix* 18.

334. 28 *Congressional Globe* 1605.

335. *Id.* 1606.

336. *See* arguments of William H. Seward on Cuba appropriation, *supra* p. 194.

337. 28 *Congressional Globe* 1605.

338. *Id.*

339. *Id.* 1531, 1609, 1621, 1669.

340. 7 *Messages and Papers* 3091; 29 *Congressional Globe Appendix* 3.

341. 27 *Congressional Globe* 2452.

342. *Id.* 2496.

343. *Id.* 2496, 2497.

344. *Id.* 2496.

345. *Id.* 2497; *see* text, *id.* 2564.

346. *Id.* 2564.

347. *Id.* 2744.

348. *Id.* 2746.

349. *Id.*

350. *Id.* 2748.

351. *Id.*

352. *Id.*

353. *Id.*

354. 27 *Congressional Globe Appendix* 1, 4 (8 December 1857); 27 *Congressional Globe* 216–17.

355. 27 *Congressional Globe* 216–17.

356. *Id.* 216.

357. *Id.*

358. *Id.* 217.

359. *Id.*

360. 27 *Congressional Globe Appendix* 4 (annual message, 8 December 1857).

361. 27 *Congressional Globe* 217.

362. *Id.* 220.

363. *Id.* 221.

364. Clingman, 17 *Congressional Globe* 179; Moore, 27 *Congressional Globe* 259.

365. 27 *Congressional Globe* 362.

366. *Id.* 278.

367. *Id.* 209.

368. *Id.* 275.

369. *Id.* 378.

370. 28 *Congressional Globe Appendix* 4–5; 29 *Congressional Globe Appendix* 4.

371. 29 *Congressional Globe Appendix* 4.

372. *Id.* 5.

373. 29 *Congressional Globe* 326–27.

374. *Id.*

375. Emphasis supplied; *id.* 1243.

376. 2 Grant, *Personal Memoirs* 545 (1885–86).

377. Bancroft 434; H.M. McCulloch, *Men and Measures of Half a Century* 387 (1888); J. Callahan, *American Foreign Policy in Mexican Relations* 305 (1932).

378. Perkins, *The Monroe Doctrine, 1826–1867* 470, 472–73; J. Rippy, *The U.S. and Mexico* 268 (1941); *Papers of Andrew Johnson*, Ser. 1, Reel 18, Library of Congress (authorization from General Marrano Escobedo to recruit armed troops in foreign countries).

379. J.M. Schofield, *Forty-six Years in the Army* 329 (1897).

380. *Id.* 380.

381. Perkins 471.

382. NARS, M-99, roll 70 (26 July 1875); Perkins 471.

383. J. McDonough, *Schofield: Union General In the Civil War and Reconstruction* 162 (1972); Rippy 269–70; Schofield 383.

384. Johnson to Napoleon III, 10 January 1866, *Papers of Andrew Johnson*, Manuscript Division, Library of Congress microfilm, Ser. 1, Reel 19; Bancroft 437–38; Van Deusen, 492.

385. Rippy 270; 36 *Congressional Globe* 1188, 2946, 3217–18, 3251 (39th Cong., 1st Sess.).

CHAPTER 4: THE EXECUTIVE CHALLENGE TO CONGRESSIONAL GOVERNMENT, 1869–1901

1. 13 Stat. 437.
2. 9 *Congressional Record* 107, 120 (1874).
3. *Id.* 594, 596.
4. *Id.* 106.
5. *Id.* 269–70.
6. 10 *Messages and Papers* 4475, 4469–80, 4481–84.
7. 9 *Congressional Record* 1928, 1943.
8. *Id.* 2144, 2176, 2180, 2199–2243.
9. *Id.* 1092–95 (125–90).
10. *Id.* 1147, 1148, 1149.
11. *Id.* 1146, 1151, 1152.
12. *Id.* 1178–86 *passim.*
13. *Id.* 1189 (33 to 23), 1267ff.
14. *Id.* 267.
15. *Id.* 1298–99 (128–97).
16. 44 *Congressional Globe* 244.
17. 44 *Congressional Globe Appendix* 71.
18. *See* Chapter 3, pp. 213–20.
19. Pierce, *supra* p. 164.
20. Johnson, *supra*, p. 182.
21. Polk, *supra* p. 143; McKinley, *supra* p. 318.
22. 44 *Congressional Globe Appendix* 49.
23. *Id.* 50.
24. 44 *Congressional Globe* 380–81.
25. *Id.* 477–78.
26. *Id.* 522, 709 (Senate vote).
27. 27 *Congressional Record* 430, 440–42.
28. *Id.* 446, 447.
29. *Id.* 634.
30. *Id.* 1358.
31. *Id.* 1902.
32. 31 *Congressional Record* 2620–21 (House); *id.* 2631–32 (Senate).
33. *Id.* 2602–20 *passim.*
34. *Id.* 3424.
35. *Id.* 3414–15, 3417.
36. *Supra* Chapter 1, p. 23.
37. *See supra* p. 267.
38. *See supra* p. 260.
39. 7 *Congressional Record* 120.
40. *Id.*
41. 10 *Messages and Papers* 4410, 4420.
42. *Id.*
43. 7 *Congressional Record* 102.

44. *Id.* 104, 105.
45. 21 *Congressional Record* 6880 (1 July 1890, qualified); *id.* 7078 (9 July 1890).
46. *Id.* 6880.
47. *Id.* 7073.
48. *Id.* 7626.
49. *Id.* 956; correspondence set forth in H.R. Exec. Doc. No. 144, 51st Cong., 2d Sess.
50. 29 *Congressional Record* 132, 168.
51. *Id.* 163.
52. 15 Stat. 223, 224 (Act of July 27, 1868).
53. *Id.* §3; 29 *Congressional Record* 166.
54. *Id.* 166; *id.* 168 (Senate passage, 15 December 1896).
55. 9 *Congressional Record* 535, 697, 681.
56. *Id.* 679.
57. *See* 9 *Messages and Papers* 3962ff.; 10 *Messages and Papers* 4210ff.
58. 4 *Congressional Record* 2158 (introduced by Joseph Blackburn (D. Ky.)).
59. 10 *Messages and Papers* 4315, 4316.
60. 17 *Congressional Record* 1585.
61. *Id.* 1587.
62. *Id.* 1901–02.
63. *Id.*
64. *Id.* 2810–14.
65. R. Tugwell, *Grover Cleveland* 133 (1968).
66. National Archives Microfilm, Department of State, *Diplomatic Instructions 1801–1906,* M77, roll 100 (Blaine to Stevens (8 November 1892), no. 62, confidential).
67. 30 *Congressional Record* 1143.
68. *Id.* 1147—49.
69. *Id.* 1143.
70. *Id.* 1147–49.
71. *Id.* 351, 463, 564, 575, 576, 580, 1004, 1119, 2524, 2629, 2753, 2940.
72. 14 *Messages and Papers* 6277, 6278.
73. 31 *Congressional Record* 3500, 3514, 3822.
74. 33 *Congressional Record* 853, 894–95.
75. *Id.* 2523–24 (5 March 1900); *id.* 3353 (27 March 1900); *id.* 4370 (18 April 1900).
76. Sofaer, *Origins* 79, 80.
77. Chapter 3, p. 190; 10 *Congressional Record* 968, 974, 1659; 11 *Congressional Record* 227.
78. H.R. 1009, 2 *Congressional Record* 1024 (43d Cong., 1st Sess.).
79. *Id.*
80. *Id.*
81. *Id.* 1023.
82. Tugwell, *Grover Cleveland* 237.
83. *Id.* 238.
84. *Id.*

85. 27 *Congressional Record* 157.

86. *Id.*

87. 13 *Messages and Papers* 5988; 27 *Congressional Record* 252.

88. 29 *Congressional Record* 500.

89. *Id.* 602–03, 578; H.R. Docs. 180, 237, 54th Cong., 2d Sess. (1897).

90. *E.g.,* 13 *Congressional Record* 398 (condition of fortifications); *id.* 546 (acquisition of sites to protect the Rio Grande frontier).

91. *E.g., id.* 687, 1245, 4556 (all related to the Clayton-Bulwer treaty).

92. 16 *Congressional Record* 7.

93. *Id.* 231 (unqualified, 15 December 1884).

94. *Id.* 299 (17 December 1884); *see also supra* p. 296.

95. S. Exec. Doc. No. 68, 50th Cong., 2d Sess.; 20 *Congressional Record* 830.

96. 20 *Congressional Record Appendix* 2–9.

97. 20 *Congressional Record* 830; *see also* S. Exec. Doc. No. 69 cited *supra,* p. 267 n.

98. 20 *Congressional Record* 1371 (Senate); *id.* 1884 (House).

99. *Id.* 1335–37 (Reagan); *id.* 1291 (Sherman).

100. 7 Bemis, *The American Secretaries of State and Their Diplomacy* 275.

101. 11 *Messages and Papers* 4684.

102. *Id.* 4684–85.

103. *Id.* 4, 7; 10 *Messages and Papers* 4573.

104. 11 *Congressional Record* 2101–05.

105. *Id.* 2101.

106. *Id.* 2105.

107. *Id.* 2099, 2107, 2154, 2158.

108. *Id.* 2193 (114 to 85, House).

109. 8 Bemis, *The American Secretaries of State and Their Diplomacy* ch. 1.

110. 11 *Messages and Papers* 4757, 4761.

111. 8 Bemis, *The American Secretaries of State and Their Diplomacy* 35–39.

112. *See supra* p. 311.

113. 13 *Messages and Papers, supra* 5615, 5621.

114. Chilean Foreign Minister Matta's note, enclosed in Egan to Blaine, 10 to 14 November 1891, in H.R. Exec. Doc. No. 91 at 137–40; Egan to Blaine, 20 November 1891, *id.* 147–48.

115. Egan to Blaine, *id.* 181–83; A. Tyler, *The Foreign Policy of James G. Blaine* 152 (1965).

116. H.R. Exec. Doc. 91, pp. 188, 288 (letters of 12 and 18 January 1892).

117. H.R. Exec. Doc. 91, p. 229 (20 January 1892).

118. *See supra* p. 272 n.

119. H.R. Exec. Doc. No. 91, pp. 193–94.

120. 13 *Messages and Papers* 5650ff., 5661 (25 January 1892).

121. Tyler, *The Foreign Policy of James G. Blaine* 159.

122. A. Volwiler, "American Foreign Policy, 1889–1893," 79 *American Philosophical Society Proceedings* 643, 646 (1938).

123. Egan to Blaine, 25 January 1892, H.R. Exec. Doc. 91 (pt. 2), pp 7-10.

124. 13 *Messages and Papers* 5662; 1892 *Papers Relating to the Foreign Relations of the United States* 64–67.

125. 23 *Congressional Record* 549.

126. 26 *Congressional Record* 127–32, 189–94, 204–06 (debate).

127. *Id.* 434, 2408–21.

128. *Supra* p. 318.

129. *See supra* p. 308.

130. 1895 *Papers Relating to the Foreign Relations of the United States* 564–65 (Salisbury to Pauncefote, 26 November 1895).

131. 14 *Messages and Papers* 6064.

132. G. Young, "The Influence of Politics on American Diplomacy during Cleveland's Administration," p. 217 (unpublished Ph.D. dissertation, 1939) (hereinafter, "Young, 'The Influence of Politics'").

133. 14 *Messages and Papers* 6087, 6090.

134. 28 *Congressional Record* 160–61, 234–35, 240, 242–45, 256, 259.

135. Tugwell, *Grover Cleveland* 248.

136. Bailey, *A Diplomatic History of the American People* 447ff; D. Perkins, *The Monroe Doctrine, 1826–1867* 187–88, 194–98 (1965); Young, "The Influence of Politics," p. 242.

137. 14 *Congressional Record* 1291; 11 *Messages and Papers* 4693 (text of message).

138. 14 *Congressional Record* 1299 (Representative Samuel Cox (D. N.Y.)); *id.* 1305 (Representative Benjamin Wilson (D. W.Va.)).

139. *Id.* 1307; 11 *Messages and Papers* 4761.

140. 20 *Congressional Record* 550.

141. *Id.* 567–68.

142. *Id.* 2698.

143. 124 U.S. 190, 194 (1888).

144. 22 *Congressional Record* 1123, 2228.

145. *Id.* 3410; for full debates, *see id.* 2224ff., 2970ff., and 3052ff.

146. 24 *Congressional Record* 1514.

147. *Id.* 1519, 1526.

148. *E.g.,* Shelby Cullom (R. Ill.), 29 *Congressional Record* 61.

149. *Id.* 355.

150. *Id.* 357.

151. *Id.* 745–48.

152. *Id.* 654.

153. 30 *Congressional Record* 615.

154. *Id.* 1153 (William Lindsay, D. Ky.).

155. *Id.* 1169–70.

156. *Id.* 1093, 1095; *id.* 562–63, 615–17, 620–21, 763, 946, 954–55, 994, 996–97, 999–1000, 1093–1101, 1153, 1169, 1172–74, 1178–86, 1459, 2936–37 (debates).

157. *Id.* 1186.

158. *Id.* 1080.

159. 31 *Congressional Record* 730, 733, 738–39.

160. *Id.* 2087 (sustained, 51–5); *id.* 2073–85 (entire debate).

161. *Id.* 3821–22.

162. *Id.* 4040.

163. *See* discussion of the shaping of these resolutions, *supra* p. 297.

164. 1 *Treaties, Conventions, International Acts, Protocols, and Agreements between the United States and Other Powers, 1776–1909*, 234–36 (Malloy ed. 1910) (hereinafter *"Treaties, Conventions* (Malloy ed.)"); 8 *Congressional Record* 1268.

165. *Id.* 1264, 1305, 1306.

166. *Id.* 1796–97.

167. 10 *Messages and Papers* 4466, 4471.

168. 19 *Congressional Record* 1580; concurring, John Morgan, *id.* 1619.

169. *Id.* 6104, 7294, 7759, 7774.

170. 25 *Congressional Record* 1161.

171. *Id.* 2483.

172. 30 *Congressional Record* 1036 (Utah governor and legislature, 12 May 1897); *id.* 1308 (citizens of Philadelphia, 28 May 1897); *id.* 2085 (citizens of North Carolina, 28 June 1897); *id.* 2527 (Knights of Labor in Nebraska, 8 July 1897).

173. 19 *Congressional Record* 2393, 4670.

174. 28 *Congressional Record* 959.

175. *Id.* 961 (Blanchard); *id.* 962 (Frye).

176. *Id.* 963.

177. *Id.*

178. *Id.*

179. *Id.* 1001 (Quigg); *id.* 1016 (Taft).

180. *Id.* 1004, 1010 (remarks on constitutionality, Representatives Robert Hitt and Robert Adams, Jr.).

181. Act of March 2, 1889, 25 Stat. 1009; *see also* 20 *Congressional Record* 2614, 1646.

182. 12 *Messages and Papers* 5450.

183. Windom to Shepard, 28 May 1889 in B. Harrison, *Papers,* ser. 1, reel 20 (Manuscript Division, Library of Congress).

184. 12 *Messages and Papers* 5533; Windom to Shepard, 26 May 1890, Harrison, *Papers,* ser. 1, reel 27.

185. Pauncefote to Blaine, 14 June 1890, in 1890 *Papers Relating to the Foreign Relations of the United States* 435–36. *See also* C. Tansill, *Canadian-American Relations, 1875–1911* 314–15 (1938).

186. Blaine to Pauncefote, 17 December 1890, 1890 *Papers Relating to the Foreign Relations of the United States* 477–501.

187. 19 *Congressional Record* 7904. Act of March 3, 1887 (the Retaliatory Act).

188. *Id.* 6253.

189. *Id.* 6901.

190. *Id.* 7167.

191. *Id.* 7900.

192. *Id.* 7901.

193. *Id.* 7909–10.

194. *Id.* 8439.

195. *See supra* pp. 278–82.

196. Tugwell, *Grover Cleveland* 276–81 *passim*.

197. *E.g.*, 30 *Congressional Record* 2452, 2581, 2754, 2803, discussing S. Res. 62.

198. *Id.* 616.

199. *Id.* 1170, 1184–85.

200. 28 *Congressional Record* 2120.

201. *Id.* 2056, 2109–10.

202. *Id.* 1978.

203. *Id.* 108–09, S. Res. 12.

204. *Id.* 529–31 (9 January 1896, Lucien Baker, R. Kan.); *id.* 783 (20 January 1896, Cushman K. Davis, R. Minn.).

205. 31 *Congressional Record* 5912, 6571.

206. *Id.* 6635.

207. *Id.* 6368 (accord, Senator William Stewart (R. Nev.)).

208. 33 *Congressional Record* 6510–11.

209. *Id.* 1304–05.

210. *Id.* 1497.

211. *Id.* 2616.

212. 15 *Messages and Papers* 6580, 6581, 6582, 6585.

213. *Supra* pp. 325–26.

214. 6 *Messages and Papers* 2564ff.

215. 11 *Congressional Record* 6, 356, 357, 361, 629, 689, 1853 (army size); *id.* 7, 73, 74, 178, 287, 1977, 2293, 2298 (fortifications, artillery).

216. Senate enthusiasm was curbed, however, when a compromise figure was adopted in conference. *Id.* 790, 791, 814, 904, 964–65, 1200, 1710.

217. 17 *Congressional Record* 7503 (Senate passage, 30 July 1886; House concurrence in amendments, 2 August 1886).

218. *Id.* 7154.

219. *Id.* 7154, 7647.

220. 23 *Congressional Record* 3390.

221. 29 *Congressional Record* 302.

222. *Id.* 303.

223. 6 *Congressional Record* 287, 288, 307–10, 322–23, 334–35.

224. *Id.* 291.

225. *Id.* 331.

226. *E.g.*, William Phillips (R. Kan.), *id.* 292.

227. *Id.* 416.

228. *Id.* 514, 560.

229. *Id.* 295.

230. *Id.*

231. *Id.* 296.

232. Schleicher's amendments were accepted, and a clause prohibiting recruitment above the army's current size was stricken. *Id.* 295, 308; *see also id.* 311, where recruitment was limited, however, to the statutory maximum of 25,000.

233. H.R. 4867; House, 7 *Congressional Record* 3877; Senate, *id.* 4303–04; 20 Stat. 151, 152.

234. 7 *Congressional Record* 4240.

235. *Id.* 4240, 4241, 4295.

236. 8 *Congressional Record* 5.

237. *Id.* 125.

238. *Id.* 2287.

239. H.R. 2175, 9 *Congressional Record* 2243.

240. *See supra* pp. 248–50.

241. 10 *Congressional Record* 2172, 2173.

242. *See* expression of this legal theory by Senator George F. Edmunds (R. Vt.), 9 *Congressional Record* 1124, 1178, 1180, 1184.

243. 100 U.S. 371, 394–95, 404; *see also* 10 *Congressional Record* 2293, 2294.

244. *Id.* 2338, 2360, 2364, 2639, 2641, 2648, 2987.

245. 9 *Congressional Record* 1609.

246. *Id.* 1465, 1466, 1606, 1659, 1683, 1862, 1911, 1948.

247. S. 554 and H.R. 1382, introduced simultaneously by Senator William W. Eaton (D. Conn.) and Representative George W. Ladd (D. Me.); 9 *Congressional Record* 1043.

248. *Id.* 1151, 1152, 1146.

249. *Id.* 1124, 1178, 1180, 1184.

250. House, 125 to 90, *id.* 1092, 1095; and Senate, 33 to 23, *id.* 1098–99, 1189.

251. *Id.* 1267.

252. *Id.* 1298, 1299.

253. 10 *Messages and Papers* 4624, 4639.

254. 11 *Messages and Papers* 4688, 4689.

255. 13 *Congressional Record* 3467.

256. *Supra* p. 266.

257. Chambers to Chandler, 9 January 1885, 72 W. Chandler, *Papers* (Manuscript Division, Library of Congress).

258. 14 *Messages and Papers* 6281, 6282; 32 *Congressional Record* 3699–3703.

259. 31 *Congressional Record* 3777.

260. *Id.* 3782.

261. *Id.* 3784, 3814, 1949, 3980–81.

262. *Id.* 3973, 3894.

263. *Id.* 3993.

264. *Supra* p. 279; 31 *Congressional Record* 3699–3702.

265. *Id.* 3732–33.

266. 10 *Messages and Papers* 4196; 2 *Congressional Record* 14; Secretary of the Navy George M. Robeson to Speaker of the House, and Robeson to James Garfield, chairman of the Committee on Appropriations, *id.* 180.

267. 10 *Messages and Papers* 4196.

268. 2 *Congressional Record* 126.

269. *E.g.,* Pennsylvania's Robert Speer (D.) and Eugene Hale (R. Me.), *id.* 128.

270. 2 *Congressional Record* 129.

271. *Id.* 184.

272. *Id.* 185.

273. *Id.* 184, 185.
274. *E.g.,* remarks of Justin Morrill (R. Vt.), *id.* 262.
275. *Id.* 265.
276. *Id.* 595–96.
277. *Id.* 498.
278. *Id.* 597.
279. *Id.*
280. *Id.* 598.
281. Nevins, *Hamilton Fish: The Inner History of the Grant Administration* 691.
282. Debate, 4 *Congressional Record* 4523, 4526.
283. H.R. Rep. No. 701, 45th Cong., 2d Sess. 241 (Ser. 1824).
284. H.R. Exec. Doc. No. 1, 45th Cong., 3d Sess. 533 (Ser. 1842, pt. I).
285. 7 *Congressional Record* 4; 10 *Messages and Papers* 4420.
286. 7 *Congressional Record* 102.
287. *Id.* 609 (letter of 27 June 1878).
288. 8 *Congressional Record* 4.
289. S. Exec. Doc. No. 90, 44th Cong., 1st Sess.
290. *See* 6 *Congressional Record* 348–51.
291. Letter, Memphis attorney Butler P. Anderson to Postmaster General D.M. Key, 14 July 1877, National Archives Microfilm, Department of War, *Records of the Secretary of War,* RG 107.
292. Letter No. 8945, 30 October 1877, *id.*
293. 6 *Congressional Record* 286, 330, 333.
294. *Id.* 330.
295. *Id.* 348 (1877).
296. *Id.* 347–48.
297. *Id.* (The secretary presented some statutory arguments to support the recruitment order.)
298. *Id.* 348.
299. *Id.*
300. *Id.* 349.
301. *Supra* Chapter 3, pp. 217–20.
302. 6 *Congressional Record* 514, 560.
303. W. Russ, *The Hawaiian Revolution, 1893–1894* 23 (1959).
304. 2 *Report of the [Senate] Committee on Foreign Relations with Accompanying Testimony and Executive Documents from January 1, 1893, to March 10, 1894* 1123, 1125, 1161–62, 1185, 1191 (1894) (hereinafter, *"Report of the Committee on Foreign Relations"*), Dispatch No. 20 (20 March 1890); Dispatch No. 46 (8 February 1892); Dispatch No. 74, "Confidential."
305. *Id.* 1162–63, Dispatch No. 48 (8 March 1892).
306. *See* Sofaer, *Origins* 346–47.
307. 3 S. Dole, *Memoirs of the Hawaiian Revolution* 85 (1936); 1 L. Thurston, *Memoirs of the Hawaiian Revolution* 249 (1936).
308. M. Tate, *The United States and the Hawaiian Kingdom: A Political History* 163-67 (1965); 2 *Report of the Committee on Foreign Relations* 1770 (statement of W.O. Smith, document no. 48, Blount Report); 1 *Report of the Committee on Foreign Relations* 448 (affidavit of William Wilder).

309. 2 *Report of the Committee on Foreign Relations* 1016 (enclosed in Stevens to Foster, 18 January 1893).

310. *Id.* 1018, 1196, 1337, 1026; Russ, *The Hawaiian Revolution* 93, 95.

311. 2 *Report of the Committee on Foreign Relations* 1207; 1050. *See also* National Archives Microfilm, Department of State, *Diplomatic Instructions,* M77, roll 100 (Foster to Stevens, 28 January, 11 February 1893).

312. 13 *Messages and Papers* 5783.

313. 2 *Report of the Committee on Foreign Relations* 1007.

314. Russ, *Hawaiian Revolution* 143; 13 *Messages and Papers* 5825.

315. Bailey, *A Diplomatic History of the American People* 432, 433.

316. C. Rogers, *The Brazilian Insurrection, 1894 Report of the U.S. Navigation Bureau* 380 (1895); 1893 *Papers Relating to the Foreign Relations of the United States* (letters to and from U.S. Minister to Brazil Thomas Thompson and Secretary of State Walter Q. Gresham, 2, 11, and 13 October and 7 December 1893).

317. National Archives Microfilm, Department of the Navy, *Area File 1775–1910,* M625, roll 27 (Benham to Secretary of the Navy Hillary Herbert, 31 January 1894).

318. *Id.*

319. An eyewitness account of the incident is presented in Rogers, *The Brazilian Insurrection, 1894 Report of the U.S. Navigation Bureau.*

320. *Papers Relating to the Foreign Relations of the United States* (Gresham to Thompson, 1 February 1894); 26 *Congressional Record* 1825.

321. *Papers Relating to the Foreign Relations of the United States* (Thompson to Gresham, 1 November 1893).

322. National Archives Microfilm, Department of the Navy, *Area Collection,* M625, roll 26 (Picking to Navy Department, 28 December 1893).

323. *Papers Relating to the Foreign Relations of the United States* (Gresham to Thompson, 11 January 1894).

324. W. LeFeber, *The New Empire* 211 (1963).

325. 13 *Messages and Papers* 5867.

326. *Id.* 5956, 5973.

327. *Id.* 5972, 5973.

328. *Hansard's Parliamentary Debates,* 23 November 1893, p. 1554; 8 December 1893, p. 1609; 2 January 1894, pp. 655–56; 5 January 1894, pp. 925–26; 11 January 1894, pp. 1346–47; 12 January 1894, pp. 1472–73; 12 February 1894, pp. 285–86; 20 February 1894, p. 849; 13 February 1894, pp. 387–88; 1 March 1894, p. 1134.

329. *See supra* p. 272. For proceedings on the charge of violation of U.S. neutrality laws see *United States v. The Steamship Itata* and *United States v. Trumbull,* 48 F. Rep. 99 (1891).

330. W. Sherman, *The Diplomatic and Commercial Relations of the United States and Chile, 1820–1914* 153 (1926).

331. Hardy, "The *Itata* Incident," 5 *Hispanic American Historical Review* 214 (1922); 2 J. Foster, *Diplomatic Memoirs* 29 (1909).

332. H.R. Exec. Doc. No. 91, 52d Cong., 1st Sess. 250.

333. Sherman, *The Diplomatic and Commercial Relations of the United States and Chile* 155.

334. S. Exec. Doc. 34, 41st Cong., 3rd Sess. 9, 10.

335. 43 *Congressional Globe* 431.

336. *Id.* 235–36, 253, 294.

337. *Id.* 194, 196.

338. *Id.* 298, 300.

339. 44 *Congressional Globe Appendix* 52–53.

340. 44 *Congressional Globe* 306.

341. 44 *Congressional Globe Appendix* 64.

342. *Id.* 43.

343. *Id.* 64–65.

344. 44 *Congressional Globe* 327. *See* Chapter 1, p. 000; Chapter 2, p. 000.

345. 44 *Congressional Globe* 327–28.

346. *See* Chapter 1, pp. 77–81.

347. 44 *Congressional Globe* 329.

348. J. Offner, "President McKinley and the Origins of the Spanish American War," pp. 25–26 (unpublished Ph.D. dissertation, 1957).

349. *Id.* 26–27; E. May, *Imperial Democracy: Emergence of America* 87 (1961).

350. May, *Imperial Democracy: Emergence of America* 84–85; 31 *Congressional Record* 2916–19 (Senator Redfield Proctor's indictment of suffering in Cuban concentration camps).

351. *Id.* 3985 (Senator George C. Perkins, R. Calif.; Senator John M. Thurston, R. Neb.); *id.* 3986.

352. L. Gould, *The Presidency of William McKinley* 189 (1980).

353. *See supra* pp. 298–99.

354. 14 *Messages and Papers* 6322.

355. Bemis, *A Diplomatic History of the American People* 505; Treaty of Paris, art. XVI, 10 December 1898; 2 *Treaties, Conventions* (Malloy ed.) 1690, 1695.

356. Bailey, *A Diplomatic History of the American People* 501.

357. H. Wayne Morgan, *America's Road to Empire* 97–99 (1965).

358. D. Trask, *The War with Spain in 1898*, at 458 (1981).

359. 32 *Congressional Record* 733 (Bacon); *id.* 503 (Hoar).

360. *Id.* 562.

361. *Id.;* complete debate, *id.* 562–63.

362. *Id.*

363. 33 *Congressional Record* 959.

364. 32 *Congressional Record* 1420; accord, John Spooner (R. Wis.), id. 1377, 1388.

365. 31 *Senate Executive Journal* 1284, 55th Cong., 3d Sess. (1899).

366. M. Storey and M. Lichauco, *The Conquest of the Philippines, 1898–1925*, at 92, 93 (1926).

367. 32 *Congressional Record* 1483–84.

368. *Id.* 1490.

369. Storey and Lichauco, *The Conquest of the Philippines* 93–95; S. Doc. No. 331, pt. 2, 57th Cong., 1st Sess. 1356. Historian David Trask's conclusion that the United States undoubtedly could have dealt more intelligently with the insurgents appears to be an understatement. Trask, *The War with Spain in 1898* 484.

370. Speech at Pittsburgh, 28 August 1899, in W. McKinley, *Speeches and Addresses of William McKinley* 211 (1900).

371. Storey and Lichauco, *The Conquest of the Philippines* 171.

372. *Id.* 161–62; 2 *Correspondence Relating to the War with Spain. Issued from the Adjutant-General's Department* 1226, 1249 (1902).

373. Storey and Lichauco, *The Conquest of the Philippines* 99; *Review of Reviews* (August 1899), 137–38.

374. Storey and Lichauco, *The Conquest of the Philippines* 99; 33 *Congressional Record* 768.

375. 34 *Congressional Record* 3020. The resolution was introduced by Senator Richard Pettigrew (R. S.Dak.); *see also* discussion *supra* at p. 324 concerning Pettigrew's inquiries into continuation of hostilities with the Filipinos on 5 February 1899, although a truce had been sought.

376. Storey and Lichauco, *The Conquest of the Philippines* 139–44; S. Doc. No. 331, pts. 1–3, 55th Cong., 1st Sess. 1603–05 (evidence).

377. 33 *Congressional Record* 4794.

378. *Id.* 5777; S. Doc. No. 387, 56th Cong., 1st Sess. 1–4.

379. 14 *Messages and Papers* 6415.

380. 34 *Congressional Record* 1549 (remarks on S.R. 155 demanding cessation of hostilities in the Philippines and recognizing the independence of the Philippine people; the resolution never came to a vote).

381. *Fourteen Diamond Rings, Pepke v. United States,* 183 U.S. 176, 178 (1901).

382. Spooner Amendment, Act of March 2, 1901, 31 Stat. 895, 910 (1901).

383. 15 *Messages and Papers* 6584–85, 6614; C. Berdahl, *War Power of the Executive in the United States* 261 (1921).

384. 4 *Congressional Record* 5531, 5533, 5538.

385. 2 T. Smith, *The Life and Letters of James Abram Garfield* 1109 (1925).

386. *See supra* p. 258.

387. 11 *Messages and Papers* 4808; 22 *Congressional Record* 1176, 2508, 3405.

388. 31 *Congressional Record* 344–46.

389. 10 *Messages and Papers* 4601–02; Act of January 16, 1883, 22 Stat. 403.

Glossary

A.S.P.
  American State Papers: Documents, Legislative and Executive (1832–1861) (38 vols.).

Bagehot
  Walter Bagehot, *The English Constitution* (1955).

Bailey, *A Diplomatic History*
  Thomas A. Bailey, *A Diplomatic History of the American People* (6th ed. 1958).

Bancroft, *Seward*
  Frederic Bancroft, *The Life of William H. Seward* (1900).

Bemis, *American Secretaries of State and Their Diplomacy*
  Samuel Flagg Bemis, *The American Secretaries of State and Their Diplomacy* (10 vols. 1927–1929).

Binkley
  Wilfred Binkley, *The President and Congress* (3d ed. 1962).

Chitwood
  Oliver P. Chitwood, *John Tyler, Champion of the Old South* (1964).

Corwin, *The President*
  Edward S. Corwin, *The President: Office and Powers, 1787–1957* (4th ed. 1974).

Curtis, *Webster*
  George T. Curtis, *The Life of Daniel Webster* (1870).

Curtis, *Fox At Bay*
James C. Curtis, *The Fox At Bay* (1970).

Ellsworth
Harry A. Ellsworth, *One Hundred Eighty Landings of the United States Marines* (1974).

Foreign Relations
Papers Relating to the Foreign Relations of the United States, 1861-1931. (71 vols. 1862–1934).

Goldsmith
William Goldsmith, *The Growth of Presidential Power* (1974).

Globe App.
Congressional Globe Appendix, 1833–1873.

Henkin, *Foreign Affairs*
Louis Henkin, *Foreign Affairs and the Constitution* (1972).

LC
The Library of Congress.

McLemore
Richard McLemore, *Franco-American Diplomatic Relations, 1816-1836* (1941).

Malloy, *Treaties*
William Malloy (ed.), *Treaties, Conventions, International Acts, Protocols, and Agreements Between the United States and Other Powers, 1776–1909* (2 vols. 1910).

Manning, *Canadian Relations*
William Manning, ed., *Diplomatic Correspondence of the United States: Canadian Relations, 1784–1860* (1943).

Manning, *Inter-American Affairs*
William Manning, ed., *Diplomatic Correspondence of the United States: Inter-American Affairs, 1831–1860 (Argentina)* (1932).

Mantell, *Johnson and Grant*
Martin Mantell, *Johnson, Grant, and the Politics of Reconstruction* (1973).

Mason
Edward C. Mason, *The Veto Power: Its Origin, Development and Function in the Government of the United States* (1890).

Messages and Papers
   A Compilation of Messages and Papers of the Presidents, 1789–1897
(J. Richardson, ed. 1896–1899) (10 vols.).

Miller, *Treaties*
   Hunter Miller (ed.) *Treaties and Other International Acts of the
United States of America, 1776–1863* (8 vols. 1931–1948).

Moore, Buchanan's *Works*
   John Bassett Moore (ed.) James Buchanan, *Works,* 12 vols. Phila. J.B.
Lippincott Co., 1908–1911.

NAM
   National Archives Microfilm
NARS
   The National Archives and Records Service, Washington, D.C.
Nichols
   Roy F. Nichols, *Franklin Pierce* (1931)

Offut
   Milton Offut, *Protection of Citizens Abroad by the Armed Forces of the
United States* (1928).

Op. Att'y. Gen.
   John L. Lott and James A. Finch (eds.) *Official Opinions of the
Attorneys General of the United States* (36 vols. 1932).

Perkins, 1826–1867
   Dexter Perkins, *The Monroe Doctrine, 1826–1867* (1965).
Perkins, 1867–1907
   Dexter Perkins, *The Monroe Doctrine, 1867–1907* (1937).
Poage
   George Poage, *Henry Clay and the Whig Party* (1936).

Quaife, *Polk's Diary*
   Milo Quaife, ed., *The Diary of James K. Polk During His Presidency,
1845 to 1849.* (4 vols. 1910).

Reeves
   Jesse S. Reeves, *American Diplomacy Under Tyler and Polk* (1907).
Register
   Register of Debates in Congress, 1825–1837 (1825–1837) (29 vols.).

Rives
   George Rives, *The United States and Mexico,* 1821–1828 (1913).

Schroeder, *Polk's War*
   John H. Schroeder, *Mr. Polk's War: American Opposition and Dissent, 1846–1848* (1973).

S. Exec. Jour.
   Journal of the Executive Proceedings of the Senate of the United States
(34 vols. 1828–1909).

Sofaer, *Origins*
   Abraham D. Sofaer, *War, Foreign Affairs, and Constitutional Power: The Origins* (1976).

War Powers Papers
   War Powers Study Papers, *Butler Library,* Columbia University.

Webster, *Works*
   Daniel Webster, *The Works of Daniel Webster* (6 vols. 1851).

Welles, *Diary*
   Diary of Gideon Welles, Secretary of the Navy Under Lincoln and Johnson (3 vols. 1911).

White, *The Jacksonians*
   Leonard White, *The Jacksonians: A Study in Administrative History, 1829–1861* (1954).

Table of Cases

Bibliography

MANUSCRIPTS

Black, Jeremiah. *Papers*. Manuscript Division, Library of Congress, Washington, D.C.

Chandler, William. *Papers*. Manuscript Division, Library of Congress, Washington, D.C.

Fremont, John C. *Papers*. Bancroft Library, University of California, Berkeley.

———. "Bear Flag Revolt in California, 1845" (narrated to Ivan Petroff, 1878). Bancroft Library, University of California, Berkeley.

———. "Fremont in the Conquest of California" (by J. Bidwell). Bancroft Library, University of California, Berkeley.

———. "Narrative of John C. Fremont's Expedition to California in 1845–46" (narrated by Thomas S. Martin to T.S. Murray, 1878).

———. "Notebook of Journey to Oregon, 1844–46" (narrated by J. Clyman to Ivan Petroff, 1878). Bancroft Library, University of California, Berkeley.

———. "Obituary for Fremont" (delivered by W. Swasey). Bancroft Library, University of California, Berkeley.

———. "Transcript of Fort Sutter Papers" (transcribed by Seymour Dunbar). Bancroft Library, University of California, Berkeley.

Gillespie, Archibald. *Papers*. Special Collections Library, University of California, Los Angeles.

Harrison, Benjamin. *Papers*. Manuscript Division, Library of Congress, Washington, D.C.

Jackson, Andrew. *Papers*. Manuscript Division, Library of Congress, Washington, D.C.

Johnson, Andrew. *Papers, Telegrams and Letters Sent, 1865–69*. Vols. 145, 146, 151, 152. Manuscript Division, Library of Congress, Washington, D.C.

381

Larkin, Thomas. *Papers.* Bancroft Library, University of California, Berkeley.

Lincoln, Abraham. *Papers.* Manuscript Division, Library of Congress, Washington, D.C.

McKinley, William. *Papers.* Manuscript Division, Library of Congress, Washington, D.C.

Polk, James K. *Papers.* Manuscript Division, Library of Congress, Washington, D.C.

Shufeldt, Robert. *Papers.* Manuscript Division, Library of Congress, Washington, D.C.

War Powers Study. Papers. American Bar Association. Summaries of congressional debates and memoranda of incidents relating to war powers. Rare Book and Manuscript Library, Columbia University, New York.

Wilson, James H. *Papers.* Manuscript Division, Library of Congress, Washington, D.C.

DOCUMENTS AND RECORDS

American State Papers: Documents, Legislative and Executive. 38 vols. Edited by W. Lowrie and M. Clarke. Washington, D.C.: Gales and Seaton, 1832–61. Varying use has been made of series of this set entitled Foreign Relations, Military Affairs, Miscellaneous, and Naval Affairs.

Annals of Congress of the United States, 1834–56. Washington, D.C.: Gales and Seaton, 1834–56.

British and Foreign State Papers, 1812–1919. London: H.M. Stationery Office, 1841–1923.

Congressional Globe, Containing the Debates and Procedures, 1833–1876. 46 vols. in 111. Washington, D.C.: Blair & Rives, 1834–73.

Congressional Record. Washington, D.C.: U.S. Government Printing Office, 1874–1902.

Correspondence Relating to the War with Spain. Issued from the Adjutant-General's Department. Washington, D.C.: U.S. Government Printing Office, 1902.

Diplomatic Correspondence of the Republic of Texas. American Historical Association Annual Reports, 1907, 1908. Washington, D.C.: U.S. Government Printing Office, 1908–11.

Diplomatic Correspondence of the United States: Canadian Relations, 1784–1860. 4 vols. Edited by William Manning. Washington, D.C.: Carnegie Endowment for International Peace, 1943.

Diplomatic Correspondence of the United States: Inter-American Affairs, 1831–1860 (Argentina). Edited by William Manning. Washington, D.C.: Carnegie Endowment for International Peace, 1932.

Diplomatic Correspondence of the United States: Inter-American Affairs, 1831–1860 (Central America). Edited by William Manning. Washington, D.C.: Carnegie Endowment for International Peace, 1933.

Freehling, William, ed. *Nullification Era: Documentary Record.* Harper & Row, 1967.

Hansard's Parliamentary Debates. 200 vols. 4th ser. (authorized ed.). New York: Kraus Reprint Co., 1969.

House of Representatives Documents. Washington, D.C.: U.S. Government Printing Office, 1861–1901.

House of Representatives Reports. Washington, D.C.: U.S. Government Printing Office, 1861–1904.

Journal of the Executive Proceedings of the Senate of the United States. 32 vols. in 34. Washington, D.C.: U.S. Government Printing Office, 1828–1909.

Journal of the House of Representatives. Washington, D.C.: U.S. Government Printing Office, 1789–1829.

Memoranda and Official Correspondence Relating to the Republic of Texas, Its History and Annexation. Edited by A. Jones. New York: D. Appleton, 1859.

Messages and Papers of the Presidents, 1789–1897 (A Compilation of the). 20 vols. Edited by James D. Richardson. New York: Bureau of National Literature, 1897.

Moore, John Bassett, ed. *A Digest of International Law.* 8 vols. Washington, D.C.: U.S. Government Printing Office, 1906.

National Archives and Records Service, Records of the State Department.

National Archives Manuscripts, Records of the Department of State, RG59. *Instructions to the U.S. Legation, Hawaii, 1892, 1893.*

National Archives Manuscripts, Records of the Department of State, RG59. *Despatches, Mexico.*

National Archives Manuscripts, Records of the Department of State, RG59. *Instructions, Mexico.*

National Archives Microfilm, Records of the Department of State, RG59. *Diplomatic Instructions, 1801–1906,* M77.

———. *Dispatches from the United States Ministers to Mexico, 1823–1906,* M97.

———. *Notes to Foreign Legations in the United States, 1834–1906,* M99.

National Archives Microfilm, Department of the Navy, RG45. *Area File of the Naval Records Collection, 1775–1910,* M625.

———. *Letters Received by the Secretary of the Navy, 1805–61, 1866–85,* M125.

———. *Letters Sent by the Secretary of the Navy to Officers,* M149.

National Archives Microfilm, Department of War, RG107. *Confidential and Unofficial Letters Sent by the Secretary of War, 1814–47,* M7.

———. *Records of the Secretary of War.*

National Archives Microfilm, House of Representatives, RG233. *Original Messages from the President, March 24 - August 14, 1848,* M .

Naval Documents of the American Revolution. 4 vols. Edited by William Bell Clark. Washington, D.C.: U.S. Naval History Division, Department of the Navy, 1961–64.

Naval Records Office, *Official Records of the Union and Confederate Navies in the War of the Rebellion.* Washington, D.C.: U.S. Government Printing Office, 1896.

Official Correspondence of the Texas Revolution. 2 vols. Edited by William C. Binkley. New York: D. Appleton-Century, 1936.

Official Opinions of the Attorneys-General of the United States. 36 vols. Edited by John L. Lott and James A. Finch. Washington, D.C.: U.S. Government Printing Office, 1932.

Papers of the Texas Revolution 1835–36, 10 vols. Edited by John H. Jenkins. Austin, Texas: Presidential Press, 1973.

Papers Relating to the Foreign Relations of the United States, 1861–1931. 71 vols. Washington, D.C.: U.S. Government Printing Office, 1862–1934.

Public Documents of the First Fourteen Congresses, 1789-1817 - Papers Relating to Early Congressional Documents. Senate Document No. 428, 56th Cong. 1st Sess. (1900).

Records of the Federal Convention of 1787. Edited by Max Farrand. New Haven, Conn.: Yale University Press, 1911–37.

Register of Debates in Congress, 1824–1837. 14 vols. in 29. Washington, D.C.: Gales & Seaton, 1825–37.

Register of the Department of State. Washington, D.C., 1875.

Report of the [Senate] Committee on Foreign Relations with Accompanying Testimony and Executive Documents from January 1, 1893 to March 10, 1894. Washington, D.C.: U.S. Government Printing Office, 1894.

Rogers, C. *The Brazilian Insurrection; 1894 Report of the U.S. Navigation Bureau.* Washington, D.C.: U.S. Government Printing Office, 1895.

Statutes at Large. 21 vols. Boston: Little, Brown, 1789–1881.

Treaties and Other International Acts of the United States of America, 1776–1863. 8 vols. Edited by Hunter Miller. Washington, D.C.: U.S. Government Printing Office, 1931–48.

Treaties, Conventions, International Acts, Protocols, and Agreements between the United States and Other Powers, 1776–1909. 2 vols. Edited by William Malloy. Washington, D.C.: U.S. Government Printing Office, 1910.

Weaver, William Augustus. *Examination and Review of a Pamphlet Printed and Secretly Distributed by Manuel Gorostiza, Mexican Minister in Washington, Entitled "Correspondence . . . respecting the passage of the Sabine, by the troops under the command of General Gaines."* Washington, D.C.: Peter Force, 1837.

LETTERS AND WRITINGS

Adams, Charles Francis. *Diary.* 6 vols. Edited by Aida D. Donald, David Donald, Marc Friedlander, and Lyman Butterfield. Cambridge, Mass.: Belknap Press of the Harvard University Press, 1964–78.

Adams, John Quincy, *Memoirs.* 12 vols. Edited by Charles F. Adams. Philadelphia: Lippincott, 1874–77.

Bates, Edward. *Diary.* Edited by Howard K. Beale. American Historical Association Report, vol. 4. Washington, D.C.: Government Printing Office, 1933.

Benton, Thomas H. *Thirty Years' View.* 2 vols. New York: D. Appleton, 1854–56.

Browning, Orville H. *Diary.* 2 vols. Edited by Theodore C. Pease and James G. Randall. Springfield, Ill.: Trustees of the Illinois State Historical Library, 1925–33.

Buchanan, James. *Works.* 12 vols. Edited by John Bassett Moore. Philadelphia: J.B. Lippincott, 1908–11.

Calhoun, John C. *Papers.* 12 vols. Edited by Robert L. Meriwether, W. Edwin Hemphill, C.N. Wilson. Columbia, S.C.: University of South Carolina Press, 1959–79.

————. *Works.* 6 vols. Edited by Richard K. Cralle. New York: D. Appleton, 1853.

Clay, Henry. *Works.* 10 vols. Edited by Calvin Colton. New York: G.P. Putnam's Sons, 1904.

Cleveland, Grover. *Letters of Grover Cleveland, 1850–1908.* Edited by Allan Nevins. Boston: Houghton Mifflin, 1933.

Ewing, Thomas. *Diary. American Historical Review,* vol. 18. New York: MacMillan, 1912–13.

Foster, John W. *Diplomatic Memoirs.* 2 vols. Boston: Houghton Mifflin, 1909.

Grant, Ulysses S. *Personal Memoirs.* 2 vols. New York: Webster, 1885–86.

Jackson, Andrew. *Correspondence of Andrew Jackson.* 7 vols. Edited by John S. Bassett and J.F. Jameson. Washington, D.C.: Carnegie Institution of America, 1926–35.

Jefferson, Thomas. *The Writings of Thomas Jefferson.* 20 vols. Edited by A.A. Lipscomb and A.E. Bergh. Washington, D.C.: U.S. Government Printing Office, 1903–04 (memorial ed.).

Lincoln, Abraham. *Complete Works of Abraham Lincoln.* 12 vols. Edited by John G. Nicolay and John Hay. New York: Francis D. Tandy, 1905.

McKinley, William. *Speeches and Addresses of William McKinley.* New York: Doubleday and McClure, 1900.

Madison, James. *The Writings of James Madison.* 9 vols. Edited by Gaillard Hunt. New York: G.P. Putnam's Sons, 1900–10.

Polk, James K. *Correspondence of James Polk.* 4 vols. Edited by Herbert Weaver, et al. Nashville, Tenn.: Vanderbilt University Press, 1975–77.

————. *The Diary of James K. Polk during His Presidency, 1845 to 1849.* Edited by Milo Quaife. Chicago: A.C. McClurg, 1910.

————. *Polk: The Diary of a President, 1845–1849.* Edited by Allan Nevins. New York: Longmans Green, 1952.

Quincy, Josiah. *Figures of the Past, From the Leaves of Old Journals.* Boston: Little, Brown, 1926.

Root, Elihu. *Addresses and International Subjects.* Edited by Robert Bacon and James B. Scott. Cambridge, Mass.: Harvard University Press, 1916.

Seward, William. *The Life and Works of William H. Seward.* 5 vols. Edited by George Baker. Boston: Houghton Mifflin, 1883–84.

Tyler, John. *The Letters and Times of the Tylers.* 3 vols. Edited by Lyon G. Tyler. Richmond, Va.: Whittet and Shepperson, 1884–96.

Van Buren, Martin. *Autobiography.* Edited by John C. Fitzpatrick. American Historical Association Annual Report, vol. 2. Washington, D.C.: Government Printing Office, 1920.

Webster, Daniel. *Letters.* Edited by C.H. Van Tyne. New York: McClure, Phillips, 1902.

————. *Papers.* 4 vols. Edited by Charles M. Wiltse. Hanover, N.H.: University Press of New England, 1974 (microfilm ed.).

————. *The Works of Daniel Webster.* 6 vols. Boston: Little, Brown, 1851.

————. *Writings and Speeches.* 18 vols. Edited by J.W. McIntyre. Boston: Little, Brown, 1903.

Welles, Gideon. *Diary.* 3 vols. Edited by Howard K. Beale, *et al.* New York: W.W. Norton, 1960.

————. *Diary of Gideon Welles, Secretary of Navy under Lincoln and Johnson.* 3 vols. Boston: Houghton Mifflin, 1911.

NEWSPAPERS

The Daily Globe (Washington, D.C.), 1831–64.
The London Times, 1829–1906.
The National Intelligencer (Washington, D.C.), 1800–70.
The New York Post, 1801–1901.
The New York Times, 1851–1901.
The New York Tribune, 1841–77.
Niles' Weekly Register (Baltimore, Md.), 1814–37.
The St. Louis Republic, 1808–1901.

SECONDARY WORKS

Adams, Ephraim D. *Great Britain and the American Civil War.* 2 vols. London: Longmans, Green, 1925.

Adams, Paul L. "The American Struggle for a Pre-eminent Position in Mexico." Unpublished dissertation, Ohio State University, 1950.

Allen, Gardner W. *A Naval History of the American Revolution.* 2 vols. New York: Houghton Mifflin, 1913.

Allen, Harry C. *Great Britain and the United States: A History of Anglo-American Relations.* New York: H. Martin's Press, 1955.

Andrews, W., ed. *Concise Dictionary of American History.* New York: Scribners, 1962.

Bagehot, Walter. *The English Constitution.* London: Oxford University Press, 1955.

Bailey, Thomas A. *A Diplomatic History of the American People.* 6th ed. New York: Appleton-Century-Crofts, 1958.

Bancroft, Frederic. *The Life of William H. Seward.* 2 vols. New York: Harper & Row, 1900.

Bancroft, Hubert. *History of California.* 7 vols. San Francisco: The History Co., 1884–90.

Bartlett, Irving. *Daniel Webster.* New York, W.W. Norton, 1978.

Bassett, John Spencer. *The Life of Andrew Jackson.* 2 vols. in 1. New York: MacMillan, 1931.

Bayard, James. *A Brief Exposition of the Constitution of the United States.* Philadelphia: Hogan & Thompson, 1833.

Bemis, Samuel F., ed. *The American Secretaries of State and Their Diplomacy.* 10 vols. New York: A.A. Knopf, 1927–29.

Bemis, Samuel F. *A Diplomatic History of the United States.* New York: Henry Holt, 1946.

———. *The Latin American Policy of the United States: An Historical Interpretation.* New York: Harcourt, Brace, 1943.

———. *Pinckney's Treaty: America's Advantage from Europe's Distress.* New Haven, Conn.: Yale University Press, 1960.

Berdahl, Clarence A. *War Power of the Executive in the United States.* Urbana, Ill.: University of Illinois Press, 1921.

Berger, Raoul. *Executive Privilege: A Constitutional Myth.* Cambridge, Mass.: Harvard University Press, 1974.

Binkley, Wilfred. *The President and Congress.* 3d ed. New York: Vintage, 1962.

Biographical Directory of the American Congress, 1774–1971. Washington, D.C.: U.S. Government Printing Office, 1971.

Braisted, William R. *The United States Navy in the Pacific, 1897–1909.* Austin, Tex.: University of Texas Press, 1958.

Brittin, Burdick H., and Lisolette Watson. *International Law for Seagoing Officers.* 3d ed. Annapolis, Md.: Naval Institute Press, 1972.

Burnette, Ollen, Jr. "The Senate Foreign Relations Committee and the Diplomacy of Garfield, Arthur and Cleveland." Unpublished Ph.D. dissertation, University of Virginia, 1952.

Callahan, James. *American Foreign Policy in Canadian Relations.* New York: MacMillan, 1932.

———. *American Foreign Policy in Mexican Relations.* New York: Cooper Square Publications, 1932.

Chitwood, Oliver P. *John Tyler, Champion of the Old South.* New York: Russell & Russell, 1964.

Church, William. *Ulysses S. Grant and the Period of National Preservation and Reconstruction.* New York: G.P. Putnam's Sons, 1897.

Cleland, Robert. *History of California: The American Period.* New York: MacMillan, 1922.

Cleveland, Grover. *Presidential Problems.* New York: The Century Company, 1904.

Corwin, Edward S. *The President: Office and Powers, 1787–1957.* 4th ed. New York: New York University Press, 1974.

Cunliffe, Marcus. *Soldiers and Civilians: The Martial Spirit in America, 1775–1865.* Boston: Little, Brown, 1968.

Curtis, George T. *The Life of Daniel Webster.* 2 vols. New York: D. Appleton, 1870.

———. *Life of James Buchanan.* 2 vols. New York: Harper & Bros., 1883.

Curtis, James C. *The Fox at Bay.* Lexington, Ky.: University of Kentucky Press, 1970.

DeConde, Alexander. *A History of American Foreign Policy.* New York: Scribner, 1963.

Dennett, Tyler, *John Hay: From Poetry to Politics.* New York: Dodd Mead, 1934.

Dole, Sanford. *Memoirs of the Hawaiian Revolution.* 3 vols. Honolulu: Advertiser Publishing, 1936.

Dowty, Alan. *The Limits of American Isolation.* New York: New York University Press, 1971.

Duane, William John. *Narrative and Correspondence Concerning the Removal of the Deposites.* New York: B. Franklin, 1965.

Duer, William A. *Outlines of the Constitutional Jurisprudence of the United States.* New York: Collins & Hannay, 1833.

Ellsworth, Harry A. *One Hundred Eighty Landings of United States Marines, 1800-1934.* Washington, D.C.: U.S. Government Printing Office, 1974.

Ettinger, Amos A. *The Mission to Spain of Pierre Soulé, 1853–1855.* New Haven, Conn.: Yale University Press, 1932.

Evans, Henry C. *Chile and Its Relations with the United States.* Durham, N.C.: Duke University Press, 1927.

Field, Edward. *Esek Hopkins, Commander-in-Chief of the Continental Navy, 1775-1778.* Boston: Privately printed, 1898.

Friedrich, Carl J. *Constitutional Reason of State: The Survival of the Constitutional Order.* Hanover, N.H.: University Press of New England, 1957.

Goebel, Julius, Jr. *The Struggle for the Falkland Islands.* New Haven, Conn.: Yale University Press, 1927.

Goldsmith, William. *The Growth of Presidential Power.* 3 vols. New York: Chelsea House, 1974.

Gould, Lewis. *The Presidency of William McKinley.* Lawrence, Kan.: Regents Press, 1980.

Graff, Henry F., ed. *American Imperialism and the Philippine Insurrection.* Boston: Little, Brown, 1969.

Griffis, William. *Matthew Calbraith Perry.* Boston: Cupples & Hurd, 1887.

Hagan, Kenneth J. *American Gunboat Diplomacy and the Old Navy, 1877–1889.* Westport, Conn.: Greenwood Press, 1973.

Hamilton, Gail (Mary A. Dodge). *The Biography of James G. Blaine.* Norwich, Conn.: Henry Bill, 1895.

Hamilton, Holman. *Zachary Taylor: Soldier in the White House.* Indianapolis, Ind.: Bobbs-Merrill, 1951.

Hart, John Seely. *A Brief Exposition of the Constitution of the United States.* Philadelphia: E.H. Butler, 1862.

Henderson, Daniel. *The Hidden Coasts: A Biography of Admiral Charles Wilkes.* New York: Sloane, 1953.

Henkin, Louis. *Foreign Affairs and the Constitution.* Mineola, N.Y.: The Foundation Press, 1972.

Holt, W. Stull. *Treaties Defeated by the Senate.* Baltimore, Md.: Johns Hopkins Press, 1933.

James, Marquis. *Andrew Jackson*. 2 vols. Indianapolis, Ind.: Bobbs-Merrill, 1933-37.

Jones, Howard Mumford. *To the Webster-Ashburton Treaty: A Study in Anglo-American Relations, 1783-1843*. Chapel Hill, N.C.: University of North Carolina Press, 1977.

Josephson, Matthew. *The Politicos*. New York: Harcourt, Brace, 1963.

Kennleyside, Hugh L., and Gerald S. Brown, 2d ed. *Canada and the United States: Some Aspects of Their Historical Relations*. New York: A.A. Knopf, 1952.

Kelsey, R. *The United States Consulate in California*. Berkeley, Calif.: University of California Press, 1910.

Kent, James. *Commentaries on American Law*. 4 vols. 4th ed. New York: published by the author, 1840.

Klein, Philip S. *President James Buchanan, A Biography*. University Park, Pa.: Pennsylvania State University Press, 1962.

LeFeber, Walter. *The New Empire*. Ithaca, N.Y.: Cornell University Press, 1963.

Leopold, Richard. *The Growth of American Foreign Policy: A History*. New York: A.A. Knopf, 1966.

Locke, John. *The Second Treatise of Civil Government*. Edited by J. Gough. New York: Barnes and Noble, 1966.

Lodge, Henry Cabot, ed. *The Federalist: A Commentary on the Constitution of the United States*. New York: G.P. Putnam's Sons, 1902.

Logan, R. *The Diplomatic Relations of the United States with Haiti, 1776-1891*. Chapel Hill, N.C.: University of North Carolina Press, 1941.

McCormac, Eugene I. *James K. Polk: A Political Biography*. Berkeley: University of California Press, 1922.

McCulloch, H.M. *Men and Measures of Half a Century*. New York: Chas. Scribner's Sons, 1888.

McDonough, James L. *Schofield: Union General in the Civil War and Reconstruction*. Tallahassee, Fl.: Florida State University Press, 1972.

McLemore, Richard. *Franco-American Diplomatic Relations, 1816-1836*. University, La.: Louisiana State University Press, 1941.

McPherson, Edward. *Political History of the United States during the Period of Reconstruction*. Washington, D.C.: D.C. Philip & Solomons, 1864.

Mantell, Martin. *Johnson, Grant, and the Politics of Reconstruction*. New York: Columbia University Press, 1973.

Marshall, Thomas Maitland. *A History of the Western Boundary of the Louisiana Purchase, 1819-1841*. Berkeley: University of California Press, 1914.

Mason, Edward C. *The Veto Power: Its Origin, Development and Function in the Government of the United States*. Boston: Ginn, 1890.

May, Ernest. *Imperial Democracy: Emergence of America*. New York: Harcourt, Brace, 1961.

Merk, Frederick. *Manifest Destiny and Mission in American History: A Reinterpretation*. New York: A.A. Knopf, 1963.

_____. *The Monroe Doctrine and American Expansionism, 1843-1849*. New York: A.A. Knopf, 1966.

Morgan, H. Wayne. *America's Road to Empire.* New York: John Wiley, 1965.

Morgan, Robert. *A Whig Embattled: The Presidency under Tyler.* Lincoln, Neb.: University of Nebraska Press, 1954.

Musser, John. *The Establishment of Maximilian's Empire in Mexico.* Menasha, Wis.: Collegiate Press, 1918.

Neustadt, Richard E. *Presidential Power: The Politics of Leadership.* New York: Wiley, 1960.

Nevins, Allan. *Grover Cleveland: A Study in Courage.* New York: Dodd, Mead, 1934.

———. *Hamilton Fish: The Inner History of the Grant Administration.* New York: Dodd, Mead, 1936.

Nichols, Roy F. *The Disruption of American Democracy.* New York: MacMillan, 1948.

———. *Franklin Pierce.* Philadelphia: University of Pennsylvania Press, 1931.

Nicolay, John G. and John Hay. *Abraham Lincoln: A History.* 10 vols. New York: The Century Company, 1890.

Niven, John. *Gideon Welles: Lincoln's Secretary of the Navy.* New York: Oxford University Press, 1973.

Oberholtzer, Ellis P. *History of the United States since the Civil War.* 5 vols. New York: MacMillan, 1926–37.

Offner, John. "President McKinley and the Origins of the Spanish-American War." Unpublished Ph.D. dissertation, Pennsylvania State University, 1957.

Offut, Milton. *Protection of Citizens Abroad by the Armed Forces of the United States.* Baltimore, Md.: Johns Hopkins Press, 1928.

Olcott, Charles S. *The Life of William McKinley.* Boston: Houghton Mifflin, 1916.

Parton, James. *Life of Andrew Johnson.* 2 vols. New York: Mason Bros., 1861.

Paullin, Charles. *Diplomatic Negotiations of American Naval Officers, 1778–1883.* Baltimore, Md.: Johns Hopkins Press, 1912.

Perkins, Dexter. *The Monroe Doctrine, 1826–1867.* 1932 Reprint. Gloucester, Mass.: Peter Smith, 1965.

———. *The Monroe Doctrine, 1867–1907.* Baltimore: Johns Hopkins University Press, 1937.

Pletcher, David. *The Awkward Years: American Foreign Relations under Cleveland and Arthur.* Columbia, Mo.: University of Missouri Press, 1962.

———. *The Diplomacy of Annexation: Texas, Oregon, and the Mexican War.* Columbia, Mo.: University of Missouri Press, 1973.

Poage, George. *Henry Clay and the Whig Party.* Chapel Hill, N.C.: University of North Carolina Press, 1936.

Pratt, Julius. *Expansionists of 1898: The Acquisition of Hawaii and the Spanish Islands.* Baltimore, Md.: Johns Hopkins Press, 1936.

Randall, James G. *Constitutional Problems under Lincoln.* 2d ed. Urbana, Ill.: University of Illinois Press, 1951.

Randall, James G., and David H. Donald. *The Civil War and Reconstruction.* 2d ed. Boston: D.C. Heath, 1961.

Rawle, William H. *A View of the Constitution of the United States of America.* 2d ed. Philadelphia: P.H. Nicklin, 1829.

Reeves, Jesse S. *American Diplomacy under Tyler and Polk.* Baltimore, Md.: Johns Hopkins Press, 1907.

Reeves, Thomas C. *Gentleman Boss: The Life of Chester Alan Arthur.* New York: A.A. Knopf, 1975.

Remini, Robert. *Andrew Jackson.* New York: Twayne Publishers, 1966.

——. *Andrew Jackson and the Bank War: A Study in the Growth of Presidential Power.* New York: W.W. Norton, 1967.

Reveley, W. Taylor, III. *The War Powers of the President and Congress—Who Holds the Arrows and Olive Branch?* Charlottesville, Va.: University Press of Virginia, 1981.

Rippy, James Ford. *The United States and Mexico.* 2d ed. New York: F.S. Crofts, 1941.

Rives, George. *The United States and Mexico, 1821–1828.* 2 vols. New York: Chas. Scribner's Sons, 1913.

Rossiter, Clinton L. *Constitutional Dictatorship: Crisis Government in the Modern Democracies.* Princeton, N.J.: Princeton University Press, 1948.

Russ, William, Jr. *The Hawaiian Revolution, 1893–1894.* Selinsgrove, Pa.: Susquehanna University Press, 1959.

Schlesinger, Arthur M., Jr. *The Age of Jackson.* Boston: Little, Brown and Co., 1945.

——. *The Imperial Presidency.* Boston: Houghton Mifflin, 1973.

——. *The Vital Center: The Politics of Freedom.* Boston: Houghton Mifflin, 1949.

Schlesinger, Arthur M., Jr., and Roger Bruns. *Congress Investigates.* New York: Chelsea House, 1975.

Schofield, John M. *Forty-six Years in the Army.* New York: The Century Company, 1897.

Schroeder, John H. *Mr. Polk's War: American Opposition and Dissent, 1846–1848.* Madison, Wis.: University of Wisconsin Press, 1973.

Sellers, Charles G. *James K. Polk, Continentalist, 1843–1846.* 2 vols. Princeton, N.J.: Princeton University Press, 1957–58.

Sergeant, Thomas. *Being a View of the Practice . . . and of Constitutional Points Decided.* 2d ed. Philadelphia: P.H. Nicklin & T. Johnson, 1830.

Sherman, William R. *The Diplomatic and Commercial Relations of the United States and Chile, 1820–1914.* Boston: Russell Publications, 1926.

Sievers, Harry. *Benjamin Harrison.* 2 vols. Chicago: H. Regnery, 1952–59.

Silverberg, Robert. *Stormy Voyager: The Story of Charles Wilkes.* Philadelphia: Lippincott, 1968.

Smith, Justin H. *The Annexation of Texas.* 2d ed. New York: Barnes & Noble, 1941.

Smith, Theodore. *The Life and Letters of James Abram Garfield.* 2 vols. New Haven, Conn.: Yale University Press, 1925.

Sofaer, Abraham. *War, Foreign Affairs and Constitutional Power: The Origins.* Cambridge, Mass.: Ballinger Publishing Co., 1976.

Soulsby, Hugh G. *The Right of Search and the Slave Trade in Anglo-American Relations, 1814-1862.* Baltimore, Md.: Johns Hopkins Press, 1933.

Sprout, Harold H., and Margaret Sprout. *The Rise of American Naval Power.* Princeton, N.J.: Princeton University Press, 1939.

Storey, Moorefield, and Marcial Lichauco. *The Conquest of the Philippines, 1898–1925.* New York: G.P. Putnam's Sons, 1926.

Story, Joseph. *Commentaries on the Constitution of the United States.* 5th ed. Boston: Hilliard, Gray, 1833; Little, Brown, 1891, 1905.

Stryker, L. *Andrew Johnson: A Study in Courage.* New York: MacMillan, 1929.

Tansill, Charles. *Canadian-American Relations, 1875-1911.* New Haven, Conn.: Yale University Press, 1943.

_____. *The United States and Santo Domingo, 1798–1873: A Chapter in Caribbean Diplomacy.* Baltimore, Md.: Johns Hopkins Press, 1938.

Tate, Merze. *The United States and the Hawaiian Kingdom: A Political History.* New Haven, Conn.: Yale University Press, 1965.

Taylor, Telford. *Grand Inquest: The Story of Congressional Investigations.* New York: Simon & Schuster, 1955.

Temin, Peter. *The Jacksonian Economy.* New York: W.W. Norton, 1969.

Thomas, Benjamin. *Abraham Lincoln.* New York: A.A. Knopf, 1952.

Thurston, Lorrin. *Memoirs of the Hawaiian Revolution.* 3 vols. Honolulu: Advertiser Publishing Co., 1936.

Trask, David. *The War with Spain in 1898.* New York: MacMillan Co., 1981.

Tugwell, Rexford. *Grover Cleveland.* New York: MacMillan Co., 1968.

Tyler, Alice Felt. *The Foreign Policy of James G. Blaine.* Hamden, Conn.: Archon Books, 1965.

Tyler, S. *Memoir of Roger B. Taney.* Baltimore, Md.: Murphy, 1872.

Upshur, Abel P. *A Brief Enquiry into the True Nature and Character of Our Federal Government.* New York: Collins & Hannay, 1833. Reprint. New York: Da Capo, 1971.

Vahle, Cornelius. "Congress, the President, and Overseas Expansion, 1897–1901." Unpublished Ph.D. dissertation, Georgetown University, 1967.

Van Deusen, Glyndon. *The Jacksonian Era, 1828–1848.* New York: Harper Bros., 1959.

_____. *William Henry Seward.* New York: Oxford University Press, 1967.

Walworth, Arthur. *Black Ships Off Japan: The Story of Commodore Perry's Expedition.* Hamden, Conn.: Archon Books, 1966.

Welles, Gideon. *Lincoln and Seward.* New York: Sheldon & Co., 1874. Reprint. Salem, N.H.: Ayer Co., 1969.

White, Leonard. *The Jacksonians: A Study in Administrative History, 1829–1861.* New York: MacMillan Co., 1954.

_____. *The Republican Era, 1869–1901: A Study in Administrative History.* New York: MacMillan, 1958.

Wilkes, Charles. *Narrative of the United States Exploring Expedition during the Years 1838–1842.* Philadelphia: C. Sherman, 1844–74.

Williams, Mary W. *Anglo-American Isthmian Diplomacy, 1815–1915.* Baltimore, Md.: The Lord Baltimore Press, 1916.

Wiltse, Charles. *John C. Calhoun.* 3 vols. Indianapolis, Ind.: Bobbs-Merrill, 1944–51.

Woodward, C. Vann. *Reunion and Reaction.* New York: Doubleday, 1956.

Wriston, Henry M. *Executive Agents in American Foreign Relations.* Gloucester, Mass.: Johns Hopkins Press, 1929.

Young, George V. "The Influence of Politics on American Diplomacy during Cleveland's Administration." Unpublished Ph.D. dissertation, Yale University, 1939.

ARTICLES

Bastert, R.H. "Diplomatic Reversal: Frelinghuysen's Opposition to Blaine's Pan American Policy in 1882." 42 *Mississippi Valley Historical Review* 653 (1956).

Blake, N.M. "The Background of Cleveland's Venezuela Policy." 47 *American Historical Association Review* 259 (1942).

Cohen, V. "Charles Sumner and the *Trent* Affair." 22 *Journal of Southern History* 205 (1956).

Cutler, L. "To Form a Government." 59 *Foreign Affairs* 126 (1980).

Golder, F.A. "The Purchase of Alaska." 25 *American Historical Association Review* 424 (1920).

Hardy, O. "The *Itata* Incident." 5 *Hispanic American Historical Association Review* 195 (1922).

Hayaski-Daigaku. "Diary of an Official of the Bakufu." In *Transactions of the Asiatic Society of Japan,* Series II, Vol. VII, pp. 98–119. Tokyo, 1930.

Henkin. L. "Some Reflections on Current Constitutional Controversy." 109 *University of Pennsylvania Law Review* 637 (1961).

Janes, H. "The *Black Warrior* Affair." 12 *American Historical Association Review* 289 (1907).

Landis, J.M. "Constitutional Limitations on the Congressional Power of Investigation." 40 *Harvard Law Review* 153 (1926).

Levitan, D.M. "The Foreign Relations Power: An Analysis of Mr. Justice Sutherland's Theory." 55 *Yale Law Journal* 467 (1946).

Lofgren, C. "War Making under the Constitution: The Original Understanding." 81 *Yale Law Journal* 672 (1972).

Note. "Congress, the President and the Power to Commit Forces to Combat." 81 *Harvard Law Review* 1771 (1968).

Rippy, J.F. "Some Precedents of the Pershing Expedition into Mexico." 24 *Southwestern Historical Quarterly* 292 (1921).

Spaeth, Carl B. "Book Review." 1 *Stanford Law Review* 178 (1948).

Stenberg, R.R. "Jackson, Anthony Butler, and Texas." 13 *Southwestern Social Science Quarterly* 264 (1932).

——. "The Texas Schemes of Jackson and Houston, 1829–1836." 15 *Southwestern Social Science Quarterly* 229 (1934).

"Taney's Letters to Van Buren in 1860." 10 *Maryland Historical Magazine* 23 (1915).

Volwiler, A.T. "American Foreign Policy, 1889-1893." 79 *American Philosophy Society Proceedings* 643 (1938).

Watson, H. Lee. "Congress Steps Out: A Look at Congressional Control of the Executive." 63 *California Law Review* 983 (1975).

Young, G.B. "Intervention under the Monroe Doctrine: The Olney Corollary." 57 *Political Science Quarterly* 247 (1942).

Index

Accessory Transit Company, 164 and n.,
165 and n.
Acts and resolutions of Congress
  Act of 1794, requiring President to
    account for use of funds, 19–20
  of 1795, authorizing President to
    use state militia for protection
    against invasion and insurrection,
    16 n., 66 n., 218–219, 229 n.
    251 n.
  of 1806, conferring broad powers
    on Jefferson, 19
  of 1807, authorizing President to
    use federal troops for protection
    against invasion and insurrection,
    16 and n., 66 n., 229 n., 251 n.,
    264
  of 1819, 1822, and 1826, conferring
    general authority to seize and
    bring pirates to justice, 52
    and n.
  of 1820, Tenure of Office, 5 n.
  of 1832, providing for payment of
    militia in case of invasion, 16
  of 1862, executive military re-
    moval authority, 176 n.
  of 1865, executive use of Army to
    maintain domestic order, 248–250
Adams, Charles Francis, 202
Adams, John Quincy, 1, 5, 15, 17, 18, 24
  and n., 31 n., 37 n., 38, 40 n.,

41 n., 43, 47, 49, 61, 63 and n., 71,
  80 and n., 92 n., 118 n., 151, 170,
  269 n.
Adrain, Garnett, 188
African slave trade, 50
Agents, executive, 6–7, 38, 75, 120, 131,
  203, 238, 240 and n., 241, 274 and
  n., 318 and n.
Aguinaldo, Emilio, 289 n., 324–325
Alaska, 185, 210
  dispute with British over Bering Sea
    fishing, 284–285
  House efforts to acquire, 212
Aldrich, Nelson, 316
Allen, William, 67 n., 90 n., 91, 124 n.,
  125 n.
Allen, William V., 264, 287 n., 289, 320,
  323
Altgeld, John Peter, 264 n.
Alvear, General Don Carlos Maria, 62
Amistad claim, 203 and n., 204
Anderson, George, 192 n., 226 n.
Anderson, Thomas, 179, 241 n.
Annexation, *see* Treaties
Appointment
  as exclusive Presidential power, 7, 89
    and n., 90, 174, 175, 327
  as war power, 3, 7, 168, 175, 227
  claimed abuse of, 7, 86, 89, 167, 227
  Congress's expansion of control over,
    4–8, 75, 89, 327

failure to transmit information on
Pacific activities, 32
negotiated treaty with England, 107 n.
and South American colonies' revolt
from Spain, 279 n.
and Yucatan Peninsula, 128 n.
Monterey
capture of, 147
incident at, 62, 63 and n.
Moore, John Bassett, 310 n., 311 n.
Morgan, John, 250, 252, 255 and n., 256
and n., 277–278, 279, 280 and n.,
281, 286, 287 and n., 288 and n.,
289 n., 296
and Nicaragua canal, 278 n.
and U.S. relations with Spain, 279 n.
and withholding of information, 260 n.
Morrill, Justin, 219 and n., 210 n.
Morton, Oliver P., 315 and n.
Muhlenburg, Henry A., 41

Nacogdoches, Fort, 69 n., 71, 73 and
n., 74
Napoleon Bonaparte, 17 n., 207 n., 243
Natchez, 48 n.
Natchitoches (town), 78 n.
Navy
appropriations, 15–16, 291 n., 292 n.
coaling stations, 270 n.
deployed to Santo Domingo, 312–315
evolution of, 290–293
executive authority to select sites, 98
and Hayes, 270 n.
increases in, *see* Military Affairs
modernization of, 292
as police force on high seas, 329
scope of, 51–52
Nelson, John, 38, 77
Neutrality Acts, 64–65, 238–239, 240
and n.
New Mexico
acquisition of, 152
executive intervention in, 87, 142,
161–163
Gadsden Purchase Treaty, 136–140
Niblack, William E., 227, 263
Nicaragua
and Buchanan's request to use force,
196
canal proposal, 252, 266, 277 n., 278,
297
Greytown incident, 56 n., 88 n., 142,

164 and n., 165 and n., 166 and n.,
167 and n., 170–171, 183
and Tigre, 107, 109, 111
and treaty negotiation, 106, 107 n.,
108, 110 and n., 111, 112 n., 196
Walker's expedition to, 236, 238–241,
245
North German Confederation, treaty
with, 276 n.
Nullification controversy, 3, 14, 28–29

Okinawa, 114
Olney Corollary, 275 n.
Olney, Richard, 263, 328
Oregon territory
boundary dispute, 41–44, 85, 119
British-American dispute over,
116–117
settlement of under Polk, 94, 126–128
Orr, James, 135
Ostend Manifesto, 122 and n., 123 and
n., 133
Otis, General Elwell, 262 and n., 323–
324, photo of, 322
Ottoman Empire and Treaty of Berlin,
284 n.

Pageot, A.J.Y., 26
Pakenham, Richard, 128 n.
Palmerston, Lord Henry John Temple,
108 and n., 109
Panama, *see* Isthmus of Panama
Panama Canal Company, 278 n.
Panchita, 234 n.
Paraguay, 186, 242, 245
Water Witch incident, 199 and n., 229,
230 and n., 231 and n., 232–233
U.S. recognition of independence,
124 n.
Paulding, Commodore Hiram, 236,
238–241
Peace power, 3, 246, 296, 326, 330
"peace at the polls," 249 n.
"peace of the United States," 250,
295
Peixoto, Floriano, 308
Pendergrast, Captain G. J., 201 and n.
Pendleton, George, 190 and n., 263
Pennybacker, Isaac, 146
Perry, Commodore Matthew, 22 n., 56 n.,
57 n., 97, 129–130
and help for Yucatan, 129 and n.

DATE DUE

APR 17 '01	